CHINA REVIEW 1993

Related titles already published

China Review
Edited by Kuan Hsin-chi
and Maurice Brosseau

China Review 1992
Edited by Kuan Hsin-chi
and Maurice Brosseau

China Review 1993

EDITED BY
Joseph Cheng Yu-shek
AND
Maurice Brosseau

The Chinese University Press

© **The Chinese University of Hong Kong** 1993

All Rights Reserved. No part of this publication may
be reproduced or transmitted in any form or by any
means, electronic or mechanical, including photocopying,
recording, or any information storage and retrieval
system, without permission in writing from
The Chinese University of Hong Kong.

ISBN 962–201–570–0

THE CHINESE UNIVERSITY PRESS
The Chinese University of Hong Kong
SHATIN, N.T., HONG KONG

Printed in Hong Kong by Magnum (Offset) Printing Co., Ltd.

Steering Committee

Maurice Brosseau
Joseph Cheng Yu-shek
Kuan Hsin-chi
Y. Y. Kueh
Paul Chun-kuen Kwong
Yun-wing Sung
T. L. Tsim

Contents

Preface ix

Contributors xi

Abbreviations xv

Chronology xix
 Willy Wo-lap Lam

1. Introduction
   Joseph Cheng Yu-shek

2. Leadership Changes at the Fourteenth Party Congress
   Willy Wo-lap Lam

3. Communist Party Orthodoxy
   Graham Young

4. Administrative Reforms in China in 1992: Streamlining, Decentralization and Changing Government Functions
   Joseph Cheng Yu-shek and Ting Wang

5. Civil Service Reform
   King K. Tsao

6. The People's Liberation Army in 1992: Political Power Plays and Power Projection
   Tai Ming Cheung

7. Economic Legal Reforms
   Wang Guiguo

8. Foreign Policy
   Gerald Chan

9. Relations with Taiwan
   C. L. Chiou

10. China's Relations with Hong Kong
    Jane C. Y. Lee

11. Economic Development in China in 1992
    Thomas M. H. Chan

12. Central-provincial Fiscal Relations
    Lok Sang Ho
13. Banking
    Luk Yim Fai
14. Market Reform and Agricultural Growth: The Dynamics of Change in the Chinese Countryside in 1992
    Andrew Watson
15. Relations between Government and Enterprises
    Lau Pui-king
16. Direct Foreign Investment in China: Trends, Performance, Policies and Prospects
    Nyaw Mee-kau
17. China's Foreign Trade and the Reform of the Foreign Trade System
    Yin-Ping Ho
18. Pearl River Delta Development
    Peter Tsan-yin Cheung
19. Population Mobility in the 1980s: China on the Road to an Open Society
    Siu Yat-ming and Li Si-ming
20. The Chinese Family and Gender Roles in Transition
    Chong-chor Lau
21. Pro-democracy Movement in the People's Republic of China and Overseas
    K. K. Leung
22. The Changing Educational System: Dilemma of Disparity
    Leslie Nai-kwai Lo
23. Slighting the Needy? Social Welfare under Transition
    Linda Wong
24. Urban Housing Reform in China amidst Property Boom Year
    Lau Kwok-yu
25. Commercialization without Independence: Trends and Tensions of Media Development in China
    Joseph Man Chan
26. A Bird-cage Culture: How Big Was the Cage?
    Sylvia Chan

Index

Preface

China Review offers once again a varied assessment of China with the publication of this third volume. The intention is to provide, from the vantage point of Hong Kong's privileged location, a yearly and up-to-date analysis of the evolution of the People's Republic of China (PRC), as the most populous nation on earth aspires to have its political, economic and social thrust recognized and respected internationally.

The metamorphosis that is taking place in the PRC often defies the observer's sense of direction. Lately, different circles have questioned the accepted criteria used to evaluate the path to modernization chosen by China and the region; a few experts are venturing the prediction that, with the participation of Hong Kong and Taiwan, China may well develop at such a speed that the size of its economy may overtake the western leading nations within the next two decades. This may beg for a theoretical and substantive rethink among social scientists, analogous to what had taken place in the early 1980s when scholars had to face the daring shedding of "politics in command" for economic reforms and the "four modernizations."

The chapters which follow try to straddle the divide between "older" and "newer" thinking, conscious that political, economic and social change in such a vast and complex country is bound to exhibit a dynamism which precludes easy generalizations, as aspirations may generate diversity, contradictions challenge orderly development and ambition tax prudence.

We wish to thank The Chinese University Press for sponsoring in early January 1993 a workshop where the draft chapters were earnestly discussed before further polishing, providing valuable assistance to our contributors. We must also acknowledge the professionalism of the staff of the Press who have again endeavoured to assure the highest quality possible in the preparation of this volume, the third of the series.

The Editors
April 1993

Contributors

MAURICE BROSSEAU is Research Officer at the Hong Kong Institute of Asia-Pacific Studies, The Chinese University of Hong Kong. He co-edited the first two volumes of *China Review*.

GERALD CHAN is a Lecturer in international relations in the Department of Politics at Victoria University of Wellington, New Zealand, and a member of the advisory board to the *New Zealand Journal of East Asian Studies*.

JOSEPH MAN CHAN is a Senior Lecturer in Journalism and Communication at The Chinese University of Hong Kong. Research interests include international communication, political communication, communications development and popular culture. He has published in various international journals and co-authored *Mass Media and Political Transition: The Hong Kong Press in China's Orbit* (New York: Guilford Press, 1991).

SYLVIA CHAN is a Senior Lecturer in Chinese at the Centre for Asian Studies, University of Adelaide. She lived in Beijing from 1951 to 1972 and taught at Beijing Teachers' College from 1961 to 1972. She did a number of English-Chinese and Chinese-English translations and worked on a dictionary and several English language textbooks in China. Since taking up a teaching post at the University of Adelaide, she has published widely on education, literature and intellectual problems in contemporary China.

THOMAS MAN-HUNG CHAN, a graduate of the University of Hong Kong, The Chinese University of Hong Kong and Flinders University of South Australia. He specializes in the economy of Socialist China; he has served as consultant to various banking and government organizations as well as the World Bank.

JOSEPH CHENG YU-SHEK is Dean, Faculty of Humanities and Social Sciences, City Polytechnic of Hong Kong. He is also Director of Contemporary China Research Centre in the City Polytechnic and Editor of its *Hong Kong Journal of Social Sciences*. His main research interests are political development in China and Hong Kong, and he has published extensively in these areas.

PETER TSAN-YIN CHEUNG is Lecturer in the Department of Political Science at the University of Hong Kong. He is completing a doctoral dissertation on

Guangdong's reforms at the University of Washington, Seattle. His research interests mainly concern central-provincial relations in post-Mao China, the political and economic development of South China, and the politics of reform in socialist countries.

TAI MING CHEUNG is a Hongkong-based correspondent for the *Far Eastern Economic Review* specializing on China, defence and Hong Kong affairs. He also undertakes academic research and writing on Chinese security affairs, including on Sino-Russian defence ties, Chinese naval modernization, Chinese defence-industrial reform, and Chinese defence policy-making.

C. L. CHIOU, Reader in Politics, The University of Queensland, Australia, has been concerned with problems of democratization in Taiwan and China for more than three decades. He has published four books and many articles on this subject matter. He has just finished a book *Democratizing Oriental Despotism: China from May 4 to June 4 and Taiwan from February 28 to June 28* and a monograph *Democratizing China and Taiwan: Cultural and Institutional Paradigms*.

HO LOK SANG, Lecturer in Economics at The Chinese University of Hong Kong, holds a doctorate in economics from the University of Toronto. Apart from studies on the Chinese economy which have been published in *China: Modernisation in the 1980s* and *Studies on Economic Reforms and Development in the People's Republic of China* (both published by The Chinese University Press), Dr Ho has published articles covering urban and regional economics, macroeconomics, social security, and bank deposit insurance.

YIN-PING HO is Lecturer in the Department of Economics at The Chinese University of Hong Kong. His most recent book is *Trade, Industrial Restructuring and Development in Hong Kong* (London/Honolulu: Macmillan Press/University of Hawaii Press, 1992).

WILLY WO-LAP LAM is the China Editor of the *South China Morning Post*. A graduate of the University of Hong Kong and the University of Minnesota. He is the author of *The Era of Zhao Ziyang* (1989) and *Toward a Chinese-Style Socialism* (1986). He is working on a book on the post-Deng Xiaoping era.

CHONG-CHOR LAU is Senior Lecturer in Sociology, The Chinese University of Hong Kong. His main research interest is the study of Chinese society. He has written extensively on China in Chinese as well as in English.

LAU KWOK-YU is Senior Lecturer in the Department of Public and Social Administration, City Polytechnic of Hong Kong. His teaching and research interest is housing and policy studies.

LAU PUI-KING is Senior Lecturer and Head of Department of Business Studies, Hong Kong Polytechnic. A graduate of The Chinese University of Hong Kong and California State University, she has specialized in the study of the Chinese economy, particularly the Chinese state enterprises and joint ventures and economic reform in Guangdong province. She has been an appointed Hong Kong representative to the Guangdong Provincial People's Congress since 1988.

JANE C. Y. LEE is a Senior Lecturer in the Department of Public and Social Administration of the City Polytechnic of Hong Kong. She obtained her MA in Public Administration at the University of Hong Kong and a PhD degree in the politics of transition in Hong Kong at the Australian National University. Her current research interest includes the evolving political groups, parties and leadership in Hong Kong, political culture of Hong Kong people, the administrative culture of Hong Kong's civil servants and the latter's relationships with the politicians.

K. K. LEUNG is President of Foundation of China Studies, Director of Centre of China Studies and Senior Lecturer at City Polytechnic of Hong Kong. His research interest is political sociology in China and Hong Kong.

LI SI-MING is a Course Leader in China Studies and Senior Lecturer in Geography at Hong Kong Baptist College. His major research interests are urban and economic geography. His recent publications include "Labour Mobility, Migration and Urbanization in the Pearl River Delta Region" (*Asian Geographer, 1990*) and "China's Open Door Policy and Urbanization in the Pearl River Delta Region" (*International Journal of Urban and Regional Research, 1990*).

LESLIE NAI-KWAI LO received his doctorate from Columbia University, specializing in Comparative Education with a research interest in the educational development of contemporary Asia and China. He has published numerous articles and chapters in scholarly journals and noteworthy books. He is presently Dean of Education at The Chinese University of Hong Kong and President of the Comparative Education Society of Hong Kong.

LUK YIM FAI is Lecturer in the Department of Economics, The Chinese University of Hong Kong.

NYAW MEE-KAU is Professor and Director of Studies in Organization and Management at The Chinese University of Hong Kong. He has authored and co-authored several books including *Export Expansion and Industrial Growth in Singapore* and *Business Operations and Management: From West to East*. He has also contributed to *Asian Survey, Journal of Management Studies, International*

Studies of Management and Organization, *World Development*, *Euro-Asia Business Review* and several other international journals.

SIU YAT-MING is a Lecturer in Sociology at Hong Kong Baptist College. His major research interests are China's human fertility and population mobility. He is currently doing a survey on population mobility and fertility in Guangdong.

TING WANG is a respected journalist and China watcher with the United Daily News Group of Taiwan. He was the founding editor of *Tide Monthly* and has published extensively on political developments in China.

KING K. TSAO is currently Assistant Lecturer in the Department of Government and Public Administration at The Chinese University of Hong Kong. He did his dissertation research on factory reforms at Peking University from September 1987 to June 1989. He is also a PhD candidate in the Department of Political Science at the University of Chicago. His research interests include: the politics of reform, policy implementation, social norms and industrial organization, and the political economy of the Soviet-type regimes.

WANG GUIGUO holds a JSD degree from Yale Law School and is Reader at City Polytechnic of Hong Kong. Visiting Professor at People's University of China and Arbitrator of China International Economic and Trade Arbitration Commission, Dr Wang has published ten books and a number of articles in the field of commercial law.

ANDREW WATSON is Professor of Asian Studies at the University of Adelaide. He works on rural development in China. He has recently published articles on China's sheep and wool production, on rural enterprise growth and on agricultural marketing reform. In 1992, he edited the book *Economic Reform and Social Change in China* (Routledge). He is currently working on a book on rural enterprise growth and on a new project on grain market reform.

LINDA WONG is Principal Lecturer in the Department of Public and Social Administration, City Polytechnic of Hong Kong. She teaches social policy, social administration and social policy in China. Her current research interests focus on social policy and development issues in the People's Republic of China, including the role of the Ministry of Civil Affairs, community care, welfare developments in Guangdong and welfare financing.

GRAHAM YOUNG is a Senior Lecturer in the Politics Department, University of New England, Australia. His main research interests include the Chinese Communist Party and its interpretations of revolution and socialism.

Abbreviations

ABOC	Agricultural Bank of China
ADB	Asian Development Bank
APEC	Asia-Pacific Economic Co-operation
ARATS	Association for Relations Across the Taiwan Strait (PRC)
ASEAN	Association of South-East Asian Nations
AUUS	Autonomous Union of University Students
BBC	British Broadcasting Corporation
BCOM	Bank of Communications
BOC	Bank of China
BOT	Build, Operate and Transfer
CAC	Central Advisory Commission
CASS	Chinese Academy of Social Sciences
CC	Central Committee
CCDI	Central Commission for Disciplinary Inspection
CCP	Chinese Communist Party
CCTV	China Central Television
CIETAC	China International Economic and Trade Arbitration Commission
c.i.f.	Cost, insurance, freight
CITIC	China International Trust and Investment Corporation
CJV	Contractual joint venture
CMC	Central Military Commission
COCOM	Coordinating Committee for Multilateral Export Controls
COO	Certificate of origin
CPPCC	Chinese People's Political Consultative Congress
CRES	Commission for the Reform of the Economic System
CSI	China Strategic Investment
DFI	Direct foreign investment
DPP	Democratic Progressive Party (Taiwan)
EBRD	European Bank for Reconstruction and Development
EC	European Community

EEC	European Economic Community
EJV	Equity joint venture
ETO	Economic and Trade Office
FEAC	Foreign exchange adjustment centre
FEER	*Far Eastern Economic Review*
FFE	Foreign-funded enterprise
f.o.b.	Free on board
FTC	Foreign trade corporation
FTU	Federation of Trade Unions
GATT	General Agreement on Tariffs and Trade
GDP	Gross domestic product
GLD	General Logistics Department
GNP	Gross national product
GPD	General Political Department
GSD	General Staff Department
HKTDC	Hong Kong Trade Development Council
ICBC	Industrial and Commercial Bank of China
IFM	International Monetary Fund
ITO	International Trade Organization
JDV	Joint development venture
KMT	Kuomintang (Nationalist Party, Taiwan)
LGEF	Leading Group on Economics and Finance
MAC	Mainland Affairs Council (Taiwan)
MCF	Multiple-channel funding
MFA	Multifibre arrangement
MFN	Most-favoured-nation (trade status)
MITI	Ministry of International Trade and Industry (Japan)
MOFERT	Ministry of Foreign Economic Relations and Trade
MOFT	Ministry of Foreign Trade
MPS	Material products system
MR	Military Region
MTV	Music Television Video
NAFTA	North American Free Trade Area
NATO	North Atlantic Treaty Organization
NIC	Newly industrializing country
NIE	Newly industrializing economy
NPC	National People's Congress
NPR	National-provincial revenue
NTB	Non-tariff trade barrier

OMELCO	Office of members of the Executive and Legislative Councils (Hong Kong)
OPD	Out-patient department
PADS	Port and Airport Development Strategy (Hong Kong)
PAP	People's Armed Police
PBOC	People's Bank of China
PCBC	People's Construction Bank of China
PECC	Pacific Economic Co-operation Conference
PLA	People's Liberation Army
PLC	Political and Legal Commission
PRC	People's Republic of China
PVF	Present value of investment
RMB	*Renminbi* (Chinese dollar)
ROC	Republic of China (Taiwan)
SAR	Special Administrative Region (Hong Kong)
SCMP	*South China Morning Post*
SDR	Special drawing right
SEC	State Education Commission
SEF	Straits Exchange Foundation (Taiwan)
SEZ	Special economic zone
SHBZB	*Shehui baozhang bao* (Social Security News)
SNA	System of national accounts
SOE	State-owned enterprise
SPC	State Planning Commission
STAQ	Securities trading automated quotation system
STAR TV	Satellite Television Asia Region Television
SWB	*Survey of World Broadcast*
TEU	Twenty-foot equivalent unit (container)
UK	United Kingdom
UN	United Nations
UNCTAD	UN Conference on Trade and Development
USA	United States of America
VAT	Value-added tax
VER	Voluntary export restraints
WFO	Wholly foreign-owned enterprise
WIPO	World Intellectual Property Organization
ZGMZ	*Zhongguo minzheng* (Chinese Civil Affairs)
ZGSHB	*Zhongguo shehui bao* (Chinese Society News)

Chronology of 1992

Willy Wo-lap Lam

JANUARY

Three Canadian parliamentarians on a visit to Beijing, Svend Robinson, Geoff Scott and Beryl Gaffney, were on the **7th** allegedly manhandled by Chinese Security after they had visited the homes of dissidents. The trio were deported from the Chinese capital the same day. Ottawa issued a formal protest to the Chinese government.

A national conference on work among the minorities was held in Beijing from the **14th** to the **16th**. Party General Secretary Jiang Zemin pledged that the central authorities would cement solidarity with members of the ethnic minorities and respect their religious and other rights. Jiang said no matter what happened abroad, all nationalities in China would remain united in their joint efforts towards modernization.

Deng Xiaoping embarked on his historic tour of the south from the **18th** to the **21st** of February, visiting cities including Wuchang, Shenzhen, Zhuhai and Shanghai. He rekindled market reform by indicating cadres should not be bothered about whether a policy was "surnamed" socialist or capitalistic so long as it resulted in economic development. He defended his "high-speed growth model," saying fast-paced development was necessary to sustain the momentum of reform. "We must enter a new threshold once every few years," he said.

On the political front, Deng coined the famous slogan: "We must raise our guard against rightism; our priority is preventing leftism." The patriarch railed against a dozen-odd leftists for blocking reform, saying those who resisted reform "should go to sleep." Deng indirectly criticized the "formalism" of General Secretary Jiang Zemin and Premier Li Peng. However, he also faulted former Party chiefs Hu Yaobang and Zhao Ziyang for failing to stem the tide of "bourgeois liberalization." The gist of Deng's remarks was disseminated to Party officials in late February as Central Committee Document No. 2.

China and Israel formally established relations on the **24th**. The joint communiqué on the setting up of full diplomatic ties was signed in Beijing by Chinese Foreign Minister Qian Qichen and his Israeli counterpart, David Levy. Tel Aviv subsequently denied reports Israel had sold military hardware or technology, including know-how behind the Patriot missile, to China.

On the **28th**, Premier Li Peng set off on a nine-day tour of Western Europe which took in Italy, Switzerland, Portugal and Spain. On the **31st**, Li broke his journey to go to New York to attend a summit of the United Nations Security Council. While the Premier was met with demonstrators in most of the cities, his largely successful visit consolidated China's re-entry into the community of nations.

FEBRUARY

On the **5th**, suspected Muslim separatists blew up a bus in Urumqi, capital of the Xinjiang Autonomous Region, killing at least six people and injuring more than twenty. Throughout the year, however, "splittist" activities were kept under control. And to defuse ethnic tensions, the central government decided to adopt the dual approach of iron-fisted repression coupled with giving more economic autonomy to Xinjiang.

In a signed commentary on the **24th**, *People's Daily* called for the "correct" and "adequate" development of the capitalistic economy. "The correct understanding and use of capitalism will benefit the modernization of Chinese socialism and expedite the progress of human society," the official organ said. "Capitalism is an extremely important historical stage in the history of mankind's social development."

The "stocks economy" was ushered into China on the **21st**, when Beijing officially approved the buying and selling of stocks on the Shenzhen and Shanghai bourses. The authorities also sanctioned the issue of the first category of B shares for foreigners. However, through 1992, Beijing turned down applications from other cities to set up the country's third stock exchange.

Seven pro-democracy activists were on the **25th** tried by the Beijing Intermediate Court on charges of "making counter-revolutionary propaganda and incitement." Wu Xuecan, an editor with the Overseas Edition of *People's Daily*, was given a prison term of four years. On 8 April, the assistant foreign editor of *People's Daily*, Qi Lin, was sentenced to four years in jail for allegedly leaking state secrets to a Taiwan newspaper.

MARCH

Beijing began its battle to join the General Agreement on Tariffs and Trade (GATT) on the **1st**, when the *People's Daily* carried Foreign Trade Minister Li Lanqing's long talk on how China's resumption of GATT membership could contribute to world trade. By the end of the year, Chinese tariffs on 3,371 types of products were reduced, representing an overall decrease of import duties by 7.3%. Beijing also indicated it would cede more of the domestic market to foreign corporations, including those which set up joint ventures or wholly-owned companies in China.

In a pivotal meeting on the **9th** and **10th**, the Politburo endorsed the spirit of the Deng Xiaoping talks in southern China. The supreme council pledged that the nation would uphold the "Deng Xiaoping line" for one hundred years. The

Politburo also promised to speed up reform, and to consider "leftist deviation" as the major threat to the Party and nation.

Beijing granted autonomous economic powers to Shanghai and Hainan on respectively the **10th** and the **13th**. Shanghai was given new authority in ten areas, including letting foreign banks open branches in the metropolis and raising funds abroad. Mayor Huang Ju quoted Deng Xiaoping as saying that he hoped Shanghai and Pudong could catch up with and overtake Shenzhen. In Hainan, the 30 sq km Yangpu zone was formally declared a bonded area where free-port policies would be practised.

The fifth session of the Seventh National People's Congress was held in Beijing from the **20th** to 3 April. Premier Li Peng's Government Work Report reflected Deng Xiaoping's exhortations about market reforms. However, Li stuck to the "conservative" growth rate of 6% a year, which was in late 1992 re-adjusted to 10%. The deputies to the Congress made an unprecedented 150 revisions to Li's report. For example, the premier was forced to insert the clause about the priority of the country being to combat "leftism."

The same session gave the approval for the controversial Three Gorges Project. The mega-scheme would be included in the Ten-year Economic Blueprint. Resettlement of the one million or so residents who would be affected by the hydroelectric project began in the latter half of the year. Several deputies, including Huang Shunxing from Taiwan, defied Beijing by openly opposing the project.

China's fledgling commercial space industry suffered a blow when, on the **22nd**, a Long March 2E rocket carrying an Australian communications satellite failed to lift off. A large explosion occurred, but luckily the satellite was not damaged. Another mishap took place on 21 December, when an Australian-owned satellite was lost in space moments after take-off. The Chinese claimed the launch was successful and that the accident was attributable to an explosion of the satellite. "It was a satellite problem, not a launch problem," an Aerospace Ministry spokesman said.

APRIL

Grain subsidies were abolished on a national scale on the **1st**. From this point onwards, the prices of staple agricultural products would to a large extent be determined by the forces of supply and demand. Aside from cutting debilitating subventions, the goal of the drastic move was to raise the enthusiasm of farmers. No major cases of consumer revolt such as demonstrations were reported in 1992.

On the **25th**, Vice-premier Tian Jiyun made a hard-hitting "anti-leftist" speech at the Central Party School. He castigated the remnant Maoists for obstructing such reform programmes as the household responsibility system, township enterprises, and renting large tracts of land to foreign corporations. Tian suggested the creation of a "leftist special zone" for the enemies of reform. In such a paradise for pariahs, food would be rationed and nobody would be allowed to go abroad. Tian's speech was interrupted by repeated rounds of applause, and video tapes of the address became a hot-selling item among intellectuals in the capital.

The country's first major horse-racing event took place in Guangzhou on the **26th**. An estimated 6,000 spectators turned up at the Wang Chuan track. Each shelled out HK$6.50 to buy lottery tickets that offered a top prize of HK$50,000. Otherwise, no gambling was allowed. Throughout the year, horse-racing events were staged in Shenzhen and other cities.

An enlarged meeting of the Central Military Commission (CMC) opened in Beijing the **last week** of the month. Top on the agenda were plans to streamline the military establishment, including the gradual demobilization of up to 700,000 soldiers for the rest of the decade. Three field armies and relatively non-essential units like academies and hospitals were abolished. CMC Vice-chairman Yang Shangkun confirmed his intention to retire from all military positions at the Fourteenth Party Congress.

MAY

Conservative elder Chen Yun indicated on the **1st** that he supported the further development of the open-door policy. While meeting with Shanghai leaders Wu Bangguo and Huang Ju, Chen said he endorsed the opening up of Pudong. It was the first time that Chen, considered the nemesis of Deng Xiaoping, had indicated his support of the new wave of reform.

United States Undersecretary of State for Political Affairs Arnold Kanter said at the end of his visit on the **8th** that the Chinese had agreed to let dissident Liu Qing and trade union leader Han Dongfang leave the country. At the end of the year, Beijing also allowed dissidents including journalists Zhang Weiguo and Wang Ruoshui to take up fellowships in American universities. However, legal scholar Yu Haocheng and Marxist theorist Li Honglin were still barred from leaving. This is in spite of Beijing's pledge to then Secretary of State James Baker in November 1991 that all dissidents not facing criminal charges would be allowed to leave the country.

Deng Xiaoping visited the Capital Iron and Steel Works (*Shougang*) on the **22nd** to give a further impetus to reform. Citing experiments in management at the plant, he seconded granting more autonomy to state enterprises. The patriarch pointed out more reformist cadres should be put in charge of the economy. He particularly heaped praise on Vice-premier Zhu Rongji as one of the few cadres "who understand how the [market] economy works." However, the patriarch complained that many of the instructions he had given during his tour to southern China had not been carried out. "There are people who burrow themselves in Zhongnanhai [Party headquarters], uttering nonsensical remarks," he said.

The Central Committee began dissemination of its Document No. 4 on the **25th**. Regarded since as the Magna Carta for market reforms, the directive extended the open-door policy to the hinterland as well as cities in the border regions. More than thirty cities, including many along major waterways such as the Yangtze River, were immediately given preferential policies on a par with those of Shenzhen and Zhuhai. Overseas corporations would be allowed to go into sectors ranging from infrastructure to the services. With the exception of departments in the police and security departments, Party and government units were given permission to operate businesses on the side.

JUNE

On the **1st**, Beijing's former representative in Hong Kong, Xu Jiatun, published a long essay in two Hong Kong newspapers entitled "Peaceful Development and Progress: Rethink in the Wake of the Low Tide in the World Socialist Movement." It was the first time Xu, 76, who defected to the United States in 1990, had spoken out. The former head of the Hong Kong branch of the New China News Agency urged the Chinese Communist Party to adopt quasi-capitalistic reforms if it is not "to sink like the setting sun." He said the 1989 democracy movement represented a legitimate demand by "all the people for comprehensive, far-reaching reform in politics and economics."

On the **3rd**, Premier Li Peng reversed an earlier decision and let dissident Dai Qing return to Beijing to visit her relatives. Dai, who was on a Nieman Fellowship to Harvard University, had been stranded in Hong Kong for a week. It was the first instance that a jailed dissident who had gone abroad was allowed to return to the mainland. Earlier in the year, Beijing published regulations welcoming overseas-based students and experts to return to China. These included guarantees of "freedom in coming and going."

Immediately prior to and after the third anniversary of the June 4 massacre, security authorities in places including Beijing, Tianjin, Hunan and Gansu arrested scores of dissidents associated with underground organizations. The latter included the Liberal Democratic Party of China, the Free Labour Union of China, the Social Democratic Party of China, the China Progressive Alliance and the All-China People's Autonomous Federation. Only a few of the detainees were put on trial as of the end of the year.

General Secretary Jiang Zemin made the only anti-leftist speech of his career when he addressed the Central Party School on the **9th**. Jiang said leftism manifested itself in a "bookish" and "dogmatic" approach to understanding Marxism, and in "taking class struggle as the key link." He indicated rightist as well as "leftist" errors would lead to the destruction of socialism. The Party chief seconded Deng's high-speed growth model, saying: "We must not lose the opportunity just because of the need to maintain stability [in the economy]."

A group of fifty-odd liberal intellectuals held an "anti-leftist" private conference at the Olympic Hotel in Beijing on the **16th**. Participants included Wang Ruoshui, Wu Zuguang, Yuan Hongbin, Lin Jingyao, Zheng Zhongbing. This was the first unsanctioned gathering of "rightist scholars" after the Tiananmen Square crackdown. Later in the year, the intellectuals published two books attacking remnant Maoism: *The Tides of History* and *Memorandum on Anti-Leftism*.

Also on the **16th**, the State Council made the decision to develop "tertiary industry," or the services sector. Their share of the national economy would be boosted. Moreover, foreign corporations would be allowed to go into tertiary sectors such as retailing and financial services. Throughout the year, major Hong Kong magnates, including Li Ka-shing, Cheng Yiu-tong, Henry Fok, and Peter Woo, made large-scale investments in areas including real estate, shopping malls and port and transportation facilities.

The Chairman of the Chinese People's Political Consultative Congress, Li Xiannian, died in the capital on the **21st**. The former state president, 83, was the first of the so-called Eight Immortals — or first-generation revolutionaries — to depart the stage completely. Li was the nominator of Jiang Zemin as Party General Secretary. Considered a hardliner, the Hubei native funnelled support to the conservative ideologues right until his hospitalization.

JULY

Bao Tong, the right-hand man of ousted Party chief Zhao Ziyang, was on the **21st** sentenced to seven years in jail. The former head of the Central Committee's Research Office for the Reform of the Political Structure, was convicted of "leaking state secrets" and making "counter-revolutionary propaganda." Bao's family said they would appeal the sentence. Influential politicians in the United States, including Senator Edward Kennedy, signed petitions protesting against what they called the trumped-up charges.

The central government announced on the **23rd** a new deal for state enterprises.

The Regulations for Transforming the Management Mechanism of Wholly-Owned People's Enterprises, which were drafted by a team under Vice-premier Zhu Rongji, gave public-sector business units fourteen major autonomous powers. They included freedoms to hire and fire employees; to engage in foreign trade; and to determine their product lines.

Shanghai's *Liberation Daily* reported on the **23rd** that the municipal authorities of Wuhan had abrogated thirteen central-government documents which were deemed incompatible with the spirit of market reforms. The documents included regulations forbidding certain categories of enterprises from becoming shareholding companies. It was the first time that a regional government had dared to challenge central edicts.

The national media published on the **24th** Chen Yun's commemorative essay on the late Li Xiannian, in which the conservative elder gave his blessings to the market reforms of Deng Xiaoping. Chen acknowledged that "practices which were effective in the past may no longer suit the needs of the new situation of reform and the open door." He added while he had never been to the special economic zones, he was concerned that "they be run well." "We must make ceaseless explorations and solve new problems," he wrote.

On the **24th**, the son of elder Bo Yibo, Bo Xicheng, became one of most high-profile officials to resign from their government posts and to join the private sector. The head of the Tourism Bureau of the Beijing municipality set up a private hotel consultancy group. "In reform, someone has to take the lead," the 41-year-old "princeling" said.

AUGUST

Official news agencies revealed on the **4th** that member of the Gang of Four and former Vice-chairman of the Communist Party Wang Hongwen had died of a liver ailment at the age of 58. A close aide of Mao Zedong and Jiang Qing, Wang had been mentioned as a possible successor to the Great Helmsman. Throughout 1992, conservative elements were busy preparing for the centenary of Mao's birth in 1993. New books, poems, films and exhibitions about the still-revered founder of the Republic were planned.

On the **4th**, the Chinese media announced that further autonomous powers would be granted the Capital Iron and Steel Works and that its experience of reformist management would be applied nationwide. In the wake of Deng Xiaoping's visit to the plant, the State Council had given the plant powers including setting up its own bank and opening branches in Hong Kong and abroad.

The first rioting since the pro-democracy demonstrations of 1989 broke out in the special economic zone of Shenzhen on the night of the **10th**. About 10,000 people gathered in the streets to vent their anger at the corruption and gross government inefficiency over the sale of application forms for new share issues. Twelve ruffians were arrested. An investigation report published in December showed more than 4,000 municipal employees, including eight mid-ranking cadres, were involved in graft and other illicit operations. Mayor Zheng Liangyu was in November transferred to the less high-profile position of Vice-governor of Jiangxi province.

Beijing's long-standing efforts at promoting "patriotic education" got a big boost during the Twenty-fifth Olympic Games, which closed in Barcelona, Spain, on the **25th**. The Chinese team romped home sixteen Golds, twenty-two Silvers and sixteen Bronzes. The Chinese Olympians became instant national heroes — and millionaires.

China and South Korea established diplomatic ties on the **24th**. The Joint Communiqué signed between Chinese Foreign Minister Qian Qichen and his South Korean counterpart, Lee Sang Ock, said the new relations "will be conducive to the relaxation of tension on the Korean Peninsula." Informally, Seoul undertook to increase investment in China as well as to boost bilateral trade. Beijing pledged to persuade North Korea to allow international inspection of its nuclear facilities.

SEPTEMBER

In the **first week** of this month, Beijing began to disseminate Central Committee Document No. 9 on policies on propaganda, the mass media and culture. The gist of the directive was that media and cultural units would be given a higher degree of freedom provided they did not break the law or go against the Party line. "So long as news and cultural workers are operating within the law and the constitution, do not interfere with them," the document said. It urged that media articles be "concise and to the point," and that they make contributions to the economy and to the increase in the flow of information.

Dissident Shen Tong was arrested on the **1st** hours before he was due to give a press conference in Beijing on the formation of the Chinese branch of his Boston-based Democracy for China Fund. A student leader of the Tiananmen Square movement, Shen had left China for the United States soon after the massacre. He returned to the mainland in late July 1992 to make contact with and to interview a large number of dissidents in Changsha and other cities. At least a dozen of these underground activists were detained after Shen's arrest. Shen was released on 24 October.

American President George Bush decided on the **2nd** to sell 150 F-16 fighters to

Taiwan. Although the jets, which would be delivered to the island in the mid-1990s, were of the less sophisticated A and B models, the move elicited strong condemnation from Beijing. In an apparent act of good will to the new administration of President Bill Clinton, however, Beijing did not take any concrete action against Washington.

The Taiwan media confirmed on the **10th** that Paris had agreed to the sale of sixty Mirage 2000-5 jets to the island. Unlike the case of the F-16 deal, Beijing reacted swiftly by first freezing the French out of commercial projects like the Guangzhou subway and then closing the French consulate in Guangzhou in early 1993.

People-to-people exchanges across the Taiwan Strait took a leap forward on the **5th** when eighteen reporters from seventeen mainland news organizations began their first-ever tour of Taiwan. A spate of famous Chinese scholars, including economist Tong Dalin and scientist Tan Jiazhen, also visited the Kuomintang-held island in 1992.

OCTOBER

The ninth plenum of the Thirteenth Central Committee was held on the **9th** to settle the question of ousted Party chief Zhao Ziyang. The plenary session upheld the decision of the fourth plenum of 24 June 1989, that Zhao was guilty of supporting the 1989 "turmoil" and "splitting the Party." However, no criminal charges would be brought against the 73-year-old leader, who lived in a guarded compound in the heart of the capital.

The Fourteenth Congress of the Chinese Communist Party was held in Beijing from the **12th** to the **18th**. Party General Secretary Jiang Zemin's Political Report laid down the fundamentals of the "socialist market economy," indicating that the role of the marketplace would be boosted. The Party chief reaffirmed the priority of combating "leftism" but also called for steps to counter the "peaceful evolution" plot of "hostile foreign forces." In a message to the Politburo four days before the Congress convened, Deng Xiaoping indicated Chief Political Commissar Yang Baibing would be relieved of all his military powers.

The Central Advisory Commission was abolished. The stage was set for a number of elders, including Chen Yun, Bo Yibo, Yao Yilin, Song Ping and Wu Xueqian, to retire from politics. The new 189 Central Committee members elected a Politburo which was notable for the number of technocrats and regional representatives. The members of the supreme council were: Jiang Zemin, Li Peng, Qiao Shi, Li Ruihuan, Zhu Rongji, Liu Huaqing, Hu Jintao (Standing Committee members); Tian Jiyun, Zou Jiahua, Li Tieying, Qian Qichen, Yang Baibing, Wei Jianxing, Chen Xitong, Wu Bangguo, Tan

Shaowen, Xie Fei, Jiang Chunyun (ordinary members); and Wen Jiabao and Wang Hanbin (alternate members).

A thorough-going military reshuffle took place immediately before and after the Fourteenth Party Congress. About 300 officers, many of whom were suspected to have ties to the Yang Clan (President Yang Shangkun and former Chief Political Commissar Yang Baibing), were removed, retired, or transferred to less sensitive positions. The composition of the Central Military Commission was announced on the **19th**. Jiang Zemin retained his position as Chairman of the Commission. The two new Vice-chairmen were Liu Huaqing and Zhang Zhen. Zhang Wannian became Chief of the General Staff, Yu Yongbo, Chief of the General Political Department, and Fu Quanyou, Chief of the General Logistics Department. The three, in addition to Defence Minister-designate Chi Haotian, were the new ordinary members of the CMC.

There were major reshuffles in the three major departments at headquarters as well as the Air Force and the Navy. The new regional line-up was as follows: Beijing Military Region (MR) Commander Wang Chengbin, Commissar Gu Shanqing (new); Chengdu MR Commander Li Jiulong, Commissar Zhang Gong (new); Guangzhou MR Commander Li Xilin (new), Commissar Shi Yuxiao (new); Jinan MR Commander Zhang Taiheng (new), Commissar Song Qingwei; Lanzhou MR Commander Liu Jingsong (new), Commissar Cao Pengsheng (new); Nanjing MR Commander Gu Hui, Commissar Liu Anyuan (new); Shenyang MR Commander Wang Ke (new), Commissar Song Keda.

Japan's Emperor Akihito made a historic visit to China from the **23rd** to the **28th**. At a banquet hosted by President Yang Shangkun, the monarch said he "deeply deplored" the "great suffering" Tokyo had inflicted upon China during World War II. However, Akihito stopped short of a formal apology, which was demanded by anti-war groups in China, Taiwan and Hong Kong. Prior to the visit, Beijing activist Tong Zeng had collected 300,000 signatures demanding a formal apology as well as full indemnities for the victims of Japanese atrocities. Tong's unofficial organization also located scores of "comfort women," many of whom were ethnic Koreans, who were forced to serve Japanese soldiers during the war.

On the **25th**, the State Council set up two specialist commissions to boost "macro-management" over the country's budding securities market. The Securities Committee, headed by Vice-premier Zhu Rongji, was charged with formulating overall policies for the development of stock exchanges and the conversion of state companies into shareholding concerns. Its executive arm, the Securities Supervison and Administration Committee, was headed by former central banker Liu Hongru.

Leung Wai-man, a reporter for the Hong Kong newspaper *Express News* was arrested by Beijing's security agents on the **25th** for "bribing" a Chinese state journalist. Leung was released on 1 November. However, her alleged informant, a reporter for the New China News Agency, remained in custody as of early 1993. One week before the Fourteenth Party Congress opened, *Express News* had published Jiang Zemin's Political Report in full.

NOVEMBER

The "Beida crisis" — or creeping doubts about the standards of China's premier institute of higher learning, Beijing University (Beida) — erupted in the **first week** of the month with the publication of a first-ever survey of college students. Of the respondents 49.4% said they were "deeply worried" about the academic standards of Beida as well as the socio-political atmosphere there. A total of 46.1% attributed the crisis to the year-long compulsory military training for first-year students. Also, 30.7% cited "administrative interference," meaning excessive political control.

The Chinese government extended an olive branch to Bill Clinton upon his election as US President on the **2nd**. The Foreign Ministry said Beijing was "ready to work with the new US administration in the improvement and development of bilateral ties." Soon after the election, Beijing announced it was buying a new instalment of American wheat. Top leaders including Jiang Zemin and Li Peng made it a point to receive almost every congressional delegation to Beijing.

A Boeing 737 jet belonging to Southern Airlines rammed into the hills of scenic Guilin on the **24th**, killing all 141 on board. Partly because the black box or flight recorder was damaged, the reasons for the worst crash in Chinese civil aviation history were not ascertained. On 31 July, another airplane crashed over Nanjing, killing 109 passengers.

On the **25th**, Beijing released on parole philosopher and historian Bao Zunxin nineteen months before his five-year term was up. Bao, 55, was suffering from a heart ailment and other diseases. The authorities claimed Bao showed "deep regrets" for his role in the 1989 democracy movement and that he had "shown his repentance." Bao denied the allegations.

Premier Li Peng began a three-day visit to Hanoi on the **30th**, the first head of the Chinese government to call on Vietnam in twenty-one years. Li signed four treaties on economic exchanges, border trade and technological cooperation. He and Vietnamese Premier Vo Van Kiet agreed not to use force to settle territorial disputes over the Spratly Islands.

Chronology of 1992 xxxi

DECEMBER

Politburo member and Deng Xiaoping loyalist Ding Guan'gen was appointed Head of the Propaganda Department on the **3rd** as part of an effort by the patriarch to clean up the leftist ideology and propaganda establishment. Other appointments in this arena included the replacement of He Jingzhi by Liu Zhongde as head of the Ministry of Culture. However, several conservative cadres either gained promotions or retained their jobs. For example, Shao Huaze was appointed Director of *People's Daily*, and former head of the Propaganda Department Wang Renzhi was made Party secretary of the Chinese Academy of Social Sciences.

On the **6th**, Beijing announced a new deal for the nation's budding private entrepreneurs. Except for a small number of product lines and resources, private-sector entrepreneurs could take part in all industrial and commercial activities. They were also allowed to do business with foreign companies or set up branches overseas. By late 1992, there were fourteen million "individual entrepreneur households" and 120,000 private companies.

During his visit to Beijing from the **17th** to the **19th**, Russian President Boris Yeltsin signed with his hosts twenty-four statements, documents and memorandums of understanding in areas including trade, military and technological cooperation, and space exploration. Troops along the 2,700-km Sino-Russian border would further be cut. In return for Chinese loans and investments, Moscow would provide further technological help for the renovation of Chinese factories built in the 1950s with Soviet assistance. The Chinese reportedly raised the possibility of buying one or two Kiev-class aircraft carriers from Moscow.

Island-wide elections were held in Taiwan on the **19th** to elect the 161 members of the Legislative Yuan. The ruling Kuomintang (KMT) suffered a setback as it got only 61.67% of the votes, which translated into ninety-six legislative seats. The opposition Democratic Progressive Party (DPP) won 36.09% of the votes, or fifty seats. It was the first time that the DPP had gained more than 35% of popular support. The opposition downplayed Taiwanese independene in its campaign and instead trained its firepower on the "money politics" of the KMT. Since a large number of unsuccessful KMT candidates were fielded by the "mainstream faction" of Lee Teng-hui, the authority of the largely popular president was dented.

In a national meeting on judicial work held in Beijing on the **21st**, President of the Supreme Court Ren Jianxin vowed to use legal means to guarantee the implementation of the socialist market economy. "The market economy is in a sense an economy [regulated by] a legal system," said Ren, who is usually classified as a conservative. "Courts of various levels should use legal means to regulate and harmonize economic relations." At the same time, the National People's Congress pledged to introduce a series of legislations to expedite the realization of a market economy. New laws under study covered areas including finance, securities, accounting and company formation.

Orders to cool down the economy were given by Premier Li Peng and Vice-premier Zhu Rongji at a national meeting on the economy on the **24th**. In an apparent reference to the "high growth model" advocated by Deng Xiaoping, Li said speed must be based on "a rational structure that matches the needs of the market and that has a good productivity." The premier said "macro-level control by the state" would be strengthened in areas including credit and infrastructure building. Earlier, Zhu had cited three areas of the economy that were particularly overheated: stocks, real estate and development zones. The economy grew by 12.8% in 1992.

Premier Li Peng affirmed the primacy of agriculture in a national meeting on agrarian work on the **29th**. "Without agriculture, there will be instability and chaos," he said. The premier expressed fears that the development of industry, commerce and particularly real estate would diminish farm land as well as capital injection into agriculture. He vowed that the state would increase investment in agriculture and guarantee the income of farmers and the stability of the prices of produce.

1

Introduction

Joseph Cheng Yu-shek

The year 1992 was a successful year for China. It achieved double-digit growth in the year and anticipated the same spectacular growth rate in the following year. Signs of an over-heated economy began to emerge in the latter half of 1992, but few would expect a repetition of the crises in the previous decade.

Economic reforms again picked up momentum after Deng Xiaoping's trip to southern China in early 1992. Deng's stand on the acceleration of economic reforms and opening to the outside world was clear and uncompromising; and he seemed to appreciate that his status in Chinese history would mainly depend on the success of the reforms. In contrast, he still assumed a balancing role in politics and on the issue of political succession. The Fourteenth Party Congress failed to reverse the verdict on Zhao Ziyang and offered no initiative on political reforms.

Diplomatically, China appeared to have accommodated itself well to the new international order. It demonstrated considerable sophistication in its trade negotiations with the United States, often making the minimum necessary concessions in the final stages. Contrary to some expectations, China successfully established good relations with members of the Commonwealth of Independent States after the breakup of the Soviet Union. Economic and military cooperation with Russia made considerable progress. China had fully recovered from the extremely difficult position in the wake of the Tiananmen Incident and the significant changes in Eastern Europe and the Soviet Union two or three years ago.

The "Peaceful Evolution" Conspiracy

In summing up China's diplomacy in 1992, the Chinese media indicated that Chinese foreign policy had been omni-directional, and they especially focused on the visits to China in the year by South Korea President Roh Tae Woo, Japanese Emperor Akihito and Russian President Boris Yeltsin.[1] The focus was explained in terms of China's central task, economic construction, which required domestic stability and a peaceful international environment. That was also why China had been paying special attention to its neighbours, including Vietnam and India. On the whole, the Chinese leaders could congratulate themselves on their diplomatic achievements in 1992 which had substantially reduced the risks of external conflicts.

On the other hand, despite the above success, the sense of insecurity on the part of the Chinese leaders had not abated. Their suspicions of a

Introduction 1.3

"peaceful evolution" conspiracy targeted against China by the western countries was exacerbated by the arms sales to Taiwan by the United States and France, as well as the political reform proposals in Hong Kong initiated by the new Governor, Christopher Patten.

In a report given by the Minister of Public Security, Tao Siju, at the Central Party School in 1991, Tao stated that "hostile international forces have made our nation a key target for stepping up all kinds of activities of subversion and destruction. They openly declare that their missions in this age are to 'advance the realization of democracy throughout the entire world' and place the Soviet Union, China and the Third World into the western order."[2] Similarly, the Chinese Communist Party (CCP) in late 1991 launched a low-key education campaign against "peaceful evolution." From the documents obtained abroad, one can see that "peaceful evolution" was considered a very comprehensive global strategy of western countries led by the United States.[3] Politically, the western countries would use human rights as an excuse to create an international anti-Beijing sentiment and would support pro-democracy organizations outside China. Economically, they would use China's most-favoured-nation status to exert pressure on the Chinese government to enhance democracy, release political prisoners, etc. Western criticisms of and sanctions against exports of prison labour products and failure to protect intellectual property rights were simply seen as political blackmail. Militarily, the western countries still used Coordinating Committee for Multilateral Export Controls (COCOM) to ban the export of high technology to China, and, diplomatically, they were continuing their attempts to isolate China too. At the same time, western media, as well as various cultural and academic exchange programmes with the West, were seen as part of an infiltration and subversion campaign against China.

The "peaceful evolution" conspiracy theory was held not only by the conservative cadres in the ideological and propaganda sphere. In the campaign against Christopher Patten's political reform proposals for Hong Kong, the entire Chinese leadership apparently subscribed to the theory in explaining the motivations behind the British administration's proposals. A very broad spectrum of the intelligentsia shared this perception too.

To some extent, in view of the recent collapse of the Soviet Union and the dramatic changes in Eastern Europe, a certain sense of insecurity and xenophobia among the leadership of the remaining major socialist country was only natural, and it did not hinder the opening of China to the outside world. Jiang Zemin, General Secretary of the Central Committee (CC) of the CCP, in his report to the Fourteenth National Congress of the Party on 12 October 1992, clearly promised "to open wider to the outside world and make more and better use of foreign funds, resources, technology and management expertise."[4] Few would doubt that this is the irreversible trend in the foreseeable future.

Despite suspicions of the West's "peaceful evolution" conspiracy, China was believed to have begun to cut back the People's Liberation Army (PLA) by nearly 10% in April 1992 to help boost a military modernization programme which had been suffering because of a lack of funds.[5] It was planned that some 260,000 of the PLA's 3.2 million troops would be demobilized over the next few years, with the bulk of reductions likely to come from the 2.3 million ground forces. Even bigger reductions might be on the way following the collapse of the Soviet Union and the relaxation of tensions along China's other borders. Admittedly, the main priority was to highlight the development of a small number of select rapid-development units. At the end of the year, however, such plans for troop reduction seemed to have been shelved as PLA leaders argued that the armed forces' existing size was the minimum required to defend the country.

The "peaceful evolution" conspiracy would help to account for any possible deterioration in China's relations with the West, and it would offer a convenient excuse to fend off western countries' criticisms of China's human rights conditions. The conspiracy theory would continue to haunt China's opening to the outside world. But the theory's most important impact would be to legitimize the Chinese Communist regime and its attempts to resist political liberalization. Together with the Tiananmen Incident of 4 June 1989, the "peaceful evolution" conspiracy scared the Chinese leaders away from their commitment to political reforms manifested in Zhao Ziyang's report to the Thirteenth Party Congress in October 1987.[6]

Political Reforms

A major theme of Zhao Ziyang's report had been that the economic reforms of recent years had added urgency to demands for political structural reform. The long-term goal had been to create a "socialist political system with a high degree of democracy" supported and underpinned by comprehensive legislation. Central to political reform had been the separation of Party powers from those of the government. Party leadership had meant political leadership. Current over-centralization of administrative, economic and cultural powers in Party committees and other organs, at both central and local levels, should have been remedied through the delegation of authority to lower levels. A spirit of competition would have been encouraged between cadres, and public supervision of their activities provided for. A system of social consultative dialogue had also been suggested. In sum, Zhao's report had concluded, "Without political structural reform, economic structural reform cannot ultimately achieve success."

In comparison, Jiang Zemin's report to the Fourteenth Party Congress had very little to offer in terms of political structural reform, his approach was rather "to reform the administrative system and the organizational structure of the Party and the government so as to bring about a change in their functions, straighten out their relations, simplify administration and improve efficiency." But even the establishment of the public service system had yet to materialize. Jiang's report specifically ruled out "a western, multiparty, parliamentary system." It declared that "democracy among the people is an essential requirement of socialism and one of its intrinsic characteristics," thus implying that no major political structural reform would be necessary. The Fourteenth Party Congress was noted for its limited access given to the domestic and international media too.

Despite the political conservatism, historians would remember that the Fourteenth Party Congress, compared with other congresses since 1949, had the least impact on people's daily life. It showed that the regime had almost completed its transformation from a totalitarian to an authoritarian one. As long as the Party leadership was not threatened, it would be willing to tolerate the expanding freedoms of the people. In the last quarter of 1992, people in mainland China were apparently more concerned with making a few more Renminbi (RMB) than with the Party Congress or the political succession issue. For once, they were "economic animals" more pressing than Hong Kong people worrying about the Sino-British confrontation over the new Governor's political reform proposals.

While the Chinese people were confident that economic reform and opening to the outside world were the inevitable trends of the future, they also had a vague fear that short-term reversals might emerge when Deng Xiaoping joined Marx. Deng obviously hoped that the trappings of a Mao-style personality cult would contribute to his political succession arrangements. Two of his hand-picked successors, CCP General Secretaries Hu Yaobang and Zhao Ziyang, had already fallen. With no convincing heir apparent left to act as his proxy, Deng had to hit the campaign trail himself before the Fourteenth Party Congress. It appeared that Deng planned to avoid sharp contradictions in the transitional period after his death and opted for a power structure which could guarantee the upholding of his policy line and balance various political forces. The arrangements also aimed to give his successors time to consolidate and establish their credentials.

Willy Wo-lap Lam's chapter offers an analysis of the new leadership line-up at the Fourteenth Party Congress. Military reshuffles aimed at terminating the influence of Yang Shangkun and Yang Baibing in the PLA continued after the Party Congress.[7] While there were many theories explaining the demise of the Yang brothers, their abdication to Liu Huaqing and Zhang Zhen reaffirmed Deng's desire for stability. Yang Shangkun's support for Deng had never been in doubt. The crucial issue was whether the Yang brothers had the prestige and credentials to control the PLA after Deng. Were this not the case, then contradictions within the PLA could well become the first point of explosion. The contributions of Liu and Zhang to the stability within the PLA were a significant asset in the eyes of Deng. The latter certainly remembered how old marshals like Ye Jianying had paved the way for his political comeback in the wake of Mao Zedong's death.

Political succession arrangements were insufficient to guarantee stability in the post-Deng era. The core of the Dengist policy line was to secure political stability and Party leadership with economic reforms. In a way, Deng offered a much larger bird cage than Chen Yun; and Deng's bird cage was in turn modelled on Singapore, South Korea and Taiwan. However, successful neo-authoritarian rule had to be backed by respectable economic performance, as the example of the "four little dragons" in Asia well illustrated. Difficult hurdles lay ahead of Deng's pursuit of political stability, and even the limited goal of reforming the administrative system and the organizational structure of the Party and the government was one of them.

A considerable portion of incumbent cadres' jobs in the Party and government were sinecures. Finding them alternative employment would be an immensely difficult task. Over the past few years, the CCP Central Committee and the State Council had issued numerous memoranda containing new regulations aimed at streamlining and cutting back Party and government organizations. However, according to Ministry of Finance figures, national administrative spending for 1980 had totalled RMB40.4 billion. By 1990, that amount had risen to over RMB140 billion.[8] The same source indicated that in 1990 national and local administrative agencies spent an average of RMB3,000 to 5,000 annually on each employee. At the end of 1991, it was estimated that administrative expenditure amounted to over 40% of total financial revenues, placing an excessive burden on the nation's finance.

Corruption

In the recent campaign to streamline Party and government agencies, the Chinese authorities encouraged the redundant cadres to move to service industries. This further exacerbated the abuses and corruption generated by Party and government cadres engaging in business and setting up companies. The combination of business and power adversely affected the normal operation and services of the Party and government agencies, as well as damaged their image and their relations with the masses. In many cases, the businesses of Party and government cadres had a detrimental influence on local commerce, disrupted normal supply and marketing operations and reduced financial revenues. Furthermore, there was no guarantee that such businesses could make money, some of them accumulating considerable debts too.[9] Under such circumstances, many senior cadres were willing to give up their "iron rice bowls" to engage in business, as they realized that wealth in China was also an important source of power, and that power and relationship networks could be exchanged for money. In the long term, this development may contribute to the emergence of a more pluralistic society in China; but the immediate impact was an enhancement of the people's skepticism regarding the Chinese leaders' determination to combat corruption.

Since Deng Xiaoping's trip to southern China in early 1992, many children and relatives of high-ranking cadres had been going southward in search of business opportunities. People in the southern provinces were worried. From March onwards, many "princelings" requested to work in Shenzhen, Zhuhai, Hainan, Fujian and other areas. It was said that the desk of Li Hao, secretary of the Shenzhen Municipal Party Committee, was piled high with such applications. Among the most notable of them were Deng Zhifang, Deng Xiaoping's second son, Chen Fang, Chen Yun's second son, and Liao Chun, Liao Chengzhi's eldest son.[10] They set up joint ventures to engage in the real estate markets and businesses of boom towns such as Shenzhen and Huizhou (a Guangdong municipality close to Hong

Kong). As the government began to ease import restrictions later in the year, a brisk trade in import/export approvals also emerged.

Local officials and entrepreneurs observed that the "princelings" were acting more independently this time. Power appeared to be less centralized, and was not consolidated in any group, as had been the case of the Kanghua Company. Many of them considered that some official graft might prove unavoidable, though it would not be possible for the economic activities of the entire region to come under the control of a small clique of "princelings." Local governments facilitated the involvement of the "princelings" in local business for two important reasons. They believed that many "princelings" would eventually inherit from their fathers senior political positions. Their participation in business activities now would encourage them to support reform and opening to the outside world once they were in power. Secondly, the "princelings" might serve as a valuable bridge of communication between the local governments and the central leaders.

Indeed, relationship networks and official graft almost became a way of life in China. Genuine efforts to eliminate corruption went against the Chinese leadership's principle of "stability takes precedence over all."[11] Like their counterparts in so many developing countries, Chinese people in the early 1990s were cynical rather than angry at corruption. Foreign businessmen certainly accepted it and were willing to absorb the costs. Arguably, corruption served as lubricant and facilitated business transactions. On the other hand, corruption when combined with ignorant and incompetent officials could easily lead to incidents such as the Shenzhen stock market scandal in August 1992. Expanding inequalities in the rapidly modernizing economy generated a lot of grievances, and corruption could be the catalyst for another Tiananmen Incident.

The Shenzhen stock market scandal also demonstrated the extent of incompetence of the officials in the Special Economic Zone which had been boasting of its ability to attract talents from all over China. The success of neo-authoritarian rule in the "four little dragons" of Asia had all depended on the respectable performance of a highly-qualified civil service which had much to contribute in the modernization process. If Shenzhen could not develop a technocracy of a satisfactory calibre, the central bureaucracy would find it much more difficult to do so. The loss of tens of thousands of overseas students to western countries after the Tiananmen Incident would exact a heavy price on China's modernization process. With the changing values in the Chinese society, the Party and government bureaucracies would have less attraction for the top graduates of the elite universities. In 1992, even Beijing University had difficulty in filling its enrolment quota. The one-year military training was an obvious handicap, but the more significant cause was the preference of university students to stay in the major cities after graduation. They thus avoided tertiary institutions which would allocate them jobs all over the country.

All these phenomena reflected the urgency for the establishment of an elite civil service which would offer a satisfactory remuneration package to attract the talents. This would also be the only effective way to combat corruption among cadres.

Supervisory Mechanisms

In his report to the Fourteenth Party Congress, Jiang Zemin pledged to "improve the work of the organs supervising law enforcement and government administration, recognize the importance of supervision by public opinion through the media and gradually perfect the supervisory mechanism." However, since the Tiananmen Incident of June 1989, the National People's Congress (NPC), the Chinese People's Political Consultative Congress (CPPCC) and the mass media had been performing poorly in their supervisory role. Compared with the two or three years before the crisis, these supervisory mechanisms had considerably less room for manoeuvre. There were more censorship and restrictions in the annual NPC and CPPCC sessions, and the media were under pressure not to report the more severe criticisms. Covering of the Fourteenth Party Congress offered a good example. The media since 1989 were obviously under the control of the "leftists." The personnel reshuffles in the second half of 1992 simply removed the most unpopular of these "leftists," but there were few indicators that an era of liberalization would follow.

Leading literary figures did make use of the Party Congress to articulate their grievances. Their statements in the wake of the congresses were centred on how "ultra-leftist" influence had wrought havoc in China in the past four decades and had remained intact after various setbacks, as well as on the control of the literary and art circle by "ultra-leftists" after June 1989, thus leading to the poor performance in these areas.[12] But they seemed to realize too that Deng Xiaoping would continue to uphold the "Four Cardinal Principles" in the ideological sphere, and the Chinese leadership's support for freedom in literary and artistic creativity would be limited.

The most encouraging sign of the recognition of the significance of public opinion was probably the emergence of all types of hotline services in the Chinese cities for people to air their grievances and make enquiries. In 1986, Tianjin started an "Urgent Seek-Help Telephone" service and was quickly followed by many municipalities and provinces.[13] It appeared that these hotline services acting as a safety-valve to release social pressure were welcome by both the Chinese authorities and the people. In Guangzhou and Hangzhou, even the mayors offered to attend to the hotline telephone calls. According to a survey, cadres, workers, students and military personnel were among the more frequent users of the services.

Incidentally, the Chinese authorities were also inclined to allow political dissidents to leave the country and settle overseas. It was said that the Ministry of Public Security had received orders not to create artificial barriers to prevent political dissidents from leaving the country. In some cases, the influential activists involved in the Tiananmen Incident might even have been persuaded to go abroad after their release from prison. Family members of the political dissidents would also be given the same green light to leave China. The Chinese authorities believed that political dissidents could make little impact in western countries, whereas they would be a serious element of political instability if allowed to stay in the major cities such as Beijing, Shanghai and Tianjin.[14]

Socialist Market Economy

Perhaps, the greatest contribution of Deng Xiaoping's southern tour in early 1992 and the Party Congress was the affirmation of the theme of socialist market economy. In the absence of the development of a market economy, without confirmation that the socialist economy also had to adopt a market economic structure, economic reforms could no longer make much headway at this stage in China. Deng Xiaoping's personal charisma and prestige naturally assumed an important role in securing the acceptance of the theme. In fact, since 1979, Deng himself had used the concept of market economy a few times as the equivalent of a commodity economy, although the concept had yet to be adopted in formal Party documents. In Deng's speeches during his southern tour, he severely criticized the controversies regarding the distinction between capitalism and socialism. He instead presented the following three pragmatic criteria: beneficial for the development of productivity, beneficial for the raising of the people's living standards, and beneficial for the growth of comprehensive national power.

The official recognition of the concept of socialist market economy concluded a fluctuating development process over more than a decade. At the end of 1978, the third plenum of the Eleventh CC of the CCP advocated "the shifting of the emphasis of Party work to socialist modernizing construction"; it also appealed for the observance of economic laws and respect for the law of value. At the Twelfth Party Congress, the policy line had been re-defined as "economic planning as the mainstay, market as the supplement." The third plenum of the Twelfth CC of the CCP adopted the "Decision on Economic Structure Reform" which raised the concept of "planned commodity economy on the basis of public ownership." At the Thirteenth Party Congress, the planned commodity economy was depicted as "a structure in which planning and market are unified internally." Since the fourth plenum of the Thirteenth CC, the term "economic structure integrating economic planning and market" had been commonly used; and it was at the Fourteenth Party Congress that the concept of "socialist market economy" finally secured official recognition.

The development of concepts and theories in the past fourteen years had obviously fallen behind the actual progress of market economy. It had also reflected the hindrance imposed by politics and ideology on reforms, opening to the outside world and the development of market economy. The Chinese authorities so far had made no attempt to distinguish between socialist market economy and market economy. Probably the crux of the matter was that the word "socialist" was needed to legitimize the leadership of the Party, the most important principle among the "Four Cardinal Principles."

Despite the spectacular economic achievements (economic growth rate of 12% in 1992, and a slightly lower rate anticipated for 1993), the risks for a smooth transition to a market economy were considerable. In the first place, economic planning had been practised for almost four decades. It had imposed certain bondage and restraints on the thoughts, psychology and life of the Chinese people. It would take a lot of efforts to break from the tradition. Secondly, the state enterprises remained a huge burden. The present situation was that one-third of them were losing money, and another third were incurring hidden losses. These state enterprises were dependent on state subsidies to maintain production. Among the over one hundred million employees of the state enterprises, at least thirty million could be made redundant. Finally, as the economic reforms proceeded, social unrest emerged because of the following factors: (a) serious inflation because of price reforms; (b) unemployment because of the streamlining of Party and government organizations and the forcing of the money-losing state enterprises to go bankrupt or to reduce the labour force; and, (c) grievances among the lowly-paid civil servants and those in educational and cultural institutions in view of the worsening income inequality.

The Chinese leaders, therefore, had to demonstrate the necessary determination and commitment to complete the transition to market economy. Undoubtedly a lot of resistance existed because of general inertia and conservatism, obstruction from vested interests, transient social and economic grievances, etc. Furthermore, the Party and government had to accept a curtailment of their powers and functions and establish the necessary system and legal framework to protect the autonomy of enterprises. In the intermediate term, the Party had to initiate the adaptation of the communist ideology to the market economy. Organs in the propaganda, education and cultural spheres had to be reformed to generate a new social order compatible with and supportive of a market economy.

State Enterprises

The problems of state enterprises deserve further attention here. Rural village enterprises, which once compared themselves to "motherless children," had been expanding to such an extent that they had been able to take over state enterprises in some cases.[15] Their secret could be summed up in one word: autonomy. Autonomous rural village enterprises were run as business enterprises following the rules of market economy. They were pragmatic and free of bureaucratic red tape. They had to deliver and, therefore, had to pay attention to quality of products and efficiency. They were able to pay high salaries to attract talents and reward hard work. In many cases, they were flexible in using bribes as lubricants to facilitate rapid transactions. State enterprises were further handicapped in two ways. Many rural village enterprises were established with employees picked from the ranks of state enterprises. A high proportion of these employees still enjoyed the accommodation, health care, education funding and other benefits which came with their original positions, thus adding to the burden of the state enterprises. The latter's remuneration packages for their employees, taking all benefits into account, were much more substantial than the salaries, but such packages provided no incentive for conscientious work.[16]

Further development of the market economy would on one hand give much greater autonomy to state enterprises and, on the other, allow the failing state enterprises to be taken over or amalgamated. In both cases, it would imply curtailment of the functions and powers of the government, and a shrinking of the revenue base of the central government. The larger-scale rural village enterprises were mostly backed by local governments and enjoyed good access to local resources, and they, therefore, would be strong candidates to take over or amalgamate with state enterprises. Since most large-scale rural village enterprises were collectively owned, this would also be more palatable politically to the Chinese Communist regime, when compared with the remaining alternatives, namely, bankruptcy of the failing state enterprises or their take-over by foreign investors and individual entrepreneurs. In view of the inadequate legal framework, however, there was danger that these collectively-owned enterprises could be transformed into the private assets of corrupt officials.

Jiang Zemin's report to the Party Congress promised "to separate the functions of the government from those of enterprises. Governments at all levels should refrain from intervening in areas where the state has decreed that functions and powers belong to enterprises." In some provinces and municipalities, part of the functions and powers regarding the supervision of enterprises had been transferred to official or semi-official chambers of commerce. Enterprises simply had to report to the chambers of commerce, and the latter might not have concrete powers over enterprises. Other provinces even abolished certain bureaus responsible for economic work, and the officials were sent to work in business corporations in an effort to streamline government organization. For example, Guangdong abolished the Food Bureau some time ago, and recently it also cancelled the Commerce Bureau. At the county level and below, the trend was for organs in charge of economic production to become self-supporting centres, and administrative cadres to be transferred to rural village enterprises.[17] In the development towards "small government, big enterprise," some progressive cadres had already adopted a new mentality compatible with the socialist market economy: "You make money, I collect tax; you go bankrupt, I don't care; you break the law, I shall investigate." Admittedly, such cadres were still a minority.

Danger Signals

While the economic reforms were encouraging, worries began to emerge concerning the overheating of the economy in the second half of 1992. On the second last day of the year, the Chinese government formally announced that gross domestic product had grown at an annual rate of 12%.[18] One should remember that Premier Li Peng in his keynote address to the NPC in April had still been touting a modest growth rate of 6%, in line with the Five-year Plan projections but in defiance of Deng Xiaoping's exhortations. The Chinese government also revealed that money supply growth exceeded the original target of RMB80 to 90 billion, and that double-digit inflation would be very likely in 1993. Industrial growth of 20% in 1992 was matched by an upsurge in retail sales. But an unhealthy proportion of this turnover reflected institutional demand, while individuals still shunned shoddy consumer goods from state enterprises. As a result, the notional value of unsold inventory in the state sector rose sharply, exacerbating the intractable problem of "debt chains." A related phenomenon was the increase in total savings, which surpassed RMB1,000 billion in the year.

Despite the poor performance of state enterprises, their new investments were increasing, and they amounted to nearly RMB1 trillion in the first six months of 1992, a 20% increase over the same period of 1991.[19] The allocation as well as the magnitude of the investments was worrying. The outlays were concentrated in processing industries and local government construction. As a result, raw material prices rose, and transport bottlenecks and power brown-outs became more common. The reformists' dilemma, according to Wu Jinglian, a famous economist and an advisor to the State Council, was a result of missed opportunities. Two or three years ago, China had a golden path to further reform. Instead, the Chinese authorities put their efforts into bailing out lukewarm state industries and involving themselves in endless debates on the speed of reform. Now, when the country had reached a consensus, the favourable climate no longer existed.[20]

At the end of the year, the worsening agricultural problems caught the attention of the State Council too. Premier Li Peng planned to call a national telephone conference, appealing to the local governments to emphasize the agricultural issues, and avoid being blindly absorbed by the "real estate fever" and the "development zone fever."[21] The reasons for this attention were simple: peasants who made up about 75% of the

Chinese population had strong dissatisfaction because of their increasing financial burden and slow growth in income. Since the price reforms in 1991, prices of industrial inputs for agricultural production had been rising substantially. At the same time, food grain prices had been in decline and in some cases, coarse grain could not even be sold. Furthermore, though agricultural taxes were not heavy, all kinds of levies and charges in the rural areas had been increasing rapidly. The Chinese authorities hoped that the streamlining of the sub-provincial government structure would help reduce the peasants' burden, and that diversification of agricultural products would enhance their income. The distribution system presented a problem too. Since the rural reforms, each county, township and village had become its own centre for distributing agricultural products. Conflicts of interest and authority often occurred between the local agencies and the state enterprises holding the national monopoly, and the peasants were the usual victims of such conflicts.[22]

Danger signals continued to become more conspicuous concerning the long-term issues of the ecology and "quality" of population. According to the *Bulletin on the State of the Chinese Environment* released by the State Bureau of Environmental Protection, 1991 had seen no reduction in the amount of air pollution in China produced by the burning of coal.[23] The Chinese authorities also revealed that there was an increasing number of condemned rivers.[24]

It was estimated that China had around 250 million illiterates, almost 30% of the world's total. Moreover, this enormous army of illiterates was still growing. The number of parents taking their children out of school, especially in the rural areas, had been increasing. At the same time, the practice of taking over school facilities for non-educational purposes had been continuing unabated. These phenomena reduced universal education to an empty slogan. Lack of funds was often the excuse for not running schools properly and not attempting to eliminate illiteracy. In the last ten years, an average of 4 million of China's 220 million primary school pupils had dropped out of school every year. A total of 30% did so because of poverty.[25] In higher education, there was an incessant drain of young teachers who either went abroad or opted for higher salaries in business. Primary and secondary school teachers were among the lowest-paid professionals in China, and the proportion of national revenues devoted to education compared very unfavourably even with developing countries. The following statement of Li Tieying, head of the State Education Commission, almost became a mockery: "All hope for the vitalization of the

Chinese nation lies in education, and all hope for the vitalization of education lies in the teachers."[26]

Conclusion

The *Financial Times* of London named Deng Xiaoping "Man of the Year."[27] The newspaper noted: "In 1992, the flowering of Chinese capitalism that he fostered became irreversible." That and the substantial improvement of living standards for one-fifth of the world's population were certainly a remarkable contribution. While neo-authoritarian modernization appealed strongly to Deng and other Chinese leaders, they should seriously consider how the bird cage could be removed gradually and safely. Chiang Ching-kuo in his final years showed that the Taiwan experience had a lot to offer to mainland China not only in its economic take-off model, but also in its far-sighted attempt at political liberalization. Before his death in 1988, Chiang Ching-kuo removed the ban on newspapers and political parties. In the early 1990s, freedom of mass media and freedom of political association too will be the litmus tests of political reform in China.

Notes

1. *Hong Kong Economic Journal*, 27 December 1992.
2. Tao Siju, "Fangfan liuzhong didui shili — Gonganbu ruhe 'fandianfu'" (Be on Guard against Six Types of Hostile Forces — How the Ministry of Public Security "Fights Subversion"), *The Nineties* (Hong Kong), No. 264 (January 1992), pp. 26–28.
3. See the series of translated documents and articles in *Inside China Mainland* (Taipei), Vol. 14, No. 3 (March 1992), pp. 3–22.
4. For the text of Jiang Zemin's report to the Fourteenth National Congress of the Party entitled "Accelerating the Reform, the Opening to the Outside World and the Drive for Modernization, so as to Achieve Greater Successes in Building Socialism with Chinese Characteristics," see *Beijing Review*, Vol. 35, No. 43 (26 October–1 November 1992), pp. 9–32.
5. Tai Ming Cheung, "Decimated Ranks," *Far Eastern Economic Review* (*FEER*), Vol. 155, No. 8 (27 February 1992), p. 15; and the same author's "Quick Response," *FEER*, Vol. 156, No. 2 (14 January 1993), pp. 19–21.
6. For the text of Zhao Ziyang's report, see *Beijing Review*, Vol. 30, No. 45 (9–15 November 1987), pp. i–xxvii.

7. Tai Ming Cheung, "Lost in the Postings," *FEER*, Vol. 155, No. 48 (3 December 1992), pp. 16–17.
8. Beijing, Central People's Broadcasting Station, 2 December 1991, broadcast excerpts; translations in *Inside China Mainland*, Vol. 14, No. 2 (February 1992), pp. 3–6.
9. Song Fumin and Zhu Xingguo, "Business and Power — A Foul Combination" (in Chinese), *Peasants' Daily* (Beijing), 29 July 1992, p. 3.
10. *Ming Pao* (Hong Kong), 22 June 1992.
11. Liang Jia (delegate to the Chinese People's Political Consultative Congress), "Corruption, Party's Greatest Fear" (in Chinese), *Democracy and the Chinese People's Political Consultative Congress Monthly* (Beijing), May 1992, p. 9.
12. Huai Bing, "Ping Zhongguo zuojia de fan 'zuo' yanlun" (Comments on Chinese Authors' Anti-"Left" Statements), *Cheng Ming* (Hong Kong), No. 183 (January 1993), pp. 76–78.
13. Mao Sen, "Dalu 'rexian' re — duojige chuqikong" (Mainland China's "Hotlines" Fever — More Safety-valves), *The Nineties*, No. 270 (July 1992), pp. 35–37.
14. Xiang Da, "Liufang yijifenzi de miling" (Secret Order on Exiling the Dissidents), *Cheng Ming*, No. 183 (January 1993), pp. 29–31.
15. Liang Xuechu, "Xiaoyu chi dayu: suoyouzhi bianhua de qushi" (Small Fishes Devouring Big Fishes: Trend of Change in the Ownership System), *The Nineties*, No. 274 (November 1992), pp. 36–39.
16. *Economic Daily* (Beijing), 31 July 1992.
17. Yu Jiwen, "'Xiaozhengfu, daqiye' — changyizhong de tizhigaige" ("Small Government, Big Enterprise" — Proposed Structural Reform), *The Nineties*, No. 274 (November 1992), pp. 34–35.
18. *Ming Pao*, 31 December 1992.
19. Lincoln Kaye, "Too Hot for Comfort," *FEER*, Vol. 155, No. 31 (6 August 1992), pp. 58–59.
20. *Ibid.*
21. *Ming Pao*, 29 December 1992.
22. "Agriculture Suffering from Poor Adjustment to Reforms" (in Chinese), *Agricultural Economic Problem* (Beijing), November 1991, pp. 21–22.
23. *Wen Wei Po* (Hong Kong), 7 June 1992.
24. *Ming Pao*, 7 June 1992.
25. *Economic Daily*, 22 February 1992.
26. Yang Lieyu, "A Massive Disappearing Act" (in Chinese), *Popular Tribune* (Beijing), May 1992, pp. 16–17.
27. *South China Morning Post* (Hong Kong), 30 December 1992.

2

Leadership Changes at the Fourteenth Party Congress

Willy Wo-lap Lam

The Fourteenth Party Congress was Deng Xiaoping's last hurrah. However, the outcome of the pivotal conclave, specially changes in the leadership line-up and structure, reflected the desires and political needs not just of the 88-year-old patriarch and his fellow octogenarians but the mainstream opinion of the Chinese Communist Party (CCP): to pursue market reforms at a steady pace while preserving the CCP's supremacy through beefing up the police-state apparatus.

There is, of course, a contradiction between the requirements of the marketplace and the need to safeguard the CCP's monopoly of power. This explains the extent to which the leadership that was endorsed by the Congress seems to lag behind economic realities, the aspirations of the people, and indeed, criteria set forth in Deng's own speeches during his *nanxun*, or "imperial tour to southern China" in early 1992.

Put simply, a solid majority of Chinese — not just the free-wheeling, irreverent denizens along the Gold Coast — want leaders who no longer spout Marxist-Leninist platitudes and who dare to take radical steps down the quasi-capitalistic road. After all, while he was in Shenzhen, Zhuhai and Shanghai, didn't Deng mothball orthodox Maoism and spin out the new theory of the "three so-long-as," namely, a policy is correct so long as it expedites economic growth, promotes productivity and boosts the comprehensive strength of the nation? Didn't the New Helmsman tell cadres who resist reform "to go to sleep"?[1]

As the following sections will argue, however, the new leadership line-up does not seem to pass muster. The collective leadership with Party chief Jiang Zemin as its "core" is in general committed to market reforms. However, in terms of economic policy it is also a cautious team that is always ready to rein in the centrifugal tendencies of the regions and the non-state-sector entrepreneurs, two of the most dynamic forces in Chinese society.

In politics, Deng managed to shove aside a token number of Maoist ideologues. However, the political straitjacket remains. In addition, the CCP has beefed up the security apparatus: representatives of the People's Liberation Army (PLA) and the legal and security establishment have gained ground *vis-à-vis* the other sectors. Overall, what Deng was after was a rough balance among the various factions and socio-economic forces so that gradual market reforms could be implemented in tandem with tight political control.

Is this leadership structure at variance with the vision evoked by Deng at his *nanxun*? As had happened so often in recent CCP history, however, the survival and vested interests of the Party Central soon towered above everything. A long-standing *leitmotif* of Deng's statecraft is to check and balance the various forces in the polity — in such a way that the Chief Architect of Reform can hold the balance and maintain his supremacy.

From the point of view of the entire Party, too, it is much better to proceed cautiously than risk being overwhelmed by the unpredictable, potentially chaotic forces that the marketplace could unleash. In short, having moved heaven to lay out his radical reform plans, Deng proceeded to move earth to confine the new forces within what the Party would consider safe perimeters. The size of the bird cage has increased significantly; but the bird still cannot fly free. For the near term.

The genie, however, is out of the bottle. The logic of the marketplace dictates that the subjectivist wishes of the octogenarians cannot hold sway for ever. Already, we see signs of the emergence of a different power elite that will reflect the new balance of forces in Chinese society and the economy — and the needs of the twenty-first century.

I. Balance of Power after the Fourteenth Party Congress

(i) Deng Xiaoping's Goal: To Reconcile Market Reforms with Political Stability

The Fourteenth Party Congress will go down in Communist-Chinese history as the watershed conclave that brought the "socialist market economy" to China. In socio-political matters, however, the preoccupation of the meeting was stability and the preservation of privilege, rather than radical changes that might render the CCP more in tune with the requirements of the next century. The impulse of the octogenarians and septuagenarians who guided what could have been their last congress was defence, not offence.

Improbable as it might seem, the rapidly ageing Chief Architect of Reform, Deng Xiaoping, took a hands-on approach to the preparation of the Congress, specially the licking into shape of what he called a "cross-century leadership." As the 88-year-old patriarch made it clear in the *nanxun* talks, he wanted to groom and elevate young leaders who had concrete track records in reform. "We must choose those who the people think will resolutely insist on the line of reform and the open door, and who have solid accomplishments [in reform]," he said. "We must induct more young people [to high office]."[2]

The emphasis on youth and reformist credentials was repeated many times by both moderate and conservative leaders — specially at the Fourteenth Congress. Even conservative Organization Department chief Lü Feng, a protégé of the hardline elder Song Ping, waxed eloquent about "being bold in picking talent." "We must break through the old concept of just respecting seniority, making special provisions [for people with connections], and being too perfectionist," he said. "We must liberate our thoughts and go through various channels in selecting people from different modes."[3]

The Fourteenth Congress saw the removal of several diehard conservatives and the elevation of a relatively large number of young technocrats, including those from the regions. However, the over-riding concern of Deng was the promotion of stability through a time-honoured balancing of the various factions.

By late 1992, the increasingly frail and senile patriarch was a lion in winter. With the generally solid support of the army and regional leaders — as well as that of the intelligentsia, entrepreneurs and international opinion — the patriarch could have manoeuvred for the kill and wiped out the "leftists." Yet, as had happened so many times since Deng grasped power in late 1978, the self-styled Great Balancer did not go the whole hog.

Firstly, in spite of the media hype surrounding the *nanxun* — and the apparent support that Deng's Second Wave of Reform had garnered among moderates and liberals alike — Deng had to sue for compromise with the conservative octogenarians as well as the bureaucrats in the Party Central and the State Council. As in past Party congresses, there was a fair amount of give and take among the various sectors and cliques of the CCP.

More important, however, Deng consciously gunned for a balance of power among the various "mountain strongholds." As he made clear in a message to the Politburo four days before the Congress opened on October 12, the leadership should reflect the "five lakes and four seas," meaning that none of the factions should assume a preponderant position.[4]

Throughout the 1980s, Deng's basic statecraft was to strike a balance between "rightists" led by former Party chiefs Hu Yaobang and Zhao Ziyang, on the one hand, and leftist ideologues and central planners led by Deng Liqun and Chen Yun, on the other. Specially in light of the crumbling of the Soviet Union and the East Bloc, Deng saw in this balancing act the key to stability. Thus, as the following sections will make clear, the leftist faction had a new lease on life in late 1992. The "radicals," as represented by the remnants of the Zhao Ziyang faction, were precluded from the centre of power.

At the same time, again taking into consideration the lessons of the East Bloc, Deng beefed up the security, or police-state, apparatus. The concern for security was reflected in Central Committee Document No. 7, which was promulgated a month before the Congress. The document warned against subversion and sabotage that might come in the wake of economic reform. Specially targetted were students, workers, and members of underground organizations. Saying that the nation must "prevent security problems from turning into political events," the document called for riot squads, fast-response units, more security on campus, and command centres for security forces in all large and medium-sized units.[5]

The obsession with stability was fully reflected in the line-up that was endorsed by the Congress. In his anxiety to pre-empt the emergence of a new strongman, Deng removed the military powers of the Yang Clan — President Yang Shangkun and General Yang Baibing — just days before the Congress opened.[6]

And in spite of his reservations about Jiang Zemin's commitment to reform, Deng continued to shore up the latter's "core" status. In effect, the New Helmsman was aiming for a collective leadership with Jiang as the putative standard bearer. While Jiang would be first among equals, power would be shared among the other members of the Politburo, specially its Standing Committee. Again, Deng hoped that the built-in checks and balances within the new team would minimize destabilizing factors.

Politics being what it is, however, it is obvious that the octogenarian's subjectivist — and very non-Marxist — concern with stability will be shattered by fast-shifting reality. Already at the Fourteenth Congress, we see certain political forces — and personalities — gaining at the expense of the others. New alliances are being formed as factions and cliques that no longer match the requirements of the "socialist market economy" fall by the wayside.

Specifically, power blocs and socio-economic forces on the ascendency include the following: modernization-minded technocrats; the army and security establishments; local-level leaders; and the cadres-turned-businessmen and private entrepreneurs. It is likely that the leaders of these factions and social blocs — many of whom do not fall within Deng's category of "cross-century cadres" — will guide China into the early twenty-first century.

Before we examine how these trends and currents played themselves out at the Fourteenth Party Congress and the rest of 1992, however, let us examine the composition of the new line-up.

(ii) The New Leadership Structure

The following line-up was announced for the Party and army at or immediately after the Congress. The 1,989 delegates endorsed a twenty-member Politburo in addition to two alternate members of the supreme body. The Politburo Standing Committee was expanded from six to seven members. In order of seniority, they were: Jiang Zemin (66 at the time of the Congress); Li Peng (64); Qiao Shi (68); Li Ruihuan (58); Zhu Rongji (64); Liu Huaqing (76); and Hu Jintao (49). Senior Vice-Premier Yao Yilin and organization chief Song Ping, both 75, retired from the top council.

The rest of the Politburo was made up of the following members: Tian Jiyun (63); Li Tieying (56); Ding Guan'gen (63); Li Lanqing (60); Yang Baibing (72); Wu Bangguo (50); Zou Jiahua (66); Chen Xitong (62); Jiang Chunyun (62); Qian Qichen (64); Wei Jianxing (61); Xie Fei (60); and Tan Shaowen (63). The two alternate members were Wen Jiabao (50); and Wang Hanbin (67).

Aside from Yao and Song, quite a number of heavyweights also departed from the Politburo. They either left active politics then and there — or were expected to step down at the first session of the Eighth National People's Congress (NPC) in March 1993. The retirees were: Yang Shangkun (85); Wan Li (76); Qin Jiwei (78); Wu Xueqian (71); Li Ximing (65); and Yang Rudai (65).[7]

An equally radical change of personnel took place at the Central Committee Secretariat. The new line-up was, in order of precedence: Hu Jintao; Ding Guan'gen; Wei Jianxing; Wen Jiabao; and Ren Jianxin. Hu Jintao replaced Qiao Shi as the *de facto* head of the Secretariat, which runs the Party apparatus and issues major documents. The "top morality squad," the Central Commission for Disciplinary Inspection (CCDI) also had a facelift. The fast-rising star in the Politburo, Wei Jianxing, took the place of Qiao Shi as chief of CCDI. His deputies were Hou Zongbin; Chen Zuolin; Cao Qingze; Wang Deying; and Xu Qing.

As we shall see in a later section, Deng masterminded a veritable "purge" of the so-called Yang Clan both at and soon after the Congress.

The Central Military Commission (CMC), which is the country's highest military organ, had a thorough reshuffle. The Chairman remained Jiang Zemin. The two Vice-Chairmen were incumbent General Liu Huaqing (76) and newcomer General Zhang Zhen (78). There were four ordinary CMC members: Generals Chi Haotian (63); Zhang Wannian (64); Yu Yongbo (61); and Fu Quanyou (62).[8]

Before we proceed with a full-scale analysis of this elite, as well as the political forces it represents, let us briefly examine whether the new team satisfies Deng's imperative about the elevation of young and reform-minded cadres. After all, the Congress Report again underlined "the principle of making cadres more revolutionary, younger, better educated and more competent, with both professional ability and political integrity."[9]

It is obvious that Deng and the "selection committee," which included Bo Yibo, Jiang Zemin, Song Ping and Hu Jintao, had only acquitted themselves — and partially too — on the score of the youth criterion. The much-maligned Central Advisory Commission (CAC), long regarded as a bastion of conservatism, was finally abolished. During preparatory conferences for the Congress, the deputies got into a fierce discussion on whether to replace the CAC with a similar — but smaller and less powerful — Central Advisory Group. That proposal was shot down at the eleventh hour.[10]

Out of the 189 full members of the Central Committee, 81 or 46.7% were newcomers. Of these inductees 61% were under 55 years of age. However, the average age of the Committee was 56.3, which was slightly higher than the figure of 55.2 for the Thirteenth Central Committee. Moreover, the re-appointment of septuagenarians Liu Huaqing and Zhang Zhen — who had belonged to the CAC — to the Central Committee looked particularly jarring.[11]

Aside from the youth criterion, Deng Xiaoping and the supreme headhunting committee apparently made good on another promise: that the "princelings," or offspring of the senior cadres, be barred from the Central Committee. To the surprise of analysts, odds-on favourites for the top such as Deng Nan (daughter of Deng Xiaoping), Chen Yuan (son of Chen Yun), Fu Rui (son of Peng Zhen), Wang Jun (son of Wang Zhen) and Bo Xicheng (son of Bo Yibo), failed to gain promotions at the Congress. Deng was quoted by insiders as having given specific instructions that the sons and daughters of Party veterans not be considered for high positions.[12]

However, it would be naive to assume that the overall political influence of the princelings is on the wane. They still hold down some of the most senior positions in both Beijing and the regions. As we shall see in a later section, a major reason why the princelings do not seem to be doing particularly well in politics is that most have shifted their interest to business. Since the *nanxun*, hundreds of the offspring of Party elders and senior officials have set up businesses — and are parlaying their connections into lucrative deals.

Summing up the post-congress leadership, the Chinese media claimed that in terms of education, professionalism and experience, the new team was reformist in nature. Thus, 83.7% of the 189 most powerful men and women in China had college education or professional training. And, 44.5% had mid- or upper-ranking professional qualifications in engineering or economics. "The great majority of the new Central Committee members are backbone cadres in different positions, including experts and scholars," the Chinese-affiliated *The Mirror* magazine pointed out. "There are numerous cadres who have proven themselves in the reform and open-door policy."[13]

Yet, as will be evident in the ensuing sections, factions and sectors that block the path of reform and that may be prejudicial to the early realization of the socialist market economy have held their own. It would take at least one or two more congresses before the forces of reform and modernization can attain a secure majority in both the CCP and the country.

II. The Rise and Fall of Major Factions and Sectors

(i) The Left: Still a Force to Be Reckoned with

When, at the height of the *nanxun*, Deng Xiaoping raised the battle cry of "anti-leftism," intellectuals in Beijing were beside themselves with joy. They were hoping that the patriarch would leave the political stage in style by dealing one last, lethal blow against the remnant Maoists.[14]

By late 1992, however, the anti-leftist campaign had petered out. This is despite the fact that the Political Report to the Congress had a pro forma reference to fighting leftism: "while we must raise our guard against rightism, the priority is combating 'leftism'."[15] It is clear that, as on various occasions in the past, the patriarch sued for compromise with the hardliners to preserve his economic reforms. Deng was also convinced that however out of step with the times the leftists were, he needed to use them to prevent the Party and nation from lurching too far to the right. If not,

China — and the CCP — risked being swept away by a wave of "bourgeois liberalization."

At least on the surface, 1992 saw the leftists suffering setbacks in the ideological and, more critical, the personnel front. The patron saint of the left, Chen Yun, was forced to "recant" his beliefs in "pure upon pure" Marxism and in the bird cage theory of central planning. In his message of condolence for the late president, Li Xiannian, Chen admitted he had "to learn new things" in order to catch up with the 1990s. "Some ways of doing things in the past no longer apply under the new situation of reform and the open door," he said. "We must ceaselessly explore and solve new problems." The conservative patriarch also indicated, while he had never been to the Special Economic Zones, he was concerned about their development.[16]

At or around the Fourteenth Party Congress, a relatively small number of key leftists were forced out. They included the two influential members of the Politburo Standing Committee, Yao Yilin and Song Ping, both considered henchmen of Chen Yun's. Vice-Minister of the State Education Commission He Dongchang and the Party Secretary of the Beijing municipality, Li Ximing, were obliged to resign. Both He and Li played a key role in persuading Deng Xiaoping to wipe out the 1989 democracy activists through armed suppression.[17]

It soon became apparent, however, that Deng's anti-leftist crusade was half-hearted at best. During the *nanxun*, the patriarch had, both by name and implicitly, cast aspersions on a dozen-odd senior leftists for blocking his reforms, for failing to promote reform-minded cadres, and for stopping the dissemination of his instructions. Aside from Yao Yilin, Song Ping, Li Ximing and He Dongchang, these included the large corps of ideologues who held sway over the ideological and propaganda establishment.[18] By late 1992, the bulk of these leftists either remained in their positions or just received a slap on the wrist.

Firstly, several well-known leftists remained in the new Central Committee. The most notable of these was Hua Guofeng, the "whateverist" former chairman of the Party who enjoyed a high popularity. Other Maoists and hardliners on the new Central Committee included organization chief Lü Feng; former minister of water resources Qian Zhengying; Party boss of Jiangxi Mao Zhiyong; Minister of Radio, Film and Television Ai Zhisheng; trade unionist Ni Zhifu; the Vice-Party Secretary of Beijing, Wang Jialiu; and head of the Central Committee Research Office Wang Weicheng.

Secondly, Deng's avowed objective of revamping the ideological and propaganda establishment evaporated into thin air. The new line-up of this crucial sector, as announced in early December 1992, represented only a lily-livered effort at flushing out leftist influence. The Propaganda Department itself underwent a minimal facelift with the appointment of Ding Guan'gen and Zheng Bijian as head and vice-head of department. Xu Weicheng, the noted Gang of Four holdover, remained as an executive vice-head of department. Many department- and bureau-level posts in the department were still held by cadres loyal to conservative patriarch Deng Liqun.[19]

Similarly, cosmetic changes took place in the Ministry of Culture, another stronghold of leftism. The ailing Maoist poet, He Jingzhi, retired as Acting Minister, making way for Liu Zhongde. Many departments of the ministry remained pockets of Maoist influence.[20]

At the same time, head of the Propaganda Department Wang Renzhi was "rewarded" with the position of Party Secretary of the Chinese Academy of Social Sciences (CASS), deemed a "disaster zone" of bourgeois liberalization. It was reported that Wang, still young at 59, was manoeuvring to become CASS President, replacing conservative historian Hu Sheng. The CASS presidency is half a rung above an ordinary minister in seniority. Other changes included the promotion of former vice-chief of propaganda Zeng Jianhui as head of the Central Committee's Leading Group on Overseas Propaganda and head of the Information Office of the State Council.[21]

It is unlikely the new line-up would make for a liberalization of policies on ideology and the media. While not considered conservatives, cadres such as Ding Guan'gen, Liu Zhongde, Zheng Bijian and Zeng Jianhui are reckoned as fence-sitters who will generally abide by Deng's precept of freeing the economy while tightly controlling ideology.[22]

Compared with such former arbiters of the field as Hu Yaobang, Zhu Houze — or even Li Ruihuan — the likes of Zheng Bijian and Liu Zhongde can be deemed conservatives. For example, while Zheng, whose last posting was CASS Vice-President, is sometimes classified as a liberal because of his having worked for Hu Yaobang, he played a role in the purge of CASS "miscreants" in the wake of the June 4, 1989 massacre. Likewise, the liberal reputation of Liu is dubious. He was close to Li Peng when both worked at the State Education Commission (SEC) during the mid-1980s. It is mostly unlikely that Zheng, Liu and their ilk would change the hard-line agenda already set by Deng Liqun, Wang Renzhi and their allies.

Thirdly, as a compensation for their leaving the historical stage, Deng apparently allowed the likes of Yao Yilin and Song Ping to "pick their successors." This is particularly evident with Song, the Politburo member in charge of personnel who heads the so-called Gansu Faction. Among Song protégés who got promotions at the Congress were new Politburo members Hu Jintao and Wei Jianxing.[23]

By the end of the Congress, it was apparent Deng had called off his campaign against leftism. Qiao Shi and Tian Jiyun — about the only two senior cadres who had responded to Deng's call for undermining leftist influence — remained mum. Tian, who missed out on a membership in the Politburo Standing Committee, was slated for the No. 2 slot at the National People's Congress. Analysts said he had alienated Party elders by saying in a speech at the Central Party School in April that Maoists be banished to a "special leftist zone" where food is rationed and where inhabitants will not be allowed to go abroad.[24]

By late 1992, Deng Liqun, or Little Deng, as he is known to most observers in Beijing, was celebrating with his cohorts. The leftists were holding boisterous banquets at the new Da San Yuan Restaurant near Zhongnanhai over the fact that they had emerged from Deng's anti-leftist campaign unscathed. They had scuttled the promotion prospects of Tian Jiyun. Their *bête noire*, Li Ruihuan, was giving up his ideological and propaganda portfolio for the largely ceremonial post of Chinese People's Political Consultative Congress (CPPCC) Chairman. Moreover, they had blocked the elevation of Zheng Bijian to head of the Propaganda Department. Four bureau chiefs of the Propaganda Department, who were appointees of Deng Liqun and Wang Renzhi, petitioned the Politburo not to appoint Zheng. This is doubly ironic given the fact that, in the eyes of the Beijing intelligentsia, Zheng hardly came across as a liberal.[25]

There were even signs that the leftists were regrouping for a counter-attack. Little Deng, who at 77 was as energetic as ever, formed a China National Historical Society of which he became President. The Society would play the role of the disbanded CAC, that of a base for the hardliners. Its membership read like a who's who of the world of leftism. The five Vice-Presidents were: He Dongchang; retired State Planning Commission vice-chief Fang Weizhong; editor of *Seeking Truth (Qiushi)*, You Lin; vice-chief of the Research Office of CCP History Sha Jianxun; and Director of the Press and Publications Administration Song Muwen.[26]

Even though it would seem most unlikely the Maoist ideologues would resume their prominence, they remained by late 1992 a force to be reckoned with. One is reminded of the fact that during ballotings for delegates to the Congress, Hua Guofeng received one of the highest votes. With the nation fairly solidly anchored on a course towards the socialist market economy, however, support for the remnant Maoists mainly comes from "twilight sectors" that are left behind by modernization. And instead of trying to revive the Maoist utopia, leftists would likely play negative and "destructive" roles, such as shooting down efforts by "bourgeois-liberal" intellectuals to rekindle political reform.[27]

(ii) The Decline of the Bureaucrats and Central Planners

The Fourteenth Party Congress confirmed the inexorable decline of the political bloc that, perhaps next to the People's Liberation Army, had wielded the most power since 1949. While political stars and ideological gurus like Chairman Mao, Jiang Qing and Deng Liqun might have hogged the limelight at one time or another, it is the bureaucrats in the State Council who oversaw the running of the economy — and the country. Disciples of such heavyweights as Chen Yun and Li Xiannian, these central planning-oriented cadres marched to the tune of Stalinist or "bird-cage" economics.

No more. With the advent of the "socialist market economy," the role of the diktat school of planners is set for drastic reduction. A key decision of the Congress was "the separation of government and business," which would be accomplished through the large-scale curtailment of the size and power of government departments. In tandem with the increase of the role of the marketplace, the state would only exercise "macro-economic control" over the economy. The functions of government departments of various levels will change from control and regulation to providing non-mandatory guidance and services.[28]

"The major work of economic departments should be transformed to strengthening macro-level regulation and adjustments," the Congress document said. "Professional economic departments whose functions overlap or whose jurisdictions are similar should be dismantled or merged. Staff establishments should be streamlined." The shrinkage of government and reorientation of its functions would be accomplished in three years.[29]

While Beijing has not disclosed the extent of the bloodletting, it has been reported that at least one-third of the 30-million strong staff establishment of the Party and government apparatus will be cut. Hardest hit will be the State Planning Commission, the Ministry of Foreign Economic

Relations and Trade (MOFERT), the Ministry of Light Industry, the Ministry of Textile Industry, and the Ministry of Radio, Film and Television. Plans in late 1992 called for the slashing of up to 70% of the staff of MOFERT and 80% of that of Light Industry.[30]

Most illustrative of the shrinking clout of the central planners is the State Planning Commission (SPC), traditionally the most important organ of the central government. Right after the Congress, the scope and quantity of its directives and production quotas began to be whittled down. For example, in 1993, 37% of the fiats would be cut in the fields of agriculture, industry and commerce. The role of the SPC would shift from direct control over production and distribution to laying down long-term plans and forecasts for economic activities.[31]

In an article in November 1992, the official *China Daily* described the SPC as a "think tank." SPC Vice-Minister Wang Chunzheng indicated that instead of "administrative intervention," his unit would "mainly adopt economic leverage to attain its goals of effective macro-regulation over the nation's economic performance." He added that, by late 1992, only 10% of state enterprises were still subjected to mandatory plans imposed by the commission.[32]

Given the CCP's determination to bring in market forces, the handwriting is on the wall for the central planners. However, it would be naive to assume that they would just fade away. Unlike Eastern Europe, China's transition to a market economy would be a long drawn-out process. For example, by late 1992, two central planners supposed to be on their way out — Yao Yilin and Wang Bingqian — exploited the need to cool down the overheated economy to claw back some territory. At State Council meetings in December 1992, they compared the "high growth model" advocated by Deng to Chairman Mao's disastrous Great Leap Forward. Their conclusion, of course, was that the country still needed central planners to rectify economic ills.[33]

There were also signs that the SPC might get a new lease on life. In a year-end speech Premier Li Peng surprised observers when he pointed out that the SPC, "in conjunction with other ministries and commissions," would be put in charge of revising the Eighth Five-year Plan and the Ten-year Economic Blueprint. The retooling of the plan and the blueprint — which had already been approved by the National People's Congress (NPC) in 1991 — had been ordered by Deng during his *nanxun* in view of their conservative nature. Up to mid-1992, it had been assumed that two ministries dominated by moderate cadres — the Economic and Trade

Office and the State Commission for the Reform of the Economic System (CRES) — would be given the authority over this vital task.[34]

At the same time, a large number of bureaucrats were seeking a reincarnation as the heads of the thousands of corporations that were being set up to "take over" the functions of the economic departments. Theoretically, these business units are supposed to be independent of the government and to be run like western-style corporations. In reality, there is a high degree of fusion between government and business, and many so-called cadre-businessmen still run these Chinese-style crown corporations along traditional lines, in the process obstructing the progress towards a market economy.

(iii) The Rise of the Moderate Technocrats

A major beneficiary of the Fourteenth Party Congress were the politically neutral technocrats. By late 1992, they were poised to take the place of both the Maoist ideologues and the central planners in the Party and government headquarters. A large number of such moderate technocrats were at the same time appointed at the local level, although, as we shall see later, the regions were also a stronghold of radical reformers many of whom are followers of Zhao Ziyang.

In economic matters, the technocrats are cautious reformers or moderate free-marketeers. While they are convinced that the Stalinist command economy should be dismantled and many economic activities be guided by the market, they also believe in the perseverance of indirect, macro-economic control by the state. At the same time, the technocrats avoid politics and ideology like the plague. As theorist Lu Jiamin sees it, at the Congress, Deng elevated a large corps of "middle-of-the-roaders whose political orientation is blurred. They are not connected with the June 4 Incident and they assume low profiles."[35] Unlike the followers of Hu Yaobang or Zhao Ziyang, they have no agenda for political liberalization.

These modernization-minded but moderate technocrats are led by Vice-Premier Zhu Rongji. They take up a large chunk of the "cross-century cadres," officials in their forties and fifties on whose shoulders fall the task of ushering China into the twenty-first century. Unlike the Soviet-trained central planners, the bulk of the technocrats were educated in local universities. Qinghua University is the alma mater of such first-tier leaders as Zhu Rongji and Hu Jintao and such regional honchoes as Shanghai

Party Secretary Wu Bangguo, Jiangxi Governor Wu Guanzheng, and Qinghai Governor Tian Chengping. Twenty-nine full or alternate members of the new Central Committee are alumni of "China's MIT," and Zhu is the acknowledged chieftain of the Qinghua Faction.[36]

Zhu's Economic and Trade Office (ETO), which was set up in the spring of 1992, has replaced the SPC as the nerve centre of the State Council. Being the only central-government unit which saw major expansion, the ETO has eleven Vice-Directors and as many departments looking after most aspects of the economy. The philosophy and methodology of both Zhu and his ETO yield a good insight into the statecraft of the moderate technocrats.

In general, the "mini-State Council" would concentrate on macro-economic guidance such as the drafting of industrial policies, trade strategies, and the coordination of the harnessing and use of rare resources such as oil and transport. Zhu and his cohorts have made it clear that China would not go down the road of capitalism. While talking to Swedish businessmen in Stockholm in late 1992, Zhu denied China would embrace capitalism. He said Beijing would hold on to such socialist trappings as "public ownership as the mainstay, the safeguarding of social justice and egalitarian prosperity."[37]

In contrast to the young turks working under Zhao, Zhu looks to Japan and Singapore instead of the West for inspiration. While briefing delegates to the Fourteenth Congress, Zhu heaped praise on the "Japanese model." He was talking about a synthesis of free-wheeling market forces and a relatively tight control by the government, meaning patriarchal clans within Japan's Liberal Democratic Party. "We can learn a lot from Japanese institutions," Zhu said. "On the one hand, there is market economics. On the other, there is a very strict macro-economic control." The Vice-Premier said specifically that ETO would be modelled on Japan's famous Ministry of International Trade and Industry (MITI). "MITI alone is a match for a dozen-odd of our ministries," he said.[38]

The way the ETO handled the development of the "stocks system" in the second half of 1992 provided a good example of the approach of the technocrats. Zhu and his colleagues shot down applications by Guangzhou, Tianjin, and a host of other cities to set up the country's third stock exchange. Moreover, the Stocks Commission, which Zhu set up in late 1992, laid down severe restrictions on the type and number of companies that could publicly sell or float their securities.[39]

It also became obvious soon after the Congress that a fair number of technocrats would be posted to the non-economic departments, including units handling ideology and propaganda.

Instead of "liberalizing" the ideological and propaganda units, as is demanded by "rightist" intellectuals, the technocrats would seek to implement the CCP strictures in a more institutional and legalistic manner. Take censorship for example. In the past, ideologues in the Propaganda Department would ban whatever they subjectively considered to be "bourgeois-liberal." However, an administative department in charge of censorship was due to be set up in 1993. And technocrats running the unit would enact specific regulations proscribing pieces of writing that would be deemed prejudicial to the interests of the state.[40]

Aside from the Qinghua Clique, the so-called Shanghai Faction — cadres who were born in or who spent parts of their career in the East China metropolis — also formed the backbone of the ranks of the moderate technocrats. A number of key players in both the ETO and the State CRES had worked in Shanghai either with Zhu or before Zhu. Prominent players affiliated with the faction include CRES chief Chen Jinhua; Foreign Minister Qian Qichen; and Vice-Chief of the General Office of the Central Committee Zeng Qinghong.[41]

The political fortune of the technocrats is tipped to expand because they suit the golden rule of moderation espoused by Deng and other major leaders. Moreover, even hard-core central planners and ideologues would find them more acceptable than the "all-out westernisers" who worked for Zhao Ziyang. And their innate cautiousness especially in waging economic reform would make them less prone to the kind of mistakes committed by the Zhaoists in early 1988.

(iv) The Zhao Ziyang Faction of Radical Reformers: Conserving Their Strength

Broadly speaking, the "Zhao Ziyang Faction" refers not just to cadres and intellectuals who worked for Zhao but the legions of "bourgeois-liberal" officials and scholars both in and out of the CCP establishment. Economically, they are "closet capitalists" who unashamedly clamour for the quasi-capitalistic road. They want the problematic qualifier "socialist" taken out of the Fourteenth Congress ideal of the "socialist market economy." Politically, they want real political reform in the sense of "power sharing" between the CCP and other sectors of society.

The seemingly effortless way in which Deng Xiaoping and the

conservative factions dumped Zhao after the massacre might give the impression that the Zhao faction was lightweight at best. However, one must be reminded that, at the height of the pro-democracy crusade in late May 1989, thousands of Party and government functionaries hit the streets in support of radical reforms. Moreover, Zhao's economic and political programmes have generally found favour with intellectuals in Beijing and other large cities. In short, the Zhaoists have been able to co-opt the bulk of the "right wing" of the Party and the intelligentsia.

Even during Deng Xiaoping's *nanxun*, it became obvious there would be no rehabilitation for Zhao Ziyang — or large-scale reinstatement of his faction of radical liberals and closet capitalists. In his talk to cadres in Guangdong, Deng praised Zhao for making contributions to fast-paced reform. However, he pointed out that former Party general secretaries Zhao and Hu Yaobang had erred in the area of ideology: both failed to stem the tide of bourgeois liberalization.[42]

More specifically, Deng could not have revived Zhao for reasons of political exigency. And this has more to do with the fact that rehabilitating Zhao would send the wrong signal that the Party might be ready to overturn the verdict on June 4. The fact of the matter is: Deng was in effect following "a Zhao Ziyang policy without Zhao Ziyang." Were Zhao cleared of his "guilt," it should be he, not Deng, who should be leading the nation.

Therefore, it came as no surprise that at the ninth plenum of the Thirteenth Central Committee on October 9, 1992, the Party decided to uphold the fourth plenum verdict of late June 1989: that the former Party chief supported the 1989 "turmoil" and split up the Party.[43] Three illustrious associates of Zhao failed to get promotions — or full rehabilitation — at the Fourteenth Party Congress. They were former member of the Politburo Standing Committee Hu Qili; and former members of the Secretariat Rui Xingwen and Yan Mingfu. Up to early October, there had been intense speculation that Hu would make it into either the Politburo or the Secretariat.

Even more disappointing for the liberal camp, however, was the unexpected failure of Xiao Yang to be inducted to the Politburo. The Party chief of Chongqing and Zhao ally was "earmarked" to be promoted Party secretary of Sichuan as well as Politburo member. However, largely owing to opposition from his conservative colleagues in Sichuan, Xiao did very poorly during ballotings for the Central Committee. The reformer was barely elected an Alternate Member of the Central Committee.[44]

As we shall see in a later section, however, the Zhaoists were by no means a spent force. As the economy continues to lurch towards the right, many in the country, specially regional leaders and entrepreneurs are again picking up the threads of Zhao's quasi-capitalistic experiments. The followers of Zhao are particularly well represented in middle and upper echelons in Guangdong and Hainan provinces, which had been the power base of the former Party chief of Guangdong.

Such of Zhao's former aides as Hu Qili remained intensely popular. A late October 1992 article in the mass-circulation *China Youth Daily* attested to the staying power of the Vice-Minister of Electronics. "You can say that the hero has a place to exercise his martial skills," the paper said, adding Hu was generally known as the "hardest-working minister." The homage was unusual given the fact that, until early 1992, hard-line ideologues had ruled that Hu be "banned" from the national media.[45]

(v) More Muscle to the Regions

The political aggrandizement of regional leaders — and to some extent, entrepreneurs — began with Deng's *nanxun*. Taking a leaf from Mao's book, Deng was mobilizing local-level cadres to "bombard the headquarters," that is, to clobber mandarins in the central Party and government authorities. At the National People's Congress of March–April 1992, Li Peng and other central planners were subjected to the merciless "bombardment" of provincial deputies, who demanded, among other things, that the Premier upwardly adjust the growth rate and enshrine "anti-leftism" as a national task. And most humiliating of all, the foster son of Zhou Enlai was forced to make nearly 150 amendments to his NPC Government Work Report.[46]

Representatives from the provinces and the cities won big at the Party Congress. This was assured from the very beginning: 1,401 or 70.43% of the 1,989 delegates to the conclave were from the regions. This compared with merely 329 delegates — or 16.54% of the total — who spoke for the central and Party organs. The unprecedented predominance of local-level cadres at the Congress was made possible through the insistence of Deng. Before the *nanxun*, the authorities had decided to allocate as many as 50% of the delegate slots to central-level bureaucrats.[47]

Since a major function of the delegates was to vote in the new Central Committee, it is not surprising that provincial and municipal chieftains took home 62, or 33%, of the 189 seats on the supreme council. Also at the insistence of Deng, the "warlords" had an unprecedentedly heavy representation on the Politburo. In addition to the slots traditionally assigned to the Party bosses of the three centrally administered cities of Beijing, Tianjin and Shanghai, Politburo membership was offered Xie Fei and Jiang Chunyun, the secretaries respectively of Guangdong and Shandong. As discussed earlier, Xiao Yang narrowly missed being elected the Politburo member representing Sichuan. Reflecting the fast-shifting economic realities of the country, politicians from Guangdong and Shanghai did particularly well at the conclave. Seven Guangdong cadres became either full or alternate members of the Central Committee. The figure for Shanghai was six.[48]

The regions' new clout has best been reflected in economic policy: autonomous powers that provinces and cities have gained at the expense of central authorities. The turning of the tide in favour of the regions had begun, of course, very soon after the *nanxun*. For example, the now-famous Central Party Document No. 4 of late April extended the open-door policy from the coast to both the heartland provinces and the border regions. In practice, this means around 100 cities and zones all over the country would acquire autonomous powers akin to those enjoyed by the Special Economic Zones (SEZ).[49]

Emboldened by the patriarch's instructions, various localities took the unheard-of step of unilaterally abrogating national policies they deemed behind the times. A case in point was Wuhan, which in July 1992 invalidated thirteen "out of date" regulations imposed by Beijing. These strictures had to do with financial and business activities, such as the ability of enterprises to get loans and to be transformed into joint-stock concerns.[50]

The bones of contention between the regions and the centre consisted largely in two areas: the speed of growth and the freedom to "do their own thing," specially raising funds both locally and from overseas sources. Citing the instructions of the patriarch, many localities were by late 1992 revising their own Eighth Five-year Plan and Ten-year Economic Blueprint to reflect their particular needs and aspirations.[51]

The year 1992 could become the watershed year in which the central government lost the power to regulate the pace of growth of the localities, specially cities along the Gold Coast. After all, Deng Xiaoping indicated during the *nanxun* that, if it was based on efficiency, a high rate of growth was desirable. This dictum has been repeated by almost every local Party secretary and mayor to justify their rapid expansion programmes.

The "high-speed model," at least for Guangdong, has been defended by such national-level leaders as Zou Jiahua, Ye Xuanping and Ren Zhongyi.[52]

A pitched battle was fought between practically all the open cities and the central leadership over the right to issue and float stocks. This has become a matter of life and death for the nation's most dynamic cities and enterprises. The right to sell shares publicly means the power to tap into the vast savings of 1.15 billion people, estimated at over RMB1.20 trillion.[53] Moreover, the freedom to issue B-shares and to be listed on stock exchanges in Hong Kong and elsewhere means the ability to raise money overseas.

The development of the "stocks economy" received a severe blow on the occasion of rioting — the first since June 4, 1989 — that broke out in Shenzhen after the problem-plagued sale of "lottery tickets" for buying new shares. Prior to that, the stock markets in both Shenzhen and Shanghai had experienced abrupt ups and downs. These incidents persuaded the central authorities to exercise caution in granting permission to companies to float their shares. In late 1992, President Yang Shangkun warned that the stocks experiment might be rescinded if it proved unsatisfactory.[54] However, by early 1993, local governments and entrepreneurs were putting tremendous pressure on Beijing to relax the restrictions.

The success with which the regions had clawed back the initiative was attested to by the dire warnings Beijing gave the localities for having gone too far. For example, the State Council issued an order in August saying that the levels of taxes to be imposed on foreign companies would be determined by Beijing alone — and local governments must not try to lower them in a bid to attract investment.[55] In November, Vice-Premier Zhu Rongji called on the regions and cities to cool the runaway development of stock companies as well as real estate speculation. "Areas of the economy which should be hot have not heated up; those that should not be hot have boiled over," he said.[56]

By late 1992, the regions were still a long way towards redressing the balance of power, which since 1949 had been tipped in favour of the centre. After all, the full Politburo does not meet very often, and the Central Committee is only convened once or twice every year in plenary session. And in spite of the gradual atrophy of central authority, regional politicians have yet to pose a frontal threat to Beijing's powers in formulating national policies.

(vi) The Non-state Sector: Power Play by the "Red Capitalists"

Both the economic and the political powers of the non-state-sector are poised for marked expansion with the gradual maturation of the "socialist market economy." By late 1992, Beijing had promulgated regulations which made possible the untrammelled development of the private sector. Political discrimination against private-sector practitioners that were introduced soon after the June 4 crackdown were gradually being lifted.

At the time of the Fourteenth Congress, China boasted over 14 million "individual entrepreneur households," which provided employment for some 23 million workers. There were 120,000 fully fledged private companies, which had more than 2 million staffers. More than 11,000 of these private concerns were companies with limited liabilities, a jump of 71.65% over the 1991 figure. The fixed assets of these private business units were mushrooming: the largest one had assets of RMB45 million.[57]

In early December, the State Council passed measures that amounted to a new deal for the private sector. For example, aside from "strategic" product lines and raw materials that the state must go on monopolizing, private entrepreneurs could engage in every kind of industrial and commercial production and management. Private companies were allowed to take up border trade and overseas commerce, including setting up branches overseas. Earlier, different provinces and cities had given permission to private concerns to form joint ventures with foreign corporations.[58]

On the political level, the Party rescinded an order given in late 1989 which forbade individual and private entrepreneurs from becoming CCP members. By the end of 1992, there were nearly 2 million CCP affiliates who were either the bosses or employees of private enterprises.[59]

The biggest break for the non-state sector, however, occurred with the passage of Central Committee Document No. 4, which gave the green light to Party units and cadres to operate businesses. As discussed earlier, quite a number of officials merely formed quasi-governmental corporations that were in practice no different from state companies. However, many set up private companies or joint ventures to take advantage of the new opportunities of the marketplace. On a massive scale, people with clout and high-level connections, including a host of "princelings," are joining the ranks of the private businessmen.[60]

By the time the Fourteenth Party Congress closed, there was no palpable evidence that private entrepreneurs might actually be inducted into policy-making bodies. No "red capitalists" made it into the Central

Committee. They were not even invited into advisory or consultative councils. One of the most talked about innovations during Zhu Rongji's tenure as Shanghai mayor was his having formed a council of business advisers, which was made up of foreign executives based in the East China metropolis. Zhu did not think of picking the brains of China's private entrepreneurs.[61]

As we shall see in a later section, however, the political prowess of the non-state-sector businessmen could grow exponentially. Somewhat echoing the development of democracy in western Europe in the nineteenth century, groups and associations of businessmen would first demand a share of political power to ensure fair competition in the embryonic marketplace.

(vii) The People's Liberation Army: More Power to the "Pillar of Socialism"

For Chairman Mao Zedong, power grew out of the barrel of a gun. Likewise, Deng Xiaoping relied on the PLA to ensure his absolutist rule. It was the support of the army, long a bastion of Deng's influence, that made possible the success of the *nanxun*. On the one hand, Deng is wary of military interference in politics. Hence the oft-repeated rule that "the Party must have absolute control over the gun." On the other hand, the patriarch wants the army to safeguard the longevity of his reign as well as the future of economic reform. In the words of disgraced Chief Political Commissar Yang Baibing, the army would "provide an escort for the emperor and protect his voyage."[62]

At the Fourteenth Congress, the PLA gained an unprecedentedly high level of representation on the full Central Committee — 22%, up from 18% in 1987. Moreover, for the first time since the Cultural Revolution, one Politburo Standing Committee seat was made available for an army representative, General Liu Huaqing, a Deng crony.[63]

The Political Report of the Congress made it clear the PLA would fulfil three major functions: to protect territorial integrity; to safeguard the socialist system; and to take part in socialist construction. The Central Committee vowed to "strengthen the army and increase the country's defence capabilities so as to guarantee the smooth progress of reform, the open-door policy and economic development."[64]

That the PLA would play sizable civilian roles was evident from two secret orders given by Deng soon after the Congress. Ten generals, including CMC members Zhang Zhen, Chi Haotian, Zhang Wannian, Yu Yongbo, and Fu Quanyou could sit in on politburo meetings. Besides, commanders and commissars of military regions and districts could join local party committes in policymaking. Military elements were instrumental in the hawkish stand that the CCP had taken towards the sale of hardware to Taiwan by the United States and France. In November 1992, a dozen odd retired generals reportedly wrote a letter to Jiang Zemin and Li Peng urging a "stern reaction" against the sale of jet fighters to Taiwan by Washington and Paris.[65]

However, inasmuch as Deng wanted the PLA to function as a bulwark for reform, he also took steps to prevent the army from being excessively politicised. In view of the role played by the army and the police in the disintegration of the former East Bloc, Deng was paranoid about coups. For example, in 1991, Deng loyalist Liu Huaqing set up a high-level military committee to study the mechanism of *coups d'état* with a view to preventing them from happening on home ground. The committee studied in detail the history of coups in such countries as Thailand and the Philippines.[66]

Various theories have been put forward for Deng's decision about a week before the Congress to rid the Yang Clan — as well as the large corps of veteran commissars in the PLA — of their military powers. The major reason seems to be that the Yang family, specially Yang Baibing, was exhibiting too overt a propensity for power-grabbing. The last straw appears to have been a series of secret meetings the chief political commissar held in the summer to allegedly plan for a "peaceful transition" after Deng's death. The patriarch was not informed of the meetings. And the Yang Baibing caper was interpreted as a precursor to a *coup*.[67]

In the communication to the Politburo on October 8 revealing his decision to sack Yang Baibing, Deng referred to the principle of the "five lakes and the four seas," or the need to avoid factionalism. From 30 October to 14 December, the *Liberation Army Daily* published twelve commentaries on how the army leadership should handle itself under Deng's military ideals. The commentary on personnel matters stressed "appointing cadres who have both morals and ability — and solely on the merits [of the candidates]." "Leaders must not substitute this [personnel] criterion with their personal likes and dislikes and their prejudices," the *Daily* warned. There can be little doubt the commentary was targetted at the empire-building efforts of the Yang Clan.[68]

This means the next crop of leaders in the PLA must come from disparate political and professional affiliations — and even geographical locations. Two criteria seemed to be at work for picking the officers who replaced the nearly 300 military men sacked or demoted because of alleged association with the Yang Clan. First of all, they must not have records of factionalism. Secondly, they must be professionals, not political commissars like Yang Baibing.

To lay the ghost of factionalism to rest, Deng also resorted to three major strategies in the thorough personnel shifts of late 1992. First of all, he inducted a large number of affiliates of the Third Field Army to top positions. In the dozen-or-so years since Deng assumed power in 1978, it was alumni from the Second and Fourth Field armies who had monopolized the bulk of the senior posts. In the post-congress PLA, the top representative of the Third Field Army was Zhang Zhen, who was resurrected from semi-retirement to be the CMC Vice-Chairman.[69]

The second strategem that Deng apparently adopted was to bring in the navy as a counterpoise to the army. At the Party Congress, six naval representatives were promoted full or alternate members of the Central Committee — more than any other branches of the PLA. While the aggrandizement of the navy reflected the growing clout of Liu Huaqing, it also mirrored the fact that a major portion of the power projections of the country would in the 1990s take place over the deep blue seas.[70]

Thirdly, a number of officers who gained major promotions were well-respected professionals who did not have a "horizontal" personal network. A good example is the new Logistics Chief, Fu Quanyou. The much-decorated general began his career with the First Field Army, which was virtually dissolved soon after 1949. Fu is not known to have a power base of his own. Perhaps to a lesser extent, the same could be said of Chief of the General Staff Zhang Wannian.[71]

To a degree, then, Deng seems to have succeeded in eating the cake and having it. The PLA will only "interfere" in politics the way he wants it. However, it is also clear that the country as a whole has to pay a stiff price. With its lopsided representation on the Central Committee and other major bodies of Party and state, the PLA will likely get its way in the demand for a larger slice of the economic pie. Already, the military versions of the Eighth Five-year Plan and Ten-year Economic Blueprint, which were laid down in 1990 and 1991, provided for an annual increase in the budget of 10% discounting inflation.[72]

(viii) The Creeping Influence of the Legal-security Establishment

Yet another winner at the Fourteenth Party Congress was the so-called legal and security establishment. In a move that may appeal to western governments, the Communist authorities decided to boost their legal arm to ensure the development of the socialist market economy: a spate of laws will be enacted to underpin the nation's transition to a market system. At the same time, the police and law courts have been strengthened to help safeguard the dominance of the Party. Again reflecting Deng Xiaoping's obsession with balance, politicians in this arena who received hefty promotions at the Congress were representatives of the hardline factions. A number of the protégés of conservative elders Song Ping and Peng Zhen rose to senior perks.

The legal-security establishment covers the following areas: the police, the secret police, the courts and procuratorates as well as the anti-corruption and "disciplinary-inspection" organs. The nerve centre of this labyrinth comprises two leading bodies of the Central Committee, namely, the Political and Legal Commission (PLC) and the Central Commission for Disciplinary Inspection (CCDI). On the government side, the commanding organs are the Ministry of Public Security, the Ministry of State Security, the Supervision Ministry, the Ministry of Justice, the Supreme People's Court, and the Supreme People's Procuratorate. In addition, the PLC also has some say over the People's Armed Police (PAP). This is despite the fact that after the June 4 bloodbath, the Central Military Commission has assumed general leadership over the PAP.[73]

The practice of lumping together the legal and police functions goes back to the early 1950s. First of all, there is no tradition of the independence of the judiciary in China. Secondly, like the PLA, the police and the law courts are deemed "tools of the dictatorship of the proletariat." As in the case of the army, the functions of the police and the courts have been expanded to diffuse post-June 4 dissent.

By late 1992, there were signs that this legal-and-security behemoth might also have swallowed the National People's Congress. The top leadership had decided that Qiao Shi would take over the Chairmanship of the NPC when its Eighth Session began in March 1993. The CCP needs tighter control over the legislature in view of the growing importance of law-making.[74]

Firstly, the success of the introduction of the "socialist market economy" hinges on whether those much-heralded statutes on company formation, stock companies, accounting, and auditing would be put into place. Secondly, as can be seen from the post-1989 legislations on public assembly and demonstrations, the party has looked upon the NPC as another tool for enforcing proletarian dictatorship. In December 1992, the NPC moved a *State Security Law* which was targetted at "behaviour that harms state security." Minister of State Security Jia Chunwang said on the occasion that even as reform ran its course, the "struggle against subversion" by foreign and local-based agents had become "sharper and more complex."[75]

The expanding clout of the legal and security network is evident from the line-up at the Party Congress. Cadres looking after law and order got an unprecedented number of seats on the Politburo and the Secretariat. They included the titular head of the establishment, member of the Politburo Standing Committee, Qiao Shi; newly promoted Politburo member Wei Jianxing, the Minister of Supervision who had taken over the leadership of the CCDI from Qiao; newly elected Alternate Politburo Member Wang Hanbin, who is a Vice-Chairman of the NPC; and the new member of the Secretariat, Ren Jianxin. President of the Supreme People's Court since 1988, Ren was in December given Qiao's job of Secretary of the PLC.[76]

The new calling of the legal-security apparatus was laid down by Party chief Jiang Zemin at a national meeting of cadres who specialized in "political and legal work." On the one hand, new laws were required for the new economic system. "Whether [they are geared towards] market adjustments or macro-economic adjustments and control by the state, [policies] need to be put on the legal track," Jiang said. "Without a healthy and comprehensive socialist legal system, there won't be a good socialist market order."

On the other hand, Jiang stressed the "dictatorship" role of the police and the courts. The Party chief urged them to provide "political guarantees" for further reform, meaning "ensuring political stability and social stability." It is noteworthy that Jiang evoked the slogan that was raised *ad nauseam* during the one year after the June-4 massacre: "Without a stable and united political situation, nothing can be accomplished."[77]

Top judge Ren Jianxin headed the list of conservative law-enforcement officers who were promoted at the Congress. A well-known leftist, Ren impressed the leadership soon after the Tiananmen Square crackdown with his iron-fisted approach to the law. The senior legal official has shocked international opinion by insisting that the Party, not the law books, should guide judicial work. As late as September 1992, Ren pointed out that "political and legal departments must self-consciously insist upon and accept the leadership of the Party." Sources in the legal establishment said Ren had a habit of calling up judges of various levels to give them instructions on how major cases should be handled.[78]

The rising star of the Politburo, Wei Jianxing, is considered a protégé of Song Ping. The two had worked together in the Organization Department. Yet another Song associate is Wei's senior deputy at the CCDI, Hou Zongbin. A former Party chief of Henan province, Hou had worked under Song in Gansu province. The new Alternate Politburo Member, Wang Hanbin, is a long-time follower of hard-line elder Peng Zhen, who is Qiao Shi's predecessor as head of the legal and security establishment.[79]

III. Collective Leadership with Jiang Zemin as Its Core

In sharp contrast to the fire-spitting speeches of his *nanxun*, Deng opted for a safe course at the Fourteenth Party Congress: a collective leadership — as manifested in the Politburo Standing Committee — with Jiang Zemin as its core. The patriarch was convinced this team was best suited to waging market reforms, on the one hand, and for maintaining an ideological and political straitjacket, on the other.

After more than three years of observation, Deng was by late 1992 apparently persuaded that Jiang, who had in June 1989 been nominated to the top Party post by the late Li Xiannian, was the best person to hold the fort. While conservative by nature, Jiang was quick to profess loyalty to Deng's market-oriented gambit. Most important, Jiang could be trusted to put the supremacy of the CCP before everything. The former Shanghai Party boss would not commit the same errors of Hu Yaobang or Zhao Ziyang by "succumbing to bourgeois liberalization."[80] Moreover, Deng was a hostage to history. Having already dumped two of his chosen successors, the patriarch would be hard put to replace Jiang with another heir-apparent.

What Deng seemed to have been willing to overlook, however, was that, in terms of economics, Jiang was closer to the central planners led by Li Peng than to the moderate technocrats led by Zhu Rongji. Moreover, he had more than once openly sided with Deng's nemesis, the leftists.

Within the Politburo Standing Committee, however, it is apparent that Jiang is at most a first among equals. Jiang's brief is that of a goal-keeper, not a centre forward. As will be argued in the following section, both because of his mediocrity and his lack of vision, the Party chief's role is not to hack out new paths but to preserve the line of the Fourteenth Congress as laid down by the patriarch.

The Politburo Standing Committee as a whole, which represents some of the disparate sectors as laid out in the previous sections, rules China. With the removal of the military prowess of the Yang brothers, Deng made sure there would be no supreme chieftain in the mould of Mao — or himself — after his rendezvous with Marx. While it can be argued that a collective leadership runs counter to millennia of Chinese history, Deng is apparently convinced that built-in checks and balances within such a leadership carry the best safeguards against chaos.

(i) The Role of Jiang Zemin

After the Fourteenth Congress, Deng again indicated his total support for Jiang as the centre of the new leadership. Jiang was promised the position of state president at the NPC in early 1993. Even more intriguing was Deng's decision to reactivate the Leading Group on Economics and Finance (LGEF) and to appoint Jiang as its head. While the LGEF does not meet regularly, it is in theory the nation's highest authority on economic decision-making. Moreover, the exalted position made it possible for Jiang to act as a counterpoise to both Li Peng and Zhu Rongji, who were named deputies of the top organ.[81]

More important, in a meeting with Jiang soon after the Congress, Deng reportedly reinforced his support for the Party boss. The patriarch vowed he would use whatever resources and energy he had to ensure that his protégé remained the "core" of the leadership. "What more can I do for you in the next few years?" Deng told Jiang. While Jiang was not effusive in his demands, the paramount leader apparently said the Party and military chief would have more say in the personnel reshuffles that were going on both in the civilian and military sectors.[82]

However, Jiang would seem to have serious flaws that preclude him from becoming a bona fide Helmsman. And this has less to do with the fact that, in Communist-Chinese history, none of the anointed successors — be it Lin Biao or Hua Guofeng — managed to last long after the demise of their patron.

First of all, Jiang had dubious credentials as a reformer. During Deng's *nanxun*, the patriarch criticized what he called the "formalism" of the top echelon, principally Jiang and Li Peng. The criticism was repeated during the paramount leader's tour of the Capital Iron and Steel Works in May 1992, when he complained that certain leaders in Zhongnanhai failed to implement the spirit of the *nanxun*. He even hinted that the so-called Jiang-Li system might have to be fine-tuned.[83] Indeed, Jiang, who has an unfortunate propensity for showing off his ungrammatical and accented English and Russian, is often ridiculed for "empty words, foreign words, and nonsensical words."[84]

The debate on how to achieve the "socialist market economy" has been focussed on whether one should emphasize market forces or "non-mandatory" macro-level control by the state. While liberal economists have almost made a fetish out of the market, there is no mistaking the fact that the Party boss wants stronger macro-level regulations. In spite of its homage to the "invisible hand" of Adam Smith, Jiang's Political Report at the Congress highlighted the need for "macro-level regulation and control" to rectify the "innate weaknesses" of the market.[85]

In a later context, Jiang also made known his largely conservative approach to "synthesizing" market forces and non-mandatory planning. He said in a December 1992 speech that "[various] markets had to be propagated and their functions developed." However, the Party chief added: "We must use economic, legal and whatever executive means as are required, to strengthen the macro-level regulation and control by the state."[86] By the end of 1992, there were signs Jiang had joined the chorus of Li Peng and Yao Yilin in decrying Deng's high-growth model.

Jiang has been able to win over the octogenarian leadership, including Deng, with his uncompromising stand against "liberalization." Compared with Tian Jiyun and Qiao Shi, Jiang's effort at "fighting leftism" was lukewarm at best. In his much-hyped speech to the Central Party School on 9 June 1992, the Party boss repeated the conservative line that "leftism" was a matter of cognizance ("taking a bookish, doctrinaire approach to Marxism"), while "rightism" was a matter of political standpoint ("negating the Four Cardinal Principles").[87]

Perhaps reflecting the views of the patriarch, the Party chief stopped making references to "anti-leftism" soon after the Congress. During a visit to Shanghai in late November, he scandalized the intelligentsia by apparently departing from the criterion of "taking economic construction as the core" of national work. "The main theme of our society should be patriotism, socialism and collectivism," he said.[88]

To the dismay of the liberal intellectuals, Jiang sided with the Maoists on repeated occasions after the *nanxun*. For example, on questions of ideology and propaganda, he funnelled support to *People's Daily* Director Gao Di — who was finally ousted in late 1992 — against Deng protégé Li Ruihuan. The Party boss was also instrumental in blocking the promotion of Zheng Bijian as head of the Propaganda Department.[89]

There are, however, clear indications that the mantle apparently thrust on him by Deng is way too large for Jiang's ability. For example, can Jiang really control the PLA? Analysts have given the CMC Chairman high marks for trying to cultivate the top brass. For example, on the more than twenty trips that Jiang had made to the regions in the three years up to the end of 1992, he huddled with local military leaders in an effort to build up a network of his own.[90]

And after seeing how the Yang brothers had blocked efforts by Jiang to consolidate his military influence, Deng put Liu Huaqing and Zhang Zhen in charge of the day-to-day administration of the army. Both being in their late seventies, neither Liu nor Zhang were expected to challenge the CMC Chairman. However, there is a consensus among Chinese and western military analysts that Jiang is held in very low regard by the professional officers.

Most fatal for Jiang's prospects of becoming a real supremo, however, is his abiding mediocrity. Not for nothing has Jiang been compared to Hua Guofeng, who was a lacklustre minister of public security before he was named Chairman of the Party by a dying Mao. A look at his career shows Jiang was a most undistinguished minister of electronics in the early 1980s. His track record in Shanghai is inferior to that of such other Shanghai mayors or Party secretaries as Wang Daohan or Zhu Rongji.

Moreover, it would be naive to think that Deng had not adopted mechanisms to check and balance the preponderance of Jiang. For example, the patriarch had earlier thwarted efforts by Jiang to promote a large number of Shanghai cadres to Beijing. In late 1990, Jiang and other affiliates of the Shanghai Faction sent fifty-odd mid- and senior-ranking officials from the East China metropolis for a spell in the Central Party School. The idea was that these officials would soon be transferred to key Party and government posts in Beijing. However, the bid for power fizzled out. About the only protégé that Jiang managed to install in Beijing was the former Vice-Party Secretary of Shanghai, Zeng Qinghong, who became Vice-Chief of the General Office of the Central Committee.[91]

(ii) Other Principal Players for the Mid-1990s

Zhu Rongji

At least in the economics department, Zhu Rongji was Deng's fourth chosen successor after Hu, Zhao and Jiang. During his visit to the Capital Iron and Steel Works in May, the patriarch openly praised Zhu's ability to propagate the market economy. He also expressed regrets about "not having elevated comrade Rongji sooner."[92] For, if Jiang Zemin and Li Peng had somehow let him down in economic reform, Deng was convinced the former Shanghai mayor would more than make amends. It was at the insistence of Deng that Zhu took the "helicopter ride" from alternate member of the Central Committee to member of the Politburo Standing Committee at the Fourteenth Congress.

Even before the Congress, Zhu had assumed effective control over most aspects of the economy, including the distribution of resources; production; circulation of products; foreign trade; the transformation of state enterprises; and the development of the stocks system and stock exchanges. Earlier in the year, the Vice-Premier had presided over the drafting of State Council regulations giving an unprecedented level of autonomy to public-sector business units. The main goal of such regulations was "pushing state enterprises to the marketplace."[93] Zhu also played a key role in speeding up the development of shareholding companies.

Reflecting his colours as a relatively cautious technocrat — as opposed to the radical reformers of the Zhao Ziyang school — however, Zhu's calling had by late 1992 turned from offence to defence. In some speeches, the Master Reformer began sounding a bit like Li Peng when he cracked the whip on "excessively ambitious" cadres and entrepreneurs in the localities.

In the last months of 1992, Zhu practically issued an ultimatum to regional cadres and managers to cool off their investment binge. The Vice-Premier pointed out at a State Council meeting that bank loans for the year had gone up by 20% and currency in circulation an incredible 200%. He specifically targetted three areas in his criticism of over-ambitious expansion: real estate, the issuing of stocks, and the opening of development zones. "The extent of loans and credit and the issuing of currency should be restricted within prescribed limits," he said. "Whoever goes beyond these limits has to be held responsible."[94]

Zhu was of course justified in sounding the alarms. Excessive capital investment and inflation were real dangers. Moreover, as in 1988, there were signals that the central planners were taking advantage of the need to "cure and restructure the economy" to choke off Deng's fast-paced reforms. However, as has been argued earlier, Zhu and other moderate technocrats were also doing their Li Peng act for political reasons: the regions and the entrepreneurs were whizzing away from the orbit of central Party authorities.

Whether the moderate technocrats led by Zhu can become the dominant force in Chinese politics, however, depends as much on whether they can cool down the economy, as on whether they can lay down fair and judicious rules for the growth of the market economy. The laws and regulations promised for 1993 — in areas like banking, accounting, auditing, company formation, stocks and shares — will be crucial. Equally important is the ability of Zhu and his colleagues to withstand political interference.

Such interference comes from two quarters. The first comprises ideologues and central planners who baulk at going further down the quasi-capitalistic road. The second comes from ingrained interests. Many senior officials and offspring of Party elders are trading their positions and connections for business deals. They will resist to the death efforts by any reformer to ensure fair competition in an open marketplace.

Li Peng

Perennial speculation about his imminent fall notwithstanding, Li Peng was by late 1992 destined for another term as Premier. In spite of Li's long-standing opposition to the "high speed growth model," Deng had to acquiesce in his continued stewardship of the central government. Li still had the support of the conservative elders as well as the central planning-oriented bureaucrats. Moreover, Deng found it possible to stomach the foster son of Zhou Enlai for the familiar reason: the Premier has a fairly good record for promoting stability.

Overall, Li's powers as head of government were reduced because of the preponderance of Zhu Rongji, to the extent that the latter chaired quite a number of major State Council conferences in the latter half of 1992. However, of all the sectors of the economy, Li is believed to have retained control over the purse-strings — specifically the Finance Ministry and the People's Bank of China.[95] Such major finance officials as the two Finance Ministers of 1992 — Wang Bingqian and Liu Zhongli — as well as central

Leadership Changes at the Fourteenth Party Congress 2.33

bankers Li Guixian and Chen Yuan are considered fiscal conservatives and Li allies.

In December 1992, Li Peng, who had seldom made major pronouncements on the economy since the summer, apparently got a new lease on life thanks to signs of the economy overheating. In a speech at a year-end economic conference, Li repeated the familiar arguments that the economy must grow under the premise of "stability, balance and harmony." While referring to Deng Xiaoping's plea, made at the *nanxun*, that "the economy should enter a new threshold once every few years," the premier warned: "The speed that we are after should be a speed that is based on a rational structure, that matches the needs of the market, and that is high in efficiency." On price reform, Li said it would only be implemented bearing in mind "the ability of society to cushion [the shocks]."[96]

Moreover, Li succeeded to retain his hold on foreign policy, including policy towards Hong Kong. His position as the head of the Central Committee's Leading Group on Foreign Affairs seemed secure. In spite of his relatively poor image overseas, Li earned the respect of Deng and other elders for successfully enhancing China's diplomatic leverage.

As the "successor" of such central planners as Chen Yun and Yao Yilin, the Premier would at least up to the mid-1990s go on being the spokesman of the huge body of central planning-oriented bureaucrats. Li also carried the brief for the so-called Soviet Faction in the State Council, or cadres trained in the East Bloc in the 1950s.

Qiao Shi

Political analysts in Beijing were by the end of 1992 divided as to whether the powers of Qiao Shi had been diminished by virtue of his having given up two key portfolios at the Fourteenth Party Congress: the head of the Central Commission for Disciplinary Inspection and the Secretary of the Political and Legal Commission. According to one theory, this was Deng Xiaoping's way of putting in check Qiao's growing influence.

However, another theory goes that Qiao's powers had in fact been augmented because of his having been designated Chairman of the National People's Congress. Thus, Qiao was well placed to become another Peng Zhen-like kingmaker — only that he would likely be stronger than Peng. After all, when Peng was NPC chief in the early 1980s, he retained his influence over the entire security establishment.

Even assuming he had lost effective control of the security apparatus to Ren Jianxin and other protégés of Peng Zhen, however, Qiao is a potential successor to Jiang as the "core" of the collective leadership. After all, he is the most senior among the civilian Politburo members, having first entered the top-most rung — the Central Committee Secretariat — at the Twelfth Party Congress in 1982. More important, Qiao is the head of the fairly large clique of student leaders who were active in Shanghai in the mid-1940s. This relatively little known cabal include Jiang Zemin, Wu Xueqian and Qian Qichen. Both Wu and Jiang reported to Qiao in those heady days of campus radicalism.[97]

Yet another basis for Qiao's claim to be top dog — should Jiang's hold falter — is his liberal credentials. In spite of his stern front as secret police chief, Qiao is a moderate who is markedly more liberal than either Jiang Zemin or Li Peng. It is well known that he cast an "abstention vote" during the meeting of the Politburo Standing Committee in May 1989 that deliberated over whether to use troops against the students. After the crackdown, Qiao urged a relatively lenient treatment of the "counter-revolutionaries" as well as bourgeois-liberal cadres and intellectuals suspected of involvement in the democracy movement. In early 1992, he reportedly proposed in the inner councils of the Party that the jail terms of several big-name dissidents be commuted.[98]

After the *nanxun*, Qiao was, together with Tian Jiyun, one of the few senior cadres who actively preached the need to fight "leftism." In various speeches to the Central Party School, Qiao warned that, as much as "rightism," "leftism" could lead to the demise of the Party and country. He zeroed in on the need to "jettison old concepts" and to "liberate one's thoughts."[99] Should the fortune of the Zhao Ziyang faction improve, Qiao could become the bridge between the establishment and the radicals.

Liu Huaqing

The old general and Deng loyalist has been given the brief to ensure stability within the PLA and also to provide military and political support to economic reforms. As we discussed earlier, in return for the military support, the PLA would be given *carte blanche* to upgrade its weapons. As a key professional and expert in research and development, General Liu will give a mighty push to military modernization. "Our major task is to strengthen the 'quality construction' of the PLA, to positively implement reforms and restructuring, and to go down the path of building up an elite corps according to Chinese characteristics," he said at the 1992 NPC.[100]

If Liu were to help his old friend Deng ensure political stability, however, he has to tame two military forces that might upset the power equilibrium in the run-up to the mid-1990s. One is the preponderance of the corps of retired generals, who included Zhang Aiping, Li Desheng, Xiao Ke, Yang Dezhi and Ye Fei. These members of the old guard, some of whom do not see eye to eye with Deng, had displayed their prowess in May and June 1989, when they expressed reservations about using military force to crush the student demonstrators. In late 1992, they had through their representative, Zhang Zhen, once again "intervened" in government by expressing opinions in areas such as diplomacy and geopolitics. As we have seen, the retired generals were a factor behind Beijing's decision to "punish" France for its sale of Mirage fighters to Taiwan.[101]

Of more lasting influence, however, will be the larger corps of relatively young officers who are the product of military reforms in the early 1980s. Graduates of formal military academies, they are sympathetic to western military doctrines as well as reform in general. Many of these young turks, who are in their forties, are considered sympathisers of Zhao Ziyang, who was CMC Vice-Chairman for a brief period before his downfall. By late 1992, however, there were no signs of their emergence as a power bloc. When they eventually throw their weight around, however, these military modernizers are expected to exert a positive influence on reform.[102]

IV. A Leadership for the Twenty-first Century

In apparent contradiction to the Marxist theory of dialectical materialism — that the political "superstructure" changes in accordance with shifts in the underpinning economic forces — Deng Xiaoping and other Party veterans hope the leadership with Jiang Zemin as its core would preserve CCP supremacy forever.

However, it is clear that the leadership structure as defined at the Fourteenth Party Congress is not a line-up that can answer the needs of the twenty-first century — or even those of the mid-1990s. Jiang Zemin and Li Peng speak with the vision and vocabulary of the 1950s and 1960s. At 64, Zhu Rongji seems to be a transitional figure rather than a Deng-like architect for yet another major round of reform.[103]

By early 1993, however, seasoned analysts see the emergence of new power blocs and new leaders that could nudge the country further to the right of the political spectrum. Presented below are three major groupings that should see the most gain — and make the most contribution to reform — in the run-up to the next century. They are the regional cadres, the private entrepreneurs, and the followers of Zhao Ziyang and Hu Yaobang. However, as will be evident from the last section, this does not mean that "twilight sectors" such as Maoist ideologues and central planners will stop playing sizeable roles, be they positive or negative. Moreover, the three forces that will render China more in tune with the requirements of a market economy must learn to appease and win over the CCP's gatekeepers, namely the army and the police.

(i) The Followers of Zhao Ziyang and Hu Yaobang

Business realities of 1992 dictated that many of the old economic theories of Zhao Ziyang and Hu Yaobang were revived. Take, for example, Zhao's much-maligned "coastal strategy" or the "theory of the big cycle" — that coastal areas will develop best if they suck in foreign capital and raw materials, make use of and process them, and then re-export them on a large scale.[104] Also reinstated was Hu's much-criticised theory that consumerism should be encouraged to spur production. The late Party chief was also given credit for having the foresight to pick Heihe in the Heilongjiang-Russian border as the "northern Shenzhen."[105]

For political reasons, of course, the followers of Hu and Zhao did not dominate the Fourteenth Congress — not by a long shot. However, there were unmistakable signs that a surprisingly large number of the remnants of Hu's so-called Communist Youth League Faction maintained their positions. This is a tribute to the empire-building prowess of Hu, a former chief of the Organization Department. Hu Jintao, who is considered "half a CYL affiliate" — he being also a protégé of Song Ping — was inducted into the Politburo Standing Committee. Other "Huists" still in power include the new head of the United Front Department, Wang Zhaoguo, and the vice-chief of United Front, Wan Shaofen.[106]

And in spite of Deng's determination to circumscribe the influence of the Zhao Faction, the patriarch elevated a number of them at the Fourteenth Congress. Head of the Party Central Committee's General Office, Wen Jiabao, was made an Alternate Member of the Politburo. The most high-profile among the Zhaoists, however, was the Party chief of Chongqing, Xiao Yang. While he missed out the chance to succeed fellow

Zhaoist Yang Rudai as both Sichuan Party chief and Politburo member, Xiao was given the governorship of the populous province. Xiao had by late 1992 impressed western businessmen with this dictum on reforming state enterprises: "to study well how the board of directors of capitalistic companies stem wastage and losses."[107]

Other examples of the staying power of the Zhaoists are Lei Yu and Zhang Wei. The hero, or anti-hero, of the "Hainan Car Scandal," Lei, who was Vice-Mayor of Guangzhou at the beginning of 1992, would have been promoted either Mayor of Guangzhou or Vice-Governor of Guangdong had it not been for sabotage by his enemies in the province. In mid-1992, he was transferred to his home province of Guangxi as Vice-Governor. Zhang is the former head of the Technological Development Zone of Tianjin. He "resigned" from the Party immediately after the massacre and was put under tight surveillance for almost two years afterwards. By 1992, however, he had been rehabilitated in a major municipal position.[108]

As we shall see in the following section, Zhaoists are particularly strong in government and business circles along the southeast coast. This has to do with the fact that soon after the June 4 crackdown, a large number of Zhao's followers — particularly cadres and social scientists in their thirties and forties — repaired to Guangdong to either serve the local administrations or to make waves in the market economy.

(ii) The Regional Leadership

It is unrealistic to assume that all or most regional leaders are "reformers." However, it is generally true that specially after the passage of Document No. 4 — which permits cadres and Party units to set up businesses — the fast-paced development of the local economy is intimately tied up with the personal well-being of regional cadres.

Partly as a check-and-balance mechanism, however, Beijing has a tradition of deliberately appointing cautious, unambitious leaders to vibrant areas. The reason is obvious: consider what would happen if a dynamic cadre were posted to a free-wheeling province like Guangdong or Fujian. While that region may develop by leaps and bounds, it may zoom out of the CCP's purview. Ren Zhongyi and Xiang Nan, the former Party boss of respectively Guangdong and Fujian, were very liberal and popular. They both had inordinately short reigns. Former Guangdong Governor Ye Xuanping, one of the few local leaders who dared openly confront the central planners in Beijing, had a relatively long tenure because of the special relationship between his father, Marshal Ye Jianying, and Deng Xiaoping.[109]

It is, therefore, not surprising that the leaders of Guangdong are, from the point of view of Beijing, safe bets who can be trusted not to stray from central edicts. Both Party boss Xie Fei and Governor Zhu Senlin are not known for their bush-whacking style of reform. In policy speeches, they have a tendency of repeating what has already appeared in central-level documents. The only exception among the top layer in the province might be the Mayor of Guangzhou, Li Ziliu. By late 1992, however, there were signs that Li might be stymied in his efforts to bring about fast-paced reforms.[110]

Economic exigencies — namely the need to fight increasingly tough competition from such other open cities as Shanghai — however, will prevail and precipitate the phasing out of the inept top rung. The succcessors of Xie Fei or Zhu Senlin could well be mid-echelon cadres in Guangdong and Guangzhou — as well as the mayors of most cities in the free-wheeling Pearl River Delta — who have enviable track records as bold reformers.

A case in point is the Party Secretary of the boom city of Foshan, Ou Guangyuan, who was praised by Deng when the latter toured the Pearl River Refrigerator Factory during the *nanxun*. Ou, 44, was the youngest among the seven Guangdong cadres elevated to the Central Committee. He won his fame for implementing the stocks system as well as for rendering the government from being a "mother-in-law-type *yamen*" to a centre of services for enterprises.[111]

The Special Economic Zone of Shenzhen yields a specially good insight into the dichotomy between a crust of cautious, even conservative, cadres at the top and a corps of radical reformers occupying positions just one or two rungs below. At the very top are officials in the old mode like Party Secretary Li Hao, Mayor Zheng Liangyu, and, since October, Mayor Li Youwei. (Liang Xiang, the former Shenzhen Party Secretary and Hainan Governor who is an unrepentent Zhaoist, had weathered corruption investigations and spends his retirement in Shenzhen. He lives in a house in the CCP compound and still exerts a "moral influence.") Below Zheng and Li are a group of radical modernizers. They include the head of the Shenzhen Committee for Restructuring the Economy, Xu Jing'an; the Secretary General of the municipal Party committee, Ren Kelei (who is the son of Ren Zhongyi); and the Secretary General of the municipal government, Li Luoli. Both Xu and Li belonged to think-tanks close to Zhao Ziyang.[112]

(iii) The Private Entrepreneurs

By the end of 1992, there was as yet no compelling evidence that the "new class" of private entrepreneurs, managers and professionals might creep close to the centre of power. However, there are reasons to believe that, if, as most projections say, the non-state sector takes up at least half of the economy by 2000,[113] the middle and professional classes would assume a political clout that is commensurate with their economic power.

The influence of the private entrepreneurs became even more pronounced as political heavyweights began joining their ranks in 1992. In mid-1992, Bo Xicheng, the son of venerated elder Bo Yibo, raised eyebrows when he resigned from his post of head of the Beijing Tourism Bureau to start a semi-private hotel management company in the capital. "In reform, someone has to take the lead," said the 41-year-old "princeling." "We must learn to be independent and to earn our own bread," he said.[114]

By late 1992, it was common knowledge that the sons, daughters and in-laws of the following CCP elders and senior ministers had, to use the Chinese expression, "gone to [the] sea [of business]": Deng Xiaoping, Chen Yun, Bo Yibo, Ye Jianying, Yang Shangkun, Wang Zhen, Peng Zhen, and so on. So many cadres had been lured away to the exciting world of Adam Smith that the Organization Department reportedly had difficulty filling the leadership positions in poor and remote provinces and areas.[115]

By the early 1990s, there were inchoate signs of the entrepreneurs and managers setting up business — though not as yet political — organizations. In line with such western institutions as chambers of commerce, practitioners in different sectors and product lines began forming trade associations. By 1992, there were at least several hundreds of such outfits. Shanghai alone boasted thirty-seven associations based on trade and product lines, and thirteen based on geographical affliations.[116]

At least in the embryonic phase, the red capitalists will be demanding a fair share of political power not for its own sake but to ensure equal competition with the state sector. This is apparent from official and unofficial reports about the second-class citizenship of the non-state-owned sector.

A survey of 117 private businesses reported by the New China News Agency in late 1992 showed the entrepreneurs grousing about "discrimination." They had difficulty getting credit, finding sales outlets, and hiring well-trained people. They suffered from a poor social status as well as a negative image in the press. And they were subjected to "unfair taxes." Only 11.1% among entrepreneurs surveyed who had assets of over RMB1 million said they were optimistic about the prospects of their businesses. The figure was higher — 41.8% — for "private bosses" with assets of over RMB10 million.[117]

Yet another study by the pro-Beijing Hong Kong daily, *Ta Kung Pao*, showed that private businesses laboured under severe handicaps. Many managers were worried about their status and future, to the extent they wanted to re-register their concerns under a state unit. Others were subjected to taxes, levies and "forced contributions" of up to 70 categories. They generally had difficulty getting raw materials, finance, and technological help.[118]

The semi-official Hong Kong China News Agency quoted managers in the Beijing-based Nande Economic Group — one of the country's largest private enterprises — as saying the government should scrap the distinction between public-sector and private-sector business units. "In reform and economic policy, we have stopped asking whether it is surnamed socialist or capitalist," one Nande executive ventured. "Similarly, we should no longer classify enterprises into government or private ones."[119]

In its report on the plight of "red capitalists," *Ta Kung Pao* said: "There is not one administrative department or organization to harmonize the relationship between [private] enterprises and government units in the areas of industry, commerce, tax or planning and construction, in such a way as to safeguard the proper and legal rights of private enterprises."[120] It is, therefore, not surprising that private businessmen might band together to demand such political power as is necessary to protect their economic rights.

Moderate economist Yang Peixin pointed out the inevitable trend of history when he advocated "electing" more entrepreneurs and managers to the NPC, the putative "organ of the highest power." Yang, who also works in the economic think-tank of the State Council, indicated that more entrepreneurs in the NPC would ensure the orderly progress of the socialist market economy. "What the NPC discusses in the main is economic legislation and policies in order to pull down the obstacles for enterprises," he said. "It will not do if we do not invite entrepreneurs [to join the legislature]."[121] One thing, of course, leads to another. If there is a justifiable need to induct entrepreneurs into the legislature, why not the councils of government?

(iv) Contours of a New Coalition

The upwardly mobile forces mentioned above could, for economic if not political reasons, put together temporary or long-term coalitions to bid for power. For example, it is conceivable that the Zhaoists — or cadres who identify themselves with the radical economic and political reforms of 1987 and 1988 — might form the core of a fairly broad-based coalition with regional leaders and private entrepreneurs.

Broadly speaking, private entrepreneurs are sympathetic with the economic and political reforms of Zhao Ziyang and his followers. On a small scale, a trial run of the Zhaoists cooperating with private-sector practitioners already took place during the pro-democracy crusade of 1989. Large non-state-owned companies like the Stone Computer Company of Beijing as well as individual enterpreneurs contributed heavily to the 1989 movement.[122]

The year 1992 also witnessed signs of a fledgling "coalition" between the liberal cadres and intellectuals, on the one hand, and entrepreneurs, on the other. It was the bosses of both state and private corporations who sponsored the growing number of private conferences held by rightist intellectuals throughout the year. Topics in these unsanctioned meetings included "fighting leftism" as well as modernization in general.[123]

It is no accident that, by late 1992, the elite among rightist cadres and intellectuals had openly called for the improvement in the status of private entrepreneurs, who were seen as a "new class" that could expedite the nation's modernization. In two major meetings in December, liberal scholars and cadres heaped praise on efforts by private businessmen Chen Jinyi and Wang Xianglin to amass capital and to take over government concerns. They argued that the state should no longer monopolize production — and that the socio-political status of private entrepreneurs must be enhanced. Participants in those conferences included Zhu Houze, Yu Guangyuan, Hu Jiwei, Li Chang, Wu Jinglian, Wu Mingyu, Wu Xiang and Dong Fureng.[124]

It is easy to explain the affinity between regional cadres, on the one hand, and Zhaoists and private entrepreneurs, on the other. As explained earlier, the southeast coast has a large concentration of radical-liberal officials some of whom used to work for Zhao. Moreover, it is obvious that officials along the Golden Coast see their future inextricably linked with how well their private-sector businessmen are doing.

Moreover, it is conceivable that depending on the development of the market economy, members of the "twilight sectors" mentioned above might join the action through ways including a pro-market self-transformation. For example, by the second half of 1992, quite a number of central planning-oriented cadres had emulated their more free-wheeling counterparts along the coast and severed relations with the government to become private-sector taipans.

Conclusion and Epilogue: Stability before Reform

(i) Deng's Bid to Ensure Stability after His Death

By early 1993, there were no signs that the senior leadership of the CCP was smoothing the way for socio-political forces that were in line with the requirements of the market economy. Instead, there were disquieting signals that factions and sectors representing the *ancien régime* might have clawed back some territory.

At least from the perspective of patriarch Deng Xiaoping, there is no doubt stability had been put before fast-paced reforms. Buffeted by whispers of mortality, the patriarch took the following steps to attain the new — and old — goal of "unity and stability" in the aftermath of his rendezvous with Marx.

First of all, a veritable personality cult was erected around Deng Xiaoping. While it was uncertain whether such of Deng's underlings as Jiang Zemin or the patriarch's children were reviving a Maoist-style personality worship to enhance their own power, it was beyond doubt Deng himself acquiesced in it. After all, Deng Thought would provide the centripetal force for holding together the nation.

Dengism had by late 1992 practically replaced Maoism — and Marxism-Leninism — as the state religion. China's socialist market was inundated by a tidal wave of Deng books, films, videos, TV movies, and other memorabilia. The lionization of Deng culminated in the publication in January 1993 of the 200,000-word tome *Deng Xiaoping on Building Socialism with Chinese Characteristics*, which contained all his words of wisdom from 1977 to 1992.[125]

Secondly, by late 1992, Deng had called off his eleven-month-old campaign against the leftists. Beijing was abuzz with reports about three new instructions given by the patriarch: "We cannot overturn the verdict on June 4; we must never cease combatting bourgeois liberalization; we must help relocate those cadres who stepped down at the Fourteenth Congress because they were not reformist enough or because they were leftist in ideology."[126] Deng obviously feared that a new round of bourgeois liberalization would break out after his death. And the leftist fire-fighters should still be put in reserve to snuff out the next manifestation of the pro-democracy movement.

Thirdly, having consigned the Central Advisory Commission to limbo, Deng was again trying to rally the elders. The patriarch, of course, was hoping against hope that, at a time of declining faith in Marxism, he could coax the last iota of "revolutionary legitimacy" out of the likes of Chen Yun, Wang Zhen or Peng Zhen. The trio, who were all in one way or another ideological enemies of Deng, made public appearances before the arrival of the Year of the Rooster (23 January 1993). They were quoted by the media as giving full support to reform and to the leadership of Deng.[127]

And the post-congress leadership took special pains to massage the egos of the elders. In a New Year's gathering, Politburo member in charge of Party organization Hu Jintao even indicated that the veterans would have a hand in the selection and training of cross-century talents. "We hope the old comrades would continue to show concern towards the propagation of the successors of the socialist enterprise, and that they would give inspiration and help to the neophytes," he said.[128]

Fourthly, as unity and stability would best be guaranteed by men in uniform, the profile of the People's Liberation Army continued to rise. By early 1993, the Party and army were celebrating the fiftieth anniversary of Chairman Mao's launch of the Movement of the Two Supports, which translates roughly into "army-government and army-civilian solidarity." At a gathering honouring the Maoist ideal, Liu Huaqing claimed that the full interdependence between the civilian and military spheres was indispensable for the "long-term security and stability" of the nation. Total army-civilian solidarity, the *People's Daily* editorialized, was "a gigantic spiritual force for unifying the Chinese nation as well as a gigantic material force for pushing forward social progress."[129] Needless to say, the Movement of the Two Supports also gave the PLA a god-sent pretext to interfere in civilian life.

Most significant, however, was Deng's revival of his so-called "major theoretical invention": "steer clear of controversy" or "let's move on without being bogged down by things we cannot solve in the near term." The "no-controversy credo" was affirmed as national policy by the new propaganda chief, Ding Guan'gen, at a meeting of propaganda cadres in early 1993.[130] This essentially means that to promote unity and stability, touchy questions like whether leftists should be punished for obstructing reform, or whether the official verdict on June 4 should be re-examined, will be shelved. In terms of personnel issues, this means that "non-controversial" figures or politicians who are acceptable to all factions should occupy centre stage.

In anticipation of leadership changes at the NPC, the *People's Daily* and the New China News Agency published in January 1993 near-identitical commentaries on the type of cadres who should be promoted to the various levels and branches of government. The commentaries stressed the need to elevate officials who were "knowledgeable about economics and modern management." However, it is instructive to note the order in which the two official organs listed the five major criteria for "cross-century cadres": "firmness in politics; boldness in reform; conduciveness to unity and harmony; cleanliness and practicality; conduciveness to a rational [cadre] structure."[131] The criteria of "firmness in politics" and "conduciveness to unity and harmony" imply relatively cautious cadres who will not rock the boat while waging market reforms.

With such requirements in mind, it is little wonder that the collective leadership with Jiang Zemin as its core would be strengthened at the first session of the Eighth National People's Congress. Jiang Zemin was poised to gain two additional titles: State President and Chairman of the State Central Military Commission. And Li Peng, another politician who is "firm in politics," would be awarded with another term as Premier.

By contrast, Tian Jiyun and Li Ruihuan would effectively be shoved out of the power centre with their appointment to respectively the First Vice-Chairman of the NPC and the Chairman of the CPPCC. In spite of their unquestioned reformist credentials, both were not deemed to be "conducive to unity and harmony." The two liberal leaders had incurred the ire of the remnant Maoists with their fiery speeches against leftism.

(ii) Changing the Colour of the Party

What would happen if the patriarch were to suddenly forsake his 1.15 billion charges? Analysts agree that the prospects for major upheavals —

street demonstrations in tandem with deep splits and internecine warfare among the the Party's different factions — are not high. To a large extent, Deng was right when he pointed out during the *nanxun* that the CCP had to draw the right lesson from the dissolution of Eastern Europe and the USSR: that if the economy is developing well and the people's standard of living is improving, the chances for a popular revolt will be minimized.[132]

Analysts also agree, however, that what is known as peaceful evolution is succeeding in spite of the CCP's determined efforts to wipe out the seeds of liberalization. In the Pearl River Delta region, peaceful evolution had by 1992 well-nigh run its course.

As dissident Wang Ruowang pointed out, however, it would be naive to think that the implementation of the market economy would necessarily bring about political liberalization.[133] At this stage, the prospect of China peacefully evolving into a "western-style," multi-party system seems remote.

It is, however, not unrealistic to expect the flowering of some form of inner-Party democracy. What dissident journalist Liu Binyan used to call the "healthy forces" within the CCP — and within Chinese society in general — seemed to be growing by late 1992. A large number of regional cadres and non-public sector enterpreneurs were for the first time tasting economic — and some political — power.

It is improbable that members of this "new class" would clamour for the end of the CCP. However, if only to ensure the viability of the socialist market economy, they would opt for a more pluralistic approach to politics. For example, they would lobby for the inclusion of more disparate elements — entrepreneurs, professionals, and liberal intellectuals in general — into the Party's higher echelons. The CCP's liberal wing — which incorporates the remnant followers of Hu Yaobang and Zhao Ziyang — might by the mid-1990s have another shot at power. And over time, to use the memorable clause of rebel astrophysicist Fang Lizhi, the colour of the Party would be changed.

Notes

1. There were different versions of the speeches Deng Xiaoping made while touring southern China in early 1992. See *Wen Wei Po* (Hong Kong), 17 April 1992; *Wah Kiu Yat Po* (Hong Kong), 15 March 1992; and *Hong Kong Economic Times*, 12 March 1992.

2. *Ibid.*
3. *Wen Wei Po*, 14 October 1992.
4. *South China Morning Post* (Hong Kong, *SCMP*), 20 October 1992; *Far Eastern Economic Review* (*FEER*), 10 December 1992.
5. Reuters, 14 October 1992.
6. For a discussion of the "purge" of the Yang clan, see, for example, *The Mirror* (Hong Kong), January 1993, pp. 38–41; *Contemporary* (Hong Kong), November 1992, pp. 22–23; Reuters, 15 December 1992.
7. For a complete line-up of the new leadership, see *The Mirror*, November 1992, pp. 30–32; and *Contemporary*, November 1992, pp. 14–16.
8. *Ibid.*
9. *Ta Kung Pao* (Hong Kong), 26 October 1992.
10. *SCMP*, 15 October 1992.
11. For the role played by Liu Huaqing and Zhang Zhen, see for example, *Wide Angle* (Hong Kong), 16 December 1992, pp. 42–46.
12. Author's interview with sources in Beijing.
13. *The Mirror*, November 1992, p. 32.
14. Author's interviews with intellectuals and other Chinese sources in Beijing.
15. *Wah Kiu Yat Po*, 15 March 1992; *Hong Kong Economic Times*, 12 March 1992.
16. New China News Agency, 22 July 1992.
17. *SCMP*, 16 June 1992; 10 April 1992.
18. On an off-the-record basis, Deng Xiaoping also criticized leftists including Wang Renzhi, Gao Di and He Jingzhi.
19. *SCMP*, 4 December 1992.
20. *SCMP*, 11 November 1992; 8 January 1993.
21. *SCMP*, 4 December 1992.
22. See *Contemporary*, November 1992, pp. 44–45; *SCMP*, 4 December 1992.
23. For a discussion of the political orientation of Hu Jintao and Wei Jianxing, see, for example, *Hong Kong Economic Times*, 26 October 1992; *Contemporary*, December 1992, pp. 48–51.
24. See *The Mirror*, September 1992, pp. 46–47.
25. *The Standard* (Hong Kong), 28 November 1992.
26. *Pai Shing* (Hong Kong), 1 January 1993, p. 25.
27. See *Pai Shing*, 1 February 1993, p. 7, for an analysis of the activities of leftists by late 1992.
28. *Ta Kung Pao*, 26 October 1992.
29. *Ibid.*
30. *Ming Pao* (Hong Kong), 21 November 1992; *United Daily News* (Taipei), 1 December 1992.
31. *SCMP*, 28 November 1992.

32. *China Daily*, 29 November 1992; *SCMP*, 30 November 1992.
33. *Hong Kong Economic Journal*, 1 January 1993.
34. *Wen Wei Po*, 31 December 1992; *SCMP*, 1 January 1993.
35. *United Daily News*, 15 October 1992.
36. For a discussion of the Qinghua Faction, see China News Service, 12 February 1993; *SCMP*, 13 February 1993.
37. New China News Agency, 27 November 1992.
38. *Wen Wei Po*, 16 October 1992.
39. *SCMP*, 2 December 1992.
40. *SCMP*, 28 December 1992.
41. *United Daily News*, 16 October 1992.
42. *Wah Kiu Yat Po*, 15 March 1992; *Hong Kong Economic Times*, 12 March 1992.
43. New China News Agency, 9 October 1992.
44. *SCMP*, 30 November 1992.
45. *China Youth Daily* (Beijing), 27 October 1992.
46. *SCMP*, 4 April 1992.
47. *SCMP*, 13 October 1992.
48. For an analysis of the regional affiliation of new Central Committee members, see *Shisida yu Zhongguo de weilai* (The Fourteenth Party Congress and China's Future) (Hong Kong: Contemporary Press, 1992), pp. 36–41.
49. *Ta Kung Pao*, 18 May 1992; *United Daily News*, 18 May 1992.
50. *United Daily News*, 23 July 1992.
51. For a discussion of different provinces revising their development plans after Deng Xiaoping's trip to southern China, see, for example, *Wen Wei Po*, 17 August 1992.
52. New China News Agency, 7 December 1992; *SCMP*, 21 December 1992.
53. Hong Kong China News Agency, 21 December 1992.
54. *Wen Wei Po*, 14 December 1992.
55. New China News Agency, 22 August 1992.
56. *Ming Pao*, 21 August 1992; *Wen Wei Po*, 21 December 1992.
57. New China News Agency, 29 October 1992.
58. New China News Agency, 6 December 1992.
59. New China News Agency, 19 November 1992.
60. *Wen Wei Po*, 13 January 1993.
61. *SCMP*, 2 December 1992.
62. *Hong Kong Economic Journal*, 24 November 1992.
63. For a discussion of the role of Liu Huaqing, see Michael D. Swaine, *The Military and Political Succession in China* (Santa Monica, California: Rand Corp., 1992), p. 197.
64. *China Daily*, 13 October 1992; *Wen Wei Po*, 9 December 1992.

65. *Hong Kong Economic Journal*, 11 December 1992; *SCMP*, 31 December 1992.
66. *China Times* (Taipei), 15 August 1992.
67. For an account of the "offence" committed by the Yang brothers, see, for example, *Ming Pao*, 13 November 1992; *Hong Kong Economic Journal*, 24 November 1992.
68. New China News Agency, 17 December 1992.
69. *Contemporary*, December 1992, pp. 44–47; *Hong Kong Economic Journal*, 3 January 1993.
70. *Ming Pao*, 6 November 1992; *United Daily News*, 15 December 1992.
71. For an analysis of the political affiliation of the newly promoted officers, see Michael D. Swaine (Note 63), pp. 197–98.
72. *SCMP*, 19 November 1992.
73. See Michael D. Swaine (Note 63), pp. 128–29.
74. For a discussion of the political future of Qiao Shi, see *Contemporary*, January 1993, pp. 39–43.
75. China News Service, 22 December 1992.
76. *SCMP*, 16 December 1992.
77. *Wen Wei Po*, 17 December 1992.
78. *SCMP*, 2 September 1992; 10 November 1992.
79. *Hong Kong Economic Journal*, 20 December 1992; *Ming Pao*, 14 December 1992.
80. Deng Xiaoping told North Korean leader Kim Il-sung that his heart was at ease with Jiang Zemin in charge, see *SCMP*, 10 October 1992.
81. *Wen Wei Po*, 14 November 1992.
82. *SCMP*, 11 November 1992.
83. According to Chinese sources, Deng complained during his address at Capital Iron and Steel Works about "cadres in Zhongnanhai who did nothing but engage in empty talk." This is generally taken as a reference to Jiang Zemin and Li Peng.
84. Jiang has a well-known propensity for showing off his foreign language skills in front of diplomats and journalists. This was most evident in his 1991 interview with Amcrican TV personality Barbara Walters.
85. *Ta Kung Pao*, 26 October 1992.
86. China News Service, 16 December 1992.
87. *The Mirror*, July 1992, p. 29.
88. New China News Agency, 22 November 1992.
89. *SCMP*, 15 October 1992; *The Standard*, 11 September 1992.
90. *The Mirror*, December 1992, p. 36
91. Author's interviews with Chinese sources in Shanghai.
92. *The Mirror*, July 1992, p. 27.
93. *Renmin ribao* (People's Daily), 23 July 1992.

94. *Ta Kung Pao*, 21 December 1992; *China Daily*, 1 February 1993.
95. *China Times*, 11 October 1992.
96. New China News Agency, 27 December 1992.
97. For a discussion of the power base of Qiao Shi, see *Contemporary*, January 1993, pp. 39–43.
98. *SCMP*, 7 October 1992.
99. New China News Agency, 2 September 1992; *SCMP*, 11 June 1992.
100. New China News Agency, 26 March 1992.
101. See Note 65.
102. For a discussion of the relationship between Zhao Ziyang and the army, see for example, *The Era of Zhao Ziyang* (Hong Kong: A. B. Books and Stationery, 1989), p. 12, 133.
103. For a discussion of Zhu Rongji's future, see *SCMP*, 2 December 1992.
104. *The Fourteenth Party Congress and China's Future* (see Note 48), pp. 18–22.
105. *Ming Pao*, 14 November 1992.
106. *Hong Kong Economic Times*, 26 October 1992.
107. *Wen Wei Po*, 26 November 1992.
108. *Wen Wei Po*, 23 October 1992; *Sing Tao Daily* (Hong Kong), 11 July 1992.
109. According to Chinese sources, Deng Xiaoping reportedly told Ye Jianying that his son, Ye Xuanping, would be allowed to stay in Guangdong for as long as he liked.
110. *SCMP*, 1 February 1993.
111. *Ming Pao*, 7 December 1992.
112. *SCMP*, 1 January 1993.
113. New China News Agency, 24 December 1992; *Ming Pao*, 13 October 1992.
114. *Ta Kung Pao*, 24 July 1992.
115. *SCMP*, 28 November 1992.
116. New China News Agency, 30 December 1992.
117. New China News Agency, 1 December 1992.
118. *Ta Kung Pao*, 14 December 1992.
119. Hong Kong China News Agency, 29 October, 1992.
120. *Ta Kung Pao*, 14 December 1992; *SCMP*, 14 December 1992.
121. *Ming Pao*, 29 December 1992.
122. For a discussion of the role played by Wan Runnan and Stone Corp. see, for example, *SCMP*, 3 July 1989; 11 July 1989.
123. Private entrepreneurs who were sponsors of the non-official conferences paid for the hotel accommodations and in some instances the costs of publications.
124. *SCMP*, 29 December 1992.
125. New China News Agency, 15 January 1993; *The Standard*, 16 January 1992.

126. *United Daily News*, 14 January 1993.
127. New China News Agency, 20 January 1993.
128. New China News Agency, 13 January 1993.
129. *Renmin ribao*, 11 January 1993.
130. China News Service, 17 January 1993.
131. New China News Agency, 14 January 1993.
132. *Wah Kiu Yat Po*, 15 March 1992; *Hong Kong Economic Times*, 12 March 1992.
133. *Hong Kong Economic Times*, 8 December 1992.

3

Communist Party Orthodoxy

Graham Young

During 1992 the process of reformulation of Chinese Communist Party (CCP) orthodoxy which began in the late 1970s was resumed, consolidated and extended. According to Party sources, since the "shift in focus" to "socialist modernization" announced in 1978, the CCP has progressively defined the path of "building socialism with Chinese characteristics." This is claimed as the second major theoretical achievement of the Party's history — as significant as the earlier successes in understanding "democratic revolution" in China, to which Mao Zedong was the principal contributor. Deng Xiaoping is presented as the main architect of the new theory, through his contributions to evaluating the experiences of the first thirty years of the People's Republic and assimilating the results of practice in order to understand the character and course of Chinese socialism.[1]

The key to this "theoretical" development has been its use as rationalization for reform programmes, most directly economic reforms. The dominant theme has been a progressive reduction of "socialism" to objectives of economic growth, although there have also been subsidiary themes concerning other dimensions of "socialist" objectives. This sort of combination is encapsulated in the formula that the Party has "one central task and two basic points": the central task of economic development, while affirming the policies of reform and "opening up" to the outside world, and adhering to the "four fundamental principles" (the socialist road, the people's democratic dictatorship, Communist Party leadership and Marxist-Leninist-Mao Thought ideological guidance). Statements of Party orthodoxy have insisted that these several elements are mutually reinforcing, while potential inconsistencies among them have been ignored or defined away by interpreting the "fundamental principles" according to the imperatives of the "central task."

The focus of Party ideological formulations during 1992 was on shoring up this orthodoxy, primarily in support of further efforts in economic reforms. This required confronting challenges implied by alternative views, suggesting that reform programmes and the centrality of economic development infringed the "fundamental principles" and undermined "socialism." Proponents of such views pointed to political events from 1989 — the "turmoil" of April–June in that year, the collapse of Eastern European regimes soon after, and in 1991 the failure of the August coup and the demise of the Soviet Union. They regarded the "turmoil" as demonstrating the need for continuing struggle against anti-socialist or "rightist" tendencies. And in the wake of the demise of other socialist regimes, they emphasized the dangers of "peaceful evolution," claiming that international capital, intent on destroying socialism, would now concentrate its attention on China. These warnings posed an implicit challenge to the reformist approach and, thus, were the target of the renewed efforts in reformulation of Party orthodoxy.

The tone of the ideological dispute was set by the extraordinary interventions of Deng Xiaoping, despite his supposed "retirement" from official position, with the propagation of some of his remarks during a tour of South China in January. The use of this tour suggests a deliberate counter-attack. Deng went beyond defence of current policies, urging faster and more wide-ranging efforts in economic reforms. He thus suggested themes which were then taken up by Party sources, extending and making more explicit some of the main aspects of official ideological justifications underlying reform programmes. Most prominent was the reinforcement of the economistic interpretation of "socialism" and, in particular, repudiation of the notion that reforms followed a "capitalist" path. Accordingly, the principal ideological danger was "leftism," which was interpreted primarily as an anachronistic attachment to practices impeding innovations in economic reforms. The success of this Deng-inspired offensive was demonstrated at the Party's Fourteenth National Congress, which enshrined in the General Programme of the revised *Party Constitution* all of the main themes of Deng's interpretation of "building socialism with Chinese characteristics."

Peaceful Evolution and Socialism

"Peaceful evolution" can have varying connotations, which are not all necessarily uncongenial to the dominant reformist approach. It is sometimes presented in terms of a generalized conspiracy, using a range of tactics directed towards undermining the Chinese regime. Thus, the mechanisms of "peaceful evolution" can include anti-Communist propaganda from western countries or from Taiwan and Hong Kong, condemnation of Chinese policies for infringing human rights, the fostering of ethnic grievances, support for exiled dissident groups, advocacy of punitive economic measures against China, and so on.[2] As with all such conspiratorial views, this interpretation is useful in explaining away difficulties and conflicts in both domestic and foreign politics.

Other interpretations focus more specifically on ideological trends which threaten to subvert the regime. The most obvious threat is "bourgeois liberalization," defined as the negation of the socialist system and Communist Party leadership, and best exemplified by the "turmoil" of 1989. Echoing Mao Zedong's fears about "peaceful evolution" in the 1960s, a prime concern is the declining commitment to socialism among younger generations. Accordingly, the prescribed remedy is to train "revolutionary successors" through larger doses of ideological training and Party-directed political study, especially among youth. Proponents of the reformist approach may not have instrinsic objections to more intensive ideological indoctrination, but they have been sensitive to the political signals it might send. They feared a popular perception that the political environment had become hostile to reformist programmes. This was exemplified by the movement of "rural socialist education" promoted from 1991. Especially given the recollection of the "socialist education movement" of the 1960s, this could easily be seen as presaging a retreat from rural economic reforms.

The most direct threat to the reformist approach emerged from another echo of the 1960s, according to which the schemes of the external promoters of "peaceful evolution" can have effect only through degeneration of the Party itself and consequent perversion of policy direction. Some of those who warned of "peaceful evolution" traced the demise of the Soviet Union back to the triumph of "revisionism" in the Communist Party of the Soviet Union during the 1950s, and there was even a revival of the Cultural Revolution notion of "capitalist-roaders" infiltrating the CCP. Thus, it was reportedly suggested that "Party building" should be regarded as a central task, of equal importance to economic construction.[3] Most generally, the question was raised of whether the Party's reform programmes since 1978 had "practised socialism or capitalism." The significance of this question was not merely disagreement over particular policy areas (such as the reported opposition to the Special Economic Zones, as enclaves for dissemination of capitalist practices) but the implicit challenge to the whole reformist framework. It suggested inconsistency with the Party's expressed socialist objectives, in terms of ultimate goals and the criteria for assessing and validating current practice. While such views were expressed in a muted and oblique fashion, they implied fundamental criticism of the whole direction of change in China since the late 1970s.

In response, Deng[4] sought to repudiate the charge that reforms were "capitalist" by specifying three criteria for "socialism," which were later to be widely propagated in the official media and included in the revised

Party Constitution. According to Deng, something is "socialist" if it facilitates the development of "socialist productive forces," increases the "national strength of a socialist country," and improves living standards. The obvious comment on this curious formula is that, as a definition of "socialism," it is effectively useless because two parts of it are tautological, while the third is simply wrong in the absence of further elaboration. Presenting "socialist productive forces" and a "socialist country" as criteria for "socialism" necessarily assumes what is to be defined. There must be some indication of the grounds on which "productive forces" and "country" can be seen as "socialist." The third criterion, improved living standards, is wrong as stated since such improvements have been achieved in systems which are indisputably non-socialist. If this is to be a criterion for "socialism," then there must be some indication of the ways in which "socialist" improvements in living standards differ from these other cases.

While Deng's formula is meaningless as a definition, it still reveals much of his attitude to "socialism." In particular, it confirms his commitment to the absolute priority of economic goals. That is reinforced by his impatience with, or even contempt for, issues such as "socialist or capitalist." He urged that debate on such "abstract" issues should be avoided, as a distraction from attention to work for economic development. He clearly regards such debate as "empty talk" because it does not deal with "reality," which is understood as the need for economic results.

Despite their enshrinement as a key plank of Party orthodoxy, the three criteria can be used only as a starting point for analyzing the current orthodox view of "socialism," and it is necessary to probe the assumptions on which Deng's tautologies are based. On the simplest level, the term "socialist" is merely self-ascription. That is, China is a "socialist country" because it calls itself such, and its productive forces are thereby automatically "socialist." This sort of approach is obviously very crude, but still significant, as there clearly would be important implications if the CCP rejected the very label of "socialism." The same sort of positive self-identification applies in other systems (as, for example, in political systems which define themselves as "democratic"). Such positive treatment can serve to exclude questions as to the basis of the identification — if the concept is locked into the existing system, then it loses capacity to allow assessment of the characteristics and practices of that system. And this purpose is evident in Deng's formula, which attempts to render meaningless the issue of whether economic development is "socialist or capitalist" by straightforward assumption that China is "socialist."

At an extreme, such self-identification can be absurd, as in the claims to "democracy" by repressive authoritarian regimes. More usually, though, it does have at least some sort of implicit basis which identifies the principal characteristics of the system and allows assessment of when these have been infringed. Thus, self-designation of a system as "democratic" may be enough to exclude questions about the extent to which social and economic inequalities inhibit possibilities of political participation for some groups, but could still be mobilized to counter obviously "undemocratic" practices such as electoral fraud or suppression of minority opinions. If we accept that the Chinese claim to "socialism" is not (or, perhaps, not yet) absurd, there must be some specification of underlying defining characteristics, in spite of any impatience with such "abstract" questions.

The Socialist System

The usual CCP approach has been to identify three dimensions of the "socialist system" — economic, political and ideological. As almost every official Party pronouncement makes clear, the principal objectives of that system are seen as economic. But a consequence of that is the emphasis on the political as the prime defining characteristic of "socialism." The ideological has a dual role, in both facilitating economic development and supporting current political arrangements.

As suggested above, a focus of the struggle over Party orthodoxy in 1992 was to maintain the centrality of economic construction, against alternative views that the centre should become opposition to "bourgeois liberalization" and "peaceful evolution." The most important aspect of the dominant reformist treatment of a "socialist economic system" is that it seeks to remove constraints on reforms, through emphasizing expansion of the scope of what such a system can accommodate while rejecting notions of characteristics which must be maintained. In order to insulate innovations in economic reform programmes from inhibitions posed by considerations of their "socialist" character, Party orthodoxy adopts two main approaches. One is to define "socialism" itself largely in terms of economic results. It is claimed that the superiority of socialism is manifested in high labour productivity and rapid material progress. The theoretical basis of this approach is provided by the notion of "initial stage of socialism," according to which the "socialist system" in China is necessarily in an "initial stage" because of objective constraints, primarily economic backwardness. Hence, the goals of this stage of "socialism" are construed in terms of economic development, and any means conducive to that can be interpreted as authentically "socialist." The second approach is to discount, or treat as secondary, claims concerning necessary defining characteristics of a "socialist economic system." As a CCP Propaganda Department official asserted, it is necessary to avoid being entrenched in "those specific systems, forms and methods which have been proven in practice to impede the development of productive forces" on the grounds that they were once named 'socialist'."[5]

The combination of these two approaches in rationalizing economic reforms is captured in the *Party Constitution* formulation: "The basic tasks of socialist construction ... are to liberate further the productive forces, to develop the productive forces, to realize progressively socialist modernization and, to this end, to reform aspects of and links in the relations of production and in the superstructure unsuited to the development of the productive forces."[6] As Deng pointed out, the reference to "liberation" is significant,[7] suggesting a wider scope for change than mere "development." It rests on the notion that, while production might rise under present economic practices, there is potential for still greater increases as inhibitions from inherited fetters are removed — primarily fetters from practices formerly understood as "socialist." During 1992 such arguments were used to repudiate the connection between "socialism" and the former style of economic planning, and the crowning achievement was to enshrine the "socialist market economy" at the Fourteenth Congress. That was linked to advocacy of higher levels of autonomy in economic management, justification of expansion in use of foreign capital, and allowing inroads of private ownership into state-owned industry. Another prominent theme in removing restraints was the need to learn from capitalism. It was argued that China must absorb and use everything which is valuable from human civilization, including the advanced experiences of capitalist development. Various practices of capitalism were seen as inherently neutral — not just technology, but also "advanced operational and managerial methods which reflect the law governing modern socialized production."[8] So long as such practices boosted productivity, they could be employed in China's "socialist" economy.

While the removal of constraints on reform was the overwhelming emphasis in orthodox formulations, there was some subsidiary attention to inherent characteristics of a "socialist" economy. These included the dominance of public ownership, absence of exploitation, and the objective of "common prosperity." The issue of ownership was clearly salient, given the proposed further shifts away from state ownership in industry, but the treatment of it was vague and formalistic. There was no clear indication of how far changes might proceed before public ownership ceased to be "dominant." Formalism has long been illustrated in the agricultural sector; the claim that land is still collectively-owned may be technically accurate, but this may make little difference in its use for a system of peasant-household production. Thus, reference to this "socialist" characteristic may have had some rhetorical effect, but its potential to inhibit reforms is minimized.

The same applies to the perfunctory treatment of issues of exploitation and inequality. Although official sources still claim that Chinese socialism repudiates the exploitative character of capitalism, there is no avoiding the fact that expansion in private hiring of labour increases exploitation in Marxist terms. The orthodox view would appear to be that such exploitation is still limited in scope and, in any case, is justified if it produces economic results. Similarly, the objective of "common prosperity" has to be seen in the context of the continuing condemnation of egalitarianism and affirmation of the need to stimulate and reward successful economic effort. Nevertheless, it was claimed that China's "socialist" economic development will entail less "polarization" than under capitalism. In terms of regional inequalities, Deng endorsed the more rapid development in southern and coastal areas, while also suggesting that the resulting inequalities would have to be addressed, according to a notion of "common prosperity," through the state channeling resources from richer to poorer regions.[9] But he advocated that redistribution should be delayed, so as not to endanger the results of successful economic growth. Thus, a commitment to equality is affirmed, but not to the extent that it impinges upon current economic practice. There are no criteria for assessing when "polarization" has become too great. Nor is it clear on what grounds it might be expected that the objective of "common prosperity" will have more effect in the future. Although Deng suggested that regional inequalities should be addressed at about the turn of the century, presumably the same sorts of arguments concerning the need to avoid impeding the successful will still apply then.

Along the same lines, the orthodoxy claims that polarization among individuals and groups will be less than under capitalism, despite the anti-egalitarian emphasis of reform programmes and the sanctioning of "some getting rich before others." According to the report delivered by

Jiang Zemin at the Fourteenth Congress, there should be "reasonable" (*heli*) widening of income differences, but also prevention of "polarization" and progressive realization of "common prosperity."[10] Again, there are references to state redistributive mechanisms, to ameliorate the effects of a market-based economy. This would appear to suggest a type of social-democratic position, consistent with one of the charges made by those emphasizing "peaceful evolution." One reason for this undoubtedly is to counter the fears of those who will inevitably be less successful in the new economic framework, or who are losing the benefits of a minimum social wage provided in the old state sector of the economy. There are again no stipulated criteria for determining when these dimensions of inequality are no longer "reasonable," and when this issue should be given priority over the need to encourage those who are economically successful. Claims of superiority over capitalism in this regard must also take into account the resources available for redistribution in favour of the disadvantaged. Anything resembling a social-democratic platform may have less to build upon in China than in richer capitalist countries.

In sum, Party orthodoxy on the inherent content of a "socialist economic system" is framed in vague and rhetorical terms. But it also contains another strand which suggests that what is crucial is not so much the content of the system but the context in which it operates. In particular, the political system is seen as a guarantee of "socialist character," whatever economic practices prevail. Thus, Deng asserted that foreign ownership of industry should not be feared because it is "constrained by overall political and economic conditions in our country." As well as the dominance of public ownership, "still more importantly, we hold political power in our hands."[11]

Such views are consistent with the tendency to identify the defining characteristics of "socialism" principally in political terms — in particular, "the core of the four fundamental principles is to uphold CCP leadership."[12] There are thus clearly fundamentally different approaches to political and economic dimensions of reform. While the main emphasis has been on removing constraints on economic reforms, innovations in political reforms have been very limited and cautious. In terms of the understanding of "socialism," these different approaches appear to be linked, in that the caution in political reform is a condition for expanding the scope of economic reform. If the "socialist" character of the sys-tem is guaranteed by political arrangements, then economic innovations can be more effectively insulated from assessment according to "socialist" standards.

Hence, Party orthodoxy retains a strict conception of a "socialist political system." The approach to political reform is correspondingly restrictive and remains instrumental, with the notion that political reform is necessary to the extent that it facilitates economic reform. The emphasis is thus primarily on processes of institutionalization — that is, encouraging the regularity of political institutions, in order to provide the stability and predictability which are seen as essential for economic development. This is linked especially to the need to separate institutional structures. The doctrine of a "socialist market" requires less direct state intervention in economic decision-making. And the state administration itself should be concerned primarily with efficiency, as shown in the repetition of several long-standing themes — elimination of corruption, reduction of bloated organizational structures, and introduction of a regularized "public service" system. Party organizations should also operate according to the demands of institutionalization, by reducing direct involvement in both administration and economic decision-making. Another main orientation is a type of corporatist approach, according to which principal social groups should be more fully incorporated into processes of policy-making. Consistent with the overarching economism, such groups are defined primarily in economic terms, and this again is seen as a type of political change necessary for fostering economic development. It suggests a recognition that wider political participation is beneficial in a modernizing economy, but in the sense of consultation of economically significant groups within mechanisms established by the state rather than more generalized autonomous participation. Despite references to expanding "democracy," CCP orthodoxy remains rigorously authoritarian, with little tolerance of political activity outside of the Party-dominated framework.

The third dimension of a "socialist system" refers to acceptance of the guiding role of Marxism-Leninism, combined with the promotion of "socialist spiritual civilization." Following from the current treatment of the economic and political dimensions of "socialism," Party orthodoxy specifies two main tasks of Marxist-Leninist guidance. One is obviously to support the economistic interpretation of "socialism" and its rationalization of economic reform programmes. In 1992 the key theme was that of further "emancipating the mind," through "seeking truth from facts." Those tainted by "leftism" were seen as being in most urgent need of emancipation, since their vestigial attachment to former understandings of a "socialist" economic system could impede innovations to "liberate the productive forces."[13] This formulation did meet some resistance, such as the attempt to distinguish a genuine leftism (defined as the upholding of Marxism) from "leftism" (defined as acting in defiance of objective constraints), which was linked to criticism of those who ignored issues of "socialism or capitalism" in their emphasis on economic development.[14] Thus, it was implied that economic reforms could be criticized from a genuine leftist perspective, as infringements of Marxism, and that those who retained former understandings of characteristics of a "socialist economy" were not "leftist." But any such views were overwhelmed by the dominant trend of insulation of economic practices from "socialist" standards and definition of "socialism" itself in terms of economic construction.

The Party's own efforts in ideological guidance were clearly to be oriented towards economic goals. As the revised *Constitution* asserted: "In leading the socialist cause, the CCP must persist in taking economic construction as the centre, and all other work is subordinated to and serves this centre."[15] The extent of subordination was suggested by Li Ruihuan's comment: "Ideological and political work should be for economic and vocational purposes only" — if not, it would be "aimless."[16] This was consistent with the repudiation of "empty talk" on "abstract" issues. And the recommendations for study of Marxist-Leninist theory suggested that very few works should be consulted, and those should be ones which either propagated Deng's views or were consistent with the line of "seeking truth from facts."[17]

At the same time, though, Party sources identified a second main task for Marxist-Leninist ideology, the opposition to "rightism." Deng Xiaoping suggested that the struggle against "bourgeois liberalization" would be longer than the twenty years he had formerly predicted.[18] The theme of such a struggle is straightforward defence of the "socialist system," and especially its political structure. While Party sources see this task as intrinsically important, they are also careful that it should not impinge upon the centrality of economic construction. It was constantly asserted that "leftism" is the principal danger. And "rightism" is interpreted as a deviation referring to political and not economic matters. As part of the insulation of economic practices from assessment according to "socialist" standards, the dominant formulations of orthodoxy have rejected suggestions of links between economic reforms and anti-socialist trends. This has meant not only repudiating or precluding any notion that reforms are themselves anti-socialist, but also insisting that ideological tendencies cannot be attributed to changes in economic practices. These sorts of linkages had been made by some of those who warned of the dangers of "peaceful evolution."

During 1992 some officials in propaganda and culture organs fell into disfavour for "leftism," as their opposition to "rightism" was not restricted to a defence of the political system but transgressed on areas of economic reform.

The formulation of "socialist spiritual civilization" refers to a diverse array of ideological and cultural characteristics. Included is the promotion of "socialist" values such as "collectivism," with little consideration of how these might be reconciled with the contrary tendencies promoted by economic reforms. Some aspects of "spiritual civilization," such as increasing levels of education and technological understanding, are more clearly appropriate to economic modernization goals. Another dimension concerns issues of morals and public order, which are again seen as desirable for economic development, through reinforcing social stability. To that is added a puritanical strand, in the repudiation of forms of behaviour regarded by sections of the leadership as unseemly. It is interesting that the promotion of public order has sometimes taken as a model Singapore — which suggests the extent to which the "socialist" part of "socialist spiritual civilization" is dispensable.

Legitimation

The issue of regime legitimacy in China must take into account the interrelationship of the CCP's own self-definition and the levels of popular acceptance or support of the regime. The CCP, of course, still asserts self-legitimation, which is most directly and forcefully expressed in insistence on the inviolability of "Party leadership." That is, the merits of the regime are construed according to notions of the objective interests of the Chinese people, and the CCP's own "leadership" is based upon claims concerning its "vanguard" character which allows it to define and realize those interests. But clearly self-legitimation is conditioned by a wider conception of "legitimacy" in terms of the extent to which such assertions are accepted by the Chinese people. Concern with that interrelationship has been important to the whole reform period since the late 1970s. Reform programmes have sought to address various sources of popular dissatisfaction, especially those deriving from legacies of the Cultural Revolution. And the issue of legitimacy was given sharper focus by the collapse of regimes in the Soviet Union and Eastern Europe.

It is a commonplace observation that the overarching framework of

Chinese politics for more than a century has been the search for "wealth and power." Current CCP orthodoxy fits very easily here. Deng's three criteria of increases in productive forces, living standards and national strength are a straightforward restatement of that framework. And this provides the main orientation of the CCP's efforts to establish regime legitimacy. Other factors such as "democracy" or "socialism" itself may be salient to some extent, but they are subordinated to the emphasis on "wealth and power."

The most obvious legitimation mechanism is economic development. The economistic interpretation of "socialism" is inseparable from a calculation that popular support will be achieved through material betterment, and that was reinforced by the demise of other "socialist" regimes. According to Party orthodoxy, those who suggested that economic reforms posed the danger of "peaceful evolution" were fundamentally wrong. On the contrary, it is asserted that China has remained stable and avoided the difficulties of the other regimes precisely because of the successes of economic reforms. And in the longer term, "peaceful evolution" will be prevented as the superiority of the socialist system is demonstrated by successful economic development, which will ensure continuing popular support.

A second obvious mechanism of legitimation is state-nationalism. In most ways this is not new, as nationalist appeals have long been invoked by the CCP. But a significant trend of current Party orthodoxy is the greater emphasis on national power for its own sake, with little reference to Marxist-Leninist justifications. It is easy to imagine Marx's reaction to Deng's suggestion that "socialism" can be defined in terms of increasing "overall national strength" of a particular country! The most useful means for reconciling Marxism with nationalism has usually been analysis of international relations according to a notion of imperialism, since nationalism could be presented as a necessary defence against international capital. Thus, the founding of the PRC was construed as "liberation," as the removal of Chinese subjection to foreign powers, which was understood primarily in terms of eliminating foreign capitalist domination. But the "opening up" plank of the reformist programme since the late 1970s has discounted the dangers of foreign economic penetration, consistent with the insulation of economic practices from any assessment in terms of "socialist" criteria. There are some echoes of former concerns with imperialism, as in the view that "peaceful evolution" is a plot by international capital and that China is now central to any world Communist movement following the demise of other regimes. These sorts of themes are rather muted, however, and national power is presented as an intrinsic objective, framed in a way which might appeal to all Chinese no matter whether or not their other political views were informed by Marxism-Leninism.

Apart from economic development and nationalism, the CCP also attempts to mobilize aspects of political reform to bolster legitimation. Its strongest appeals refer to political stability, as both an end in itself and a pre-requisite for economic development. This reciprocal relationship was neatly summarized in the report delivered by Li Peng to the 1992 session of the National People's Congress: "... the fundamental purpose (of social and political stability) is to further reform and development. Only if there is uninterrupted deepening of reform, uninterrupted development of the economy, and uninterrupted raising of the people's living standards, can a solid foundation for society's long-term public order be established and the superiority of the socialist system be fully demonstrated."[19] This sort of appeal is attractive as it strikes a chord with popular distaste for instability, especially given the experience of the Cultural Revolution. It is also clearly advantageous for the CCP to emphasize stability since, by definition, that means persistence of the existing system in which it is dominant.

Other aspects of legitimation through political reforms are, however, more problematic. Consultation and cooperation are presented as means of increasing effective participation in the regime's political processes. And there are constant claims concerning the "democratic" basis of the state, as expressed through elections and representative institutions. But such claims must be limited so that they do not conflict with the Party's fundamental self-legitimation. CCP orthodoxy refuses to countenance any notions, such as those categorized as "bourgeois liberal," which suggest sources of legitimation apart from "Party leadership." The inherently restrictive approach to political reform thus limits its utility as a focus of appeal for popular support.

The results of proposed political reforms may also do little to enhance the regime's popular standing. Thus, there have been constant official calls for reducing inefficiency and waste in state administration, but the very repetition indicates the lack of success. Most damaging have been the intractable problems of corruption. There is ample evidence of popular dissatisfaction with official corruption, which easily translates into a generally cynical attitude to the regime. The CCP's demands for "clean" government are no doubt widely supported, but if they are perceived to be insincere, or if they fail to achieve results, regime legitimacy is bound to be damaged.

The greatest threat to the regime from failures is, of course, in economic policy, since the Party has tied legitimacy, and its own "leadership," so closely to "economic construction." Hence, the regime is immediately vulnerable to disaffection should economic development falter, or should some groups perceive themselves as disadvantaged by reforms. It is hard to imagine that the Party could then resort to appeals to "socialist" objectives in mobilizing support, given its own economistic interpretation of "socialism."

This illustrates an underlying tension in the CCP's overall legitimation strategy. While still asserting self-legitimation, the main emphases of the Party's efforts to gain popular support are not closely tied to its own "vanguard" status. Objectives of economic development are stated in terms of increased production, with little attention to specifically "socialist" characteristics. National strength is also presented as an intrinsic objective, largely independent of any Marxist-Leninist interpretation. There is thus little in the formulations of Party orthodoxy firmly connecting economic and nationalist objectives to the characteristics of the CCP itself, apart from mere assertion. Thus, the self-legitimation evident in assertions of the inviolability of "Party leadership," and underlying resistance to political change, is not reinforced by other parts of CCP's own approach. In that case, the emphasis on stability could be especially important, as that may become a crucial prop for the regime and for the Party's role within it.

Conclusion

The most distinctive trend in CCP ideological orthodoxy during 1992 was the renewed vigour of an economistic approach, with further attenuation of "socialism" as an intrinsic and substantive ideological framework. An overwhelming emphasis on economic construction was supplemented by an eclectic set of tendencies, including nationalism, social democracy, puritanism, authoritarianism, corporatism. The triumph of economism was achieved against contrary currents, which implicitly challenged reformist programmes by suggesting inconsistency with "socialist" objectives. With Deng Xiaoping's direct intervention, the response to that challenge which came to dominate formulations of Party orthodoxy effectively rendered irrelevant the question of whether reforms were "socialist or capitalist."

There remain some notions of "socialist" characteristics and objectives, but, with the crucial exception of "Party leadership," these are vaguely formulated and dissociated from current economic practices. This has two main implications for the content of ideological dispute within the Party. One is that the parameters of allowable difference are narrowed. It is difficult to use ideological arguments against reforms, without a radical rejection of the orthodox approach (which is certain to be labelled not only as "leftism" but also as infringement of the Party's "basic line"). On the other hand, the very vagueness of "socialist" characteristics provides grounds for limited disagreement. Thus, the battle between "reformers" and "conservatives" may not be over whether reforms are consistent with "socialism" but over interpretations of issues such as when the "dominance" of public ownership is threatened or what levels of inequality are acceptable. With the decline of identifiable intrinsic characteristics, the contents of "socialism" become what is attributed by political authorities.

If those who warned of "peaceful evolution" were anxious about the CCP retaining its position as the ruling party, they can take comfort from the continuing assertion of "Party leadership." But if they were concerned with the demise of "socialism" in China, then it could be suggested that Party orthodoxy has already provided the framework for "peaceful evolution," while giving little indication of how its progress might be checked.

Notes

1. Deng's theoretical contributions were emphasized in Jiang Zemin's Report to the Fourteenth Congress: *Renmin ribao*, 21 October 1992, pp. 2–3; and *Renmin ribao* editorial, 19 October 1992, p. 2.
2. See, for example, excerpts of a speech by Tao Siju at the Central Party School, in *The Nineties* (Hong Kong), No. 1, 1992, pp. 26–28.
3. For example, the comments attributed to Chen Yun and Deng Liqun in response to Deng's southern tour, in *Cheng Ming* (Hong Kong), April 1992, pp. 8–9.
4. The following is based upon "Document No. 2 on Deng Xiaoping's Talks during his Southern Tour," in *Cheng Ming*, April 1992, pp. 23–27.
5. Gong Yuzhi, "Emancipate the Mind, Liberate the Productive Forces," *Wenhui bao* (Shanghai), 15 April 1992, p. 1.
6. *Renmin ribao*, 22 October 1992, p. 1.
7. See also Li Junru, "Reform Is Also Liberation of Productive Forces," *Wenhui bao*, 27 March 1992, p. 6.

8. *Beijing Review*, 13–19 April 1992, p. 4. Cf. Wu Shuqing, "Three Standards for Determining the Success or Failure of Reform and Opening Up," *Renmin ribao*, 3 July 1992, who points to the "dual character" of capitalist management of production.
9. "Document No. 2 on Deng Xiaoping's" (see Note 3), p. 24.
10. *Renmin ribao*, 21 October 1992, p. 2.
11. "Document No. 2 on Deng Xiaoping's" (see Note 3), p. 24. Gao Di, under pressure for his "leftist" views, argued that, while exploitation would exist under reform programmes, it differed from exploitation in the old society, as the workers involved are still "masters of the state, and masters of the economy owned by the whole people," *Renmin ribao*, 22 June 1992, p. 5.
12. *Renmin ribao*, 1 July 1992, p. 3.
13. See the *Renmin ribao* editorial "On Emancipating the Mind," 4 July 1992, p. 1.
14. As reported in *Contemporary* (Hong Kong), 18 March 1992, excerpted in British Broadcasting Corporation, *Summary of World Broadcasts Part III The Far East* (*SWB* FE) 1337 B2/2 and 1354 B2/4.
15. *Renmin ribao*, 22 October 1992, p. 1.
16. *SWB* FE/1397 B2/2.
17. See the comments in Jiang's Report to the Fourteenth Congress, that the "core content" of the study of Marxism-Leninism is to study Deng's "theory of building socialism with Chinese characteristics," *Renmin ribao*, 21 October 1992, p. 3; and the reported remarks by Qiao Shi in *SWB* FE/1477 B2/6.
18. "Document No. 2 on Deng Xiaoping's" (see Note 3), p. 26.
19. *Renmin ribao*, 6 April 1992, p. 1.

4

Administrative Reforms in China in 1992: Streamlining, Decentralization and Changing Government Functions

Joseph Cheng Yu-shek and Ting Wang

In early 1992, Deng Xiaoping, the paramount leader in China, in his visit to Guangdong, Shanghai and other places, sent a strong signal to "re-launch" a campaign to deepen economic structural reforms.[1] Major strides in economic reforms were achieved in the year. The central and local governments expanded their absorption of the experiences of contemporary market economies in developing productivity. In mid-October, the Fourteenth Party Congress basically announced the replacement of the planned economy with a market economy, marking a new milestone in China's economic reforms.[2] In line with the substantial increases in investment, China's gross domestic product (GDP) grew at the rate of 12% in the year, twice the planned rate of economic growth.

The Chinese leaders, however, remained conservative regarding political reforms while pushing for the liberalization of the economy. Despite the breakthroughs in economic reforms, the Chinese leaders still stubbornly rejected western-style democracy. Until then in fact, little had been done in the cultivation of an environment for socialist democracy, and political structural reforms discussed in the very early 1980s had not made much progress at all. The Party Congress did mention political structural reforms, but their genuine contents were no more than administrative reforms based on the reform of the Party and government organizations.

This chapter intends to discuss the administrative reforms in 1992 under the following headings:

a. the definition of political structural reforms;
b. the contents of administrative reforms;
c. the rationale for administrative reforms; and
d. the problems and prospects of administrative reforms.

The Definition of Political Structural Reforms

From Deng Xiaoping to Zhao Ziyang and Jiang Zemin

In the early 1980s, the Chinese leaders began to initiate reforms of the "leadership systems of the Party and the state." In August 1980, at an enlarged meeting of the Chinese Communist Party (CCP) Political Bureau, Deng Xiaoping gave a long address, entitled "Reform of the Leadership Systems of the Party and the State," which was subsequently to be considered a blueprint for political structural reforms. The reforms which Deng had in mind then far exceeded the reform of the administrative structure and improvement of cadres' work styles. Deng pledged "to create in politics a higher level and more practical democracy than that in capitalist countries." The promise was soon forgotten in favour of stability. Deng also opted to avoid antagonizing the other Chinese leaders as well as the cadres while trying to mobilize their support for economic reforms.

Deng, however, pointed out that the major problems of the leadership and the cadre systems were: bureaucratism, over centralization of power, patriarchism, life appointments for cadres and "all kinds of phenomena associated with privileges." On the lack of consultation and intolerance of criticisms and alternate views under patriarchism, Deng stated : "In many localities and units, patriarchal type of figures exist. Their power has no limits, others simply have to follow their orders, and depend on them as their protégés.... They generate privileges, and act in a privileged way, leading to dissatisfaction among the masses."[3]

In October 1987, CCP General Secretary Zhao Ziyang presented his report to the Thirteenth Party Congress on behalf of the CCP Central Committee. His report, entitled "Advance Along the Road of Socialism with Chinese Characteristics," discussed in relatively concrete terms the issue of political structural reforms. Some of his proposals symbolized the germination meaningful to political structural reforms, including the separation of the Party from the government, a system of consultation and dialogue with the society, elections which would reflect "the will of the voters," etc. Zhao further stated: "Without political structural reforms, economic structural reforms cannot ultimately achieve success."[4]

The sad reality was that Zhao's ideas never materialized. In the report to the Fourteenth Party Congress delivered by Jiang Zemin five years later, political structural reforms as conceived by Zhao had simply disappeared. Yet the kind of phenomena severely criticized by Deng Xiaoping certainly had not faded. In fact, most of them had become even more serious.

Political Structural Reforms and Administrative Reforms

Since documents of the CCP Central Committee and other Party organs have claimed that political reforms have been implemented, it would be useful to examine the contents of political reforms.

Political structural reforms and administrative reforms are different concepts. Political structural reforms include administrative reforms, but the latter cannot be equated with the former. Political structural reform means reforms and innovations regarding the ossified traditional system, involving changes to the political system and macro-power structure, to a certain extent leading to changes in the nature of the regime. Administrative reforms do not involve changing the nature of the regime, they are reforms within the existing political structure.

It was hopeless in 1992 to expect from the Chinese Communist regime political reforms based on the model of western countries since it had specifically rejected multi-party parliamentary democracy and the separation of powers. However, at this stage, there were certain social demands which would shape the essential contents of a political reform package along with the "special characteristics of Chinese socialism." Such social demands mainly came from two sources:

 a. the expectations regarding political structural reforms among the elites of the intelligentsia, the reformists within the political elites, and the opinion leaders in various social strata;[5]
 b. the representative political demands in Chinese society as perceived by public opinion. In sum, political structural reforms intended to democratize the existing socialist system and to attach to it a "human face."[6]

Essential Contents of Political Structural Reforms

The law would be the key to political structural reforms. In the absence of an established and adequate legal framework and in the subsequent unsupported cultivation of respect for the rule of law, political structural reforms could not succeed. The latter would have to include the replacement of the all-embracing authority of the Party and the gerontocracy by a legal system, which would be able to guide the functioning of the political system. In time, this legal system would have to be backed by the independence of the judiciary, i.e., the interpretation and adjudication of law would not be interfered with by the Party and the Chinese leaders. Further, the legal system would have to protect the rights of the people and facilitate the articulation of their interests. In the foreseeable future, the emphasis would be on the observance of the law by governments and cadres of all levels, and the containment of all abuses of power and privileges.[7]

Guarantees of democratic rights in the Party Constitution and State Constitution should be gradually implemented too. So far these guarantees only existed on paper. Within the Party, power was in the hands of a small group of gerontocratic leaders who no longer held any formal positions in the Party hierarchy. Within the government, the Party was above the state, and the Party controlled the National People's Congress (NPC), which could not even function as an effective means of checks and balances. The first important step of political structural reforms would consist in clearly stating in the State Constitution that it would be above the Party and allowing the NPC to function more independently. Some progress had been made in the two or three years before the Tiananmen Incident for the NPC to play a more significant role in supervising the work of the government. Despite the setbacks triggered off by the Tiananmen Incident, the NPC should be developed as the most authoritative organ offering some checks and balances *vis-à-vis* the state and the Party. To strengthen the NPC's role, its elections should be democratized and more candidates be allowed so as to enforce some accountability. This would be the very minimum of socialist democracy.[8]

Limiting the functions of both the Party and the government and strengthening the transparency of the political process would be important components of political structural reforms. The theory of the dictatorship of the proletariat and the related Leninist doctrines would have to be reappraised. They should be criticized in particular for generating a monopolistic, closed and privileged power elite. The establishment of a civil service with open and fair recruitment as well as clear criteria of appraisal would be an important step towards creating a more open political system. At the same time, recognition in practice of the people's right of access to information, their right to participate in and to supervise the government, and their right to protest would be the obvious means to enhance the transparency of the political process.[9]

The concepts of liberty and equality and the measures to put them in practice should be absorbed into the political structural reforms. A young research scholar in politics stated in Shanghai that "political development should be the development of humanization" and "the process of improving the people's livelihood."[10] The development of humanization referred to respect for the individuality of human beings, respect for the equality of human beings and their right to liberty, and effective guarantee of basic human rights. Dictatorship of the proletariat (or people's democratic dictatorship) rejected the equality of classes, of professions and that before the law. It implied the arbitrary removal of the constitutional right of freedom, including freedom of choice in career vocation and marriage.[11] Naturally, a system to guarantee clean government, to curb privileges and the abuse of power, as well as the guarantee of freedom of mass media to enforce supervision of government by public opinion would all be significant components of political structural reforms.

On the basis of the above, one can find no meaningful progress in political structural reforms in China in 1992.

The Development of Organizational Reform and Its Content

Administrative reforms in 1992 were mainly organizational reforms, and their special features were simplification, decentralization and change of functions.

Messages of Organizational Reforms in 1992

In 1982 and again in 1988, the regime launched an organizational reform at the central Party and government level to simplify structure, reduce sinecures, and pass on some management authority to local Party and governments organs as well as enterprises.

The first reform campaign had reduced the ninety-eight ministries and their equivalents in the State Council to fifty-two, and the establishment had been reduced from almost 50,000 people to 32,800.[12] However, expansion soon resumed, and a similar campaign was repeated in 1988 which also ended in failure.

In 1989, the regime changed its strategy and emphasized a reform at the county level in an attempt to break the vicious circle. In early 1992, as a result of Deng Xiaoping's visit to Southern China and his push to accelerate reforms, organizational reforms at the county level achieved some significant development at the testing sites. In November, over 350 counties were listed as testing grounds for organizational reforms, i.e., about 20% of the counties in China.[13]

In July 1992, the State Council promulgated the *Regulations on Changing the Operational System of Industrial Concerns under State Ownership* (hereafter referred to as the *Regulations*).[14] The document demanded the change of functions on the part of some government organs to meet the changing operational system of state enterprises. It not only promoted organizational reforms at the county level, government organs at the provincial and central levels also felt the pressure to respond. Jiang Zemin's report to the Party Congress in October 1992 stated: "If we are to reform the political structure, deepen the economic reform, establish a market economy and accelerate the modernization drive, we must make it our urgent task to reform the organizational structure and to simplify administration." This was certainly a strong signal to the Party and government leaders at all levels.

In sum, organizational reforms stayed at the counties chosen as testing sites. The document *Regulations* had not yet been fully implemented. Organizational reforms at the provincial and central levels had not yet started either, they were still at the deliberation and preparation stages. It did not appear that organization reforms at all levels could be rapidly implemented in 1992, or 1993.

Organizational Reform Experiments at the County Testing Sites

The general orientation of organizational reforms at the county testing sites was "small organization, big service." The establishments of Party and state organs at the county level and their functions were to be reduced, while maintaining the provision of productive and social services.

Such organizational reforms had three major elements. The first was the reduction of their personnel and the simplification of the administrative departments. The second was the separation of the government from enterprises, and the passing of authority from the government to enterprises. The government was no longer supposed to operate and manage enterprises directly, eliminating its functions relating to administrative management and political and ideological control, while strengthening its functions in providing economic, scientific and technological, information and social welfare services. The third was transforming certain economic administrative departments and institutions attached to the government into independently operated economic entities or social service entities. They were to leave the government structure completely within a transitional period of one to three years, terminating their dependence on government appropriations and achieving economic independence and financial self-sufficiency.[15]

Zhuozi county in Inner Mongolia Autonomous Region was one model of organizational reforms which had attracted much attention in the political and economic circles. Since 1984, the county had drastically reduced its Party and government organs from forty-two to twenty-one. Of the original twenty-eight government organs, only six remained. They were responsible only for administrative management and presumably no longer directly involved in the management of enterprises and institutions.

Personnel made redundant from economic, technical and administrative management departments had been given loans by the government to start economic entities gradually separated from the government and its finances.[16] Many counties in Shandong province also accumulated valuable experience in organizational reforms, and their model was similar to that in Zhuozi county in Inner Mongolia.[17]

The organizational reforms of the county testing sites learnt a lesson from the failures of the 1982 and 1988 organizational reforms at the central level. They did not concentrate solely on the nominal reduction of organs. Of the more successful cases reported in 1992, all attempted to create outlets for those made redundant in the simplification of organizational structure in terms of employment opportunities and new sources of profit to support new economic entities.

The transformation of administrative departments at the county level also affected the industrial, commercial, and scientific and technological sectors. They were pushed into becoming independently operating economic entities and social service entities; a gesture which was very similar to corporatization as practised in western countries, such as when radio and television stations, hospitals, printing presses, etc. had gradually left governments. The transformed entities had normally been given a transitional period during which they had not yet been totally abandoned by their respective governments; they could still rely on the latter's loans and appropriations to draw up arrangements for the employees made redundant. These transformed entities then had to cut costs and improve efficiency to survive. This model obviously could better avoid the pressure on the government organs to re-absorb its former employees, and could more effectively channel the labour resources to the economy.

The New Scene of Changing State Enterprises' Operational System

At this stage, the Chinese regime was still groping its way through organizational reforms. In 1992, the CCP Central Committee decided to reform the operational system of state enterprises, demanded the cutback of government functions and asked government organs at the central level to prepare for experiments in organizational reforms.

In September 1991, the CCP convened a Central Work Conference to discuss the improvement of large and medium state enterprises in industry with a view to grant more autonomy for their operations and to reform their operational system.[18] The objectives were to improve their backward management, raise low returns on investment and cut long-term losses. The latter had been a substantial burden on the state's finances. In the first half of 1991, about 37% of state enterprises had incurred losses.[19] In recent years, on average over one-third of state enterprises suffered losses.

The *Enterprise Law* promulgated in 1988 had already stipulated reforms of the state enterprises' operational system. But the law had not been effectively implemented because government organs had not changed their functions, and government had not been separated from enterprises. Much of the autonomy which should have been enjoyed by enterprises was still being confined at the hands of government.

The Chinese leaders finally realized that government functions had to be curtailed to facilitate the reform of the enterprises' operational system. In July 1992, the *Regulations* were promulgated; and the document's gist was to separate government from enterprises.

According to the *Regulations*, ownership of state enterprises remained with the government, but state enterprises had relatively complete autonomy in their operations. The government was in charge of administrative supervision at the macro-economic level, while state enterprises were responsible for their management and operations on a contract basis. State enterprises were formally provided with the means to secure from the government the authority to decide on their operations, such as setting the prices for their products and services, controlling the supply and distribution of their products, acquiring raw materials and supplies, importing and exporting materials and products, making investments, controlling the capital flow and cash flow, controlling capital assets, engaging in joint ventures and mergers, the employment of workers, the management of personnel matters, the distribution of wages and bonuses, decisions on internal organizational structures, and the right to reject arbitrary levies. Governments at various levels were not allowed to interfere with state enterprises' authority in these fourteen areas.[20] State enterprises should become independent in operations; they should be accountable for their profits and losses, responsible for their development and for self-regulation. In short, they should gradually become independent economic entities.

In view of these changes, enterprises would no longer be attached to government departments. The latter, especially those involved in administrative management of the economy, had to change their functions. The guiding principle would be "separation of government from enterprises, supervision at the macro-economic level, *laisser-faire* at the micro-economic level."[21] The government could no longer directly operate and manage enterprises and curtail their autonomy. The government's responsibilities were mainly to be adjustment and administration at the macro level, including adjusting the production structure in society, designing and implementing economic strategies as well as adapting them, establishing and improving the legal system and industrial policies, cultivating the market system while setting up social welfare services and the social security system, etc. Managerial activities at the micro level were the responsibilities of the enterprises alone.

In line with the changing functions of the government and its organizational reforms, the planning, industrial, commerce and foreign trade organs at the provincial and State Council levels would either cutback on personnel or be merged with other organs. Some of them would become economic entities or social service entities; they would not retain their economic management functions or their access to government financial appropriations after leaving the government structure.[22]

After the promulgation of the *Regulations*, each province began to identify testing grounds for transforming the operational system of enterprises. However, organizational reforms at the provincial and central levels were being implemented without an overall plan, the needed laws and regulations, and a schedule in 1992. Only a small number of ministries in the State Council, such as the Ministry of Textile Industry, were preparing for disbandment or transformation into industrial groups.

Rationale for Organizational Reforms

The Chinese Communist regime pushed for organizational reforms for the following reasons:

a. expansion of government organs leading to exorbitant budgetary expenditure;

b. serious bureaucratism accompanied by low administrative efficiency; and

c. the need to facilitate the transformation of the enterprises' operational system and the transformation of the planned economy into a market economy.

Financial Burden Created by Expansion of Government Organs

The CCP, the government, the People's Liberation Army (PLA) and the mass organizations controlled by the Party together constituted a gigantic machinery for exercising dictatorship. But, complicated and overlapping structures, too many sinecures, exorbitant yet ever increasing administrative expenditures had been perennial symptoms of the Chinese Communist regime.

Within the State Council, overlapping structures and functions were common phenomena, leading to a multiplication of co-ordinating organs. Besides ministries, commissions and bureaux directly under the State Council, there were many other offices and leading groups as well, far exceeding the stipulated nomenclature. Since the organizational simplification in 1988, staff of the State Council had increased from about 32,000 to over 47,000 by 1992.[23]

The same phenomena were afflicting the local governments. There were over 2,100 Party and government organs at the overall provincial level, averaging more than 70 in each province. On the average, there were about 45 Party and government units in every county; and the number was rising to 60 or 70 in some of them. Party and government organs at the provincial, prefectural and county levels exceeded their regulatory establishment by about 20%; and among the personnel in administrative organs at the county level, about one out of four was in surplus of the authorized register.[24] In the standing Party and government organs above the county level, more than 30,000 staff were in excess of the stipulations.[25]

The number of those who were securing their remuneration from the government budgets had risen from 15 million in 1979 to 34 million in 1991, an increase of 127%.[26] Taking into consideration those who were living off state's financial subsidies, the number had further increased to 40 million by 1992; in other words, one out of 27 or 28 people depended on the state for a job.[27]

The expenditures of administrative organs and institutions in China had amounted to RMB 40 billion in 1980. It had increased to RMB140 billion by 1990, an increase of 250%. Administrative expenditures were now absorbing about 40% of the state's revenues. In 1991, the fiscal deficit amounted to RMB 21 billion, about one-seventh of it caused by over spending in administrative expenditures.[28] In fact, huge increases in administrative expenditures had become an important obstacle to the effort at reducing the substantial budget deficits.

China was not a developed country. Per capita income per annum in the past year only reached the US$300 level, but the wastes by the Party and government bureaucracies were shocking. Apart from the substantial outlays on salaries and fringe benefits such as housing, medical care, etc. the cadres' corrupt practices of using public funds for banquets, travels and various types of "free lunches" were extremely costly.[29] In many provinces and counties, local economic poverty was not preventing the vast expansion of administrative organs and institutions. In one province, the cadre corps had increased from over 200,000 to about 660,000 between 1980 to 1990. In the latter year, remuneration for cadres had amounted to RMB2.6 billion, almost 80% of the local government revenues.[30] In some poor counties where per capita income per annum was below RMB200, there were cases of cadres diverting subsidies provided by the central or provincial governments to pay for the extravagance of the administrative organs.[31]

Bureaucratism and Low Administrative Efficiency

Bureaucratism and low administrative efficiency were certainly serious obstacles to modernization. They too adversely affected the immediate interests of the people, causing much dissatisfaction among them. Deng Xiaoping himself admitted that the high level of power concentration at the centre was "the root cause of our special type of bureaucratism."[32] Indeed, organizational reforms since the early 1980s had largely been a reflection of bureaucratism and low administrative efficiency.

Twelve years ago, an article by the editorial department of *Red Flag*, entitled "Organizational Reform Is a Revolution," depicted the phenomenon of low administrative efficiency as follows:

> Organizational overstaffing, overlapping of structures, sinecures, confusion of functions, mutual avoidance of responsibility, low work efficiency, serious bureaucratism: all these conditions have reached an unbearable level, and have become serious obstacles to our implementation of modernizing construction.... We cannot simply bear witness to this lack of enthusiasm and efficiency on the part of our Party and government organs.[33]

Unfortunately, not much improvement had been made regarding such bureaucratism and low administrative efficiency since then. On the contrary, new phenomena of corruption, privilege, abuse of power, using network of ties to open the back door, etc., had become very serious, exacerbating the people's grievances against the regime.

The Chinese leaders in the early 1990s realized this threat, and they too appreciated the impact of changing the operational system of enterprises and transforming the planned economy into a market economy. Functions of government organs had to change to face the challenge of the market as well as the trend of marketization.[34]

Problems and Prospects of Organizational Reforms

Major Problems Encountered by Organizational Reforms

Like the reform of enterprises, administrative reforms were also a major re-adjustment of power and interest relationships and, therefore, were bound to encounter formidable obstacles. They included: the breakup of existing power relationships, the difficulties of setting up a legal framework and implementing it, corruption among cadres, replacing old values and perceptions with new ones, demand for a broadly-based social security system, etc.

Administrative reforms with organizational reforms at their core required the separation of the Party from the state, and the government from enterprises. The Party and government bureaucracies had to re-examine their authority and functions in a market economy. Party committees at all levels had to simplify their structures and abandon the tradition of totalitarian control. Administrative authority had to pass from the Party committee to the government at the corresponding level, so that the latter could have an independent system regarding decision-making, management and operation. On the other hand, the government had to hand over to enterprises the operational autonomy stipulated in the *Regulations*, so that government organs would no longer be directly involved in the management and operation of enterprises.

The realities of 1992 demonstrated that it would be very difficult to alter the totalitarian control exercised by the Party. As expected, the Party and government bureaucracies resisted any attempt to deprive them of their powers. Separation of the Party from the government was not even on the agenda in 1992, and progress in the separation of the government from enterprises varied. In many cases, state enterprises faced severe resistance in attempting to act as independent economic entities. The usual pattern under such circumstances was: ownership and operational autonomy were not well delineated, government retained some measure of control over state enterprises and, in practice, no one could be made responsible for the latter's losses.

Organizational reforms should be based on a clear legal framework and well-defined systems. An important cause for the failure of past organizational reforms had been the lack of effective restraints on the subsequent establishment of government organs and their administrative expenditures. The necessary system, budgetary control and legal procedures did not materialize; or those already in existence were insufficient to deter the officials who were not used to restrictions. The organizational reforms in 1992 were equally disturbed by the "soft" constraints of the budgetary procedures and the patriarchism among senior officials.

The rampant corruption among officials was also a serious problem for organizational reforms. Power was used as a currency in exchange for favours among officials at all levels.[35] Those who were eager for privileges had many incentives to expand their organizational structures and establishments to benefit their families and friends and strengthen their own power/resource base for private interests. There had been some talk of an organization and system to combat corruption along the model of the Independent Commission Against Corruption in Hong Kong or Singapore. But no concrete plan emerged in 1992; the Chinese leaders were not even close to convincing the people of their determination to fight corruption. Once again, Chen Yun repeatedly talked about the elimination of improper work style within the Party. Such statements, however, were mainly interpreted as veiled criticisms against the reformist leaders and their economic liberalization programmes rather than as an advocation of a determined campaign against corruption.

The replacement of old values and perceptions by new ones was an important aspect of organizational reforms. The old system based on "the dictatorship of the proletariat" and related theories had generated inequalities. On the other hand, the eating-from-the-same-big-rice-bowl mentality, the worship of authority, emphasis on rank and hierarchy and the widespread abuse of power and privilege still remained serious handicaps in organizational reforms.[36]

The absence of a broadly based social security system and the low quality of cadres had an adverse impact on organizational reforms as well. For a long time, a social security net had been offered by government organs, institutions and enterprises themselves. But a social security system for the society was absent. Upon leaving an official position in government, institution or state enterprise, an individual would immediately lose his social security safeguard. Finally, incumbent officials at the county level tended to score high marks on "redness" and low marks on "expertise." They were often political commissar type of officials without the qualifications and knowledge required to serve competently either in administration or on economic and technical assignment.[37] This meant that it would be rather difficult to find alternative employment for officials made redundant in the simplification of organizational structures at the county level.

Prospects of Organizational Reforms

In early 1993, the State Council was drafting proposals on simplifying organizational structures for the consideration of the first session of the Eighth NPC in March. On the basis of the organizational experiments at the county level, reforms at the provincial and central levels would be gradually implemented in 1993. It can be expected that an attempt will be made to merge organs with similar functions, that some others will be abolished or transformed into economic consortia or social service entities.

Within the State Council, certain super ministries may expand their management authority at the macro-economic level and take over part of the authority from related ministries and commissions. For example, the existing Economic and Trade Office of the State Council may become the Economic and Trade Commission after the convening of the Eighth NPC, and it may become responsible for the overall adjustment of the economy. The authority of the State Planning Commission may thus be curtailed. Certain industrial management ministries such as the Ministry of Textile Industry, the Ministry of Chemical Industry, etc. would probably have some of their authority transferred to the Economic and Trade Commission; and, they may even be reorganized into economic corporations without administrative functions.

In some cases, short-term financial support is probably going to be provided for government departments to create enterprises. The latter may gradually become independent, and the original government officials may become owners of the enterprises. In view of their network of ties with the government bureaucracy, they would have privileged access to resources, enabling them to become members of the bureaucrat-capitalist class. The emergence of the newly rich may exacerbate the gap between the rich and the poor.[38]

In the foreseeable future, organizational reforms will be quite unpredictable. It seems that the general trend will be to facilitate the transformation of the operational system of enterprises and the cultivation of a market economy. The essential challenge, however, is to push the reforms with determination to avoid the vicious circle of expansion — simplification — expansion. But there are many variables, including the political succession crisis, which are going to be difficult to gauge.

Notes

1. In the spring of 1991, Deng Xiaoping went to Shanghai to launch a propaganda offensive against the conservatives. In early 1992, he visited Guangdong to encourage the acceleration of reforms. The visit had an important impact on the deepening of economic structural reforms. On these events and their significance, see Ting Wang, "Dierci nanbeizhanzheng: jinggai de zai chufa? — Zhonggong jinqi zhengzhi douzheng xunxi jiedu" (The Second North-South War: Re-launching CCP's Economic Reforms? — An Interpretation of the Recent Signals of Political Struggles), *Tide Monthly* (Hong Kong), No. 50 (April 1991), pp. 47–52; Ting Wang, "China: A Movement Toward Reform?" *The World & I* (Washington, DC: USA, 1991), pp. 78–83; and Ting Wang, "Deng Xiaoping nanxun yu dierci nanbeizhanzheng" (Deng Xiaoping's Visit to South China and the Second North-South War), *Hong Kong Economic Journal Monthly*, Vol. 16, No. 2 (May 1992), pp. 20–24.
2. On the debates regarding planned economy and market economy, see Wu Jinglian, "Jianyi queli 'shehuizhuyi shichang jingji' de tifa" (Proposal to Firmly Establish the Notion of 'Socialist Market Economy'), *Caimao jingji* (Beijing), No. 7, 1992, reproduced in *Xinhua yuebao*, No. 9, 1992, pp. 45–47; Dong Fureng, "Tan gaige kaifang zhong de zhenglun" (A Discussion of the Controversies on Reforms and Opening to the Outside World), *Gaige* (Beijing), No. 3, 1992, pp. 63–69; and Ma Hong, "Jianli shehui zhuyi shichang jingji xintizhi" (Establish the New Socialist Market Economy Structure), *Jingji yanjiu* (Beijing), No. 11, 1992, pp. 3–10.
3. See Deng Xiaoping, "Dang he guojia lingdao zhidu de gaige" (Reform of the Party and State Leadership Systems) (18 August 1980), in *Shiyi jie sanzhong chuanhui yi lai zhongyao wenxian xuandu* (Selected Readings of the Important Documents Since the Third Plenum of the Eleventh Central Committee), Vol. 1 (Beijing: Renmin chubanshe, 1987), pp. 215–17.
4. See *Zhongguo gongchandang dishisan jie quanguo daibiao dahui wenjian*

huibian (A Compendium of the Documents of the Thirteenth National Congress of the CCP) (Beijing: Renmin chubanshe, 1987), pp. 41–59.
5. These people included Yu Guangyuan, Hu Jiwei, Qin Chuan, Li Rui, Su Shaozhi, Wang Ruoshui, Yu Haocheng, Li Honglin, Zhang Changjiang, Xu Liangying, Li Shu, Yan Jiaqi, Zhang Xianyang, Zhang Zonghou, etc.
6. On the alienation phenomena in a socialist society as well as democratization and humanization under a socialist regime, see:
(a) Zhou Yang, "Guanyu Makesizhuyi de jige lilun wenti de tansuo" (Probing A Number of Theoretical Questions Concerning Marxism), *Renmin ribao*, 16 March 1983; (b) Wang Ruoshui, "Tantan yihua wenti" (Discussions on the Alienation Question), *Xinwen zhanxian* (Beijing), No. 8, 1980, reproduced in Wang Ruoshui, *Wei rendaozhuyi bianhu* (In Defence of Humanitarianism) (Beijing: Joint Publishing Co., 1986), pp. 186–99; (c) Wang Ruoshui, "In Defence of Humanitarianism," *Wenhui bao* (Shanghai), 17 January 1983; (d) Ru Xin, "Rendaozhuyi jiushi xiuzhengzhuyi ma?" (Is Humanitarism Revisionism?), *Renmin ribao*, 15 August 1980; (e) Xue Dezhen, "Jiefang de zhexue he zhexue de jiefang" (Liberation Philosophy and the Liberation of Philosophy), *Xuexi yu tansuo* (Harbin), No. 3, 1981, pp. 4–15; (f) Ting Xueliang, "Xin Makesizhuyi dui Zhongguo dalu de yingxiang" (The Impact of Neo-Marxism on Mainland China), *Minzhu Zhongguo* (Paris), No. 6 (February 1991), pp. 38–49; and (g) Ting Wang, "Cong 'muzhongwuren' dao renxing fugui — shehuizhuyi yihualun chutan" (From Total Disregard for the Individual to the Return to Humanism — A Preliminary Examination of the Theory of Socialist Alienation), *Ming Pao Monthly* (Hong Kong), January 1984, pp. 29–36.
7. On the expectation of using law to restrict the exercise of authority and the critique of "the privatization of public authority," see Li Zhengang and Shi Ming, "Shilun xingzheng quanli rengehua yu fazhihua" (An Attempt to Discuss the Personification of Administrative Authority and Its Incorporation into a Legal System), *Shehui kexue* (Shanghai), No. 2, 1992, pp. 36–39; Xie Hui, "Quanli sihua yu zhengzhi baiquanjiao" (Privatization of Authority and the Cult of Political Authority), *Xuexi yu tansuo*, No. 5, 1988, pp. 31–37; and Su Shaozhi and Wang Yizhou, "Weiji yu sikao" (Crisis and Reflection), *Shijie jingji daobao* (Shanghai), 24 October 1988.
8. On the expectations regarding the NPC exercising its democratic functions, see Situ Yan, "Zhongguo zhengzhi tizhi gaige de beijing yu qianjing" (The Background and Prospects of China's Political Structural Reforms), *Zhengzhixue yanjiu* (Beijing), No. 1, 1987, pp. 1–6; Cao Siyuan, "Zhengzhi tizhi gaige de anquan tongdao" (The Safe Channel for Political Structural Reforms), *Xinhua wenzai* (Beijing), January 1989, pp. 9–11.
9. On the strengthening of political procedures and the transparency of political affairs, see Bao Tong, "Dangqian zhengzhi tizhi gaige de ruogan wenti"

(Certain Questions on the Current Political Structural Reforms), *Qiushi* (Seeking Truth), No. 1 (July 1988), p. 4–9; and Yan Jiaqi, "From 'Politics without Procedures' to 'Politics Following Procedures'," *Xinhua wenzhai*, October 1988, pp. 1–5.

10. Wang Huning, "Jianli yizhong xin de zhengzhi fazhanguan" (Establishing a New Political Development Perspective), *Zhongguo qingnianbao* (Beijing), 19 August 1988.
11. On the freedom of choice, see Chen Ziming, "Gaige zhong de zhengzhi yu jingji" (Politics and Economics under Reform), *Zhengzhixue yanjiu* (Beijing), No. 1, 1987, pp. 7–11.
12. See Zhao Ziyang, "Guanyu Guowuyuan jigou gaige wenti de baogao" (Report on the Question of Organizational Reform in the State Council), *Zhongguo jingji nianjian 1992*, Part II (Beijing: Jingji guanli zazhishe, 1982), pp. 27–28.
13. "Quanguo jigou gaige shidian xian da sanbaiduoge" (Testing-site Counties for National Organizational Reform Exceed Three Hundred), *Remin ribao*, 22 September 1992.
14. *Renmin ribao*, 25 July 1992.
15. "Zhuanbian zhineng jingjian jigou, cujin shengchanli fazhan" (Change Functions, Streamline Organizations, Promote the Development of Productivity), *Renmin ribao*, 23 November 1992.
16. See "Nei Menggu Zhuozi xian tizhi gaige yantaohui" (Seminar on Structural Reform in Zhuozi County in Inner Mongolia), *Xinguancha* (Beijing), No. 8 (April 1989), pp. 4–26; and Yi Junhua, "Jingjian jigou zhuanbian zhineng — Nei Menggu zizhiqu qixian zonghe gaige de shijian yu tihui" (Streamlining Organizations and Changing Functions — Practice and Insights Concerning Comprehensive Reforms in the Banners and Counties in the Inner Mongolia Autonomous Region), *Zhongguo nongcun jingji* (Beijing), No. 7, 1992, pp. 7–10.
17. Gao Cangli, "Shandong sheng xianji jiguan gaige de huigu yu sikao" (Review and Thoughts on the County Organizational Reforms in Shandong), *Zhongguo nongcun jingji*, pp. 3–6.
18. *Renmin ribao* Editorial, "Jizhong liliang gaohao guoying da zhong xing qiye" (Concentrate Forces to Improve State Large and Medium Scale Enterprises), *Renmin ribao*, 7 November 1991.
19. Lü Dong, "Zai lun zhuanhuan jingying jizhi shi gaohao guoying da zhong xing qiye de guanjian" (Again on Changing the Operational Mechanisms as the Key to Improve State Large and Medium Scale Enterprises), *Renmin ribao*, 1 November 1991.
20. See "Quanmin suoyouzhi gongye qiye zhuanhuan jingying jizhi tiaoli" (Regulations on Changing the Operational Mechanisms of State-owned Industrial Enterprises), July 25, 1992; and Zhu Rongji, "Guanyu zhiding

zhuanhuan qiye jingying jizhi tiaoli de jige wenti" (A Number of Questions Concerning the Formulation of Regulations on Changing the Operational Mechanisms of Enterprises), *Renmin ribao*, 1 July 1992.
21. *Renmin Ribao* Editorial, "Yau qieshi zhuanbian zhengfu zhineng" (Government Functions Must Change Realistically), *Renmin ribao*, 5 August 1992.
22. *Ibid.*
23. Liu Jinghuai, "Zhongguo jigou gaige jiang quanmian tuikai" (Organizational Reforms in China Will Proceed on an Overall Basis), *Liaowang Weekly* (Overseas Edition), 21 September 1992, pp. 1–4.
24. Li Qi, "Lüelun xingzheng jigou gaige de tongbu yunxing" (Brief Discussions on the Simultaneous Operation of Executive Organizational Reforms), *Jiefang ribao* (Shanghai), 5 August 1992.
25. See Note 23.
26. Bao Xin, "Zhengzhi tizhi gaige de jinpo renwu" (Urgent Tasks of Political Structural Reforms), *Liaowang Weekly* (Overseas Edition), 7 September 1992, p. 2.
27. See Note 23.
28. See Note 26.
29. "Jijian gongzuo wei dang de jiben luxian fuwu" (Discipline Inspection Work Serves the Party's Basic Line), *Renmin ribao*, 9 September 1992.
30. Li Jianxing and Ding Jianming, "Bu 'Jingbing jianzheng' xing ma?" (Can It Work without 'Streamling and Simplifying'?), *Heilongjiang ribao* (Harbin), 26 November 1991.
31. According to CCP Politburo member Tian Jiyun: in 1992, over 80 million poor people in the rural areas could not be adequately fed and clothed or could not be so in a stable manner; they constituted about one-tenth of the rural population in China. See New China News Agency dispatch, 13 December 1992.
32. See Note 21.
33. Editorial Department of *Hongqi*, "Jigou gaige shi yichang geming" (Organizational Reform is a Revolution), *Hongqi* (Beijing), No. 6, 16 March 1982, pp. 2–5.
34. He Wei, "Zhuanbian zhengfu zhineng shi dangqian shenhua gaige de kuanjian" (Changing Government Functions Is the Key to the Current Deepening of Reforms), *Gaige*, No. 3, 1992, pp. 100–103.
35. Wan Chaoling, "Fubai xianxiang: yige duo weidu de yuanyin fenxi" (The Phenomenon of Corruption: A Factor Analysis of Multi-Perspectives), *Guangdong shehui kexue* (Guangzhou), No. 5, October 1991, pp. 57–61 and Hu Shoujun, "Quanli jingji mianmian guan" (Perspectives on Power Economics), *Shijie jingji daobao*, 31 October 1988.
36. Chen Zhun, "Lun quanli jiazhiguan" (Perspective on Power Fancy), *Shehui kexue*, No. 10, 1992, pp. 20–23.

37. Zhang Qingzhong, "Guanyu xianji jigou gaige ruogan wenti" (A Number of Questions on Organizational Reforms at the County Level), *Zhongguo nongcun jingji*, No. 7, 1992, pp. 17–19.
38. Concerning the phenomenon of corruption among cadres and the inequality of distribution in the society, see Gong Lingdong, "Lizu guoqing, jianshe you Zhongguo tese de shehuizhuyi minzhu zhengzhi" (Based on the Situation in China, Establish Socialist Democratic Politics with Chinese Characteristics), *Jiaoxue yu yanjiu* (Beijing), No. 1, January 1992, pp. 35–39.

5

Civil Service Reform

King K. Tsao

After the Fourteenth National Congress of the Chinese Communist Party (CCP) held on October 1992, the Party Congress and the subsequent announcements by the Chinese government have declared that further civil service reform[1] will take place in 1993 and beyond to meet the needs of economic and political development. These pronouncements have created the perception and the expectation that large-scale, substantial structural and governmental reforms will be conducted in the future.[2] China, as a developing and socialist country, has faced both problems. As a typical developing nation, her bureaucracy is characterized by widespread corruption which has become the norm rather than the exception.[3] China lacks properly-trained professionals and well-educated personnel. The public and private arenas remain undifferentiated. The political system has a low degree of institutionalization and routinization.[4] China is also a socialist country (with "Chinese characteristics"). The Party is above the state. There is no political neutrality for the civil servants.[5] Bureaucratic red-tape, overstaffing, overlapping, inefficiency and inertia are also the norms. As Deng Xiaoping lucidly summarized the problems of the Chinese bureaucracy in 1980:

> Bureaucracy remains a major and widespread problem in the political life of our Party and the state. Its harmful manifestations include the following: standing high above the masses; abusing power; ... overstaffing administrative organs; being dilatory; inefficient and irresponsible; ... circulating documents endlessly without solving problems; shifting responsibility to others; and even assuming the airs of a mandarin, reprimanding other people at every turn, ... deceiving superiors and subordinates, being arbitrary and despotic, practising favouritism, offering bribes, participating in corrupt practices in violation of the law, and so on. Such things have reached intolerable dimensions both in our domestic affairs and in our contacts with other countries.[6]

---

* This chapter was first presented at the *China Review 1993* Workshop held at The Chinese University Press, 9 January 1993. I appreciated the comments from the participants at the workshop, and Joseph Y. S. Cheng offered many helpful suggestions. Moreover, I would like to make use of this opportunity to extend my gratitude to the South China Programme of the Hong Kong Institute of Asia-Pacific Studies, The Chinese University of Hong Kong, for its financial support which led to the completion of this chapter. In particular, the Programme provided the necessary funding for conducting in-depth interviews with scholars and officials in Guangzhou during 1992.

Given these general features of the Chinese bureaucracy in a comparative perspective, it is worth looking at the strategies used to reform the Chinese civil service system in the post-Mao era, as well as the unsuccessful implementation of previous organizational reforms, to understand the structural and contextual problems faced by the Chinese bureaucracy. This analysis shows the limitations of the reforms and suggests future prospects for civil service reforms. This chapter is organized into four sections. Section 1 outlines proposed reforms of the civil service system and its related issues in the current context of the Fourteenth Party Congress. Section 2 traces the strategies of reform by using the drafting of the regulations of the state civil servants, the cornerstone of civil service reform, as a case to demonstrate change and continuity with the post-Mao era. Section 3 examines the previous failed attempts to streamline the governmental and administrative structure and to reduce staff. The underlying causes of failure are offered primarily as organizational survival and vested interests arguments. Finally, comments and evaluations of the current reforms are proposed, based in a comparative perspective on China's previous experiences.

Civil Service Reform and Its Related Issues at the Fourteenth Party Congress

The Fourteenth Party Congress heralded the recognition and the institutionalization of a socialist market in the years ahead. This is the first time the Chinese reformers introduce the idea of the market into the Party Constitution, making the market the guiding principle of further Chinese economic and political reforms in the future.[7] Market forces will further be introduced into the system, and this will bring simultaneous changes to the bureaucratic system as well. The key significance and implications of this Party Congress to the civil service and administrative reforms are summarized as follows:

Market forces are further accepted, integrated and interwoven into the regime. Market forces of supply and demand play an increasingly important role in most of the transactions, as the market further dominates or even dictates choice. The proportion of industrial production subject to *jihua* (mandatory planning) actually has decreased from 97% to the present 11.6% within the last fourteen years, since Deng Xiaoping initiated the reform in 1978. Furthermore, the proportion of consumer goods sold at state-set prices dropped to 21%; that of capital goods to 36% in 1991.[8]

Market forces have played an increasingly important role in the reform era, even with the co-existence of a *zhidao jihua* (guidance plan) with which the enterprises need to comply.[9] Consequently, the power and the scope of control possessed by the State Planning Commission will be further reduced. Also the number of bureaucrats in this Commission, at either the national or sub-national level (provincial and city), will be dramatically reduced. The Planning Committee of Guangzhou city of Guangdong province will be cut by 150 people.[10]

Secondly, the abolition of the Central Advisory Commission (CAC) will further decrease the roles played by the old and senior cadres, a further step towards institutionalizing the political system.[11] The existence of the CAC can be traced back to 1982, when a compromise offered retirement to senior leaders to create room for younger and more educated cadres. This was a historical solution to allow for a smooth power transition from the first generation of revolutionary cadres to the second generation. By offering those retired cadres material comforts and rewards compatible with past benefits and creating for them a new Central Advisory Commission, younger cadres could assume the leading posts. However, this kind of succession management did have its problems. Even though the old cadres did not have official and formal titles, they still exercised their power and influence through their life-long linkage with previous institutions and personal connections. For example, the removal of the late Party Secretary Hu Yaobang in early 1987 was due to the pivotal role played by senior retired cadres in ousting him.[12]

The abolition of the Central Advisory Commission signifies that those few senior retired cadres have lost their institutional base, which makes it more difficult, if not impossible, for them to intervene at the high level of policy-making and the political process. Future retired cadres will no longer aspire to any post in this Commission. This can be further regarded as a step forward towards routinization of the political system as originally envisioned by Deng Xiaoping in 1982, when he promised the Commission would be abolished in ten to fifteen years.[13]

Moreover, streamlining the functioning of the bureaucratic organization and reducing the over-sized bureaucracy have their functional implications. For example, organizational restructuring will take the film division away from the Ministry of Broadcasting, Film and Television and return it to its original home, the Ministry of Culture. Staff will be cut drastically in the following ministries: the Ministry of Foreign Economic Relations and Trade, Ministry of Light Industry, Ministry of Textile Industry, Ministry of Railways, Ministry of Communications and the Civil Aviation Administration of China. Numerically, the Ministry of Foreign Economic Relations and Trade will cut 70% of its staff; the Ministry of Light Industry, 80%.[14] According to another source, the Ministry of Supplies will be incorporated back into the Ministry of Commerce; the State Administration of State-owned Properties and the State Bureau of Taxation will be amalgamated under the control of the Ministry of Finance; many ministries and commissions of the State Council will be streamlined and over ten thousand of the officials will be leaving their departments.[15] Those who will be reshuffled from their organizations will primarily go to different *jingji shiti* "economic entities, corporation or companies" run by their respective administrative agencies. Other options include the arrangement for early retirement or finding other jobs.[16]

Fourthly, another arena affected by organizational changes at the Party Congress includes state-owned enterprises; they are going to further experiment with stock ownership to change the overall economic structure. The use of denationalization will challenge the ownership structure and property rights within the system. The full implications of this emphasis are not yet clear at the moment, but the role of the economic bureaucrats in different layers of the administrative system will definitely be reduced.

Finally, changes to the bureaucracy affect not only the higher authorities under the State Council such as the various ministries and commissions, but they extend also below, as low as the counties in order to reduce the number of bureaucratic staff across the nation.[17] Above all, the announcement that civil service reforms will be further promoted in 1993 and that by 1995 a modern civil service system will be introduced, has been the most important news on the civil service reform since the Party Congress.[18]

Strategies for Reforming the Civil Service System

I. The Origins, Evolution and the Main Characteristics of the "Temporary Regulations of the State Civil Servants"

Besides the brief announcement about the furthering of civil service reform in 1993 and beyond, many of the proposals and attempts had been laid out in the previous years already. As a matter of fact, the introduction of a modern civil service system into the Chinese administration had begun in the 1980s to meet the needs of the modernization programmes. The strategies of civil service reform are manifold. Usually, the main strategy is to draft and formulate the conditions and terms, which in turn leads to a set of rules, regulations, ordinances that finally grow into laws that applies to all the state employees at the national level.[19]

The institutionalization of a Chinese civil service system actually began in 1982, as senior Chinese cadres gradually began to retire. In November 1984, the Organization Department of the Party Centre and the former Labour and Personnel Department of the State Council, with the help of academicians and experts from the universities and research institutes, completed the first draft of *Guojia jiguan gongzuo renyuan fa* (*Law of the Working Staff of State Organizations*). The draft was gradually changed to *Guojia jiguan gongzuo renyuan tiaoli* (*Regulations of the Working Staff of State Organizations*) and *Guojia gongwuyuan tiaoli* (*Regulations of State Civil Servants*).[20] In 1987, the draft was further changed to the document by which it is still known today, *Guojia gongwuyuan zanxing tiaoli* (*Temporary Regulations of the State Civil Servants* or hereinafter *Temporary Regulations*).[21] In 1988, the former Labour and Personnel Department of the State Council was changed to Personnel Department. At that time, the *Temporary Regulations* were in their thirteenth draft already. By April 1989, the sixteenth draft was produced. In May 1989, the *Temporary Regulations* were sent to the different regions, districts, and governmental departments for further consultation.[22] The twentieth draft of the *Temporary Regulations* was completed on 4 March 1992, and the twenty-first draft was finished around September.[23] More recently, this draft was modified and approved by the State Council in February 1993; then it is soon to be sent to the Eighth National People's Congress convening in March 1993 for approval before it becomes law.[24]

The details of the *Temporary Regulations* will not be discussed here;[25] they are properly the subject of another article addressing the specific contents with regard to conditions leading to gradation, hiring, performance appraisal, rewards and punishments, promotion and demotion, assignment and dismissal, training, exchange, conflicts of interests, salary and fringe benefits, firing and retirement.[26]

Ia. The Non-distinction between Political Appointee and Career Civil Servant

There are eighteen chapters in this draft, and it has two chapters more than the sixteenth draft.[27] The twenty-first draft has been a setback, it is not as progressive as the seventeenth draft,[28] as among the setbacks, one finds the cancellation of the differentiation between two kinds of civil servants, the *zhengwu* (government affairs) and the *yewu* (professional or vocational affairs),[29] and the institutionalization of the grading system in the current draft stands out. Let us examine these two issues more closely.

In the seventeenth draft, *zhengwu* refers to ministry-level or above posts, namely the vice-premiers and ministers of the various departments of the State Council or heads of the People's Congress committees who are elected or approved by the People's Congress. They formulate policies and assume political responsibilities. These posts are roughly equivalent to the political appointees in a western political system who are affected by the outcome of party elections. The *yewu* are what we consider as civil servants, who conform to the Weberian ideal type, competent and life-tenured, a career personnel the Chinese want to adopt; they merely execute policies.[30] The idea of a sharp distinction between politics and administration, widely accepted elsewhere in the early development of public administration, has also been used as a guide to reform the Chinese civil services;[31] however, in this draft, the distinction between the two types of positions has been removed.

Ib. Stratification

In the present draft, the bureaucracy is divided into fifteen grades. The first or second grades refer to the chairman and vice-chairman of the state, and the premier of the State Council; the second and third grades refer to vice-premiers or state councillors; the third or fourth grades refer to the ministers of the State Council or the governors of the provinces; the fourth and fifth grades refer to vice ministers and vice-governors. The fifth, sixth or seventh grades refer to department heads under a ministry (*si*), department heads at the provincial level (*ting*), bureau heads (*ju*), or mayors of the provincial level. The sixth, seventh and eighth grades refer to the deputy-heads of *si*, *ting* and *ju* and the deputy-mayors. The seventh, eighth, ninth and tenth grades refer to the division heads (*chu*), county heads (*xian*) and the researchers in the institutes. The eighth to eleventh grades refer to deputy division heads, deputy county heads and associate researchers. The ninth to twelfth grades refer to section chiefs (*ke*) and responsible government employees. The tenth to thirteenth grades refer to deputy section chiefs and deputy responsible government employees. The tenth to fourteenth grades refer to section members. And finally, the eleventh to fifteenth grades refer to clerical staff. Those who have grades equivalent to or above vice-ministers are regarded as senior civil servants (*gaoji gongwuyuan*). Those who are of their fifth grade or below (department heads or below), and above the rank of deputy division heads are regarded as middle-level civil servants (*zhongji gongwuyuan*); and those under the rank of section chief are regarded as junior civil servants (*chuji gongwuyuan*).[32]

Within the drafting process, we can see a sudden, substantive disruption after the Tiananmen Square Tragedy of 1989. The work, however, was not stopped, and the twenty-first draft of the *Temporary Regulations* met the proposed completion schedule by the end of 1992.[33] At this stage, it is hard to evaluate the actual consequences of the civil service reforms as most of them are still only on paper, particularly since regulations and rules of the *Temporary Regulations* have not become ordinances that apply to all the Chinese state employees. Hence, all the proposals have been made, but only some trial experiments, for example at the State Statistical Bureau, have been performed and most of the programmes are not yet fully implemented. It is still too early to evaluate their consequences and impact upon the Chinese bureaucracy, the state and the society.

The elimination of the distinction between the two groups of civil servants is obviously a setback in the context of Chinese civil service reform. The current draft, as a whole, is a further evidence supporting the view that political reforms have not been touched upon at the latest Party Congress. The setback, again, can largely be explained by the factors of the June 4 Incident and the collapse of the former Soviet-type regimes in Eastern Europe and the disintegration of the Soviet Union; these have made the regime more cautious about reforming the civil service system, as the stability and continuity of the system, above all, are valued as the most important priorities to guide the reforms.

II. Other Strategies

Some other strategies for promoting civil service reforms within the last several years include the following:

(1) The coastal area and the southern part of the country have been chosen to adopt the civil service system first. Experiment and trial implementation are to be introduced in the coastal area and then gradually move into the hinterland.[34] A few cities have also been chosen to carry out the streamlining of governmental organizations, including Harbin, Qingdao, Wuhan, and Shenzhen.[35]

(2) Six bureaux under the State Council have been chosen to implement the civil service reforms at the beginning of 1989. These include: Auditing Administration, State Bureau of Construction Materials Industry, General Administration of Customs, State Administration of Industry and Commerce, State Bureau of Taxation and State Statistical Bureau.[36] In particular, the State Statistical Bureau has been widely promoted as a unit successfully implementing the rules of avoidance of conflicts of interests (*huibi*),[37] of promotion and demotion,[38] and of hiring and performance appraisal.[39] The reformers only use the technically-intensive departments for administrative experiments with policy implementation. This is in part due to the fact that those organizations require professional expertise and technically-oriented knowledge that can be more or less easily evaluated. Moreover, all these departments are less sensitive to cost if the experimental policy goes wrong. Few, if any, political and ideological issues are involved in these technical departments, so assessment can be more neutral. Finally, the use of experimentation prior to a possible national application has been the managing and implementation styles through the whole period of the Chinese regime.

(3) The National Administration College has been set up so that more senior administrators can be trained. This college is still under construction. The newly recruited civil servants will be trained under a curriculum offering competitive and professional courses. The idea of setting up this college, partly inspired by the modern experiences of democratic capitalist countries, such as the French *Ecole Nationale d'Administration*, is also based on the assumptions borrowed from and examples set by the National Defense University and the Central Party School. The National Defense University trains the young and professional elite military cadets who will occupy the future key positions in the

military, so does the Central Party School for Party positions. In short, the overall approach is to further delineate these three key areas of administration, military, and Party in order to have functional differentiation and effective governance. This is a further step towards differentiating the past overlapping functions performed within the system.

Overstaff Reduction — Organizational Streamlining and Reshuffling

Given the current emphasis on organizational streamlining and further civil service reforms in 1993 and beyond, a thorough understanding of the limitations and the significance of the Chinese administrative and civil service reforms is not possible without an examination of previous efforts at organizational streamlining and departmental reshuffling. A review of past efforts at reducing the number of layers of the hierarchy and cutting down the number of officials is important in the following sense: the streamlining and the reduction of redundant layers of the hierarchical structure should enhance the efficiency and the performance of the governmental organizations. The reduction or expansion of the hierarchical levels undoubtedly affect the number of staff and personnel, and this is definitely related to the crucial issues of hiring, promotion, gradation, dismissal, retirement and other issues of the civil service system. Moreover, past attempts should have a profound impact upon the proposed reforms embodied in the *Temporary Regulations* as well as on its implementation in the future. In short, they can offer us the basis on which to judge the earlier attempts and understand the causes of their failure, so to cast light on the current proposals.

Four separate attempts — in 1958, 1970, 1982 and 1988 — had taken place to reform the administrative structures and organizations.[40] While the reforms of 1982 and 1988 had primarily aimed at the restructuring of the relationship of the state and the society,[41] the previous two had concerned themselves with the functional reordering of some departments and organizations.[42] In the 1982 reform, one concern, among others, was the shift of power from the retiring elderly cadres to the new leadership. Thus, at the central level, the Central Advisory Commission and the Central Commission for Disciplinary Inspection were formed. Bureaucratic reforms were introduced to cut the number of organizations to meet the needs of the reform programmes on the separation of the Party and the state organizations, on the one hand, and of the enterprise and the public administration, on the other.[43] In 1988, ambitious reforms were introduced in the restructuring of governmental organizations, primarily by abolishing departments with economic functions and, instead, setting up corporations to replace them. Subsequently, these "corporations" were to retain the functions and decision-making power of their previous economic departments.[44]

There are differences in the nature, substance, timing, scope, and extent of these four organizational reforms. However, there is one *common* element linking all of them, namely, the reduction in the number of staff was never successful; on the contrary, the number further increased. Overstaffing has become one of the primary problems of the Chinese bureaucratic system. For example, in 1979 there were 15 million cadres who were paid out of the state budget;[45] the number reached 30 million in 1989,[46] and it grew to 34 million in 1991.[47] Though hardly conclusive the figure does indicate the trend of overstaffing.[48] Inefficiency, poor performance, redundant procedures[49] and, above all, the consumption of a large portion of public revenues are the results.[50] As the size of the bureaucracy increases, the operation of the newly-created market is hampered, and there is more bureaucratic red-tape.[51] Overstaffing has even remained the norm within the reform era, thus jeopardizing the purpose of reform policies and the professionalization of the civil service; and other goals of the "four modernizations" programmes are seriously affected. The obvious question to be asked is: why and how has overstaffing occurred? To answer briefly, there are five variables to account for this expansion.

First, the demand for the "upgrading" or "promotion" (*shengge*) of the local administrative units has propelled the expansion of the local bureaucratic organizations. The county-level town demands promotion to the level of district or regional city; the sub-bureau demands upgrading to the bureau level of the provincial government. If approved, the internal organizations and units are administratively elevated, as well as the number of bureaucrats. In turn, their pay and benefits within the organizations are augmented as their grades escalate.[52]

Secondly, even though the central government has repeatedly promulgated decrees and regulations forbidding the creation of new party and bureaucratic organizations, the local government still continues to create new organizations and assign cadres to the newly-created departments. For example, in one province there are more than seventy party and administrative organizations and 124 technical units (*shiye danwei*) in excess of the permitted establishment. Their pay and benefits are all under the budget of the local governments. It is estimated that there are more than 1.7 million institutions sustained by the state budget.[53] Local expansion and the local vested interests are the engines of further expansion, which results in overstaffing.

Thirdly, non-regular and non-establishment administrative units and organizations in local governments have increased.[54] This is related to the emphasis on particular projects or work requested by the hierarchical organizations at either the central or provincial level. Lower administrative units, hence, need to respond with newly-created organizations, committees, units, offices or groups of staff and personnel which can meet the demands from the higher administrative agencies. Once the project is over though, these non-regular units are not necessarily abolished. In fact, some *ad hoc* organizations have existed for more than ten years; some of these have become permanent and part of the local overall administrative structure.[55]

Fourthly, some governmental organizations within the local administrative structure have increased the number of their internal sub-units, divisions and institutions. According to one survey, one particular district has twenty-nine administrative departments (which in itself is too many and already exceeds the number in many other districts). Within these twenty-nine departments, there are 236 sub-units and institutions under their jurisdiction![56]

Fifthly, many departments and organizations had been created in 1982 to meet the needs of economic development and the modernization programmes. Banking, industry and commerce, ancillary revenue and tax-collecting organizations, auditing and supervising units, people's congresses, political and legal units were also strengthened. In addition, new organizations were created to perform macro-planning and management which the existing administrative organizations could not handle. Thus, new staff and personnel were needed.[57]

In sum, local-level bureaucratic expansion is responsible for overstaffing throughout the process of organizational reforms. The question of localism requires a separate discussion that I cannot touch upon here.[58] Instead, I shall concentrate on the question of bureaucratic expansion. This is akin to bureaucratic survival or expansion, fuelled by the desire to acquire more resources to deliver services and programmes. The expansion not only consolidates the power and resource bases but also increases the scope of influence and authority for the leaders within the organization. Thus, the more staff the bureaucratic organization possesses, the better off it will be as its members are more likely to have better promotion prospects, more salary, higher status and the like.[59]

In addition, the administrative system is highly hierarchical and finely divided into layers and grades as most of the governmental organizations do in other countries. Each level of the unit or layer has its own number of established staff, grades of salary, fringe benefits and treatments. These hierarchical organizations (*tiaotiao*) are divided into: ministry, departments (*si* and *ting*), bureau (*ju*), division (*chu*), and section (*ke*). The national administration is also divided into central, provincial, regional, city, county, and village levels. Each has its prescribed standing bodies, establishment of institutions and staff. The higher the layer of the unit a cadre belongs to, the better he will be treated. Moreover, the rewards and the benefits of the cadres are still well protected; they have their tenured jobs. It is ironic that even in the open, private-oriented economy of Wenzhou, there are still many applicants for the civil service posts.[60] Thus, the "bureaucratic-centricity system" (*guanbenwei zhi*) is still prevalent in China.[61] To be an official is still the best guarantee of access to power, material benefits, and other private goods as well. It is not surprising that there is a "strange cycle" (*guaiquan*), as the Chinese call it, that reducing of bureaucratic staff yields expansion and further reduction gives rise to re-expansion in all these departmental streamlining and organizational reshuffles. This has become the bureaucratic phenomenon of China.[62]

Prospects, Unintended Consequences and Limits

Using a historical perspective, the shift of the focus from politics to economics at the Fourteenth Party Congress is a further victory for the reformers. They have adopted the strategy of using non-political and non-ideological means to tackle the problems of ideology and politics. The economic approach is more "neutral" and acceptable to the top leaders, including the conservatives, so that further progress can be made with reform and open-door policy. It has been a victory for Deng Xiaoping.[63] Thus, the good news about the recent Party Congress is that more consensus has been reached, and the continuation of open-door and reform policies will be carried on in the 1990s. The reform programmes have been gradual and partial within the last fourteen years. However, the basis for a reform package has been formed which is superior and more successful than the "big-bang" approach of the Soviet Union or the comprehensive policy of reforming according to a plan, as in the former Soviet-type regimes of Eastern Europe.[64]

With the institutionalization of the socialist market, this will further push the reforms forward. More incentives will be created for state employees to seek benefits by engaging in economic and other related commercial activities. On the positive side, it will further reduce the administrative engagement of the bureaucratic organizations and cut down the strength to control the economy by streamlining their organizations. The size of the administrative staff and personnel will be considerably reduced, as will the administrative capacities and the powers of these bureaux. Regulations, decrees and administrative control will be lessened as these organizations shrink. Economic activities will be less hampered by the bureaucrats. Moreover, the trimming of the staff size can cut the state budget and save public finance as the state has been constantly facing fiscal deficits in the reform era.[65] Lastly, the opening up of the system by significantly reducing the number of officials will create the opportunities for them to have the experience of engaging in commercial and economic activities; that is important to the transition of a traditional society to a modern one, as the roles of businessmen and entrepreneurs were despised and suppressed in traditional China and the pre-reform Mao Zedong era. Suffice to say, the prospect of moving the economy into a socialist market economy is a challenging one as not much of past experience can be counted on.

This massive cutting of staff, however, may have adverse consequences on China's politics and the economy within the next several years. Based on the previous analysis of the historical experiences of cutting staff and organizational streamlining, one obviously questions whether the goal of large-scale lay-offs of officials can be attained and the intended consequences ensured. Several possible outcomes and unintended consequences may be generated from this large-scale lay-offs of staff.

First, bureaucratic organizations may make use of previous strategies to strengthen and expand staff size by creating new programmes, new needs and new divisions to survive — although these will largely be confined to their "economic entities," economic policy-making bodies, and regulation or control agencies. The central bureaucracy will be cut, but there is enough evidence to suggest that the local bureaucracy will be increased to compete with neighbouring provinces, regions, cities, counties and the like.

Secondly, with many former state employees going into business and engaging in economic activities, the market may function less well. The market is still at the nascent stage, and most of the rules of the game are either not well-defined or not elaborated, let alone vigorously enforced by a set of impartial institutions. Thus, economic activities may be carried out more or less in a hierarchical manner, depending on the power and support from background hierarchical or administrative organizations. Until now, there is enough evidence to suggest that those economic entities or corporations which have powerful support are not only assured of getting the business but also they may try monopolizing most of the business as well.[66] In the final analysis, the struggle for profit within the commercial arena will be largely a factor of support from background administrative organizations. Thus, hierarchical means are still the key to success, market share and gains. Making use of *guanxi*, personal connections, will still predominate. More companies and economic entities will be run by bureaucratic organizations. The performance of these "entities" will not only affect those staff formally working for their governmental organization but also affect the earning power and rewards of current cadres. These cadres have their vested interests as well. This creates another outlet for bureaucratic intervention, though this time in the economic arena, to protect their vested interests. Though there have been numerous state regulations and decrees to forbid state cadres from engaging in commercial and economic activities, the results are not that satisfactory. One can suspect that this time, witness the cutting of the number of state employees and staff, intervention and engaging in economic activities will be made legitimate, though indirectly.

The fundamental basis of reform is to further divorce the government from enterprises, delineate the sphere of politics and economic activities, differentiate the roles played by the central government and the local authorities and, above all, separate the Party from the state.[67] However, at the Fourteenth Party Congress, the issue has not been about the separation of the Party from the government, but primarily about the separation of politics from the administration. In short, it is intended to have effective governance.

With respect to the Four Cardinal Principles laid down in the *Temporary Regulations*,[68] there is no indication that the Party will give up its domination both within the state and the society, though its influence has been notably diminished during the reform era. Even before the June 4 Incident of 1989, there was no intention to favour political neutrality in the reformation of the civil service system.[69] The non-acceptance of the distinction between political and professional appointee is another indication of the domination exercised by the Party. *Nomenklatura* is still effective in respect of "lists of positions for which party committees traditionally held responsibility in recruitment, and lists of persons deemed suitable to fill them. In general, appointments to such posts could not be made without the sanction of the relevant party committee."[70]

Needless to say, if we use the existence of the *nomenklatura* as *the* yardstick to gauge the extent and the significance of the civil service reform within the post-Mao era, then there is not that much to say about the changes and the attempts to reform from within. By not maintaining the structure and the dominance of the *nomenklatura*, we can witness a complete system transformation but not a change from within. Professionalization and the use of modern expertise will be the key to the Chinese civil service reform. However, the importance of the Party apparatus in the regime does bring forth one fundamental and controversial question, namely: Can the civil service reform lead to the creation and the emergence of a group of efficient, competent, impartial and professionally-trained civil servants whose very existence is essential for successful policy implementation and for effective governance, as in any modern government?[71] I do not have a definite answer on this, and it is an empirical question. However, a few remarks can be made.

First, there is no positive linkage between having a competent civil service system and a democratic political regime. The regime may be undemocratic and authoritarian in nature, but it can still possess an efficient civil service system. This is what some of the young Chinese reformers, particularly before 4 June 1989, did advocate with the "neo-authoritarian" approach towards modernization — having economic liberalization but maintaining undemocratic political institutions.[72] Secondly, the issue of the existence of a group of impartial civil servants is a historical issue; it cannot be created from a vacuum or simply with the reach of a single shot at any radical changes. It cannot even be achieved merely through system transformations. This is a long historical and evolutionary process, and we need to have a longer perspective to observe this slow yet incremental transformation of the Chinese civil service system. It does take time for new institutions to be created, let alone consolidated, so that the desired results and impacts can be attained. Surely, the best choice is to have a group of competent civil servants and a democratic system at the same time, but that is a utopian option right now which is largely inapplicable to the concrete empirical realities and the systematic constraints of the regime. Lastly, whether there is the creation of a group of competent and professionally-trained civil servants, and the attainment of modernization programmes without changing the basic rules of the political game, this will essentially boil down to the trade-off between two sets of crucial and conflicting values: stability and the continuity of the regime, on the one hand, and democratic changes and human rights, on the other. Again, the answer to this issue is not an either-or choice. On this issue, Professor Tang Tsou did perceptively point out the underlying difficulties and dilemma of the post-Mao reform more than a decade ago. He said:

> For many years to come, the question will be whether a political system set within these limits (Four Cardinal Principles) can perform effectively the function of promoting controlled social change fast enough to satisfy the demands and pressures originating inside China while enabling the state to cope successfully with a threatening international environment.[73]

This was the question faced by the reformers in the 1980s, as it has been validated by the events of 1989 and their subsequent consequences. This question is more pertinent to the present reform elites as the dust of the radical changes in the former Soviet Union and the Eastern European countries has gradually settled. Thus, this is also the question to be addressed in the 1990s and, perhaps, even far beyond in the future.

In sum, civil service reform is only part of the overall changes within the post-Mao reform era, and it cannot be separated from the general picture that the Fourteenth Party Congress has painted. All in all, the civil service reform not only creates opportunities for the reform elites but also provides them with challenges as China approaches the twenty-first century.

Notes

1. The usage of the term "civil service reform" (*gongwu gaige*) indicates the attempt by the Chinese reformers to recast their governmental organizations in the light of modern experiences, and that is why this term has been used. A number of varied usages such as "state cadre" (*guojia ganbu*), "working staff and personnel of the state organizations" (*guojia jiguan gongzuo renyuan*),

"civil servant" (*gongwuyuan*), "public servant" (*gongpu*) and "bureaucrat" (*guanliao*) all refer to the same group of personnel and staff working within governmental organizations, though with different connotations and value judgements attached. Given the short history of Chinese civil service reform, these terms will be used interchangeably through this article to denote this group of personnel and staff.

2. Party Secretary Jiang Zemin delivered his report to the Congress on 12 October 1992. Section seven of chapter two of his report exclusively deals with bureaucratic and administrative reforms. *Wen Wei Po* (Hong Kong), 13 October 1992, pp. 19–20.

3. A. Heidenheimer, M. Johnston and V.T. LeVine (eds.), *Political Corruption: A Handbook* (New Brunswick, NJ: Transaction Books, 1989) and James C. Scott, *Comparative Political Corruption* (Englewood Cliffs: Prentice Hall, Inc., 1972).

4. Professor Tang Tsou has characterized the post-Mao reforms as attempts to institutionalize and routinize the political system. Tang Tsou, *The Cultural Revolution and Post-Mao Reforms* (Chicago: The University of Chicago Press, 1986), pp. 259–334.

5. The Vice-Minister of the Ministry of Personnel stated that China would not adopt the "political neutrality system" for her proposed civil service reforms. *Renmin ribao*, 11 November 1988, p. 4.

6. *Deng Xiaoping wenxuan* (Selected Works of Deng Xiaoping) (Beijing: Renmin chubanshe, 1983), p. 287.

7. This will most likely be included in the State Constitution at the Eighth National People's Congress to be convened on 15 March 1993. *Wen Wei Po*, 14 February 1993, p. 1.

8. *Beijing Review*, 9–15 November 1992, p. 4.

9. Basically, there are three forces at play: the mandatory plan, the guidance plan and the market. The guidance plan is a kind of mandatory planning, as it is imposed by local governments. The effect is the same as that of mandatory planning: compulsory. This is a sign of the increasing role played by the local governments. For more details, please refer to: Wei Wei, "Difang zhengfu xingwei de niuqu yu jiuzheng" (The Twists in the Behaviours of the Local Governments and Their Remedies), in *Anhui caimao xueyuan xuebao* (Anhui College of Finance and Trade Journal), No. 1, 1988, pp. 2–7.

10. Interview with an official from the City's Planning Committee. A scholar also stressed that the Planning Committee would be the first organization to have the cut. Author's interview conducted on 28 November 1992 in Guangzhou.

11. *Ta Kung Pao* (Hong Kong), 19 October 1992, p. 2.

12. Parris H. Chang, "China after Deng: Towards the 13th CCP Congress," in *Problems of Communism*, May–June 1987, p. 36.

13. *Zhongguo gongchandang di shier ci quanguo daibiao dahui wenjian huibian*

(The Compilation of Documents of the Twelfth National Party Congress) (Beijing: Renmin chubanshe, 1982), p. 171.
14. *Ming Pao* (Hong Kong), 21 November 1992, p. 6.
15. There are more than 100 ministries and commissions under the State Council which will be affected. See *Wen Wei Po*, 28 December 1992, p. 6. The exact figure of staff that will be cut in any specific organization depends on a number of variables such as the bargaining power of the concerned department and the overall strategy of reform at the time. Suffice to say that there is no doubt that substantial cuts amounting to one-third of the total staff under the State Council will be carried out. *Wen Wei Po*, 15 February 1993, p. 6.
16. *Ming Pao*, 21 November 1992, p. 6.
17. *Wen Wei Po*, 28 November 1992, p. 2, editorial.
18. *South China Morning Post* (Hong Kong), 26 November 1992, p. 12.
19. *Renmin ribao*, 11 November 1988, p. 4; and *Zhongguo jigou yu bianzhi* (Chinese Organization and Establishment), No. 6, 1992, p. 28.
20. *Ibid.*, p. 32; *Qiushi* (Seeking Truth), No. 8, 1989, p. 23; Professor Tong Zhimin's talk at The Chinese University of Hong Kong on 16 October 1992. Another translation of these "Regulations" as "Ordinances on State Civil Servants" can be found in Foreign Broadcast Information Service, China — Daily Report (Washington, DC: Department of Commerce) [FBIS], 18 November 1987, p. 18.
21. *Liaowang*, 12 March 1990, p. 14.
22. *Ibid.*, p. 14; *Qiushi*, No. 8, 1989, p. 23; and Professor Tong Zhimin's talk, see Note 20.
23. The difference between the twentieth and twenty-first drafts, according to Professor Tong Zhimin, is not substantial. Interviewed on 18 October 1992.
24. *Ta Kung Pao*, 27 February 1993, p. 6. According to an earlier report, the final version has become the *Guojia xingzheng jiguan gongwuyuan zhidu* (The State Executive Organizations Civil Servants System). Whether this report is accurate or not, this document still needs the endorsement of the People's Congress. *Ming Pao*, 20 February, 1993, p. 2.
25. The author has a copy of the twentieth draft of these *Temporary Regulations*. All the discussion about grading and stratification systems in the following section will be based upon this document.
26. Some of these dimensions have been addressed and touched upon in the past, though not based on the current draft proposals. See, for example, Doak A. Barnett, *Cadres, Bureaucracy and Political Power in Communist China* (New York: Columbia University Press, 1967); Michael Oksenberg, "Getting Ahead and Along in Communist China: The Ladder of Success on the Eve of Cultural Revolution," in *Party Leadership & Revolutionary Power in China*, edited by John W. Lewis (Cambridge: Cambridge University Press, 1970); John P. Burns, "Civil Service Reform in Contemporary China," in *China:*

Modernization in the 1980s, edited by Joseph Y. S. Cheng (Hong Kong: The Chinese University Press, 1989), pp. 108–19 and "Chinese Civil Service Reform: The 13th Party Congress Proposals," *The China Quarterly*, No. 120 (December 1989), pp. 739–70; King W. Chow, "The Management of Chinese Cadre Resources: The Politics of Performance Appraisal (1949–1984)," *International Review of Administrative Sciences*, Vol. 54 (1988), pp. 359–77; and Melanie Manion, "Politics and Policy in Post-Mao Cadre Retirement," *The China Quarterly*, No. 129, 1992, pp. 1–25.

27. Besides those twelve topics (chapter 3 to chapter 14), there are six more chapters in the twentieth draft. Chapter 1 is on the general guidelines; chapter 2 is on rights and duties; chapter 15 is on prosecution appeal and; chapter 16 is on the managing organizations; chapter 17 is on the legal responsibilities; and the last one is made up of supplementary articles. In the sixteenth draft, there were only sixteenth chapters. *Zhongguo jigou yu bianzhi*, No. 6, 1992, p. 32. According to a source reported by a Hong Kong newspaper, there are twenty chapters in the latest version of the draft. *Ming Pao*, 20 February 1993, p. 2.

28. Some of the regulations of the seventeenth draft can be found in Tong Zhimin's book, *Guojia gongwuyuan gailun* (Outline to the State Civil Servants) (Beijing: Zhongguo renmin daxue chubanshe, 1989).

29. For example, the Vice-Minister of the Ministry of Personnel stated the importance of the classification of these two categories of civil servants. *Renmin ribao*, 11 November 1988, p. 4.

30. *Ibid.*

31. The definitive statement of this distinction can be found in Woodrow Wilson, "The Study of Administration," reprinted in *Classics of Public Administration*, edited by Jay M. Shafritz and Albert C. Hyde (Pacific Grove: Brooks/Cole Publishing Co.,1992), pp. 11–24.

32. *Temporary Regulations*, pp. 3–5. This stratification has been kept and used as well in the *Guojia xingzheng jiguan gongwuyuan zhidu*, see Note 24.

33. On 10 November 1988, the Vice-Minister of the Ministry of Personnel declared the set date for the completion of the draft would be strived for. *Renmin ribao*, 11 November 1988, pp. 1 and 4.

34. *Qiushi*, No. 8, 1989, p. 22.

35. *Liaowang* (Outlook, Overseas Edition), 21 January 1991, p. 19.

36. *Liaowang*, 15 June 1992, p. 20.

37. *Liaowang*, No. 24, 1992, p. 201–21. The system of *huibi*, avoiding conflicts of interests, includes three dimensions: the avoidance of hiring relatives to work in the same administrative section, or to execute similar official tasks and duties, and thirdly, relatives who come from the same region or locality. See *Temporary Regulations*, pp. 13–14.

38. *Liaowang*, No. 27, 1992, pp. 16–17.

39. *Liaowang*, No. 29, 1992, pp. 11–13.
40. *Liaowang* (Overseas Edition), 21 September 1992, p. 3.
41. Tang Tsou, see Note 4, pp. 259–334.
42. I shall focus mostly on the two reforms of the 1980s. Readers can consult the following article on the earlier two attempts and their consequences. See Diao Tianding, "Zhide zhuyi jingjian jigou de lishi jingyan" (It Is Worth Paying Attention to the Historical Experiences of Organizational Streamlining), *Zhongguo xingzheng guanli* (China Administrative Management), No. 5, 1986, pp. 2–5.
43. For a more detailed treatment, refer to Xia Hai, "Zhengque renshi yijiubaernian de jigou gaige" (Correctly Understand the 1982 Organizational Reforms), in *Zhongguo xingzheng guanli*, No. 6, 1987, pp. 23–24.
44. *Liaowang*, No. 37, 1992, p. 24.
45. *Liaowang*, 7 September 1992, p. 18.
46. *Renmin ribao*, 16 September 1989, p. 1.
47. The exact figure is hard to estimate here, depending on the way one categorizes those staff and personnel. If we count the "workers who substitute as cadres" (*yigong daigan*) and the staff recruited by the institutions and organizations which are also under local budget, then the number would approach 40 million. *Liaowang*, 7 September 1992, p. 18.
48. Another example is that the number of people who are employed in state, Party and the mass organizations (such as the Women Federation and Trade Unions) has increased massively from 1978 to 1990. The data are: 4.3 million were employed in 1978, 5.77 million in 1982, 7.7 million in 1986; it reached 9.29 million in 1990. *Zhongguo tongji nianjian 1991* (China's Statistical Year-book 1991) (Beijing: Zhongguo tongji chubanshe, 1991), p. 102.
49. A factory in Wuxi needed 745 official seals from different hierarchical layers such as the bureau (*ju*), division (*chu*), section (*ke*), and the like, before it could launch a capital construction programme. *Renmin ribao*, 8 August 1992, p. 3.
50. Exact data have not been fully disclosed yet. One can have an idea of the figures in *China's Statistical Year-books*. For example, the "administrative and management fees" in 1981 was RMB7,088 million, RMB18,243 million in 1986, and it reached RMB37,581 million in 1991. *Zhongguo tongji nianjian 1992* (China's Statistical Year-book 1992) (Beijing: Zhongguo tongji chubanshe, 1992), p. 222.
51. "Bound by Red Tape," *Far Eastern Economic Review*, 9 November 1989, pp. 34–35.
52. *Liaowang*, No. 36, 1992, p. 18.
53. This allocation is also called imperial grain (*huangliang*), referring to the consuming of grains by the officials in Imperial China. *Ibid*.
54. For example, there are almost forty-thousand staff and personnel more than

the approved roster at the various levels of government in Hunan province. *Renmin ribao*, 8 July 1992, p. 5.
55. *Liaowang*, No. 36, 1992, p. 18. An interesting point of evolution for comparative purpose that is a typical example of this kind is the International Screwthread Commission which was formed in 1918 by the Congress of the United States for a life span not to exceed sixty days. It did survive until 1933 when President Franklin Roosevelt ordered it abolished. However, the commission simply reformed itself into the Interdepartmental Screwthread Commission which eventually was re-established as the present commission. see Nicholas Henry, *Public Administration and Public Affairs* (New Jersey: Prentice-Hall International, Inc., 1988), pp. 11–12.
56. *Liaowang*, No. 36, 1992, p. 18.
57. *Ibid.*, No. 37, 1992, p. 24.
58. This is one of the most important subjects to be studied in the post-Mao era as the power of the local government has increased in contrast to the central government. See, for example, Wang Chengde, "Difang zhengfu jingji quanli pengzhang de jili fenxi" (Analysis on the Mechanisms of the Economic Power Expansion of the Local Governments), *Gaige* (Reform), No. 3, 1989, pp. 132–36. Also see Note 9.
59. There is a voluminous literature on bureaucratic expansion and sovereignty, though based on different assumptions and methodologies. One can consult, for example, the following books: C. Northcote's Parkinson's Law or the rising pyramid in *Parkinson's Law and Other Studies in Administration* (Boston: Houghton Mifflin, 1957); Anthony Downs' life cycle of bureaux in *Inside Bureaucracy* (Boston: Little, Brown and Company, 1967); and William A. Niskanen's budget maximization in *Bureaucracy and Representative Government* (Chicago: The University of Chicago Press, 1971).
60. *Ming Pao*, 24 November 1992, p. 9.
61. Hu Zhengmin, "Guanyu gaige 'guanbenwei' de sikao" (Reflections on the Reform of "Bureaucratic-centricity" System), *Zhongguo xingzheng guanli*, No. 3, 1989, pp. 1–5.
62. *Liaowang* (Overseas Edition), 21 September 1992, p. 3.
63. Interview with Professor Tong, see Note 23.
64. John McMillan and Barry Naughton, "How to Reform a Planned Economy: Lessons from China," *Oxford Review of Economic Policy*, No. 1, 1992, pp. 130–43.
65. In 1978, the state had a budget surplus of RMB1.01 billion but since then it has declined. In 1981, the deficit was RMB2.55 billion; RMB4.45 billion in 1984 and RMB8.05 billion in 1988. *Zhongguo tongji nianjian 1989* (China's Statistical Year-book 1989) (Beijing: Zhongguo tongji chubanshe, 1989), p. 657.
66. A company which specializes in importing fire prevention devices has the

support of the local Public Security Bureau. This company can easily obtain a licence from the Fire Prevention Office, a branch under the hierarchical control of the Public Security Bureau, after installing devices in restaurants, hotels and shops. As a result, this is a guarantee to the customers as they are certified according to the law. On the contrary, any company which does not have this kind of connection will not have that much business. Customers may worry that, after spending the money on installation of the fire prevention system, they simply cannot get the certification from this office. Author's interview, 20 April 1992, in Guangzhou.

67. *Liaowang*, No. 38, 21 September 1992, p. 15.
68. These four principles are: upholding socialism, the dictatorship of the proletariat, the leadership of the Party and Marxism-Leninism and Mao Zedong Thought. And they are not listed out in the second section of the first chapter of the *Temporary Regulations*, p. 2.
69. See Note 5.
70. Ronald J. Hill and John Lowenhardt, "Nomenklatura and Perestroika," *Government and Opposition*, No. 2, 1991, p. 229.
71. This is a slightly modified version of Max Weber's classic formulation on bureaucracy. For the characteristics of bureaucracy, please refer to *Classics of Public Administration* (Note 31), pp. 51–56.
72. They made use of the successful experiences of the Latin American and Asian countries on their road to economic development and applied them to the Chinese context. This is what has been called "neo-authoritarianism." For details, please refer to *Xinquanweizhuyi* (Neo-authoritarianism), edited by Liu Jun and Li Lin (Beijing: Beijing jingji xueyuan chubanshe, 1989).
73. Tang Tsou, "Back from the Brink of Revolutionary — 'Feudal' Totalitarianism," in *State and Society in Contemporary China*, edited by Victor Nee and David Mozingo (Ithaca: Cornell University Press, 1983), p. 78.

6

The People's Liberation Army in 1992: Political Power Plays and Power Projection

Tai Ming Cheung

As guardian of the state and defender of the Communist Party's hold on power, the People's Liberation Army (PLA) is one of the most powerful and orthodox institutions in China. But it is not a monolithic or politically acquiescent organization. As a series of dramatic events in 1992 revealed, the military leadership was deeply split among competing factions vying for control of the armed forces. The dispute revolved around the extent of the military's continuing involvement in politics, and in particular its role in choosing a successor to ageing patriarch Deng Xiaoping.[1]

At the heart of the controversy was the personal ambitions of General Yang Baibing and, to a lesser extent, his elder and more influential half-brother Yang Shangkun. The Yangs had been gradually building up their military power base since the early 1980s when they began assuming key command posts. Yang Shangkun, Deng's right-hand man, had become Secretary General of the powerful Party Central Military Commission (CMC) in 1981, allowing him to oversee the daily running of the sprawling military establishment and pluck his half-brother from obscurity following the Cultural Revolution to a string of prestigious positions in the Beijing Military Region, the country's premier regional military command.

From 1979 onwards, the younger Yang served in various political commissar positions in the Beijing Military Region, including becoming its Chief Commissar from 1985 to 1987. He received a crucial boost in 1987 when he became Director of the PLA General Political Department (GPD), which gave him an influential voice in the selection and promotion of military officers. His department was also administratively responsible for overseeing the service records of serving PLA personnel.

The making of the Yang military dynasty accelerated following the June 1989 military crackdown — an operation that the Yangs played a prominent role in organizing and prosecuting. For their tough stance during these upheavals, they earned the gratitude of conservative hardliners who gained temporary political ascendancy after the crackdown. They were rewarded in November 1989 with promotions to top positions in the military hierarchy. Yang Baibing was made CMC Secretary General, won a place on the Party Secretariat, and remained as GPD Director, while Yang Shangkun was elevated to become CMC First-Vice Chairman as well as continuing on as state President. However, Deng is said to have only agreed to Yang Shangkun's move on condition that Yang would retire after two years to pave the way for other younger leaders.

Yang Baibing in particular moved quickly to install his supporters, including large numbers of fellow political commissars, into key command slots. He initially concentrated his efforts in the GPD which he directly controlled and the Beijing Military Region, although he soon reached out to cultivate his support across the PLA. His accumulation of power was so swift and widespread that he was regarded as a crucial arbiter of power both in the military and political systems.

But in his promotions, Yang alienated many senior and retired but still influential generals who were not only worried about his greedy empire-building efforts but also the disastrous impact on the PLA's professionalism. Having spent his entire career as a political commissar with little experience in operational military matters, Yang focused on ideological education and political reliability at the expense of professionalism. Instead of spending the majority of their time training to fight, soldiers concentrated instead on attending political classes. Professional standards and morale, which had not been high beforehand, declined, in particular among the officer corps.

Up until the beginning of 1991, the Yangs held a virtual monopoly on authority within the high command. Deng was still in political retreat from the June 1989 crackdown, and the Yangs were able to shut out Communist Party General Secretary Jiang Zemin, who succeeded Deng as CMC Chairman. This was because even though Jiang was Commander-in-Chief, his actual authority was considerably less than that derived from his position. Without a background in military affairs, lacking political clout in Beijing and without much personal charisma or leadership talent, his ability to command respect and allegiance was severely lacking.[2] Such a combination had been fatal for past leaders who had needed the PLA's backing for their political aspirations but were instead snubbed by military leaders because of their lack of military experience. This fate apparently befell Hu Yaobang, Deng's first chosen successor, in the mid-1980s.

Despite these strong misgivings over Jiang's qualities, he was still able to get the backing of a number of moderate and professionally oriented generals.[3] Among senior officers who appeared to align themselves behind Jiang included Chief of the PLA General Staff Department (GSD) General Chi Haotian, Defence Minister General Qin Jiwei, Director of the PLA General Logistics Department (GLD) General Zhao Nanqi and to a lesser extent CMC Vice-Chairman General Liu Huaqing. These officers oversaw the PLA's professionalism drive in the 1980s and were concerned that their work was being undone by Yang. But perhaps more importantly, many of them were angered that they were being sidelined in the decision-making process and that their subordinates were being left out in the promotion stakes.

This growing opposition helped to check the Yangs' empire-building, and throughout most of 1991 an uneasy balance was maintained. The Gulf War at the beginning of 1991 and the overwhelming technological superiority of the US-led coalition forces helped to add momentum to the efforts of Jiang and his supporters to blunt and eventually overturn Yang's zealous politicization campaign. Professional priorities were restored and political classes were cut back. With his policies in disarray, Yang retreated from the public spotlight and for much of 1991 maintained a low profile.

But according to informed observers, Yang remained active behind the scene to try and continue to expand his grip of the high command. With the promotion process in paralysis as the different factions sought to block the elevation of their supporters, Yang turned his attention to examining other channels with which to push his position. Among activities that Yang is believed to have been engaged in includes holding private meetings with some of his closest supporters on a variety of sensitive military topics relating to the roles of the PLA and the para-military People's Armed Police (PAP) in the internal power structure, such as the ability to deal with riots and other political disturbances. Some of these discussions are believed to have focused on how the PLA should act operationally in the event of Deng's death.

Although any military establishment has to be prepared for a wide range of contingencies, Yang's interest in these issues not only exceeded his brief as GPD Director but was also curious as he had previously shown little interest in operational matters. In addition, other senior commanders who should have attended the meetings, such as the Chief of the General Staff, were not informed that they were being held. Among officers who attended the meetings are believed to have included a Deputy-Commander of the Beijing Military Region and its chief of staff, Lieutenant-General Zou Yuqi and the PAP Commander Lieutenant-General Zhou Yushu. Although these meetings were carefully scripted to show they were brainstorming discussions on military planning, they nonetheless hinted of a *coup d'état* or a military power-grab in the making.

These private meetings initially caused few waves when they were held in the summer of 1991, either because they did not come to light or were not considered as particularly threatening. But they eventually were included among a growing wealth of evidence that Yang's opponents were amassing to present to Deng in an effort to put a stop to his power-hungry ambitions.

As the intrigues continued to be played out furiously but quietly within the military leadership, Deng remained aloof, at least for the time being. His attentions were focused instead on revitalizing economic reforms which had stalled in the aftermath of a three-year retrenchment programme and bickering between radical reformers and more orthodox policymakers. Deng made a celebrated trip to southern China in January 1992 visiting Shenzhen and other economically dynamic areas. This was followed up by a public relations effort that within a couple of months saw the pendulum of power swing decisively in favour of reformist elements.

Yang Baibing, ever the consummate opportunist and particularly aware that the key Fourteenth Communist Party Congress was just months away, saw the political advantages of jumping onto the reform bandwagon. At the National People's Congress (NPC) in late March 1992, Yang declared that the PLA would "serve as a protector and escort" for the reforms.[4] This became the rallying cry for the military for the next few months. In an effort to promote reformist thinking within the PLA leadership, senior officers from many PLA units undertook study tours to Guangdong, Shenzhen and other special economic zones and proclaimed themselves impressed and fully behind the reforms. Yang's abrupt U-turn from an uncompromising hardliner to a reformist champion was taken with strong scepticism, even by those hardened to the violent swings of Chinese politics.

Whether Deng believed in Yang Baibing's reformist reincarnation or not was left unstated until the run-up to the Party Congress. The Yangs appeared hopeful that they had done enough, and Yang Baibing in particular, to deserve a position in the Politburo and its more exclusive standing committee. Getting onto these bodies was an important objective for Yang Baibing; backed by his elder brother who already was a Politburo member, he lobbied hard. But at a series of summer meetings in Beidaihe and other parts of China, the country's top leaders appeared opposed to Yang's elevation. By at least early September, the leadership lineup for the Politburo standing committee was decided and Yang had failed to win a place. Instead, Liu, the most senior PLA officer after the Yangs, and a professional modernizer with few political ambitions, was promoted onto the Politburo and its standing committee.

Even though the leadership arrangements were in place, the Yangs apparently still persisted in their efforts to push for Yang Baibing's inclusion at the top of the political pecking order. On 4 September, Yang Shangkun wrote a letter to Deng Xiaoping saying that he would step down from his positions if his younger brother would be promoted to the Politburo Standing Committee and also to a CMC Vice-Chairmanship. There were also other reports in the Hong Kong press that said that Yang Baibing had called an unauthorised meeting of military officers on the eve of the Party congress to discuss matters following Deng's death and had also changed the central military guard that protects the senior leadership.[5]

Yang's mistakes were sufficiently serious for Deng to personally intervene in a manner not seen since the dismissal of Party General Secretary Zhao Ziyang in May 1989.[6] Some analysts believe that several influential retired military officers lobbied Deng for Yang's removal. Among the most vocal was former Military Academy Commandant General Xiao Ke, former Defence Minister General Zhang Aiping and former GLD Director General Hong Xuezhi. A television appearance in mid-November by Zhang marked the end of a three year political exile that followed his public reservations, along with several other retired generals, over the use of force in the run-up to the June 1989 military crackdown.[7]

The last straw for Deng appears to have been Yang Shangkun's letter. On 6 September, Deng passed on his reply to the Politburo which shortly afterwards convened a special meeting. In his message, Deng said that Yang Baibing was no longer to hold any military positions. As a face-saving gesture, Yang was offered a Politburo position. Deng also pointed out that he wanted to see the promotion of professional and open-minded military commanders not politically aligned to any factions. Deng's bombshell was officially endorsed by the Politburo. Besides giving up his CMC General Secretaryship, Yang also lost his GPD directorship and his place on the Party Secretariat.

It took several weeks before details of Yang's removal began to be hinted in the official press. In an unsubtle allusion to Yang's excesses of power, mainland and Beijing-backed newspapers in Hong Kong published a five-point CMC directive on 25 November that stressed the need to develop the fine traditions of the army and root out corruption in the ranks. Among the points emphasized, the directive said the "improper promotion and use of cadres must be corrected, the use of power for personal gain and the exchange of power for money must be stopped."[8] In the ultimate irony, Yang, who had fervently warned about the development of unhealthy tendencies within the ranks because of the growing increase of western influences, is believed to have been criticized himself for engaging in spiritual pollution and corrupt activities.

Despite Yang's black marks, the offer of the politburo seat, which he accepted, does suggest that Deng did not intend to completely destroy the Yangs' influence. Despite Yang Baibing's sudden downfall, his rapid rise throughout the 1980s was also done with Deng's approval. In addition, Deng's personal friendship with Yang Shangkun extends back several decades to the civil war years. Although Yang's ambitious empire-building finally forced Deng to take harsh counter-measures, this does not necessarily mean that their friendship has come to an end, although some observers believe that Yang feels bitter and betrayed by a comrade-in-arms he has served so loyally.

To what extent the Deng-Yang Shangkun relationship has been damaged, and therefore Yang's political influence, could prove a key factor in the immediate aftermath of Deng's death — assuming that Yang is still sufficiently fit to fight for power at that point. Before the Party Congress, Yang had been widely acknowledged as the country's second most powerful leader and a natural, if though transitional, successor to Deng. Although 85, Yang is in better physical shape than many of his contemporaries. As one of the few remaining Long March generation of leaders, with a long record of working within the Party bureaucracy, and responsible for the PLA's modernization efforts in the 1980s, he has built up a good reputation and close connections with many political and military insiders.

Yang's departure from all his official posts, including the CMC First Vice-chairmanship at the Party Congress and the state presidency at the eighth NPC in March 1993, means that he is now left waiting on the sideline. The only way for him to re-enter the central political arena appears to be with Deng's death, but the longer the patriarch remains active, the weaker Yang's position will be as his personal power steadily ebbs away. Nonetheless, it would be premature to write Yang's political obituary.

The Yangs' departure brought in a host of new faces and the unexpected return of some old soldiers. Most surprising was the promotion of General Zhang Zhen, a 78 year old Korean War veteran as CMC Vice-Chairman. Zhang, a loyal lieutenant of Deng, had been expected to retire because of his failing health and long tenure at the PLA National Defence University, where he had been President since its founding in 1986. Despite these considerations, Deng chose Zhang because he was one of a small number of top generals who could be trusted to follow his orders faithfully, as well as having sufficient respect within the ranks to fill the large gap left by the Yangs' abrupt departure.

Zhang's tenure at the PLA's premier educational establishment also allowed him to cultivate ties with many middle and senior officers who passed through the university for advanced studies in preparation for taking up higher posts. Such knowledge would have proved invaluable as Zhang was given by Deng a large part of the responsibility to oversee the PLA's most extensive high-level reshuffle in its history to make sure that the Yang's power-base was effectively dismantled.

As the only military representative on the Politburo and Politburo Standing Committee, Liu Huaqing should be in full command of the military establishment. But he lacks the political clout to be able to claim Yang Shangkun's mantle as the country's military strongman. Although a Deng loyalist, Liu has spent little time cultivating support from the ranks or among civilian leaders. His primary focus has been overseeing the PLA forces' modernization programme, and in particular managing arms purchases and coordinating the development of defence-related science and technology projects. As a former navy commander and student at a Russian military academy, Liu has also played a key role in pushing the navy's development and the expansion of Sino-Russian military relations. Liu, therefore, is unlikely to play a major role in any future struggle for power within the military.

Another surprise was that the CMC Secretary General's position was left unfilled, the first time this had happened. This may have been because of the abruptness of Yang Baibing's dismissal. There had previously been little discussion that Yang would leave this seat, even had he been elevated to become a CMC Vice-Chairman. The decision to leave the post vacant may have also been due to the lack of a suitable candidate. There was no suggestion, however, that the position was being abolished as it is considered a crucially important slot with which the CMC liaises with the PLA headquarters departments. It is believed that the Secretary General's work has been divided up between the two CMC Vice-Chairmen and the new Deputy Director of the GPD, Lieutenant-General Wang Ruilin.

Other officers rewarded with promotions at the Party Congress were Jinan Military Region Commander Lieutenant-General Zhang Wannian, who replaced Chi Haotian as the new Chief of the General Staff. Chi stepped aside temporarily until the Eighth NPC when he took over as Defence Minister from Qin Jiwei. Zhang's appointment was a surprise as his fortunes were seen to have suffered a setback following the June 1989 military crackdown. Zhang, 64, was rumoured to have been hesitant in backing the use of force when he was in charge of the Guangzhou Military Region and was subsequently transferred to Jinan in early 1990. Zhang's move further underlines the importance of the Jinan Military Region as a key stepping stone in the promotion prospects of military chiefs. Chi Haotian had also served in Jinan in the mid-1980s before he became GSD chief in 1987.

However, some analysts think that Zhang's move to Jinan was due more to strained relations with the military region's long-standing political commissar Lieutenant-General Zhang Zhongxian, a close friend of Yang Baibing. Zhang Wannian's command experience in the country's most economically dynamic province may prove useful as he oversees the PLA's operations at a time when military units are increasingly involved in money-making activities to make up for shortfalls in their budgetary allocations from Beijing.

General Fu Quanyou, Commander of the Lanzhou Military Region, took over control of the GLD from General Zhao Nanqi who went to become President of the Academy of Military Sciences, the PLA's top think-tank. Fu, 63, is a well-respected commander with a wealth of combat experience, having served during the civil war, the Korean War and during the 1979 Sino-Vietnamese border war. He performed well as a division commander during the Vietnam campaign and was quickly elevated to become a group army commander and then to head the Chengdu Military Region before transferring to Lanzhou in 1990. Fu has a formidable task managing the PLA's logistical operations and allocating limited financial resources, which, despite hefty budgetary increases by the government since 1990, remain inadequate to cover the PLA's needs.

Lieutenant-General Yu Yongbo, a GPD Deputy Director took over as GPD chief. The move was surprising as Yu had been considered one of Yang's protégés, although some analysts believe that Yu had begun to distance himself from Yang several months before his fall. Yu, 62, had been a Director of the Nanjing Military Region's Political Department before being picked by Yang in late 1989 to move to GPD headquarters. But Yu's promotion also meant a downgrading in the importance of the once immensely powerful GPD directorship. Yu's stature and political connections appear to be considerably weaker than any of his predecessors.

More significantly, however, was the appointment of Wang Ruilin as

Deputy GPD Director. Wang is believed to have taken the post at the same time that Yang Baibing was removed. Wang, 64, was previously a deputy director of the Communist Party General Office, head of the CMC's Disciplinary Inspection Commission and, more importantly, the military secretary to Deng since 1977. As one of Deng's most trusted lieutenants, Wang is believed to have been given the task of dismantling Yang Baibing's most important power base. Although only a deputy to Yu, Wang's personal connections make him much more powerful than the GPD Director — and by most other appearances more influential than Liu Huaqing and Zhang Zhen.

Wang, Zhang Zhen and Liu Huaqing are now the three most powerful generals in the high command following the fall of the Yangs. But they are only transitional leaders. Wang's position depends almost wholly on Deng's patronage. When the patriarch dies, then Wang's continued tenure will be in doubt. Although he joined the army in 1946, he was transferred into the civilian bureaucracy after Liberation (1949), serving most of the time as Deng's personal assistant, and only returned to military administration when he became Deng's military assistant. Liu and Zhang are too old to remain in office longer than a few more years.

The search is on, therefore, for a new generation of professionally-minded officers without overweening political ambitions. A key step in this process was a sweeping reshuffle of the senior ranks of the military leadership shortly after the end of the Party Congress. An enlarged meeting of the CMC was convened where many of the personnel changes were announced, although changes had begun to take place even before then. Zhang Zhen and Wang Ruilin were responsible for deciding the reshuffle, which is believed to have involved close to 300 generals. The Beijing-affiliated *Wen Wei Po* newspaper in Hong Kong reported that the changes, which took more than a month to complete, were the biggest since the founding of the People's Republic in 1949.[9] It even exceeded an extensive purge of Lin Biao's supporters following Lin's attempted coup in 1971. Although some of the moves are part of the normal round of service promotions and retirements, many involved the removal or transfer of officers thought to have been close to the Yangs.

Along with the drastic changes in the CMC leadership, its administrative office also saw the departure of its Director, Lieutenant-General Li Jijun. Li, who went to become a Deputy Commandant at the Academy of Military Sciences, is believed to have been replaced by his deputy, Major-General Cheng Jianing. Li, who had been behind efforts to modernize doctrinal thinking, had previously had strained relations with Yang Baibing, but the two apparently patched up their differences in mid-1991. The administrative office exercises considerable informal influence through its responsibility for the organization of top-level CMC meetings that decides key policies.

A sizeable number of senior officers in the PLA headquarters departments were also affected by the reshuffle. The GPD leadership saw a particularly heavy changeover with all three Deputy GPD Directors being moved. While Yu was promoted, his other two colleagues fared less well and were demoted. Lieutenant-General Zhou Wenyuan became a Deputy Commissar in the Shenyang Military Region and Major-General Li Jinai joined the Commission for Science, Technology and Industry for National Defence as a Deputy Commissar. Only Wang Ruilin was appointed to fill one of these vacant posts.

Three Assistant GPD Directors were appointed instead, the first time these positions have been filled since 1984. They were Major-General Zhou Siyu, a commissar at the Air Force Academy, Major-General Xu Caihou, commissar of the 16th Group Army in Changchun in Jilin province, and Major-General Du Tiehuan, commissar of the 67th Group Army in Boshan in Shandong province.

Three assistant GSD chiefs were also appointed for the first time since the early 1980s. They are Major-General Xiong Guangkai, who was previously head of military intelligence in the GSD, Major-General Kui Fulin, head of the GSD operations sub-department, and Major-General Wu Quanxu, Commander of the 1st Group Army from Nanjing. Xiong is likely to have taken over some of the functions, including overseeing intelligence operations, of General Xu Xin, a Yang supporter, who retired as deputy GSD chief. Kui is likely to have assumed the duties of another outgoing deputy GSD chief, Lieutenant-General Han Huaizhi. Another Deputy GSD Director, Lieutenant-General He Qizhong, was demoted and transferred to the Nanjing Military Region as Deputy Commander. Besides a new director, the GLD saw few other changes in its top ranks, although Major-General Wang Tailan, head of the Nanjing Military Region's Logistics Department, was promoted to become a Deputy GLD Commander.

Lieutenant-General Xu Huizi held on as Deputy GSD Commander and was joined by two new faces: Major-General Cao Gangchuan, who was previously in charge of the CMC's weapons trade office, and Vice-Admiral Li Jing, who was a Deputy Commander of the navy. Li's move was a major boost for the navy as this was one of the first times a naval officer has been elevated to such a high position within the GSD. Li's appointment may have been helped by Liu Huaqing, who is a former navy commander, but it also indicates the growing importance of the navy in overall military priorities.

Many of the commanders and political commissars in charge of the country's seven Military Regions were also changed in the reshuffle. Lieutenant-General Zhang Taiheng took charge of the Jinan Military Region following Zhang Wannian's promotion as GSD chief. Zhang Taiheng's move marks a remarkable political recovery following his dismissal as Chengdu Military Region Commander in the autumn of 1991. Zhang, a respected military thinker, was ostensibly punished by military chiefs following a helicopter crash in Tibet earlier that year which killed one of Zhang's deputies and other senior regional military commanders. Zhang's transfer out of Chengdu ended efforts by Yang Baibing to try and promote him to take over from Chi Haotian as GSD chief.

Shenyang Military Region commander Lieutenant-General Liu Jingsong, considered a Yang loyalist, was transferred to head the Lanzhou Military Region, and replaced by the commander of the Xinjiang military district, Lieutenant-General Wang Ke. Wang's move to Shenyang underlined the sometimes chaotic state of the reshuffle. Wang was assigned to Shenyang only a couple of days after he had been made Lanzhou Military Region Commander. Lieutenant-General Zhang Zhongxian, Political Commissar of the Guangzhou Military Region, retired and was replaced by Lieutenant-General Shi Yuxiao, previously Political Commissar of Nanjing Military Region. Replacing Shi in Nanjing was Lieutenant-General Liu Anyuan, Political Commissar of the Second Artillery Corps. Guangzhou Military Region Commander Lieutenant-General Zhu Dunfa was made head of the National Defence University and replaced by one of his deputies, Lieutenant-General Li Xilin.

A number of officers swapped positions in a move designed to undermine any power bases they may have been building up. This included Beijing Military Region Political Commissar Lieutenant-General Zhang Gong, who was sent to Chengdu Military Region and his place taken by the Chengdu Military Region Commissar Lieutenant-General Gu Shanqing. Although Zhang ostensibly moved to a position of equal rank as his previous post, it was clearly interpreted as a demotion as Chengdu is a less prestigious posting than Beijing.

Zhang's Chengdu move may be a prelude to his eventual retirement. Zhang's meteoric rise to take overall charge of political duties in the

Beijing Military Region in 1990 from his previous position as the Director of the Military Region's political department was due largely to his close ties with Yang that were built up during the 1980s as well as a hardline performance during the 1989 military crackdown. When Yang served as a rapidly rising Political Commissar in Beijing Military Region between 1979 to 1987, Zhang is believed to have been one of his principal assistants.

A considerable number of other officers who also served in Beijing Military Region and who had been promoted by Yang were also reshuffled or removed. Among those included Zou Yuqi, who became a Deputy Commander of the Lanzhou Military Region, also a minor reduction in his status. His colleague Major-General Dong Xuelin, also a Deputy Beijing Military Region Commander and head of the Beijing Garrison Command was given an equivalent ranking position as a Deputy Commander of the Jinan Military Region. Just before Yang's dismissal, he had apparently tried to install more than forty Beijing Military Region officers into positions in the three general headquarters' departments as well as the *Liberation Army Daily*. These transfers were stopped following Yang's fall.

Several officers managed to retain their positions, including Beijing Military Region Commander Lieutenant-General Wang Chengbin, who was disliked by Yang Baibing but had the patronage of Deng and Jiang to protect him. Long-serving Shenyang Military Region Political Commissar Lieutenant-General Song Keda also held on as did Lanzhou Military Region Political Commissar Lieutenant-General Cao Pengsheng, Nanjing Military Region Commander Lieutenant-General Gu Hui and Chengdu Military Region Commander Lieutenant-General Li Jiulong.

Another close supporter of Yang Baibing who was moved was PAP Commander Zhou Yushu, who was transferred to become Deputy Commander of the Guangzhou Military Region. His position was taken over by Major-General Ba Zhongtan. Ba was a former chief of the Shanghai Garrison command in the late 1980s and may have developed some ties with Jiang Zemin. Before Zhou took over as PAP Commander in 1990, he was commander of the 24th Group Army based near Chengde in Hebei province. His return to the PLA suggests that the PAP, although nominally separate from the military establishment and under the daily control of the Ministry of Public Security, is closely connected to the PLA command structure.[10]

Many other routine personnel moves that were delayed by the Yang power play finally went through. Air force Commander General Wang Hai was replaced by Lieutenant-General Cao Shuangming, Deputy Commander of the Shenyang Military Region and head of its air force headquarters. Second Artillery Commander Lieutenant-General Li Xuge was replaced by one of his deputies, Major-General Yang Guoliang and his Political Commissar was Major-General Sui Yongju, previously the Second Artillery's head of the political department.

Several salient features emerge from these changes. First, although many of the Yangs' associates were affected by the reshuffle, only a small number were either retired or demoted. Most were instead transferred to positions outside of Beijing. These include some of those believed to be the Yangs' most trusted allies, including Zhang Gong, Zou Yuqi, Zhang Taiheng, Zhou Yushu, Dong Xuelin and Liu Jingsong. While these officers are now in much weaker positions, having been separated from their power bases and moved to military regions far from Beijing, they nonetheless still hold active positions. Although their return to Beijing would appear unlikely while Deng is still alive and has his lieutenants in key high command posts, should Deng die within months rather than years, then the situation could drastically change. Although Wang Ruilin, Zhang Zhen and other Deng loyalists are busy building up their power bases and cultivating the support of younger officers, this process remains in its infancy. Zhang Wannian, Fu Quanyou and Yu Yongbo lack the stature of past predecessors of their positions, and they also spent much of their careers outside of Beijing.

Secondly, Jiang Zemin's influence in the high command also appears to have been adversely affected by the reshuffle. His closest supporters, Chi Haotian and Zhao Nanqi, were moved into peripheral positions. Moreover, one of the principal reasons why many officers sided with Jiang was their opposition to the Yangs. But as this cause has now disappeared, Jiang's attraction to some of these officers may also have been diminished.

Although Jiang now holds the country's top posts of CMC Chairman, Party Secretary and State President, his power base within the military has suffered a setback. This calls into greater doubt his chances for becoming paramount leader after Deng's death. This apparently contradictory action by Deng to grant Jiang more formal powers while undermining his informal support base may be because Deng still has strong misgivings over Jiang. The Party Secretary was not Deng's choice as his successor but was apparently a suitable compromise during the mid-1989 crisis when the conservative elders were in the ascendancy.

Thirdly, Deng's appointment of his chief, if ageing, supporters into the top command slots appears to have been aimed at preventing the PLA from becoming too fractured as the power-jockeying behind the scenes for his succession grows in intensity. But while the presence of Wang Ruilin, Zhang Zhen and Liu Huaqing ensures stability for the present, whether they can survive after Deng's departure is questionable. The position of Wang Ruilin, the most important of Deng's lieutenants, is being compared to Wang Dongxing, Mao Zedong's chief bodyguard who controlled access to Mao in his last years. Wang did not survive long after Mao's death and was purged by Deng. Consequently, the current military leadership lineup appears to be a stop-gap measure.

Can these arrangements survive after Deng's death? One key card Deng's lieutenants have on their side is the support of many prominent, retired generals who were close associates of Deng. The roles of Xiao Ke, Zhang Aiping, Ye Fei, Hong Xuezhi and other elderly figures could be extremely important when the institutional structures of power and succession in the PLA and the broader political process are lacking.[11] These retired generals do not appear to have much respect or support for the other factions coalesced around Jiang Zemin or the remains of the Yang empire.

The role of the new generation of commanders in the general headquarters departments and among the key military regions, such as Zhang Wannian, Fu Quanyou and Wang Ke, will become more important if they have time to settle into their positions. But at present, they are too junior to be a major force to be reckoned with in any immediate succession struggle. In addition, they appear to be less politically ambitious and more focused on dealing with professional issues.

The scene has, therefore, been set for a potentially destabilizing power struggle among different military factions following Deng's death. How intense the in-fighting will be and how it might affect the civilian succession process will depend to a significant extent on whether Deng dies sooner or later. If his death were to occur within the next couple of years, then there could be the prospects of a highly debilitating struggle. The Yangs could perceive an opportunity to make another grab for power after having come so close. But if Deng is able to live longer, then the present leadership arrangements might have a better chance of surviving intact. But whatever happens, the events of 1992 have redefined the nature of Chinese military politics, at least for the foreseeable future.

Military Modernization and Foreign Security Ties

Even as these internal upheavals took place, military chiefs still found time to concentrate on professional issues, and in particular the continuing efforts to modernize the PLA's outdated arsenal. This included a major boost to the PLA air force's firepower with the arrival of Russian advanced fighter aircraft and new generations of warships for the navy. There was also plenty of discussions on the reorganization of the high command structure and the reduction of the standing army in the post-Cold War era.

The PLA air force took delivery of twenty-six Sukhoi Su-27 combat aircraft it had ordered from Russia back in mid-1991. The aircraft, which arrived in two batches towards the end of the year, were deployed to an air force base in Wuhu in Anhui province around 100 km from Nanjing. With the building of extensive support facilities at the base, it appears that the aircraft will be permanently stationed there, though with routine deployments in southern China, including Hainan Island, to provide air cover for the South China Sea and the disputed Spratly Islands some 1000 km from the mainland. The sophistication of the aircraft, which is at least a couple of generations more advanced than any of the latest Chinese fighters, will mean that it will take several months before the aircraft become fully operational.

The regiment of Su-27s may be followed by another order for a similar number of aircraft by the Chinese. There were reports in March 1993 that the Chinese were negotiating for twenty-six more Su-27s, having dropped their initial interest in MiG-31 high-altitude interceptors. The costs of the Su-27s are high though, with the first deal estimated to be more than US$1 billion. The Chinese have been particularly interested in acquiring the licence production rights for the aircraft or other technology transfers to help its problem-plagued defence-industrial sector, especially in the aerospace sector.

The Su-27 sale provoked US President George Bush, also in the midst of an election, to approve the sale to Taiwan of up to 150 General Dynamics F-16 fighters in September, which was later followed by France's sale of sixty Mirage 2000 fighters. The sales were ostensibly aimed at maintaining the air-balance across the Taiwan Straits, but also to provide contracts for the shrinking arms industries in the West. Beijing was angered by these sales, and while taking little action against the US decided to diplomatically and economically retaliate against Paris by closing its Consulate in Guangzhou and banning French companies from large-scale infrastructural projects.

Another major Sino-Russian arms deal signed in late 1992 or early 1993 was China's purchase of close to 100 SA-300 long-range surface-to-air missiles.[12] According to western military analysts, the PLA began to take delivery of these missiles in early March with the arrival of a Russian merchant freighter carrying the first consignment at a northern Chinese port. The weapons are expected to be deployed around Peking to provide high-altitude air defence. With a combat range of up to 100 kilometres and a limited capability to intercept in-coming cruise and long-range ballistic missiles, the SA-300s will help fill many of the holes in the antiquated air defence network. The missiles are expected to be fitted into an over-the-horizon radar system the Chinese are also negotiating to buy from the Russians.

The Su-27s, and maybe also the SA-300s, helped to account for the US$1.8 billion worth of arms sales that Russia concluded with China in 1992. The figure was disclosed by Russian President Boris Yeltsin during a visit to Beijing in December 1992. The amount would have been higher if discussions between China and the Ukraine on the sale of the partially completed 67,000 tonne Varyag aircraft carrier had been successful. China's interest in the carrier first surfaced in early 1992 when the Soviet Union's break-up meant that the Soviet navy could no longer afford to purchase the ship. With hundreds of millions of roubles owed to the Ukraine by the Russian government, which had taken over the bulk of the Soviet navy, the Ukrainian government began to look for potential customers. Among those interested was China.

Beijing's interest was initially fuelled by reports that the Ukrainian authorities were offering bargain terms for the carrier. Chinese military officials contacted the Ukrainian government and sent a technical delegation to evaluate the ship in June. But the initial discussions over financial terms stalled over the high prices the Ukrainians were demanding for the vessel, with some Japanese newspapers reporting at least US$2.4 billion. These same reports said that the deal was close to completion.[13] But Ukrainian officials denied any deals were being worked out. Valeriy Kazakov, a Deputy Ukrainian Defence Industry Minister, said that "there has been no concrete proposals from the Chinese or anyone to buy" the vessel, although he added that "we want to sell the vessel."[14] Unwilling to pay the price asked for, the Chinese pulled out of negotiations and the deal was eventually aborted.[15] Nonetheless, Chinese interest in acquiring a

Russian aircraft carrier had not completely disappeared. Chinese leaders are believed to have asked Yeltsin when he was in Beijing about the availability of the older and smaller Minsk-class carriers which have been phased out of the Russian navy.[16] But a Chinese naval delegation that visited one of the carriers was disappointed at its state of disrepair[17] and Chinese interest in Russian carriers appears to have finally subsided.

Yeltsin also signed a treaty during his trip on troop reductions along the Sino-Russian border, although this was only a revised version of a 1990 agreement in principle on the demilitarization of the Sino-Soviet border concluded when Li Peng went to Moscow. Details on substantial cutbacks are still being contested between Russian and Chinese military negotiators in their regular working group meetings. Although Chinese defence planners no longer regard Russia as an immediate military threat, they are still concerned at military, internal security and other developments in that country that could have adverse implications for China's security.

One source of anxiety comes from the massive transfer of former Soviet weapons and forces from the European theatre to east of the Ural Mountains as part of the Conventional Forces in Europe Treaty that was signed in late 1990. China has not voiced any public concerns so far over these redeployments so as not to create tensions that may disrupt the relationship. But Chinese defence planners privately express worries that these forces could quickly be moved to the Sino-Russian border should relations between the two countries again deteriorate. They point out that this happened in the mid-1960s following the rupture in Sino-Soviet relations.

There are hints that strategic cooperation between the two military establishments may be underway. Western military attachés in Beijing believe that since mid-1992 there have been at least two visits by Russian military intelligence delegations to China.[18] The development of an intelligence relationship, especially if it includes the sharing of classified data, usually indicates that ties between two countries are becoming increasingly intimate. Although the nature of this military intelligence interaction is so far unclear, it would make most sense for the two countries to exchange information on strategic issues of common concern, such as the volatile ethnic situation in Central Asia or developments in North Korea.

China's efforts to get Russian defence technology and know-how has increased substantially since the latter half of 1992. This topic, for example, dominated the agenda when Russian Deputy Defence Minister

Andrey Kokoshin visited China in October 1992. Kokoshin held talks with senior Chinese officials from the Commission on Science, Technology and Industry for National Defence, which oversees research on defence science and technology, and with Liu Huaqing. Among installations that Kokoshin visited included a missile factory in Shanghai.[19]

During Yeltsin's Beijing visit, he signed a memorandum of understanding at the urging of Chinese leaders on the principles governing future defence technological and industrial exchanges, and said that the two countries' defence ministries would work out a more detailed cooperative agreement within a month. Yeltsin pointed out that Russia "is prepared to cooperate in all sectors, including the most sophisticated armaments and weapons." He added that "China is one of the most solvent countries in the world" and that "we will be able to provide China with the best technology and equipment."[20]

Although bargain-priced, former Soviet military technology and arms represent an attractive quick fix solution to the PLA's present equipment problems in some high priority areas, Chinese military planners remain committed to a gradual modernization based on indigenous resources. To do otherwise would see China become over-reliant once again on Russian military assistance.

Although the air force is the prime beneficiary of the Sino-Russian arms relationship, the navy is also receiving considerable resources in its modernization efforts. Shipyards in Shanghai and other port cities have rarely been so busy. At present, several new types of warships are close to completion in Shanghai, including a new class of destroyers known as the Luhu, a new Jiangwei-class frigate and logistics support ships that will help the Chinese navy's efforts to eventually become a blue-water force.[21] These new warships have enhanced air-defence capabilities and can carry a helicopter each for anti-submarine work. The Chinese are also believed to have approached Russia over the possibility of purchasing Kilo-class conventional submarines to upgrade their obsolete force of 1950s generation Romeo and Ming-class submarines.[22]

This growing naval capability is already being employed by China to back up claims over maritime territory it is disputing with several neighbours, in particular Vietnam and other Southeast Asian countries over the Spratly Islands. Although senior Chinese officials have expressed willingness to negotiate peaceful settlements of these disputes, several developments in 1992 sent shock waves around the region. These included the NPC's passing of a law on its territorial waters in April that claimed all of the Spratlys and control over the area's sealanes. In May, China signed an agreement with a US oil company, Crestone Energy Corporation, to explore for oil close to an offshore Vietnamese oil and gas field. The company's president later said his operations would be protected by the Chinese navy. In June, Vietnam protested that China had landed troops on a reef in the Spratlys. These developments were one of the main issues discussed by Asean foreign ministers at their annual meeting in Manila in July. They issued a statement urging a settlement to disputes in the areas without resorting to force.

While the air force and navy are upgrading their outdated weapons, the PLA also decided at a CMC enlarged meeting in April 1992 that it would trim the size of its 3 million-strong establishment. This included a consolidation of its general headquarters' departments, the merger or closure of twenty academies and military schools, and other primarily administrative cuts. There were also proposals for a cutback of frontline forces and the elimination of the Jinan Military Region. A total reduction of between 300–500,000 troops was said to have been under consideration.

Military chiefs, however, eventually decided against demobilising combat units and the reorganization of the seven military regions, but approved the closure of the military schools and a consolidation of the PLA general staff headquarters totalling around 100,000 personnel. Defence planners said that the decision against reducing frontline forces was because the PLA's present size was the minimum required to defend the country. Military commanders supported their claim by pointing out that the post-Cold War world order is even more unstable than in the past.

The trimming of the ranks will eventually lead to some small savings and ease the heavy burden being placed on the defence budget by growing arms purchases and the spiralling costs of upkeeping troops in a more affluent economy. This is despite substantial annual increases in defence appropriations since 1990. The defence budget grew by 12% in 1992 to RMB37 billion, and rose by another 13.5% in 1993 to RMB42.5 billion, almost double the level of funding in 1989. Much of the arms acquisitions from Russia, however, is believed to come from extra-budgetary resources not included in the official budget.

Notes

1. The information on the power struggle inside the military comes from

extensive interviews conducted in Beijing and Hong Kong. Those interviewed requested anonymity.
2. For an assessment of Jiang Zemin, see Tai Ming Cheung, "Channels of Support," *Far Eastern Economic Review* (*FEER*), 15 June 1991.
3. See Tai Ming Cheung, "Gun Barrel Politics," *FEER*, 17 January 1991.
4. See *Deng Xiaoping nanxun hou de Zhongguo* (China after Deng Xiaoping's Southern Tour) (Beijing: Gaige chubanshe, 1992.)
5. "'Ming Pao': Yang Baibing, Jiang Zemin Both Called Meetings When Deng 'Ill'," *Ming Pao*, 1 December 1992, in *BBC Summary of World Broadcasts: Far East* (Hereafter BBC/*SWB*/FE), 1558/B2/3, 8 December 1992. This and other reports had both indicated that Deng was ill on the eve of the Party congress, although he did make a public if feeble appearance at its conclusion.
6. See also Tai Ming Cheung, "Back to the Front," *FEER*, 29 October 1992.
7. "Veterans Return in Military Reshuffle," *South China Morning Post* (Hong Kong, *SCMP*), 23 November 1992.
8. *Wen Wei Po* (Hong Kong), 25 November 1992.
9. *Wen Wei Po*, 15 December 1992.
10. On the functions of the PAP, see "People's Armed Police," *China News Analysis*, April 1993.
11. For an argument on the importance of these senior retired military officers and their connections to the field army system, see Michael D.Swaine, *The Military and Political Succession in China: Leadership, Institutions and Beliefs* (Santa Monica, CA: Rand Corporation, 1992).
12. See Tai Ming Cheung, "Sukhois, Sams, Subs," *FEER*, 8 April 1993.
13. "Beijing Buys Aircraft Carrier," *The Standard* (Hong Kong), 5 August 1992.
14. Interview, Kiev, July 1992.
15. See "Varyag Doomed as Sale Collapses," *Jane's Defence Weekly*, 21 November 1992, and "Ukraine Denies Carrier Deal with China," *SCMP*, 1 November 1992.
16. Interview with western military analyst, Hong Kong, January 1993.
17. Interview with western military analyst, Hong Kong, March 1993.
18. Interview with western Military Attaché, Beijing, October 1992.
19. "Russian Military Delegation Arrives in Beijing," *TASS News Agency*, in *SWB*/FE 1508 A2/3, 10 October 1992.
20. Lena Sun, "For Moscow, A 'New Stage' with Beijing," *International Herald Tribune*, 19 December 1992.
21. Interview with western naval analyst, Hong Kong, June 1992.
22. Interview with western naval analyst, Hong Kong, March 1993.

7

Economic Legal Reforms

Wang Guiguo

Law is defined in China as the total sum of the codes of behaviour enacted or approved by the state to be implemented with the guarantee of the state's power of enforcement in accordance with the interest and will of the ruling class.[1] This concept, however, has in practice undergone significant changes with the incorporation of the western legal thinking and principles in the last fifteen years. Currently, both the Chinese government and jurists seldom talk about the traditional viewpoint of law. This demonstrates the growing realization by China of the outdatedness of the orthodox Marxist legal theory, which paves the way for further development of the legal system. It does not mean, however, that there is no difference between the law on paper and its implementation.

The evolution of legal theory and the restructuring of the legal system or legal reforms in China influence each other. With the changes in legal thinking, new laws have been adopted to regulate the life and activities of the people and entities.

The legal reforms, however, have always lagged behind the economic reforms, because legal reforms are considered a means to accommodate and spur economic reforms. The inexperience and lack of adequate knowledge of the law drafters in connection with international commercial practices[2] have also contributed to the slow progress of legal reforms. So has also the conservative attitude of the legal circle.

With regard to economic legal reforms, because of the conservative policies adopted by the Chinese government since June 4 of 1989, the law-drafters had been reluctant to take bold steps until Deng Xiaoping, the paramount Chinese leader, visited the southern part of China to boost the economic reforms in the spring of 1992. Thereafter, the law-drafters in Beijing speeded up their legislative work and adopted a number of laws and regulations covering a wide range of fields including protection of wildlife,[3] urban planning, foreign trade, customs and tariffs, taxation, maritime matters,[4] matters relating to enterprises,[5] etc. The most important laws adopted in the year include the regulations concerning the state-owned enterprises and other business concerns which have been the focus of the economic reforms in 1992. This chapter will be confined to the examination of the regulations adopted in 1992 in connection with the domestic enterprises, taxation, intellectual property and foreign trade, while leaving other aspects of the legal reforms aside.

I. Reforms Pertinent to Enterprises

China does not have a comprehensive corporation law, though there are laws and regulations dealing with the establishment, registration and licencing of enterprises. Such laws and the forms of enterprises are, however, quite complex. For instance, according to ownership, enterprises are divided into state, collective, private, foreign, and Chinese and foreign jointly-owned enterprises plus domestic companies with mixed ownership. Based on the number of shareholders, enterprises may be divided into stock companies and limited liability companies. There are also administrative companies incorporated by administrative bodies as their arms to supervise other business entities. In addition, there have been enterprises without legal personality.[6]

The confusion about the forms of enterprises in China to some extent is due to the nature of China's economy and economic reforms introduced since the late 1970s. Prior to 1979, most of the enterprises had been state-owned. Thereafter, were created other forms of enterprises including foreign and private concerns which were not in compliance with the traditional socialist ideology. With the development of the economic reforms, however, business entities of various types were set up.

The adoption of laws and regulations governing the rights and obligations of the business enterprise did not speed up until Deng Xiaoping's boost for the economic reforms early this year. Soon after Deng's visit to southern China, the Chinese government promulgated regulations in connection with the reform of state-owned companies and the establishment of limited liability companies and stock companies.

1. Reforms re the State-owned Enterprises

Four years after the enactment of the *Industrial Enterprise Law*,[7] the State Council promulgated the *Regulations for Converting the Management Mechanisms of the Industrial Enterprises Owned by the Whole People* on 23 July 1992 (hereinafter the *Industrial Enterprise Regulations*) to implement the Law. Article 2 of the *Industrial Enterprise Regulations* provides that the objectives of the *Regulations* are to convert, in accordance with the development of a market economy, the companies owned by the whole people (the "state companies") into enterprise legal persons which are, in compliance with the law, to operate, develop and manage their business, and take responsibility for their profits and losses independently and into entities for the production of merchandise.

The separation of ownership from its management is considered a means to achieve the above objectives. Accordingly, the state companies have the right to possess, utilize and dispose of their property which is owned by the state (§6). This stipulation manifests the Chinese law drafters' misunderstanding of the concept of legal persons.[8] Although of good intent, this provision will in effect serve to disregard the legal person status of the state companies. The solution to the problem is to allow the state, the sole owner, to own the state companies; at the same time, to let the state companies own, operate and utilize the property they have. Without such a clear provision the legal person status can hardly be effectuated, and the Chinese company laws will remain incompatible with those of most other countries.

(A) *The Rights of State Companies*

Under the *Industrial Enterprise Regulations*, a state company has the right to decide the business affairs of the company, including the formulation of production plans, arranging for the procurement of materials, marketing and selecting a management style (§8). To be specific, the rights over business affairs include: (a) arrangement for manufacturing products and providing services; (b) requesting for adjustment of state plans and rejecting production orders given by non-planning organs; (c) marketing its own products in the market and for the prices it desires, except where the State Council provides otherwise; (d) procuring materials and parts from the suppliers of its own choice; (e) taking a decision regarding merger or forming an association with another entity or investment in a project or an entity; (f) selecting import-export agents and participating in negotiations with foreign parties; and (g) allocating and distributing profits and disposing of properties (§9 to §16).

The above rights are important to state companies. The provision of these rights represents a major step forward for China's reforms. The effects of such provisions, however, will depend on their actual enforcement. In the last few years, the *Industrial Enterprise Law* had not been properly enforced when the policy of the State Council had appeared to reduce the power of the state companies. The *Industrial Enterprise Regulations* contain more detailed rules which should be helpful for the release of the state companies from the government's control.

Another aspect of the state companies' rights under the *Industrial Enterprise Regulations* is personnel management. This includes the right to employ and dismiss staff members and workers and to decide the organizational structure and the size of the personnel. Article 18 of the *Regulations* stipulates that the employment of personnel must be in accordance with the merits of the applicant. It further provides that a state company may adopt an examination system and may hire technicians and administrators from areas outside the locality where the state company is situated. It also gives the general manager of a state company the right to appoint and remove the mid-level officials of the company and to recommend appointment and removal of his deputies. A state company is also given the power to grant technical titles to its technicians.

The rights of a state company over personnel, after the enactment of the *Industrial Enterprise Regulations*, are quite comprehensive. Taking into consideration the Chinese culture and the tradition of government interference in personnel matters of business entities, the effective enforcement of these rights will not be possible in the near future. One of the difficulties facing the Chinese government is that the public in general supports the reform programme, but when one's own interest is affected, e.g., being fired by the employer, the individual may withdraw his support. The complicated nature of personnel issues is illustrated in the Zhang Zhiping case.

Zhang Zhiping was an employee of the Nanjing Number 24 Plastics Factory (the "Plastics Factory"). The Plastics Factory was one of the twenty-three entities in Nanjing facing bankruptcy. In order to save the entity, the Number Two Light Industry Bureau of Nanjing Municipality (the "Light Industry Bureau"), a government body in charge of supervising the Plastics Factory, decided to experiment with reform measures at the Plastics Factory by delegating powers to the general manager and deputy general managers of the Plastics Factory, among which was the power to hire and fire.

Having taken up the responsibility, Mr Yan Nian, the general manager and Mr Guo Haiqing, a deputy general manager, together with other officials, adopted rules to get rid of the "iron rice bowl" system. According to the new rules, each employee was under a contract and was, therefore, subject to penalties in case of breach of contract. According to one of the measures, the employees were required to produce a medical certificate which had to be confirmed by the medical centre in the factory, should they ask for a sick-leave. With the new measures being enforced, the Plastics Factory began to do better.

One day in 1991, the husband of Zhang Zhiping submitted a sick-leave application on Zhang's behalf. Zhang's husband and Mr Yan started arguing soon thereafter. They then started to fight. When the local police department learned about what was going on at the Plastics Factory, it dispatched some police officers to take Zhang's husband to the police station. Zhang, together with her mother and sisters, then went to Mr Yan's office for a sit-in protest which lasted for four days and nights. Eventually Zhang was dismissed.

Being dissatisfied with the decision of dismissal, Zhang appealed to the local labour dispute arbitration body, which decided in Zhang's favour. Yan and his four deputies considered the arbitration body's decision to have constituted an interference with their right to hire and fire and, therefore, submitted a collective resignation.

The Plastics Factory suffered a serious disorder. The employees of the factory started a sit-in protest first at the arbitration body, then at the city government, requesting the reappointment of Mr Yan and his deputies. Under pressure from the employees, the city government held a joint meeting with the labour bureau, the arbitration body, the Light Industry Bureau and the Plastics Factory. Three days later, Mr Yan and his deputies resumed duty as general manager and deputy general managers respectively.

The dispute, however, did not end. The last decision was appealed to the central government in Beijing. The Light Industry Bureau and the Plastics Factory took one side. The labour bureau, the arbitration body and the trade union took the other side. The issues surrounding the case were whether the factory manager should have the power to dismiss Zhang under the circumstance and whether the rules adopted by the factory in connection with labour discipline were essential for reforms.[9]

Another right of the state companies under the *Industrial Enterprise Regulations* covers the determination of the amount and forms of wages of employees and methods of bonus distribution. Article 19 stipulates that a state company has the right to determine the salary and bonus of its employees while taking into account the level of skill, the amount of labour required and the responsibility of the employees, the working conditions and the contribution made by the employees.

The right to determine salary and bonus schemes is not without restrictions. First, the general manager and employees are responsible for the performance of their company. Secondly, according to Article 24 of the *Industrial Enterprise Regulations*, the level of increase of the total income of employees must not be higher than the growth level of productivity and revenue of the company. The total income includes the salary, bonus, compensations and other incomes of the employees. Any increase of salary must be approved by the workers' congress of the company. In case a state company performs poorly, the income of the employees should be reduced.

A state company may decide the salary scheme, including the promotion scheme and criteria independently. It may also reject any suggestion by a government body to promote the state company's employees.

(B) The Responsibilities of State Companies

Under the *Industrial Enterprise Law*, the most important responsibility of the state companies is to fulfil the mandatory plans of the state. The *Industrial Enterprise Regulations*, however, make no mention of this obligation. This omission can hardly be interpreted as an oversight on the part of the lawmakers. The logical explanation may be that, when the *Industrial Enterprise Regulations* were drafted, the Chinese government had already decided to establish a market economy. Therefore, it would be contrary to the government policy for the *Regulations* to emphasize state plans. This omission, however, does not mean that the state companies have no such obligation, because the *Regulations* are of a lower hierarchy than the *Industrial Enterprise Law*.

The main responsibility of the state companies under the *Industrial Enterprise Regulations* is to bear civil liabilities (§23). That is, the state companies must be independently responsible for their profits and losses. In this regard, the leading officials and employees of a state company are jointly responsible. The *Industrial Enterprise Regulations* provide in detail the economic consequences of poor performance of the state companies. For instance, if a state company suffers losses for one year because of poor management, the general manager and other leading members of the company are disqualified for bonuses and the total amount of the salary of the employees should be decreased. If the company continues to suffer losses in the year to follow, no bonus may be distributed to any employee and the general manager's and leading members' salary must be reduced, and they may be demoted or removed from their posts (§29). At the same time, good performance of a state company entitles the general manager and other employees to bonuses or promotions (§25 to §26).

A state company's responsibilities also include ensuring the normal maintenance of its fixed assets and upgrading and renewing its equipment, guaranteeing the quality of its products and services and being responsible to users and consumers, implementing the system of safe production, improving labour conditions, etc.[10] The *Industrial Enterprise Law* contains a clause requiring state companies to "strengthen ideological and political education, legal education, national defence education, scientific and cultural education." The *Industrial Enterprise Regulations* have again omitted this clause.

(C) The Relationship between the Government and State Companies

With regard to the relationship between the government and state companies, the *Industrial Enterprise Regulations* contain clear-cut rules. Article 40 of the *Regulations* prescribes that the functions of the government are to coordinate, supervise and administer the state companies in accordance with law and serve the latter. The *Regulations* provide for the first time that the State Council on behalf of the state exercises the rights of ownership over the state companies (§41). For this purpose, departments and government organs under the State Council are to perform the functions of (a) examining the maintenance of the property of the state companies; (b) determining the allocation of profit between the state and the companies; (c) making a decision on merger, separation, establishment of a branch or a subsidiary, and termination of the state companies; (d) appointing and removing from post the general managers of the state companies, etc. (§42). Clearly from the wording of the *Regulations*, the government, except in decision on important matters, should refrain from participating in the daily business decisions of the state companies so that the latter can manage their business affairs independently.

The government is to employ macro-economic measures and adopt policies to revitalize the economy, such as strategic development plans, interest rates, exchange rates and taxation, and formulating accounting standards, etc. The government is also required to set up a welfare system and to provide market information, etc.

Needless to say, it will take some time before an adequate and accurate assessment of the effect of these rules on the state companies can be made, especially taking into account the novelty of these rules and the traditional relationship between the government and state companies.[11]

2. Share Companies

On 15 May 1992, the State Commission for the Reform of the Economic System (CRES), the Planning Commission, the Ministry of Finance, the People's Bank of China and the Production Office of the State Council jointly issued *Measures on the Experiment for Share Companies* (the *Measures*). On the same day, the State CRES also promulgated the *Opinion on the Standardization of Limited Liability Companies* (the *Limited Company Rules*) and *Opinion on the Standardization of Stock Companies* (the *Stock Company Rules*). The announcement of the *Measures* and *Rules* filled the gap in the laws regulating enterprises and companies.[12] The *Measures* and *Rules* mutually reinforce each other by prescribing the general principles and specific standards for share companies. In this regard, the *Measures* serve as guidelines whilst the *Rules* set up detailed provisions.

The purposes of the *Measures* are: (1) to convert the management mechanisms of the enterprises; (2) to separate the government from the enterprises; (3) to realize the goal of independent management, becoming independently responsible for losses and profits, self-control and development of enterprises; and (4) to create new channels for fund raising. The establishment of a share company must follow the principle of maintaining the majority ownership of the state, must not transfer the state assets to collectively-owned enterprises and individuals in the form of shares and must strictly observe the provisions of the *Limited Liability Company Rules* and *Stock Company Rules* (§2). The principle of equality, i.e., each share representing the same rights and obligations, also holds. Under Article 6 of the *Measures*, however, no share company may be established in the following fields: enterprises involving the security of the state or sophisticated technology for defence, rare metal projects of strategic significance and enterprises in the trades exclusively conducted by the state.

The *Measures* subdivide share companies into limited liability companies and stock companies. The basic features of the limited liability companies include: (1) the company may issue investment certificates but not stocks to the shareholders; (2) the transfer of shareholding is restricted; (3) the number of shareholders is restricted; and (4) each shareholder enjoys rights and bears obligations in proportion to his investment. The stock companies are not subject to such restrictions, except that they must make public their statement of accounts after examination by a registered accountant (§3).

Procedures for the approval of the establishment of limited liability companies and stock companies are also provided in the *Measures*. Among government departments involved, the State CRES is empowered to play the leading role.

When the State CRES promulgated the *Limited Liability Company Rules* and *Stock Company Rules*, many were surprised. It was the first time for the Commission to issue rules. Some wondered whether the Commission had the legislative power. If the answer to the question was "yes," why had it issued such *Rules* in the form of opinions rather than regulations? Some of the Chinese officials and legal scholars argued that, for the purpose of unifying the formation of limited liability companies and stock companies, it was important for the local government and enterprises to have guidelines to follow.[13] Nevertheless, since the State CRES played an important role in stock issues, before the formal adoption of a company law in China which is being drafted, these *Rules* would play an important role in the near future.

As to why a distinction has been made between a limited liability company and a stock company in China, there is no logical explanation. Based on the opinion gathered from Chinese scholars and government officials, the major difference between the two kinds of companies is the number of shareholders, to be discussed later. Most of the Chinese law drafters are not well equipped with the knowledge of company laws which are prevailing in the industrialized countries. To them, although the liability of the investors or shareholders of both kinds of companies is limited, if a given company is not a stock company it should be forbidden from issuing stocks to the public. In fact, whether a company should be permitted to issue shares to the public depends, in addition to the number of shareholders, on a number of other factors including the performance and the history of the company in question. Such issues should be dealt with by the rules regarding listing of stocks at stock exchanges. In this regard, the adoption of these *Rules* has further complicated such basic company law issues.

(A) Limited Liability Companies

According to the *Limited Liability Company Rules*, a limited liability

Economic Legal Reforms 7.11

company refers to a company with two or more shareholders; each shareholder is liable for the company's debts only to the extent of the amount he has invested with the company, and the company is liable for its debts to the full extent of its assets (§1). Article 9 of the *Limited Company Rules* further provides that a limited liability company must have two or more shareholders but not more than thirty shareholders. In special circumstances, with the approval of the competent government authorities a company may have more than thirty shareholders but in any event may not have more than fifty shareholders.

With regard to the requirement of registered capital of a limited liability company, it depends on the nature of the business in which the company intends to engage. The required minimum amount of the registered capital of each kind of company is as follows (§10):

a. for production companies, RMB500,000;
b. for commercial and wholesale business companies, RMB500,000;
c. for commercial and retail companies, RMB300,000;
d. for scientific and technological development, consultancy and service companies, RMB100,000.

Autonomous regions and poor areas may, with the approval of the State Administration of Industry and Commerce, reduce the minimum amount of the registered capital up to 50%. Investment by shareholders may be in the form of cash, materials, intellectual property, know-how, the right to use land, etc. Except cash, every other form of investment must be assessed on a cash value. In any event, the total amount of investment in the form of intellectual property and know-how should not exceed 20% of the registered capital (§12). Other conditions for the establishment of a limited liability company are similar to those applicable to stock companies, to be discussed later.

A limited liability company may make an investment in other business entities. But its total investment in other entities should not exceed 50% of its net assets. This rule, however, does not apply to investment companies or holding companies which obtain a special approval of the competent government departments. A limited liability company is not permitted to become a member with unlimited liabilities of another economic entity. The effect of this provision is to exclude limited liability companies from becoming partners of any partnership enterprise. The policy behind this provision is that, if a limited liability company is allowed to become a member of a partnership with unlimited liabilities, it may eventually transfer its assets to the partnership or to the creditors of the partnership. Since most of the limited liability companies under the *Limited Company Rules* will be state-owned companies, it is necessary to have such a provision in order to safeguard state property.

Shares or stocks of a limited liability company are transferable. The transfer of shares must be approved at a shareholders' meeting or a board of directors' meeting. If no consensus can be reached, those who are not to transfer their shares must purchase the shares offered for transfer. Even if the shareholders' meeting or board of directors' meeting approves the transfer of shares, the existing shareholders still have the right of first refusal.

The management structure of a limited liability company is similar to that of a stock company to be discussed later.

(B) *The Establishment of a Stock Company*

Under the *Stock Company Rules*, a stock company may be established through promotion or the method of prospectus. The establishment of a stock company through promotion is that only promoters subscribe to the shares of the company, which shares are not open to subscription by other people. This method can only be used for the establishment of stock companies for large construction projects (§7). In other words, most of the stock companies should be established through the method of prospectus which includes private placement or specific offering and public offering. Article 25 of the *Stock Company Rules* provides that the ownership of stock companies is represented by stocks; at the same time, stock companies established through private placement or specific offering may not issue stocks and, therefore, ownership of such companies is not identified by stocks. The problem is that Article 7 of the *Stock Company Rules* permits a stock company established through specific offering to be converted into a stock company instituted by public offering after operation for one year. Since a stock company set up by specific offering is not allowed to issue stocks, how can it offer stocks to the public after one year? In addition, such provisions are contrary to the basic principles of company law in most countries.

Under the *Stock Company Rules*, three promoters are in general required for the establishment of a stock company. In the eventuality of a large state company being converted into a stock company, with special approval of the competent organs of the government, the state company

Economic Legal Reforms

alone may be the sole promoter (§9). The subscription by all the promoters to shares should not be less than 35% of the total number of shares to be issued (§8). A promoter must be a Chinese legal person operating on the Chinese territory. Privately owned enterprises or wholly foreign-owned enterprises are not qualified to serve as promoters. In cases where Chinese-foreign joint ventures or contractual ventures serve as promoters, they may not account for more than one-third of the total number of promoters. Natural persons are not allowed to be promoters. These provisions apparently aim at ensuring that state companies will retain a substantial number of shares of a stock company. With such a provision, when a state company is converted into a stock company for public subscription, the resistance from the orthodox Marxists may be smaller.[14]

Promoters are required to enter into an agreement among themselves for the establishment of a stock company. They have the responsibility of submitting an application to the relevant government bodies, subscribing for the shares they are required to purchase and for the establishment of the company. After entering into an agreement, one of the promoters may be appointed as representative to go through the establishment procedures which include securing approval from the competent organs of the government and registration with the State Administration of Industry and Commerce (§10 and §13).

The competent organs of the government in charge of establishing stock companies are the relevant departments at provincial, autonomous region and city levels with the CRES at the same level as the leading body. Documents to be submitted include the agreement between the promoters, the application form, the feasibility study report, articles of association, the report on the assessment of assets, the report on the examination of assets, prospectus and an opinion letter of the relevant department in charge of the company. The application must include:

a. the name, location and the legal representative of the promoters;
b. the name, aims and objectives of the company;
c. the investment purpose and business scope;
d. the method of establishment of the stock company, total investment, registered capital, subscription by the promoters, method and the sphere for distributing the prospectus;
e. the total number of shares, the total number of each kind of shares, par value of the shares and composition of the shareholders;
f. basic information about and credit worthiness of the promoters;

g. other matters that need to be explained.

The feasibility study report must describe the operation and credit worthiness of the promoters including the basic information regarding the promoters' business for the previous three years. An assessment of investment returns and public demand for the products or services to be provided by the company should also be included. In general, a feasibility study report should be able to convince the decision-makers that the company to be established will have a good future, be profitable and can contribute to the national economy. The *Stock Company Rules* require that the minimum registered capital of a stock company should be RMB10 million. If the company includes foreign investment, in other words, if foreign companies or individuals have subscribed to the shares, the minimum registered capital should not be less than RMB30 million (§12).

Article 7 of the *Stock Company Rules* gives a detailed listing as to what items should be included in the articles of association. The most important items include:

a. the name, objectives and scope of business, method of establishment and distribution of shares of the company;
b. the registered capital, total number of shares and face value of each share;
c. methods regarding the transfer of shares;
d. the rights and obligations of shareholders;
e. rules in respect of shareholders' meetings;
f. the legal representative of the stock company and the authorities thereof;
g. the organization of the board of directors, the authorities of the board of directors and the rules regarding the board of directors' meetings;
h. the organization of the supervisory board and the authorities of the board;
i. methods for the distribution of profits;
j. accounting principles;
k. procedures for the amendment of the articles of association;
l. procedures for the termination and liquidation of the company;
m. notice and announcement.

Having secured all the necessary government approvals and after the shares have been fully subscribed and paid, within forty days, a

Economic Legal Reforms 7.15

shareholders' meeting for the establishment of the company should be called by the promoters. The quorum is two-thirds of the shares (§19). At the meeting, the shareholders are to examine and approve the report by the promoters in connection with the establishment of the company, approve the Articles of Association, elect members to the board of directors and supervisory board. If the meeting is successfully held, within thirty days, the board of directors should register with and apply for a business licence at the State Administration of Industry and Commerce. Upon the issue of a business licence, the stock company becomes a legal person and is legally established.

(C) Shares of Stock Companies

As in the case of limited liability companies, investors of a stock company may contribute cash, materials, intellectual property, etc. in exchange for shares.

A stock company may have common shares and preference shares. The rights and obligations of such shares are similar to those applicable in the market economies.

The *Stock Company Rules* sub-divide the shares in accordance with the nature of the shareholders. Therefore, there are state shares, legal person shares, natural person shares and foreign investor shares (§24). State shares are the shares held by the state government and in general should be common shares. Such shares should be held by government bodies authorized by the State Council. There is no restriction whatsoever with regard to state share holdings.

Legal person shares are held by a legal person. According to the *Stock Company Rules*, if one company owns 10% of the shares of another company, the latter is not allowed to hold any shares of the former.

With regard to natural person shares or shares held by individuals, they are subject to several restrictions. In the first place, no person is allowed to hold more than 0.5% of the shares of a stock company. Secondly, employees of the stock company which issues shares through private placement may not hold more than 20% of the total shares of their company. Thirdly, the total holding by employees of their company shares issued through prospectus may not exceed 10% of the shares subscribed by the public. Fourthly, the total holding of shares by the public should not be less than 25%, unless otherwise approved by the government. No ceiling is imposed on the public holding of shares.

Shares held by foreign investors or investors from Hong Kong, Macau and Taiwan are referred to as foreign investor shares or *Renminbi*-denominated special shares which are also known as B shares. Under Article 29 of the *Stock Company Rules*, B shares may only be issued by those companies which have been approved by the relevant government departments to have foreign investment and with the approval of the People's Bank of China. B shares may only be purchased by foreigners with foreign currency. They are created for the investors from foreign countries and Taiwan, Macau and Hong Kong. Such investors are not allowed to purchase *Renminbi*-denominated ordinary shares or A shares.

Except for promoters, any shareholders owning more than 10% of the shares of a stock company must notify the company. This provision is similar to the report requirement of the securities laws of some western countries. Nevertheless, the holding of shares in excess of 10% must be approved by the People's Bank and government organs in charge of economic reforms.[15] The *Stock Company Rules* stop short of providing for the operation of this provision. Therefore, it is unclear whether approval should be secured in advance of or subsequent to the actual transaction. Presumably, the approval should be obtained before such transactions take place. At the same time, government officials involved are bound by the rule of secrecy.

With regard to dealings in shares, such as transfer, mortgage, or making a gift, Article 30 of the *Stock Company Rules* contain detailed provisions. Firstly, shares of a stock company set up through promotion can only be transferred among legal persons. Shares issued through private placement may only be transferred among legal persons and employees of the issuer. Thirdly, legal person shares and state shares as well as share warrants may not be allocated to employees of the issuer as bonuses. Fourthly, shares subscribed to by the promoters may not be transferred within one year. Fifthly, shares held by employees may not be transferred within three years, except when a given shareholder leaves the issuer or dies. Sixthly, shares held by the board members and the general manager of the issuer may not be transferred within three years. Thereafter, with the consent of the board of directors, 50% or less of the shares held by a board member or the general manager may be transferred. Seventhly, no shares may be transferred starting from the date of announcement of liquidation of the issuer.

Under the *Stock Company Rules*, all shares must have their holders' name stipulated. The name of a shareholder must be the registered name,

Economic Legal Reforms 7.17

i.e., the name on the ID card or passport or the registration documents in case of legal person shareholders.

(D) Management of Stock Companies

The shareholders' meeting is the highest authority of a stock company; it is composed of all the common shareholders. If the company fails to distribute dividends to the preference shares for three years consecutively, the preference shareholders are entitled to participate in the shareholders' meeting along the common shareholders (§39). A shareholders' meeting should be held once every year. Special shareholders' meetings may be held for matters arising between the annual shareholders' meetings.

Resolutions of a shareholders' meeting are divided into common resolutions and special resolutions.

The quorum for a common resolution is 50% of the total number of shares. The adoption of a common resolution requires 50% or more of the shares present at the meeting. The quorum for a special resolution is two-thirds of the total number of shares. The adoption of a special resolution also requires two-thirds of the shares present (§46). Shareholders may vote by proxy. The following items must be adopted by special resolutions:

a. increase or decrease of the registered capital, changing subscription method or transfer method of shares;
b. borrowing money;
c. merger, separation, termination or liquidation of the issuer; and
d. amendment of the articles of association.[16]

For a decision on the following items a common resolution is sufficient:

a. examination and approval of the report by the board of directors and the supervisory board;
b. approval of allocation of profits and losses;
c. approval of the budget, revenue report, balance sheet, profit report and other accounting reports;
d. election and removal of directors and members of the supervisory board; and
e. examination of proposals made by 5% or more shares issued.

The executive body of a stock company is the board of directors which is accountable to the shareholders' meeting. A board must have at least five members with a term of three years (§52 and §53). A director may be re-elected. The *Stock Company Rules* give the board of directors broad power in business decision-making which are similar to those under the company laws of western countries.[17] For instance, the board of directors is authorized to call a shareholders' meeting and report to the shareholders' meeting, implement decisions adopted by the shareholders' meeting and prepare development plans and annual plans for the company. The board of directors is also charged with retaining and dismissing senior managerial members of the company and determining their remunerations. In fact, most of the items for a decision by the shareholders' meeting are to be recommended by the board of directors. The chairman of the board of directors is the legal person of the issuer and is elected by two-thirds of the members of the board.

A stock company may also have a supervisory board with three or more members for a term of three years. Members of the supervisory board may also be re-elected. One-third to 50% of the supervisory board members may be elected and removed by employees of the company. The rest of the members should be elected by the shareholders' meeting. Members of the supervisory board may not serve as directors or take any other senior posts in the company (§64).

The main function of a supervisory board is to supervise the work of the board of directors. The supervisory board may also suggest the holding of a shareholders' meeting or, on behalf of the company, deal with the directors including the institution of a lawsuit. When exercising its functions, the supervisory board may retain lawyers, registered accountants, auditors and other specialists as assistants or advisors. Every decision of a supervisory board requires a two-thirds majority (§64).

The most noticeable feature of the *Stock Company Rules* is the relaxed control by the government in respect of management of stock companies. For instance, there is no provision requiring a stock company to carry out the state plans. Of course, this does not mean that a stock company may ignore state plans and price policies completely, especially taking into consideration the fact that state companies will be major shareholders of the stock companies. The only major restriction on a stock company imposed by the *Stock Company Rules* is that a stock company may not become an unlimited liability member of any other economic entity. The policy reason behind this provision is the same as that for the limited liability companies discussed earlier. A stock company may invest in another economic entity as an investor with limited liability.

The maximum amount of investment a stock company may make in other economic entities is 50% of its own net assets (§4). Apparently, the policy behind such liberal provisions is to speed up the economic reforms, particularly the reforms with regard to converting the current management mechanisms of the state-owned companies and redefining the relationship between the state-owned companies and the government.

II. Taxation

There are two tax systems in China, one applicable to the situations involving foreign interests and the other to domestic circumstances. Efforts are being made to establish a unified tax system so that both Chinese taxpayers and taxpayers involving foreign interests are treated equally.[18] Other issues that China faces include tax evasions and open refusal by taxpayers to pay taxes.[19] To cope with the situation, the Standing Committee of the Seventh National People's Congress adopted the *Law of the People's Republic of China on the Administration of Taxes* (*Law on the Administration of Taxes*) and the *Supplementary Provisions on Punishment of the Crimes of Evasion of and Refusal to Pay Taxes* (*Supplementary Tax Provisions*) at its twenty-seventh session on 4 September 1992.[20]

The adoption of the *Law on the Administration of Taxes* constitutes the first step and paves the way for the unification of the tax laws. The *Law on the Administration of Taxes* applies to "the administration of all taxes to be collected by the tax authorities in accordance with the law" (§2). Hence, Chinese enterprises and enterprises with foreign investments will be treated equally, for instance, with regard to tax registration, preparation and keeping of account books, filing tax returns, payment of taxes, exemption from taxes and liabilities.

The most obvious feature of the *Law on the Administration of Taxes* is the well-defined powers of the tax authorities. Tax authorities are required to implement the tax laws strictly. They must collect taxes according to law and may not levy new taxes, stop the collecting of any taxes, authorize tax reductions or exemptions in violation of law (§18).[21]

The tax authorities are given important powers for the enforcement of tax laws. They are authorized to assess the tax liabilities and seize the products or properties of those refusing to pay taxes (§25). The tax authorities may also notify the banks with which a taxpayer in question has an account to freeze an adequate amount of the taxpayer's money for tax payment or to notify the bank to deduct an amount from the taxpayer's account as tax payment (§25 to §27). In addition, the tax authorities may, by notifying the immigration authorities, stop a taxpayer who has failed to pay taxes due from leaving the country (§28).[22]

With regard to transfer pricing, the *Law on the Administration of Taxes* contains provisions similar to those of the *Income Tax Law of the People's Republic of China on Enterprises with Foreign Investment and Foreign Enterprises*.[23] Article 24 of the *Law on the Administration of Taxes* requires associated enterprises to transact with each other at arm's length. Otherwise, the tax authorities may make adjustment to their incomes and expenditures.

Both the *Law on the Administration of Taxes* and the *Supplementary Tax Provisions* provide for severe punishments for tax evasion and refusal to pay taxes. Such punishments may be in the form of a fine, criminal prosecution or both.

III. Intellectual Property

The legal mechanism pertinent to intellectual property has been established after examination of the systems in western countries. For instance, China's *Trademark Law*[24] and *Patent Law*[25] were drafted under the obvious influence of the laws of former West Germany. When drafting these laws, the Chinese government sent delegations to West Germany and other western countries as well as international organizations such as World Intellectual Property Organization (WIPO) to study their experience, and the latter also offered help by dispatching their experts in intellectual property law to China. The drafting of the *Copyright Law*[26] followed a similar pattern. Therefore, the Chinese legal system on intellectual property is quite close to the international standard and has not been subject to much criticism. No substantial amendment had been made to the laws on intellectual property until 1992 when China was motivated by the United States' threat to impose the Special Section 301 sanction against Chinese exports and China's desire to resume its contracting party status of the General Agreement on Tariffs and Trade (GATT).

1. *Patent Law*

One of the major complaints of the United States and other countries was the scope of protection offered by China's *Patent Law*.[27] In response, the

Standing Committee of the Seventh National People's Congress amended the *Patent Law* at its twenty-seventh session on 4 September 1992 (hereinafter the *Amendments*),[28] which has brought the law in line with the international standards. The revision has impacts on the scope of protection of patented rights, terms of a patent, compulsory licences, publication of patents, etc.

(1) Scope of Protection. The scope of patent protection was the central issue of the controversy between China and the United States in 1991. The *Amendments* sanction the granting of patent right to food, beverages, flavourings, pharmaceutical products and substances obtained by means of a chemical process which were excluded from the patentable items under the old law.[29] The exclusion of those items from the patentable categories was apparently because of the concern that the infant domestic chemical and pharmaceutical industries might be adversely affected.[30] Indeed, the domestic chemical and pharmaceutical industries strongly resisted the revision of the *Patent Law* in 1991. Nevertheless, taking into account the fact that these industries are far behind those of the industrialized countries and the necessity of harmonization of the *Patent Law* with the international practice, the opinion supporting the changes prevailed. Accordingly, Article 25 as amended has reduced the items precluded from being qualified for a patent to (a) scientific discoveries; (b) rules and methods for mental activities; (c) methods for the diagnosis or treatment of diseases; (d) animal and plant varieties; and (e) substances obtained by means of a nuclear transformation. Such items are in general not patentable under the laws of industrialized countries. The *Amendments* have also effectively extended the scope of patent protection to micro-organisms and biological products.

The protection of process patents under the *Amendments* is also significant. The old law only prohibited the use of patented processes. According to this provision, the selling of and dealing with the products obtained from a patented processes did not constitute an infringement. Thus, the protection offered was of little value in practice. The *Amendments* have extended the protection in respect of patented process and have enabled patentees to prevent others from use or sale of "the product directly obtained by the patented process."[31] A patentee has also "the right to prevent any other person from importing, without its or his authorization, the patented product, or the product directly obtained by its or his patented process."[32] In disputes involving process patents, the burden of proof is on the defendant.[33]

(2) Term of Protection. Under the *Amendments*, the term of protection for invention patents and for utility model and design patents is increased from fifteen to twenty and from eight to ten years respectively. This extension of the protection period has also brought the *Patent Law* into line with the international standard. This revision does not apply to the cases where an application for patent is made prior to 1 January 1993.[34]

(3) Compulsory Licences. Provisions in respect of compulsory licences under the old law were criticized for being too rigid on the exploitation of a patented right. Under those provisions a patent holder was required to develop his/its invention in China within three years from the date of granting the patent right unless justifiable reasons were adduced; otherwise, the State Patent Office may order a compulsory licence. The immediate effect of the rule was that a patent holder had to manufacture products with the patented technology and that mere importation of the patented product could not satisfy the development requirement. Foreign manufacturers generally want the Chinese government to guarantee that their products incorporating a patent right will be protected under Chinese law, whereas the Chinese government is concerned that foreign manufacturers may elect to export their products rather than produce the same in China. Although the *Amendments* fail to provide positively that importation will constitute "development" of a patent right, the omission of the positive requirement to develop a patent in China has a similar effect.[35] It is believed that, when the *Regulations for the Implementation of the Patent Law* are amended,[36] more detailed provisions regarding compulsory licencing will be incorporated by which importation of a patented product will be considered to be a means of exploiting patent rights.

(4) Publication and Request for Revocation of Patents. Important changes have also been made by the *Amendments* in connection with publication and revocation of patents. The revised Article 34 authorizes the Patent Office to publish patent applications after the expiration of eighteen months from the date of filing and its satisfaction with the result of the preliminary examination, while the old Article 34 permitted publication "within eighteen months of filing." Needless to say, the amended Article 34 offers more adequate protection to applications from foreign countries. China recognizes the right of priority on the basis of reciprocity or in accordance with international obligations,[37] the period for which is twelve months. At the same time, the validity period for exceptions of disclosing an invention or creation without losing novelty is six months.[38] Thus,

publication of a patent "within" rather than "after expiration of" eighteen months may have deprived a foreign applicant of the right of priority.

The right to file an application for revocation of a patent under the revised Article 41 serves a similar purpose by granting more rights to foreign applicants. The old Article 41 allowed any individual or entity three months after the publication of a patent to file an "opposition," whilst the revised Article 41 extends the period to six months and allows a request for "revocation" of patents.

2. Copyright Law

The *Copyright Law* of China[39] went into effect on 1 June 1991.[40] The *Regulations for the Implementation of the Copyright Law* were promulgated by the National Copyright Administration on 30 May 1991. Thus, a copyright system was established for the first time in the history of the People's Republic. Further steps were taken in 1992 for the building of a copyright system reconcilable with that recognized by the international community. On 15 and 30 July 1992, China submitted its decision to accede to the *Berne Convention for the Protection of Literary and Artistic Works* and the *Universal Copyright Convention* respectively.[41] Both became effective three months thereafter. The accession to the *Berne Convention* aligns China's copyright system concerning foreigners on the international standard.[42] Article 142 of the *General Principles of Civil Law* provided that "If any international treaty concluded or acceded to by the People's Republic of China contains provisions differing from those in the civil laws of the People's Republic of China, the provisions of the international treaty shall apply, unless the provisions are ones on which the People's Republic of China has announced reservations." In fact, as far as the *Universal Copyright Convention* is concerned, it does not add much to the copyright system of China, for China's *Copyright Law* offers a higher level of protection than the *Convention* does.

For the purpose of implementing the *Berne Convention*, the State Council promulgated the *Regulations for the Implementation of International Copyright Treaties* on 25 September 1992 (the *Regulations*). Through the *Regulations*, the *Berne Convention* applies to works of the enterprises with foreign investment in China. At the same time, unpublished works of foreigners will be protected under the *Copyright Law*.

The most important feature of the *Regulations* is protection in connection with public performance. Article 11 of the *Regulations* stipulates that

"The copyright owner of a foreign work may authorize other persons to perform their works publicly or to disseminate the performances of their works publicly in any form and by any means." Article 12 of the *Regulations* provides: "Copyright owners of foreign cinematographic, television and videotaped works may authorize other people to show their works publicly." Accordingly, the copyright owner of a work may authorize by licencing or otherwise public performance of films, musical works, etc.

The *Regulations* recognize the exclusive right of a copyright owner to prevent importation of works infringing his/its copyright. Protection of computer software is also provided for in the *Regulations* under the category of literary work.

The introduction of these *Regulations* has, on the one hand, raised the level of copyright protection in China to the international standard and, on the other hand, has created "two systems" in the country. Foreigners will in essence enjoy a higher standard of protection in accordance with the international treaties. The Chinese copyright owners' rights, however, will still be governed by the *Copyright Law*. It is understood that this situation of "one country, two systems" serves as a transitional period through which provisions of the international treaties to which China is a party will be incorporated into the Chinese law.

IV. Foreign Trade

For a long time the foreign trade system in China has been subject to criticism both within and without China. Since the late 1980s, China has been trying to resume its contracting party status of the GATT. As part of the effort to rejoin the GATT and also as part of the economic reforms, the Chinese government has speeded up the reform of its legal system in respect of foreign trade.[43] A senior Chinese official in charge of foreign trade recently stated that within two years the import of most of the goods would not require licences and that within one year China would promulgate all the regulations in respect of foreign trade which would then be regulated only by the publicly promulgated laws and regulations.[44] Measures in this regard have been taken. Over the last few months, China has promulgated the *Regulations of the People's Republic of China on Import and Export Duties* (the *Import and Export Duties Regulations*)[45] and the *Rules on Place of Origin of Export Goods of the People's Republic of China* (the *Origin of Goods Rules*).[46] In addition, in early December, the

Economic Legal Reforms 7.25

Chinese government again adjusted the customs rates for import and export goods so as to make them more reconcilable with the requirements of the GATT.

(A) Import and Export Duties

The *Import and Export Duties Regulations*, as revised, have clarified several important issues. Article 2 of the *Regulations* stipulates that importation of goods which were originally manufactured in China is subject to import duties. This provision has resolved one of the most difficult problems which China had been facing in recent years. The reforms of foreign trade have led to the diversity of business transactions with foreign concerns and the increase of foreign trade companies. With or without intent, such foreign trade companies sometimes imported products from foreign countries, which products were later discovered to have been manufactured in China. The question was whether they should be subject to import duties. Some customs authorities insisted on imposing duties whilst some others felt it was wrong to do so. In addition to stopping the disorder of the customs in such circumstances, this rule will have a deterring effect on importing Chinese made goods to China, for the importers will not have the luck of escaping the customs duties.

It is also significant that the *Import and Export Duties Regulations* contain detailed rules for valuation of the imported goods. No assessment is needed if the value of the imported goods can be ascertained.[47] In case the value of the imported goods is unascertainable, Article 11 of the *Regulations* stipulates the basis and order of priority in assessing the duty-paying value of the goods for import as follows:

   a. the transaction price for the identical or similar goods imported from the same country or region;
   b. the transaction price for the identical or similar goods in the international market;
   c. the wholesale price for the identical or similar goods in the domestic market, minus the import duties levied and other taxes paid in the process of importation, the normal charges on transportation and storage after importation, the business expenses and the profit; and
   d. the price obtained from other reasonable methods of valuation by the Customs.

This article has brought the customs valuation rules of China in line with the international practice and more importantly with the provisions of the Customs Valuation Agreement under the GATT.[48] Therefore, it is a concrete step taken by China to rejoin the international organization. Under this provision, importers and exporters will be able to plan their transactions with more certainty.

The tariff rates have also been re-classified under the *Import and Export Duties Regulations*. Prior to the revision, there were general tariff rates and minimum tariff rates. Currently Article 6 of the *Regulations* provides for two categories of tariffs, i.e., general and preferential tariff rates, which are adopted by most of the countries.

(B) Determination of the Origin of Goods

Prior to the promulgation of the *Origin of Goods Rules*, there had been no rules for determining the place of origin of exported goods in China. With China being more and more integrated into the international community and especially having often faced the problems of export quotas, and dumping and subsidy charges in foreign countries like the United States and Europe, it is crucial for China to have such rules to protect the Chinese manufacturers and exporters. In the past, the place of origin had been the most difficult issue in disputes involving goods processed in mainland China but exported by enterprises in Hong Kong or Macau. Since China had no law for determining the place of origin of exported goods, the matter had to be decided by the laws of the importer's home country.[49]

Under the *Origin of Goods Rules*, the Certificate of Origin (COO) is the document to prove that the related exported goods have China as the place of origin (§2). COOs may be issued by local import and export merchandise inspection offices, branches of the China Council for the Promotion of International Trade and other organs designated by the state government. The supervision and control of the administration of COOs are the responsibility of the government departments in charge of foreign economic relations and trade at provincial and municipal level. Enterprises established in China and authorized to engage in foreign trade or processing and assembling business for foreign clients "may" apply for COOs (§5). The use of the permissive word "may" implies that an exporter in question has the discretion not to apply for a COO. This provision is quite helpful, because in practice identification of the place of origin may not be necessary and the exporter should be relieved from the obligation of securing a COO in such case.

Two categories of products are considered to have China as the place of origin, i.e., products entirely produced or manufactured in the territory of China and products mainly and finally made or processed in China with partially or entirely imported raw materials, spare parts and components. The products entirely manufactured in China include: (a) minerals extracted from the territory of China and continental shelf; (b) plants harvested or gathered in China or their products; (c) animals bred and raised in China and their products; (d) products obtained by hunting or fishing in the Chinese territory; (e) marine and other products obtained by ships or other means of China from the sea and their processed goods; (f) scraps and waste materials recycled in the course of manufacturing or processing in China; and (g) products entirely made from the above-mentioned products or from other non-imported raw materials in the territory of China. The criterion for determining whether a given product mainly or finally made in China should have China as its place of origin is a substantive change in appearance, nature, form or use. In other words, if after processing in China the product in question is not substantively changed, it will not be considered a product of China. The interpretation of the word "substantive" is significant to the enterprises engaged in processing business for foreign concerns. The Chinese organs in charge of issuing COOs are required to apply the principle of "focusing on the manufacturing or processing procedure and supplementing it with the composition ratio" (§6).

The *Origin of Goods Rules* contain provisions to deal with offenses against the *Rules* such as submitting false information, forgery, illegal transfer of COOs, etc. Punishments include administrative measures and prosecution according to the criminal law. Officials from the organs in charge of issuing COOs are also subject to administrative punishment or criminal prosecution for abuse of power, neglect of duties, etc. Such measures are seen as part of the efforts of China to suppress the corruption of government officials and to raise the efficiency of government.

V. Conclusion

Tremendous efforts have been made by China to reform its economic legal system over the last fifteen years, which have brought the Chinese system in most of its major aspects in line with those adopted by most of the industrialized countries. With the deepening of the economic reforms and especially the decision to build a market economy, legal reforms again have speeded up after Deng Xiaoping's visit to southern China in the spring of 1992. Currently, the Chinese law drafters are busy with the preparation of new bills for adoption by the Standing Committee and the National People's Congress. Among them are the *Law on Product Liabilities*, *Company Law*, *Economic Contract Law* (to be re-promulgated after major revision), *Arbitration Law* and *Securities Law*. It is understood that veteran lawmakers are eager to have more laws adopted before their formal retirement at the completion of the current Congress ending in April 1993.

Notes

1. This definition is given in "The Study of Law," *China's Great Encyclopedia* (1984); see Byron S. J. Weng, "China's Concept of Socialist Law," in *Introduction to Chinese Law*, edited by Byron S. J. Weng and Chang Hsin (Hong Kong: Ming Pao Press, 1989), p. 9.
2. For political and ideological reasons, over the last fourteen years, substantial progress has been made mainly in private laws or legislations regulating commercial transactions and relations between the government and business enterprises, between business entities and between business entities and individuals. Although reforms in the public law sector have also been carried out, they are in general of lesser significance and on smaller scales.
3. On 1 March 1992, *Regulations of the People's Republic of China on the Protection of Wildlife* were promulgated to implement the *Law of the People's Republic of China on the Protection of Wildlife* effective as of 1 March 1989.
4. For the first time in its history, China promulgated the long awaited *Maritime Law of the People's Republic of China* on 7 November 1992. The *Maritime Law*, adopted by the Standing Committee of the Seventh National People's Congress at its twenty-eigth session and effective on 1 July 1993, contains 278 articles representing the most comprehensive law China has ever enacted.
5. Several sets of regulations in respect of business enterprises have been issued by the Chinese government in 1992. Such regulations will be discussed in detail in this chapter.
6. For a detailed account of the nature, establishment, rights and obligations of

Chinese enterprises, see *Zhongguo jingjifa jiaocheng* (Textbook on Economic Law of China), edited by Fei Zongyi (Beijing: The People's Court Publishing House, 1990).

7. Formally known as *Law of the People's Republic of China on Industrial Enterprises Owned by the Whole People* adopted at the first session of the Seventh National People's Congress and promulgated on 13 April 1988, effective as of 1 August 1988.

8. For example, Article 2 of the *Industrial Enterprise Law*, on the one hand, provides that the state is the owner of the property of the state company and, on the other hand, requires state companies to obtain legal person status.

9. In another case, a Mr Wang entered into a labour contract with a refrigerator company for a term of five years in October 1989. Starting in 1990, Mr Wang accepted gifts and bribes from the customers and often stole parts of refrigerators from the company. Upon discovering his misconduct, the refrigerator company dismissed Mr Wang on 5 April 1991. Wang appealed to the local labour arbitration organ arguing that his contract had not yet expired and, therefore, he should not have been dismissed. The labour arbitration organ decided in favour of the refrigerator company on the basis that Mr Wang's conduct, although being short of committing a crime, constituted a breach of contract and thus the dismissal was justified. See *Zhonghua Renmin Gongheguo Shierfa Anli Huibian* (A Collection of Cases of the Twelve Laws of the People's Republic of China), edited by Cai Cheng (Beijing: China's University of Politics and Law Press, 1992), p. 692. On 12 July 1986, the State Council promulgated the *Interim Regulations on the Labour Contract System in State-owned Enterprises*, amended on 18 May 1992, which provide, *inter alia*, that employees of state-owned enterprises, except as otherwise provided by the state, must conclude a labour contract with the enterprise where they are employed. These *Regulations* also stipulate that an employee is entitled to an advanced notice of dismissal and that he/she may not be dismissed during sickness.

10. Article 30 of the *Industrial Enterprise Regulations* provides that state companies must observe the laws and regulations on the management of state properties and must assess and examine such properties on a regular basis. State companies are also required not to use the funds allocated for major repairs and development of new products and depreciation funds to pay salaries or bonuses.

11. In this regard, the T City Xinhua Book Store case is instructive. On 3 October 1988, the Xinhua Book Store entered into a purchase and sale contract with Dong Sheng Trading Company for the purchase of fifty automobiles. Because the superior department in charge of the Xinhua Book Store believed the latter had no authority to conduct automobile business, the performance of the contract was interrupted. Then, Dong Sheng Trading Company sued the

Xinhua Book Store for breach of contract. The local court decided that the defendant Xinhua Book Store must pay damages to the plaintiff. At the same time, the court ruled that the superior department inappropriately interfered with the normal business of the Xinhua Book Store (the contract was not in violation of any law) and, therefore, must be responsible for the breach of contract by the defendant. See Cai Cheng (Note 9), pp. 686–87.

12. In the past, China enacted laws and regulations such as the *Law on Industrial Enterprises Owned by the Whole People*, the *Law on Enterprise Bankruptcy*, the *Law on Chinese-foreign Joint Ventures*, the *Law on Chinese-foreign Contractual Ventures*, the *Law on Foreign Capital Enterprises* and the *Regulations on Private Enterprises* to govern the establishment and activities of the state-owned enterprises, enterprises with foreign investment and private enterprises. Although establishment of share companies and issuing of stocks began several years ago, there had been no regulations at the national level.

13. Some Chinese scholars consider the promulgation of the two "Opinions" as a milestone for the development of the company law in China. See Zhang, "The Formation of the Company Law of Our Country and the Two Opinions on Companies," *Falü xuexi yu yanjiu*, May 1992, pp. 59–63.

14. Apparently, Chinese scholars and government officials are of the view that the state should be the majority shareholder of the stock companies. At the same time, some scholars argue that stock companies should be classified into state owned, collectively owned and private stock companies in accordance with the composition of the ownership. For instance, if the state holds the majority share of a given stock company, the latter should be considered a state company. See Guo Feng, "Gufen youxian gongsi yuanli yu shiwu" (Theory and Practice of the Limited Stock Companies) (Beijing: Xiandai chubanshe, 1990).

15. There has been established a commission for the reform of the economic system or office at each level of government in China. These commissions and offices play a key part in the development of the stock system.

16. Article 46 of the *Stock Company Rules* provides that the articles of association may require other items to be adopted by a special resolution.

17. Article 55 of the *Stock Company Rules* provides in detail the items to be decided by the board of directors.

18. Under the current system, Chinese taxpayers are subject to a higher income tax. As a result, many Chinese companies have formed fake joint ventures with foreign concerns to reduce their tax obligations.

19. With regard to open refusal to pay taxes, the problem is essentially confined to Chinese taxpayers. It was reported that officials from tax authorities were beaten by the local people who did not believe that they owed taxes or owed that much taxes as demanded by the tax authorities.

Economic Legal Reforms 7.31

20. Both the *Law on the Administration of Taxes* and the *Supplementary Tax Provisions* became effective on 1 January 1993.
21. In the past, complaints were filed about the tax authorities' abuse of power in tax collections, including over-levying of taxes and unlawful or arbitrary tax reductions and exemptions.
22. The same Article permits a taxpayer to secure a guarantee in lieu of tax payment before leaving China.
23. This law was adopted at the fourth session of the Seventh National People's Congress on 9 April 1991.
24. The *Trademark Law* of the People's Republic of China was adopted at the twenty-fourth session of the Standing Committee of the Fifth National People's Congress on 23 August 1982.
25. The *Patent Law of the People's Republic of China* was adopted at the fourth session of the Standing Committee of the Sixth National People's Congress on 12 March 1984.
26. The *Copyright Law of the People's Republic of China* was adopted at the fifteenth session of the Standing Committee of the Seventh National People's Congress on 7 September 1990.
27. For a discussion on the theory and practice of China's *Patent Law*, see Tang Zongshun, "Protection of Industrial Property," in *Chinese Foreign Economic Law: Analysis and Commentary*, edited by Rui and Wang (Washington, DC: International Law Institute, 1991).
28. The *Amendments* adopted on 4 September 1992 became effective on 1 January 1993.
29. Article 26 of the *Patent Law* prior to its amendment prohibited granting of a patent right to such items.
30. It is understood that the technology employed by the Chinese chemical and pharmaceutical industries is about twenty years behind that of the industrialized countries.
31. See Article 11 of the *Patent Law* as amended.
32. *Ibid.*
33. Paragraph 2 of Article 60 of the *Patent Law*, as amended, states that "When any infringement dispute arises, if the patent for invention is a process for the manufacture of a new product, any entity or individual manufacturing the identical product shall furnish proof of the process used in the manufacture of its or his product."
34. The *Amendments* explicitly provide that patent applications filed before 1 January 1993 are to be dealt with in accordance with the existing law.
35. The revised Article 51 provides that: "Where any entity which is qualified to exploit the invention or utility model has made requests for authorization from the patentee or an invention or utility model to exploit its or his patent on reasonable terms and such efforts have not been successful within a

reasonable period of time, the Patent Office may, upon the application of that entity, grant a compulsory licence to exploit the patent for invention or utility model."

36. At the time this chapter was written, amendments to the *Regulations for the Implementation of the Patent Law* were being considered by the Chinese government.
37. See Article 29 of the *Patent Law* as amended.
38. Article 24 of the *Patent Law* as amended provides for the circumstances where disclosure of an invention or creation will not disqualify such invention or creation from being patented. Such circumstances include disclosure at international exhibitions and academic or technological meetings and disclosure by a third party without the consent of the applicant for patent.
39. The *Copyright Law of the People's Republic of China* was adopted by the Standing Committee of the Seventh National People's Congress at its fifteenth session on 7 September 1990.
40. For discussions on the legislative history and interpretation of the *Copyright Law*, see He Shan and Xiao Shui, *Zhuzuoquanfa gaiyao* (An Introduction to the Copyright Law) (Beijing: The People's Publishing House, 1991).
41. Apparently the fifteen-day delay for China to join the *Universal Copyright Convention* was caused by a technical problem in transmitting the accession document which was approved by the Chinese government on the same day the accession to the *Berne Convention* was to be made.
42. For a detailed comparative analysis of the international copyright system, see Zheng Chengsi, *Banquanfa* (Copyright Law) (Beijing: People's University of China Press, 1990).
43. For a detailed account of the reforms in China's foreign trade system, see Feng Datong, "Foreign Trade Laws and the Foreign Economic Contract Law," in *Chinese Foreign Economic Law: Analysis and Commentary* (see Note 27).
44. See *Ming Pao* (Hong Kong), 14 February 1992, p. 20. China has been criticized for applying secret or unpublicly issued rules in the administration of foreign trade.
45. The *Regulations of the People's Republic of China on Import and Export Duties* were revised and re-promulgated by the State Council on 28 February 1992. The *Regulations* were first promulgated on 7 March 1985 and then revised in 1987. The current revision became effective on 1 April 1992.
46. These *Rules* were adopted by the Executive Meeting of the State Council on 28 February 1992, effective from 1 May 1992.
47. Article 10 of the *Import and Export Duties Regulations* prescribes that the duty-paying value of the goods to be imported should be assessed according to the c.i.f. (cost, insurance and freight) price based on the normal transaction value verified by the Customs.

48. The *Customs Valuation Agreement* also known as *Customs Valuation Code* was adopted by the contracting parties of the GATT at the Tokyo Round in 1979. Its formal title is "Agreement on Implementation of Article VII of the General Agreement on Tariffs and Trade." Article 11 of the *Import and Export Duties Regulations* contains provisions almost identical to those of the *Customs Valuation Agreement*.
49. In anti-dumping and countervailing duties litigations and for the implementation of quotas, the determination of the place of origin of the goods in question is essential. For discussion of the anti-dumping and countervailing duties rules under the GATT, see G. G. Wang, *International Trade Order: Economics, Politics and Law* (Beijing: Law Publishing House, 1987), Chaps. 7 and 8; for discussion of the anti-dumping law of the United States, see G. G. Wang, *Sino-American Economic Exchanges: The Legal Contributions* (New York: Praeger Publishers, 1985), Chap. 6.

8

Foreign Policy

Gerald Chan

> Quand la Chine s'éveillera, le monde tremblera.
> (When China awakes, the world will tremble.)
> — Napoléon Bonaparte, 1817

Is China today a global power or a regional power? Why? How does China maximize its national interests in an increasingly regionalized world? Those who argue that China is a global power often give these reasons: China is a big country with 1.1 billion people, constituting a fifth to a quarter of humankind. It is nuclear-armed with three million soldiers. It is a permanent member of the United Nations Security Council. It has a huge, growing consumer market and is the world's ninth-largest economy. All these reasons are valid, but if we take a deeper look, as do a few scholars such as Samuel Kim, we are likely to get a clearer picture which may help us to better understand the situation.

In making an assessment of China's national power in 1991, Kim says that:

> China belongs easily to the top-five category in global pecking order only in demographic size, strategic nuclear warheads, and global arms trade. After having established an all-time global record in doubling per capita output in the shortest time period (1977–87), China still ranks ninth in GNP, fifteenth in merchandise exports (even behind Taiwan and South Korea), eighty-second in the United Nations Development Programme's "Human Development Index Ranking," and one hundred and fourth in per capita GNP. China is not even included in the category of top fifteen patent powers.[1]

Although there is no universally acceptable way to measure national power, it would be appropriate to regard China as a formidable regional power in Asia with a potential but as yet limited global reach. Most Chinese leaders would agree to this, as Deng Xiaoping said in 1985 that "China is both a major country and a minor one. When we say it is a major country, we mean it has a large population and a vast territory.... But at the same time, China is a minor country, an underdeveloped or developing country. It is a minor one in terms of its ability to safeguard peace and deter war...."[2] Obviously, Deng was referring to China's limited capability to influence events relating to international war and peace. With his statement as a caveat it would be useful to analyze China's foreign relations in

---

I wish to thank Professor Herbert Yee of the University of Macau and Dr K. K. Leung of the City Polytechnic of Hong Kong for reading an earlier draft of this chapter.

global and regional terms and to draw some linkages between these two spheres of China's activities. For reasons of scope, importance and direct relevance to China, I propose to investigate the developments of two triangular relationships which are gaining prominence against the background of the dramatic decline of Russia's role in international affairs: one involving China, the United States and Japan at the global level; the other involving China, Japan and South Korea at the regional level.

How have these triangular relationships come about? With the collapse of the Soviet Union, the great power triangle involving the United States, the Soviet Union, and China in the Cold War days has given way to new sets of global and regional relationships. Europe, for example, is in the throes of economic and political integration and is set to become one of the most important power centres in world politics. The United States, a superpower in relative decline, is trying hard to arrest its fall. The establishment of the North American Free Trade Area (NAFTA), which brings together the United States, Canada and Mexico, is mainly an American initiative to protect and promote its economic interest. Newly-elected American President Bill Clinton is determined to make American economic recovery his top priority. Asia, because of its political, economic and cultural diversity, is more fragmented than Europe or North America. However, most Asian leaders realize that their countries share some common features — their colonial past and their dynamic economic growth in recent times.

From a global as well as regional perspectives the most important bilateral relationship is the one between Japan and the United States. Together these two countries contribute about 40% of the world's total economic output. To many countries in the Asia-Pacific region, their security relationships are the prime factor for peace and stability in the region. Within Asia itself the most important bilateral relationship is arguably that between China and Japan. From these two important bilateral relationships, a new triangular relationship involving China, the United States and Japan is developing. According to Singapore Foreign Minister Wong Kan Seng, Chinese strategic thinkers have already informally mooted the idea of this new triangle taking the place of the old triangle of the United States, China and the Soviet Union.[3] This new triangle draws Asia and the US closer together through interactions of various kinds across the Pacific. It may, therefore, be called the *Pacific power triangle*.

The effect of the ending of the Cold War is felt as sharply in East Asia as in other parts of the world. In addition, the rising standard of living and public awareness have changed the configuration of international political relationships in the region. From China's perspective, the establishment of diplomatic relations with South Korea in August 1992 has changed not only the nature of their bilateral relationship but also their relations with North Korea, Japan and Taiwan. A new regional power triangle is in the making, involving China, Japan and South Korea. This may be called the *Asian power triangle*.

The scopes of the Pacific and the Asian triangles are not as clear-cut as described above because of the numerous linkages that exist between these two triangles and between them and the outside world. Likewise the simple dichotomy between China's regional and international perspectives may not reveal the full extent of complexities involved. However, for analytical reasons and reasons of manageability, it is desirable to pitch at the chosen level of generality.

In order to understand the dynamics of the Pacific power triangle and the Asian power triangle, it would be useful to analyze, first of all, the changing global environment in which Chinese foreign policy operates and, then, the constituent parts of these two power triangles: the bilateral relationships between China on the one hand and the United States, Japan and South Korea, on the other.

The Changing Global Environment

It has become increasingly apparent that the world is evolving towards the formation of a three-bloc system. The balance of power dominated by the superpower rivalry between the United States and the Soviet Union in the past is being replaced in part by the balance-of-power among three blocs: North America, Europe and Asia.[4] The old balance was primarily built on military-strategic interests whereas the present balance is based mainly on economic strengths. This new international order holds good in general terms despite the difficulties that might be involved in explaining some anomalies such as the exact alignment or non-alignment of Africa or the Middle East to this new system.

The division of labour in the new international order at various dimensions of trade, development, peace-keeping, politics, and economics justifies the assertion of such a tripolar world, the main characteristics of which are summarized in the following table.

The political dimension can be taken as representative of the military

Foreign Policy

Table 1. The Present Tripolar World

	America	Europe	Asia
Trade	NAFTA	EC	APEC, PECC
Development	World Bank	EBRD	ADB
Peacekeeping	UN (USA) in the world	NATO in Europe	UN (Japan?) in Asia
Politics	USA	France, UK, Germany	China, Japan
Economics	USA	Germany	Japan

Abbreviations:
EC   European Community
APEC Asia-Pacific Economic Cooperation
PECC Pacific Economic Cooperation Conference
EBRD European Bank for Reconstruction and Development
ADB Asian Development Bank

dimension with the addition of Russia which straddles Europe and Asia. In this tripolar world the United States is still the most powerful nation.

How does China fit into this order? Apart from holding a permanent seat in the United Nations Security Council, China's influence in this new global order is small compared with countries such as the United States, Japan, Germany, France, or the United Kingdom. Its role in the World Bank, the Asian Development Bank, the Asia-Pacific Economic Cooperation, and the Pacific Economic Cooperation Conference is more of a beneficiary or follower than a donor or leader. Even in the Security Council China, these days, tends to go along with the other four permanent members or abstain from voting on issues in which it wants to express reservations or misgivings, especially issues that affect its relations with the developing world. Although China has the potentials of a world power, its present reach is rather limited. It is still on the whole a very poor country trying to modernize and catch up with the developed world. Its human rights and environmental records are poor; its political and legal systems leave a lot to be desired; and these aspects sometimes spill over into China's trading, economic, and even political relations with other countries. Its influence is felt most strongly in Asia, and it is feared by many of its neighbours.

Despite these and other limitations, the Chinese government has worked hard at building or restoring its perceived rightful place in the world. Three years after the 1989 Tiananmen Incident Chinese foreign policy is back in full swing, this time with greater vigour than at any time since the opening up of the country to the outside world in 1978 and the subsequent establishment of diplomatic ties with the United States in 1979. Prime Ministers Kaifu of Japan and Major of Britain came as guests, so did US Secretary of State Baker. Chinese Premier Li Peng toured Europe and visited the United States. Diplomatic ties were established with Indonesia, Singapore and Israel. The year 1992 saw not only the establishment of diplomatic relations with South Korea, but also the visit of Emperor Akihito of Japan to China, the first time by a Japanese monarch. Japan and South Korea are two of China's most important Asian neighbours. Their newly-forged relationships certainly herald a new pattern of political and economic development in Northeast Asia.

On the economic front, China's performance for the past three years has been extremely remarkable, considering that most parts of the world are experiencing one kind of economic recession or another. The economic growth in South China, including the provinces of Guangdong and Fujian, is among the highest in the world, averaging some 25% in 1991. Real GNP for the whole country has grown by an average of almost 9% a year since 1978. Foreign companies are eager to rush in to get a share of the market. Labour is relatively cheap in China, and the consumer market is expanding, fuelled by the growth of a new middle class. Foreign dignitaries, politicians and businessmen are gradually finding their way back to Beijing.[5] Herein lies the dilemma faced by many countries in their dealings with China. The China market is full of potentials. It is increasingly attractive and hard to ignore. However, China's growing assertiveness and nationalistic behaviour are difficult to handle. How to balance one's political and economic interests when dealing with China remains a delicate and challenging task.

China and the USA in the Pacific Power Triangle

Subsequent to the collapse of the Soviet Union, both China and the United States recognize the diminishing value of using each other against Russia or using Russia against each other in the pursuit of their national interests. The great power triangle has lost its strategic significance. Bilateral relations between China and the United States, henceforth, have to rely on their abilities to settle amicably a host of substantive issues that stand in the way of improved relations, including the balance of trade, human rights, intellectual property rights, the sales of Chinese arms, technology transfer and the case of Taiwan.

Foreign Policy 8.7

The recent trade friction between China and the United States worsened on 10 October 1991 when the then American President, George Bush, instructed the office of the US Trade Representative to investigate how China's trade laws and practices affected market access for American exporters. As a result of the investigation, the United States determined that China's trade practices constituted significant barriers to American exports. Consequently, Washington began calling on Beijing to liberalize its trade policies and to improve its commercial practices.[6] The United States drew up a list of its imports from China worth about US$3.9 billion to be subjected to increased duties of up to 100% if Beijing did not open its market by 10 October 1992. In response Beijing prepared its hitlist of American goods with US$4 billion.[7] (All currencies quoted in this chapter are in US dollars unless otherwise stated.)

On 10 October 1992, the deadline set by the United States, a trade agreement was finally reached between the two countries which helped to avert a possible trade war. Under the agreement China promised to take measures to liberalize its trade policies and to eliminate some trade barriers. China hopes that this concession may win the support of the United States for its entry to the General Agreement on Tariffs and Trade (GATT).

The trade dispute between the two had its origin mainly in their balance of trade. In 1991 China exported $19 billion worth of goods to the United States and imported $6.3 billion in return, running a trade surplus of $12.7 billion.[8] This was by no means a small sum compared with Japan's $48.6 billion and Taiwan's $9.7 billion trade surpluses with the US in the same year.[9] American businessmen as well as human-rights activists began to question China's most-favoured-nation (MFN) trading status.[10] The American Congress voted to deny Beijing unconditional MFN status, but was vetoed by George Bush.

China's MFN status comes up for review every year and is a thorny issue in Sino-American relations unless China can find a permanent way to satisfy the American demand or become a contracting party to the GATT. In any case China needs the support of the United States to gain entry to this world trade body. Apparently, Bill Clinton is less sympathetic towards China than George Bush. During his election campaign Clinton criticized China's human rights record and classified Chinese leaders as "tyrants." He was against giving MFN status to China without gaining concessions from it on its human rights and trade records.[11] However, he acknowledged that China had made phenomenal progress in recent years and said that he did not want to isolate China.[12]

China's relations with the United States has plummeted to a new low. The impending sale of 150 American F-16 jet fighters to Taiwan has infuriated Chinese leaders. They have accused the United States of violating the Joint Communiqué of 1982 in which the United States agreed "that its arms sales to Taiwan will not exceed, either in qualitative or in quantitative terms, the level of those supplied in recent years since the establishment of diplomatic relations between the United States and China." As a retaliatory gesture China has announced that it will withdraw from the talks among the big powers to ban nuclear weapons. In a way Bill Clinton's election to the American presidency has provided a chance for both countries to take stock of their relationship and to make any adjustments necessary. What Clinton does after he assumes the presidency may not correspond with his campaign rhetoric. Although Clinton is known to be less sympathetic to China than Bush, his policy towards China after taking office depends a lot on his policy advisers on Asia, the Democratic Party platform, the attitudes of the Congress, businessmen and interest groups, and the changing mood of the American public towards China. At least, he is expected to push ahead with the sale of F-16s to Taiwan. China's top leaders, on the other hand, have sent telegram congratulations to Clinton, and a Chinese government spokesman has said that China "is ready to work with the new US administration in the improvement and development of the bilateral ties on the basis of principles enshrined in the three Sino-US Joint Communiqués (of 1972, 1979, and 1982)."[13] Also, as a gesture of goodwill to the president-elect, China has affirmed its purchase of two millions tons of wheat and civilian aircraft from the United States.

Despite the relative decline of American power and the rough Sino-American relations, the importance of the US market to Asia cannot be underestimated. As far as China is concerned, the United States is the third most important trading partner after Hong Kong and Japan. In a conference speech in Beijing in September 1992 Singapore's Lee Kuan Yew pointed out that "the US will remain the main absorber of the exports of China and of all other countries of East Asia for the next ten to fifteen years."[14]

As the great power triangle sinks into oblivion, so emerges a new one among China, the United States and Japan. The United States and Japan are military allies. Their relationship has endured well since the end of the Second World War and is fundamentally strong, although increasingly they may not see eye-to-eye on all matters, especially economic ones. The demise of the Soviet Union has undermined the base upon which their security treaty has been built. To justify the continuation of the security treaty, Japanese strategic planners have to look for new targets to justify the maintenance of Japan's formidable military establishment. How much is Russia a security threat? Is North Korea the new arch enemy? Is China another one in the future? Is the overall military build-up in the Asia-Pacific region a security threat? To what extent can peacekeeping and disaster relief activities serve as substitutes for security functions? These are some of the uncertain factors which are likely to affect the future shape of the military alliance between Japan and the United States.

On the other hand, the worsening trade relations between Japan and the United States and the formation of the NAFTA which excludes Japan and many other Pacific Rim countries mean that Japan has to prepare itself against possible US trade protectionism.

The establishment of NAFTA and the adoption of trade protectionist measures by the United States and Europe tend to force Asian countries to look more towards themselves for mutual economic support, thus stimulating commercial activities within Asia. Already intra-Asian trade has surpassed cross-Pacific trade. In 1991 intra-Asian trade stood at $362 billion compared with $347 billion across the Pacific,[15] and $257 billion across the Atlantic.[16] Japan is already the largest investor and aid donor to Asia, and it is natural that it will take a fresh look at opportunities in its neighbourhood as Asia's economies are booming and the developed world is becoming more protectionist. A modernizing China is a very important partner. Japan has all along tried to maintain a cordial relationship with China, and very often it is the United States that provides the impetus for Japan to take momentous steps to improve its relations with China. The Nixon Shock of 1972 led to the establishment of diplomatic relations with China later in the same year. And the setting up of NAFTA, the worsening trade relations between the United States and its two Asian trade partners, the relative power shift between the United States and Japan in favour of the latter, and the growing importance of China all add up to a force strong enough to shock Japan into taking further steps to improve its relations with China.

China and Japan: A New Power Axis in Asia

Politically, economically and culturally, China and Japan have regarded each other as important neighbours. China is the most populous nation while Japan is an economic superpower. Despite the traditional distaste that the Chinese and the Japanese have of each other and the lingering problems between the two countries such as territorial dispute over Diaoyutai (Senkaku to the Japanese), the revision of Japan's history textbooks, and the rise of Japanese nationalism, leaders in both countries recognize that a good neighbourly relationship is essential not only for the future well-being of both but also for the Asia-Pacific region at large. China needs Japan's capital, trade and technology, while Japan wants China's natural resources, market and cheap labour. Their economic complementarity is clear.

Emperor Akihito's visit to China in October 1992 symbolizes an important step towards improving bilateral relations, normalized twenty years ago when diplomatic ties were established. The timing of the visit is interesting. Coming a week after the conclusion of the Fourteenth Chinese Communist Party Congress, it can be construed as the lending of legitimacy by the Emperor to the Chinese government. To the Japanese government, the visit helped to stablilize and improve bilateral relations. Japan has an interest in seeing that China proceeds smoothly with its modernization programme, at least in the foreseeable future. Whether or not Japan would like to see a strong and modernized China in the long term remains doubtful. At the moment, a politically and economically stable China is not only conducive to the strategic interests of Japan, but also to peace and stability of the whole Asia-Pacific region.

Japan was the first among the industralized countries to resume aid to China shortly after the Tiananmen Incident, amounting to $6.5 billion (Y810 billion) in 1990. Its most recent aid package to China comprises $6.2 billion worth of concessional loans to build the country's infrastructure.

Although Japan's total investment in China is low compared with other Asian countries such as Indonesia, it has soared to new heights. Japanese direct investment in China is estimated to reach $1.8 billion in 1992, against $580 million in 1991 and $439 million in 1990. This dramatic increase runs counter to Japan's overall foreign investment, which has been falling for the past two years. According to one financial estimate, China is close to becoming Japan's third largest offshore manufacturing base after Thailand and Malaysia.[17] Bilateral trade is growing: a record high of $23 billion was reached in 1991, with a $5.6 billion surplus in Chinas' favour. In the first six months of 1992, trade grew at an annual rate of 26% to $12.8 billion. It is expected to reach $26 billion in 1992.[18] China is likely to overtake South Korea in 1992 to become Japan's second-largest trading partner, after the United States. For China, Japan is its second-largest commercial partner. The trade agreement signed on 10 October 1992 between the United States and China could help to boost Sino-Japanese trade further as the opening up of the Chinese market to foreign goods will benefit Japan as well.[19] Japan, however, is worried about the trade protectionist tendencies of the Clinton administration. Japanese Foreign Minister Watanabe Michio is reported to have said in a public speech on the American election day that "the Democratic Party is trade protectionism."[20]

Of course, Japan is not all angels to China; it has its own self-interests too, as attested by Inoguchi Takashi of Tokyo University. In an interview with the British Broadcasting Corporation on Emperor Akihito's visit to China, he said that it was important for Japan to keep in touch with China, to monitor its developments and to manipulate its relations with China.[21]

In a speech in Beijing the Emperor deeply deplored the sufferings of the Chinese people during the Japanese occupation of the 1930s and 1940s, referring to it as an unfortunate period in history. However, he stopped short of giving a full apology, which had been demanded by many ordinary Chinese. The Chinese government, however, made it a condition for the visit that the Emperor would not be asked to make an apology. To many Chinese, especially those overseas, the Chinese government had simply knuckled under the mighty *yen*.

The timing of Emperor Akihito's visit has another interesting aspect. Coming one week before the American presidential election, it can be seen as a sign of Japan's growing assertiveness and independence in its foreign policy. Japan is taking greater strides to improve relations with China, in face of worsening trade relations with the United States. The attitude of the United States towards China in the new Pacific power triangle has so far been ambivalent. On the one hand, the US is worried about its declining power relationship with Japan and would like to strengthen its relations with China in order to put a check on a growing Japan. On the other hand, it is also hindered by its not so cordial relationship with China and has enraged China by selling arms to Taiwan. This leaves room for China to play off one against the other in this triangular relationship. However, since Japan and the United States are China's major trading partners and sources of capital and technology, it will not be easy for China to play this power-balancing game.

Japan's drive to improve its relations with China is not without competitors. South Korea, for one, is trying very hard to develop better links with China after the establishment of formal diplomatic ties in August 1992. China is also eager to count South Korea as a bargaining chip against the United States and Japan, and as a way to further its economic interests and to isolate Taiwan diplomatically. There lies the motivating force that drives the dynamics of the new Asian power triangle in Northeast Asia involving China, Japan and South Korea.

China and South Korea in the Asian Power Triangle

China and South Korea established diplomatic relations after a freeze of more than four decades. This was followed by a state visit to Beijing in late September by the then South Korean President, Roh Tae Woo. Roh said his visit marked a "turning point in the removal of the cold war in Northeast Asia and the formation of a new world order based on reconciliation and cooperation."[22] Roh discussed bilateral trade and the issue of nuclear weapons in North Korea with Chinese leaders.

China's policy towards the two Koreas is entering a period of transition. On the one hand, it has said that its policy towards North Korea would not change, while on the other it has established diplomatic relations with South Korea, a long-time adversary of the North. China now supports dialogue between the two and has expressed willingness to cooperate with them to lessen their mutual tension so as to bring peace and stability to the Korean peninsula.

Trade between China and South Korea has been increasing quite dramatically over the years, which partially explains why China decided to normalize its relations with South Korea. The establishment of diplomatic relations will further stimulate bilateral trade, communications, investment and aid flows. Two-way trade was worth $5.8 billion in 1991, with China running a surplus of $1.1 billion. It is expected to rise to $10 billion, and China is expected to become South Korea's biggest trading partner after the US and Japan in 1992.[23] China is now the third most popular place for South Korean investment after Thailand and Indonesia.[24] Samsung Electronics has signed a $60 million joint-venture project with the Tianjin communications board to assemble video cassette recorders and Daewoo will participate in a $200 million venture in Shandong province.[25]

The Tumen Delta development project, sponsored by the UN Development Programme to the tune of $30 billion, brings together not only China and South Korea, but also North Korea, Japan, Russia and Mongolia to stimulate growth and development in the region.

The Sino-South Korean normalization has several ramifications. First, it serves as a balance to Japan's economic dominance in Northeast Asia. Both Japan and South Korea are investing heavily in Northeast China. A point might be reached in the near future when their investment interests clash with each other. In such an eventuality Beijing will have the option to play off one against the other in order to maximize its national interest. Secondly, it might either force North Korea into adopting a more conciliatory stance towards its neighbours or produce the opposite effect of pushing North Korea into speeding up its nuclear weapon programme to defend itself. The latter possibility will then trigger off a chain reaction in Asia: South Korea and Japan will reconsider their nuclear policies and other countries will take precautionary defensive measures. This might intensify the mini-arms race now going on in the Asia-Pacific region. However, it seems that the former scenario is more likely to happen because of China's influence over North Korea, North Korea's compliance with international inspection of its nuclear facilities and the on-going inter-Korean dialogue. Thirdly, Taiwan will be further isolated diplomatically in Asia forcing it to further strengthen its economic diplomacy — to use its economic power to harness political gains — and its military defence. Apart from 150 American F-16s, Taiwan intends to buy sixty advanced Mirage 2000 jets from France and other sophisticated weaponry from other European countries. Fourthly, how is China going to manage the Asian power triangle involving Japan, South Korea and itself? Can China play off South Korea against Japan, and Japan against the United States?

Conclusion

Chinese foreign policy today is increasingly pragmatic. It is geared towards developing friendly relations with all countries, irrespective of their ideological or political orientations. The forging of a trading link with South Africa in the absence of diplomatic relations is a good example. The aim is to cultivate a peaceful international environment conducive to its economic growth and development. This kind of policy bears some resemblance to the so-called "comprehensive national security strategy" adopted by Japan since the late 1970s to maximize its national interests by taking an omnidirectional approach. However, in terms of development and strategic priorities, it is becoming apparent that Chinese foreign policy is undergoing a fundamental shift from its traditional or classical strategic thinking of *yuanjiao jingong* (befriend the distant [state], attack the near [state]) to the present *jinjiao yuangong* (befriend the near, attack the distant). In the contemporary context "attack" rarely means a military offensive but refers mostly to a check-and-balance or a maintenance of the *status quo* relationship. This policy shift is based on two premises, according to China's perception: first, the recognition that Asia (the near) will remain an important region of economic growth in the foreseeable future and that China should align itself with this region and, secondly, the need to contain the United States (the distant), now the sole hegemon in the world after the collapse of the Soviet Union.[26]

As a regional power with a limited global reach, China's foreign policy is necessarily regionally based but interspersed with occasional posturing in the international arena, especially in the United Nations, when circumstances require. Its overall national concern is modernization and economic development, and its foreign policy is so crafted as to achieve such an aim within a peaceful environment, regionally and internationally.

In regional terms, China is taking steps to bring about reconciliation between the two Koreas and hence peace and stability in Northeast Asia. It is also trying to facilitate the peace process to settle the conflict in Cambodia. It has expressed willingness to settle the dispute with the other six claimants over the Spratly Islands in the South China Sea by putting aside the issue of sovereignty for the time being so that joint exploration of natural resources in the area can take place. Li Peng's visit to Vietnam in November–December 1992 helped to nurture Sino-Vietnamese relations so damaged in the past seventeen years. However, Asian neighbours are worried about China's intention to modernize its military forces and its long-term move to project its naval power.

China's increasing assertiveness in its military and foreign policies is not the only one in the Asia-Pacific region. Other countries such as Japan, South Korea and the ASEAN countries are doing the same. In general terms, the balance-of-power among the countries in the region remains quite stable despite the onset of a mini-arms race in the region,[27] while the balance-of-power between Asia as a whole and the rest of the world has tilted in favour of the former. China and Japan, the two great East Asia powers, will certainly take on a greater role in world affairs as they grow stronger.

In global terms, China is at present still a relatively weak country. Its nuclear capability, however, remains a significant qualification for its global power status. Its permanent membership of the United Nations Security Council is a trump card with which it can play sometimes to the delight of the Third World. Its sheer demographical size and potential resources remain an attraction to other countries who can ill afford to ignore the China factor or the China market in their political-economic calculations.

Provided the post-Deng leadership in Beijing remains committed to market reform and openness and is able to maintain domestic stability, it is likely that the post-Cold War era will see China increasingly reaching out beyond its regional concerns.

Notes

1. Samuel S. Kim, *China in and out of the Changing World Order* (Princeton, New Jersey: Center of International Studies, Princeton University, 1991), p. 74. See also his "China as a Regional Power," *Current History*, Vol. 91, No. 566 (September 1992), pp. 247–52.
2. Deng Xiaoping, *Fundamental Issues in Present-day China* (Beijing: Foreign Language Press, 1987), p. 98.
3. His speech to the Asia Society, New York, 1 October 1992, mimeograph, pp. 9–10. In an address hosted by the New Zealand Institute of International Affairs in Wellington on 3 December 1992, Wong said that these Chinese strategic thinkers were Chinese scholars who expressed their views at a conference in the United States in 1992. In a reply to a question about the role of Russia, Wong said that he did not think that Russia, Japan and China formed another power triangle because of the territory disputes between Russia and Japan and the problems arising along the Sino-Russian border. In a seminar on "China and the Uncertain New World Order" at the Centre for Asian Studies, University of Hong Kong, on 10 December 1992, Dr V. P. Dutt, a China specialist, thought that Russia's potential power should not be underestimated and that it has committed itself to increase its interaction with the Asia-Pacific region.
4. Economist Lester Thurow narrows this tripolar formation to the United States, Europe and Japan and calls it the new strategic triangle. See his *Head to Head: the Coming Economic Battle among Japan, Europe, and America* (New York: William Morrow and Co.), 1992.
5. For a bold projection of China's economic strength well into the next century, see the special China survey in *The Economist*, 28 November 1992.
6. *Far Eastern Economic Review* (*FEER*), 8 October 1992, p. 78.
7. *The Economist*, 3 October 1992, p. 25.

8. *Asian Wall Street Journal*, 28 July 1992, p. 8.
9. *Asiaweek*, 13 November 1992, p. 37.
10. *The Economist*, 3 October 1992, p. 25.
11. *Asiaweek*, 9 October 1992, p. 33.
12. *FEER*, 12 November 1992, p. 11.
13. *China Daily*, 6 November 1992, p. 1.
14. At the China International Trade and Investment Corporation Conference on 29 September 1992, mimeograph, p. 17.
15. *Asian Wall Street Journal*, 23–24 October 1992, p. 3.
16. This figure is obtained by projecting the 1990 GATT figures reported in *FEER*, 8 October 1992, p. 70. Considering that the intra-Western European trade amounted to a staggering figure of $1,164 billion in 1990, there is a lot of work that Asian countries can do to bolster their own intra-regional trade.
17. *Australian Financial Review*, 26 October 1992, p. 5 supplement.
18. *FEER*, 22 October 1992, pp. 53–54; 5 October 1992, pp. 13–14; *Asiaweek*, 6 October 1992, p. 30.
19. *FEER*, 22 October 1992, p. 54.
20. *Hong Kong Economic Journal*, 5 October 1992, p. 25.
21. BBC world news, 22 October 1992.
22. *Time* magazine, 12 October 1992, p. 8.
23. *The Economist*, 3 October 1992, p. 25.
24. *Ibid.*, 29 August 1992, p. 17.
25. *Australian Financial Review*, 12 October 1992, p. 38.
26. *Ming Pao* (Hong Kong), 9 September 1992, p. 30.
27. For an interesting analysis of the Asian arms race, see *Asiaweek*, 13 November 1992, pp. 28–36.

9

Relations with Taiwan

C. L. Chiou

Introduction

In 1992, China's relations with Taiwan markedly improved on economic and cultural fronts. On the political front, both sides of the Taiwan Straits tried hard, at least openly and officially in their policy pronouncements, to separate politics from economics; however, in the cold reality of long historic animosity and mistrust between the Chinese Communist Party (CCP) and Kuomintang (KMT) and despite the dramatically changed political circumstances across the Straits, "politics in command" was applied by both with equal skill but without discernable success. The political relations between the two historic antagonists advanced little in substance.

On the Chinese side, since his return to power for the third time in 1978, Deng Xiaoping had designed a master plan, so-called "one country, two systems," to achieve reunification with Taiwan. The policy was officially announced by the Standing Committee of the National People's Congress (NPC) in an open letter to Taiwan on 1 January 1979. The letter called for "*san tong*" (three links, namely commerce, air and sea transport and post communication). On 30 September 1981, Marshall Ye Jianying proposed his "nine-point" Taiwan policy, basically specifying in details Deng's "one country, two systems" model. On 26 June 1983, on the eve of the Sino-British negotiations on the future of Hong Kong, Deng held a lengthy talk with US-based Professor Winston Yang of Seton Hall College and made known his "six-point" proposal.

Since, China's political position on the reunification issue has been consistent and unchanged.

On the Taiwanese side, on 4 April 1979, President Chiang Ching-kuo had spelt out the Republic of China's (ROC) position of "*san bu*" (three nos — no talk, no contact and no compromise) policy. Taiwan's "three nos" policy was rigidly maintained until July 1985, when the ROC government was forced by increasing indirect trade across the Straits to relax its tough position and adopt a new "three nos" trade policy, namely "no contact, no encouragement but also no interference," and on 16 July 1987, shortly before his death on 13 January 1988, Chiang Ching-kuo lifted martial law that he and his father, Chiang Kai-shek, had imposed on Taiwan since 1949; and on 2 November 1987, he allowed Taiwanese residents to visit their relatives on the Chinese mainland.

On 4 May 1989, during the Tiananmen crisis, Shirley Kuo, Taiwan's Minister of Finance, led a delegation to attend the annual meeting of the Asia Development Bank in Beijing. On 7 October 1990, soon after he was re-elected President, Lee Teng-hui set up his National Unification Council to map out Taiwan's new policy towards China. The cabinet-level Mainland Affairs Council (MAC) was established on 18 October, and the semi-official Straits Exchange Foundation (SEF) which would be authorized by MAC to carry out "unoffical" contacts with the People's Republic of China (PRC) authorities to deal with "non-governmental" matters was founded on 21 November.

Finally, on 23 February 1991, Lee's National Unification Council announced its "National Unification Guidelines" in which short-, intermediate- and long-term policies towards China were clearly set down. Then on 1 May 1991, Lee officially abolished the "Temporary Provisions during the Period of Mobilization against the Communist Insurgency" and, in effect, announced that the CCP was no longer a "bandit" organization and the PRC no longer an "illegitimate" government.

To counter these dramatic changes in Taiwan, China set up its Association for Relations Across the Taiwan Straits (ARATS) to deal with Taiwan's SEF. Thus, the stage and the rules of the game had been set by the two sides to play their cat-and-mouse economic-cultural-political games across the fairly auspicious waters of the Taiwan Straits in 1992.

"Economics in Command"

Ever since the ROC government relaxed its tight control of Taiwanese businessmen's trade and investment activities in China in 1985, economic relations across the Taiwan Straits, particularly indirect trade and investment through Hong Kong, increased to such a great extent that, by the end of 1992, fears of economic dependency and potential "political blackmail" became a real worry to many people in Taiwan, including both the KMT and the Democratic Progressive Party (DPP) leaderships. In spite of the 4 June 1989 Tiananmen Incident, Taiwanese businessmen and entrepreneurs had continued to trade, invest, form joint ventures, set up factories, buy property, shares and stocks, and carry out other business operations on the mainland.

Most across-straits trade has been carried out through Hong Kong. Thus, China–Hong Kong–Taiwan economic relations have been tightly intertwined. According to Taipei's official data, in 1991 the three-way trade reached US$473 billion, about 6.6% of total world trade, and could reach US$500 billion in 1992, that would rank number four in the world.

On 19 October 1992, Kao Kung-lien, vice-chairman of Taiwan's MAC, said that in 1991 the indirect trade between Taiwan and China had amounted to US$5.6 billion, and in 1992 he expected the trade to grow to about US$7.8 billion. He also expressed the view that, other than the transshipments through Hong Kong, the trade through other entrepôts was difficult to estimate. His rough calculation was that the total indirect trade between China and Taiwan could reach US$10 billion in 1992.

According to an article witten by a *Free China Journal* staff:

> It appears that the island is now more dependent on the mainland market. Taiwan's exports to the mainland through Hong Kong surged to US$3.93 billion in the first eight months of this year. This represents 7.28 percent of Taiwan's total exports in the eight-month period, according to statistics from the Economics Ministry. Imports from the mainland, on the other hand, amounted to US$740 million or 1.56 percent of the island's total imports. The US$4.67 billion indirect two-way trade accounted for 4.6 percent of Taiwan's total foreign trade in the first eight months of this year.[1]

Exports to the mainland have assumed a greater role in Taiwan's foreign exchange earnings according to Taiwan's Board of Foreign Trade. The trade surplus over the mainland accounted for more than half of the island's US$6.98 billion global surplus in the January–September period. According to Taiwan's Central Bank of China, Taiwan's balance of international payments registered a US$2.53 billion surplus in the year's first nine months. When deducting the mainland trade surplus, the balance of payments would become a US$1.1 billion deficit.

On the investment front, the CCP Fourteenth Party Congress' new emphasis on socialist market economy has further encouraged Taiwanese investment on the mainland. Taiwanese investment in China started in 1988 and reached a new height in 1992. By October 1992, there were more than 5,000 Taiwanese investment projects in more than twenty provinces and municipalities on the mainland, which amounted to about US$4.2 billion. According to Taiwanese sources, by July 1992, China had become the third largest overseas investment destination for Taiwanese entrepreneurs.

Taiwan's ministry-level Council for Economic Planning and Development released a report in early November, showing that more than 32% of the surveyed manufacturers had investment abroad. Up to 41.9% of these overseas projects were in China while the US and Malaysia got an equal share of 22.6% each, the report said. Running against the ROC government policy of a more stable and prudent pace on mainland ventures, some 80% of Taiwan's businesses were targeting China for their overseas investment.

Taiwanese authorities watched closely the growing interest of Taiwanese businessmen in investing on the mainland, fearing that this would have a negative impact on the island's economy in the long run. Officials said that Taiwanese businessmen's so-called "mainland fever" could run out of control.

Even the Chinese government acknowledged on 14 November that the ROC officials were deeply troubled that increasing Taiwanese investment on the mainland would create "hollowing out" effect in the island state's economy. Beijing was not happy that the ROC government had warned the Taiwanese businessmen and even legally prohibited large enterprises and technology-intensive industries from investing in China. The PRC sources said that in 1988 only 200 Taiwanese enterprises had gone to the mainland and invested about US$200 million, but by November 1992, more than 5,000 enterprises had invested in twenty-four provinces and cities in China with capital totaling more than US$4 billion.

In mid-November, a SEF fact-finding team led by the foundation's deputy secretary-general, Shih Chi-ping, toured the Yangtze delta and met with Shanghai officials. It was told that Taiwan's private investment in Shanghai's stock and real estate markets had grown rapidly, with some 200 companies opening offices in Shanghai in the first nine months of 1992. In the Pudong area alone, Taiwanese investors had agreed to invest more than US$100 million. Some Taiwanese companies, one in wheat processing and one in synthetic fiber manufacturing, had decided to issue shares on the Shanghai Stock Exchange.

On 21 November, according to Shantou Special Economic Zone officials, four major Taiwanese enterprises formed a joint-venture company to build the 7,400 metre bridge linking Nan'ao and Chenghai in Guangdong province and to develop the mountain region of Nan'ao.

As early as August, the Taiwanese government began to put political pressure on some of Taiwan's largest entrepreneurs.

When Tsai Wan-lin, head of the Cathay Insurance and Construction Group, announced his intention in mid-August to launch a number of projects in China that ranged from a cement plant to property development, the government hit back sharply. Economics Vice-Minister P. K. Chang vowed to block the plan or punish Tsai if he tried to go ahead with his plans. Steering a careful course between defiance and compliance, Tsai set off on a highly publicized tour of Chinese cities to investigate market potentials, but said he would not yet test the government's resolve by launching his investment ventures.[2]

Taipei authorities also managed to block plastics tycoon Wang Yung-ching from implementing his proposed US$7 billion petrochemical project in Xiamen's Haicang, just across the Taiwan Straits. "Wang's investment would take away one third of our industrial base," claimed Ma Ying-jeou, vice-minister of MAC, adding "this we cannot permit."[3]

At the end of November, the ROC authorities further tightened Taiwan's trade and investment policies towards China. Approval of major entrepreneurs' investment applications to start up projects on the Chinese mainland would be based on how the proposed ventures would affect Taiwan's industrial stability. The new "interrelation" policy of MAC aimed at maintaining local industry's technological superiority over the mainland. To do so would also ensure the island's competitive advantage over the Chinese manufacturers and traders.

MAC's economic department Director, Chen Ming-chang, said on 26 November that the council would develop a formula for measuring a proposed mainland project's interrelation with Taiwan's industrial climate. The formula would serve as the basis for approving the mainland proposals of large Taiwanese enterprises. The approval system was the latest move by the ROC government to make sure that local firms' enthusiasm for investment in China did not rage out of control. Authorities feared that the island's manufacturing sector could become too reliant on the unpredictable Chinese economy.

MAC's action followed the 23 November announcement by Wang Yung-ching's Formosa Plastics Group that, instead of the larger Haicang project in Xiamen which it had decided to discard, it planned to build a multibillion-dollar petrochemical complex along the Yangtze River region. Many small and medium-sized Taiwanese enterprises have already set up factories on the mainland. However, large firms are capital- and technology-intensive. ROC officials felt that their funds and advanced equipment and technology could be better utilized at home to boost Taiwan's economic potential. By the end of 1992, it was still uncertain whether the government would allow Wang Yung-ching's Yangtze project to go ahead.

On 10 December, President Lee Teng-hui was forced to take a more drastic action by announcing that the ROC government would wait until 1993 when the new US President, Bill Clinton, clarified his China policy before he would decide what to do with Taiwan's mainland China investment policy. This announcement was seen by Beijing as a delaying tactic by Lee to slow down Taiwanese businessmen's gowing investment in China.

Still, according to the statistics released by Taiwan's Ministry of Finance in December, Taiwan's surplus in trade with Hong Kong, an entrepôt for across-straits trade, rose 41.6% to US$1.42 billion in November, bringing the January–November figure to US$12.4 billion. In November alone, Taiwan's transshipments to Hong Kong exceeded US$1.57 billion, accounting for one-fifth of the island's total exports. As such, the British colony had become the top source of Taiwan's trade surplus.

On 27 December, according to the figures issued by Hong Kong Customs Office, in the first ten months of 1992, the indirect trade between Taiwan and China through Hong Kong totalled more than US$6.04 billion. Thus, Hong Kong's Taipei Trade Centre estimated that the indirect across-straits trade in 1992 could reach US$7 billion. Taiwanese business sources estimated that, by including the across-straits trade that was not carried out through Hong Kong and listed by the Hong Kong Customs Office, the total indirect trade between Taiwan and China could amount to US$9–10 billion.

On 31 December, *China Times* referring to ROC government statistics said that, in spite of the slow-down of economic growth in Taiwan, the indirect trade between Taiwan and China continued to increase for the third consecutive year in 1992. According to the statistics, the across-straits trade in 1992 should reach US$7.3 billion, an annual growth of about 30%, as compared with the 1991 growth rate of 40%. In 1992, through Hong Kong, Taiwan's exports to the mainland amounted to US$6.2 billion, a growth of 35% over 1991, while imports from China reached US$1.1 billion, slightly lower than 1991, clearly due to Taiwan's mini-recession.

Clearly, the above figures, even the official ones issued by PRC or ROC authorities, are not always congruous, they are even confusing at times. Due to the complex nature of the China–Hong Kong–Taiwan triangular trade relations and the illegal nature of many trade and investment activities carried out by Taiwanese businessmen, most economists agree that the figures are on the conservative side. The real figures could be much higher than the official ones.

Cultural Contacts

Nineteen Hundred and Ninety-two was surely a busy year for the pro-unification artists, movie makers, writers, academics, scientists and other cultural workers on the two sides of the Taiwan Straits. The exchange programmes, visits, seminars, symposia and conferences carried out on both sides were just too numerous to count. The following are just some of the examples of such cultural contacts:

On 3 January, Shanghai set up its Association for Taiwan Studies which immediately called for increasing academic exchange with Taiwan. On 7 January, China's sports Minister, Wu Shaozu, called on his Taiwanese counterpart to push for more direct sport exchange programmes.

On 3 February, the well-known Chinese painter, Shi Yu, began his exhibit in Taiwan. On 9 February, the famous Dunhuang Technological Artifacts Collection was put on show in Taipei and instantly attracted large audiences. Even President Lee Teng-hui attended the exhibit.

On 3 March, the ROC government relaxed its rule and allowed Taiwan's university and college presidents to visit China. On 7 March, Taiwanese singer Wu Shih-kai began his mainland tour.

On 10 April, a science conference to discuss research and teaching cooperation attended by both Chinese and Taiwanese scientists was opened in Nanjing. On 13 April, 300 pieces of duplicates of ancient palace paintings and calligraphy, part of Taiwan's massive Palace Museum collection, were put on exhibit at Beijing's Historical Museum. On 15 April, the publisher of *Chinese Industry and Commerce Times* completed his visit to Taiwan. On 24 April, Taiwan's MAC in principle permitted student exchange programmes to be initiated between the two sides of the Straits.

On 10 May, a Taipei-Shanghai-Beijing marathon run attended by runners from both sides started in Taipei. On 13 May, the former ROC Economics Minister, Chao Yao-tung, led a group of economists to attend a conference in Beijing and to meet Chinese officials, including Premier Li Peng and General-Secretary Jiang Zemin, to discuss problems related to trade and investment issues between China and Taiwan. On 31 May, a Chinese physics conference attended by Taiwanese scientists was convened in Beijing.

On 8 June, the first group of seven eminent Chinese scientists and their spouses, including Tan Jiazhen, an internationally renowned genetic scientist, to visit Taiwan arrived in Taipei and began meeting Taiwanese scientists led by Wu Ta-yu, president of the Academia Sinica. In addition to meeting Wu's people, the Chinese scientists also held seminars at National Taiwan University and other institutions. Five of the seven scientists were members of the CCP, who would have been banned from coming to Taiwan previously. On this occasion, due to the pressure put on the ROC government by Professor Li Yüan-che, a Nobel prize winner in chemistry, an exception was made. On arriving in Taipei, the Chinese scientists called on the scientists on both sides to cooperate in their work to create a brighter future for the Chinese people. They said that science and politics should be separated. They, however, urged that direct air and sea links between China and Taiwan be established as soon as possible.

On 30 June, a group of Taiwanese academics, including Auyang Hsün, former president of National Chengchi University, on a study tour on the mainland met and held talks with Vice-Premier Wu Xueqian. During the meeting, Wu Xueqian, as one of the top leaders in charge of the CCP united front work, told the group that the most urgent task facing both sides was to start CCP-KMT Party-to-party talks on the peaceful national reunification issue. He said, "when we sit down and talk, everything can be raised, including the questions of national flags and names." He, however, stressed that such talks had to be carried out in accordance with the principles of "one China" and "one country, two systems." He was adamant that China would refuse to sign any mutual non-aggression treaty with Taiwan. He said that under the principle of "one China" there was no possibility of signing such a treaty and Taiwan's raising such an issue was totally useless.

Auyang Hsün expressed the view that although Wu's showing flexibility on the flag and name questions was interesting, his proposal on CCP-KMT talks, insistence on "one China" and "one country, two systems" and unwillingness to recognize Taiwan as an equal political entity and to sign a non-aggression pact between the two governments still showed how little Wu really knew of the political reality in Taiwan.[4]

On 2 July, for the first time, a group of eighty Taiwanese travellers was allowed to fly, via Manila but on the same plane, to Xiamen and then obtained their entry visa at the Xiamen airport. The exercise was regarded as an attempt to create a "direct" air link between China and Taiwan. According to the ROC law, this trip was illegal. However, the Taiwanese authorities did not stop it.

On the same day, Vice-Premier Wu Xueqian again met another group of Taiwanese academics, led by Professor Chu Hsin-min. He suggested that the two sides should start out with one of the "three transportation links" first, such as the postal communication. He again reiterated China's unyielding position on "one China" and arms sales by the US and France to Taiwan. He also refused to accept Taiwan's "dual recognition" proposal in which countries would simultaneously set up diplomatic relations with Beijing and Taipei. He pointed out that the KMT's "National Unification Guidelines" made a mistake by putting the "three transportation links" in its second "intermediate," rather than first "short-term," stage.[5]

Between 2–4 August, the second conference on "Straits Relations" was held in Beijing. Many former ROC officials, including Professor Shaw Yu-ming (former government spokesman), Professor Chang Chien-han (former minister without portfolio) and Professor Chao Ching-chi (former vice-minister of education) attended the conference.

On 22–24 August, more than 200 Taiwanese economists, scientists, technologists, industrialists, bankers and businessmen, led by Liu Tai-ying, director of the Taiwan Institute of Economics, with their Chinese counterparts held a large "Conference on Cooperation and Exchange of Industry, Science and Technology" at the People's Great Hall on Tiananmen Square. On 22 August, Liu and some of his colleagues met with President Yang Shangkun and were reported to have been involved in a heated debate on the unification question. Yang reportedly told Liu, a confidant of President Lee Teng-hui, that Lee should curb the rising voice of Taiwan independence advocates and open up more contacts with the mainland. Liu responded by asking China to stop isolating Taiwan in the international community. Liu said that the PRC's attempts at isolating Taiwan and its continued threat to use force to attain national reunification had only further alienated the Taiwanese people and given the Taiwan independence advocates more legitimacy. Liu urged Yang to accept Taiwan's "National Unification Guidelines" as a basis for improving relations across the Taiwan Straits. Yang was reportedly not happy with Liu's views, and the exchange turned rather nasty. On 26 August, Liu also met with Premier Li Peng.[6]

On 5 September, the first officially invited group of eighteen Chinese journalists flew into Taipei, via Hong Kong, to begin their reporting activities. With the arrangement of the SEF, they were able to carry out a series of interviews, including rare interviews with Marshall Chang Hsüeh-liang, the principal actor of the 1936 Xi'an Incident, and Ch'en Li-fu, one of the KMT's elder statesmen. On 14 September, after the journalists had completed their "work" and returned to China, *Renmin ribao* published a special commentary on the event, "Open the Two-Way Exchange Door between the Two Sides of the Straits." The article praised the Taiwan government for allowing such a media exchange. It pointed out that since

1987 about 2,000 Taiwanese journalists had toured the mainland, but, other than the eighteen, only two Chinese journalists and one newspaper publisher had been allowed into Taiwan. It called on the Taiwanese authorities to allow more media people to report on events taking place in the island.

On 29 October, Li Ruihuan, a CCP Politburo member in charge of ideological work, met Taiwanese and Hong Kong journalists and journalism scholars who were attending a conference on "Asia-Pacific Print Media, Science and Technology and Social Development" in Beijing. He told Taiwanese media representatives that it would be possible for Taiwanese news media to set up branch offices in China and to go into joint ventures with Chinese counterparts to publish newspapers or journals in the mainland. Li was reported to have also said that China would never lessen its opposition to Taiwan independence and would stop such a separatist movement even if they had to "spill blood." The report of Li's words was widely circulated and created a political storm even at the top of the KMT. At a KMT Central Standing Committee meeting, Lee Teng-hui reportedly told the committee members that it was wrong for some media and some people in Taiwan to use Chinese Communist threats to scare the Taiwanese people.[7]

On 29 October, more than fifty artists from Shanghai's famous *Kun Ju* Theatre Group began their performance tour in Taiwan. However, due to his official NPC deputy status, one of the principal actors was not allowed to enter Taiwan.

On 12 November, the ROC's MAC decided at an extraordinary council meeting to push for more cultural and educational exchanges with mainland China and to expedite the implementation of more than 100 proposals for private exchange. MAC held its first mainland affairs conference in September, when a total of 375 propositions were approved, setting a new direction in across-straits exchange. They included: setting up an across-straits crime-prevention hotline; relaxing the qualifications and quotas for mainland spouses to Taiwanese residents to relocate in Taiwan; drafting a regulation allowing the introduction of mainland Chinese manufacturing technologies into Taiwan; permitting Taiwan's financial institutions to remit funds directly to mainland China; simplifying entry procedures for mainland reporters; building a mainland information and research institution; allowing certain government personnel to conduct fact-finding missions on the mainland; and setting up the "China Development Funds" to promote across-straits cultural exchanges.

On 13 November, a Taiwanese official source said that, from January to October 1992, more than 1.2 million individual trips were made by Taiwanese residents to the Chinese mainland. Since November 1987, when the ROC government allowed the mainland trips, more than 4 million visits had been made. The Taiwanese visitors had also spent more than US$10 billion on their mainland tours, including gifts to their relatives in China.

On 23 November, for the first time, a conference on law was held in Taipei and was attended by eleven distinguished Chinese legal scholars, including Chen Guangzhong, head of the University of Law and Politics. Issues of legal education, property ownership, contract, intellectual property, company law, taxation law and other legal problems between the two sides of the Taiwan Straits were discussed by the legal experts.

Between 28 November to 5 December, invited by Taiwan's Centre for Mainland China Studies, four senior researchers from the Institute of Taiwan Studies, Xiamen University, led by its director, Chen Kangli, were in Taiwan to attend conferences and seminars and to exchange views with Taiwanese scholars. This was the first time these Chinese Taiwan specialists were able to carry out field trips in Taiwan.

On 12 December, a fifteen-member team of movie makers and stars led by the famous movie director, Xie Jin, was for the first time invited to attend the official "Golden Horse" (Taiwan's Oscar) award presentation ceremony. During the visit, they also carried out a series of exchange programmes with Taiwanese movie makers.

From 25 to 28 December, a conference on industrial development policies in China and Taiwan was held in Xiamen. More than thirty Chinese economists and industrialists led by Liu Guoguang, Vice-President of the Chinese Academy of Social Sciences, and more than twenty Taiwanese industrial policy experts led by Yu Chung-hsien, Director of Taiwan's Chinese Institute of Economics, attended the meeting. The conference dealt with the developmental problems of high-technology industry, energy and mineral industry and other economic and industrial matters.

Finally, China Travel Services in Hong Kong revealed on 31 December that in 1992 more than 1.5 million entry permits were issued to Taiwanese residents, as compared with 994,000 in 1991, an increase of more than 50%. According to the news release, more than 90% of the Taiwanese travellers were tourists and businessmen and two-thirds were aged between twenty and fifty. Taiwanese visitors had thus become the largest tourist group to the mainland, accounting for one-third of the total number of foreign travellers in China.

Although only in a brief chronological form, the list above is impressive enough to show how far the cultural exchange programmes between China and Taiwan developed in 1992. There was a widely circulated joke in Taiwan that some pro-unification defence scientists had actually suggested that Taiwanese nuclear scientists should carry out cooperative work with their Chinese counterparts to develop Taiwan's nuclear weaponry.

Still, it must be pointed out that just as the reported confrontation between Professor Liu Tai-ying and President Yang Shangkun and the reported disagreement between Vice-Premier Wu Xueqian and Professor Auyang Hsün, cultural and academic exchanges between the two sides were certainly not immune to "political interference." Although both sides claimed to be willing to separate cultural and political issues, both sides were equally guilty of often committing the "crime" of "politics in command."

"Politics in Command"

In spite of "political interference" at times, both economic and cultural relations between China and Taiwan in 1992 certainly advanced and improved remarkably. It was in the political arena that both sides failed to achieve any meaningful breakthrough. In fact, in 1992, due to the tension created by US sales of F-16 fighters and French sales of Mirage 2000-5 jets to Taiwan and South Korea's severing diplomatic relations with the ROC and setting up official ties with the PRC, the political relations between China and Taiwan deteriorated to some extent.

As already mentioned above, the Chinese political position on Taiwan had been clearly spelt out in Ye Jianying's and Deng Xiaoping's "one country, two systems" statements as early as 1981 and 1983. What Ye and Deng had said and what was contained in October 1992 in Jiang Zemin's political report to the Fourteenth CCP Party Congress on the Taiwan question were fundamentally the same.

Before 1992, on the other hand, Taiwan's China policy had been ideologically confusing to say the least. It had been so anachronistic that no one had really taken it seriously. Even when Lee Teng-hui set up his National Unification Council, MAC and SEF in 1991, not many people knew exactly what were their constitutional or legal bases and what they could and would do. Many people, especially the DPP, simply regarded them as another set of anachronistic institutions set up by the KMT to fool the Taiwanese people.

However, on 10 May 1992, Cheyne Chiu, the ROC presidential spokesman, indicated a change of tone at a MAC conference on the "National Unification Guidelines" (that had been adopted on 23 February 1991). Chiu proposed to sign a "mutual non-aggression treaty" with the PRC, similar to the one signed between West and East Germany two decades earlier; at once the KMT China policy as spelt out in the "Guidelines" began to be looked at more favourably and taken more seriously. The political intention of the KMT government to attain political recognition for Taiwan as a political entity equal with China before "three transportation links" could be established, as specified in the "short-term" goals of the "Guidelines," became a clearer, firmer and more acceptable policy stand to the Taiwanese people.

Yang Shangkun responded ten days later and officially rejected the proposal. He reportedly said that, if China accepted the non-aggression treaty, it would amount to recognizing two governments. He stressed that any talks between the two sides that were regarded as talks between two governments would not be acceptable to China.[8]

On 19 June, Niger's Foreign Minister, Hamidou Diallo, and the ROC Vice-foreign Minister, John Chang, signed an agreement in Taipei to resume diplomatic relations between the two countries after an eighteen-year break. On 28 June, an *Agence France-Presse* report said that, because of pressure from Beijing which also had formal ties with Niger, a tiny African nation, the Niger Government had backed out of the deal forged nine days earlier. However, on 29 June, Niger's Prime Minister, Amadou Cheffou, denied the report and reconfirmed the resumed ties with Taiwan. Although the ROC Foreign Minister, Frederic Chien, announced on 29 June that, when Taiwan and Niger resumed diplomatic relations, Taiwan did not ask Niger to sever its official ties with China, thus officially acknowledging Taiwan's new position on "dual recognition," the PRC immediately declared its displeasure and broke off diplomatic relations with Niger.

On 8 July, *Renmin ribao* (overseas edition) attacked Taiwan's "National Unification Guidelines" and accused Taiwan's attempts at creating an "equal political entity" and "coexistence in international community" as violating the "one China" principle. It pointed out that Taiwan's plot to have separation before reunification would not work and that the attempt was in essence a Taiwan independence scheme.

Although both the CCP and KMT talked about the principle of "one China," clearly both sides meant different "Chinas." After a great deal of confusion and debate, finally on 1 August, Taiwan's National Unification Council produced its version of "one China," basically reiterating the KMT position that their "one China" was the "Republic of China," not the "People's Republic of China" and their "national unification" was to be attained under a "free, capitalist, prosperous and democratic China." On 27 August, in an interview with the New China News Agency, an official from ARATS rejected the proposal from Taiwan to discuss the issue of the "meaning of one China." He said that China did not agree with Taiwan's interpretation of "one China." He reiterated China's policy of opposition to "two Chinas," "one China, one Taiwan," and "two equal political entities." He said that, when his ARATS met Taiwan's SEF, they should accept the basic principle of "one China" without questioning the meaning of "one China." He expressed the Chinese wishes that, after accepting the principle of "one China," they should proceed to deal with the general non-political matters between the two sides.

The PRC was to win its biggest diplomatic victory, and the ROC to lose its most important cold-war anti-Communist ally, on 24 August, when South Korea's Foreign Minister arrived in Beijing to sign an agreement of normalization of relations with the PRC Foreign Minister. On 23 August, Taiwan was told by South Korea about this diplomatic blow; Taipei immediately announced its break of official ties with Seoul and severed its air link with South Korea. Although Taiwan managed to increase the number of countries that recognized the ROC to thirty-one in 1992, the countries such as Niger, Vanuatu and Grenada were poor and small, and the loss of South Korea left Taiwan with only South Africa as a country of international importance.

The ROC and South Korea had been staunch anti-Communist allies since 1950 when the bloody Korean War had started. The end of the cold war with the collapse of Communism in the former Soviet Union and Eastern Europe was seized quickly by the South Koreans as a chance to set up economic-political ties with their former ideological and political enemies. Taiwan, still under "military" threat from the PRC across the Taiwan Straits, reacted more slowly and could not accept the swift change in Seoul's foreign policy. Thus, Taipei was bitterly disappointed and angered by South Korea's "betrayal," especially since Taipei was given notice only one day before the switch in diplomatic recognition and was not given enough time to take care of its valuable embassy building and other real estate properties.[9]

In August, the General Agreement on Tariffs and Trade (GATT) issue became dominant. On 28 August, Chinese trade officials said that Beijing had reached a policy decision that the two sides of the Taiwan Straits should simultaneously join GATT although the PRC application should be dealt with first and Taiwan should be admitted according to the "Olympic formula" by using the name of "Chinese Taipei." Taiwan, on the other hand, wanted to join GATT under the name of "Separate Customs Territory of Taiwan, Penghu, Kinmen and Matsu." In Chinese, "separate" here was literally translated to mean "independent." Again, the PRC tried to foil Taiwan's attempt to have any "separate" or "independent" wording in its name in international affairs.

In early October, the ROC was informed that the GATT had granted it observer status as a separate customs territory. However, Taiwan was annoyed that, under PRC pressure, the name "Chinese Taipei" was also used, and it was placed on the level of a colony, the same as Hong Kong and Macau. Hong Kong and Macau joined GATT with the recommendations of Britain and Portugal respectively, based on GATT's Article 26. Their highest officials stationed in GATT are thus referred to as "permanent representatives" and not "ambassadors," as is the case for sovereign nations.

GATT's "Statement by Council Chairman, Ambassador B. K. Zutshi, on Access of Chinese Taipei, Agenda Item No. 2" decided by the GATT Council of Representatives meeting on 29 September stated:

> I have carried out extensive consultations during recent months on the subject of establishing a working party to consider the possible accession to the GATT of Chinese Taipei, in GATT known as the Separate Customs Territory of Taiwan, Penghu, Kinmen and Matsu (hereafter referred to as "Chinese Taipei").
>
> All contracting parties acknowledge the view that there is only one China, as also expressed in the United Nations.
>
> General Assembly's Resolution 2758 of October 25, 1971. Many contracting parties, therefore, agree with the view of the People's Republic of China (PRC) that Chinese Taipei, as a separate customs territory, should not accede to the GATT before the PRC. Some contracting parties do not share this view. There is, however, a general desire to establish a working party for Chinese Taipei.[10]

Relations with Taiwan 9.17

Taiwan was not happy with this decision but had no choice but to accept. The people in Taiwan again saw this as a political interference in purely economic affairs by China to "Hongkongize" and isolate Taiwan in the international community.

In the midst of his tense presidential campaign and under pressure from the US economic recession, President George Bush announced on 4 September that the US would sell 150 F-16 fighter aircraft to Taiwan. After having sought to buy the advanced jet fighters for more than a decade, naturally, Taiwan was delighted, while China reacted angrily and lodged an immediate protest. The ROC Defence Minister, Chen Li-an was quoted as saying, "Washington's decision is not only a major political breakthrough but will also ensure the security of Taiwan and the Asia-Pacific region." The Chinese Vice-foreign Minister, Liu Huaqing, on the other hand, summoned the US Ambassador, J. Stapleton Roy, to tell him that, despite many approaches by the PRC government, the US still went ahead to make the sales, thus in total violation of the "17 August" (1982) Sino-US Communiqué, rudely interfering in Chinese internal affairs, seriously damaging Sino-US relations, and interfering with and hurting China's peaceful reunification work. Liu further warned that Bush's decision would "inevitably cause negative impact on Sino-US cooperation in the United Nations and other international organizations." "Pending a reversal of this decision by the US side, China would find it difficult to stay in the meeting of the five (permanent members of the United Nations Security Council) on arms control issue."[11]

Although *Renmin ribao* continued to blast the US decision for four consecutive days, 4–7 September, other than strong rhetoric, there was in *realpolitik* terms little China could do to retaliate, because the Sino-US economic ties had developed rapidly in favour of China and Beijing needed to have the most-favoured-nation trade status from the US government. On 15 September, the US State Department was informed by Beijing that China was boycotting multilateral talks on arms control in the Middle East which began in Moscow that day.

To make the situation worse for China, long negotiations between Taipei and Paris on sales of sixty French Mirage 2000-5 fighters were also on the verge of fruition. Although the US might have put some pressure on Taiwan not to buy the Mirages, the deal eventually went ahead and was approved by the French government on 10 September. In spite of the fact that at the same time China had quietly purchased advanced SU29 jet fighters from Russia, Beijing reacted even more violently to the French case.

On 23 December, to show its rage, Beijing closed down the French Consulate-General in Guangzhou. The Sino-French relations had thus hit the bottom since diplomatic relations were established between the two nations more than three decades before.

On 25 September, China denounced a US plan to sell twelve anti-submarine helicopters to Taiwan and warned Washington of serious consequences if it did not revoke the plan. The verbal protests from Beijing was to continue for the rest of the year.

Another case of economic-political mix-up was the membership of the Asia-Pacific Cooperation (APEC). On 9 September, the PRC Foreign Minister, Qian Qichen, refused to countenance the ROC's presence as a member with equal status (according to the rules of the Cooperation) at the proposed APEC summit. Taiwan, China and Hong Kong were simultaneously inducted into the regional trade body last November. The Chinese government allowed Taiwan to enter as an equal entity under the name "Chinese Taipei" but did not want it to appear that any Taiwanese government leader attending an APEC summit would rank equally with Beijing representatives. Australian Foreign Minister Gareth Evans had been soliciting support for such an APEC summit meeting to bring together high ranking heads of member states. ROC Economics Minister Vincent Siew, attending a high-level 10–11 September APEC ministerial forum in Bangkok, said Taipei was not assuming any special stance in regard to the proposed summit "as long as the ROC is treated equally," and he would only consider the best interests of Taiwan, if Evans approached him on the subject. Siew said the main task of his delegation at the Bangkok conference was to conduct bilateral talks with ministers of the US, Canada, Australia, New Zealand, Japan and the ASEAN nations. He said he did not anticipate any talks with Chinese APEC representatives. Beijing's Foreign Minister was quoted as saying he would not exchange views with Taipei officials on any substantive issues.

After some months of studies, Taiwan's MAC finally issued its long-awaited report on "Issues and Prospects of Direct Transportation Links across the Taiwan Straits" on 13 September. The report stated that the ROC was not opposed to opening direct air and sea links with the Chinese mainland. It said, however, that such direct transportation links would be established when, and only when, the Chinese Communists renounced the threat of force against Taiwan and recognized the ROC as an equal political entity.

Again, clearly based on its "National Unification Guidelines," Taiwan was using economic issues to attain political goals. It was a kind of "politics in command." Like their counterparts on the mainland, the Taiwanese political elite had learnt to play the same political game, and the more they played, it seems, the better they became at it.

Thus, on 18 September, Taiwan convened its "Mainland Affairs Conference." Premier Hau Pei-tsun in the opening speech said that the security and welfare of Taiwan and Taiwanese people was the foundation on which Taiwan's economic, political and other developments were based. He also urged ROC officials to work hard to cause "changes" on the Chinese mainland to make the life of Chinese people more and more liberalized and democratized, exactly the notion of "peaceful evolution" that the Dengists disliked most. The Chairman of MAC, Huang K'un-hui, in his speech, declared that "peaceful and democratic reunification" was the only way to reunify the nation. He said that, during the process of reunification, although Taiwan wanted to coexist peacefully, even compete peacefully, with China, they had to be aware of the Chinese united front policy and military threat. He called on the Taiwanese people to be vigilant and oppose China's strategic moves to "annex Taiwan in fact, while using peaceful reunification only as a pretext."

Taiwan's chief of the National Security Bureau, Sung Hsin-lien, used even stronger terms in his warning that the CCP was applying their "one country, two systems" model to make Taiwan "politically illegitimate, economically hollowed, internally divided and externally isolated."

In his political report to the Fourteenth Party Congress entitled "Accelerating the Reform, the Opening up to the Outside World and the Drive for Modernization, so as to Achieve Greater Successes in Building Socialism with Chinese Characteristics," General Secretary Jiang Zemin touched on the question of Taiwan only briefly:

> We have put forward the creative concept of "one country, two systems" — the proposition that, on the premise that there is only one China, for a long time to come the main part of the country should adhere to socialist system while Hong Kong, Macau and Taiwan maintain their original capitalist system. In accordance with this principle, we shall work for the peaceful reunification of the motherland.
>
> To accomplish the reunification of the motherland is in the fundamental interest of the Chinese nation, and it is the common aspiration of the entire

> Chinese people, including our compatriots in Taiwan, Hong Kong and Macau and those residing overseas. We shall work steadfastly for the great cause, adhering to the principles of peaceful reunification and the "one country, two systems...." Taiwan is an intergal part of the sacred territory of China. We absolutely oppose in any form the notion of "two Chinas," "one China, one Taiwan," "one country, two governments" and any acts aimed at bringing about the independence of Taiwan. We shall continue to work for direct links for postal, air and shipping services and trade between the two sides of the Taiwan Straits and to promote people-to-people exchanges and cooperation in various fields. In particular, we shall work for greatly expanded economic cooperation between the two sides in an effort to revitalize the economy of the whole nation.[12]

Then, he went on to call:

> We reiterate that the Chinese Communist Party is ready to establish contact with the Chinese Kuomintang at the earliest possible date to create conditions for the talks on officially ending the state of hostility between the two sides of the Taiwan Straits and gradually realizing peaceful reunification. Representatives from other parties, mass organizations and all circles on both sides of the Taiwan Straits could be invited to joint in such talks. On the premise that there is only one China, we are prepared to talk with the Taiwan authorities about any matter, including the form that official negotiations should take, a form that would be acceptable to both sides. We hope that the Taiwan authorities will comply with the wishes of the people and help remove the artificial obstacles to the reunification of the motherland, as to make it possible for relations between the two sides to enter a new stage of development.[13]

Political Impasse

Although Taiwan had been relaxing its regulations to allow more economic and cultural contacts with China, the KMT was not able to accept the CCP proposal to hold Party-to-party talks under the principle of Dengist "one country, two systems," in which no matter how generous Deng had sounded in allowing the capitalist socio-political systems in Taiwan to continue, Taiwan would be only a special administrative region, a local government, of the PRC. Taiwan would allow direct *"san tong"* to take place but would do so only after China recognized Taiwan as an equal political entity, a separate government, and stopped threatening a military solution. Thus, Lee Teng-hui's "one country, two governments" model was an anathema to Deng's "one country, two systems."

In Lee's "National Unification Guidelines," to make China politically recognize Taiwan as an equal entity and cease military threat to attain peaceful and friendly relations was the goal for the first "short-term" stage. "*San tong*" was the goal for the second "intermediate" stage that could be pursued and achieved only after the goals of the first stage were achieved. Peace talks to discuss reunification had to wait for the last "long-term" stage. In 1992, Taiwan was only at its first stage of "national unification."

In addition, although both KMT and CCP agreed on the principle of "one China," their interpretations of or meanings for "one China" were different. The KMT's "one China" was the ROC, not the PRC. On the other hand, China liked to keep the meanings of "one China" purposely blurred, to avoid dealing with the ROC government as an equal political entity, to isolate and to prevent Taiwan from getting any international political recognition, but to welcome with open arms increasing economic and cultural exchanges with Taiwan, to give Taiwanese industrialists and businessmen every opportunity and every help to invest and trade on the mainland and, then, skilfully applying pressure, to force Taiwan into initiating and accepting "*san tong*" and CCP-KMT Party-to-party contacts and talks. In short, in 1992, the CCP wanted to force the KMT into Lee Teng-hui's second-, even third-stage "national unification" game, without really wanting to go through the sticky first stage.

Both of them played "one China" card, but without an agreement on what "one China" meant. Both of them played the "politics in command" game, but the rules, the procedures of the game were different, and even the basic nature of the game was not the same.

Thus, the demarcation between political and non-political matters was extremely difficult, if not totally impossible. For instance, on the question of direct air link, since the 1990 Beijing Asian Games, the issue had been discussed almost every time the two sides had met, yet no solution was in sight. On 30 September, a *Free China Journal* article declared:

> Before travellers on both sides of the Straits complain any further, we should point out that there are serious political considerations that need to be addressed before direct flights can be introduced. The ROC government does not enjoy having people make pointless detours, turning a normal three-hour flight into a two-day trip. Rather, it is the Chinese Communist authorities who, when addressing the issue of establishing direct sea and air links between the mainland and Taiwan, have expressed little willingness to recognize the ROC government's due political status. A spokesman for the Chinese Communist State Council's Taiwan Office last week made Beijing's first

official comments on a booklet, published ten days earlier by the ROC's Mainland Affairs Council, which detailed Taipei's position on the direct transportation issue. The spokesman accused Taipei of attempting to create "political obstacles" in talks over direct links by demanding that Beijing first treat the ROC as an existing political entity on an equal footing with Beijing. The fact, as ROC authorities have repeatedly pointed out, is that since 1949 when the Communists overrun the mainland, Beijing and Taipei have been two separate political entities on an equal footing. That is the only fact that Taipei is asking Beijing to recognize. The establishment of direct transportation links between Taiwan and China, or between any two other political entities in the world, is a political issue, no matter how strongly Beijing denies it.

To see how complicated and how difficult were the political games they had been playing, one needed only to take a look at the ongoing deadlock of negotiations on verification of documents between the two "united front" organization, China's ARATS and Taiwan's SEF. In spite of the facts that more than four million trips to China had been made by Taiwanese residents since 1987, and more than US$7 billion (a conservative figure) indirect trade was done across the Taiwan Straits and more than US$4 billion (also conservative) investment was made by Taiwanese businessmen in 1992 alone, by the end of 1992, there was still no official procedures and regulations acceptable to both Bejing and Taipei authorities on how to verify legal documents, such as marriage licenses, birth certificates, business contracts, property ownerships, court decisions, government papers, etc. The situation was ludicrous to say the least.

Both sides, of course, recognized the serious nature of the problem. However, due to the "official" or "governmental" nature of the documents that needed to be verified, since the two sides could not recognize each other as legitimate governments of their respective domains, the legal dilemmas they faced were neither domestic nor international, thus they were totally powerless, or simply not ready, to deal with the crux of the matter and settle their differences.

On 21 January 1992, in a well orchestrated press interview by *Remin ribao*, the "responsible person" of China's Documents Verification Association expressed the urgent need for finding a way to verify the increasing number of documents that had to be verified to facilitate the increasing economic, cultural and other exchanges between the two sides of the Taiwan Straits. However, for the first half of the year, although both sides did raise the issue many times and the preliminary low-level meetings between the two semi-official "united front" organizations, ARATS and SEF, did take place, no progress was made.

In desperation, on 6 August, ARATS Chairman Wang Daohan, a former mayor of Shanghai, sent a warm personal letter to his counterpart in Taiwan, SEF Chairman Ku Chen-fu, an influential member of the KMT Central Standing Committee, asking him to hold a meeting to exchange views on trade and other "general matters," presumably including the deadlocked talks on documents verification. Ku responded favourably to the invitation but was not keen about Beijing as the venue for such a high-level meeting and was not sure about when the meeting could be held.

On 27 August, a "responsible person" for ARATS gave an interview to the New China News Agency, rejected Taiwan's proposal to discuss the question of the "meaning of one China," saying that China did not agree with Taiwan's interpretation of "one China," and instead, invited once more SEF to hold talks on non-political "general matters." Again, the Chinese were evidently trying to avoid the issue.

Finally, on 17 September, SEF Secretary General Chen Jung-chieh, went to Xiamen, via Kinmen, rather than Hong Kong, to meet his counterpart, ARATS General Secretary Zou Zhekai, to hold talks on the procedure of sending back Chinese illegal workers and visitors and on the long delayed decision on how to certify documents between the two sides. No progress on the latter was made.

More than one month later, from 28 to 30 October, both sides finally held a "real working meeting" in Hong Kong to discuss the documents verification question. Afterwards, the Chinese side said that, although both sides could not agree on how to deal with the interpetation of "one China," they had made some gain in the area of documents verification. However, Taiwan's official MAC did not think they had made any headway. It said the two-day meeting ended without any agreements after Chinese representatives persisted on discussing political matters. MAC pointed out that issues involving documents verification were general affairs that the two agencies could tackle without touching on political issues. "The Chinese Communists attempted to achieve a breakthrough of their so-called 'one country, two systems' tactics by insisting on discussing the 'one China' principle," said MAC. "It was an obvious cover-up of a political blackmail."[14]

The Taiwanese said that the meeting in Hong Kong between the representatives of SEF and ARATS was the second time this year they had tried to find out ways to deal with general "civilian" matters, particularly the process of verification of documents necessary in cross-straits non-official exchanges. They claimed the Chinese had wrecked the talks.

On 17 December, on the anniversary of the establishment of ARATS, SEF Chairman Ku Chen-fu said that the two organizations had not done enough to serve the people on the two sides of the Taiwan Straits. He urged the two sides to do more but indicated that the long-awaited meeting between him and Wang Daohan would have to wait until 1993. He said that, before such a meeting could take place, general non-governmental issues, such as the verification of documents, had to be settled and regular communication channels set up.

Conclusion

Thus, the end of 1992 did not bring about the most important "political" encounter, the Ku-Wang meeting, between the two historic antagonists across the Taiwan Straits. Had the Ku-Wang meeting officially taken place, whether in Beijing or Singapore, it would have been the political *coup* of the year for the CCP and KMT as well as for the pro-unification people on both sides of the Straits. Although it would have been only a high-level semi-official contact, it would have had profound political implications.

After Taiwan's 19 December Legislative Yuan elections in which the opposition DPP won 36% of the votes — regarded by most political commentators as both a moral and political victory[15] — the political ecology in the island state became more democratized, and a two-party system emerged to become a political reality. China's proposition for CCP-KMT Party-to-party reunification talks consequently became less and less relevant and attractive. Taiwan's "one China" concept was also inevitably further complicated by this momentous development. Deng Xioaping's "one country, two systems" not only did not gain much support in Taiwan in 1992 but probably began to lose some of its limited appeal in the aftermath of the elections.

In 1992, economic and cultural relations across the Taiwan Straits improved remarkably. With marked successes, China encouraged more trade and investments from Taiwan and supported more cultural, from art and sport to scientific and technological, exchanges. Taiwan, on the other hand, tried to control "mainland fever" and discourage Taiwanese businessmen and entrepreneurs from trading and investing too much on the mainland, but with only limited success.

Both CCP and KMT played "politics in command" games and wanted to use their economic muscles: abundant raw material and cheap labour and huge market on the Chinese side and, on the Taiwanese side, advanced technology and abundant capital and business knowhow; to attain their respective political goals, in the long run a "one country, two systems" reunification for the Chinese, an immediate recognition of Taiwan as an equal political entity for the Taiwanese. In these complex political games, both sides fared poorly in 1992, because what China wanted Taiwan could not give, while what Taiwan wanted China could not deliver either. Some political commentators even concluded that on the political front, in 1992, the relations between the two sides of the Taiwan Straits had not only had no improvement but had in fact suffered some setback.[16] The relations were certainly at a serious political stalemate, which would require a great deal of political wisdom in 1993 to break.

Epilogue

According to a *Far Eastern Economic Review* article (14 January 1993, pp. 10–11), in a dramatic policy shift, China had decided to invite the Taiwan government to hold direct official talks on the reunification of the island with the mainland. Beijing's new policy was to be announced by Jiang Zemin in late December 1992 but had been postponed at the last minute, because the Chinese leaders had judged "the timing to be premature." Now, it was expected that Beijing would make the offer within the next couple of months.

However, Taipei officials in charge of mainland affairs said they were unaware of Beijing's change of heart and insisted that the offer would be credible only if it was made public. Such scepticism arose from the fact that in the forty-four years of acrimonious confrontation across the Taiwan Straits, Beijing had steadfastly refused to recognize Taiwan as a separate equal political entity. "I would be sceptical," said Ma Ying-jeou, Vice-Minister of the MAC. According to Ma, China's past refusal to hold government-to-government talks was based on the fact that the talks would "legitimatize" Taiwan as a separate, even independent, political entity, thus creating "one China, one Taiwan," "one country, two governments," or simply "two Chinas," a political situation totally in contradiction with

Deng Xiaoping's "one China" principle and "one country, two systems" formula.

Notes

1. Song Su-feng, "Mainland Still Hot Investment Spot," *Free China Journal*, 20 November 1992; see also Julian Baum, "Flags Follow Trade," *Far Eastern Economic Review (FEER)*, 17 September 1992, pp. 20–21; Lincoln Kaye, "Myopic Vision: Lack of Direction Marks China's Attitude to Taiwan," *FEER*, 17 September 1992, p. 22.
2. Carl Goldstein, "The Bottom Line: Taiwan Capital, Factories Pour into China," *FEER*, 17 September 1992, p. 23.
3. *Ibid.*
4. For details on this debate, see *China Times*, 1 July 1992.
5. *China Times*, 3 July 1992.
6. *China Times*, 25, 26, 27 August 1992.
7. *United Daily News*, 30 October 1992; *China Times*, 30, 31 October 1992.
8. For more details, see *Wen Wei Po* (Hong Kong), 30 May 1992.
9. *China Times*, 24, 25 August 1992.
10. *Foreign China Journal*, 2 October 1992.
11. For more details on arms sales, see Julian Baum, "A Foot in the Door: US Decision Opens New Options to Taiwan Military," *FEER*, 17 September 1992, pp. 12–13; Susumu Awanohara and Julian Baum, "Pork Barrel Roll," *FEER*, 17 September 1992, pp. 12–13. For China's strong reaction, see also "Proposed F-16 Sale Draws Strong Protest" and "A Grave Move to Sabotage Sino-US Relations," *Beijing Review*, 14–20 September 1992, pp. 4–5; "US Prepared Fighters Sale Criticized," *Beijing Review*, 21–27 September 1992, p. 4; Zhang Xiaodong, "US Jet Sales Denounced Worldwide," *Beijing Review*, 21–27 September 1992, p. 11; "China Won't Attend Arms Control Talks," *Beijing Review*, 28 September–4 October 1992, p. 8.
12. *Beijing Review*, 26 October–1 November 1992. pp. 31–32.
13. *Ibid.*, p. 32.
14. *Foreign China Journal*, 10 November 1992.
15. "Taiwan Breaks the Mould," *The Economist*, 26 December 1992–8 January 1993, pp. 27–28; Julian Baum, "The Hollow Centre: Poll Result Undermines President's Power," *FEER*, 7 January 1993, pp. 14–15.
16. For details, see a series of articles on China published by *China Times*, 1–6 January 1993.

10

China's Relations with Hong Kong

Jane C. Y. Lee

Introduction

Since the signing of the Sino-British Joint Declaration on the future of Hong Kong, China and Hong Kong have been getting closer to each other, yet they have undergone several stages of ups and downs, ranging from friendly dialogue, consultation and cooperation, to accusations, wars of words, open condemnation and even periodic no-contact as in the few months after the June 4 events of 1989 in Beijing. Nevertheless, Hong Kong's generous contribution to East China's (*Hua Dong*) rehabilitation from a serious flood in the summer of 1991 was appraised by the Chinese officials as a sign of Hong Kong's patriotism and loyalty to China.[1] Hong Kong businessmen and government officials have also played an important role in lobbying the United States President and the Congress to renew China's most-favoured-nation (MFN) status in the three years since 1990. Still, China has remained critical of Hong Kong's support for Chinese dissidents and has kept on warning Hong Kong not to become a subversive base for "counter-revolutionaries."[2] Controversies over the Port and Airport Development Strategy (PADS) in Hong Kong's Lantau Island since 1989–1990 have further overshadowed the Sino-Hong Kong relations with a constant atmosphere of uneasiness, mutual scepticism and distrust.

This chapter intends to analyze China and Hong Kong relations. It will focus on the issues which have been raised after the conclusion of the Sino-British Memorandum of Understanding of July 1991 in which both diplomatic powers agreed "to intensify consultation and cooperation over Hong Kong issues in the approach to 30 June 1997."[3] The Memorandum of Understanding incidentally marked the beginning of a new era in Sino-Hong Kong relations. First of all, Hong Kong was entering the second stage of the political transition. Chinese officials logically demanded that Chinese government should be consulted more frequently on any major issues affecting the post-1997 administration. Secondly, there were major changes in political leadership both in Britain and Hong Kong in 1991–1992 as evidenced by John Major's new leadership in the British Conservative Party in July 1991, the emergence of the liberals in Hong Kong's Legislative Council after the first direct elections in September 1991 and the appointment of a new Governor, Christopher Patten, in July 1992. Moreover, despite the signing of the Memorandum, China still disapproved of the financial package of the PADS proposed by Hong Kong government and continued to complain about the dominance of British-led companies in winning the awarding of the PADS contracts. The policy proposal of the new Governor in October 1992 even aroused severe criticism from major Chinese officials as disrupting the *status quo* in the existing political system.

Before discussing these major issues affecting China's relations with Hong Kong, this chapter first intends to address two fundamental questions. On what basis are China's relations with Hong Kong established and developed? With whom and on what issues can China's relations with Hong Kong be considered as good or bad?

Basis of China's Relations with Hong Kong

The basis of China's relations with Hong Kong is founded upon the Sino-British agreement of 1984 (the Sino-British Joint Declaration) which legitimizes China's recovery of Hong Kong's sovereignty on 1 July 1997. In return, the Chinese government has agreed to cooperate with the British administration in the pre-1997 period through a Sino-British Land Commission and a Sino-British Joint Liaison Group. The Land Commission is responsible for overseeing the implementation of the Joint Declaration relating to land leases, while the Joint Liaison Group is responsible for discussing matters relating to the smooth transfer of government in 1997. In the first few years of the transition, the Joint Liaison Group was primarily concerned with ensuring Hong Kong's continued participation as an independent member in international economic agreements, such as the General Agreement on Tariffs and Trade (GATT). Gradually, China kept on emphasizing that Britain was obliged to consult China on all important matters straddling 1997 because the Joint Declaration had provided for closer cooperation and intensified consultation especially in the second half of the transition.

The Sino-British agreement had provided for China's supremacy over the post-1997 Special Administrative Region (SAR) government in the territory. The setting up of the Joint Liaison Group had further paved the way for China's involvement in Hong Kong's internal affairs even in the pre-1997 period. The ultimate question is whether or not the Chinese leadership is ready to interfere with Hong Kong's internal affairs even before 1997 by interpreting rigidly the terms of reference of the Joint Liaison Group.

Academics, such as Norman Miners, argue that the extent to which China is prepared to get involved in Hong Kong's internal affairs depends on a presumably unofficial understanding with and consent of Hong Kong government in maintaining mutually beneficial relations. Miners believes that China prefers to take over a stable, prosperous and contented society in 1997 and does not intend to directly get involved in Hong Kong's administrative process. Hong Kong government has also been very cautious about a powerful neighbour who can put an end to the existing arrangements at any time, and so has adopted a policy of avoiding unnecessary provocations against China. Sometimes, Hong Kong government even seeks to be as accommodating as possible to all China's reasonable requests, both great and small.[4]

The argument of Miners is based on the assumption that by maintaining the *status quo* in Hong Kong, China actually benefits from an increasingly closer economic relation with the territory. Since the conclusion of the Sino-British agreement in 1984, China's economic connections with Hong Kong have been growing unprecedentedly fast with over 30% of Hong Kong's trade being conducted with China in 1991–1992. By early 1992 China constituted 27% of Hong Kong's exports and surpassed the United States to become the largest market for Hong Kong's products. China also became the most important country for Hong Kong's re-exports, with 49% of Hong Kong's re-exports being supplied by China and 31% of Hong Kong's imports being re-exported to the Chinese markets. Moreover, Hong Kong has been playing an important role in mediating the Sino-United States trade disputes, including the renewal of MFN since 1989–1990 and the tension over Section 301 in October 1992. In both instances, Hong Kong's business lobbying in Washington among the United States Congressmen has become very active and well-organized, thus playing an informal role but providing a significant source of support to Chinese negotiators. Miners therefore believes that the Chinese leadership group is always very careful of maintaining the confidence of the Hong Kong people as well as the overseas investors, and thus prefers to tolerate Hong Kong's separate existence.

Miners' argument, however, does not help answer the question why China does not tolerate the demands from Hong Kong for more direct elections and democracy. His argument also does not explain why Hong Kong government repeatedly makes some decisions which cause embarrassment to the Chinese government. A decision not to repatriate a student dissident, Yang Yang, in 1989 is an example. Another decision to allow an ex-director of Hong Kong Xinhua News Agency, Xu Jiatun, to leave mainland China through Hong Kong's Kai Tak airport without the permission of Beijing is also an example. Some academics, therefore, argue that China's relations with Hong Kong should rather be described as mutual distrust and scepticism. Joseph Y. S. Cheng, for example, considers that Beijing's perception of Hong Kong is dominated by a belief in a conspiracy theory.[5] Accordingly, Beijing representatives in the Land Commission have tried to ensure that the British administration would not sell land beyond certain limits before 1997. China's criticism of the controversial second airport in Hong Kong since 1989–1990 has also been overwhelmingly concerned with whether or not the future SAR government would be bearing the financial burden of the remaining infrastructural project development. Indeed, when the then Hong Kong Governor, David Wilson, announced in October 1989 the intention to construct a HK$127 billion airport, he simply regarded it as Hong Kong's internal affairs and did not consult over the decision with the Chinese government through the Joint Liaison Group. Thereafter, Chinese officials have strongly protested against the unilateral decision of the British administration on the ground that the airport project would have important implications for the finances of the future Special Administrative Region's government after 1997. Finally, the Chinese government has succeeded in interfering with what had originally been regarded by Hong Kong government as its sphere of internal autonomy. According to the Memorandum of Understanding, Hong Kong government is required to consult the Chinese side on all major airport-related franchises or contracts straddling 1997.

What can be derived from the two different perspectives in analyzing China's relations with Hong Kong? It is argued in this chapter that, even though China is the future sovereign power, its ultimate concern is whether or not it is practically capable of exercising effective control over Hong Kong, both economically and politically speaking. In other words, China's attitude depends on whether or not its government is able to benefit from sharing Hong Kong's economic as well as political interests. Yet, China is not able to do so, at least before 1997, primarily because of the presence of the British administration. The apprehension of Hong Kong people over the territory's ultimate incorporation into the communist regime further reduces Beijing's tolerance of a high degree of local autonomy for the SAR government. Even though Beijing has been exercising a degree of self-restraint and tolerance towards maintaining Hong Kong's autonomy, its relations with Hong Kong remain overshadowed by the leadership's distrust of the British and Hong Kong politicians.

There has been evidence indicating that Chinese officials have attempted to exercise stronger control over Hong Kong's internal affairs. For instance, although China has agreed to let Hong Kong enjoy a high degree of local autonomy, Hong Kong representatives have never been allowed to become involved in negotiating detailed transitional arrangements for the territory. At the same time, Chinese officials have refused to recognize the Legislative Council as representing the wishes of the Hong Kong people and have claimed that it is merely an advisory machinery. Such a claim has justified the legitimacy of the Chinese government to representing Hong Kong's interests and negotiating with the British government over whatever issue concerns Hong Kong's future. Non-recognition of the representativeness of the Legislative Council, however, has meant that China does not have official communication with Hong Kong, which has merely been developed indirectly through the Joint Liaison Group, the Land Commission and other Sino-British diplomatic channels. Until now, China has not established any official liaison office with Hong Kong government, either in Beijing or in Hong Kong, apart from limited contacts between relevant departments over some practical issues like cross-border crimes and repatriation of illegal immigrants to China.[6] The Xinhua News Agency in Hong Kong operating under the State Council's Hong Kong and Macau Affairs Office is the *de facto* representative of Chinese diplomatic agency in the territory. Yet, it basically serves to implement Beijing's policy in Hong Kong. By transmitting messages to and from Beijing officials, Xinhua News Agency can best exert diplomatic pressures on Hong Kong government's major decisions rather than govern the territory. The Sino-British Memorandum of Understanding over the airport has allowed for the first time the Director of the Hong Kong and Macau Affairs Office and the Governor of Hong Kong to hold regular meetings to discuss matters of mutual concern.[7] Yet, the Governor is regarded by China as representing the British administration rather than the people of Hong Kong. Lack of direct official communication with Hong Kong people indicates that China is not capable of effectively controlling the developments in the territory in the transitional period before 1997.

In 1991–1992, China has become primarily concerned with the development of two major issues which it cannot comfortably control. First, despite the signing of the Memorandum of Understanding, China has been unable to exercise control over the approval of business contracts by Hong Kong government relating to the airport projects, which has also had important implications for the decisions on other economic contracts before 1997. Secondly, China has also been unable to control the overall political development in the territory, especially the newly-elected Legislative Council and appointments to the Executive and the Legislative Councils. These two major problem areas have become the stumbling-block to a smooth Sino-Hong Kong relation in the second half of the transition.

What Beijing's leadership can do is to exert pressures on the major decisions of the Hong Kong government on an issue-by-issue basis and keep on reminding the people in Hong Kong that China is the ultimate sovereign power, and any intention to prevent China's control will only be wishful thinking. Also, through a series of united front strategies, Chinese officials have been developing a fairly systematic and widespread liaison network with different groups in the territory. Through various social and economic connections, Chinese officials are gradually extending their informal influence, if not control, over the opinions of various groups of Hong Kong people. Through such connections, Chinese officials also hope to develop a significant group of supporters in the territory, who would emerge as a dominant group of political actors in the run-up to 1997 and beyond.

Liaison Network

Apart from appointing some Hong Kong members to the National People's Congress (NPC) and the Chinese People's Political Consultative Congress (CPPCC), China's connections in Hong Kong are primarily social and economic. While its economic connections have been expanding very rapidly through the cooperative joint ventures both in China and in Hong Kong, the traditional social network of the Chinese Communist Party (CCP) in Hong Kong has been established through such leftist papers as *Wen Wei Po* and *Ta Kung Pao* and a few residual leftist schools. Yet, the political influence of these pro-China organizations has been diminishing since the 1970s and 1980s. The Federation of Trade Unions (FTU), which in 1992 has claimed to have a membership of 180,000, is comparatively more influential. Since 1985, FTU has had one member in the Legislative Council representing the labour constituency.

Apart from these social and economic networks, China also made various attempts to widely enlarge in the post-agreement period its liaison with various groups of in the territory. During the five years of the Basic Law discussions, for example, China appointed twenty-three Hong Kong members to the drafting committee and 180 members to the consultative committee. Such connections were temporarily disrupted by the 1989 Tiananmen Incident in Beijing. At that time, even some individuals in FTU and *Wen Wei Po* also condemned the suppression by the Beijing administration. China soon re-established friendly relations with these local pro-China groups or individuals, with the latter declaring their loyalty to the Chinese government and expressing a sense of patriotism towards the mother country.[8]

By 1991-1992, China's informal networking in Hong Kong had got re-established and had even become increasingly active on various occasions. For example, five candidates, who were known to be pro-China, contested in the electoral campaign to the Legislative Council in September 1991, although none of them got elected. Besides, China also made some attempts to further widen its formal and informal connections with various social and political groups in Hong Kong. A group of leading businessmen, called the Professional and Business Federation, was set up in July 1991 and quickly went to Beijing to give advice to the leadership sector concerning Hong Kong's economic and political problems. In the Sino-British Memorandum of Understanding on PADS, China was also able to convince the British counterpart to agree to the establishment of a Hong Kong Airport Consultative Committee and, thus, allow China to formally consolidate its liaison network with fifty Hong Kong individuals outside the formal governmental structure. (For a membership list of Airport Consultative Committee, see Appendix A.) By March 1992, China had made further efforts towards strengthening its local connections by appointing forty-four advisers, among them there being twelve NPC and CPPCC Hong Kong delegates, some leading business figures and other prominent pro-China individuals in different economic and professional sectors. (For a membership list of Hong Kong's Beijing Advisers, see Appendix B.) In his visit to Hong Kong in January 1992, Lu Ping, director of the Hong Kong and Macau Affairs Office, even openly urged the territory's pro-Beijing bodies to organize themselves into political parties to gear up for the 1995 elections.[9] It was intended of course as an encouragement to pro-China individuals to emerge and seek a dominant position in Hong Kong's political process. By July 1992, a new organization called the Democratic Alliance for the Betterment of Hong Kong was established, which consisted of a CPPCC delegate, Tsang Yok-sing, FTU members (Tam Yiu-chung, Chan Yuen-han, and Yip Kwok-chung) and a leftist school teacher, Cheng Kai-nam. It is widely believed that, even though these individuals may not be able to win many seats through the direct election exercises in the future, they may be the most favoured group of people for appointment to the Election Committee in the 1995 legislature.[10] Whether or not these activities have been part of China's united front tactics, it is obvious that its strategy towards Hong Kong has been to strengthen its liaison network while attempting to encourage its loyal supporters to consolidate themselves and prepare for the 1995 elections and, hence, the transfer of power in 1997.

Despite all these different efforts to set up liaisons in the Hong Kong community, Beijing's suppression of the student leaders in June 1989 has served as a stumbling-block to its increasingly closer relations with the Hong Kong community. The Hong Kong Alliance in Support of Patriotic Democratic Movement in China was formed in 1989 which managed to mobilize more than one million people in the territory to strongly criticize the Chinese government for suppressing the student dissidents. It also called for the non-recognition of the Li Peng administration. Since it has continued to organize various mass protests to demand the release of the imprisoned students in Beijing, it has become a constant source of annoyance and irritation to the Chinese leadership. The Hong Kong Alliance, therefore, has been reprimanded by China as being subversive and counter-revolutionary. Its major leaders, Martin Lee and Szeto Wah, also resigned from the Basic Law Drafting Committee in 1989 and formed a political group, the United Democrats of Hong Kong, in December of the same year with about 220 founding members. Contrary to the wishes of the Chinese leaders, the United Democrats have become the leading group of liberals calling for more democracy and political reforms in Hong Kong, after its having very successfully contested twelve out of the eighteen directly-elected seats in the territory's Legislative Council elections in September 1991. As of late 1992, Chinese officials are still refusing to establish a dialogue with the United Democrats. Obviously, the issues relating to political reforms and direct elections have become the major obstacle to good Sino-Hong Kong relations.

Relations with the Directly-elected Legislature

It was written down in the Basic Law that twenty seats would be allowed to be constituted by direct elections in the Legislative Council of 1997. Accordingly, China also agreed with the British diplomats that eighteen seats would be directly elected in the Legislative Council of 1991. In the period between 1991–1994, other legislative seats would then be occupied by twenty-one indirectly elected functional representatives and eighteen appointed members. The Hong Kong government also reserved the right to appoint three official members. The 1991 Legislative Council elections were carried out in September. The various groups of liberals succeeded in sixteen of the eighteen directly elected seats contested and got five seats in the functional constituencies. Together with a few liberal-oriented appointed individuals, the liberal camp quickly emerged as a significant political force, which clearly altered the political balance existing in the pre-1991 Legislative Council.

The landslide victory of the liberal-oriented candidates in the territory's maiden direct elections in September 1991 was regarded as evidence of Hong Kong's "disapproval" of the pro-China candidates and, hence, distrust of the Chinese government.[11] During the electoral campaign, a major bone of contention had been: what should be the style and attitude of the political representatives in handling the thorny China relations? Among the fifty-four candidates, thirteen of them had tried to offer a "rational" and "pragmatic" approach in order to contrast themselves with what they had identified as the "radical" and "confrontational" style of the liberals. These thirteen "pragmatists" had been mainly comprised of the five pro-China individuals and the conservative candidates, who had commonly reminded the voters not to accept the uncompromising approach of the liberals towards the Chinese government. Logically, they had argued that Hong Kong's future elected legislative members should be acceptable to China and should be capable of establishing close dialogue with the senior authorities in Beijing. The liberals, however, had emphasized their consistent commitment to speak up for the interests of the people in Hong Kong, especially their track record of condemning Beijing's suppression of the 1989 democracy movement. They had also kept on reminding the voters that their opponents' pragmatic approach would result in a sell-out of Hong Kong's interests.[12] Chinese officials, therefore, claimed that those elected members who were not acceptable to China would not be allowed to remain in the post-1997 Legislative Council. Yet, even though voters had been reminded not to choose those candidates who were detrimental to good Sino-Hong Kong relations,[13] the voters had remained inclined to support those candidates who had demonstrated their record of speaking up against the pressures of the Chinese authorities. Consequently, none of the pro-China candidates got elected.

Nevertheless, China's relation with Hong Kong was generally positive in view of the signing of the Sino-British Memorandum on PADS in September 1991, the same month the direct elections to the Legislative Council were carried out. China tolerated the strategies of the liberal camps in arousing public sentiments with respect of the 1989 Tiananmen Incident against the pro-China candidates. China also did not openly ask the Hong Kong government to stop candidates of the United Democrats from standing for the elections. China's dealing with the 1991 direct elections was basically quite cautious and lenient.[14] In any case, China only mildly claimed that the 39% turnout rate was too low, hence justifying its earlier claim that the Legislative Council could not be considered as representative of the opinion of the Hong Kong community. Chinese officials also warned that some people, such as members of the United Democrats, would not be allowed to remain in the post-1997 SAR legislature. More significantly, the then Governor, David Wilson, skilfully handled the China factor in making appointments to the new Legislative Council. First of all, the Governor did attempt to maintain the original balance in the Legislative Council by appointing eighteen outstanding but independent-minded individuals from various commercial, industrial and professional elites. Secondly, the Governor only appointed one directly-elected member, Andrew Wong, to the Executive Council, who was regarded more as a moderate than a liberal. Thus, none of the leaders of the major liberal camps were appointed to the Executive Council, let alone the United Democrats. Soon, twelve appointed members and eight functional representatives quickly aligned themselves and formed the Cooperative Resources Centre within the Legislative Council, with a view to forming into an effective bloc against the liberals. So, even though the liberals had won a landslide victory in the general poll, they were yet unable to dominate the Legislative Council.

The newly-formed Legislative Council inevitably became more critical of the Chinese authorities. A motion debate, for example, was initiated to discuss the decision of the Joint Liaison Group to fix the proportion of overseas and local judges to a ratio of one to four in the future Court of Final Appeal. Simon Ip, the lawyers' representative in the Legislative Council, initiated the motion calling for greater flexibility in the proportion between the local and overseas judges, which was passed by a vote of thirty to eleven in December 1991. It not only represented an attempt of the members of Legislative Council to get themselves involved in Sino-British diplomatic negotiations, the vote also signalled the Legislative Council's rejection of a Sino-British bilateral agreement. The Hong Kong Bar Association and Law Society, in particular, accused both governments of breaching the spirit of the Joint Declaration and the Basic Law. China, of course, accused the Legislative Council of not having the power to interpret the stipulations of the Joint Declaration while the right of interpreting the Basic Law should rest with China's NPC.[15] Hong Kong government also echoed the warnings of the Chinese government by emphasizing that what had been agreed by both powers should not be revoked by the Legislative Council. Having secured the support of Hong Kong government, Chinese officials felt nothing more than minor irritation at the debate in the Legislative Council.

The newly-created Legislative Council also became more reform minded. The debate on a Committee System in the first four months was an example. By allowing the committee to study and vet the government's policy proposals, the liberals intended to enhance the monitoring function of the council. Beijing apparently claimed that such a change would alter the political system fundamentally from executive-led to legislative-led. Yet, the debate ended up in January 1992 with a decision on a model, which was proposed by a conservative Cooperative Resources Centre member, to formalize the *ad hoc* groups and the in-house meetings and, thus, resulted in merely preserving rather than revising the existing system. The debate on the number of directly elected seats to the 1995 Legislative Council was another example. In June 1992, a liberal-oriented commerce representative, Jimmy McGregor, initiated a motion calling for Britain and China to accept a 1989 Office of Members of the Executive and Legislative Councils (OMELCO) consensus that had supported thirty seats to be directly elected to the Legislative Council of 1995. The McGregor motion was finally defeated by a margin of twenty-four to twenty-two. As long as the conservative forces remained dominating, China's relations with Hong Kong was generally not damaged by a directly elected Legislative Council.

Despite all these fairly positive relations with different sectors in the Hong Kong community, signs of uneasiness and distrust continued . By the first quarter of 1992, Hong Kong government began to persuade the Chinese authorities, through the British diplomats, to allow an increase in the number of directly elected seats from eighteen to twenty in the 1995 legislature. In May, Lu Ping ruled out such suggestion by claiming that it was incompatible with the Basic Law. Negotiations over the new airport's development was not very promising either. In the same month, China refused to agree upon the ten airport's core project proposed by Hong

Kong government beyond the agreeable one-month limit based on the Memorandum of Understanding. When the Financial Secretary, Hamish Macleod, introduced a concept of callable equity as an additional assurance to lenders, China rejected it as another form of debt. China continued to express worries about the escalating costs and the possibility of substantial cost overruns which would overburden the future SAR government. China also complained about the tendering decisions on the major airport related projects as unfair and biased in favour of the British-led companies. While Governor David Wilson failed to settle the deadlock, his term of office came to an end in July 1992. Although the British Prime Minister, John Major, attempted in June to resolve the airport issue with China's Premier, Li Peng, in a diplomatic meeting in Spain, the deadlock was not eased off before the new Governor arrived.

Relations with the New Governor

The name of the new Governor, Christopher Patten, was publicly announced soon after the Conservative Party, under the leadership of John Major, got re-elected to office in April 1992. Signs of a shift in British policy became evident after the general elections. In his first press conference in London, Christopher Patten emphasized the maintaining of "liberty and freedoms" in Hong Kong, a stance which was very much different from what had been stressed in July 1991 by Lord Caithness, then British Minister responsible for Hong Kong, as "stick to the agreement" and "long term stability and no change."[16] In May, Hong Kong's liberals, such as the United Democrats, began to lobby the Governor-designate for more democracy by presenting him a letter signed by all eighteen directly-elected members calling for increasing the number of directly elected seats to thirty in 1995. It now became clear that the airport's financing controversy could not be resolved separately from the question of direct elections and other related questions of political reform. By 20 June, the newly appointed British Minister responsible for Hong Kong, Alastair Goodlad, even openly protested against the Chinese government having raised the question of Executive Council appointment at the Joint Liaison Group meeting, which, he claimed, should not interfere with the internal administration of Hong Kong. While the British government insisted that the appointment to the Executive Council should be the decision of the Hong Kong Governor alone, the Chinese side also stood firm on the airport project funding plan. At the same time, China kept on warning the Governor not to appoint leaders of the United Democrats to the Executive Council. Upon Patten's arrival in Hong Kong in early July 1992, leftist papers in Hong Kong also reminded the new Governor that his priority should be to maintain a good relation with China and to ensure convergence with the Basic Law.[17]

The new Governor finally appeared to make a compromise on China's demand about the appointments to the Executive Council. By separating the membership of the Executive and the Legislative Councils, the Governor appointed neither members of the United Democrats nor the influential conservative senior members of the Cooperative Resources Centre. Even though the appointments to the Executive Council were no longer a controversial topic, China's relations with Hong Kong drastically deteriorated soon after the Governor announced on 7 October 1992 the proposals for political reforms in the next five years of his administration. Among the various suggestions, China was most unhappy with three major subject areas relating to the composition of the 1995 Legislative Council, including: (a) an expansion of the franchise of the Functional Constituencies by five times to include 2.7 million voters, (b) an increase in the number of directly elected seats from eighteen to twenty; and (c) the introduction of a fully elected District Board system whose members would elect among themselves ten representatives to the Election Committee as required by the Basic Law. These proposed changes, which were emphasized by the Governor as totally consistent with what had been stipulated in the Joint Declaration and the Basic Law, were nevertheless quite different from the existing practices in a number of ways. Firstly, the expansion of the voting rights of the Functional Constituencies were practically to "give every single worker in Hong Kong the opportunity to elect to the Legislative Council a member to represent him or her at the work place."[18] Such a change was clearly altering the previous accent of the Hong Kong government officials who had justified the elitist nature of the functional representatives as necessary to ensuring the availability of "specialist knowledge and valuable advice" in the Legislative Council.[19] Secondly, the issue concerning the number of directly elected seats has been an on-going item of discussion between the British and Chinese governments through the Joint Liaison Group, of which the Governor is not a member. The same procedure would then be applied to discussing the issue relating to the composition of the 1995 Election Committee, the outcome of which, as Chinese officials have insisted from time to time, should be consistent with what had been stipulated in the Basic Law. The composition of the Election Committee of the 1995 Legislative Council had not been stipulated in the Basic Law, but the membership of the second term of the Legislative Council Election Committee had been clearly specified and was to be similar in membership to the Election Committee for the future Chief Executive. Accordingly, it should consist of 800 members from various community sectors and should not be composed exclusively of members of the district boards. (See Table 1 below.) Thus the proposals of the Governor were obviously not violating any terms of the Basic Law in a legal sense, yet, their outcomes, if implemented, would be against the original intentions of the Basic Law drafters.

After Patten's policy proposal was made known to the general public in Hong Kong, spokesmen in the Hong Kong and Macau Affairs Office indicated that they were "extremely worried" about Patten's proposal because he paid no attention to the repeated warnings of the Chinese government.[20] By citing what had been stipulated in the Sino-British Joint Declaration, Chinese officials emphasized that there should be closer cooperation and intensified consultation between two sovereign powers in the second half of the transition to 1997. Accordingly, they reprimanded the unilateral proposal of the Governor as in breach of the spirit of the Joint Declaration as well as the Basic Law. On 15 October, Lu Ping made it clear that "it was not sufficient [for the Governor] to just 'inform' China" about the proposals, but he should have also discussed the matter with the Chinese government through the diplomatic channels established by the

Table 1. Composition of the Election Committee for the Second Term of the Legislative Council 1999–2002

Composition	Number
Industrial, commercial, and financial sectors	200
The professions	200
Labour, social services, religious and other groups	200
Members of the Legislative Council, representatives of district-based organizations, Hong Kong deputies to the National People's Congress, and representatives of Hong Kong members of the National Committee of Chinese People's Political Consultative Congress	200
Total	800

Source: *The Basic Law of the Hong Kong Special Administrative Region of the People's Republic of China* (April 1990), Annex One, p. 57.

Joint Liaison Group.[21] In other words, the Governor should have first discussed with China, and obtained approval for, whatever changes he intended to introduce in Hong Kong before they were made known to the Hong Kong community.

In the few months after Patten's policy proposal was announced, China's attitude towards Hong Kong changed from one of warning to one of accusations, open criticisms, rejections and even threats of sanctions. In a meeting of the Airport Committee on 16 October 1992, China simply rejected all proposals being put forward by members of the British team, thus, resulting in a complete suspension of the progress in the airport project negotiation. Then, Hong Kong officials indicated that Hong Kong government might go ahead alone with the airport project if China did not cooperate. The Chinese stance became obviously hardened after Patten returned from his visit to Beijing in late October. In a press conference of 23 October, Lu Ping heavily criticized Patten for initiating "confrontation" instead of "cooperation."[22] He also warned that should both sides not arrive at a mutually acceptable agreement, Chinese government would not honour any contract being signed by Hong Kong government unilaterally. Lu Ping even threatened that the Land Commission would apply sanctions by not approving any additional land being requested by Hong Kong government in the future. In early November, the Hong Kong issue was raised to the ministerial and congressional levels of Chinese politics. At a meeting of the Standing Committee of the National People's Congress, the Hong Kong problem was the major item on the agenda, and a senior member, Li Hou, emphasized that if Patten did not back down from his proposals, China would establish a new system of legislative, executive and judicial organizations for the SAR government.[23]

China's increasingly harsh stance over Hong Kong was partly a result of the strong backing of the British government and the Parliament but was further hardened by an unfavourable atmosphere both in Hong Kong as well as in the international community. In Hong Kong, China's supporters, such as the Democratic Alliance for the Betterment of Hong Kong, the New Hong Kong Alliance, the Beijing advisers and the Business and Professional Federation, joined into the war of words and accused Patten of upsetting the prosperity and stability of Hong Kong. Liberal-oriented members in the Legislative Council, however, threw their full support behind Patten's proposal. In a debate of 10 November 1992, the Legislative Council even voted overwhelmingly in favour of a motion which called for giving "general support to the package of proposals on electoral reforms relating to 1995 elections to the Legislative Council put forward by the Governor."[24] In a number of surveys conducted in Hong Kong, public opinion was also supportive of Patten's policy change. In a poll conducted a few days after the policy speech was delivered, 73% claimed to agree with Patten's plan for Hong Kong, while 60% of the respondents agreed that Patten had gone far enough to meet the aspirations for democracy in Hong Kong, and 48.8% believed that Hong Kong government should proceed with Patten's proposal even if China rejected it.[25] In another survey conducted after Patten's return from his unsuccessful trip to Beijing, 59% of the respondents still agreed that Hong Kong should go ahead with the political reform even if China objected.[26] In the international community, Patten naturally obtained the support of the governments of the United States, Canada and Australia.

By November 1992, China's position was very much isolated by the lack of support from Hong Kong's public opinion, the directly elected Legislative Council and the international community. What China could do was to reiterate the non-recognition of the Legislative Council and to challenge its constitutional position in deciding on whatever political reforms to be introduced in the territory. Chinese officials then denounced Patten for lobbying the support of the overseas governments as a conspiracy to establish allies in the West. On 30 November, China retorted by claiming that any contract being signed with Hong Kong government straddling 1997 had to be first approved by Beijing. Accordingly, Beijing declared that a most recent contract concerning the construction of Container Terminal Number Nine, which was being granted to a British-led company, was void and would be ineffective after 1997. More significantly, China claimed that it would establish a separate organization responsible for approving the renewal of the existing franchise contracts straddling 1997. On 1 December, a list of ten such contracts extending beyond 1997 was published in a pro-China newspaper, *Ta Kung Pao*; the list included Hong Kong Electric, China Light and Power, China Motor Bus, Kowloon Motor Bus, Hong Kong Air Cargo Terminal Services, Hong Kong Telephone Company, International Telecom, Cross Harbour Tunnel, Eastern Harbour Crossing and City Bus.[27] While some of these contracts with China Motor Bus, Kowloon Motor Bus, Hong Kong Electric, and Hong Kong Air Cargo Terminal Services were due to expire before 1997, others were to expire a few years soon after 1997. China's declaration quickly aroused unexpected uproar in Hong Kong's community who was shocked by China's unprecedented move to threaten the stability of the economy. It was also widely speculated that, if a separate organization were established to make independent approval to any contracts straddling 1997, China was in fact creating another power centre intended to challenge the legitimacy of the existing government.

The position of the British side was also firm. While the British Foreign Office protested against China's interference in Hong Kong's internal administration, the Governor repeated his contention that Britain had not violated the Basic Law and that the British government also had a moral responsibility over Hong Kong in the post-1997 period. By December 1992, China's position had become extremely inflexible and rigid. Chinese officials refused to accept the initiatives of the British foreign office to re-open the negotiations at the Joint Liaison Group level. By insisting on having the sole power to interpret the Basic Law, China demanded Patten to totally back down from his proposal before any diplomatic discussion could further proceed.

Concluding Remarks

What could be observed from the drastic deterioration in Sino-Hong Kong relations in the second half of 1992? It is obvious that since 1991–1992, China has begun to emphasize the need of intensified cooperation and discussions with the British government concerning any matter affecting the second half of Hong Kong's transition to 1997. However, even with the signing of the Sino-British Memorandum of Understanding over the airport in which both governments have agreed to cooperate more closely with each other, China has yet been unable to exercise control over two most important issues, namely the membership of the Executive and Legislative Councils and the approval of major business contracts by Hong Kong government. More significantly, the new political leaderships in both Britain and Hong Kong have not been ready to succumb to whatever pressure being exerted by the Chinese government. In Hong Kong, government officials have been increasingly concerned with maintaining an effective administration in the second half of the transition to 1997, hence expressing their grievance towards China's intended interference with its internal affairs. When the new Governor assumed duty in mid-1992, he found that the job of governing Hong Kong was extremely difficult. On the one hand, an executive-led government was increasingly criticized by a new Legislative Council and, thus, by implications being confronted by the society at large. On the other hand, could also be discerned the concern of the civil servants over China's demand for more cooperation and intensified consultation, which practically meant less autonomy and less effective government. The Hong Kong government had become inevitably split between the demands for accountability to the Hong Kong public as well as accountability to the future sovereign power.

The proposals of the new Governor to reform the political system were obviously an attempt on the part of the Hong Kong administration to regain leadership over Hong Kong's governing process in the second half of the transition to 1997. By performing a more open style of government, Patten claimed that an effective executive-led government should be accountable to a popularly elected Legislative Council. Since October 1992, Patten began to regularly attend special sessions of the Legislative Council to answer questions raised by the members. Patten also asserted that should members of the Legislative Council endorse his policy blueprint, he would implement it despite China's objections. Patten's move inevitably enhanced the political accountability of the non-elected administration to the general public of Hong Kong, which, China argued, would mean the creation of a semi-independent territory, and hence a challenge to China's *de facto* sovereign power over the territory.

Chinese officials now claimed that the Hong Kong Governor had infringed upon China's sovereign authority over Hong Kong. It seemed that China was ready to regain political control at the expense of economic and social stability. It also looked as if China was no longer entrusting the British government to administer Hong Kong and was ready to take over the transitional administration in case negotiations broke down. In the three months between October and December 1992, the tactics of the Chinese officials could be summarized as: (a) continuing attacks on the Governor of violating the Basic Law and breaching the spirit of the Joint Declaration; (b) mobilizing the cause of nationalism through its liaison network in Hong Kong; (c) retaliating on the economy and the airport project; (d) cancelling formal and informal contacts between Hong Kong and Chinese officials;[28] (e) threatening to set up a separate power centre in Hong Kong before 1997; (f) mobilizing their supporters in the Legislative Council in an attempt to delay the passage of the policy proposal in the form of bills, and (g) warning the Hong Kong public to reject Patten's proposal, while persuading them to choose what is acceptable to China. In addition to employing these various tactics, spokesmen of Xinhua News Agency claimed that the doors remained open for negotiations. There were also signs indicating that Chinese government was not yet prepared to totally ruin the economy and the confidence of the business investors.

By December 1992, the ultimate test rested with the Hong Kong people: how were they to respond to China's retaliation and sanctions? China's tactics resulted in short-term fluctuations on Hong Kong's stock market and in public opinion. In December 1992, more people began to withdraw the original support they had once given to the Governor because they were increasingly worried about the effect of Sino-British hostility on the confidence of the businessmen, hence the economy of the territory. In a survey published on 7–8 December 1992, 38.9% of the respondents felt that they were less confident about Hong Kong's economy. In the same survey, only about 50% of the respondents considered that Patten's proposal for the 1995 elections should be followed upon, while only 59% were satisfied with the performance of the Governor and 55% believed that he was trustworthy. A general lack of confidence towards the existing government, however, did not allow China to gain any credit in the opinion poll. When being asked whether they agreed or disagreed with China's denunciation of the Container Terminal Number Nine Contract, 32% and 63.9% respectively said that they strongly disagreed or disagreed with China's move.[29] Therefore, China's effort to regain control over Hong Kong's internal administration not only served to discredit the existing government, but also led to further damage China's legitimacy in the eyes of the Hong Kong people.

Chinese officials soon recognized that their tactics of persuasion and intimidation had only limited success. The Legislative Council was scheduled to debate the policy proposal in February 1993 and, were it passed by the third reading, the Governor indicated that he would implement it in Hong Kong. China's trump card had been to resume sovereign power, i.e. political control, over the Hong Kong administration even before 1997. China may have considered undertaking military action and then setting up its own political structure in the territory. Yet such effort would not merely upset the smooth running of the existing political system but would also discourage economic investments in Hong Kong. By early 1993, another confidence crisis had been triggered off in the Hong Kong community, with the public's apprehension about the Communist takeover being reactivated. The Chinese authorities have been revising their strategies in handling the volatile Hong Kong relations. What they have to do is to re-establish the confidence of the Hong Kong people towards the Chinese leadership. Otherwise, the various sanctions applied by the

Chinese government may cause greater difficulty in Sino-Hong Kong relations, which may ultimately affect China's exercise of sovereignty over Hong Kong in 1997.

Notes

1. It was reported in various newspapers that, by July 1991, donation from Hong Kong amounted to HK$400 million. See *Ta Kung Pao* (Hong Kong), 16 July 1991, p. 1; *Hong Kong Standard*, 10 July 1991, p. 1.
2. The term was first used by Ji Pengfei, then director of Hong Kong and Macau Affairs Office, when he openly indicated that China would not tolerate people in Hong Kong taking part in any movement against the CCP's leadership. See *People's Daily* (Overseas Edition), 21 July 1989, p. 2. It was repeatedly applied by Chinese officials on subsequent occasions to remind the Hong Kong people not to get involved in overseas Chinese democracy movements. See for example *Hong Kong Standard*, 20 June 1991, p. 1, and *Hong Kong Economic Journal*, 25 June 1991, p. 5.
3. Sino-British Memorandum of Understanding Concerning the Construction of the New Airport in Hong Kong and Related Questions, 3 September 1991, Article G.
4. Norman Miners, *The Government and Politics of Hong Kong* (5th ed.; Hong Kong: Oxford University Press, 1991), p. 228.
5. Joseph Y. S. Cheng, "Introduction," in *The Other Hong Kong Report 1992*, edited by Joseph Y. S. Cheng and Paul C. K. Kwong (Hong Kong: The Chinese University Press, 1992), p. xx.
6. *Ibid.*, p. xxv.
7. Sino-British Memorandum of Understanding (see Note 3), Article G.
8. "Qinzhong renshi de shunliu niliu" (Distrust amongst the Pro-China Individuals), *Pai Shing* (Hong Kong), No. 217 (1 June 1990), p. 17. See also *Hong Kong Standard*, 19 June 1990.
9. *South China Morning Post* (Hong Kong, *SCMP*), 14 March 1992, p. 6.
10. Louie Kin-sheun, "Politicians, Political Parties and the Legislative Council," in *The Other Hong Kong Report 1992* (see Note 5), p. 72.
11. Joan Leung and Rowena Kwok, "Electorates' Perception of Political Groupings in Hong Kong," in *A Report of the Conference Proceedings on Politics and 1991 Elections*, edited by Jane C. Y. Lee, W. N. Ho and Jermain T. M. Lam (Hong Kong: City Polytechnic of Hong Kong, April 1992). See also Rowena Kwok and Elaine Chan, "Issue Voting: Policy Positions and Voting Inclinations," *Asian Journal of Public Administration*, Vol. 13, No. 2 (December 1991), p. 105.

12. Jane C. Y. Lee, "Campaigning Themes of the Candidates in the 1991 Direct Elections," a paper presented at a Workshop on 1991 Elections held in Hong Kong (13 October 1992).
13. *SCMP*, 1 September 1991, p. 1.
14. Tsang Tak-shing, "On Chinese Official Attitudes towards Legislative Council Elections 1991," in *A Report of the Conference Proceedings* (see Note 11), pp. 44–47.
15. *Wen Wei Po* (Hong Kong), 11 November 1991, p. 1.
16. See Frank Ching, "The Implementation of the Sino-British Joint Declaration," in *The Other Hong Kong Report 1992* (see Note 5), p. 90; *Hong Kong Standard*, 25 July 1991, p. 1.
17. See *Wen Wei Po*, 9 July 1992, p. 1; *Ta Kung Pao*, 10 July 1992, p. 1.
18. *Our Next Five Years: The Agenda for Hong Kong*, Address by the Governor The Right Honourable Christopher Patten at the Opening of the 1992/93 Session of the Legislative Council (7 October 1992), paragraph 136, p. 39.
19. Green Paper, *The Further Development of Representative Government in Hong Kong* (Hong Kong: Government Printer, July 1984), p. 13.
20. *Wen Wei Po*, 9 October 1992, p. 2
21. *SCMP*, 16 October 1992, p. 2.
22. *Express News* (Hong Kong), 24 October 1992, p. 3.
23. *Ibid.*, 8 November 1992, p. 1.
24. The motion debate was passed with a vote of 32 against 21. For a description of the debates, see for example *SCMP*, 11 November 1992.
25. *SCMP*, 10 October 1992, p. 10.
26. *Ibid.*, 20 October 1992, p. 3.
27. *Ta Kung Pao*, 1 December 1992, p. 12.
28. It was reported on 14 December 1992 that the scheduled visit of the Attorney-General to China was cancelled. On an earlier occasion, a conference on "Hong Kong in Transition" which was originally scheduled for 28–30 October 1992 and was organized by a pro-China One Country Two Systems Economic Research Institute was also cancelled abruptly upon the arrival of Lu Ping and Ji Pengfei on 27 October. Apart from the participation of important Chinese officials, the conference also invited important officials from Hong Kong government.
29. *Ming Pao* (Hong Kong), 7 and 8 December 1992, p. 1.

Appendix A Airport Consultative Committee Membership List
(As of November 1991)

1.	Wong Po-yan	Chairman, United Overseas Enterprises
2.	Cha Mou-sing	Director, HKR International
3.	Chan Hung-kwan	Land Development Corporation
4.	Chan Man-hung	Senior Lecturer, Department of Economics, Hong Kong Baptist College
5.	Chan Yuen Yin-ling	Supervisor, Hong Kong Christian Service
6.	Chau How-chen	Director, Chau's Brothers Holdings
7.	Cheng Hon-kwan	Partner, HK Cheng and Partners
8.	Cheng Wai-chee	Managing Director, Wing Tai Garment International
9.	Cheng Yiu-tong	Chairman, Hong Kong Federation of Trade Unions
10.	Cheung Bing-leung	Senior Lecturer, Department of Public and Social Administration, City Polytechnic of Hong Kong
11.	Cheung Hon-kau	Partner, T. Y. Lin, HK Consulting Engineers
12.	Cheung Wing-lam	Deputy Commercial Director, Cathay Pacific Airways
13.	Cheung Yau-kai	Professor, Department of Civil Engineering, University of Hong Kong
14.	Chong Kim-loong	Deputy Group Managing Director, Gammon (HK)
15.	Chow Chun-fai	Manager, United Art
16.	Choy Wai-shek	General Manager, Realty Art Supplies
17.	Chu Yu-lin	Managing Director, Upswing Company
18.	Fok Chun-wan	Director, Yau Wing
19.	Fung Kwok-lun	Managing Director, Li and Fung
20.	Fung Shiu-wing	General Secretary, The Methodist Centre
21.	Gerry Higginson	Managing Director, Wharf (Holdings)
22.	Ho Chung-tai	Director, Maunsell Consultants Asia
23.	Ho King-on	President, HK Federation of Education Workers
24.	Hu Fa-kuang	Chairman, Ryoden (Holdings)
25.	Kan Fook-yee	Director, Knight Frank Kan and Baillieu
26.	Ho Kam-chuen	Director, Jardine Pacific
27.	Kwok Ping-kwong	Director, Sun Hung Kai Property
28.	Lam Wai-keung	Executive Director, Lee Yan Investment
29.	Lau Hon chuen	Solicitor, Chu and Lau Solicitors and Notaries
30.	Lau Kong-wah	Johnston and Ray
31.	Lau Ting-chung	Director, Hong Kong Ferry Holdings
32.	Lee Lin-sang	President, New Territories Association of Societies
33.	Leung Chun-ying	Director, Jones Lang Wootton
34.	Leung Kwong-cheong	Supervisor, Kwai Shing Christian Social Service Centre
35.	Li Tzar-kuoi	Executive Director, Cheung Kong Holdings
36.	Henry Litton	Queen's Counsel
37.	David Austin Morris	Chairman, David Morris Associates
38.	Ng Chee-siong	Chairman, Sino Land
39.	Poon Chung-kwong	Director, Hong Kong Polytechnic
40.	Heinz Rust	Managing Director, Professional Projects Co., Ltd.
41.	Shao You-bao	Deputy General Manager, Bank of Tokyo
42.	Sit Fung-suen	Reader, Department of Geography, University of Hong Kong
43.	Tan Man-kou	Kwan, Wong, Tan and Fong

Appendix A (continued)

44.	Wan Sek-luen	Director, Enviro-chem Engineering and Laboratory
45.	Wang Liang-huew	Senior Lecturer, Department of Geography, University of Hong Kong
46.	Wong Hong-hin	Senior Staff Tutor, University of Hong Kong
47.	Wong Shou-yeh	Chairman, Dah Sing Bank
48.	Wu Ying-sheung	Managing Director, Hopewell Holdings
49.	Yeung Yue-man	Professor, Department of Geography, The Chinese University of Hong Kong
50.	Yip Wah	Supervisor, Che Yan School

Appendix B Beijing's Hong Kong Advisers Membership List
(As of March 1992)

1.	Ann Tse-kai	Member of Basic Law Drafting Committee; Chairman of Basic Law Consultative Commitee and Head, One Country Two Systems Economic Research Institute; CPPCC delegate
2.	Cha Chi-man	Former Basic Law Drafter and head of China Dyeing
3.	Chan Yat-sun	Vice-chairman of Heung Yee Kuk
4.	Alice Cheng	Vice-chairman, Chinese General Chamber of Commerce; CPPCC delegate
5.	Cheng Kai-nam	Chairman of Federation of Education Workers and Teacher, Pui Kiu Middle School; member of Basic Law Consultative Committee
6.	Cheng Wai-kin	Director, One Country Two Systems Economic Research Institute
7.	Cheng Yiu-tong	Chairman, Federation of Trade Unions; NPC delegate and member of Basic Law Consultative Committee
8.	Chu Yau-lun	Director, Aircraft Technology
9.	Chung Sze-yuen	Chairman, University of Science and Technology; former member of Executive and Legislative Councils
10.	Fok Ying-tung	Former member of Basic Law Drafting Committee; NPC/CPPCC delegate
11.	Fong Wong Kat-man	Accountant and former Legislative Council member
12.	Hu Fa-Kuang	Chairman, Royden (Holdings)
13.	Kan Fook-yee	Director, Knight Frank Kan and Baillieu; member of Basic Law Drafting Committee; CPPCC delegate; member of New Hong Kong Alliance
14.	Kwong Kong-kit	Anglican Bishop of Hong Kong and Macau and member of Basic Law Drafting Committee
15.	Lau Ting-chung	Adviser to the Hong Kong and Yaumati Ferry Co
16.	Lau Wong-fat	Head of Heung Yee Kuk and member of Legislative Council; member of Basic Law Drafting Committee
17.	Leung Chun-ying	Director, Jones Lang Wootton and member of Basic Law Consultative Committee
18.	Li Fook-sean	Former Justice of Appeal and member of Basic Law Drafting Committee
19.	Li Ka-shing	Chairman and Managing Director, Cheung Kong and member of Basic Law Drafting Committee
20.	Li Kwok-po	Legislative Council member and Chief Executive, Bank of East Asia; member of Basic Law Drafting Committee, and founder of One Country Two Systems Economic Research Institute
21.	Liao Poon-huai	Former Hong Kong government official and former member of the Joint Liaison Group
22.	Henry Litton	Queen's Counsel; member of Basic Law Consultative Committee; member of New Hong Kong Alliance
23.	Liu Yiu-chu	Solicitor and NPC delegate
24.	Lo Hong-sui	Managing Director, Shui On and member of Basic Law Consultative Committee

Appendix B (continued)

25.	Lo Tak-shing	Former Executive Council member; member of New Hong Kong Alliance
26.	Mun Kin-chok	Dean, Business Administration, The Chinese University of Hong Kong; CPPCC delegate
27.	Ng Chee-siong	Chairman, Sino Land
28.	Ng Hong-man	Supervisor, Pui Kiu Middle School; NPC delegate and member of Basic Law Drafting Committee
29.	Shao You-bao	Deputy General Manager, Bank of Tokyo
30.	Run Run Shaw	Film magnate
31.	Sik Kok-kwong	President, Hong Kong Buddhist Association
32.	Tam Wai-chu	Barrister; Former member of Executive and Legislative Councils; Member of Basic Law Drafting Committee and member of Liberal Democratic Federation
33.	Tang Hsiang-chien	Managing Director, Soco Textiles (HK)
34.	Tong Yat-chu	Executive Director, Construction Industry Training Association
35.	Tsang Hin-chi	Managing Director, Goldlion; NPC delegate and member of Basic Law Consultative Committee
36.	Tso Wung-wai	Senior Lecturer, Department of Biochemistry, The Chinese University of Hong Kong; member of Basic Law Drafting Committee and member of New Hong Kong Alliance
37.	Tsui Tsin-tong	Head of China Paint and Citybus
38.	Tung Chee-wah	Director, Orient Overseas Container Line and member of Basic Law Consultative Committee
39.	Wong Po-yan	Chairman, United Overseas Enterprises
40.	Wong Yu-hong	Legislative Council member and former deputy-Chairman of Stock Exchange.
41.	Wu Wai-yung	Member of Basic Law Consultative Committee; Vice-Chairman of Liberal Democratic Federation
42.	Wu Ying-sheung	Managing Director, Hopewell Holdings
43.	Xu Si-min	Publisher, *The Mirror* magazine, and CPPCC delegate
44.	Zee Sze-yung	Professor of Botany, University of Hong Kong; NPC and CPPCC delegate; Member of New Hong Kong Alliance

11

Economic Development in China in 1992

Thomas M. H. Chan

Introduction

Since 1985, the radical implementation of a market-oriented economic reform has transformed the decentralized, administratively controlled planned economy of China into a primary market economy. Even though the administrative element of the old economic regime survived under the planned track of the new double-track system, this planned track has gradually shrunk by the intrusion of the market track through various attempts at price liberalization and enterprise reform after 1985. This has culminated in 1991 and 1992 in the merging of the two tracks into one that is dominated by market mechanisms in most of the product markets and has made China's economy in the early 1990s resembling more the typical market economy of the world capitalist system. And as such, it is subject to the structurally inherent cyclical fluctuations in demand and supply, in prices and, therefore, in growth that are found in market economies in general.[1]

However, as the Chinese proclaim their new market economy keeps a socialist nature, the legacy of central planning and socialist property of the last four decades still has a strong effect on the present functioning and performance of the Chinese economy. This should not be seen as inadequacy and incompleteness of the current economic reform or systemic transformation, something portrayed by the western media as the product of resistance against market reform from "conservative" or "communist" elements in China's economic administration. Even in the West market economies have not uniformly achieved the same scale and extent of marketization; they are subject to frequent non-economic interventions by government and society as well as cultural constraints through traditional norms and values that are internalized by or imposed upon economic actors in their economy. The present "socialist" distortions of the Chinese market economy should be compared with government interventions for welfare purposes and/or for anti-cyclical measures of growth stimulation in established market economies. The methods and policy tools used may be different, but the difference is more of degree than of nature, despite the socialist distinction of their policies always emphasized by the leaders of the Chinese Communist Party.

This chapter will try to examine the performance of the Chinese economy in 1992 in the context of the cyclical pattern of development that has been determined by both the emergence of the new market system and government interventions and structural impediments, which are not directly related to the consequence of the market-oriented reform but are commonly found, albeit in different forms, in other more established market economies.

Background to 1992

The anti-cyclical government interventions in the "socialist" market economy of China in 1992 have tampered with the trend pattern of the present economic cycle.

The cyclical downturn in industrial and economic growth started in 1989 but bottomed out in 1990, when industry resumed growth in March and retail sales ended their nominal negative growth in June.[2] Yet, there were still large growth differentials between industrial production, on the one hand, and retail sales and investment, on the other, which may be seen as representing an imbalance between aggregate supply and demand in the economy. In 1990 industrial output increased in real terms by 7.53% over the previous year, while the annual growth rates for retail sales and fixed assets investment were respectively 0.34% and 5.32%.[3] Aggregate supply appeared to outgrow demand. The shortfall was probably filled up partially by the emergence of net exports in the year, in sharp contrast to the net imports in previous years of economic overheating and high growth. Compared with retail sales, the net exports were equivalent to about 5% of sale volume, if converted from US dollars at the official exchange rate. Such a size of net external demand was rather small and should not have been sufficient to maintain the excess supply represented by the increase in gross industrial output, even if one takes into account the double counting inherent in the compilation of output statistics of industry. The source of support for the moderate industrial growth of 7.53% should therefore lie elsewhere.

Driven by the political concern of avoiding any downturn in economic growth, the Chinese government had since September 1989 reversed its tight monetary policy and had started to pump large amount of credit money into the state sector by the state banking system through a relaxation of credit control and two reductions of interest rates. This had led to a rapid growth in net increase in bank loans and other aggregates of money supply. The 22% growth at current prices (or about 19% if deflated by the rise in retail price index) in net increase in bank loans contrasted sharply with the real annual growth of 5% of GNP and 7.53% of gross industrial output. The net increase of about RMB273.1 billion in bank loans[4] was closer to the net increase in gross industrial output of RMB190.7 billion at current prices. Of the net increased amount of loans, as a result of the deliberate policy of the government, a large majority (76.7%) was devoted to working capital loans, used mainly for financing current production of state enterprises. While growth in consumption demand, in terms of retail sales, was still very sluggish, the working capital loans offered state enterprises the means to maintain or even expand their current production regardless of whether there was demand in the market or not. The result was, therefore, that almost all of the net increase in working capital loans (93% in a sample of 40,000 state industrial enterprises) was used for building up inventory and in the form of receivable revenues as goods sold to clients had little chance of payment because of the lack of demand in the market or by users. The latter became bad debts among enterprises. It was estimated that in 1990 alone the abnormal increase in industrial and commercial inventories amounted to RMB100 billion.[5]

The economic situation in 1991 improved significantly, but the engine of growth was investment rather than market demand and consumption. Fixed assets investment rose in real terms by 20.32%, 15 percentage points higher than in the previous year. The change was prompted by a shift in government's monetary policy. As the injection of working capital loans could not revive the state sector, sales by state enterprises covered by the state budget — the core of the state sector — remained in decline in 1990;[6] the central government focused loans on investment with the target of raising final demand for industrial products in the economy. This provided the impetus for the expansion of investment in the state sector, which in turn and in an indirect fashion stimulated increase in investment in the collective and private sectors, which had suffered from real declines in the previous two years. As current industrial production and state investment were financed by easy bank credits, this led to two consequences: with the rapid expansion, workers in the state sector received larger income including bonuses which were tied to increase in the scale of economic activities, and this in turn generated a larger purchasing power. Yet, contrary to the expectation of the government, retail sales did not rise accordingly. Its real annual growth rate was 10.24%, substantially higher than a year ago by a large margin of 10 percentage points; but retail sales still lagged behind the high growth in investment and in industrial output, the latter registering 14.52% for the year or doubling the growth rate in 1990. The debt-driven growth or economic recovery (with GNP growth of 5%) in 1990 was

Economic Development in China in 1992

superseded by an investment-led and even higher growth in 1991 (7.7%), which continued to be founded upon an accumulation of bad debts in the state sector and a very lax monetary policy that would have long term inflation implications. External demand (net exports) did not change from the level of the previous year, and its contribution to aggregate demand in the year diminished further and was inconsequential for the higher growth of 1991.

Growth Acceleration in 1992

The year 1992 began with modest economic growth targets. Initially, probably as decided upon by the State Council at the annual planning and economic conferences at the end of 1991, GNP growth was targeted at 5.5%,[7] more than 2 percentage points lower than the level attained in 1991. It might reflect the worries of State Council's technocrats about the underlying inflationary pressure of the investment-led and debt-driven higher growth of 1991. However, political intervention by Deng Xiaoping, the patriarch still wielding final veto-power over every major policy-decision in the Party, forced the State Council to revise the growth target upward at the March meeting of the National People's Congress to half a percentage point higher at 6%.[8] The move was more symbolic than it appeared and in fact gave the green light to local authorities to pursue a higher growth than

Table 1. China's Year-on-year Real Growth in Gross Industrial Output by Months in 1992

January	12.9%
February	22.0%
March	20.1%
April	18.2%
May	16.7%
June	18.2%
July	21.8%
August	21.2%
September	20.7%
October	22.4%
November	26.1%
December	32.2%

Sources: *China's Latest Economic Statistics* (Hong Kong: CERD Consultants Ltd.), 1992 and 1993, various issues.

they were approved for by the central government in their annual plans. Central government's monetary policy was eased at the beginning of 1992[9] in an open effort to support the call for higher growth and bolder reform by Deng.[10] The pattern of forced economic growth by investment and loose credit since late 1989 was thus maintained and even with a greater vigour and political devotion than before with the full backing of Deng. The timid attempt of the central economic bureaucracy to arrest the deterioration because of bad debts in the state sector and out-of-control money expansion was abandoned completely after March. Replacing it was an intense local competition for economic acceleration and a scramble for loans from the state banking system based on ill-prepared financial innovations in fund-raising. The central government and its technocrats became passive onlookers bound in a political strait-jacket that forbade any intervention from them.

In the first half of the year, China's economic growth continued the pattern that had been set up earlier. GNP growth was 10.6%, exceeding both the growth target approved by the National People's Congress in March and the actual growth achieved in 1991. Industrial growth reached 18.2%, still faster than that of last year, but the relationship between heavy and light industries changed. In 1991, the two industrial sectors expanded at more or less the same pace, with annual growth rate of 14.6% and 14.4% respectively. Probably as a time-lag consequence of the investment-led nature of economic growth or a much stronger investment growth in 1992, heavy industrial growth outgrew light industry in the first six months of 1992 by 4.4 percentage points, to reach 20.4% and 16% respectively.[11] The slower growth of light industry, which included production of consumer goods, reflected the sluggish increase in retail sales in the period, which stayed at about 9% in real terms with little improvement over 1991. Since the growth differential between industrial production and retail sales had widened, investment in the form of fixed assets was expected to expand much faster than in 1991. It increased by 28.5%, or 22.5% after correction for the rise in retail price index. However, the ratio of real growth in investment to that of industrial production and the ratio of retail sales expansion to industrial growth showed significant drops, indicating that aggregate demand increased more slowly than aggregate supply. The first set of ratios for 1991 and the first half of 1992 were 1.39 and 1.24, while the second set gave 0.70 and 0.50. If aggregate supply in the first six months of 1992 was not supported by corresponding rise in aggregate demand, the need for finance from state banks and the piling up of inventory should be larger than in 1991. Unfortunately, there is no information on the latter, but the net increase in bank loans in the period was RMB1,255 billion, doubling the original target set by the central bank, and was over RMB60 billion larger than a year ago.[12] Money expansion in the period was indeed very impressive and should probably be regarded as the real driving force behind economic acceleration. External factors did not change the picture; an increase in direct foreign investment in the period was less than RMB9 billion, approximating only about 5% of the rise in fixed asset investments, and net exports of China also experienced a large shrinking to US$2.5 billion. Contributions from both external funding sources or external demand still remained marginal to China's domestic growth.

Imbalance in aggregate demand and supply did not give rise to any visible economic difficulty in the middle of 1992. Rise in retail price index for the nation as a whole stayed at the low level of 4.9% and actually fell from the much higher inflation at the beginning of the year, thanks to another bumper harvest of food grains in the early and summer crops.[13] However, the acceleration in investment and industrial production did not proceed without impact on the underlying inflation trend in the economy. Prices of industrial raw materials and intermediate goods moved up under heavy demand. In the first six months, the existing stock accumulated under the government induced recession in investment in the preceding three to four years was used up, and current production was unable to catch up with the rapid expansion in demand, even though output of heavy industry jumped to a 20% plus growth in the period. As a result, the price index of industrial materials rose by 6.4%,[14] only slightly higher in appearance than the inflation rate in retail prices, but with a much stronger upward spiral that led to faster increase in subsequent months. In July and August the retail price index continued on the slow climb, below an annual rate of 5% (4.3% and 4.8% respectively),[15] whereas the price index of industrial materials rocketed by increases of 14.1% and 18.3%.[16] Although it usually takes some time before price fluctuations in industrial materials ripple through the economy to cause cost-pushed inflation in retail prices, that inadequate supply of industrial materials for investment and current industrial production should very obviously underpin the potentially volatile nature of prices and, therefore, the economic stability of the economy.

Unfortunately, the Chinese leadership under the ideological persuasion of Deng for a strategy of speedier growth and bolder reform was impressed by the high growth and low inflation of the first half of 1992; they did not take heed of the warning sent by the sudden upsurge in industrial material prices. On the contrary, the central government regarded the high-growth-and-low-inflation condition as offering the ideal timing for price liberalization, in particular for the more sensitive prices of energy, raw materials and transport charges. Starting from July, a series of price liberalization and price adjustments were implemented. And as expected, the move sent prices flying. The price index for industrial materials then entered a much stronger upward spiral. It was reported that, by the end of 1992, the index had risen by between 20 to 25%.[17] There was also a corresponding rise of the indices of retail prices and living-of-cost prices, though tracing behind with the time lag of a few months and a large differential. The biggest rise in inflation took place in the two months of September and October, which showed respective increases of 1.6 and 3.1 percentage points in retail price and cost-of-living price indices, and coincided with the jump in industrial material prices.

Rising Inflation and Government's Readjustment Attempts after August

The sharp increase in domestic prices and the resulting huge pressure on imports, which had probably by that time led to an alarming reversal of China's trade surplus into a real deficit[18] (a final balance after discounting exports, which have long suffered from a low level of remittance of foreign exchange earnings), forced the more conservative (with an overriding preference for economic stability and sustainable growth) economic leadership of the State Council to apply the brakes to the out-of-control economic acceleration. In fact as early as in late July, probably alarmed by the loss of its control over government monetary policy, the People's Bank of China had called for a suppression of credit expansion in the third quarter of the year,[19] but without active support from the economic leadership[20] the call had not been heeded by any one, including the local branches of the People's Bank. It was only in mid-August, when monetary figures revealed a serious problem of money overhanging and excessive expansion, that the central leadership began to address directly the issue of economic overheating.[21]

The market-oriented reform by economic devolution has reduced the number of macro-economic policy tools available to the central government to only credit control of the state banking system. It was through the exercise of this policy tool that it was able to revive economic growth from the bottom in 1990, although at the cost of a number of far-reaching structural problems in the economy. When economic overheating became threatening to the goal of sustainable economic growth, the central government once again resorted to this proven measure. The immediate result was a drastic cut in credit in the economy. In September, the increase in loans issued by state banks was merely RMB10.6 billion, which was over RMB20 billion less than the average sum of the preceding months, and 38 billion lower than the amount achieved in the same month a year ago. By the end of October, the accumulated net increase in the outstanding amount of loans stood at RMB238.1 billion, about RMB51.6 billion more than the level attained in the same period in 1991.[22] Compared with the RMB247.17 billion by the end of August,[23] the two months of September and October witnessed a decline in loans extended. This was very unusual as the third and fourth quarters of a year were normally characterized by the usual increase in demand for bank loans. The reverse occurring in these two months represented a very determined and indeed very effective turnaround in central government's monetary policy. At the end of the first half of 1992, the outstanding amount of bank loans in China was 22.6% higher than a year before. The drastic brake of the subsequent months were to force the increase rate down to 19.9%.[24]

Despite the effective brake on credit creation, economic acceleration did not abate in the remaining months of the year. Investment, contrary to past experience, did not undergo any slow-down in growth under the constraints of credit from the state banking system. Investment in the first three quarters increased by about 36.3%, but, by the end of the year, the annual growth remained at 37.6%, with a further increase of pace.

The main reason for the ability of investment spending to continue along the acceleration path regardless of the credit squeeze imposed by the central government might have been the availability of surplus capital in the coastal regions because of the financial deepening and liberalization of the Chinese economy. Through transfers in inter-bank capital market and the attraction of the higher profit return from the newly emergent speculative markets (stocks, property, foreign exchange and commodity futures markets) in the coastal regions (in Shanghai and Guangdong in particular), a large stock of surplus capital had been accumulated there. For instance, by June the state banking system in Shanghai had a surplus in deposits of over RMB5 billion, a reversal from the previous long-standing pattern of imbalance in deposit-loan accounts.[25] This eased the credit supply in the local and neighbouring capital markets (in Jiangsu and Zhejiang, capital flow across the provincial boundaries were frequent and on a very large scale) and provided the necessary funding for the many new and ongoing investment projects in the region. Shanghai's surplus deposits was rather small when compared with Guangdong's. By the end of June, surplus deposits in Guangdong's state banking system amounted to RMB44.52 billion,[26] a sharp rise of 33.26 billion in the five months since just before the Chinese New Year in February.[27] Central Bank's credit squeeze policy could only affect loans granted by banks. It could not be applied to controls on deposit withdrawal from banks. With the huge surplus deposits in high growth provincial economies like Shanghai and Guangdong, mere withdrawals from the banks would generate a multiplying effect on deposits that could be and were taken out to finance investment and consumption locally and/or in nearby areas. As in the present financial system of China capital could be easily transferred from one place to another, the restrictive loan policy could only have effect on local economies heavily dependent on central bank's credit support; and this policy would, therefore, have contributed further to regional disparity in economic growth as the interior region that was now suffering from a deficit in deposits would not have the funds to support growth-inducing investment.

In addition to the proliferation of inter-regional inter-bank transfers of capital funds and surplus savings, 1992 also saw the rapid development of many other forms of capital markets, including the two regional stock markets in Shanghai and Shenzhen and the STAQ system (Securities Trading Automated Quotation System) in Beijing, foreign exchange swap markets; and various types of future markets, foreign exchange spot and futures markets became widespread towards the end of the year in the coastal regions despite their illegal status. Moreover, property markets also entered a phase of drastic expansion when foreign firms were allowed to take part, with the immediate outcome of land prices rocketing up. The return rates appeared to be much higher than normal saving interest rates and profit margin offered by industrial and commercial investment. It was quite natural for capital from the interior provinces to be attracted to the coastal region, further increasing the available supply of capital, which had already become over-abundant there from revenues generated under the persistent much higher growth. At the same time, the influx of massive foreign direct investment from overseas, in particular Hong Kong and Taiwan, was boosted by the call for speedier growth and bolder reform by

Deng Xiaoping; the relaxation of foreign entry into China's services sector, including the unexplored property market, focused overwhelmingly on the coastal region, especially Guangdong and Shanghai; it offered the local investment projects with alternative funding sources. Of the total amount of US$11.16 billion (about RMB60 billion), about 40% went to Guangdong,[28] and probably a total of 80% of this large sum was delivered to the coastal region.

The ineffectiveness of the credit squeeze policy on constraining investment, and hence economic growth, was clearly reflected in the further expansion of industrial growth in the Chinese economy. In the first three quarters of the year, gross industrial output growth averaged 19.3%, but in the remaining three months it was up by 22.4%, 26.1% and 32.2% respectively, indicating a yet very strong accelerating trend. However, the accelerating trend in the last quarter showed a greater concentration in coastal provinces than before. Of the nine provincial economies that experienced an above-national-average growth in the first three quarters, seven of them, with the exception of Anhui and Jiangxi, were coastal provinces south of the Yangtze river, excepting Shandong which is north of the river. Shanghai was not counted among the nine as it had only an average growth. The greater concentration of growth did not only take place in the coastal region as a whole but also within it: growth was further concentrated in the three highest growth provinces, Jiangsu, Zhejiang and Guangdong. Among them, they shared 40.83% of the net growth of the national industrial production in the first nine months. Their share moved up to 48.55% or about half of the nation's newly created industrial output. Of the three, Jiangsu was most outstanding. Its annual growth was an amazing 43.1%, about 10 percentage points more than the second placed Guangdong and over 20 percentage points above the national average. Its year-on-year monthly growth in the last three months of the year showed a triple jump from 46.7% in October to 57.8% in November and even to 75.8% in December. Its contribution to the national growth in the last quarter was 26.2%, significantly above the 19.5% attained in the preceding three quarters. Such an increasing concentration of growth in a few provinces reduced to six the number of provincial economies with growth above the national average in December (with a strange sudden upsurge in growth by Jilin to 44% from below 20% in the preceding months of the year), with not a few provinces struggling with a growth rate less than half of the national average. In terms of annual performance, there were still four provincial economies, three in the northwest and one in the northeast,

Table 2. China's Year-on-year Real Growth in Gross Industrial Output by Provinces in 1992

	January–December	October	November	December
National average	21.7%	22.4%	26.1%	32.2%
Jiangsu	43.1%	46.7%	57.8%	75.8%
Guangdong	33.3%	39.9%	42.6%	45.8%
Zhejiang	29.5%	34.4%	36.6%	42.8%
Hainan	28.9%	19.0%	46.4%	39.7%
Guangxi	26.9%	30.7%	36.5%	20.8%
Fujian	25.6%	26.0%	26.6%	48.0%
Shandong	23.1%	26.1%	22.5%	28.6%
Jiangxi	18.9%	12.0%	20.5%	19.2%
Henan	18.9%	16.5%	21.7%	27.7%
Shanghai	18.6%	14.3%	21.5%	16.9%
Anhui	18.4%	11.1%	11.3%	17.6%
Sichuan	17.6%	16.5%	23.1%	26.1%
Hebei	17.3%	17.6%	16.7%	23.3%
Tianjin	15.9%	17.4%	16.5%	23.5%
Yunnan	15.5%	23.9%	22.7%	11.4%
Beijing	15.0%	16.6%	14.2%	28.0%
Hunan	14.8%	13.2%	19.9%	18.8%
Jilin	14.6%	13.6%	20.0%	44.0%
Hubei	14.4%	17.8%	19.5%	24.8%
Xinjiang	14.2%	–3.7%	8.7%	17.2%
Liaoning	14.1%	15.0%	14.8%	22.7%
Guizhou	13.5%	7.5%	10.9%	9.9%
Ningxia	13.2%	18.7%	20.8%	15.8%
Gansu	12.2%	15.4%	18.1%	32.3%
Shaanxi	11.6%	13.0%	15.2%	16.1%
Inner Mongolia	9.3%	0.8%	9.1%	12.4%
Shanxi	9.2%	9.6%	12.0%	16.8%
Qinghai	4.8%	6.6%	20.5%	17.8%
Heilongjiang	4.3%	0.6%	5.8%	5.1%

Sources: *China's Latest Economic Statistics* (Hong Kong, CERD Consultants Ltd.), various issues.
Note: Tibet is not included.

that suffered from a below 10% growth in their industry. The persistent acceleration in industrial production towards the end of the year was basically the working of coastal provinces and cities, which were fortunate to enjoy an unconstrained supply of capital for financing their investment and investment-induced production as well as consumption arising from the income generated from both investment and production expansion.

The regional pattern of retail sales growth also confirmed the worsening regional disparity under the high growth of the Chinese economy. Corresponding to the acceleration in industrial production and investment in the last quarter, retail sales experienced a similar upward trend, albeit less dramatic than that of industrial production. Year-on-year monthly increase was 16.5% in October, 17.1% in November and 23.1% in December. However, if deflated by the rise in retail price index, the growth was not impressive at all, except for December, when the real growth broke beyond the 10% mark and reached 15.26%. Behind the rising sales in these months was a wide discrepancy in consumption between the urban and rural sectors. The gap in the real growth rates in retail sales in the two sectors was close to 4 percentage points in the last quarter. If provincial difference is entered into the retail trade scene, one should expect the discrepancy in consumption between urban and rural sectors in the interior region to be larger than the national average. Regional disparity has in a way produced the foundation for its worsening as the vicious circle of lower economic growth/capital shortage and, then, low income increase/lower consumption/still lower demand for raising growth drags further down the growth performance of the low-growth interior and northern provinces. Without the support of a mass consumption in the interior and northern China, the high growth of the coastal region, despite its heavy dependence on exports and imports, can not be sustained for too much longer, both for the market of its industrial products and for supply of capital supplementary to local and foreign sources.

The imbalance in national aggregate demand and supply and in regional disparity sustained economic acceleration in the coastal region by means of massive imports. Imports rose much faster in the last quarter at 36.93%, about 14 percentage points more than that of exports. It led to a reversal from the trade surplus of the preceding months of the year or of the same quarter in 1991 into a trade deficit of US$0.6 billion. If December alone were counted, the size of the trade deficit would be a huge US$2 billion. The lapse into a negative trade balance was quite an expected consequence of the persistent economic acceleration, as the rising prices of industrial materials close to and above international market price levels would easily induce users in China to turn to imported goods. It was probably because of the availability of imports that the coastal region was able to have the continuous material supplies for its growth acceleration and that inflation in China in general remained at a considerably lower level (stabilized at around 6.5% in the last three months of 1992) than what was normally expected from such a high economic growth.

Conclusion

By the end of 1992, the upward thrust of economic acceleration in the present cycle in China did not yet reach its peak, thanks partly to the open-door policy, which gave China access to the international markets for industrial materials and consumer goods, and partly to the very skewed regional pattern of economic growth, which prevented an explosion in aggregate demand in the whole of China. The high growth in 1992 was characterized by a heavily investment-led and therefore credit-supported pattern, while personal consumption in the form of retail sales lagged by a very large margin behind, distinguishing it from the double expansion in investment and consumption of 1987–1988. However, retail sales in the coastal regions and the urban sector were pulled up by the excessively high growth there; and because of the domination of the high income group of the urban population in this wave of consumption growth, retail sales unleashed a strong pressure for imported consumer goods, which, coupled with the excess demand for industrial materials arising from investment and production, in turn led to a fast building up of trade deficits, similar to the phenomenon in 1987–1988. Prices were also under a strong pressure to move up fast. The retail price index moved up in a spiral from an average of 4.9% in the first half of the year to 5.4% for the entire year with about 6.5% for the last quarter. The upward movement extended into 1993 to jump to 8.5% in January and February. If the trend continues into the latter months of 1993 — which is very likely given the strong upward trend in investment, production and prices — the peak of the present cycle will take place in 1993, perhaps in the first half of the year. But the imbalance of demand and supply has worsened so much that the foundation of sustainable growth has already been removed. Under the twin pressure of inflation and trade deficits, one may easily expect the kind of deflation experienced in recent years can occur again ushering the economy into a down-swing phase of the economic cycle, very much resembling the situation in 1989, albeit of a less abrupt nature.

Notes

1. See the discussion in Thomas M. H. Chan, "Industrial Development in China, 1977–1989," in *A Decade of "Open-door" Economic Development in China, 1979–1989*, edited by E.K.Y. Chen and T. Maruya (Tokyo: Institute of Developing Economies, 1991), pp. 29–55.
2. Cited in Ma Hong and Sung Shangqing (eds.), *Economic Situation and Prospect of China, 1990–1991* (in Chinese) (Beijing: China Development Press, 1991), pp. 3, 5.
3. Figures in current prices were deflated by the increase in the retail price index to give the annual real growth rates.
4. Ma and Sung (see Note 2), p. 8.
5. *Ibid.*, pp. 9–12.
6. *Ibid.*
7. Announcement made by the State Planning Commission, cited in *Economic Information* (Beijing), 31 January 1992, p. 2.
8. Li Peng, "Government Work Report," 20 March 1992.
9. Liu Guoguang (ed.), *Analysis and Projection of Economic Situation in 1993 China* (in Chinese) (Beijing: Chinese Academy of Social Sciences Press, December 1992), p. 23.
10. The call was made during Deng Xiaoping's southern tour in January and February 1992. The central Party organ issued a "Central Document Number 2" to make Deng's instruction an official policy instruction of the Party and government.
11. The growth rates are not comparable with those of 1991 listed above, as the latter refer to gross industrial output of the whole economy while the figures for the first half of 1992 are output at the *xiang* (town) level and above. Figures for 1991 come from *Statistical Year-book of China 1992*, and the 1992 data from *China's Latest Economic Statistics* (Hong Kong: CERD Consultants Ltd.), July 1992, part 1. Statistics of 1992, if not noted otherwise, are quoted from various issue of *China's Latest Economic Statistics*.
12. *Zhongguo jinrong* (China Finance), No. 12, 1992, p. 56.
13. Liu Guoguang (see Note 9), pp. 71ff.
14. *Ibid.*, p. 104.
15. *Ibid.*, p. 185.
16. *Ibid.*, p. 77.
17. See reports in *Economic Daily* (Beijing), 18 December 1992, p. 2; and *Economic Information* (Beijing), 13 January 1993, p. 1.
18. An official of the Research Office of the State Council revealed the emergence of a deficit in the foreign exchange balance in China's trade account in October 1992. See Liu Guoguang (see Note 9), p. 54.
19. *Financial Times* (Beijing), 5 August 1992, p. 1.

20. Premier Li Peng did not show his active support for the call of the People's Bank, nor did he express any concern for the liberal credit policy and rising inflation. See his remarks as reported during the period in *Economic Daily*, 21 July 1992, p. 1; 30 July 1992, p. 1, and *Economic Information*, 30 July 1992, p. 1.
21. It was said that a central work conference was held in the middle of August with most of the top of the Party and government participating. The outcome of the discussion at the conference was the "Central Document Number 8," which called for a rectification of the credit policy and inaugurated another round of credit squeeze in the economy.
22. Qiu Xiaohua, "Current Economic Situation in China and the Thinking for the 1990s," paper presented at the conference on China's Economic Development in the 1990s, February 1992, Hong Kong.
23. Liu Guoguang (see Note 9), p. 77.
24. Qiu Xiaohua (Note 21).
25. See the various sources in *People's Daily* (Overseas Edition), 18 September 1992, p. 2; *Economic Information*, 17 September 1992, p. 1; and *Liberation Daily*, 21 July 1992, p. 2.
26. *Guangdong Economic Analysis — Monthly Report* (Hong Kong: CERD Consultants Ltd.), July 1992, part 2.
27. *Guangdong Economic Analysis — Monthly Report*, February 1992, part 2.
28. Estimated from the over US$3 billion received by the province in the first eleven months in 1992. *Guangdong Economic Analysis — Monthly Report*, December 1992, part 2.

12

Central-provincial Fiscal Relations

Lok Sang Ho

Introduction

The study of central-provincial fiscal relations is interesting on three grounds. It represents an important aspect of the economic relationship between central government and provincial government, and can reveal past tensions and future developments. As central-provincial fiscal relations is an avenue for interregional equalization of economic disparities, it also inevitably represents an important aspect of inter-provincial economic relations. From this perspective the study of central-provincial fiscal relations is both a case study of the economics of regional disparity and a case study of intergovernmental politics. At the same time, it is an important determinant of the economic development of regions. From the economic point of view, regional investment can only be financed in any of three ways: reliance on own savings, including private sector savings and fiscal savings; reliance on private capital inflows; or reliance on intergovernmental fiscal transfers.[1] As investment is the engine of economic growth, an understanding of central-provincial fiscal relations will throw light on the future economic development of a province.

Strictly speaking, fiscal policy consists of only two components: policy on government spending and policy on taxes. Government spending has three effects, all of which must be spatially defined and thus have regional implications: it boosts *local* incomes which in turn stimulate private consumption and investment; it improves the level of *local* public services (consumption); it contributes directly to *local* fixed capital formation (investment). Taxes, on the other hand, draw down disposable income, again spatially different in incidence, and distort private sector incentives, leading to what economists call "excess burden" — a deadweight loss in terms of efficiency. Different taxes are levied on different tax bases, which are also different across different regions. While these aspects of fiscal policy are interesting, a fuller understanding of intergovernment fiscal relations must not narrowly focus on these issues. Discretionary power, depending on whether it is assigned to the provinces or to the central government, has different consequences on the tax revenues and spending of the different levels of government. Thus, we find it necessary in this chapter to discuss also the assignment of discretionary power, in addition to the narrowly defined fiscal policy issues.

According to *China Statistical Year-book*, the central share of budget revenue had declined steadily to 14.3% by 1979 but since then it has risen back, peaking in 1986 at 40.56% to decline moderately before rising again and breaching that percentage to reach 41.29% in 1990. The figure for 1991 was 38.76%. These figures, however, are misleading, first, because they represent revenues the collection of which was the responsibility of the central government and not revenues that accrue to central government. Moreover, it is widely recognized that extra-budget (*yusuanwai*) revenues as well as "extra-establishment" (*zhiduwai*) revenues have grown dramatically in recent years. Extra-budgetary revenues are revenues outside the purview of the state budget and collected by local governments, government agencies, enterprises, or administrative units according to set rules for specific purposes. Chinese sources admit that the figures reported officially (Table 1) understate the real picture. "Extra-establishment" revenues are revenues collected locally not according to established rules mutually agreed to between the central and the local governments. It is believed that budgetary revenues account for only one-quarter of total revenues collected by the entire government sector.

Overall, there seems to be little doubt that during the 1980s there was a real decline in the central government's relative fiscal position. According to Xiang Huaicheng (ed.),

> A series of budgetary deficits had arisen from the late seventies through the entire eighties.... According to the western way of calculating deficits which does not count money raised through external or internal loans as income, every single year in the eighties was a deficit year.... These fiscal deficits were essentially central government deficits. Total national deficits from

Table 1. Central/Local Shares of Extra-budget Revenues and Expenditures (RMB million)

Year	Central extrabudgetary income	Local extrabudgetary income	Central extrabudgetary expenditure	Local extra budgetary expenditure
1982	27070	53024	22705	50748
1983	35990	60778	30038	57543
1984	47054	71794	42024	69450
1985	63610	89393	56205	81298
1986	71663	102068	64094	93743
1987	82803	120077	74161	109914
1988	90715	145362	84286	130241
1989	107228	158655	97587	152723
1990	107328	163536	103769	166937

Source: *Zhongguo tongji nianjian 1992* (China Statistical Year-book 1992).

1981 through 1990 amounted to RMB 58.19 billion, of which the central government had RMB 68.658 billion of deficit while the local governments had RMB 10.468 billion of surplus. The central government's fiscal deficit would have been even larger if money raised from debt had not been counted as income....[2]

While the central government's fiscal position deteriorated, the provinces' fortunes were quite diverse. Some provinces and localities enjoyed a rapid increase in their command of resources; other provinces faced serious and aggravating problems. In some ways, the economic reforms of the 1980s had aggravated the problems of some provinces while benefiting others. Pricing policy, in particular the practice of suppressing prices for key industrial inputs, while allowing industrial output to fetch market prices, clearly benefited the more industrialized provinces at the expense of the raw material producing provinces. Measures were taken in the early 1990s to rectify some of these problems.

Most of these developments were not altogether planned.[3] Since 1979, the main concern of the central government had been economic growth. Fiscal policy and economic reform had been aimed at promoting economic efficiency, subject only to the constraints that any resulting fiscal imbalance be "manageable," and that inflation, social crises and regional grievances stay within acceptable limits. Pursuance of the main objective of economic efficiency underlay the trade reforms, price reforms, market reforms, as well as fiscal reforms throughout the 1980s. Considerations of the constraints underlay the fiscal transfers across regions, the ongoing negotiations with the provinces over fiscal arrangements, and the various attempts at checking and enforcing tax compliance and tightening up loopholes and the effort to experiment with new tax initiatives in carefully selected regions. Yet one thing led to another. Dynamics came into play, and the evolution of central-provincial relations soon had a momentum of its own.

Discretionary Power and Economic Development

The kinds of discretionary power that are of most interest to us include the power to issue bonds and, otherwise, to borrow; the power to raise taxes, to grant tax relief and to levy various kinds of charges; the power to release land for development and to determine the terms of release; the power to invest directly and to approve investments. The rapid economic growth of regional economies that have enjoyed the special status of "special economic zones," "open cities," or have opened up areas gives witness to the hypothesis that discretionary power at the regional level has been the key to good economic performance for the relevant regions. Yet, an important question is whether these special status regions have been gaining at the expense of other regions, or at the expense of the central government. Indeed the Governor of Shanxi made this remark recently: "Already there is disparity between the north and the south and the coastal regions as opposed to the inland regions. If the experience of the coastal regions and the special economic zones has been billed as successful why can the same policy apply to the inland regions? This would be favourable to productivity growth and fair competition. The coastal regions already are more favourably located than the inland regions. If they continue to enjoy more favourable policies the tensions between them and the inland regions will grow in a few years."[4]

It should be noted that the higher the value of these discretionary powers is, the fewer the provinces that enjoy them. When one province enjoys a discretionary power not shared by others it is in a better position to attract investment from foreign investors. Its gain in terms of larger tax base and employment may well be at the expense of other provinces.

In more recent months, China has begun to open up the more inland and more remote areas, first beginning with the regions along the Changjiang and later extending to truly inland areas. After considerable negotiation the central government has now promised to invest some RMB 77 billion in Hubei, an inland province, by 1995 and to grant it a status matching that of the special economic zones (SEZs).[5] Similarly, the border provinces of Heilongjiang, Yunnan and Xinjiang are also opening up to foreign investment and are seeing an upsurge in trade with neighbouring countries. Heihe and Suifenhe are two border cities that just recently received province-level status in regard to trade and economic cooperation matters. They are also allowed to open up economic cooperative areas with status similar to that of the special economic zones. Hunchun city, located in the Tumenjiang development region of Jilin, has been granted status at least matching that of the SEZs. These developments suggest a rather dramatic change in the relative fiscal positions of the provinces in the 1990s.

The Background of Fiscal Reform

Understanding fiscal reforms in China has to be predicated on understanding the dynamics of its economic reforms. For a long time China could claim that almost no Chinese citizen needed pay the income tax, but because wages were artificially depressed to well below workers' marginal products they were actually subjected to very high tax rates, but instead of paying them directly, the enterprises where they worked were able to derive huge artificial profits which were in turn remitted to the coffers of the government. In this process very serious "excess burden" had resulted: that is, the social loss caused through distorted incentives and output declines far exceeded the revenues raised. An important aspect of economic reform is thus to allow wages and prices to find their market levels, restore incentives and reinstitute more direct forms of taxes to recoup the otherwise lost revenue.

Quite apart from the "profit turned tax" (*li gai shui*) and the wage and price reforms that this transformation has required, the opening up of the Chinese economy has introduced much competition into Chinese markets, creating new challenges for China's state enterprises. In the product markets, state enterprises have had to face competition from enterprises set up by collectives, individuals, as well as foreign investors. In the labour market, they have had to compete for workers, whose total remuneration — wages, bonuses, and benefits included — have risen spectacularly. In principle, personal taxes should rise to replace eroded profits tax from state enterprises. In actual fact, however, few new personal taxes have been raised, while profit remissions to the state and profit taxes have sagged. At the same time, many winners in the competition — the newly rich business operators, private enterprises, and foreign companies — have been sheltered from either profit tax or personal tax because of a lack of tax collection and auditing ability and tax privileges. Unrecorded profits and earnings, as well as earnings from various illicit activities have been astounding.[6] Given China's circumstances, to include these incomes in the tax net would have required an expansion and consolidation of China's indirect tax system. In the absence of a successful tax effort in this direction, government revenues fell dramatically, from 31.2% of gross national product in 1978 to 18.1% in 1991.[7]

The decline in tax revenues accruing to the provinces may appear to be somewhat less dramatic, but their fiscal responsibilities have been rising throughout the 1980s and into the 1990s. In desperation, three authors from the provincial fiscal branch of Sichuan had this to say:

> Under the present system, the provincial fiscal situation is marked by the

absence, in a fundamental sense, of a direct revenue source that it can call its own. Because of this it is losing its ability to maintain itself as an independent fiscal entity. Dependence on both higher and lower levels of government for revenue has replaced independent discretion over revenue.[8]

Against this background there has been rising pressure to tap new tax revenues from all levels of government. Because of the lack of discretion by provincial governments to raise formal taxes that are on budget they have tried to raise revenue through off-budget levies of various sorts. As mentioned above, local governments resort to extra-budgetary and extra-establishment levies for this purpose. The former are mainly user charges and special levies raised by local government agencies in accordance with stipulated rules agreed to with the central government to meet specified needs. Extra-budgetary revenue as a percentage of budgetary revenue grew from 31% in 1978 to 79.5% in 1991. The latter are *ad hoc* charges, lawful at times and unlawful at other times but always levied under legitimate pretexts. Lawful or otherwise, it most certainly contributed to what has been called consumption by the social entities (*shehui jituan xiaofei*). Its excesses prompted a recent call for a formal legal framework to limit the various anomalies.[9]

Caution in Implementing Reforms

The central government has always been very cautious about introducing fiscal reforms, particularly those that affect local interests. Recognizing that much of the fiscal problems during the 1970s was traced to the ineffective control of spending at the local level, given the ease with which deficits could be passed to the central government, the central government introduced a system of fiscal contracts with the local governments in 1980 with the purpose of building up a sense of fiscal responsibility at the local level. This represented the first serious attempt at fiscal decentralization in the post-Mao period.[10] But in fact most of the reforms had precedents in fiscal experiments implemented at various times during the previous two decades.[11] The basic philosophy was to use the system of fiscal contracting to force the provincial governments to assume greater responsibilities for their own affairs.

Under this system revenue sources generally fell into three categories: central government revenue (e.g. profits of centrally controlled enterprises, industrial and commercial taxes or *gongshang shui* and tariffs); local government revenue (e.g. profits tax, salt tax, agricultural taxes, etc.); and shared revenue (either at fixed or adjustable ratios). On the expenditure side, "regular expenditures" were designated according to the lines of responsibility while "special category items" were covered from central revenue through special appropriations. Guangdong and Fujian, however, were allowed to remit a lump sum to the centre and retain the rest.[12] Shanghai, Beijing and Tianjin, on the other hand, had to remit a large fraction ranging from about two-thirds to 90% of all revenues collected.[13]

Since then, more major reforms were implemented in 1985 and 1988. The 1985 reform was designed to address the problem of differences in fiscal capabilities among provinces. A province may fall under any of four different models. It may retain an assigned percentage of total revenue collected, with the retention rate varying from 23.54% in the case of Shanghai in 1986 to 1987 to 100% in the case of Sichuan and Hubei during the same years. It may retain all revenues collected *and receive* an agreed subsidy from the centre, as in the case of Inner Mongolia. It may retain all revenues collected and pay an agreed amount to the centre. Finally, it may negotiate a custom-made contract with the centre in terms of revenue delivery. These options provided considerable flexibility in dealing with any province. The 1988 reforms represented a continuation of the same philosophy.[14] For fourteen provinces and autonomous regions designated as in-deficit according to baseline revenue and expenditure measures (Jilin, Jiangxi, Shaanxi, Fujian, Inner Mongolia, Guangxi, Tibet, Ningxia, Xinjiang, Guizhou, Yunnan, Gansu, Qinghai and Hainan), fixed transfers were given regardless of possible improvement in the fiscal position achieved by austerity measures or by revenue mobilization.[15] For two provinces and one municipality (Shandong, Heilongjiang and Shanghai) with a fiscal surplus, the revenue transfers to the centre were independent of new tax efforts. For five provinces (Hebei, Liaoning, Jiangsu, Zhejiang and Henan) and five municipalities (Beijing, Shenyang, Harbin, Ningpo and Chongqing), the marginal retention rate was to become 100% when revenue grew beyond specified levels. For two surplus provinces (Guangdong and Hunan), remissions to the centre were to grow yearly according to stipulated rates. These reforms were clearly designed to preserve the incentive of local governments to raise revenues.[16]

In 1990, after a lengthy consultation period, the seventh plenum of the Thirteenth Chinese Communist Party Central Committee resolved to leave intact the prevailing system of fiscal contract system and the enterprise contract responsibility system unchanged in the Eighth Five-year Plan period, rather than introduce the much-discussed tax sharing and tax-profit separation systems.[17] These latter systems, introducing a totally new mechanism of revenue collection and sharing, were regarded as more drastic than measures such as raising the base of existing fiscal contracts for local governments and tightening up the terms of responsibility contracts for enterprises. Partly as a result of growing fiscal stress, and partly in recognition of the merits of a well-defined tax sharing system, however, the central government decided to go ahead with experimentation with the tax sharing system (*fenshuizhi*) in nine provinces and cities, including Zhejiang, Liaoning, Xinjiang, Tianjin, Wuhan, Qingdao, Dalian, Shenyang and Chongqing. It is expected that the same system will be extended to other provinces and municipalities in 1993 and 1994.

The Salient Features of the Experimental "Tax Sharing System"

Just as in 1980, taxes are put into three categories: those designated as central government revenue, those designated as provincial government revenue, and those designated for sharing between the two levels of government. However, the emphasis is on providing a greater self-sufficiency at the local level and on departing from the fiscal contracting system. Any excess of revenues over expenditures is to be remitted to the centre, at an incremental rate of 5%, while any deficit over baseline expenditures is to be covered through a lump-sum subsidy from the central government. Baseline expenditures are drawn from actual expenditures in 1989 with adjustments when necessary.[18]

Under the new system, fifteen taxes are designated provincial tax categories for the first time. Among others, they include: agricultural and pastoral taxes, local state-owned enterprise income taxes, collective enterprise income taxes, local joint venture and foreign-owned enterprise income taxes, etc. The major departure from the prevailing practice is that the central government gives up any claim to state enterprise incomes. This enhances the incentives of the local governments to promote good economic performance of the enterprises. In general, the provincial governments are expected to derive more stable income under the proposal.

Under the new system, the fiscal contract system is to be gradually replaced by a system of tax sharing. The taxes to be shared are mainly indirect taxes, including the product tax, the value-added tax (VAT), business tax, the consolidated industrial and commercial tax, and the resource tax. These revenue sources have been expanding rapidly. Under the contract system, the percentage of tax revenues going to the central government has been on the decline. The new system, with the sharing ratio set at 5 : 5 for most provinces and at 2 : 8 for regions inhabited predominantly by minorities, is intended to rectify this trend.

The central government will retain all customs duties and all VAT and product taxes collected at customs. As well, income taxes derived from central government-owned state enterprises and from off-shore oil companies are 100% central.

That the Chinese government is fully committed to the tax-sharing system can be seen from the provisions in the *State Budget Management Regulations* (State Council Order No. 90), which took effect on 1 January 1992. There, four important principles were enshrined:

1. revenue sources are to be categorized as fixed central budgetary income, fixed local budgetary income and shared budgetary income while expenditures are to be categorized as central budgetary expenditures, local budgetary expenditures and special appropriations by the central government in favour of local expenditures (§17);
2. local budgetary surpluses are to be remitted to the centre; local budgetary deficits are to be covered with subsidies from the centre (§18);
3. the State Council will determine how the actual revenues and expenditures are to be categorized; similarly the State Council will determine how remissions and subsidies are to be made (§19);
4. higher levels of government must not appropriate funds of lower levels of government beyond what is provided by the budget; lower levels of government must not encroach upon funds of higher levels of government (§22).

In the absence of a formalized system of tax-transfer system that is regarded fair and is respected it is not clear how these principles can be put into practice. The immense complexity of the prevailing tax system will make such a system hard to work out.

The Urgent Need for Tax Simplification

From the fiscal reform initiatives of the 1980s through the recent attempt of "tax sharing," we can see that Chinese leaders are aware of the key principles of fiscal reform:

1. local expenditures earmarked for local benefit should be mainly funded locally (the 1980, 1985, 1988, and 1992 reforms);
2. the preservation of enterprise incentives requires that enterprises retain as much of their marginal profits as possible: the *de facto* marginal tax rate is what matters (under the *li gai shui*, enterprises were to pay a series of taxes designed to strip away all unearned income accruing to them, after which they were to be given greater autonomy in disposing of their residual earned income);[19]
3. fiscal equalization between the rich and the poor provinces;
4. preservation of the local tax effort.

Yet, the Chinese tax-transfer system is generally too complicated with too many *ad hoc* "add-ins" implemented from time to time to function effectively. For instance, there are four kinds[20] of enterprise profit taxes: the state enterprise profits tax, the collective enterprise profits tax, the private interprise profits tax, and the foreign-funded and foreign enterprise profits tax. Tax rates vary, with a proportional tax at 55% for the middle-sized and large-sized state enterprises and a progressive tax structure for small state enterprises and collective enterprises. Private enterprises are taxed at 35% while foreign-funded and foreign enterprises are taxed effectively at 33%. There are all sorts of exemptions.

On the other hand, various "adjustment" taxes or surtaxes can be imposed, and foreign enterprises in some special economic zones such as Shenzhen, are able to pay a profits tax of only 15%.[21] Similarly indirect taxes are equally, if not more complicated. While there are only two main categories of indirect taxes: the product tax and the value added tax, within the category of product tax, there are 24 types of products subject to different treatment with a total of 250 individual items. There are, moreover, 24 tax rates with the top at 60% and the lowest at 3%.[22] The value added tax is also immensely complicated, providing for various kinds of exemptions and with more than 10 tax rates applicable.[23] The tax system has not been effectively simplified by the tax reforms that have occurred since the late 1950s. Some taxes, such as the business tax, had been incorporated in 1958 in the "consolidated industrial and commercial tax" but were revived in subsequent reforms.[24] Such an intricate tax system is extremely unfavourable to the setting up of a credible tax-transfer system.

It has been recently reported that China is about to embark on a significant tax system simplication drive, consolidating various direct taxes and indirect taxes.[25] In particular, the personal income tax, the personal income adjustment tax and the individual business income tax are to be unified into one tax; as well, the various profits taxes will also move towards unification; while the intricate indirect tax system will be simplified. This should be an important step towards a less *ad hoc* tax-sharing-revenue-transfer system.

A Proposed Tax-transfer System

The current fiscal system provides considerable room for negotiation between the central and provincial governments. While these negotiations do allow much needed flexibility, the result of the negotiations may also reflect differences in political clout which may have little to do with the economic reality. At the same time, the tremendous regional differences and discrepancies in fiscal practices make monitoring and enforcement very difficult. Certain localities, for example, have reportedly ignored central government's stipulated rules and have included indirect taxes in fiscal contracting, eroding central government revenues.[26] A rational tax-transfer system designed from the national perspective should make the system fairer and more efficient. Moreover, in view of the serious intra-provincial inequalities that exist and of the fact that spending programmes, such as investment in industrial projects, may aggravate rural-urban disparity,[27] a tax-transfer system is superior to a tax-spending system in dealing with regional disparity. Governments of the poorer provinces will be in a better position than the central government to work with the transfers to help the poorer communities within their jurisdictions.

With very rapid economic growth, China's consumer market has been growing very strongly in recent years; it is projected to breach the RMB 1.1 trillion level by the end of 1993. In view of the very large underground economy and artificially depressed nominal incomes for a large segment of the population, indirect taxes should be central to the tax-transfer system.[28]

Suppose total national taxes collected is RMB K in a year. The central government retains a fixed percentage α of this revenue to cover its expenditures. Let us refer to the leftover revenue as national-provincial revenue (NPR). This NPR is subject to equalization among the provinces. NPR per capita for the nation is then K $(1 - \alpha)/N$ or RMB X per year, where N is the national population. If a province i has a population of n_i, and gross taxes collected are k_i, after remission to the central government it has $(1 - \alpha)k_i$, which averages out to x_i per capita. Suppose, for the sake of argument, this is smaller than X.

The transfer to province i can be calculated as

$$X \cdot n_i[1 + \beta(D - d_i)] - x_i \cdot n_i$$

where D is an average index of agglomeration for the nation while d_i is the index of agglomeration for province i. In general, the lower the index of agglomeration is, the more revenue is required to maintain a given level of government services. The first term is a measure of the amount of revenue required to maintain the supply of government services at an acceptable level and to alleviate poverty in the province. β is positive so that a high agglomeration index locally is assumed to reduce revenue requirements while a low agglomeration index is assumed to increase revenue requirements. Transfers/remissions are called for if the local revenues collected net of remissions fall short of/exceed local requirements. In practice, transfers receivable are paid via the central government while transfers payable are paid to the central government. To apply the formula one will have to work out the parameter β as well as the agglomeration indices for each of the provinces, self-administrative regions and directly administered cities.

Regionalism and Regional Balance of Payments

During the early 1980s, the economic and fiscal reforms failed to narrow the disparities existing between different regions of the country. "In 1979 the main regions East, Central, and West had per capita incomes of RMB451, RMB271 and RMB254 respectively, at the ratio 1 : 0.6 : 0.56. In 1987, per capita incomes for the same regions stood at RMB1,156, RMB672 and RMB591 respectively, at the ratio 1 : 0.58 : 0.51.... To an extent, the rapid development of the eastern seaboard was a result of the unequal economic relationship among the three regions and particularly between the coastal region and the inner provinces."[29] From 1981 to 1988 fixed capital formation for state enterprises in the inland areas as a percentage of the national total fell from 46.4% to 41%, a fall of 5.4 percentage points. During the same period the share of Guangdong, Shandong and Jiangsu's fixed capital formation for state enterprises rose by 6.5 percentage points. As the inland provinces were less able to attract foreign investment their relative decline was further accentuated. A similar story applies to infrastructural investment. The level of infrastructural investment in the coastal regions by the state was about the same as that in the inland provinces in 1984. The ratio rose to 1.26 in 1986 and 1.36 in 1988.[30]

The discontent of the inland provinces has been further exacerbated by the lack of support for education and medical care by the state.[31] Under the current system basic education and medical care are both the responsibility of the local government. As a result of fiscal contracting down to the level of the village (*xiang*) certain localities did not have enough financial resources to maintain adequate supply of educational services. A recent report, for instance, showed that 10 out of 12 counties (*xian*) in the Nanchong area of Sichuan owed 2 to 6 months of teachers' salaries. In Yilong county, as of November 1992, seven thousand teachers had not been receiving salaries for seven months, and the enrolment of new students had dropped from 2,500 in 1989 to 1,200 in the spring of 1992.[32]

Table 2 shows the *absorption* of the regional product in each province, autonomous region and directly-administered cities in selected periods. Absorption refers to the sum of consumption and investment in both private and public sectors. An excess of absorption over output is possible only through capital inflow or fiscal injection from out of the region. Thus, Qinghai, Ningxia and Xinjiang, not being popular spots for foreign investment, were the largest net recipients of fiscal injections in the list during the 1986–1989 period, while Shanghai and Jiangsu were clearly the major sources of fiscal outflows. Guangdong, being a favourite destination region for foreign capital, appeared to be a moderate source of fiscal outflow. The figures seem to suggest that Shanghai was at a significant disadvantage relative to Guangdong in terms of fiscal remissions to the central government since inauguration of the People's Republic of China.

As with any large country, considerable fiscal redistribution can be observed from the following Table. The problem with the Chinese fiscal transfer system is the lack of a systematic approach in dealing with the regional disparity problem. *Ad hoc* make-do programmes are both unfair and a source of uncertainty. One complaint recently lodged against the central government is that, instead of providing rural population the support that they need, the central government, strained by fiscal problems, let

Central-provincial Fiscal Relations

Table 2. Absorption as a Percentage of Regional Output*

Region	First Five-year Plan	Fifth Five-year Plan	Sixth Five-year Plan	1986–1989	Total 1950–1989
Beijing	201.1	73.6	92.3	114	98.1
Tianjin	65.2	68.5	76.1	96.2	76.9
Hebei	99.1	97.1	99.9	112.1	102.4
Shanxi	99.3	97.1	99.9	112.2	102.4
Inner Mongolia	80.9	129.4	127.3	121.9	115.5
Liaoning	82.3	73.4	81.9	91.9	81.9
Jilin	102.1	106.9	107.4	106.3	103.5
Heilongjiang	93	80	89.6	97.8	89.8
Shanghai	58.1	39.3	57	25.6	35.2
Jiangsu	89.1	85.8	86.5	67.2	77.1
Zhejiang	90.7	91.4	91.5	98	94.4
Anhui	100.2	96.5	99.5	100.3	99.5
Fujian	102.6	107.9	105.1	106.1	106.8
Jiangxi	94.2	106.4	106.1	104.6	104.7
Shandong	98.4	92.5	90.3	95.4	93.1
Henan	103	99.2	97.1	96.6	98.6
Hubei	108.2	96.7	91.3	n.a.	n.a.
Hunan	96.5	91.3	97.7	98.8	95.8
Guangdong	103	91.7	99.7	100.8	98.6
Guangxi	109.9	110.6	110.5	107.9	109.4
Sichuan	99.9	104.5	102.5	104.4	105
Guizhou	108.9	124.6	114.4	109.9	117.8
Yunnan	103	122.9	117.1	108	114.2
Shaanxi	111.4	104	118.7	119.3	118.2
Gansu	141.1	90.8	100.6	117.5	108.4
Qinghai	n.a.	125.8	131.4	136.9	131.4
Ningxia	112.7	125.8	131.4	136.9	131.4
Xinjiang	105.4	136.8	134	128.5	128.9
Nation	84.1	99.4	102.8	104.7	102.2

Source: Jiang Yue and Liu Yin (eds.), *Zhongguo diqu jingji zengzhang bijiao yanjiu* (A Comparative Study of Regional Economic Growth in China), (Shenyang: Liaoning People's Publishers, 1991). The editors quote these statistics drawn from China Statistical Publishers, *A Historical, Statistical Almanac of Provinces, Autonomous Regions, and Directly Administered Cities, 1949–1989*; data for Hainan and Tibet missing.

n.a. = not available

* These statistics are based on the MPS (material products system). The MPS differs from SNA (system of national accounts) principally in its treatment of services; the MPS does not count services as output; see *Zhongguo jingji tongji shiyong daquan* (Practical Manual on Chinese Economic Statistics), (Beijing: People's University Press, 1989), pp. 161–62.

the provinces with no choice but to issue IOU's (*da baitiao*) in their purchases from farmers, who had already been hurt by strong input prices that outstripped output procurement prices.[33] Rural provinces, such as Jilin, Hubei and Hunan, are especially affected by the central government's agricultural policy, which often imposes losses on such agricultural output as food grain. According to Zhou Jianwei, Secretary General of Hubei government, the loss on each kilogram of food grain in 1992 averaged RMB 0.2, and the fiscal deficit had to be borne by the provincial government. Hubei was the largest net borrower among all provinces; accumulated food production losses amounted to RMB 5 billion by the end of 1992 while unsold inventory of food had tied up an additional RMB 4 billion of funds.[34] The aggravation of the problem of regional disparity is a potential source of social instability and certainly is an important reason behind the "blind current" (*mangliu*) of migrants to the more prosperous cities.

It was against this background that Deng Xiaoping on his tour of the southern coastal cities earlier in 1992 "reportedly exhorted the coastal areas to pay some more taxes to the central government in the future in order to help out the less developed areas in the west."[35] Over the long run, as Ho Lok Sang (1993) argues,[36] a shortage of investment tends to jeopardize the ability of a region to export competitively, making it more dependent on central transfers.

Figure 1

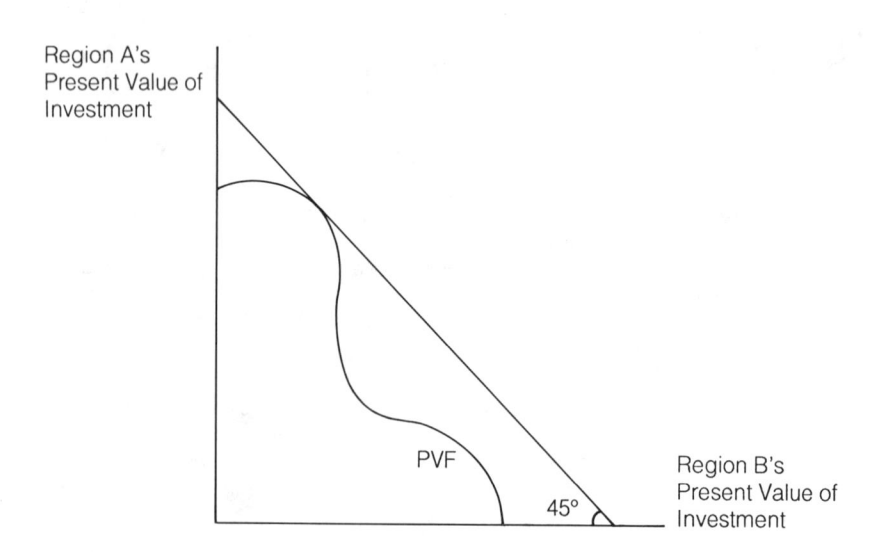

To a certain extent, the same problem has also characterized the traditional industrial heartlands of the country, such as Shanghai and Liaoning. Their industrial production rose respectively by 6.87% and 8.64% annually during the period 1981–1988, by only 57.5% and 72.4% of the national average. This was attributed to a stagnation of investment caused by excessive fiscal remissions to the centre. Shanghai had been required to remit in excess of 75% to the central government every year, as compared to less than 20% for the southern provinces.

From the nation's point of view, maximizing the "bang" for the "buck" requires that any investment be channelled to the locality where the return is highest. Put in another way, the nation wants to maximize the national net present value by allocating the investment funds spatially across regions. Figure 1 shows the maximization problem graphically. Suppose there are two regions, and the frontier of present values of capital invested in the two regions is shown by the line present value of investment (PVF). Because of local increasing returns the PVF line features a valley in the middle, suggesting that equal division of investable funds between the two regions may not be in the best interest of the nation. Maximization of present value, as required by efficiency considerations alone, however, means that region A will enjoy much faster economic growth than region B. In practice, a stronger infrastructure base will continue to attract private and foreign capital for a long time, leading to further disparity in the revenue bases of the two regions. In his much-reported tour to the south early in 1992, Deng Xiaoping was reported to have "exhorted the coastal areas to pay some more taxes to the central government in the future in order to help out the less developed areas in the west."[37] Table 3 shows that the open coastal cities and the special economic zones generally enjoy a fairly strong fiscal position. From this analysis, the need for a formal system of regional equalization payments and transfers is evident.

Conclusion

In 1992, foreign-related (*shewai*) taxes amounted to RMB10.7 billion, up a hefty 52.3%. Yet, it is generally recognized that tax evasion among the so-called *sanzi qiye* or foreign-funded enterprises (FFE) is rampant. Artificial losses, as well as the exhausting of all tax holidays and then the winding up of the enterprises, are common. There is also evidence that some foreign-funded enterprises artificially boost their import prices to

Table 3. Local Budgetary Revenue and Expenditure for Open Coastal Cities and Special Economic Zones 1990–1992 (in thousand RMB)

City	Local budgetary revenue/expenditure 1990	Local budgetary revenue/expenditure 1991	Local budgetary revenue/expenditure January–June 1992
Dalian	2595040	2713410	1301860
	1951100	2028380	732420
Qinhuangdao	407310	452430	238500
	292550	321010	131610
Tianjin	4808710	4900080	2396040
	3820430	3957970	1740000
Yantai	1032720	1135700	537940
	899730	916030	363810
Weihai	360760	398130	208500
	348060	363250	148230
Qingdao	2278040	2482960	1358890
	1163960	1233020	555510
Lianyungang	398080	383380	182770
	385840	419110	152850
Nantong	1259490	1229000	629020
	714630	763220	332910
Shanghai	16270000	16508610	8552000
	7536830	8285590	3843720
Ningbo	1589100	1756720	1074400
	971330	1040260	469710
Wenzhou	889290	993820	658370
	4531050	935570	383210
Fuzhou	1094470	1199600	695070
	828160	956840	412100
Guangzhou	3784010	4170330	2161720
	2291170	2500980	1163260
Zhanjiang	697670	829130	314820
	627800	779880	289180
Beihai	158730	194860	93730
	182370	216660	105160
Total for open coastal cities	37623420	39348160	
	26545010	24717770	
Shenzhen	2169630	2731570	2097510
	1979930	2430610	1404850
Zhuhai	444340	592420	n.a.
	554250	678690	
Shantou	840840	1073420	458010
	1020810	1244630	340510

Table 3. **Local Budgetary Revenue and Expenditure for Open Coastal Cities and Special Economic Zones 1990–1992 (in thousand RMB)** (continued)

City	Local budgetary revenue/expenditure 1990	Local budgetary revenue/expenditure 1991	Local budgetary revenue/expenditure January–June 1992
Xiamen	1029820	1183620	662600
	939790	1012870	363650
Hainan	738940	921010	572950
	1742470	1934560	804130
Shenzhen (SEZ)	1951250	2454810	n.a.
	1804890	2207580	
Zhuhai (SEZ)	389510	480500	n.a.
	489590	568130	
Shantou (SEZ)	148740	213740	n.a.
	148860	199060	
Xiamen (SEZ)	982110	1125300	n.a.
	870170	932330	
Fangchen Port	8950	28990	n.a.
	15710	32490	

n.a. = not available

bring about losses and thus to reduce their tax liability.[38] Moreover, there are many "false *sanzi qiye*" that are really indigenous but assume a false identity simply to obtain favourable treatment. In general, these practices are mainly at the expense of the central government. Standardizing the tax system by removing the differential treatment applicable to FFE and local enterprises will simplify matters and plug an important loophole in the tax system. It is unlikely that removing the favourable treatment for FFE will significantly reduce capital inflow, as the price of land will adjust to retain China's attraction for foreign capital. The government has already announced its policy of levelling state enterprises and private enterprises. Levelling FFE and indigenous enterprises is in the same spirit and will promote efficiency.

As of December 1992, the total number of approved foreign-funded enterprises stood at over 83,200. With the policy of taking the market economy route officially entrenched and the establishment of a sounder legal system, there is no doubt that foreign-related taxes will continue to grow rapidly, outpacing most other sources of revenue. Another rapidly growing category of taxes is indirect taxes (product tax, value-added tax, and business tax), which rose RMB 19 billion to reach RMB 205.3 billion in 1992.[39] Simplifying these taxes and using a national perspective in restructuring the tax-transfer system regionally in the way we have proposed will improve efficiency, reduce regional disparity and minimize tax evasion. In recent years, China's fiscal deficit problem has not improved notwithstanding rapid economic growth. Tax simplification is an important first step towards dealing with the fiscal deficit problem. At the same time, we have argued that equalization transfer payments should provide the formal mechanism to deal with the regional disparity problem, while infrastructure investments should be dictated by considerations of efficiency alone. Regional equalization should be incidental to, rather than a main consideration behind, infrastructure investment.

Epilogue

During the upcoming Eighth National Peoples' Congress the problem of fiscal relation is on the agenda and is said to be a focal point of discussion. Total government sector deficit in 1992 amounted to some RMB90.5 billion. Internal debt should cover RMB21.2 billion of the total deficit and external debt RMB23.7 billion. The central government is expected, in addition, to borrow some RMB20.6 billion from the People's Bank of China, while local governments are "to find their own ways of resolving the deficit of 3.1 billion yuan."[40] That central-local conflicts and interregional conflicts will come to the forefront in national debate has been clear from the very beginning, and it is high time that the central government addresses this problem with determination and economic sense. Because the local governments are generally very much circumscribed in their ability to borrow, and they do not have access to the printing press as does the central government, their fiscal problems are potentially more acute than that of the central government. It has even been reported that some local governments have been unable to fulfil their obligations paying their staff. The signs indicate that Beijing is well aware of the grievances of local governments and the potential risks. It is hoped that Beijing will soon use a systematic rather than the *ad hoc* approach which has been prevalent thus far in tackling this problem.

Notes

1. For a discussion, see L. S. Ho, "Regional Balance of Payments: An Interpretation," *Regional Studies*, forthcoming.
2. See *Jiushi niandai caizheng fazhan zhanlue* (Strategy of Fiscal Development

Strategy in the 1990s) (Beijing: Zhongguo caizheng jingji chubanshe, 1991), pp. 16–17.
3. Wong argued that the pervasive use of extra-budgetary funds by local governments was a "dysfunctional outcome of fiscal reform rather than ... an intended product" (p. 693). See "Central-Local Relations in an Era of Fiscal Decline: The Paradox of Fiscal Decentralization in Post-Mao China," *The China Quarterly*, No. 128 (December 1991), pp. 691–715. Unintended though this may be, I would argue that this generally conforms with the *quid pro quo* principle of taxation, whereby user charges of various kinds are used to finance local expenditures and, therefore, is not altogether inefficient. See Christine P. W. Wong, "Fiscal Reform and Local Industrialization: The Problematic Sequencing of Reform in Post-Mao China," *Modern China*, Vol. 18, No. 2 (April 1992), pp. 197–227.
4. He Pin, "Regional Lords Each Showing His Power — A Brief Outline of Regional Powers in China" (in Chinese), *Hong Kong Economic Journal Monthly*, August 1992, pp. 78–81.
5. He Pin (see Note 4), p. 80.
6. See Lu Xianchang and Yang Yunyan, "The Erosion of Revenue by the Underground Economy," *Caimao jingji* (August 1992), pp. 44–49, for a study of the development of underground economy in China. According to an estimate they cited, tax evasion amounted to RMB8.82 billion in 1989, 200% higher than the 1986 level.
7. *A Statistical Survey of China, 1992*.
8. Li Dachang, Wang Bin, Wang Yingsong, "A Discussion of the State of Fiscal Position of the Provinces and the Directions of Reform," *Caizheng yanjiu*, June 1992, pp. 22–27.
9. See Wu Lihua and Wang Qingjian, "Strengthening the Supervision of Extra-budgetary Funds Requires a Legal Framework," *Caizheng* (June 1992), pp. 25–26. The discussion clearly applies to extra-establishment funds which are seldom formally discussed in official publications.
10. An outline of the earlier developments can be found in Audrey Donnithorne "Central-Provincial Economic Relations in China," *Contemporary China Papers*, No. 16, 1981, Contemporary China Centre, Research School of Pacific Studies, Australian National University; and Nicholas Lardy, "Centralization and Decentralization in China's Fiscal Management," *The China Quarterly*, No. 61 (March 1975), pp. 26–60.
11. Michael Oksenberg and James Tong, "The Evolution of Central-Provincial Fiscal Relations in China 1971–1984: the Formal System," *The China Quarterly*, No. 125 (March 1991), pp. 1–32.
12. Guangdong submitted RMB 1 billion each year from 1979 to 1984. Submission rates were raised from 1985. See Zhu Jiajian, "Guangdong's Economic Relationships with Central Government and with Other Provinces/

Municipalities," in *Guangdong: 'Open Door' Economic Development Strategy*, edited by Toyojiro Maruya (Hong Kong: Centre of Asian Studies, University of Hong Kong and Tokyo: Institute of Developing Economies, 1992), pp. 98–125.
13. See Christine Wong, Note 3, p. 208.
14. See Yan Bin, "Correctly Dealing with the Fiscal Relationship between Local and Central Governments: Gradual Implementation of the Tax-sharing System," *Caizheng jinrong yanjiu*, Vol. 4, No. 113 (1991), pp. 3–10.
15. Hubei and Sichuan, excluding Wuhan and Chongqing, were designated as in-deficit and received subsidies out of revenue remissions of the two cities to the centre.
16. More special, "custom-made" arrangements were reached for Tianjin, Shanxi, Anhui, Dalian, Qingdao and Wuhan.
17. See "Opinion," *China Economic News*, Vol. XII, No. 3 (21 January 1991).
18. *Caizheng*, August 1992 and *Ta Kung Pao*, 20 June 1992.
19. Christine Wong, see Note 3, p. 215.
20. A more detailed categorization would be four profits taxes for domestic enterprises and two profits taxes for firms with foreign connections.
21. For some of the problems, see Liu Xingyi and Shi Jian, "Unify the Enterprise Profit Tax and Establish an Equitable Tax Environment," *Caizheng yanjiu*, July 1992, pp. 43–45. See also Zhuang Xianwen, "Reform the Enterprise Profits Tax by Learning from Foreign Tax by Conventions," *Caimao jingji*, Vol. 5, No. 125 (May 1992), pp. 31–34 and 37.
22. See Song Shuhai and Xia Jinliang, "The Product Tax and the Value-added Tax: A Comparison," *Caimao jingji*, No. 109, January 1991, p. 32.
23. See Chen Gong, "Some Thoughts on Rejuvenating the Fiscal System," *Caimao jingji*, No. 11, 1991.
24. For an overview of reforms see Deng Ziji (ed.) *Caizheng yu xindai* (Finance and Credit) (Beijing: Central Television Broadcast University Press 1985), and World Bank, *China: Revenue Mobilization and Tax Policy* (Washington DC: 1990).
25. *Hong Kong Economic Times*, 30 (circa) December 1992.
26. *Ming Pao* (Hong Kong), 14 November 1992.
27. See Kai-yuen Tsui, "Decomposition of China's Regional Inequalities," *Journal of Comparative Economics*, forthcoming. An indicator of the great income inequality in China is savings figures. While the top less-than-3% of the Chinese population accounted for 28% of total savings deposits, 800 million rural population dependent on agriculture accounted for only 26%. Richer families in cities and townships, including mainly the individual business operators, have an average savings deposit of RMB5400, 6 times the national average and 18.3 times that of the rural population, *Ming Pao*, 12 February 1993.

28. See Lu Xianchang and Yang Yunyan, Note 6, pp. 44–49.
29. See Jiang Yue and Liu Yin (ed.), *Zhongguo diqu jingji zengzhang bijiao yanjiu* (A Comparative Study of Regional Economic Growth in China), (Shenyang: Liaoning Peoples' Publisher, 1991), p. 36.
30. See Regional Economic Policy Study Group, "Regional Economic Policy in the 1990s," *Guomin jingji jihua yu guanli*, June 1990, pp. 18–23.
31. It was recently reported that Yilong county in Sichuan had owed teachers seven months of salary totalling RMB7 million in November 1992. With fiscal contracting down to the *xiang* (village) level economic backward areas like Yilong and Nanchong had been severely affected by the shortage of funds.
32. *Ming Pao*, 21 January 1993.
33. *United Daily News*, 10 February 1993.
34. *Ming Pao*, 30 January 1993.
35. *China Economic News*, Vol. XIII, No. 43, 9 November 1992.
36. See Note 1.
37. See "Opinion," *China Economic News*, Vol. XIII, No. 43.
38. In Shenzhen, it is estimated that 60% of the *sanzi qiye* engage in some form of tax evasion. Nationally, at least half of state enterprises evade taxes; some 60% of collective enterprises and 80% of private enterprises and individual business operators evade taxes, *United Daily News*, 17 February 1993.
39. *United Daily News*, 19 January 1993.
40. *United Daily News*, 14 March 1993.

13

Banking

Luk Yim Fai

Introduction

Since Deng Xiaoping's celebrated tour to the south early last year, China's economic reform started to move at a much faster pace. Economic activities expanded rapidly and the official growth rate reached 12.8% in 1992, more than double the planned figure of 6%. Nevertheless, there have not been much inspiring reform in the banking sector in the past year or so, except may be the presence of an increasing number of foreign financial institutions in wider geographical areas. Within the financial system, any significant change in the banking sector, if at all, was overshadowed by the development of the share-holding system and the stock exchanges in Shanghai and Shenzhen. The sharp fluctuations in stock prices, the listing of new enterprises in the exchanges, as well as the issuance of the so-called "B" shares for foreigners all caught the attention of domestic and foreign investors alike. In comparison, banks still operated in more or less as in the mid-1980s, lagging behind other aspects of economic reform.

In a market economy, banks serve two broad categories of functions. First, they are involved in the credit process as intermediaries, channelling funds from households and enterprises with surpluses to those currently in need. In doing so, banks perform the role of "delegated" monitors: they evaluate the prospects and risks associated with the loans they grant to the borrowers. The latter are not in a good position to judge the loans themselves because they lack the appropriate expertise. Moreover, the amount of their individual deposits is usually not large enough to justify spending resources on acquiring the relevant information to screen the loans and monitor the payback. Banks, on the other hand, can handle loans better because of economies of scale and the possibility of risk-pooling. In other words, one social function of the banking sector is to help channel funds to those areas that are most worthwhile. Secondly, banks are involved in the monetary process. Monetary policies by the central bank for macroeconomic control are typically carried out through the banking sector. As such, a well-functioning banking sector is instrumental in the maintenance of macroeconomic stability.

Despite the effort spent on the reform of the banking sector in the past decade or so, banks in China are still far from being able to carry out the above functions well. The following sections give a brief review of the earlier reforms of China's banking system, examine the current situation and some recent development, as well as discuss the possible changes that will take place in the near future.

Earlier Banking Reforms

Before 1979 when central planning was the rule in organizing economic activities, production and investment were carried out by command and were allocated the necessary financial capital. As a result, it was not the responsibility of financial institutions to oversee and determine the flow of funds: banks did not serve as banks but merely as cashiers. They did not perform the functions of risk assessment and loan monitoring. Since economic activities typically carry over from the present to the future, and since no one knows for sure what will happen in the future, there have got to be risks and uncertainties associated with current economic decisions. In a market economy, such risks are born by the corresponding investors and suppliers of funds, or transformed and traded in the financial markets. However, the pre-reform banking system of China ignored such risks and, as a result of resource allocation by command, risks were born by the economy as a whole.

There were other shortcomings as well. For one, there was a lack of distinction between state budget policy and monetary policy. For another, it was basically a system with no diversity and no competition. Indeed, since the job was primarily that of cashiers, there was no need for diversity nor competition. With regard to macroeconomic concern, there was little problem of macroeconomic instability, at least on the surface. Aggregate demand was highly constrained by administrative means and by the low levels of income. After all, basically all prices were controlled. Any inflationary pressure was suppressed so that it did not show up in official statistics.

As long as the economy remained controlled and dominated by central planning, the incompetence of the banking system continued to be concealed. However, since the late 1970s, reforms such as the devolution of economic decision-making power, the opening up to foreign trade and direct investment, the increasing reliance on the market mechanism, etc. have drastically transformed the Chinese economy. Yet, banking reform has not made sufficient progress to keep pace with other reforms.

At the outset of reform, the People's Bank of China (PBOC) was basically the only national banking institution. The major part of banking reform in the 1980s involved the breaking up of the national banking system into a few specialized banks serving different sectors of the economy. The first of these specialized banks was the Agricultural Bank of China (ABOC) which had previously been set up and abolished a few times. It was re-established in February 1979 to handle the financing of rural development and was instrumental in the success of rural reform, the first phase of Chinese economic reform.

The second specialized bank instituted was the Bank of China (BOC) which was made independent of the PBOC in March 1979. It specialized in foreign exchange dealings and helped finance the opening up of China in both trade and investment. At the same time, the State General Administration for Foreign Exchange was set up to supervise exchange control and exchange rate policy.

The People's Construction Bank of China (PCBC) had been shouldered with the responsibility of handling the country's construction investment since its establishment in 1954. However, what it had been doing was to distribute state funds to state enterprises in the form of non-repayable, non-interest bearing loans according to planning and under the direction of the Ministry of Finance. Since the reform, the PCBC has had more independence in the management of both its assets and liabilities. It can expand its deposit base to build up its source of funds, and its loans for construction investment have become repayable and interest-bearing. In addition, the China Investment Bank was set up in December 1981 to specialize in channelling foreign funds such as those from the World Bank to domestic fixed investment.

The earlier mono-banking system under the PBOC was further dismantled in late 1983 when the State Council announced that the PBOC would give up its commercial banking functions of lending and deposit-taking. Instead, PBOC would become a central bank in the western sense of the term, being responsible for macroeconomic control of money and credit, the regulation of other financial institutions and the provision of banking services for the government. The original commercial lending and deposit-taking businesses of the PBOC were taken over by the newly created Industrial and Commercial Bank of China (ICBC). The ICBC has since become the largest of the specialized banks and is responsible for the financing of industrial and commercial activities in urban areas.

As a result of the above changes, by mid-1980s China's banking system mainly consisted of a central bank and a few major specialized banks, each catering to the needs of different sectors of the economy. The next stage of banking reform involved the introduction of a series of comprehensive and regional banks in 1987. The most prominent comprehensive bank is the Bank of Communications (BCOM), which was re-instituted in April 1987. The BCOM is a joint-stock bank, with 50% of its shares held by the state represented by PBOC, and the rest by municipal governments, enterprises and private investors. Unlike the specialized banks, it is not restricted in its business to any particular regions, sectors or activities. It provides more or less full banking services and can deal both in *Renminbi* (RMB) and foreign currencies. Another important comprehensive bank is the one under China International Trust and Investment Corporation (CITIC) called the CITIC Industrial Bank which started business in August 1987.

A few regional banks owned by government and government enterprises have also been set up to promote regional economic development. These include the Shenzhen Development Bank which is a commercial bank serving various types of enterprises in the Special Economic Zone of Shenzhen. Other important examples of regional banks are the Guangdong Development Bank, the Fujian Industrial Bank and the Xiamen International Bank. The Shanghai Pudong Development Bank has also been licenced to do business in Pudong, the new focus of China's economic reform in the 1990s.

Besides banks, numerous credit cooperatives have also developed in both rural and urban areas. These are under supervision of the ABOC and ICBC respectively and both aim to serve small enterprises, collective and private. By the end of 1991, there were over 58,000 rural and over 3,400 urban credit cooperatives.[1]

The breaking down of the mono-banking system into one with various institutions necessitated a mechanism for the flow of funds among these institutions. In 1986, interbank lending was authorized and encouraged, and since then, regional and nationwide interbank markets have developed with centres in major cities such as Beijing, Shanghai, Wuhan, Chongqing and Guangzhou.[2]

The diversification of China's banking institutions in the 1980s was accompanied by rapid expansion in the volume of banking business, due mainly to the overall success of economic reform. The total sources of funds to the state-owned banks and the rural credit cooperatives as a whole multiplied from RMB220.5 billion in 1979 to RMB1,821.3 billion in 1990, with an annual growth rate of 21.2%. Total deposits increased from 136.2 to 1,302.9 billion and total loans from RMB208.2 to 1,654.1 billion in the same period, with annual growth rates of 22.8% and 20.7% respectively.

There have been some slight changes in the structure of the asset side of the consolidated balance sheet. Total loans accounted for 94.4% of total use of funds in 1979. The percentage dropped to 90.8 in 1990. Loans remained the predominant uses of funds simply because little alternative assets such as securities were available domestically. As international transactions increased, foreign assets became possible forms of fund holding. The total shares of foreign exchange holdings and assets in international financial institutions rose from 0.9% to 4.7% of total uses of funds.

Changes on the liability side, however, were more distinct. In 1979, only 61.7% of total sources of funds came from deposits from various sectors; by 1990 the figure rose to 71.5%. In particular, urban savings deposits and rural household savings deposits accounted for 14.9% and 5.7% of total deposits in 1979; by 1990 the figures were 39.9% and 14.1% respectively.[3] This rapid increase in household deposits was the result of fast economic growth and the greater degree of economic autonomy on the part of the private sector, as well as the lack of alternative forms of assets. One implication of this change in the debt structure of the banks was that banks had to face increasing market pressure from the private sector.

Thus, earlier reform in China's banking system was focused on the diversification of the financial system. The progress was quite impressive in comparison with the situation before the reform. More varieties of institutions were handling rapidly increasing volumes of banking activities. Nevertheless, in terms of the needs of the economic reform, the system hitherto had been far from being able to serve the functions of efficient channelling of funds and the maintenance of monetary and credit control.

The Current Situation

Earlier banking reforms in the mid- and late 1980s resulted in a more diversified system of financial institutions, but diversification of financial institutions by itself did not imply that these institutions had emerged as independent and competitive entities. Banks in China are still subject to excessive government control, the need to make substantial amounts of loans for policy rather than economic consideration, non-performing loans to loss-making state enterprises and the lack of sufficient market competition, etc., conditions which characterized banking before the reform. In addition, the reform and its accompanying devolution of economic power have weakened the central government's ability to perform its macro-economic control. Thus, on the one hand, funds are still not allocated efficiently; on the other hand, macroeconomic instability has become a recurrent phenomenon. As in other aspects of reform, but to a greater extent, banking reform in China has not been successful in arriving at the delicate balance between appropriate control and sufficient deregulation.

Unlike other aspects of the economic reform where the private sector has been able freely to participate and sometimes even take the initiatives, very little private sector participation has been allowed in the realm of finance. The provision of banking services has basically been confined to the state sector. While non-state enterprises now account for half of output in industry, China's state banks still hold more than 85% of all financial assets.[4] There have been reports of private banks emerging in cities like Wenzhou, Zhejiang province, but these account for a negligible share of national banking business. Besides, they have recently been highly regulated in their activities.[5] The lack of voluntary private sector input means that banking reform in China has to proceed from top to bottom in a planned manner and be always under strict government control.

The most immediate effect of state dominance in banking is the large amount of policy loans, that is, loans made as a result of policy consideration. In most cases the loans are granted to poorly managed state enterprises which would not be able to get any alternative source of funds. Officially, 30% of loans offered by specialized banks are policy loans, although it has been recognized by a bank director that the true proportion is probably higher than that.[6] State banks do not have to worry about the performance of policy loans since it is understood that they are to be bailed out by the government in case they run into trouble, while state enterprises can count on getting funds from the banks as policy loans irrespective of their own productive efficiency. This problem of super-moral hazard results in large amounts of bad debts. It has been estimated that perhaps 20% of the loans on the books of the state banks are bad.[7] And according to PBOC, 46% of fresh bank loans in 1992 only created unmarketable goods.[8]

As loans are allocated by administrative means, there is no necessary relationship between the amount of deposits and the amount of loans. Banks are given quotas on the amount of loans they can make. Once the quotas are used up, banks have very little liberty to extend further loans even with more deposits. Idle funds in the economy simply become idle funds in the banks, not channelled into more productive use. On the other hand, banks that do not attract enough deposits can still make loans of large amounts, the shortfall being covered by the authorities.

The transformation of the earlier mono-banking system into a more diversified one might introduce some elements of competition to help enhance banking efficiency. However, this is not obviously true since the specialized and regional banks that were instituted were all assigned their own business areas with little overlapping. Only the comprehensive banks, which are much smaller both in number and in the size of their balance sheet, can generate some form of competition. In fact, it could be argued that monopoly tendencies in banking have strengthened. The savings deposits of the four major specialized banks — the ICBC, the ABOC, the BOC, and the PCBC — rose from 65% to 74% of the national total in 1991. Moreover, 95% of all central bank low interest loans went to these four, and they enjoyed preferential treatment in their business, as well as in the establishment of branches.[9]

Thus, despite the earlier banking reforms, banking activities in China still remain highly susceptible to intervention by the state. In addition, as economic reform results in some degree of decentralization of economic decision-making power, banks have to accommodate the requests of the local governments as well. Policy loans are also made on the initiative of local officials in addition to that of the central government.

Economic decentralization has also given rise to a new series of bank and nonbank institutions. Both the Everbright Bank of China and the Huaxia Bank, set up in 1992, have been affiliated with large national enterprises, the latter being under the Capital Iron and Steel Corporation. The former, free from some of the directives that govern lending of most institutions, was able to quadruple its assets in the span of just a few months. Most large enterprises are thinking of doing the same thing, moving into the lucrative business of banking and finance irrespective of their primary business concern. Besides banks, numerous nonbank financial institutions have also been established. Most of these are involved in speculation in the recently opened markets of stocks and real estates; the supervisory responsibilities of such institutions are vague.[10]

The long history of administrative control of bank credit has deprived the banking system of the opportunity to develop more efficient ways of channelling funds. Economic reform itself has, on the other hand, weakened the ability of the authorities to regulate. A large part of bank credit is simply appropriated by the powerful at various levels. Short-term loans are turned into long-term loans, long-term loans into indefinite loans, and credit funds are taken as fiscal budgets.[11]

The lack of credit control is partly reflected in the interbank market. Interbank loans have relatively long terms to maturity. They are not borrowed to augment required reserves or for short-term liquidity needs, but as a source of loan funds. The volume of interbank loans has been high despite the fair amount of bank reserves. At the end of 1991, the specialized banks had 12.7% more reserves than required, and yet they borrowed over RMB211 billion from the PBOC, the central bank.[12]

Under the present system, central bank credit is coveted by everyone. Each year, billions of *Renminbi* of new central bank credit are distributed among banks, regions, and institutions. The process is extremely arbitrary. Branch banks at all levels seek larger sizes of funds and do all possible to exploit the interest rate differentials. Some large nonbank financial institutions have tied up central bank credit for a long period of time to make profits in such a way.[13]

Due to the inefficiency of the bank loan market, the extending of policy loans and the appropriation of loans at both the central and local levels, credit planning has ceased to be effective in itself and as a means of macroeconomic policy. Credit plans are typically based on planned growth rates, planned degree of increase in prices and constant interest rates when, in fact, changes in the economic system have rendered these variables unaffected by means of control. As a result, readjustments in planning have to be constantly made throughout the year. For example, total new loans planned at the beginning of 1990 were RMB170 billion, the actual figure at the end of that year turned out to be RMB273.1 billion. The corresponding figures for 1991 were RMB210 and RMB289.5 billion respectively.[14] In 1992 actual new loans rose to RMB360 billion and the money supply grew by 30%.[15] The rapid growth in money and credit has sparked concern of rekindled inflation. In fact, the annual inflation rate for the first quarter of 1993 was 8.6% for the economy as whole, but reached 15.7% in the major cities.[16] Such high inflation rates are reminiscent of the previous high inflation in 1988, when the authorities had no policy tools to tackle such problem but to resort to austerity measures. Unfortunately, should such measures be again adopted to fight inflation, their effectiveness will be doubtful. The devolution of economic power as an integral part of reform has made it more difficult to contract the economy by administrative means.

Overall, earlier banking reforms in China have not gone far enough to handle the changing needs of the economy. Instead of facilitating economic reform, the banking system has become the restraining factor for further economic development with stability. Ultimately banks have to assume the functions of the efficient allocators of credit and the guardians of macroeconomic stability.

The Commercialization of Banks

The present state-dominated banking system has to be transformed into one with a large share of banks that can make decisions on commercial rather than policy grounds. Commercial banks are free from the restrictions currently placed on the specialized banks and are subject to less government control.

The BCOM is often cited as a successful commercial bank in China today. It has learned to use the kinds of asset and liability management methods of foreign banks. It was listed in the June 1992 issue of *Euromoney* as among the 1,000 largest banks in the world, with a net return on capital of 31.5%, the seventh highest in the world.[17] The BCOM is a joint-stock bank and aims to be listed on the Shanghai stock exchange in the future. It has succeeded because it has been less influenced by the government than the specialized banks. Its president, Mr Dai Xianglong, claims that the bank makes no policy loans and faces no credit quota. Yet, like the other banks, interest rates are fixed and it cannot use the rates to adjust for different risks and maturity of loans and deposits. As a result, one-third of BCOM's loans turns over every 40 days, and 95% of the loans have maturities less than one year.[18] This shows that the commercialization of banks by itself is not sufficient if the whole system is heavily regulated. Nevertheless, the separation of commercial and policy activities is still necessary.

After the Communist Party's Fourteenth Congress last October, the central government announced that the specialized banks should be commercialized. The difficulty lies in the way to transform their assets and liabilities. Zhao Haikuan, Director of the Research Institute of Finance and Banking under the PBOC, proposed the set-up of a government bank to shoulder the special loan items now within the central bank, the policy loans by the specialized banks, as well as the small amount of loans currently made by the treasury. At present, the central bank takes up quite a certain amount of business, with organizations at all levels down to the county level. This is not conducive to macroeconomic control. Once the government bank shoulders the businesses of the central bank, the latter will have less conflict with the specialized banks. It can then focus on macro control and monetary policy, stabilize the exchange rate, etc.[19] It has even been reported that the government had already decided to establish a government development bank to shoulder the task of investing in and lending to the state's key construction projects and infrastructural facilities. The PCBC will in due course specialize in long- and medium-term commercial loans and will not be responsible for policy loans.[20]

Tong Zengyin, Vice-president of PBOC, expressed that, as a first step towards commercialization, all specialized banks beginning this year would keep separate accounts for loans that are commercial and those that are for policy purpose. In three to five years, banks will be set up to take up the policy loans so that existing specialized banks can all change into commercial banks. The investment companies under the State Planning Commission will serve as the basis for the new policy banks and will be given tax breaks or advantages.[21] Premier Li Peng said earlier this year that based on practical consideration, the four major specialized banks would for a long time to come have to accommodate both policy loans and commercial loans, though the ratio of policy loan business had to decrease gradually.[22] It seems, though decision-makers agree on how to further reform, they differ on the speed of implementation.

In addition to the insulation of commercial banking business from the intervention of policy concerns of the government, commercialization of banks also requires changes in the ownership structure of the banks. Commercial banks are likely to become joint-stock companies themselves, as in the case of BCOM. Moreover, efforts have to be made to clean up the current balance sheets of state banks. One possibility is to change long-term loans to enterprises into investments to ease the burden of enterprises, many of which face difficulty servicing their debts. This amounts to a debt-equity swap, so that if the firms become joint-stock companies the bank loans will become shares held by banks. The investments in the firms that do not have a share-holding system can be regarded as long-term and low-interest bonds. Furthermore, it has been advocated that the PBOC should be under the jurisdiction of the legislature, that is, the Standing Committee of the National People's Congress, instead of the State Council so that it can have independence from the administration.[23] However, when it comes to monetary and credit control, central bank independence is not enough. At present, there is a complete lack of policy instruments in this respect.

Monetary and Credit Control

The only existing way of monetary and credit control in China has been credit planning and administrative allocation of credit, which has become increasingly ineffective. Unfortunately, it is not quite certain when China can develop more effective and flexible central banking techniques in the maintenance of macroeconomic balance. In the near future, loan quotas seem to be the only instrument available.

The most direct way for a central bank to alter the amount of money and credit in the economy is open market operation. However, this requires an appropriate instrument with a deep and sophisticated market. The natural candidate for such an instrument is national debt. China did not begin to issue any national debt until 1981, and the market is still underdeveloped. As at the end of 1990, national debt outstanding was RMB75.9 billion, only about 4.2% of the consolidated assets of the state-owned banks and rural credit cooperatives.[24] The private sector does not hold and trade large amounts of national debt. Besides, while the PBOC is not an independent central bank, the redemption of national debt upon maturity from the Ministry of Finance might pose problems.

The use of rediscount policy is hampered by the lack of a well-developed market in commercial bills for rediscounting. Statistics show that, in the first quarter of 1992, there were RMB4.3 billion worth of commercial bills nationwide, but there were only a little over 10,000 transactions, and only RMB1.3 billion worth were rediscounted by the PBOC, compared to the nearly RMB2 trillion in total bank loans.[25] More importantly, rediscount policy aims to use the rediscount rate as a guide to market interest rates. This presupposes that interest rates are flexible and market-determined, which is not the case in China now.

China has adopted reserve requirement policies since the mid-1980s, but the purpose has not been monetary control. Since the PBOC acts as an administrator in the distribution of central bank credit, it makes use of the reserve by lending it out again in order to balance surpluses and shortages of funds among different regions and agencies. Another way to control money and credit is to auction a given amount of central bank credit periodically and let all financial institutions bid for the credit competitively. The problem here is how to determine the correct amount of credit to be auctioned.

Yet another possibility is to decontrol interest rates and let the market determine the amount of credit under flexible interest rates. Sooner or later

Banking

this has to be an integral part of financial reform, but the government is not yet willing to relinquish such control. There is the worry that high demand for loans might not be curbed by rising interest rates if state enterprises can avoid being disciplined by the market mechanism and still count on getting funds from the state through the banks. High loan rates would drive out mainly borrowers from the private sector and lower the quality of bank balance sheets.

Thus, it seems loan quotas will continue to be imposed to control the total amount of credit in the near future, but the policy will become increasingly difficult to implement. Credit plans are more difficult to chart due to changing economic environments, and plans cannot be carried out easily due to the inability to enforce. The lack of monetary and credit control will persist in China.

Foreign Banks in China

Foreign banks could be a significant means to introduce competitive elements into the the banking system in China. The first financial institution established by a foreign bank since 1949 was the Long-Term Credit Bank of Japan which opened its office in China in 1979.[26] By early 1993, financial institutions from 29 countries and areas have had over 230 representative offices in 15 cities, and about 70 foreign bank branches in 8 cities.[27] Previously, branches of foreign banks had been restricted to the Special Economic Zones, but by June 1992 the State Council had given approval for foreign banks to set up business in Dalian, Tianjin, Qingdao, Nanjing, Ningbo, Fuzhou and Guangzhou.[28] By late 1992, four banks had started branches in Guangzhou: Nanyang Commercial Bank Ltd., Bank of East Asia, Société Générale, and Sumitomo Bank Ltd. It has been reported that the second group of foreign banks permitted to do business in Guangzhou would amount to 15.[29]

No individual foreign bank has set up branches in all major cities open to foreign banking in China. This is aimed to preserve competition among foreign banks. Moreover, dominance by any individual foreign bank will mean too much competition for domestic banks should RMB dealings be allowed in the future.

Besides branches of foreign banks, joint venture banks have also been approved in China. The first of this kind was the Xiamen International Bank established in 1985 by the ICBC and a Hong Kong group; it was subsequently injected with capital by other foreign banks as well. While branches can benefit from the financial support from parent banks, joint venture banks can benefit from the connection network of the local partner.

In terms of business, as of now, foreign banks have not been allowed RMB dealings — except for the very few which stayed in the mainland after 1949 — and have not been allowed to accept RMB deposits. Their business consists of mainly serving foreign-owned enterprises and joint ventures, dealing in foreign currency, acting on real estate deals in South China in large part for clients in Hong Kong, and "B" shares trading and clearing.

The current main issue in contention with regard to foreign banking in China is the opening of RMB business to foreign banks. There are a few concerns in this respect. The participation of foreign banks in RMB dealings can introduce further competition to the domestic banking system and speed up the commercialization of domestic banks. However, since domestic banks have not been used to competition, especially that from outside, they simply are not in a position to compete with foreign banks on an equal footing. It is very likely that some protective measures will be adopted, such as restrictions on branching for foreign banks. On the other hand, bank depositors have implicitly been insured in the past decades since domestic banks have not been allowed to fail. Such protection, however, would not be extended to foreign banks, and depositors will have to learn to make a judgement about different banks. The most important consideration with opening RMB business to foreign banks is the implication for domestic macroeconomic control. The authorities cannot easily impose loan quotas on foreign banks should it prove necessary to restrict credit. Foreign bank RMB operations could be a major loophole in the already loose control mechanism. Another worry is that, under the present highly protective nature of banking in China, bank profits are high. Sixty percent of bank profits go to the state in the form of taxes which are to be redistributed by the state to society. The opening of RMB business to foreign banks will affect this mechanism.[30]

Conclusion

The banking system is the dominant financial system of a modern economy. Even in the US where equity finance has had a long history and the stock market has been well developed with relatively highly sophisticated investors and increasingly innovative financial instruments, stock market shares account for around 2% of external finance for non-financial businesses. On the other hand, for countries including the US, the UK, France, Germany and Japan, around 60% of external finances of non-financial businesses come from bank loans.[31] It is true that, as of now, direct finance (through the issue of securities) has been underdeveloped in China and should be greatly promoted. However, compared with the stock market and given its sheer size, it seems that the banking system has received unduly little attention. Banking reform in China has not been that successful in the past decade in properly restoring to banks their commercial or central banking functions. There is still a long way to go, and it seems drastic changes are impossible in the near future.

Notes

1. "China's Financial System Reform during the 1990s" (in Chinese), *Gaige* (Reform), No. 5 (20 September 1992), pp. 24–33.
2. Liu Hongru and Wang Peizhen (eds.), *Complete Work on China's Reform (1978–1991): Volume on Financial System Reform* (in Chinese) (Dalian: Dalian Publishing Company, 1992), p. 48.
3. Calculated from figures in *Almanac of China's Finance and Banking*, various issues.
4. "Still in the Middle Kingdom," *The Economist*, 12 December 1992, p. 90.
5. "Entrepreneurs Banking on Loans in the Private Sector," *Sunday Morning Post* (Hong Kong), 28 February 1993.
6. "Building Site," *The Economist*, 27 March 1993, p. 84.
7. "Out of the Wilderness," *Far Eastern Economic Review*, 14 January 1993, p. 41.
8. "Banks' Lending Policy to Favor Sound Firms," *China Daily*, 1 February 1993, p. 4.
9. See Note 1.
10. See Note 7.
11. "Moves in the Reform of China's Financial System" (in Chinese), *Outlook Weekly* (Overseas Edition), 22 February 1993, pp. 14–16.
12. See Note 2, p. 412.
13. See Note 1.
14. Ma Hong and Sun Shangqin (eds.), *Economic Situation and Prospect of China (1991–1992)* (in Chinese), (Beijing: China Development Publishing Company, 1992), p. 179.

15. "Li Moves to Rein in State Bank Sector," *South China Morning Post* (Hong Kong), 19 January 1993.
16. *Hong Kong Economic Journal*, 20 April 1993, p. 2.
17. "Foreign Banks Are Coming" (in Chinese), *Jinrong Shibao* (Financial Times), 8 September 1992, p. 1.
18. See Note 6, p. 84.
19. "Set Up Government Bank to Reform the Financial System" (in Chinese), *Hong Kong Economic Journal*, 14 March 1993.
20. "State to Set Up Government Development Bank" (in Chinese), *Jingji daobao* (Economic Reporter), No. 3 (18 January 1993), p. 28.
21. *Hong Kong Economic Journal*, 20 March 1993.
22. *Hong Kong Economic Times*, 22 March 1993.
23. "Banking Reform Will Eliminate Central Planning," *China Daily*, 10 December 1992.
24. Calculated from figures in *China's Securities Markets (1991)* (in Chinese), edited by Jin Jiandong, Xiao Zhuoji and Xu Shuxin (Beijing: China Finance Publishing Company, 1991), p. 68.
25. "Several Issues on Improving the Macroeconomic Financial Control Mechanisms" (in Chinese), *Jingji ribao* (Economic Daily), 10 October 1992, p. 3.
26. "Foreign Banks Are Coming — What Shall We Do?" (in Chinese), *Jinrong Shibao*, 8 September 1992, p. 1.
27. *Hong Kong Economic Journal*, 13 February 1993.
28. *Hong Kong Economic Journal*, 13 August 1992.
29. *Hong Kong Economic Times*, 21 December 1992.
30. *Hong Kong Economic Times*, 26 February 1993.
31. Frederick S. Mishkin, *The Economics of Money, Banking, and Financial Markets* (3rd ed.; New York: Harper Collins, 1992), p. 158.

14

Market Reform and Agricultural Growth: The Dynamics of Change in the Chinese Countryside in 1992

Andrew Watson

Until the reforms began in late 1978, the terms "agriculture" and "rural economy" were virtually synonymous. By definition, China's peasants lived in the countryside and derived their livelihood primarily from agriculture. This rural economy was distinguished from the industrial and urban sectors in many distinct ways. Its ownership was collective rather than state. Its population was confined to the countryside by the operation of the household registration, rationing, employment and welfare systems. Its main activities were crop and animal production. And its interaction with the urban economy, including both the exchange of products and of the factors of production, was mediated through state agencies operating according to quotas, plan volumes and administrative prices. In effect, the rural agricultural sector and the urban industrial and commercial sector operated like two separate economies, with distinct labour, capital and other resources and a set of trading relations determined by state financial, planning and commercial systems.[1]

After 1978, the reforms gradually transformed this situation. Despite the many inevitable debates, hesitations and policy adjustments, the process of rural reform was one continuous trend towards relaxation of state controls, commercialization and privatization.[2] The state progressively reduced the number and volumes of products it attempted to control. The power of the collectives to determine the ownership and use of the factors of production declined. And the producers achieved increasing autonomy in production and consumption.[3]

Within that process, the growth and evolution of markets played a central role. Markets and market prices increasingly influenced the allocation of resources for different types of production. They also generated the incentives to encourage producers to increase their efficiency and to diversify output. Despite the fact that the organization of the markets and their scale were varied and unstable, that state institutions continued to intervene in ways which modified market behaviour, and that smoothly-integrated national market networks were not yet developed, there can be no doubt that the growth of marketing systems was one of the most dynamic forces bringing change to the rural economy.[4]

In many ways, 1992 marked a new high point in this process. The fanfare given to Deng Xiaoping's southern tour at the beginning of the year signalled the resurgence of reform policies. Subsequent decisions by the State Council and its ministries reinvigorated marketing reforms which had been slowed down by the deflationary policies of 1988 and the aftermath of June 1989. A period of uncertainty characterized both by an urgent need to restore macroeconomic stability and by debate and conflict over the orientation of reform was, thereby, brought to an end in favour of a further intensification of the long-term trends of change set in motion in 1978. As discussed below, during 1992 state institutions began to reduce their remaining areas of direct intervention in the marketing and pricing of agricultural products. Even in the case of grain, the most crucial commodity in the edifice of planned production and supply, a multitude of reform experiments were launched, heralding the possibility of the final removal of the remaining direct state controls over agricultural products and of a shift to a more indirect regime.

By the beginning of 1992, the consequences of the process of marketization which had taken place over the preceding years were profound. To begin with, it was no longer possible to consider the rural economy as purely agricultural. Driven by the set of opportunity costs created by the new market relationships, the allocation of labour, land and capital in the rural sector had been transformed and had moved sharply away from a primary emphasis on agricultural production. The role of agriculture in the rural economy and as a source of peasant income had declined, underlining both the high costs of increasing output in an agriculture characterized by high yields and limited land resources and the benefits to be gained by diversification into non-agricultural production. The rural economy had thus become much more complex, with greater labour mobility, booming industrial and service sectors and increasing inter-regional linkages. By the end of 1991, agricultural and animal production accounted for only 42.9% of total rural output value.[5]

A second major consequence flowing from these changes was the impact on the dual economic structure. The rural economy had become a complex mixture of activities. It was still, however, marked by a distinct set of boundaries from the state urban system, especially in terms of ownership, pricing policies, employment conditions, labour and capital management and population status. Statistical and sectoral definitions based on systems of ownership and administrative location maintained, and still maintain, a clear distinction between the urban and rural sectors, creating administrative and managerial barriers which complicate an analysis according to economic function. While the reforms mean that the boundaries between the two sectors are blurring, the continued existence of a dual structure in a much more complex economy is a source of further tension and change.

Finally, given the dual structure, by 1992 the market reforms had transformed the nature of urban-rural exchange. Despite the co-existence of different types of markets and prices (planned, negotiated and free) and despite the many fluctuations in the prices of agricultural products and their relative level against industrial products and services, rural producers had experienced considerable improvement in the returns obtained from their output. The price increases of the initial years of reform brought substantial benefits after a long period in which the price mechanism had functioned to transfer resources from the rural to the urban economies. The diversification of production stimulated by the opening up of the markets enabled a switch to higher-value products, with greater profits. And the existence of a variety of market channels gave producers flexibility in how they organized the flow of their goods to urban consumers. The corollary of such changes were that the prices faced by urban consumers also changed. While the state attempted to stabilize the supply and prices of key commodities such as grain, oils and meat by using a mixture of subsidies and fixed contracts, there was an inevitable inflation in the prices paid both for foods and for the economic crops used for industrial production. As a result there was an intensification in the competition between the urban and rural sectors for the benefits flowing from economic growth. Such competition was reflected in the increasing pressures of agricultural and food subsidies on the state budgets, the backlash from consumers faced by worries over inflation, and the fluctuations in agricultural output as the government's efforts to ensure the production and supply of key commodities at controlled prices resulted in shifting incentives to producers. The marketing reforms of 1992 thus marked the latest stage in the government's attempts to resolve the underlying problems.

This chapter focuses primarily on developments in 1992. Any analysis of the nature of marketing and pricing in Chinese agriculture, however, must be seen in the context of the issues outlined above. The following sections will, therefore, address a number of key themes. To provide a framework for understanding the events in 1992, I shall begin with a brief discussion of some fundamental issues in China's market reforms. This will be followed by a discussion of the market reform policies adopted during 1992 and the general consequences for agriculture. These themes will be illustrated by reference to reforms in three types of markets: vegetables, as an example of full marketization; wool, as an example of an industrial raw material; and grain, as the most politically-sensitive of all crops. The analysis of these three commodities will enable us to draw some conclusions about the orientation and impact of market reforms during

1992. In the final section, I shall address some of the consequences of these changes for peasant autonomy, regional interaction, agricultural growth and the future role of agricultural commodity markets in China's rural reforms.

The Role of Market Reform in the Rural Economy

The introduction of market reforms in agriculture after 1978 were intended to improve efficiency, both allocative efficiency in the use of resources for production and so-called "x-efficiency" in terms of the incentives for producers to work harder. These assumptions about the efficiency of markets were derived from a fairly orthodox view of market function and supported by arguments about the inefficiencies of collective agriculture and planned production.[6] In addition, it was argued that market forces would help diversify production, encourage specialization, raise incomes and simplify managerial procedures. While the initial experiments were introduced within the framework of continued strong government intervention in production and marketing, the logic of the policies adopted and of the forces released by the introduction of markets, inevitably led to an acceleration in market growth and a broadening of their scope.

This transition to a greater role for markets raised three key questions: the appropriate speed of the transformation, the sequencing of change, and the role of the government and the state sector in the process.[7] Unlike the "big bang" approach of Russia, China opted for a gradual process of change, characterized by experiment and *ad hoc* adjustments. Such a process not only implied friction and conflict between old and new systems but also risked distortion of the overall target as old and new vested interests attempted to influence the direction of change. In some ways, this might be seen as a trade-off between the short-term benefits of cautious change and the long-term risks of failing to achieve the desired goal. Given the high costs of sudden large-scale change and the inevitable problems of institutional adaptation, however, China's experience in agricultural marketing reform demonstrates the pragmatic advantages of evolutionary change. In practice, China's leaders did not adopt any dogmatic definition of the ideal goal and, instead, allowed the new system to evolve. The new wave of reform introduced in 1992 underlines that the economic pressures generated by partial market reform continue to push towards the logical conclusion of an ever greater role for markets.

The sequencing of reform is significant because a market economy relies on an interdependent relationship between many facets such as systems of ownership, pricing mechanisms, the organization of commodity and factor markets, institutional structures for such things as banking and financial services, a legal framework, a range of technological services, and the development of appropriate human skills. This does not mean that only one type of combination of such things can be a "true" market economy. As is often noted, there is considerable variation in the settings for such things among all the market economies in the world. The point is that, in moving from a command to a market economy, all these areas are affected.

In China's case, the initial reforms liberalized the management of labour, increased state purchase prices and reintroduced small, local free markets. The set of economic incentives for producers created by such reforms then called forth further changes which, ultimately, led to the reinstitution of private ownership of everything except land, a steadily increasing role for market prices as an allocatory mechanism, the growth of commodity and factor markets, and new ways of providing financial, technical and other services. Nevertheless, as China's experience has shown, as well as creating demand for further change, partial and uncoordinated reforms in the different aspects of markets can be a source of friction, uncertainty and corruption. By 1992, therefore, the utility of and need for further market improvement was clear.

Finally, the market transition of the 1980s also involved the issue of the role of state institutions. The underlying goal was to reduce the role of the state and to allow market forces to predominate. Ironically, however, the transition required firm state action to manage the change and also created the conditions for different parts of the state (local government and state units, for example) to intervene in markets in their own interests. It was this aspect of reform which generated the most problems. The fluctuations in output and prices and the "commodity wars" that characterized agriculture after the mid-1980s were, to a large extent, reflections of uncertainties over government policies, of attempts by the local arms of the state to influence the production and marketing of particular commodities by the use of subsidies and quotas and of failures by the government to anticipate how producers might respond to the new environment they faced. In many ways, the further retreat of the state from direct market management which occurred in 1992 reflected the negative lessons gained from the fluctuations of the period after 1984, the high costs of state subsidies and the increasing maturity of the marketing institutions which had evolved in the meantime.

By late 1991 and the beginning of 1992, therefore, market reforms were deeply entrenched in the rural economy and were becoming more and more significant for the process of urban-rural exchange. With the stability in agricultural production of 1990–1991, the commitment to the growth of agricultural product markets was reaffirmed, and the CCP issued a statement at the end of 1991 which stated that "except for a small number of major agricultural goods whose procurement and trading are centralized by the state according to regulations, the trading of all other agricultural goods should be decontrolled and regulated by the market."[8] Free markets already dominated or were very significant for many products, including fruit, vegetables, eggs, fish and aquatic products, meat and milk. Nevertheless, state agencies still intervened in the marketing of a number of the key basic commodities, primarily grain, oils, cotton and a small number of industrial products such as tobacco, silk and wool. The state also retained a very significant role in input markets for such things as fertilizer, diesel oil, energy and plastics, with a proportion of such goods supplied to producers at subsidized prices and the rest being sold at much higher market prices. The situation was thus still characterized by expensive subsidies and potential conflict. Against this background the relative stability in prices and agricultural production of 1991 provided the context for a renewed approach to market reforms which was launched in early 1992.

Policy Developments and Market Changes in 1992

The year began on the basis of the relatively successful production of 1991. Grain output, though down on 1990, was still over 435 million tonnes.[9] Cotton, oil crops, sugar, tobacco, meat, milk, wool and many other products all achieved significant increases. The trend towards diversification out of agriculture was also maintained, with 57.7% of total rural output value coming from non-agricultural rural enterprises. The decision of late 1991, cited above, signalled that more market reform was anticipated, and the process was given impetus by the publicity given to Deng Xiaoping's remarks on his tour of the south.[10] During 1992, therefore, a series of reforms and experiments were introduced into those remaining aspects of the marketing system where the state still maintained an important role.

In March, during the period of the fifth session of the Seventh National People's Congress (NPC), the State Council issued a circular on structural economic reform.[11] This called for the vigorous development of markets in the countryside. It suggested that edible oil and sugar should be exempted from mandatory planning and that, after quotas were filled, there should be a further relaxation of grain marketing. The document still, however, envisaged a continuing role for state intervention in some commodities:

> Except for a few products subject to unified state management, all farm products can be sold freely through multiple channels of circulation, with their prices fluctuating according to market demand.

Premier Li Peng's speech to the NPC also reflected this sense of balance between further liberalization and the maintenance of a role for the state as a player in the market.[12] He argued:

> Deepening the reform of the pricing and circulation systems of agricultural products is the key to further developing the rural commodity economy. We should actively promote the reform of the grain purchase and marketing pricing system, further set up and perfect the reserve and regulatory system of cotton, grain, edible oil, and other major agricultural products and develop wholesale and futures markets. We should practice multi-channel circulation. *While giving play to the main channel role of state-run commerce and the supply and marketing cooperatives*, we should support the peasants in carrying out commodity circulation and in vigorously developing tertiary industry. (My emphasis)

Even as Li Peng spoke, however, experiments were under way which pointed towards a much smaller role for state institutions.[13] One of the most significant developments was the increase in grain selling prices of 40%, introduced on 1 April. Coming on top of an increase of around 50% in May 1991, this meant that the subsidy provided by the difference between the government's purchasing and selling prices was eliminated. It also meant that the state price was brought into line with the market price. There was thus less likelihood of consumer resistance to a complete shift to market management. The increases in urban incomes during the 1980s, the decline of food expenditure as a proportion of total expenditure, and the decline in direct grain consumption by the urban population also made such a change less politically difficult.

Meanwhile, experiments were also occurring in places such as Guanghan county in Sichuan and in Guangdong province with ways to abolish the state grain ration system and to rely on market distribution. The implications of these changes were spelt out by Vice-Premier Tian Jiyun in an article produced in late March. He said:

> We should gradually change the way we manage grain — from managing grain using the product economic method to managing grain using the commodity economic method and using market regulation as the means.[14]

He concluded that "grain commercialization and market-oriented operations are, therefore, the fundamental solution to the grain problems." In other words, while the official position remained one where direct state intervention in the marketing of key products was still envisaged, the actual practice of the reforms was leading to a further decline of the role of the state.

This trend towards further change in the few remaining commodities under state controls was exemplified by the complete liberalization of the Xinjiang wool market in May–June[15] and by mid-year reports that the State Council was urging complete relaxation of controls over grain prices.[16] A meeting in the Ministry of Agriculture in July also called for further loosening of controls over agricultural product prices, especially grain,[17] and reports of further experiments with deregulation continued during the rest of the year. These developments eventually culminated in the State Council's "Decision on Developing a High-Yielding, High Grade and Efficient Agricultural System" issued on 25 September.[18] Noting that "since the mid-1980s China has decontrolled the trading of most agricultural goods, including aquatic products, fruits, vegetables, livestock, poultry, eggs and milk," the decision stated:

> We must seize current opportunities to speed up the restructuring of the grain purchasing and marketing system so that more commodity quality grain can be produced and traded on the market. We should, through the decontrolling of the purchasing and marketing price of grain, arouse the enthusiasm of grain producers — and especially the major grain producing areas — to produce more good quality grain and give full scope to these areas' capacity for grain production, so that there will be a rational regional division of labour.

In other words, market reform was not only seen as a solution to problems in grain distribution but also as a spur to changing the nature and distribution of production. The decision thus went on to argue that "guided by the market, continual efforts should be made to restructure agricultural production," thereby spelling out that the "socialist market economy" endorsed by the Fourteenth National Party Congress in October really implied a full transition to a market economy in agricultural products. The significance of this for agriculture can be illustrated more clearly by examining in a little more detail the changes as they affected vegetables, wool and grain.

In the case of vegetables, the switch to free market management began with the initial reforms in 1978.[19] Peasants rapidly developed sideline vegetable production, which they sold directly to consumers in the expanding rural and urban markets. This process was given added impetus by the reforms of 1984, which completely liberalized fruit marketing and accelerated the growth of wholesale markets in fruits and vegetables. Nevertheless, at great cost in terms of subsidies to both producers and consumers and waste of poor quality vegetables, the state continued to manage the production and distribution of key seasonal vegetables, relying on production bases in suburban areas. The symbol for this system was the so-called "patriotic cabbage," produced in the suburbs of Beijing during autumn and sold in large quantities to the local population for consumption over winter.

By the early 1990s, this state system was breaking down. Apart from the cost to urban budgets of maintaining local state production, the competition from the free market in terms of quality and variety was becoming intense. Large-scale free wholesale markets were being developed in all major cities and in key rural locations, and the state distribution centres were handling a declining proportion of consumption.[20] While these changes had many implications for such things as inter-regional trade, with the abandonment of efforts to promote local self-sufficiency and the acceptance of reliance on distant sources of fresh vegetables, and for the relationships between the different state institutions originally involved in vegetable production and marketing, the pressures created by surging consumer demand for quality and variety and the increased opportunity costs facing suburban producers meant that the subsidized suburban production system could not be maintained. Already by 1992 many small cities, and even some large ones like Guangzhou, had abandoned any efforts to sustain planned production and distribution, and long-distance free market trade was intensifying. The surge in marketing reform during 1992 thus marked an acceptance that the complete liberalization of vegetable production and distribution should spread to the remaining centres. In Beijing, for example, it was announced in October that, after the sale of the 1992 cabbage crop, price controls would be withdrawn.[21] The eventual decision also liberalized all remaining Beijing local government intervention in the purchase and selling prices of eggs, vegetables, pork, beef and mutton.[22] The end of 1992 thus saw the completion of a transition from the planned production and supply system to free market distribution not only for vegetables but for most of the non-staple foods of urban consumers. While this was generally associated with a one-off increase in cash subsidies to the urban population, it marked a significant reduction in the role of state institutions in the agricultural marketing system and an acceptance that market signals would guide the allocation of production resources and the trading relationship between town and countryside.

In the case of wool, the liberalization of the market in 1992 came at the end of a cycle of boom and bust in wool production and processing.[23] Originally one of the most tightly controlled rural products, wool production and prices began to accelerate upwards during the mid-1980s. Demand for wool came from both the established coastal industries and from the new processing capacity developed in the wool-producing regions to increase local value-added and income. The result was intense competition for domestic supplies, a loss of control over marketing with consequent upwards pressure on prices and a surge in imports, leading to a rise in international prices. Embedded within these supply and demand relationships was regional competition between the pastoral wool-producing provinces and the coastal processing provinces. It was not until the deflationary policies of 1988 were introduced and the economic slowdown of 1989 and 1990 ensued that this competition for raw wool ceased. The collapse in raw wool demand led to a collapse in prices which, in turn, enabled a reassertion of order in the market. In places like Xinjiang, the state purchasing agencies were able to stabilize their position (though the number and types of state participants were much broader than before), the private merchants began to play a more minor role again, imports were controlled, and, in order to sustain production, efforts were made to stop state purchase prices falling too far.

Although these developments brought greater stability to the market and encouraged renewed efforts to improve raw wool quality, the market remained flat. The lack of demand for end products also meant that processors were keen to hold raw material prices down and to enforce stronger quality requirements. In the context of this (from the producers' point of view) unpromising but relatively stable market environment, the renewed emphasis on market reforms at the beginning of 1992 offered administrators the opportunity to implement a thorough-going change without the dangers associated with the overheating of the "wool war" period. In May–June, therefore, when the new season planned prices and marketing arrangements are normally announced, the regional authorities (who by 1992 were empowered to take the key decisions in wool marketing) decided to liberalize both wool prices and wool marketing channels completely.[24]

As a result of this decision, producers were free to sell their wool to any purchaser, private merchants were able to re-enter the market, state agencies were free to intensify their competition with each other, and processors were also able to diversify their sources of supply. This change, however, entailed a number of consequences, the effects of which have yet to be digested. From the producers' point of view, the removal of controls over prices and of obligations to sell to state agencies introduced new choices for marketing and new opportunities for price bargaining. It also increased the significance of the opportunity costs of production, especially in terms of the relative price between meat and wool. For the wool handlers, it reintroduced competition between private and state dealers. The latter are subject to various tax and mark-up regulations, whereas the private merchants can try to avoid product taxes and compete by reducing handling charges and costs. During 1992, this situation enabled them to offer the producer a higher price and the processor a lower price, while still clearing a good profit compared to the state agencies. Meanwhile, the state agencies were under pressure to abandon their "iron rice bowls" and to become more efficient and competitive. In 1992 in Xinjiang, all the state commercial departments experienced a large drop in the volume of wool they handled. At the same time, the enforcement of grading and handling standards became more difficult as wool dropped out of the established handling network and moved from producer to processor through the private dealers. Finally, the processors found that, although wool quality was threatened and the wool delivered by private traders was more mixed, they were able to adjust their raw material supply by buying from different sources at different price levels. The switch to a totally open market situation, therefore, generated changes in behaviour which now require further reforms in marketing institutions, in grading and handling standards and techniques, and in the trading relationship between rural producers and industrial users. While the producers are gaining increasing autonomy, it will take some time to evolve a stable and efficient marketing structure.

The final example of market reform considered here, the changes to the grain marketing system, represents the most profound change to the rural product marketing system in China. Until the reform process began, the planned production and supply of grain was the cornerstone of agricultural planning. Grain was the key commodity in the agricultural system, and plans for the output of other products were subordinate to the requirements for grain. Throughout the reform period, therefore, relaxation in the controls over grain has been the most cautious. In the initial phase, the unified purchase and sales system was maintained, with the consequence that increases in grain purchase prices by the state without associated increases in selling prices led to substantial increases in state subsidies. These rose from RMB1 billion in 1978 to RMB39 billion in 1990, imposing a substantial burden on the 1990 state budget of around 330 billion.[25] At the same time, however, producers were granted the freedom to trade in grain, once their state quotas were met. From 1978 to 1984, therefore, there was a steady growth in free market sales and in sales of surplus grain to state purchasers at negotiated prices.

The next stage in the reforms came in 1985, when the unified purchase and sales system was abolished and replaced by a contract system. The aim was to provide producers with greater freedom to plan production and also to reduce the state's obligation to purchase all grain offered for sale. Producers had to fulfil their contractual obligations, but other grain trading and production could be decided according to their own consumption needs and market demand. This change was prompted by the successful harvests in the years before 1985 and the growing belief that China's chronic grain shortage was being overcome. Producer response, however, was influenced by rising opportunity costs for grain production. During the late 1980s grain output fluctuated substantially. The central and local governments responded by enforcing contracts strictly, by attempting to increase the supply of subsidized inputs and by maintaining state subsidies to consumers. Combined with further increases in state purchase prices, these policies led to a revival of grain production in 1990 and 1991. Nevertheless, the free market in grains continued to develop, grain wholesale markets were established in different centres, and these began to influence the price of free market grains.[26]

As discussed above, the significant increases in state grain selling prices introduced in 1991 and 1992, created the opportunity for a further round of reforms in grain marketing. The March 1992 comments by Li Peng and Tian Jiyun on the need to increase the commercialization of grain production and marketing were, therefore, followed by State Council decisions in June and September which heralded the complete liberalization of the grain market. One report of 28 September, for example, indicated that experiments with deregulation now embraced some 300 counties in sixteen provinces and around 180 million people.[27] Eventually by early December a national conference indicated that the reform of grain marketing would accelerate, with marketization as the key goal, and that the experiments had spread to some 400 counties, affecting over 200 million people.[28] Clearly the situation was a very fluid one. Reforms were taking place with increasing speed, and local areas were beginning to push for change from below.

Over this period, the experiments in methods of grain marketing embraced two main approaches.[29] One was the full liberalization of all aspects of grain marketing, by removing all controls over production, sales and prices. This was done, for example, in Guangdong province at the end of March 1992. It was claimed that this improved incentives and incomes for producers, forced greater efficiencies on the state grain handling systems (though these still received some subsidies), encouraged producers to shift to better seeds to suit market demand and, through increased prices to consumers, encouraged less waste.

The alternative was to introduce reform in stages by such things as liberalizing market prices but retaining production quotas, liberalizing quotas but retaining a role for the state in market supplies or getting rid of ration quotas but still guiding prices. These initial changes were seen as preparing the way for full-scale deregulation. Most of the experimental areas tried variations of this second approach during 1992. The aim was to develop a more cautious and gradual programme of change which would ensure stability and avoid risk. In practice, however, it was found that the one-step approach worked fairly successfully, and this encouraged an acceleration in the process and a rapid spread to other regions.

In this process, the problem of the stock of grain ration coupons in people's hands (estimated to have a trade-in worth of around 20 million tonnes in mid-1992) disappeared. Originally, there was concern that if these coupons were presented, China's grain stocks would be depleted. In practice, the "market" price of a coupon roughly equalled the difference between the subsidized grain price and the free market price. At its highest this had been RMB0.30. By mid-1992, it had shrunk to RMB0.02–0.03, underlining the new relationship between the state and the market price. Local governments were thus in a position to "buy back" the coupons and to cancel any further issues. Furthermore, such a buy-back would liberate the stock held against the coupons for selling on the market.

At the same time as this process was occuring, however, warning notes were being struck about the consequences for output and producer behaviour. In many places market prices were now below state prices, and that high opportunity costs meant that grain cropping remained in an unfavourable position. This implied that farmers might well shift resources away from grain. Problems to be resolved included such things as the potential for a reduction in grain sown area, the appropriate policies to adopt for input supplies and input prices, the methods needed to manage state stocks and to balance fluctuations in market supplies and prices, and the way domestic prices might link to world prices. At year-end, therefore, a series of speeches and meetings in Beijing underlined the perceived need to continue to encourage grain production.[30] At a national television hook-up conference, Li Peng listed a series of policy initiatives aimed at encouraging continued growth in grain output.[31] These policies included proposals to guarantee state purchases and to stop the issuing of IOU's,[32] to put an end to the excessive fees, levies and charges imposed on peasants, to maintain preferential policies for input supplies to grain producers, to help grain-producing areas to develop other aspects of their economy, to streamline the state grain management system, to stabilize sown area, to increase investment, to control input prices, to establish a guaranteed minimum grain price and to adjust the agricultural tax system. Once again, therefore, the orientation and problems of the grain marketing reforms thus underlined the increasing autonomy of the producers and the need for further changes in institutions and marketing systems. At a deeper level, they also indicated the important shift in government policy towards the use of economic incentives to encourage farmers to produce grain. In other words, after a long period in which planned agriculture had been used as a source of accumulation for economic growth, the government was becoming more concerned to use economic incentives in a market framework in order to protect and stimulate production which might not occur under existing opportunity costs. Chinese policy was thus moving towards increasing protection for agricultural producers.

The above discussion has demonstrated how the market reforms of 1992 further intensified the reform process in agriculture, with major consequences for the output of agricultural products and the behaviour of rural producers. The discussion of the examples of vegetable, wool and grain marketing also illustrated four key points. First, continued marketization of agricultural production presents many problems for existing government agencies and marketing institutions. Such institutions are loosing their original functions, but the new market systems are often incomplete and unstable. These problems will continue to call forth further changes in market structures. Secondly, producers are gaining increasing autonomy in production and are, thereby, much more sensitive to changing opportunity costs and market conditions. This is forcing government to reconsider its incentives and other policies and to try to manage the market economy by using economic incentives. Thirdly, the changes in prices for rural products is leading to a new trading relationship between urban and rural areas, with consequences for food and raw material prices. Finally, the uncertainties in this situation are likely to lead to continued fluctuations in output of different products and will require careful management to minimize any further imbalances and dislocations caused by the transition. The likely consequences of these trends for producer autonomy, regional specialization and agricultural growth are examined in the concluding section below.

Conclusion

Against this background of further reform, agricultural production in 1992 remained relatively good.[33] Total grain output was just over 442 million tonnes, up over 1991 but still slightly below the 1990 record. Increases were reported for tobacco, wool, hemp, fruit, vegetables, meat and aquatic products, the latter two recording substantial gains. Cotton and oil seeds, however, both crops still influenced by state marketing policies, performed less well. Cotton declined by as much as 20% and oil crops were static. At the same time, the growth of rural enterprise output was reported to have gone up by nearly 37%, with non-agricultural rural employment topping 100 million. There was also a claimed 5.9% real increase in rural per capita incomes. Apart from the relative security this background provided for the introduction of further reforms in 1993, the results underlined that the shift towards free marketing systems was continuing to have a positive impact on output.

As the above discussion has demonstrated, the process of market reform in 1992 and the years before have generated increasing producer autonomy in production. Producers are sensitive to the opportunity costs of their land, labour and capital, with the result that agricultural production has diversified. The effects of this process have been most pronounced in such things as meat, eggs, vegetables, fruit and aquatic products, where state intervention is now considerably reduced. It is also becoming increasingly important in industrial raw materials like wool. The reforms of 1992 have spread the effects even more deeply into the key area of grain production.

Such changes are creating significant new problems for the government. On the one hand, it remains concerned about ensuring supplies at reasonable prices, and, on the other hand, it has to encourage the growth of new marketing institutions, while reforming the old planning systems, which, in reality, are loosing their role. In other words, the government has to find the appropriate economic mechanisms to manage the market economy. In this respect, it is important to note that the "producers" are now a complex mix of private and collective activities.[34] At the basic level, the peasant households take many of the key decisions about land management, labour input, and agricultural accumulation and investment. In many ways, they operate as independent economic agents. At the same time, however, the households have a complex relationship with local village government and collective economic undertakings. In agricultural production, this might include cooperative work on pre- and post-production activities and, in some cases, even village control of cropping patterns and decisions. In both cases, however, the producers are increasingly functioning in response to market signals. Even where the village economy remains strongly integrated, the producers are still much more autonomous *vis-à-vis* state and government agencies.

A second consequence of these marketing changes is the encouragement of regional specialization. While the effects on grain production remain relatively limited,[35] the influence on wool, fruits and vegetables, for example, has been strong. In wool production, the pastoral production regions have emphasized output growth and investment in value-adding processing industries. In vegetable production, the old planned system of urban self-sufficiency has given way to extensive inter-regional trade and the evolution of specialist horticultural areas, aiming at supplying distant urban consumers.[36] Further marketing reform is thus likely to see continued efforts to develop regional specialization.

Finally, the process of marketization has been accompanied by significant growth in output, especially in products where state intervention has declined the most rapidly. Nevertheless, whether this will continue in an even more deregulated system remains debatable. To some extent the booms in output of various products may have reflected distortions in opportunity costs created by state intervention, either through production quotas or pricing policy. The removal of those distortions might well change many of the current relationships. In addition, in the absence of stable marketing institutions, production choices will remain difficult. The concerns expressed over the future of grain production at the end of 1992, for example, implies a potential for a drop in output as producers respond to price signals and opportunity costs. In addition, new issues on the horizon include the implications of the General Agreement on Tariffs and Trade (GATT) membership and of a closer relationship between domestic and world prices. It is likely, therefore, that the Chinese government will continue to seek ways of protecting or influencing the market in order to sustain production of key commodities.

Overall, the changes of 1992 have further entrenched the role of agricultural commodity markets in China in guiding agricultural production. While, as the preceding discussion has suggested, many problems still remain and the government will continue to seek a role in influencing production decisions, the growth of such markets has the potential to lead to more integrative regional economic interaction. Specialization by region and reliance on inter-regional trading links may thus tend to produce economic forces which can counteract some of the pressures in the fiscal and political areas portending greater fragmentation. While agricultural regions achieve greater independence from the centre in their economic decisions, their economic interdependence provides countervailing pressures to help mitigate any divisive forces at work.

Notes

1. This issue is explored further in Christopher Findlay and Andrew Watson, "Surrounding the Cities from the Countryside," in *Economic Reform and Internationalisation, China and the Pacific Region*, edited by Ross Garnaut and Liu Guoguang (Sydney: Allen and Unwin, 1992), pp. 49–78.
2. The strength of those debates and hesitations should not, however, be underestimated. A useful reminder of the transitional nature of the Chinese economy in the late 1980s is found in Y. Y. Kueh, "Growth Imperatives, Economic Recentralization and China's Open-door Policy," *The Australian Journal of Chinese Affairs*, No. 24 (July 1990), pp. 93–119.
3. This latter point is a complex one since the new production system involves a variety of contractual and other relationships between individual households and villages. Nevertheless the underlying principle is clear. The rural producer, whether individual household or village community, has much

greater autonomy *vis-à-vis* the state and its institutions than existed under the commune system.

4. For an analysis of the evolution of agricultural markets during the early 1980s, see Andrew Watson, "The Reform of Agricultural Marketing in China since 1978," *The China Quarterly*, No. 113 (March 1988), pp. 1–28.
5. *Zhongguo tongji zhaiyao 1992* (A Statistical Survey of China 1992) (Beijing: Zhongguo tongji chubanshe, 1992), p. 54.
6. A useful summary of the critique of collective, planned agriculture is found in Michael M. Ellman, "Agricultural Productivity under Socialism," *World Development*, No. 9/10 (1981), pp. 982–88. The issue of x-efficiency is discussed in Nicholas Lardy, "State Intervention and Peasant Opportunities," in *Chinese Rural Development*, edited by William L. Parish (New York: M. E. Sharpe Inc., 1985), p. 34.
7. This discussion draws on Louis Haddad, "From Central Planning to a Market Economy: What are the Questions?" in *Market Reform in the Changing Socialist World*, edited by Hans Hendrischke (Sydney: Macquarie University, Centre for Chinese Political Economy, 1992), pp. 133–51.
8. CCP Central Committee, "Decision on Agriculture and Rural Work," November 1991, *SWB* FE/1268/C1/1–12, p. 4.
9. Xinhua News Agency, 28 February 1992, *SWB* FE/W0222/C1/1.
10. *Cheng Ming* (Hong Kong), 1 April 1992, *SWB* FE/1346/B2/1–7.
11. Xinhua News Agency, 26 March 1992, *SWB* FE/1341/C3/1–5.
12. Xinhua News Agency, 3 April 1992, *SWB* FE/1349/C2/1–12.
13. Shwu-eng H. Webb and W. Hunter Colby, "China's Agricultural Marketing System in the 1980's," *China Agricultural and Trade Report*, RS-92-3, United States Department of Agriculture, Economic Research Service (July 1992), pp. 46–54.
14. Xinhua News Agency, 28 March 1992, *SWB* FE/1344/B2/1–3.
15. *Zhongguo fangzhi bao* (China Textile News), 2 June 1992, p. 1.
16. *Wen Wei Po* (Hong Kong), 2 June 1992, p. 2.
17. *Jingji ribao* (Economics Daily), 19 July 1992, p. 1.
18. Xinhua News Agency, 8 October 1992, *SWB* FE/1525/B2/7–11.
19. For a discussion of the process of vegetable marketing reform, see Andrew Watson, *Conflict over Cabbages: The Reform of Wholesale Marketing in China*, USC Seminar Series No. 6 (Hong Kong: Hong Kong Institute of Asia-Pacific Studies, The Chinese University of Hong Kong, 1992).
20. See "Woguo shucai pifa shichang gaikuang" (An Outline of Wholesale Vegetable Marketing in China), *Zhongguo wujia* (China Prices), No. 3, 1992, pp. 10–14 for an outline of the situation in early 1992.
21. *South China Morning Post* (Hong Kong), 9 October 1992, Business, p. 9.
22. *Shoudu jingji xinxi bao* (Capital Economic News), 1 December 1992, p. 2.
23. For an analysis of the "wool war" and its aftermath, see Andrew Watson and

Christopher Findlay, "The 'Wool War' in China," in *Challenges of Economic Reform and Industrial Growth: China's Wool War*, edited by Christopher Findlay (Sydney: Allen and Unwin, 1991), pp. 163–80.

24. Interviews, Xinjiang, July 1992. See also *Zhongguo fangzhi bao*, 2 June 1992, p. 1.
25. Shwu-eng H. Webb and W. Hunter Colby, see Note 13.
26. For an example of a study of Zhengzhou grain market prices, see Qiao Linxuan and Mao Heying, "Zhongguo Zhengzhou liangshi pifa shichang jiage tantao" (An Exploration of Prices on the Zhengzhou Grain Wholesale Market), *Zhongguo wujia*, No. 3 (March 1992), pp. 6–9.
27. Xinhua News Agency, 28 September 1992, *SWB* FE/1504/B2/4.
28. *Jingji cankao* (Economic Reference News), 10 December 1992, p. 1.
29. Interviews with Guo Shutian, July 1992, and Luo Yousheng, February 1993.
30. See, for example *Renmin ribao* (People's Daily), 9 December 1992, p. 1, and speech by Jiang Zemin, Xinhua News Agency, 26 December 1992, *SWB* FE/1579/B2/6–8.
31. Speech by Li Peng, 29 December 1992, *SWB* FE/1579/B2/1–4.
32. A widespread practice of local state purchasers who defer cash payments to peasants by issuing promissory notes.
33. *Renmin ribao*, 19 February 1992, p. 2.
34. For a discussion of the relevant issues, see Andrew Watson, "The Management of the Rural Economy: The Institutional Parameters," in *Economic Reform and Social Change in China*, edited by Andrew Watson (London: Routledge, 1992), pp. 171–99.
35. See the discussion in Li Qingzeng, Andrew Watson and Christopher Findlay, "Grain Production and Regional Economic Change in China," Chinese Economy Research Unit, University of Adelaide, Working Paper Series No. 13 (1991).
36. On the latter, see Andrew Watson, *Conflict over Cabbages*, see Note 19.

15

Relations between Government and Enterprises

Lau Pui-king

The philosophy behind the enterprise reform in the People's Republic of China (PRC) is to improve economic efficiency of the state enterprises by organization and management reforms while maintaining state ownership.

In the Chinese centrally planned economy, allocation of natural resources, capital, agricultural output for production and consumption are in the hands of those bureaucrats in charge of responsible ministries and bureaux under the State Council. State-owned enterprises were established as subordinate units of the government administration, or the so-called leadership units (*lingdao danwei*), and required to fulfil the planned targets in production. In return, the enterprises received guaranteed supply of raw materials and fuel, capital for fixed assets investment, liquidities from the central planning bodies. Both input and output prices were fixed. Revenue received by the enterprises were submitted as budgetary revenue of the government, and as a result profits and losses of enterprises turned out to be a composite of the state's budgetary surplus and deficit. The State Council and its ministries were principals which decided the appropriation of funds for investment in fixed assets for each enterprise based on the economic development strategy of the state and the appropriation of revenue for the enterprise.

Of the state enterprises, key industries were directly under the control of the State Council or ministries. They had to stick to the instructions from their leading units in finance, production, pricing, distribution and personnel management. The local state enterprises whose property rights were held by provincial and municipal governments could have more freedom, especially after the launch of the reform programme. In fact, they could engage in extra-plan production after the fulfilment of planned targets. These local state enterprises have had the freedom to decide on investment, production, product pricing and profit appropriation for their extra-plan output.

The planners had believed in the Soviet-type economic thinking which had presumed that investment in heavy industry might accumulate growth resources faster. In 1979, China called for the reverse of investment strategy by placing more weight on agriculture and light industry. Yet statistical data for investment in productive assets since 1980 indicate that the redistribution has not corrected the balance; agriculture has received 4%, light industry 15%, heavy industry 63%, and communication and transport 18%.

The State's strategic investment plan which placed emphasis on directed heavy industry at the wrong location and scale, instead of market demand, resulted in serious hidden cross-subsidization between industrial sectors and between enterprises, in the form of capital and resource appropriation, and price control or subsidies from the state budget.

The state exercised its supervision and control over state enterprises via commissions and ministries of the State Council. The leading bureaucratic units would set targets of production and investment for state enterprises according to the state's annual and five-year plan. Other supporting bureaux, such as the Bureau of Material Supplies, the State Planning Commission, the Ministry of Energy, etc., were responsible for providing raw materials and energy to guarantee the fulfilment of production targets. State enterprises received funding for fixed capital investment and current working capital directly from the state budget. Sometimes, they received financial support from the regional government to fulfil local targets in addition to the central assignment. Under such circumstances, these central state enterprises were jointly supervised by their multilevel principals as stated in Granick's model.[1]

The gross output value based in national income accounting on stipulated price instead of sales volume based on market price still recorded growth in those years. In order to achieve a higher growth, state enterprises were competing for the scarce — and yet free of charges — capital for investment, and over-expansion was the common phenomenon among them. The corollary of employing excessive labour added to the financial burden of the enterprises. As a consequence, the piling-up inventories of heavy industries and the shortage of agricultural and light industrial products persisted over the years, and explicit and hidden subsidies from the central budget and local authorities distorted the income distribution between urban and rural population.

Profit and loss of enterprises were distorted by the fixed prices controlled by the Price Bureau. Most of the state enterprises were in the red due to inefficiency and/or regulatory measures of the planning and control units. Under the system, budgetary surpluses and deficits of the state were mainly attributed to the performance of state enterprises.

In the Chinese planned economy, state enterprises performed their role the same way bureaucratic units do under government, they were budget maximizing, not output or profit maximizing. The lack of market mechanism in the allocation of resources, including capital, land, raw material and labour and in the redistribution of products finally led to imbalance in industrial structure and to heavy burden on government budget. Managers of state enterprises behaved cautiously as bureaucrats concerned about avoiding political mistakes and pleasing the supervisors rather than being risk-taking entrepreneurs.

Economic reforms broke the interlocking barriers to trading activities as the exchange of factor inputs and products emerged, and a competitive market environment developed. The introduction of price reform cut off the privilege of price subsidies enjoyed by state enterprises. In 1983, state enterprises were required to adopt the tax-for-profit (*ligaishui*) scheme. Some of them were asked to pay a contracted amount of tax per annum based on mutually agreed growth factor. Budgetary capital and liquidity appropriation were replaced by bank loans. From 1986, financial subsidies for loss-making enterprises were recorded separately on the public account; the amount stood at RMB32.5 billion in 1986 and reached RMB51 billion in 1991.

The difficulties encountered by state enterprises raised the concern of the Chinese leaders. The ideological belief in state ownership was the last rooted stronghold of socialism in China. Instead of seeking reform in property rights, they sought to resolve the problem by management reform in the 1980s and adopted market reform in the 1990s. The enterprise reform in the minds of Chinese political leaders meant the adoption of the western management practices and the introduction of market mechanisms under state ownership. Yet, the practice was different from the idea of separation of management from ownership in a capitalist society. The experiments with a share-holding system entrusted to the leading government ministries and bureaus the property rights of state enterprises. The monitoring of state enterprises was ineffective without a stock market for the free transfer of property rights.

Alongside this management reform, the parallel development of the economy in the forms of collective ownership, private ownership and joint ventures, however, has also nurtured the competitive market environment in the economy. The extra-budgetary and extra-planning economic activities have grown rapidly. As a result, the significance and the influence of the state-owned sector have diminished as the relative weight of the state-owned economic activities has decreased.

Internal Enterprise Reform without Matching Environment, 1983–1988

At the start, to provide incentive for managers and employees in state enterprises, a contracting system which allowed enterprises to share incrementally in profits with the control units was introduced. At the same time, liquid capital was allocated through the banking system instead of the leading units in the government via government budget. Managers were given greater autonomy in the distribution of wages, bonuses and other fringe benefits in kind, such as housing. Price control was gradually relaxed, especially for extra-plan output. Very soon, the government realized that the managers and employees, as agents of state property, were taking advantage of the policy, and without fail were using retained profits to increase wage fund and product prices. As Table 1 indicates, after 1984, both general price and wage indexes of state enterprises increased.

Table 1. Indexes of General Retail Price and Wage Level (Preceding Year = 100)

Year	Retail price	Wage
1981	102.4	101.1
1982	101.9	103.0
1983	101.2	103.5
1984	101.7	119.5
1985	109.4	117.3
1986	106.5	116.6
1987	107.4	109.3
1988	119.0	119.9
1989	117.5	110.9
1990	101.6	111.1
1991	102.9	108.5

Source: *China Statistical Year-book 1992.*

In 1983, collective enterprises owned by municipal and county authorities were encouraged. But, at the start, the number of newly established collective enterprises was not large enough to play a supplementary role in market supply. As the state enterprises were given some autonomy in price setting and appropriation of profits under the state monopoly, without market competition and property rights reform, the loosening monitoring role of the government via the leadership units in the State Council could lead to only an increase in economic rent from price rises, not economic efficiency in production. The excess profits became the source of bonus for management and workers instead of capital accumulation for re-investment.

To remedy the weakness of management autonomy without market environment and property rights reform, the central government tried to strengthen the link again by introducing corporate income tax and "adjustment tax," which was a surcharge on excessive bonuses. The "tax-for-profit" scheme was introduced in 1984 as the second stage of tax reform, in which enterprises were levied on a variety of taxes, including product tax, value added tax, sales tax, and resources taxes, etc.

There are three categories of taxes in terms of recipients in the new scheme:

1. taxes levied by the central government;
2. local taxes levied by local government; and
3. taxes shared between central and local governments.

Income taxes are paid to the central or local government via the leading units according to the level of supervisory authority to which they belong. For example, central state enterprises pay the central government via the leading ministries of the State Council and local state enterprises pay the provincial or municipal governments. Other taxes, such as product tax, sales tax, value added tax, resource tax, construction tax, salt tax, personal income tax, state enterprise bonus tax, industrial and commercial tax and income tax from foreign firms and joint ventures are shared between central and local authorities. Based on the categorization, different arrangements have been negotiated between the central and provincial governments on tax revenue and public expenditure sharing.

The tax and profit revenues from rapid growth in the number of local collective enterprises, as part of extra-planning accounts, have helped to build up the "small safe box" or the reserve of local governments. Taxes and charges by local governments for various specific purposes caused financial difficulty for enterprises. In 1986, the State Council had to prohibit any additional levies on enterprises by local authorities without prior approval. Without any effective measures of control, the share of public finance going to the local government has kept expanding.

The percentage in gross industrial output value reflects the changing relative importance of state, collective and private enterprises in the economy. (See Table 2.)

In order to cope with the increasing need of the state budget, the payment of profit and tax by state enterprises could not be released or reduced. In 1992, state enterprises pay for about 60% of total revenue of the state budget.

In 1986, the government drew regulations for plant managers of state

Table 2. Percentage of Gross Industrial Output by Types of Enterprise

Year	State	Collective	Private
1981	74.76	24.62	0.62
1982	74.44	24.82	0.74
1983	73.36	25.74	0.90
1984	69.09	29.71	1.20
1985	64.86	32.08	3.06
1986	62.27	33.51	4.22
1987	59.73	34.62	5.66
1988	56.80	36.15	7.06
1989	56.06	35.69	8.24
1990	54.60	35.62	9.77
1991	52.94	35.70	11.36

Source: *China Statistical Year-book 1992.*
Note: Not all percentages add up to 100 due to rounding.

enterprises. Under the regulations, plant managers were monitored by various government departments, Party units and employees. At the same time, they were given the freedom to develop other business in addition to the state output targets. For state enterprises which had privileged supply of resources, local or imported, they tended to hold up the stocks for those buyers who could offer higher prices. The development of informal markets immediately cut off the guaranteed supply of raw materials for utilizing units and enabled the state enterprises to compete for economic rent under the monopolized environment. The enlarging private sector was more flexible and had an edge in the price competition compared with the state enterprises. Yet, hoarding by monopolists and rapid fluctuations in market prices for resources and final products aroused discontent among the masses and led to the outburst of emotions which resulted in the ordeal of 1989.

The different consequences of agricultural and enterprise reforms were rooted in the different structures of the two sectors. The agricultural sector, composed of the 800 million rural population, was able to redistribute key components of ownership (except land, held by collectives) so that individual farmers reacted quickly to supplement the planned state supply and successfully built an adjustment mechanism against the pressure of inflation. The industrial sector was highly concentrated and nationalized. As bureaux and state corporations realized their monopoly power over the supply of scarce resources, they all turned out to be a rent-seeking privileged class in the informal market.

Immediately after the June 4 Incident, some people blamed the reforms in prices and the emergence of private enterprises for the failure of the state-owned sector, and the discussion of share-holding system was criticized as the signal for the rise of capitalism. State enterprises blamed the price reform and its effect on resource allocation for their slow-down in production and their losses.

To solve the incentive problem of state enterprises, many distribution schemes were experimented with. For example, Shekou Industrial Zone used a complicated formula in the calculation of bonus spread between the leading unit and the staff. The objective was to provide incentive for minimization of costs and maximization of profits in the local enterprises.

In 1984, Zhao Ziyang, the then Premier, had called for the formation of conglomerates to develop economies of scale and synergy as a means to enter the international market. Many firms thus formed conglomerates with short-term contractual relations covering the supply of raw materials and the distribution of products. They could also benefit from preferential treatments granted by the government. The policy proved to be short-lived as the economy was volatile. Many firms failed to honour their contracts under the austerity programme, and their conglomerate relationship has either come to a halt or has been entangled in debt.

During the first stage of reform, political leaders in China did not realize the significance of nurturing a competitive market environment as a means to adjust prices and to encourage enterprise reform. They believed that economic efficiency could be attainable under public ownership. Enterprise reform meant the building of large state-owned corporations. The problem of monitoring enterprises without clearly defined property rights was not recognized. In fact, what the Chinese political leaders had in mind in the reform programme was state capitalism instead of a competitive free market.

Enterprise Reform by External Growth, 1985–1992

In 1988, the *State-owned Industrial Enterprise Law* was promulgated by the National People's Congress whereby plant managers were given more autonomy and responsibility, and enterprises were regarded as legal entities separate from their leading units. Yet the leading units in the government maintained the power of appointing key management personnel. State enterprises still had to fulfil the state plan as their first priority duties. Before the law could be implemented, the June 4 Incident broke the momentum of the reform, and China turned to the austerity policy for inflation control.

The impact of the political disturbances on state enterprises was a renewed emphasis on Party leadership. The plant manager of a state enterprise would have to consult the Party Secretary in decision-making on financing and personnel management.

The triangular debt problem emerged in the state enterprises at the time of recession under the austerity policy. Among the state enterprises, two-thirds fell into deficit. Because of the stringent credit control, many enterprises could not get liquidity as working capital for production. Purchasing and supply contracts among firms were breached. Even firms with sound financing were affected by the debt chain. In 1990, the State Council decided to increase credit supply to the state enterprises, to initiate the clearing of debts. The exercise extended until the end of 1991. Debts were cleared up to a certain extend but the poor performance of state enterprises remained.

The major cause of triangular debt was the deficiency of the money and capital market. Banks in China did not have autonomy in the extension of loans and the setting of interest rates. Financial instruments were scarce. Enterprises had to make financial arrangement outside the banking sector, mainly with their trading partners.

The central government was concerned about the difficulty faced by the large and medium-sized state enterprises. To protect state properties, leading units were required to audit all state assets by present value, replacement value, market price or clearing price. In 1991, the Management Bureau of State Assets was established to keep an account of all state enterprises. This was important as the transfer of assets by the merging of activities and the forming of share-holding companies were under experiment. The Bureau for the Administration of Industry and Commerce was given the authority to monitor the operation of all enterprises, including state enterprises.

In the course of 1992, the reform of management in state enterprise was marked by a change in vocabulary: the previously used expression *guoying qiye* (state-managed enterprise) was officially changed to *guoyou qiye* (state-owned enterprise); it signified, in symbolic terms, the passage of a crucial and determinant stage of the reform. Moreover, the regulations for changing the management mechanisms of enterprises under the *Industrial Enterprise Law*, which had gone unimplemented for close to four years because of the impossibility of enforcement, were finally approved by the State Council on 23 July 1992. This gesture enforced during the rest of 1992 and early 1993 a gradual and complementary elaboration into particular self-limiting regulations by ministries, agencies and provincial governments having the power of supervision (and substantive ownership rights).

Under the regulations, state enterprises are empowered to make decisions on production in addition to state directed plan, pricing, marketing, investment, purchase of raw materials, import and export, the takeover of other units, employment, wages and bonuses. State enterprises are to be responsible for their losses. The management and labour of an enterprise may have their wage fund cut back if the account goes into deficit.

The State Council, on behalf of the state's interests, will be responsible for the auditing of the assets of state enterprises, the proportion and amount of income distributed between government and enterprises. All changes in ownership, transfer of assets, new establishments and corporate integration, liquidation and auction must have the approval of the State Council. The responsible departments of the State Council will also monitor the hiring and firing of plant managers and protect the right of management in the enterprise.

By granting autonomy to management in enterprises, the government is responsible for the promulgation of laws and regulations relating to the management of state enterprises, such as industrial policy, interest rates, exchange rates, tax rates which become tools of macro-economic adjustments. Other areas of laws and regulations to be improved are related to accounting and financial system, wage system, cost and depreciation system, distribution of income and tax system.

In addition, the government is also responsible for the establishment of a market environment such as the building of markets for raw materials, labour, capital, technology and information, the elimination of regional trade barriers and illegal practices. The government will also help build a sound social security system. If the Chinese economic reform are to succeed, the function of the government in China will be similar to its counterpart under a market economy.

At the second stage of enterprise reform, the Chinese government has tried to spell out measures to implement the *Industrial Enterprise Law*.

The reform at this stage has encouraged state enterprises to exert themselves to make a profit. Many of the large state enterprises, taking advantage of preferential treatments and connections with higher authorities, have diversified into business not yet open to free competition, such as retailing, trading, import and export, restaurant and hotel trade, and industrial processing and assembling of restricted products. The move has immediately improved the financial situation of the state enterprises. The Capital Iron and Steel Works has been an example. The general manager of this state enterprise has been regarded by Deng Xiaoping as a model manager leading his enterprise reform.

It is fair to say that those state enterprises which have claimed success in enterprise reform have not achieved it through raising efficiency in their operation, but by making use of the freedom granted to them and extending the diversification of their business in a market environment not regulated by the government.

Another measure to vitalize the state enterprises has been to allow the state enterprise to form joint ventures with foreign investors. Those state enterprises must have an acceptable accounting and auditing system in order to form a joint venture. The move has helped the state enterprises to modernize their accounting and follow the rules of the market in their operation.

A third measure to vitalize state enterprises has been the forming of enterprise groups in China. It is the continuation of the policy which encouraged the forming of conglomerates in the mid-1980s. Instead of the 1,600 loosely connected groups formed at that time, fifty-five large enterprises were selected for the experiment with management integration aimed at the optimization of operation and the rationalization of organizational structure. These enterprise groups were granted favourable terms with regard to management and finance, etc.[2]

Premier Li Peng has been quoted as saying at a national working conference held on 23 September 1992:

> The most important thing in building socialism with Chinese characteristics is to continuously enhance the vitality of large and medium-sized state-owned enterprises and raise their efficiency.[3]

The Rise of Local and Private Enterprises

In 1981, of 381,500 enterprises existing nationally, 22.1% were state enterprises which produced 78% of the total industrial output value. The remaining 78.7% were collective enterprises which produced 21% of the total industrial output value. About 50% of the enterprises were located in the rural area. At the beginning of the reform programme, state enterprises were larger in scale, and their share of output was larger than that of collective and private enterprises. After ten years of reform, in 1991, many rural industrial enterprises have been set up and their output included in the industrial statistics. The industrial output of state enterprises has dropped drastically to 53% of the total and that of collective enterprises has increased to 36%. The statistics for private enterprises remains incomplete, and the actual output could be larger than what has been reported.

The change in output value under different ownerships has also affected the revenue of the central government. After 1983, enterprises were required to pay industrial and commercial taxes instead of remitting revenues and profits. Government revenue from state enterprises, as a result, has decreased. The tax and profit of enterprises had increased quickly as the reform programme got underway in the early 1980s but they slowed down significantly in the late 1980s going into the 1990s. Government subsidies to enterprises have also had the same trend, increasing rapidly in the 1980s and starting to decrease in the 1990s. (Table 3.)

Table 3. Taxes and Subsidies of Enterprises in China

Year	Industrial and commercial taxes	Enterprise income	Enterprise subsidies
1985	1197.69	43.75	—
1986	1299.69	42.04	324.78
1987	1385.38	42.86	–376.43
1988	1577.16	51.12	–446.46
1989	1877.33	63.60	–598.88
1990	1970.87	78.30	–578.88
1991	2035.51	74.69	–510.24

Source: *China Statistical Year-book 1992.*

As the proportion of total output by state enterprises decreased, their share of the total tax burden increased from 70% to about 80%. The increase in output by collective enterprises did not bring about a proportional income to government revenues. Due to the strong link between central government revenues and state enterprises, and the difficulty with levies from collective enterprises which are known to have a poor accounting system, the development of collective and private enterprises has resulted in a weakening of control by the central government.

Most of the collective enterprises are township or county-owned. The local leaders are the decision-makers in financing and personnel management. Collective enterprises are required to turn in a contracted amount of tax and profits which has become the major source of revenue for the local government. These governments reserve their right to exact other levies from the collective and private firms. In return, managers of collective enterprises are given a free hand in management and decision about remuneration for their staff, either in money or in kind. The collective enterprises are basically similar to state enterprises with regard to the form of ownership. However, some of them are simply managed by family members or relatives of the political leaders in charge. The close relationship with the local officials make monitoring easier and collusion possible. To show that the collective enterprises are socialist in nature, some of the collective enterprises have built up a social welfare system similar to that of state enterprises. We may predict that the problems with monitoring these collective enterprises will become more numerous as the size of enterprises grows.

The increasing number of township and village enterprises, collective or private, and joint ventures further serve to enlarge the scope of enterprises' activities out of the reach of the central government.

A corollary is the effort to realize the separation of government administration from business activities. In the future, income available to the central government will be linked to the performance of the large and medium-size state enterprises and a few enterprise groups directly under the control of the State Council. The relative size of their output will diminish as the local and non-state-owned sectors grow.

Deepening Enterprise Reform

In view of the changing relationship between the government and enterprises, the state has proceeded by step to develop administrative measures and to legislate forms of relations and protection; Table 4 provides a select list of such decisions and measures over the last decade or so. Worthy of note, in addition to the motivation of the large and medium-sized enterprises to improve their productivity, two areas of further reform were put forth by the State Council.

Table 4. Selection of Major Documents on the Reform of Enterprises 1981–1992

Sources	Topic	Date
1. Party Central State Council	Decisions on Opening Avenues to Invigorate the Economy and Solve Urban Employment Problems	17 October 1981
2. State Council	Provisional Decisions on the Collective Economy in Cities and Towns	14 April 1983
3. State Council	Approval of the Report by the People's Bank of China on State Enterprises' Liquid Assets and Its Unified Management by the People's Bank	25 June 1983
4. Ministry of Finance	Regulations on State Enterprises Income Tax	18 September 1984
5. State Council	Approval of the Ministry of Finance's Report on the Second Stage of the Tax-for-profit Reform in State Enterprises	18 September 1985
6. State Council	Regulations on Manager's Work in State Enterprises	15 September 1986
7. State Council	Provisional Regulations on the Management Responsibility Contract System in State-owned Industrial Enterprises	27 February 1988
8. State Council	Provisional Regulations on Private Enterprises Provisional Regulations on Private Enterprises' Income Tax	25 June 1988
9. National People's Congress	*State-owned Industrial Enterprise Law*	1 August 1988
10. State Council	Circular on the State Economic System Reform Commission on the Salient Points of Economic Reform in 1989	3 March 1989

Table 4. Selection of Major Documents on the Reform of Enterprises 1981–1992 (continued)

Sources	Topic	Date
11. State Council	Regulations on Rural Village Collective Enterprises	11 May 1990
12. State Council	Regulations on the Administration of Industry and Commerce Office	1 April 1991
13. State Council	Regulations on Rural Township Collective Enterprises	21 June 1991
14. State Council	Measures on the Evaluation and Management of State-owned Assets	June 1991
15. State Council	Approval of the List of Large State Enterprises to Experiment with Consortium Formation	14 December 1991
16. State Council	Provisional Decision on Financial Management for Enterprises Experimenting with Share System	6 June 1992
17. State Council	Rules on the Reform of the Management Mechanisms in State Industrial Enterprises	23 July 1992
18. State Council	Regulations on the Implementation for Commerce of the *Law on Urban Collective Enterprises*	10 August 1992
19. State Council	Implementation Rules for the Change of Management Mechanisms in State Commercial Enterprises	6 November 1992

Firstly, the promulgation of laws and regulations on taxation and registration and the monitoring of collective and private enterprises have been speeded up since 1988. Private enterprises have become legal entities under state's legislation.

Secondly, in line with the experiment with a share-holding system, new laws, such as the *Accounting Law* and *Regulations on Registered Accounts* for share-holding companies have been implemented in 1992. If the new accounting system is well received and adopted, the relationship between the government and enterprises will be no more than legal supervision and taxation levies.

Conclusion

The enterprise reform in the Chinese economy is crucial for the building of an efficient market economy. It involves market reform which means the building of free enterprise system and price mechanism, on the one hand, and property rights reform which separate managment from ownership of enterprises, on the other. China has adopted the market reform gradually, but it has become much more secure with the endorsement of Deng Xiaoping in his visit to southern China in early 1992. The reform of property rights in the name of a share-holding system and the setting up of a stock exchange are still at the experimental stage. Many enterprises have recorded success in performance, but they have either been earning some form of monopoly profit or operating efficiently in a market environment.

It is unrealistic to ask for improvement in productivity and efficiency by managerial reform alone. The separation of management from the leading bureaucratic units without a mechanism for effective monitoring may lead to utility maximizing by the management and to corruption. In a capitalist society, the management is monitored by shareholders' active stock trading in an environment where market information is relatively close to perfect and the stock market is close to efficient. In China, information on the stock markets in Shanghai and Shenzhen is far from perfect, and the markets are far from efficient in term of size and volume of trading. It is impossible for the shareholders, either individuals or institutions, to monitor the management through the limited and incomplete information found in the published accounts of the enterprises.

The enterprise reform in China during the past ten years, however, has had a significant impact on the relationship between the government and state enterprises. The decreasing relative share of output by state enterprises indicates the diminishing influence of the previous industrial policy which placed emphasis on investment in heavy industry. Revenues and profits of state enterprises will be replaced by more diversified taxes and charges as the major source of government revenue, given successful tax and accounting reforms.

Due to the rapid growth of collective, private and joint venture enterprises, state enterprises will be merged with them. The existence of state enterprises, in terms of number and size, will be relatively unimportant. The government might insist on the protection and subsidization of a few in the key industries but their effect on the government budget and the national economy will be negligible.

Notes

1. David Granick, *Chinese State Enterprises* (Chicago: The University of Chicago Press, 1990).
2. Yao Jiangguo, "Experimenting with Enterprise Groups," *Beijing Review*, 11–19 May 1992, pp. 14–19.
3. *Beijing Review*, 21–27 October 1992.

16

Direct Foreign Investment in China: Trends, Performance, Policies and Prospects

Nyaw Mee-kau

Introduction

At the third plenum of the Eleventh Central Committee of the Chinese Communist Party (CCP) held in December 1978, China adopted an "open-door policy" that opened its economy to foreign investment. This was a major shift from its past self-reliance policy that had resulted in a closed economy. During the fourteen-year period of 1979–1992, China made great strides in its domestic economic development and foreign trade relations by establishing five special economic zones (SEZs) — Shenzhen, Zhuhai, Shantou, Xiamen and Hainan — fourteen open-trade coastal cities, coastal economic development zones, inland development areas, and, most recently, the new Pudong area in Shanghai.[1] They are designated as target areas for attracting foreign direct investment.

In its quest for economic modernization, China has suffered from two severe bottlenecks: lack of savings for capital formation and foreign exchange constraints. Consequently, China has sought an inflow of foreign capital to increase its capital formation, and it has attracted export-oriented industries to increase its foreign exchange earnings, thereby alleviating the two constraints. In addition, foreign investment has facilitated the transfer of technology and management techniques, both badly needed by the modernization drive.

According to the classification used in China, utilization of foreign capital takes the following three forms: (a) "foreign loans" by foreign governments and international development agencies such as World Bank and Asian Development Bank (ADB); (b) "direct foreign investment" (DFI) which includes "equity joint ventures" (EJVs), "contractual joint ventures" (CJVs), "wholly foreign-owned enterprises" (WFOs), and "joint development ventures" (JDVs) which relate mainly to oil exploration; and (c) "other foreign investment" which includes compensation trade, export processing and international leasing. In this chapter we will (1) examine the trends and structural features of foreign investment in terms of forms, sources of investment, and geographical and sectoral distribution during 1979–1992; (2) analyze the performance of foreign-invested firms; (3) discuss development strategies and foreign investment policies through 1992; (4) investigate major developments in 1992; (5) examine problems and obstacles encountered; and (6) assess the prospects for future foreign investment in China. We will specifically focus on three forms of foreign direct investment, EJV, CJV and WFO enterprises, and briefly examine "other foreign investment."

Trends and Structural Features, 1979–1992

Among the various forms of foreign investments, there are four that need some explanation. An EJV, officially called a Sino-foreign joint venture, is a limited company jointly funded through equity by two or more investors. It has the status of a legal person, and the investing companies share risk profits or losses in proportion to their respective equity shares. A WFO is a branch funded by a foreign firm, or it can be an independent enterprise formed by a foreign company or a group of individuals outside China. It is wholly responsible for profits or losses. The third form, a CJV, is sometimes called a "cooperative venture," and it is probably unique to China. A CJV is a loose form of enterprise where Chinese and foreign partners cooperate in operations and management as prescribed in the contract. The Chinese side often provides land, natural resources, labour, local equipment, or facilities but does not contribute equity funds. The foreign partners often provide funds, technology, major new equipment and materials. Under a CJV, profits or losses are split according to a ratio that both parties have agreed upon beforehand. Finally, a JDV is a joint investment by Chinese and foreign interests that is limited primarily to exploration of off-shore oil resources. The purpose of the venture is not to share profits but to share oil resources. Output, once produced, is divided between both sides according to contract terms.

Table 1 shows the utilization of foreign capital from 1979 to 1992. During this period, total contractual or pledged DFI and other foreign investment totalled US$126.2 billion, while total realized value of DFI was US$34.5 billion. In addition, there was US$64 billion in pledged foreign loans (realized value of US$52.8 billion) for the period 1979–1992. In the early years, foreign investment followed a zig-zag path. It grew slowly in the initial years then suffered a drastic decline in 1986 due to the deterioration of the investment climate. When the Chinese government started to take serious actions to rectify the situation, foreign investment began to gradually recover until the outbreak of the pro-democracy movement in Beijing in 1989. After the Tiananmen Incident in June 1989, China was sanctioned by a number of western countries. In addition, an economic retrenchment programme initiated in 1988 to curb high inflation rates had an adverse effect on DFI in 1989. According to the data published by the Ministry of Foreign Economic Relations and Trade (MOFERT), renamed as the Ministry of Foreign Trade and Economic Cooperation at the Eighth National People's Congress in early 1993, the pledged DFI projects had

Table 1. Utilization of Foreign Capital, 1979–1992

(Unit value: US$100 million)

	Foreign loans[1]		Direct foreign investment[2]		Other foreign investment[3]		Total	
	Projects	Value	Projects	Value	Projects	Value	Projects	Value
I. Contractual:								
1979–1989	510	517.34	21,776	337.65	—	44.93	22,286	899.92
1990	98	50.99	7,273	65.96	—	3.90	7,371[4]	120.85
1991	108	71.61	12,978	119.77	—	4.45	13,086[4]	195.83
1992	—	—	47,000	575.00	—	110.00	—	—
II. Realized:								
1979–1989	—	393.21	—	154.95	—	29.69	—	577.85
1990	—	65.35	—	34.87	—	2.68	—	102.90
1991	—	68.88	—	43.66	—	3.00	—	115.54
1992	—	—	—	111.60	—	—	—	—

Sources: *Zhongguo tongji nianjian* (China Statistical Year-book) (various years); *Zhongguo tongji zhaiyao 1992* (A Statistical Survey of China 1992), *Zhongguo jingji nianjian* (China Economic Year-book) (various years); *People's Daily* (Beijing), 19 February 1993.

Notes: (1) Include loans by foreign governments and international development agencies;
(2) direct foreign investment includes the following forms: equity joint ventures, contractual joint ventures (cooperative ventures), wholly foreign-owned enterprises and joint development ventures (petroleum);
(3) includes compensation trade, export processing and international leasing;
(4) excluding projects in "other foreign investment" category.

declined from 5,945 in 1988 to 5,779 in 1989, representing a negative growth rate of –2.8%. Total commitments in 1989 recorded only a moderate growth of 6.1% as compared to 1988, and the number of EJVs and CJVs declined by 6.4% and 27.3% respectively.[2]

In the second half of 1990, foreign direct investment in China began to recover as western countries gradually normalized their relations with China, in particular after the lifting of economic sanctions by France which had adopted a tough stance against China's crack-down on the pro-democracy movement. Foreign investors flocked back to China after a cooling-off period, and DFI continued to increase in 1991. It surged even further in 1992, and the momentum seems unabated. The latest released data show that there were 47,000 foreign-invested projects committed with a pledged value of US$57.5 billion in 1992, and the realized value made by foreign investors was US$11.16 billion.[3] This represents a growth rates of 262% for pledged projects and 380% for contracted value as compared to 1991. Both pledged projects and the value of DFI in 1992 surpassed the figures for the entire previous period of 1979–1991! This record is truly impressive by any standard. The high growth rates in 1992 were partially due to the huge investments in real estate from overseas. Certainly the optimism of DFI in China was spurred by Deng Xiaoping's visit to southern China in January 1992, when he argued for more rapid development of the "open-door policy." It was also helped by the adoption of the "socialist market economy" doctrine at the Fourteenth CCP Congress held in October 1992. According to a report by Reuter News Agency, total commitments of foreign investment to China during the first nine months of 1992 had far surpassed that of Indonesia, Malaysia and Thailand, three of the booming Southeast Asian countries which compete with China for foreign direct investment.[4]

The relative shares of various forms/types of foreign investment have changed over the years in China. As presented in Table 2, in the first few years of opening to the outside world, China's utilization of foreign funds was realized mainly through contractual joint ventures, joint oil development ventures and compensation trade and export-processing ventures. Together, these accounted for 82% of foreign investment during 1979–1984. EJVs and WFOS were relatively unimportant during that period. CJVs and compensation trade and export processing ventures in particular were generally smaller in scale and of low-skill labour-intensive industries which were located mainly in four SEZs and the Guangdong province. A majority of the foreign investors are mainly from neighbouring Hong

Table 2. Percentage Shares of Various Form of Foreign-invested Enterprises to Total Foreign Investment, 1979–1992 (contractual values)

Year	EJVs	CJVs	WFOs	Joint development	Other investment*	Total foreign investment (in US$100 million)
1979–1984	13.4%	45.6%	4.6%	23.5%	12.9%	103.3 (100%)
1985	32.1	55.2	0.7	5.7	6.3	63.3 (100%)
1986	41.3	40.8	0.6	2.4	14.9	33.3 (100%)
1987	45.2	29.7	10.9	0.01	14.1	43.2 (100%)
1988	50.6	26.2	7.8	1.0	14.4	61.9 (100%)
1989	42.3	17.2	26.3	3.2	11.0	62.9 (100%)
1990	38.7	17.9	35.0	2.8	5.6	69.9 (100%)
1991	49.0	17.2	29.5	0.7	3.6	124.2 (100%)
1992	—	—	—	—	—	575.0 (100%)

Sources: Computed from *Almanac of China's Foreign Economic Relations and Trade* (various years).
* Includes compensation trade, export processing and international leasing.

Kong, that took advantage of low wages and cheap land prices. In addition, the forms of CJVs and export processing ventures were quite flexible which usually required no cash outlay by Chinese partners. These types of ventures were more than welcomed by China which lacked capital funds for economic development.

As shown in Table 2, EJVs have become increasingly important since 1985. The number of WFOs also surged after 1987 whereas CJVs and "other investment ventures" declined. The increase of WFOs was due mainly to three factors. First, there was a huge surge of DFI from Taiwan in the late 1980s (see pattern of investment flows below). Taiwan investors usually were inclined to control their own companies rather than to cooperate with partners. Secondly, considerable costs and time involved in the coordination of technology and management deemed essential in EJVs and CJVs was avoided by establishing WFOs.[5] And thirdly, there was greater acceptance by the Chinese government of WFOs which are export-oriented and bring into China much needed foreign-exchange earnings. It is worth noting that many EJVs and WFOs have been established by well-known multinationals and conglomerates from all over the world. China has been quite successful in attracting large-scale, high-tech foreign enterprises to invest in the country in recent years.

By 1992, investors from over fifty countries or areas had invested in China. Table 3 presents the direction of flows of direct investment into China by leading countries/areas. Hong Kong/Macau have been the largest investor area taking up 62.2% of total direct investment during 1979–1991. Before 1990, the State Statistical Bureau of China did not separate Hong Kong from Macau in its published foreign investment figures. Despite this, it is known that most of the flow of foreign investment is from Hong Kong whereas Macau accounts for only a minute share.

It should be stressed that published DFI figures for Hong Kong are overstated. Part of the investment flow from Hong Kong is in fact originating in Southeast Asia. Some overseas Chinese and Taiwan businessmen invest in the mainland through subsidiaries registered in Hong Kong to avoid scrutiny from their home countries. Investing in China by wealthy overseas Chinese businessmen is politically sensitive in some Southeast Asian countries such as Indonesia. Indonesia broke diplomatic relationship with China after the Indonesian Communist Party was linked to the *coup d'état* in 1965. The two countries re-established diplomatic ties in 1990; it is only in 1992 that the Indonesian government has taken a more positive attitude towards its ethnic-Chinese citizens investing in China. In Taiwan,

Table 3. Shares and Sizes of Direct Foreign Investment by Leading Countries/Areas, 1979–1992

(Unit: US$100 million)

Countries/Areas	Projects (1979–1991) Number	Percentage	Contractual values (1979–1991) Amount	Percentage	Average value per project (US$ million)
Hong Kong/Macau	31,453	75.1	325.7	62.2	1.03
USA	2,000	4.8	50.1	9.6	2.51
Japan	1,891	4.3	39.1	7.5	2.07
Germany	111	0.3	10.9	2.1	9.81
Singapore	558	1.3	9.1	1.7	1.63
United Kingdom	132	0.3	7.3	1.4	5.53
Australia	181	0.4	3.4	0.6	1.88
Canada	187	0.5	3.2	0.6	1.71
Sub-total	36,513	87.0	448.8	85.7	
All Countries/Areas	42,036	100.0	523.4	100.0	

Taiwan	Projects 1983–1991	1992*	Contractual values 1983–1991	1992*	Realized values 1991	1992	Average size (US$m) 1983–1991	1992*
	3,815	3,750	34.3	30.0	8.5	—	0.9	0.8

Sources: *Zhongguo jingji nianjian* (various years); *Almanac of China's Foreign Economic Relations and Trade 1991/92, 1992/93*; Taiwan's data are from *China Daily* (Beijing), 30 December 1992.

* Figures for January to September 1992.

investors were legally prohibited from investing in China prior to 1990, although Taiwanese businessmen found ways to circumvent government restraints by registering ventures through Hong Kong. The rule was relaxed in 1990 to allow Taiwanese firms to invest in the mainland through proper registration with the Taiwan government. Consequently, future accounting for DFI through Hong Kong/Macau will be more accurate, but data on investment flow for previous years coming from Hong Kong and Macau include Taiwan and other Southeast Asian interests.

Moreover, there are some China-funded firms in Hong Kong and Macau that have established joint ventures with other domestic Chinese firms. The so-called "bogus blue-eyed" joint ventures have been established to take advantage of the preferential treatment given to joint ventures. Clearly, the existence of the "reverse investment," as it is often called by the Chinese, overstates the flow of foreign investment funds from Hong Kong. However, its magnitude is unknown as there have been no official data published by China.

After Hong Kong, the second largest foreign investor in terms of DFI value for the period 1979–1991 was the United States, followed by Japan and then Germany. Taiwan's DFI should be noted here. China began to publish investment figures from Taiwan only in 1990. According to the figures released by *China Daily*, there were 3,815 foreign-invested projects with contractual or pledged value of US$34.00 billion for 1983–1991. Pledged investment increased significantly in 1992, which was equivalent to 87.5% of that pledged during the period of 1983–1991 (Table 3). The relative position of Taiwan increased from fourth in 1991 to second in 1992, only after Hong Kong.[6] According to a report published by the Chung-Hua Institution for Economic Research, a semi-government think-tank based in Taipei, there were over 10,000 cumulative Taiwanese-invested projects in the mainland with a total contractual value exceeding US$68 billion.[7] This surpassed the United States. Investment flow from South Korea also became increasingly important. In 1991–1992, South Korea's investment position climbed from obscurity to fifth place after Hong Kong, Taiwan, US and Japan.[8] China established full diplomatic relations with South Korea in 1992, which marked the end of hostility between the two countries following the Korean War. This breakthrough will certainly have a positive effect on the flow of Korea's direct investment into China due to geographical proximity of the two countries. Historically, South Korea had close ties with Shandong province, which, today, is the key recipient of DFI from South Korea, and it is expected to remain so in the future.

As illustrated in Table 3, investment projects made by Taiwan and Hong Kong are small in scale, with an average value of US$0.9 million (1983–1991) and US$1.03 million (1979–1991) respectively. The average size of DFI from Germany is the largest with US$9.81 million, followed by the United Kingdom (US$5.53 million) and the USA (US$1.51 million). The average Japanese DFI project is quite small with a value of US$2.07 million, but the Japanese DFI in China accounts for only 1.1% of Japan's total overseas investment and 6.3% of its total Asia investment for the period 1982–1984.[9] In view of Japan's huge economic power, its proximity to and its traditional cultural ties with China, the relatively small total DFI has been disappointing. This can be explained partially by the relative difficulty in transferring Japanese technological know-how to China, and partially by the huge bilateral trade surplus in Japan's favour. China has been critical of Japan's reluctance to invest more, particularly when good performance of Japanese DFI is taken into consideration.[10] Given the improved investment climate in China in recent years, Japan needs to respond more positively to China's demand.

China's foreign direct investments by geographical distribution in terms of both amounts and percentage shares are presented in Tables 4 and 5 respectively. Four SEZs accounted for 20.2% of total DFI during 1979–1989. Shenzhen, the first SEZ established in China, topped the list and absorbed 13.2% of DFI. This was partly due to its proximity to Hong Kong. Apart from the SEZs, DFI was concentrated in the nine "open coastal provinces" which accounted for 61.7% of DFI. Guangdong province alone took 42.2% of that total (Table 5).

As DFI surged during the period 1990–1992, there were some shifts of geographical distribution. In the special economic zones, Shenzhen declined whereas Shantou increased. As a whole, the performance of the SEZs remained strong after 1989. In the "open coastal cities," Dalian recorded the largest increase in terms of percentage share (i.e., from an average share of 1.6% during 1979–1989 to 6.9% in 1991). Although Guangzhou's DFI increased in absolute terms throughout the period, its relative share remained rather stable at about 5.5%. "Open coastal provinces" continued to absorb the lion's share of DFI with larger percentage shares in 1990 and 1991 as compared to the period 1979–1989. After being promulgated a separate province in 1987, Hainan was able to attract an increasing share of DFI, and Guangdong continued to remain vibrant. On

Table 4. Direct Foreign Investment in China by Geographical Distribution (realized values)

(Unit: US$ million)

	1979–1989	1990	1991	1992 (Realized)	1992 (Contractual)
SEZs	3,152.05	654.63	969.18	—	—
Shenzhen	2,045.76	388.94	398.75	70[1]	2,510[1]
Zhuhai	497.37	69.10	134.33	—	—
Shantou	175.25	123.86	303.10	—	—
Xiamen	433.67	72.73	133.00	—	—
Open coastal cities	2,823.53	642.16	816.54	—	—
Dialian	250.16	201.29	261.11	—	—
Tianjin	313.89	36.93	132.16	—	—
Qingdao	97.37	45.88	46.47	—	—
Shanghai	1,248.74	177.19	145.19	—	2,260
Guangzhou	913.37	180.87	231.61	—	—
Open coastal provinces†	9,537.15 (11,117.78)*	2,711.44 (2,925.56)*	3,367.32 (3,644.67)*	—	—
Liaoning	435.40	257.31	348.88	—	—
Hebei	97.63	44.47	44.37	—	—
Shandong	455.39	185.70	179.50	—	3,150

Table 4. Direct Foreign Investment in China by Geographical Distribution (realized values) (continued)

(Unit: US$ million)

	1979–1989	1990	1991	1992 (Realized)	1992 (Contractual)
Jiangsu	406.22	133.97	212.32	1,410	7,190
Zhejiang	219.07	49.14	91.62	—	2,910
Fujian	799.78	319.89	466.29	1,410	6,550
Guangdong	6,541.68	1,582.31	1,822.86	4,860[(2)]	19,870[(2)]
Hainan	302.22	103.02	176.16	—	2,260
Guangxi	279.76	35.63	25.32	—	—
Beijing	1,517.66	278.95	244.82	—	2,510
PRC total	15,495.00	3,487.00	4,366.34	11,160	57,500

Sources: Figures for 1979–1990 are derived from Y. Y. Kueh, "Foreign Investment and Economic Change in China," *The China Quarterly*, No. 131 (September 1992), Table 3, p. 649; 1991 figures are from *Almanac of China's Foreign Economic Relations and Trade 1992/93*; 1992 figures are from various sources such as *People's Daily*, 9 February 1993; *Ta Kung Pao*, 15 January 1993 (note 1) and *Sing Tao Daily*, March 11 1993 (note 2).

* Bracketed values include DFI in Tianjin and Shanghai;
† PRC total is less than the sub-totals as figures for open coastal provinces include values in other sections.

Table 5. Shares of Foreign Direct Investment in China by Geographical Distribution (realized values)

	1979–1989	1990	1991	1992 (Realized)	1992 (Contractual)
SEZs	20.5%	18.9%	22.2%	—	—
Shenzhen	13.2	11.2	9.1	6.2	4.4
Zhuhai	3.2	2.0	3.1	—	—
Shantou	1.3	3.6	6.9	—	—
Xiamen	2.8	2.1	3.1	—	—
Open coastal cities	18.2	18.5	18.7	—	—
Dalian	1.6	5.8	6.0	—	—
Tianjin	2.0	1.1	3.0	—	—
Qingdao	0.6	1.3	1.1	—	—
Shanghai	8.1	5.1	3.3	—	3.9
Guangzhou	5.9	5.2	5.3	—	—
Open coastal provinces	61.5	77.8	67.5	—	—
	(71.8)*	(83.9)*	(83.5)*	—	—
Liaoning	2.8	7.4	8.0	—	—
Hebei	0.6	1.3	1.0	—	—
Shandong	2.9	5.3	4.1	—	6.1
Jiangsu	2.6	3.8	4.9	12.6	12.5
Zhejiang	1.4	1.4	2.1	—	5.1
Fujian	5.2	9.2	1.1	12.6	11.4
Guangdong	42.2	45.4	41.7	43.6	34.6
Hainan	2.0	3.0	4.0	—	3.9
Guangxi	1.8	1.0	0.6	—	—
Beijing	9.8	8.2	5.6	—	4.4

Sources: Computed from Table 4.

the other hand, Beijing's DFI declined in relative terms over the period 1979–1992. Another notable recent development is that inland areas have been attracting more DFI, although their relative values are not very significant. Traditionally, businessmen from Hong Kong and Taiwan have concentrated their investments in the Pearl River Delta and Fujian province, although there is a notably new trend that more investors from Hong Kong and Taiwan are seeking investments in the Yantze River Delta and some inland areas.

The sectoral distribution of DFIs for 1979–1991 is shown in Table 6, but a brief explanation of the classification for economic sectors is necessary. According to the United Nations' standard classification of economic sectors, "mining and quarrying" is considered a primary sector whereas in China it is included in the "manufacturing" group as a secondary sector. Also, in China only primary sectors (e.g., agriculture, forestry, husbandry and fishing) and secondary sectors (e.g., industry, transportation, posts and construction) are considered "productive" sectors while categories under the services sector (e.g., commerce and catering) are classified as "non-productive." Before 1984, economic sectors were broken down into twenty-one sub-groups. This was later consolidated into ten sub-groups. As illustrated in Table 6, there were fluctuations in the relative share of economic sub-sectors throughout the period 1979–1991. When China first opened its economy to foreign investors, one of its primary objectives was to attract import-substituting industries to the country. Thus, it attracted a significant amount of DFI in the industrial sector during the initial years (Table 6). On the other hand, China also absorbed a substantial amount of direct investment in the hotel industry. During 1983–1984, the tourism and hotel industry accounted for 21.6% of total DFI with a value of US$103,440 million.[11] With respect to EJV investment, 36.8% came from the tourism and hotel industry with a value of US$50,857 million.[12] Foreign investors concentrated on the services sector during those early years because the investment climate in industry was less than satisfactory. At the same time, the payback period for investment in hotels was shorter than in industry, which was attractive to many investors.

With the promulgation in 1986 of the "Provisions of the State Council for the Encouragement of Foreign Investment" (the so-called twenty-two article provisions), the industrial investment climate improved. Also, the "Regulations on Guiding Foreign Investment Operations," approved by the State Planning Commission in 1987, played a role in attracting investors to venture in the industrial sector. Consequently, there has been a larger share

Table 6. Direct Foreign Investment by Economic Sectors (on contractual basis)

Economic Sectors	1979–1989	1985	1986	1987	1988	1989	1990	1991	Average size per projects (US$m) 1979–1989	1990	1991
Agriculture, forestry, husbandry and fishing	3.1%	2.0%	2.2%	3.4%	3.9%	2.2%	1.8%	1.8%	$0.99	0.54	0.68
Industry	52.9	43.4	27.7	47.9	75.9	83.3	84.4	80.3	1.14	0.85	0.83
Building	1.6	2.1	1.9	1.5	2.2	1.2	2.7	1.1	1.03	4.19	1.69
Communications, post and telecommunications	1.3	1.7	1.2	0.5	1.7	0.9	0.6	0.8	0.85	0.78	1.45
Commerce and catering	4.7	8.3	3.5	0.8	1.2	1.2	1.7	1.4	1.51	1.16	0.12
Real estate, public utilities and servicing	25.2	35.9	57.1	39.7 (28.0)*	10.0 (6.3)*	9.4	6.8	12.6	5.44	2.85	3.77
Hygiene, sports and social welfare services	0.4	0.8	0.6	0.3	0.1	0.6	0.6	0.5	2.07	2.67	2.14
Education, culture and arts	0.4	0.1	1.4	0.4	0.9	0.1	0.09	0.5	1.75	0.40	1.20
Science, research and general technical services	—	0.1	—	—	0.1	0.06	0.5	0.2	0.33	1.12	0.30
Others	10.5	5.7	4.5	5.7	3.8	1.0	0.8	0.8	2.89	0.88	0.96
Total: Value (US$100 mill.)	$337.6	$63.3	28.4	37.1	53.0	56.0	$66.0	$119.8	$1.55	$0.91	$0.92
Percentage**	100.0	100.0	100.0	100.0	100.0	100.0	100.0	100.0			

Sources: Computed from *Zhongguo Jingji Nianjian* (various years); *Almanac of China's Foreign Economic Relations and Trade 1991/92, 1992/93*.

* Figures in brackets refer to direct investment in hotels.
** Total percentage figures may not add up to 100 due to rounding.

of DFI in the industrial sector (47.9% in 1987), but direct investment in the tourism and hotel sector was still substantial (28% for 1987). Because of the glut of hotel rooms from earlier investments, China temporarily halted further investments in hotels in 1988. Thus, foreign direct investment in industry continued to increase significantly both in terms of relative share (over 80% after 1989) and absolute value. The Tiananmen Incident in 1989 dealt a serious blow to tourism, and DFI in hotels shrunk even further, but as people's memory faded, tourism had fully returned to normal by 1992. DFI in manufacturing was concentrated in low-end, labour-intensive industries rather than capital or skill-intensive enterprises. This was generally demonstrated by the small size of projects. In 1991, the average size of an industrial project was US$0.83 million. Larger-scale projects were normally found in the real estate, public utilities and services sub-group which includes hotel development. There are indications that China has been able to attract more capital-intensive projects in recent years. According to a high-ranking Chinese official, "productive" (i.e., non-services related) projects accounted for 90% of total projects approved, "most of them are either technically advanced or export-oriented."[13] Reports in the press showed that an increasing number of projects of this kind were being signed with foreign investors. For example, a joint venture automobile plant in Changchun was signed with Volkswagen and a large-scale petrochemical plant with Royal-Shell Dutch in 1991. The former was designated as a "state project" by the Chinese government.[14]

Performance of Foreign-invested Enterprises

In a questionnaire survey of thirty-four EJVs located in Shenzhen SEZ in 1986, Henley and Nyaw found that the performance of the EJVs was rather mixed. Empirical findings of firms with regard to planned profit targets were as follows: surpassed target (9.4%), achieved target as planned (40.6%), failed to achieve target (31.3%), some losses (15.6%), and heavy losses (3.1%). With regard to foreign exchange earnings, 23.5% of firms indicated that there were net gains, 44.1% achieved a balance, and 32.4% had deficits. As far as the overall performance of EJVs was concerned, the following findings were given: "very successful" 3.0%, "basically successful" 24.2%, "cannot tell yet" 24.2%, "not very successful" 9.1%, and "basically a failure" 9.1%.[15]

If EJVs in the Shenzhen Special Economic Zone are indicative of the nation as a whole, it seems that one-third of China's EJVs have not performed well. This was substantiated by a remark made by Yu Xiaochong, Vice-Minister of MOFERT in late 1991. According to Yu, China's *san zi* enterprises (i.e. three forms of foreign-invested enterprises, or EJV, CJV and WFO) had reversed their earlier trend of low-performance to one characterized by "normality" in 1987. By the first half of 1991, however, about 70% of the nation's 16,000 *san zi* enterprises under actual operation were profitable, remitting RMB4.35 billion of taxes to the state's treasury.[16] The number of enterprises running at a loss was decreasing.

Based on a 1991 survey conducted by the Foreign Investment Management Bureau of MOFERT, economic efficiency of *san zi* enterprises did not differ much among the various open coastal areas and inland provinces. Differences in economic efficiency were related to different lines of industry, forms of investment, orientation of marketing or managerial capabilities. The survey showed that ventureship between foreign investors and large state-owned enterprises had generally performed better. Based on another survey of 1,000 foreign-invested enterprises conducted by Fujian's Provincial Statistical Bureau, performance by technologically advanced/large-scale capital-intensive enterprises was significantly superior to that of smaller enterprises in the same industry.[17]

The poor performance of foreign enterprises could be attributable to several reasons. Firstly, new enterprises in the surveys had only been in operation less than a year, and their profit picture was not yet known. Secondly, in order to avoid taxes, enterprises could resort to "transferring" profit elsewhere (often in dubious ways), thus showing net losses in their income statements. Some enterprises evaded tax payments by outright fraud and deception. Thirdly, enterprises had genuine difficulties. The second reason, that of hiding profits through transfers, seemed to be predominant in China. Given the widespread corruption among Chinese officials and the unreliably low standard of accounting systems in China, it was extremely difficult to unearth malpractices.

Performance of foreign-invested enterprises at the national level for the year 1992 was not yet reported for verification here; however, based on scattered data released so far, performance in 1992 was probably among the best since the open-door policy was launched in 1979. For example, in Guangdong province foreign enterprises accounted for over 40% of the total national value of DFI in China (Table 5), and in mid-1990, 46.6% of the province's 2,569 foreign-funded enterprises were losing money. Lack of raw materials, energy shortages, stagnant domestic demand, inconsistent policies and other reasons were cited for such poor performance.[18] By the end of 1992, however, this trend had been reversed. In a survey conducted by the Guangdong Foreign Economic Relations and Trade Commission in 1992, it was shown that about 90% of the 6,505 *san zi* enterprises under survey were making profits. Net profit for the first half of 1992 was RMB1.28 billion, an increase of over 20% compared to the same period in 1991.[19] This may demonstrate the experience gained by both foreign and Chinese partners in operating *san zi* enterprises, ultimately resulting in greater economic efficiency. In particular, Chinese managers had learned many of the intricacies of a market economy, such as market pricing of products and operations management of enterprises.

Compared to the outstanding performance of Guangdong and other coastal provinces, the inland Sichuan province did not perform well. Sichuan had only 1,600 foreign-invested enterprises in 1992, which are only 24.6% of the number in Guangdong. According to a survey of 118 *san zi* enterprises in Sichuan, only 46% were profitable while more than 50% were losing money. A poor investment climate and an inadequate infrastructure were certainly important factors contributing to less-than-satisfactory performance; in addition, many foreign partners were not remitting their investment funds to their enterprises as pledged.[20] This has become equally serious in other areas as well in recent years.

Development Strategies and Foreign Investment Policies

We now turn to the discussion of development strategies and foreign investment policies which play important roles in shaping the current state of foreign investment in China. Before the adoption of the open-door policy in 1979, China's socialist modernization programme had generally adhered to the principle of "self reliance" to the exclusion of "assistance from outsiders." This principle was based on an important speech made by Mao Zedong in 1952 on China's economic development. Principle of self-reliance was self-explanatory, i.e., funds for development were to be generated domestically. However, assistance from outsiders did occur and had various connotations in different periods. In the 1950s, China received low interest loans from the Soviet Union and, with Soviet technical assistance, built 149 large industrial projects. Soviet assistance came to an abrupt stop in 1960 when relations between the two countries deteriorated over ideological conflicts. Subsequently, China began actively soliciting assistance from several western countries. During 1963–1968 it imported over eighty technological items and industrial projects (52% were "turnkey" or complete projects) from Japan, the United Kingdom, France, West Germany, Sweden, Italy and Austria. These were valued at over US$100 million, and they were financed mainly by export credits and deferred payment systems of the exporting countries.[21] Importation of foreign technology was seriously hindered during the Cultural Revolution which commenced in 1966.

With the downfall of Gang of Four in 1976, Hua Guofeng, a Maoist who succeeded Mao Zedong as Chairman of the Party, launched the so-called "Leap Forward with a Foreign Character" (*yang yuejin*). Within a short span of one year in 1977, China signed contracts with western countries worth more than US$780 million, 70% of which were "turnkey" industrial projects.[22] However, such drastic change, and at such a fast pace, strained China's foreign reserves, and project importation was scaled down. Then in 1978, Hua was out-manoeuvred by Deng Xiaoping and his associates at the third plenary session of the Eleventh CCP Central Committee. Dengist reform and the open-door policy were established as guidelines for long-term, systematic economic development.

China had basically followed an inward-looking industrialization strategy from 1952 until then; in recent years liberalization allowing foreign investment occurred. In the early years, China had imported only high-end, technologically advanced equipment in the petrochemical, mechanical, steel and fabrics industries which could not be produced domestically. Contribution to the modernization programme had been the sole criterion for importing these items regardless of their economic efficiency. This had usually resulted in misallocation of resources. During Hua Guofeng's years (1976–1978), China embraced a more "liberal" foreign economic policy than during the Cultural Revolution period, yet it still vehemently defended the Maoist position on foreign direct investment, declaring that China would never embark on joint ventures with foreign capitalists.[23]

Before the open-door policy, Chinese cadres had probably never heard of the concept of "joint ventures." This, of course, changed when Dengists came into power. The motives behind Deng's reversal of China's foreign economic policy is beyond the scope of this study, although much has been written on the subject.[24] However, the great success of China's neighbouring "Four Little Dragons" (South Korea, Hong Kong, Taiwan and Singapore) certainly had a great impact on Deng and his associates. One common feature of the phenomenal economic growth of the "Four Little Dragons" during the last two decades was the openness of their economies. In the Dengist view, China would have to follow suit or lag behind and remain poor. The latter could be detrimental to the future stability of the nation.

The open-door policy called for utilization of foreign capital and a speeding up of the process of economic development in China. However, policy-makers were careful not to inhibit the development of local industries by driving them out of the domestic markets at the initial stage. Four special economic zones were first set up to attract foreign investment. Later, other economic and technological development areas, open coastal cities and open coastal provinces were also established to tap the mature, high-accumulation economies.

The Chinese government also formulated a set of strategic targets for guiding foreign investment in light of state industrial planning and specific situations of the recipient areas or regions. State industrial planning has changed over the years. Prior to 1978, the Stalinist or Maoist strategy had emphasized the development of heavy industry. During the early 1980s, in spite of the new reform programme, investment allocation was still "strongly skewed towards the preferential growth sector of heavy industry."[25] The current planning is aimed at achieving a more diversified industrial base with transfer of new technology and managerial capability from abroad. Because of capital shortage, foreign investors are expected to bring in machinery, equipment and raw materials while their Chinese counterparts are expected to provide cheap labour and land for production destined for export. In addition, foreign-invested firms are expected to balance their own foreign exchange.

In order to generate hard currency needed to finance various industrial plans, Zhao Ziyang launched a new initiative in 1987 arguing that Chinese coastal areas should participate in the international division of labour, or what he called the "international great cycle" or "two heads outside, pursuing big import and big export" (*liangtou zaiwai, dajin dachu*).[26] Essentially this meant that development in the coastal areas would rely entirely on the outside world for both inputs and manufactured exports. This approach was different from the import substituting strategy pursued by some developing countries which solicited foreign investment into industry destined predominantly for the domestic market and resorted to protectionist high tariffs or non-tariff trade barriers. In contrast, the "international great cycle" approach linked China more closely to the international economy. Although Zhao was replaced by Jiang Zemin after the June 4 Incident in 1989 and his "international great cycle" approach has been rarely mentioned since then, this does not imply that the approach has been abandoned; rather, the strategy has been amended by discarding the big-push overtone. It should be pointed out that, unlike the export-led strategy of the "Four Little Dragons," China did not open up its vast domestic market to foreign competition during the period of 1979–1990. Since 1990, however, China has begun to liberalize its policies and open domestic markets in response to international pressure and because of China's strong desire to resume its seat in the General Agreement on Tariffs and Trade (GATT). China's development strategy, nevertheless, is inherently inward-looking, although it is bound to evolve gradually towards a more open economy.

Against the background of the above macro development strategy we now turn to the discussion of foreign investment policy. China's foreign investment policy is comprised of various laws, regulations and provisions which have been formulated to change the industrial mix of the country, to effect investment flows to certain designated geographical areas, to target particular forms of investment and to protect the interests of foreign investors. Since 1979 more than 200 laws and regulations have been introduced which, today, constitute a complex web of regulating mechanisms.

The first piece of legislation on foreign investment in China was the *Law of the PRC on Chinese-Foreign Joint Ventures* (hereafter referred to as the *Joint Venture Law*) promulgated by the State Council in July 1979. It was very brief with only fifteen articles, and it lacked substance. Subsequent laws and regulations were passed on income tax, company registration, labour management, trademarks, contracts, advertising and various other matters relating to foreign-invested firms. Then, in September 1983, the Chinese government adopted the *Regulations for the Implementation of the Law of PRC on Chinese-Foreign Joint Ventures*. This occurred more than four years after the promulgation of the *Joint Venture Law*; it contained 118 articles which codified and elaborated the 1979 *Joint Venture Law* and other laws and regulations that had been issued since 1979. Essentially, the *Joint Venture Law* spelled out the following preferential treatments or salient features of an EJV:[27]

(a) an EJV in SEZs, economic and technological development zones and Hainan pays an income tax of 15%; a new joint venture may

be exempted from income tax in the first two years and allowed a 50% reduction in taxes for the third to the fifth years;
(b) it is exempted from import duties on advanced equipment;
(c) it can repatriate abroad all its profits as well as funds it receives upon expiration or early termination of the venture;
(d) its foreign employees can remit all after-tax income abroad;
(e) there is no fixed export ratio for the products it produces (but normally a JV is expected to balance its foreign exchange budget with its own resources);
(f) it has the right to hire its own staff and workers based on individual merits;
(g) it can seek arbitration by judicial means in China or in a third country if a dispute between the concerned parties cannot be resolved.

These apparently attractive investment incentives were not without problems. For example, foreign investors found out that they ran into a host of problems with the Chinese bureaucracy. It was widely reported in the Hong Kong and overseas media that overseas investors were dismayed by the practice of Chinese officials of levying fees indiscriminately or making up arbitrary rules. The influential *Time Magazine* reported that Chinese cadres "often made up taxes, rules and regulations as they went along, rather than following any written policy."[28] As a result, foreign-invested firms in China found that their profits were eroded by hundreds of unforeseen expenses. The incident of Beijing Jeep, a joint venture of American Motors and a Chinese state-run automaker, was a case in point. Because of a serious foreign-exchange crisis caused by a consumer-product buying spree in 1985, China launched an across-the-board clampdown on import purchases which affected AMC's import of parts from its Canadian factory. The financial problem was finally resolved only after Zhao Ziyang personally intervened to allocate financial resources to Beijing Jeep.[29] Consequently, the confidence of foreign investors was seriously damaged, and total DFI in China dropped significantly in 1986 (see Table 6).

In view of the very negative response from overseas investors, China acted swiftly to enact the *Provisions of the State Council for the Encouragement of Foreign Investment* (twenty-two article provisions) in October 1986. This was intended to rectify the inadequacies or limitations of past laws and regulations on foreign investment. Furthermore, it provided additional incentives to foreign-invested firms. The provisions were definitely one of the most important documents on foreign investment in China. Essentially, the provisions granted strong incentives to both "export enterprises" and "technology enterprises" which gained priority in allocation of water, electricity, transportation and communication equipment. This infrastructural support has been critical to the success of foreign-invested enterprises because of the prevailing unreliable and underdeveloped infrastructure of the nation. If a "technology enterprise" is an EJV, the pre-existing tax holiday is extended by three additional years at half the tax rate. In addition, lower land-use fees are granted to the two forms of enterprises if they are not in busy urban sectors of large cities. They also have priority in obtaining short-term loans in foreign exchange or *Renminbi* from the Bank of China and other Chinese financial institutions. In addition, foreign-invested enterprises have gained protection against unreasonable charges as local governments are required to comply with the *Notice of the State Council on Resolutely Curbing the Indiscriminate Levy of Charges on Enterprises*, which is applicable to both state-owned and foreign-invested enterprises. This has been, of course, a welcome move by the State Council as far as foreign investors are concerned.

As indicated earlier, foreign investment policies have been formulated to achieve an optimal industrial mix in China. Vice-Premier Tian Jiyun, in a speech to senior MOFERT officials on 24 December 1991, stated that "the important work at present is to strive for improving the quality of foreign investment projects (including economic efficiency and technical standards) to make them develop to a higher level." He reiterated that preferential policies should be used to lure foreign investment from export-oriented and technologically advanced foreign enterprises, particularly transnational corporations and large conglomerates with advanced management experience and world-wide networks.[30] This can be characterized in economic development terms as an unbalanced growth strategy. It is a strategy of selecting key industries for development to spark a reaction in other industries that are affected by, or are part of, the key industry's value chain.

In the twenty-two article provisions, "advanced technology" is broadly defined to include technology that China lacks in all economic sectors except the services industry. This is extended to technology that can help China develop new export products or technology needed by an import substitution industry. These are broad guidelines, but they have been useful in granting favourable incentives to enterprises through credit, taxation, tariffs and the supply of raw materials.

In 1987, the State Planning Commission adopted the *Regulations on Guiding Foreign Investment Operations* which outlined the general principles and administrative procedures in dealing with foreign investments. Investment in so-called "productive industry" was generally welcomed. The 1987 regulations also provided a detailed list of industries as guidelines in directing the flow of foreign investment into China. The list may change to reflect need and the specific situations of various provinces, cities or areas, but generally industries fall under the following three subgroups: preferred group, restricted group, and prohibited group. The preferred group includes primary industries such as textiles, chemicals, petroleum, machinery, automobile, scientific equipment, nuclear plant or equipment and building equipment. The restricted group includes certain industries such as fisheries, beverages, shipbuilding, real estate, finance and insurance. The prohibited group includes projects in arts and crafts, mail communication, airlines and airport management, foreign trade, storage, broadcasting and military equipment. In recent years, China has emphasized that foreign investment policy should direct the flow of capital to sectors of agriculture, energy, transportation and urgently needed raw materials. Vice-Premier Tian Jiyun made this policy statement clear in December 1991.[31] Based on the broad definition of "advanced technology," would be included any technology related to energy and transportation, and thus incentives would be awarded accordingly.

Protection of investment is a major concern of foreigners investing in China and this is due to two obvious reasons. Firstly, the PRC is a socialist country, and when the CCP took power in 1949, it confiscated properties of both the so-called Chinese bureaucratic capitalists and western companies. Nationalization of foreign investors' properties also has occurred in third-world socialist countries, resulting in tremendous losses. These recollections are very much in the minds of foreign capitalists or multinational managers when they consider investments in China. Secondly, foreign investors are fearful of drastic political changes that could affect the existing open-door policy. This is understandable, as in the past, PRC policies have oscillated between radicalism and pragmatism. In order to allay these fears, Article 2 of the *Joint Venture Law* in 1979 asserted that "The Chinese Government protects, in accordance with the law, the investment of foreign joint ventures, the profits due them and their other lawful rights and interests in a joint venture." Unfortunately, there were no clear provisions or mechanisms stipulated. In enforcing the law, other Asian countries have more specific laws and provisions for protecting the interests of foreign investors. To strengthen the confidence of foreign investors, China moved one step forward to legitimize foreign investment in the country by including a new article in the revised *Constitution of the People's Republic of China*, adopted at the fifth session of the Fifth National People's Congress in December 1982. Article 18 of the revised constitution stipulates that "The PRC permits foreign enterprises, other foreign economic organizations and individual foreigners to invest in China and to enter into various forms of economic cooperation with Chinese economic organizations in accordance with the law of the PRC." The article further stresses that the "lawful rights and interests of all foreign-invested enterprises are protected by the law of PRC." Obviously, such recognition of the legitimate rights of foreign investors has great symbolic value.

China has taken concrete actions to sign bilateral agreements on investment protection with a number of countries since 1982. The first two bilateral investment protection pacts were signed in 1982. More pacts were signed in subsequent years. In 1992, China signed a record number of seventeen protection pacts with other countries. During 1982–1992, it signed a total of 47 pacts with 48 countries (Belgium and Luxembourg shared one pact with China), including the United States, Canada, Japan, Australia, European Economic Community (EEC) members, and countries in Latin America, the Middle East, Eastern Europe, Africa, Southeast Asia and the Commonwealth of Independent States. Another 13 agreements are now under negotiation or in the planning stage.[32] Signing bilateral agreements on investment insurance and protection with other countries would imply that China is willing to adopt the practice of international rules for dealing with flows of DFI between two countries. Admittedly, this would boost the confidence of foreign investors.

On the organizational level, the *Joint Venture Law* stipulates that disputes between the signing parties should be resolved, if possible, internally by the board of directors. This is the preferred procedure, but should it fail, disputes could be referred to a Chinese arbitration organization. The *Joint Venture Law* also permits foreign partners to choose arbitration outside China. In the early years of China's open-door policy, foreign investors were very hesitant to submit disputes to arbitration because it was felt that this may jeopardize their business relations with China. This attitude has changed, and more and more disputes have gone to arbitration in the last few years.

Inside China, arbitration cases are handled by the China International Economic and Trade Arbitration Commission (CIETAC). This organization is based in Beijing under the auspices of the China Council for the Promotion of International Trade. China is a signatory to the *New York Convention on the Recognition and Enforcement of Foreign Arbitral Awards*, and, consequently, arbitration results are currently recognized by over eighty countries or areas. Arbitration by CIETAC has increased significantly in the last few years. It has become the second busiest arbitration centre in the world, handling about 900 cases in 1992.[33] This is second only to the tribunals under the famous Institute of Arbitration of the Stockholm Chamber of Commerce. Although CIETAC is widely credited as a relatively inexpensive, fair and expeditious forum for resolving disputes, many foreign investors have found that it is very difficult to enforce arbitration awards in China. Many cases have been reported in which regional courts in China have refused to enforce awards against local economic interests. For example, a British company won a case against a Ningxia company. Yet the Ningxia local court refused to enforce awards even under the Beijing court's repeated requests for immediate settlement.[34] This makes a mockery of the entire legal system in China which badly needs changing. Unless the arbitration awards are enforceable, foreign investors may become less willing to go to CIETAC for arbitration.

Major Developments in 1992

There were several major developments of DFI in China during 1991 and, in particular, during 1992. We will highlight these developments in this section.

First, China relaxed its restrictive policy by permitting greater foreign participation in its services industry. This created an euphoria for foreign investment opportunity, and many firms turned to China in large numbers to invest in the lucrative services sector, including retailing, accounting, consulting and advertising industries. In the retail sector, China now allows foreign companies to establish department stores in selected cities on a case-by-case basis. There is a stipulation that foreign products can not exceed 50% of the store's sales volume, and the firms must balance their foreign exchange accounts.[35] Some famous department store companies in Hong Kong, such as Sincere, Wing On and Giordano, and Japan's Yaohan and Seibu established joint-venture stores in 1992. Sun Hung Kai Property

Ltd., a giant property development company, signed an agreement with a Beijing company valued at US$255 million to redevelop Dong An Market, a famous department store in the busy Wangfujing area of Beijing.[36] In addition, chain restaurants and stores such as Cafe-de-coral, Fairwood, McDonald's, Park-N-Shop, Wellcome, 7-Eleven, and Watsons, among others, entered China's domestic market in 1992 or earlier. International accounting and consulting firms, such as Arthur Anderson and Price Waterhouse also established footholds.[37] China has been seriously considering a provision to allow foreign insurance companies to operate in China. During the past few years several commercial banks from Hong Kong and elsewhere have been permitted to open branches, although they are prohibited from taking *Renminbi* deposits, which are restricted to state Chinese banks. Restrictions on *Renminbi* deposits may also be liberalized in due course, and if this occurs, it will be a significant shift in policy away from state controlled currency transactions.

Secondly, there was a great surge of property investment by foreigners in 1992 subsequent to China's adaptation of a land-leasing experiment modelled after Hong Kong's land system. This began in 1987, and under the experiment, the state retained ownership of land but could lease to developers. Since the experiment has been introduced, it has generated US$6 billion in official revenue.[38] Hong Kong's land developers have been the active players with Tian An China Investment Co. leading the group by focusing its property business solely in China. Hong Kong's giant real estate developers, such as New World Development Co., Hopewell, Wharf Holdings, and Cheung Kong Holdings, have enlarged their interests. The later two companies have entered the China market with major investments in 1992.

In 1992, one-fourth of China's total contractual foreign investment of US$45 billion has been destined for property development in residential, commercial and industrial projects.[39] Hong Kong firms have gained an estimated 200 million sq. ft. of lease-rights on land by late 1992, and total projects have been valued between US$1.5–2.5 billion.[40] Without question, a large percentage of these leases are being held for speculative purposes. Yet there are active development projects in the Pearl River Delta, Hainan, Shanghai, Beijing, Fujian and Yangtze River Delta areas.

Thirdly, China has signed many huge projects with foreign investors for infrastructure projects such as highways, power plants, harbours and ports in 1992. One of the top priorities of China's modernization programme is to inject funds into infrastructure development; and due to shortage of domestic funds, China has been actively soliciting funds from abroad to bridge the gap. So far, most private investment in infrastructure projects has come from Hong Kong. Gordon Wu of Hopewell Holdings has led the way by investing in the Guangzhou-Shenzhen-Zhuhai highway and power plants in Shajiao of Guangdong province. China Light and Power has also made a significant investment in a nuclear power plant in Daya Bay. By 1992 New World Development Co., Hutchison-Whampoa, Wharf Holdings, and China Light and Power have signed major contracts for investment in highways, power plants, electrified railways, liquified gas and various other infrastructure projects.

In April 1993, Vice-Premier Zou Jiahua announced that China would adopt the international "BOT" form (build, operate and transfer) as a means to channel investment into infrastructure projects. The "BOT" scheme allows foreign investors to have contractual rights in managing and operating projects while the Chinese state only collects taxes. When a contract expires (usually after fifteen years), the entire project would be turned over to China. According to Zou, China has plans to liberalize the existing monopolistic market structures in the energy, telecommunications and transportation industries.[41] Demand for infrastructural facilities is immense as China continues its existing market reform. This will provide additional opportunities for foreign investors to tap this expanding sector.

Fourthly, there has been an attempt by the Chinese government to "privatize" some of its state-owned enterprises. This has been accomplished by converting enterprises to Sino-foreign joint ventures, establishing new shareholding companies with foreign participation or by simply leasing them to foreign investors. Poor performance by state-owned enterprises, whether large or small in size, is no secret. Currently, there are about 100,000 state enterprises, one-third of them operating at a loss, and another third only breaking even. These figures are probably understated as a result of a low depreciation policy and poor accounting standards that fail to capture many hidden costs. Due to this dismal record, the Chinese government has had to allot nearly 20% of its budget expenditure and 80% of its bank loans to prop up state-owned enterprises. In 1991, the state industrial sector incurred a loss of US$5.30 billion, and losses have continued to increase.[42] This has been a very heavy burden for the central government to bear. A reform policy meant to invigorate the inefficient state enterprises by various means, including expansion of enterprise autonomy, has been less-than satisfactory. The contract responsibility system has also had significant problems, but these issues are beyond the scope of this chapter. Suffice it to say, the problems of the state industrial sector are far from being resolved.

In 1992, the Chinese government launched a variety of "marketization" schemes for participation by foreign investors in state-owned enterprises on an experimental basis. The most notable case occurred in the city of Quanzhou, in Fujian, which signed a joint-venture agreement with Hong Kong-based China Strategic Investment Ltd. by selling 41 of its 42 state-run industrial firms in December 1992. If the forty-second enterprise had not been engaged in a joint venture with another foreign company, it would have been a total "sale"! It was reported that China Strategic Investment Ltd. is injecting RMB240 million for a 60% controlling share of the newly-created company called Quanzhou CSI (Holdings) Ltd.[43] The latter is currently restructuring the 41 enterprises by closing down some of the inefficient firms and expanding the more profitable ones. In another example, a Hong Kong firm took a 51% controlling share in Wuhan Number 2 Dyeing and Printing Factory in July 1992. This was the first time in PRC history that a foreign enterprise had taken a controlling share of a state-owned factory.[44]

Apart from Quanzhou, Wuhan city in Hubei was negotiating with Taiwan and Hong Kong investors in late 1992 to sell thirty of its state enterprises. Earlier, a bankrupt textile-dyeing firm was sold by Wuhan to a Hong Kong entrepreneur.[45] In Qingdao, the city has recently selected several state enterprises for possible joint ventureship with foreign investors.[46] It is envisaged that the trend to "sell" state enterprises will accelerate in the next few years.

Another form of foreign participation in existing state-owned enterprises is by leasing them to foreign investors. In Sichuan province, one of its fourteen prime enterprises in passenger-car manufacturing has been leased to a Hong Kong-based firm for a rental of RMB63 million to be paid annually for a contract period of fifteen years. The contract stipulates that the Hong Kong firm is to inject funds and transfer modern technology to the leased firm whilst the latter is solely responsible for its profit and loss. The firm has been the first of its kind in China, the lease taking effect in July 1992.[47]

Another form of foreign participation in state-run enterprises is through establishment of new shareholding companies. One of the large-scale ball-bearing industrial enterprises in Harbin with about 20,000 staff and workers signed a shareholding contract with a Hong Kong-based firm in April 1993. The foreign investor injected RMB108 million to the newly established company for a share of 45%.[48] This is the first case where a large-scale state industrial firm has established a partnership with a foreign firm.

China also welcomes foreign investors interested in buying state enterprises that are declared bankrupt. Last year, a state printing equipment firm in Shenzhen was declared in receivership through a court order. Later it was announced that the firm would be sold through auction and foreign investors were welcome to bid.[49]

Various forms of foreign participation in Chinese state-owned enterprises as illustrated above seem to indicate that China is endorsing a process of "privatization," particularly for less efficient firms. However, it would be unrealistic to expect that a great number of state-run enterprises will follow suit in the next few years. Some sensitive problems, such as job arrangements for employees who are used to the security of the "iron-rice bowl" policy, need to be resolved, and privatization procedures must be resolved to avoid social instability.

Last but not least, since 1991, the State Council has approved the establishment of twelve "bonded zones" (or free trade areas) to further encourage trade and investment. These run from the northeast to the south along the coast, including Dalian, Tianjin, Waigaoqiao (Shanghai), Zhangjiagang, Futian, Shatoujiao, Guangzhou, Haikou, Qingdao, Ningbo, Xiamen and Fuzhou. Shantou, Yantai and Beihai also have submitted applications for bonded zones to the State Council for approval.[50] Among the twelve bonded zones, Shatoujiao is the first, and it is the smallest one beginning operation in 1991. The bonded zones, modelled after other successful free trade zones in Asia, are established mainly in the economic and technological development areas or the SEZs.

A bonded zone allows free mobility of capital, goods and executives. This mobility has a significant impact on luring foreign investments. Industries related to foreign trade and exports such as processing, storage, re-export, trading, finance and property development are targeted for development in the bonded zones. Each of the twelve bonded zones has developed its own preferential policies for investments, but a national policy for all bonded zones has yet to be formulated.[51] Generally speaking, foreign-invested enterprises established in the bonded zones enjoy all privileges available to other economic and technological development zones. In addition, they are exempted from import and export duties, production taxes and industrial consolidated taxes if their products are exported. In Guangzhou's bonded zone, there is free convertibility of foreign currency, and companies enjoy a 50% reduction of taxes on tobacco and liquor. The bonded zone in Guangzhou has attracted US$130 million in foreign investment, including construction of a US$80 million exhibition centre.[52] Given additional preferential treatments, the bonded zones should appeal to many export-oriented foreign firms. Xiamen's free trade zone, for example, should have great appeal to Taiwanese investors in light of its geographical proximity, reduced hostility and closer economic ties between the two sides of the Taiwan Straits.

Problems and Obstacles

This section will briefly discuss some of the current problems of foreign direct investment which have surfaced in China. These problems have received increasing attention from Chinese officials in charge of DFI policies. We shall focus on the following five aspects: "fake" joint ventures, evasion of taxes, appraisal of properties, preferential policies in different areas, and the status of "high-tech zones."

Chinese officials have become increasingly concerned about the rising number of "fake joint ventures." These become apparent when, after signing a contract, foreign investors' pledged capital fails to materialize. During 1991–1992, Guangdong province cancelled several hundred fake foreign-invested enterprises.[53] The problem in Sichuan province is more serious with approximately 50% of pledged capital by foreign investors unaccounted for during 1992; in 1991 it was 30%.[54] Some of the "fake" ventures are due to poor feasibility studies, poor management, conflicts among partners, or, in some instances, fraud. There are also some investors who actually have no capital of their own but rather seek to utilize the newly-established foreign firm as a vehicle to borrow funds from domestic financial institutions, thus passing the risks entirely to Chinese partners. In addition, some foreign-invested firms that are losing money have decided no longer to inject additional funds, thus making their ventures inoperative.

Tax evasion by some foreign-invested enterprises has also been quite serious, particularly in smaller companies. These companies incur "losses" by taking advantage of loopholes in tax laws, such as artificially raising prices of imported raw materials or lowering prices of exported products. Another tactic has been to "wind up" the original company, replacing it with a newly-registered company, thereby continuing to enjoy tax benefits after the initial tax-exemption period has expired. Some companies also resort to moving their enterprises to new areas, allowing them to apply for new tax holidays with local authorities.[55]

Whether value of land and other state assets have been properly appraised is another major concern. Many state assets have been appraised at artificially low prices by local authorities in order to attract joint ventures. Some local authorities even set ceilings on state assets to attract foreign investment. According to an official of the Bureau of State Owned Property, less than 10% of the state properties are properly appraised.[56] On the other hand, some foreign investors import old or unwanted equipment and then price the equipment as new to artificially increase the book value of the joint ventures. These investors have been mainly from Japan, Hong Kong and Taiwan.[57] How much revenue has been lost due to these unethical tactics may never be known. According to a crude estimate by a state official, revenue loss to the state treasury resulting from overpricing of equipment amounted to several hundred million RMB in 1992.[58]

Another problem encountered by China in attracting foreign investment is related to the discrepancy of preferential treatment in different areas. In order to attract foreign investors, local authorities compete with each other by offering a variety of favourable terms. Many of these are in violation of state provisions and tax laws. In August 1992, the State Council issued a stern warning to local authorities to abide by the state laws.[59] Earlier, this issue had been specifically highlighted in the Outline of the Ten-year Programme (1991–2000) and the Eighth Five-year Plan (1991–1995) for National Economic and Social Development which was adopted at the fourth session of the Seventh National People's Congress in March 1991.[60] Although competition among local authorities may work to the advantage of some foreign investors, confusion may arise due to the ambiguity of national and local regulations. Foreign investors are generally more concerned with factors other than tax incentives in assessing the investment climate.

Since 1984 China has established economic and technological development zones (sometimes referred to as "development zones" or "high-tech zones") to attract foreign investment. This was discussed early in the chapter. Development zones are designed either by the state, province or county. State-level development zones are approved by the Science and Technological Commission. Forty-seven development zones had been established by 1992, mainly located in the coastal open cities.[61] There are, however, many development zones designated by local authorities. According to the New China News Agency, there are close to

2,000 development zones throughout the country, taking up 15,000 sq. kilometres of land.[62] Many of these zone's however, are not approved either by state or provincial authorities. Local authorities are generally over-zealous and jump into the fray to attract foreign investment without careful prior planning. Therefore, many have been found to under-perform or simply stay idle after establishment. For example, one county in Sichuan appropriated 2,000 acres of farm land, offering it to Taiwan investors, hoping that the latter would invest NT$2 billion in development capital. But the investment funds were never remitted, and consequently the land remained idle for many years.[63] This case is certainly not an isolated one. Steps are now being taken by the State Council to assess all development zones in accordance with stipulated criteria, such as projects and work completed, amount of pledged and realized capital, management capabilities and other factors, etc. Under this new assessment system, development zones which fail to meet the criteria can be closed, and "life-time" status of the zone is no longer guaranteed. Zones in local counties without proper approval from provincial authorities will be closed.[64]

The problems outlined above are presented from the perspective of Chinese authorities. A different set of problems emerge when viewed from the perspective of foreign investors. They are concerned more with obstacles that inhibit foreign investment in China. For example, the existing regulatory framework remains unsatisfactory, and unpublished rules and regulations continue to influence company operations. Some rules and regulations, published or otherwise, are inconsistent thus leading to ambiguity. In addition, the scope of authority and responsibility in various government departments is often vague, thus inhibiting foreign investment. Apart from the regulatory environment, other obstacles to investment include inadequate protection of property rights; existence of arbitrary fees imposed by some local authorities; excess barriers to local markets; lack of a national liquidation law; and bureaucratic interference in the wage-setting process which hampers the ability of foreign-invested enterprises to practice market-oriented policies, i.e. their prerogative to recruit, retain and motivate employees.[65] All these issues need to be carefully evaluated and the problems resolved.

Conclusion and Prospects

Without question, China has made great strides in attracting foreign direct investment since 1979. The impressive growth of DFI has impacted on structural changes of many segments of the Chinese economy, especially the industrial and services sectors. Many of the economic changes were probably inconceivable before 1979. In the initial years of the open-door programme, however, China was fraught with problems of building a framework conducive to attracting foreign investment. Broadly speaking these problems could be viewed as either "hard" and "soft" sides of the investment environment. On the "hard" side, the infrastructure bottleneck has been a disincentive to foreign investment. Some improvements have been made over the years, but it is not expected that the problems will be solved quickly. A high priority is attached by both central and provincial governments to improve China's physical infrastructure. Coupled with an enthusiastic participation by private-sector interests during 1991–1992, China could alleviate the development bottlenecks significantly. In the final analysis, a long-term commitment is required by the government to build up a modern infrastructure over the next several decades.

Strengthening the "soft" side of the investment environment seems to be crucial for China in the short-run, and it may influence infrastructure development. Improving the "soft" side of the investment climate can be accomplished mainly through policy adjustments that address the problems in and obstacles to attracting foreign direct investment. Investment laws also need to be uniform among constituent areas and consistent in their application. Although laws governing foreign investment are important, attitudes towards the rule of law is even more crucial. A case in point is the non-enforcement of arbitral awards in China.

The most important change since the adoption of the open-door policy is perhaps the "market mentality" which now deeply imbues Chinese cadres. Ideological conflicts between Chinese officials and foreign investors seem to be fading as dogma is replaced by a sense of pragmatic "economism." These will facilitate "marketization" to take root in China. Clearly this is the trend that is currently taking place, and China seems prepared to further open its domestic economy to foreign investment. For example, in a joint venture contract, the standard ratio between exports and domestic sales has been 70%, but now it is possible to negotiable the ratio downward to as low as 50%.[66] In addition, Shenzhen and Hainan are adopting the international practice of company registration, i.e. to register a company directly without going through various levels of bureaucratic red-tape.[67] The liberalization trend is likely to spread to other coastal open cities in the next few years. Furthermore, China's impending accession to

Direct Foreign Investment in China 16.35

GATT will provide further impetus to liberalizing the domestic economy. This will appeal to more and more foreign investors, given the sheer size of the country and improved income level of the Chinese people.

Notes

1. Shenzhen, Zhuhai, Shantou and Xiamen were proclaimed SEZs in 1980. Hainan Island, formerly part of Guangdong province, gained provincial status in 1987 and has since been designated a SEZ, the largest among the five. In 1984, the following fourteen coastal port cities were opened to the outside world: Dalian, Qinhuangdao, Tianjin, Yantai, Qingdao, Lianyungang, Nantong, Shanghai, Ningbo, Wenzhou, Fuzhou, Guangzhou, Zhanjiang and Beihai. Economic and technological development areas were set up within them. In 1985, China further opened the Yangtze River Delta, the Pearl River Delta and the Minnan Delta to foreign investors.
2. Calculated from MOFERT, *Almanac of China's Foreign Economic Relations and Trade 1989/90* and *1990/91*.
3. *Ming Pao* (Hong Kong), 4 January 1993 and *Wen Wei Po* (Hong Kong), 6 January 1993.
4. *Sing Tao Daily* (Hong Kong), 4 October 1992.
5. K. Hiraiwa, "Foreign Investment in PRC, 1990–91," *China Newsletter* (JETRO), No. 96 (January–February 1992), p. 11.
6. *China Newsletter*, No. 96, p. 12.
7. Reported by *Wen Wei Po*, 18 April 1993.
8. See *Wen Wei Po*, 6 January 1993.
9. *The World and Japan's Foreign Direct Investment* (various years) (Japan), quoted in Fan Yongmin, *Industrialization and Foreign Direct Investment in China* (Shanghai: Shanghai Institute of Social Sciences, 1992), p. 179.
10. *Ibid.*, pp. 173–78.
11. *Almanac of Foreign Trade and Economic Relations*, 1984 and 1985.
12. *Zhongguo tongji nianjian 1985* (China Statistical Year-book 1985).
13. Wu Sufen, "China's Absorption of Foreign Investment Achieves Remarkable Results," in *Almanac of China's Foreign Economic Relations and Trade, 1992/93*, p. 51.
14. K. Hiraiwa (Note 5), p. 12.
15. John S. Henley and Nyaw Mee-kau, "The System of Management and Performance of Joint Ventures in China: Some Evidence from Shenzhen Special Economic Zone," in *Advances in Chinese Industrial Studies*, edited by Nigel Campbell and John S. Henley, Vol. 1, Part B (Greenwich, CO and London: JAI Press, 1990), pp. 277–95.

16. Quoted by Xinhua News Agency, 20 November 1991, reported in *Ta Kung Pao* (Hong Kong), 21 November 1991.
17. *Ta Kung Pao*, 21 November 1991.
18. *South China Morning Post* (Hong Kong), 12 June 1990.
19. *Ta Kung Pao*, 30 December 1992.
20. *Sing Tao Daily*, 22 April 1993.
21. Fan Yongmin (Note 9), pp. 1–4.
22. *Ibid.*, p. 5.
23. Frederick Wu, "Realities Confronting China's Foreign Investment Policy," *World Economy*, Vol. 7, 1984, pp. 296–97.
24. See for example studies by Samuel P. S. Ho and R. Huanemann, *China's Open-Door Policy: The Quest for Foreign Technology and Capital* (Vancouver: The University of British Columbia Press, 1984); and Y. C. Jao and K. C. Leung (eds.), *China's Special Economic Zones: Policies, Problems and Prospects* (Hong Kong: Oxford University Press, 1986).
25. Y. Y. Kueh, "Foreign Investment and Economic Change in China," *The China Quarterly*, Vol. 131 (September 1992), p. 638.
26. This coastal development strategy was first proposed by Wang Jian, a research fellow associated with the Institute of Economic Planning at the State Planning Commission.
27. See *Regulations for the Implementation of the Law of PRC in Chinese-Foreign Joint Ventures*, 30 September 1983; and Chu Baotai, *Foreign Investment in China: Questions and Answers* (Beijing: Foreign Language Press, 1986).
28. See *Time Magazine*, 2 June 1986.
29. See the story by Jim Mann in his *Beijing Jeep: How West Business Stalled in China* (New York: Simon & Schuster, Inc., 1989).
30. Tian Jiyun's speech was delivered at the National Working Conference on Foreign Economic Relations and Trade on 24 December 1991. His speech was reprinted in *Almanac of China's Foreign Economic Relations and Trade, 1992/1993*, pp. 13–17.
31. *Ibid.*, p. 15.
32. *China Daily* (Beijing), Business Weekly, 10–16 January 1993.
33. *Ta Kung Pao*, 7 April 1993.
34. This case was mentioned in a speech by Lee Kuan Yew, former Prime Minister of Singapore, at a World Economic Forum held in September 1992 in Beijing. See *Sing Tao Daily*, 1–3 October 1992. The case was more fully discussed in a paper by Barsani. See Matthew D. Barsani, "Enforcement of Arbitration Awards in China," *The China Economic Review* (May–June 1992), pp. 6–10.
35. So far, Ministry of Commerce has allowed fourteen cities including Beijing, Shanghai and Guangzhou to discuss joint-venture retail deals. See "Trend and

Issue," *China Business Review* (September–October 1992), p. 4.
36. Liang Bosong, "An Analysis of the Current Status of Foreign Enterprises," *Hong Kong & Macao Economic Digest* (15 January 1993), pp. 32–33.
37. *Express News* (Hong Kong) (9 December 1992).
38. M. C. Ross and K. T. Rosen, "China's Real Estate Revolution," *China Business Review* (November–December 1992), p. 44.
39. *Ming Pao*, 4 January 1993.
40. M. C. Ross and K. T. Rosen, "The Great China Land Rush," *China Business Review* (November–December 1992), p. 51.
41. *Wen Wei Po*, 24 April 1993.
42. See Kathy Chan, "Hong Kong–China Venture Overhauls State-run Firms," *Asian Wall Street Journal*, 22 December 1992; and James McGregor, "China's State Enterprises Think Private," *Asian Wall Street Journal*, 8–9 January 1993.
43. *Asian Wall Street Journal*, 22 December 1992.
44. *United Daily News* (Hong Kong), 13 July 1992.
45. *Asian Wall Street Journal*, 8–9 January 1993.
46. *Ta Kung Pao*, 23 January 1993.
47. *Ta Kung Pao*, 27 July 1992.
48. *Ta Kung Pao*, May 1993.
49. *Hong Kong Times*, July 1992.
50. *Ming Pao*, 24 December 1992; and *China Daily*, Business Weekly, 10–16 January 1993.
51. *Wen Wei Po*, 24 November 1992.
52. *Ming Pao*, 24 December 1992.
53. *Ta Kung Pao*, 10 February 1993.
54. *Sing Tao Daily*, 22 April 1993.
55. *Ming Pao*, 7 December 1992; 10 February 1993.
56. *Ming Pao*, 21 December 1992.
57. *Ming Pao*, 3 May 1992.
58. *Ta Kung Pao*, 10 March 1993.
59. *Ta Kung Pao*, 23 August 1992.
60. Li Peng, *Report on the Outline of the Ten-Year Programme and the Eighth Five-year Plan for National Economic and Social Development* (Beijing: People's Press, 1991), p. 134.
61. *Ming Pao*, 23 December 1992.
62. This high figure probably includes those under planning by the local authorities, but it was not stated in the news item. See New China News Agency, 9 March 1993.
63. *Sing Tao Daily*, 22 April 1993.
64. *Ming Pao*, 17 February 1993.
65. Some of the obstacles are discussed in a US–China Business Council's report

presented to China. The report was published in *China Economic Review* (September–October 1992), pp. 6–10.
66. *South China Morning Post*, 28 December 1992 and *Hong Kong Economic Times*, 7 December 1992. According to a well-known Hong Kong business leader heavily investing in China, it is possible to sell all products of a joint venture in the domestic market if there is a demand.
67. *Ta Kung Pao*, 8 December 1992.

17

China's Foreign Trade and the Reform of the Foreign Trade System

Yin-Ping Ho

Introduction

After three years of arduous counter-cyclical puffing, China's international trade and direct inward investment activities have been pressing ahead with gathering momentum since Deng Xiaoping's historic tour of South China in January and February 1992 and his subsequent political campaign to entrench economic reforms and opening to the outside world.[1] The drive for faster reforms and greater openness towards building a "socialist market economy," as officially proclaimed in the political report by General Secretary Jiang Zemin at the Fourteenth National Congress of the Communist Party (CCP) in mid-October 1992, pushed China's total national industrial output upward to reach an all-time high of RMB2.8 trillion (US$487.6 billion) last year, representing a hefty increase of 21.7% in real terms over 1991.[2] Correspondingly, while the West struggled with recession, China's real gross domestic product (GDP) grew by a staggering 12.8%,[3] more than twice the original target rate of 6% per annum for the Eighth Five-year Plan (1991–1995),[4] and real per capita income in most coastal cities were up by over 10%, undoubtedly the fastest rates in the world.

That China has today the most dynamic and the fastest growing economy can hardly be doubted. Despite stop-go cycles, real GDP in China has grown at almost 10% per annum over the period 1979–1992. *Per se*, this growth rate has been high not only by China's own historical standards but also internationally. In fact, for the coastal provinces, from Guangdong in the south up through Fujian, Jiangsu, Zhejiang to Shandong in the north, the annual growth rate has averaged over 12% for the same period. With hindsight, China's growth performance during the last reform decade would not look out of place amongst the records of the legendary "hyper-growth" East Asian newly industrializing economies (NIEs) of Hong Kong, Singapore, South Korea and Taiwan. The achievement stands out all the more if one takes into account the fact that China has the most populous and diverse economy on earth.[5]

All of this has led to predictions by western experts that China's domestic economy could become the world's dominant economy by the turn of the twenty-first century. For instance, Lawrence H. Summers, former chief economist of World Bank, recently extrapolated that, if the growth differential between China and the United States during the 1980s continues, China could surpass the United States to become the world's largest economy in eleven years.[6] "If Chinese per capita income reached

Taiwanese levels," says Summers, "China's GDP would exceed that of the entire Organization for Economic Cooperation and Development!"[7] To be sure, should China continue to succeed over the next decade or so in duplicating the success of Taiwan, then the economic impact on the global economy could scarcely be exaggerated. Seen in the same vein, a recent, well-researched survey article on the awakening of China by Jim Rohwer for *The Economist* claims that "China's economic performance in the fourteen years since then has brought about one of the biggest improvements in human welfare anywhere at any time."[8] If China maintains the impetus of the Dengist 1978 reforms, says Rohwer, China's current economic boom could herald the greatest metamorphosis the world has seen since the Industrial Revolution.[9]

Yet, in contrast to the pre-reform era, no sector in the Chinese economy has undergone as dramatic a change as foreign trade and international production of consumer tradables via direct inward investment, otherwise known as direct foreign investment (DFI). Since December 1978 when the history-making third plenary session of the Eleventh Central Committee of the CCP was held, China has made tremendous headway in attracting DFI capital,[10] mostly in industrial processing and export-oriented manufacturing. Between 1979 and 1991, according to the reckoning of the Hong Kong Trade Development Council (HKTDC),[11] China had approved DFI contracts amounting to US$121.5 billion, of which US$79.6 billion were actually utilized; the number of DFI projects approved totalled 42,178. By the end of 1991, some 37,000 DFI enterprises were registered in China, comprising 22,000 joint ventures, 8,500 cooperative undertakings and 5,900 wholly foreign-owned enterprises.[12] More eventfully, the number of newly-signed DFI projects in 1992 exceeded 40,000, almost equal to the approved total in the previous thirteen years; and actual investment from them was over US$16 billion, while pledged volume hit a record US$58 billion, more than triple that in 1991.[13]

In the early reform years, DFI activities were basically domiciled in coastal regions, particularly in Guangdong and Fujian provinces. Since the mid-1980s, however, DFI enterprises have been spreading geographically, covering virtually all provincial capitals and their surrounding areas in the interior as well as border areas in the west and the north. As has been well reported, Hong Kong, and to a lesser degree Taiwan, have played a crucial role about DFI proliferation in China. It is estimated that between 1979 and 1992 some three-fifths of all DFIs in China have been made by Hong Kong entrepreneurs. In particular, as high as 80% of DFIs in Guangdong have come from Hong Kong; and over three million workers in the Pearl River Delta are now employed by Hong Kong companies, compared with a manufacturing workforce in Hong Kong of only some 660,000. The central role played by Hong Kong in the modernization as well as internationalization of China's economy goes without saying.[14]

As to China's trading position in the world economy, in the pre-reform and closed-door era China had traded little with the outside world for a country of its size. Since 1979, however, China's foreign trade has expanded significantly, and increasingly so over time. In the relatively short span of fourteen years, China has emerged as an important trading nation exporting and importing a wide range of products of substantial volume to cause concerns over problems of industrial adjustment in the world's major industrial countries, especially in the United States. By 1992, China's total foreign trade volume ranked eleventh in the world, an impressive surge from thirty-second in 1979, the years the reforms and open-door policy actually began. The marked rise of China's international trading position mirrors the fact that foreign trade has grown over the past decade or so more rapidly than the domestic economy.

It would seem obvious that foreign trade and DFI have become twin engines of growth behind China's rapid economic advance, accelerating not only the speed of industrial development but the pace of economic transformation as well.[15] As the subject matter of DFI is discussed elsewhere in this edited volume, the focus of this article will be on issues pertaining to China's foreign trade and its whereabouts.

Open-door Policy and International Trade

Trade theorists as well as development economists have long argued that countries, whether resource-poor or otherwise, pursuing outward-looking, externally-oriented development strategies, tend to achieve a higher rate of economic growth, for obvious reasons of improved efficiency and comparative advantage.[16] The experience of China's open-door policy constitutes another case in point. The open-door policy (while open to some conflicting interpretation) consisting of export promotion and trade liberalization (albeit still modest in scope) has attracted foreign capital and resorted to foreign loans; it has played a central role in the rapid growth of China's international trade.

By any measure, the growth of China's foreign trade volume since

1978, as Table 1 shows, has been little short of phenomenal. The money value of China's merchandise exports of US$85 billion in 1992 was about 8.8 times the US$9.7 billion of 1978, representing a compound growth rate of 16.8% per year; while imports of US$80.6 billion in 1992 were 7.4 times the US$10.9 billion of 1978, at a compound growth rate of 15.4% per year. Taken together, the volume of China's two-way trade grew from US$20.6 billion in 1978 to US$165.6 billion in 1992, at an average growth rate of more than 16% a year, almost three times as fast as world trade.[17] If such a growth trend persists, the dollar value of China's total external trade in 1997, the year British sovereignty over Hong Kong expires, should be approaching US$350 billion. In fact, both the actual and the projected figures for China's exports and hence total trade volume would be larger under calculations used by western countries, which include Chinese re-exports through Hong Kong as part of China's total exports.

Following the continued expansion of merchandise exports, China's

Table 1. China's Foreign Trade, 1978–1992 (in US$ billion)

Year	Total	Exports	Imports	Balance
1978	20.6	9.7	10.9	–1.2
1979	29.3	13.7	15.7	–2.0
1980	37.8	18.3	19.6	–1.3
1981	44.0	22.0	22.0	0.0
1982	41.6	22.3	19.3	3.0
1983	43.6	22.2	21.4	0.8
1984	53.5	26.1	27.4	–1.3
1985	69.6	27.4	42.3	–14.9
1986	73.8	30.9	42.9	–12.0
1987	82.7	39.4	43.2	–3.8
1988	102.8	47.5	55.3	–7.8
1989	111.7	52.5	59.1	–6.6
1990	115.4	62.1	53.4	8.7
1991	135.6	71.8	63.8	8.1
1992	165.6	85.0	80.6	4.4

Sources: Figures for 1978–1979 are Ministry data: Editorial Board of the Almanac of China's Foreign Economic Relations and Trade, *Almanac of China's Foreign Economic Relations and Trade 1989* (Hong Kong: China Resources Advertising Company, 1989); figures for 1980–1991 are from General Administration of Customs, the People's Republic of China (PRC), *China's Customs Statistics* (Hong Kong: Economic Information and Agency, selected quarters); and the 1992 figures are from *South China Morning Post*, "China Slashes Trade Surplus to US$4.4b" (8 January 1993).

Note: Exports are valued on a f.o.b. basis while imports on a c.i.f. basis.

trade and current account balances as well as its international balance of payments which had been in deficits over most of the 1980s turned into surpluses in 1990. Despite strong import demands, in 1992 China still enjoyed a trade surplus of some US$4.4 billion, compared to the US$8.1 billion high of 1991, and the historic height of US$8.7 billion in 1990. Thanks to export successes, China's foreign exchange reserves, as Table 2 shows, also continued to climb, reaching a record of US$42.7 billion by 1991, the world's sixth largest stock of hard currency.[18] These sizable reserves serve well to meet China's external debt obligations. It is interesting to note that, since the discarding of the previous watchword of "self-reliance" and the subsequent acceptance of loans from international agencies and foreign governments to facilitate infrastructural developments and other modernization needs in late 1970s, China's external debt has increased more than tenfold between 1980 and 1991 from US$4.5 billion to US$52 billion, growing especially fast between 1985 and 1988.[19] Yet, given its present gross external reserves level, almost equivalent to about eight months of imports, China does not face a significant debt servicing problem.

In terms of economic growth and the expansion of foreign trade, the Chinese economy during the last fourteen years of reforms and open-door policy seems to be repeating the East Asian NIEs' pattern. Today, large segments of the Chinese economy are dependent on international trade, and small-scale rural industries and DFI ventures are two important, coexisting sources of export expansion and employment creation in China, not only in the five special economic zones (SEZs) and the fourteen open coastal cities.[20] The emergence, particularly the subsequent proliferation, of small rural industries, otherwise known as "township and village enterprises" (TVEs), is unique to China. In 1983, there were some 1.1 million TVES, mostly engaged in export-oriented manufacturing, in the countryside, employing some 29.3 million people; by 1991 there were 19.9 million TVEs employing 94.7 million people.[21] According to *The Economist* figures by Rohwer,[22] the output of these TVEs has been growing by an average of almost 30% a year for over a decade; their exports grew by a torrid 65% a year in the latter half of the 1980s. By the early 1990s, says Rohwer, the TVEs were responsible for nearly 40% of China's industrial employment, more than 25% of industrial output and nearly a quarter of total exports.[23]

What is even more intriguing is that during the state retrenchment policy of 1989, a large number of TVEs went under or were taken over,

Table 2. China's Current Account Balance and International Reserves, 1986–1991 (in US$ billion)

	1986	1987	1988	1989	1990	1991
Merchandise trade balance, Customs basis	-8.4	0.2	-3.2	-1.7	13.1	13.4
Exports f.o.b.	30.9	39.4	47.5	52.5	62.1	71.9
Imports f.o.b.	39.3	39.6	50.7	54.2	48.9	58.5
Services, net, IMF basis	1.4	1.7	1.1	0.9	2.6	2.8
Other current transactions	-0.4	-1.2	-1.7	-3.5	-3.7	-3.8
Current account balance	-7.3	0.3	-3.8	-4.3	12.0	12.4
International reserves						
Foreign exchange reserves	10.5	15.2	17.5	17.0	28.6	42.7
Reserve position with IMF	0.4	0.4	0.4	0.4	0.4	0.4
Special drawing rights (SDRs)	0.6	0.6	0.6	0.5	0.6	0.6
Total including gold (national valuation)	12.0	16.9	19.1	18.5	30.2	44.3
Total including gold (London price)	16.4	22.5	23.8	23.1	34.5	48.2

Source: World Bank, Country Operations Division, China and Mongolia Department, and East Asia Pacific Region, *China: Country Economic Memorandum — Reform and the Role of the Plan in the 1990s*, Report No. 10199-CHA (19 July 1992), Tables 1.9 and 2.5.

Notes: Figures of current account balance are net of grants. For current account balance and balance of payments statistics, imports are customarily valued on a f.o.b. basis. National valuation is at SDR 35 per fine ounce.

resulting in nearly three million workers losing jobs in 1990; but, with the political pendulum swinging back in favour of deeper reform and growth promotion, 1991 witnessed a hefty increase of some 4.5 million TVE workers.[24] These sheer numbers of incessant entry and exit indicate an amazingly high degree of flexibility in TVEs to withstand bad times and bounce back quickly. There is no gainsaying that the same Darwinian "survival-of-the-fittest" process that has been working on small-scale enterprises in Hong Kong's "crude capitalism" over the postwar years is now at work in China's TVE sector.

So far as the performance of China's 80,000 DFI enterprises is concerned, the most recent statistics from China's General Customs Administration[25] show that the export volume of these ventures stood at US$17.4 billion last year, up 44% over 1991, accounting for one-fifth of the nation's total; their imports grew by 56%, to reach US$26.4 billion in 1992. The combined foreign trade volume arising from these DFI firms totalled US$43.8 billion in 1992, accounting for more than a quarter of the national total. In terms of production arrangement, more than 88% of the DFI exports originated from outprocessing activities last year, according to the same Customs source.

In virtue of the open-door policy and encouraged by a series of concessionary measures, the fourteen open coastal cities have seen a robust DFI-pushed, export-led growth over the reform years. By 1992, the fourteen cities' exports amounted to US$16.4 billion, up 16.2% over the 1991 figure, while their imports grew by 36.6% to reach US$12.8 billion last year.[26] Of their total trade volume of US$29.2 billion in 1992, some US$10.9 billion were attributed to the DFI ventures.[27] As regards the five SEZs, which have served as the models in China's opening, they reaped a US$24.3 billion worth of foreign trade in 1992, representing 14.7% of the national total. During the year, their exports rose by 24.2% to US$12.4 billion and imports hit US$11.9 billion, up 16.6% over 1991.[28] According to China's Customs data, some 47.9% amounting to US$11.7 billion of the SEZs trade volume were generated by DFI businesses; this was a 23% increase over 1991 and 26.6% of the total foreign trade created by all DFI ventures in China.[29] In terms of individual contributions, the significance of Shenzhen SEZ, which commanded some 52.6% — US$12.8 billion — of the total trade volume associated with the five SEZs in 1992, needs little saying.[30] Much of these hectic developments in China's coastal cities and SEZs, and Shenzhen SEZ in particular, is attributed to the escalation of outprocessing trade by Hong Kong investors.

Export Promotion and Changing Export Structure

It is no exaggeration to state that, prior to the 1979 open-door policy, especially before the early 1970s, China's foreign trade was by and large harnessed to the development of a heavy industrial sector by exporting natural resource-based goods, mostly agricultural products, to the Soviet Union and East European countries in return for capital goods. Central to the open-door policy is a shift from the Stalinist import-substitution development strategy towards more emphasis on export promotion. The main concern of China's export promotion policy is to earn foreign exchange, acquire foreign technology and managerial expertise and strengthen the industrial base. On top of its robust growth performance in international trade, as noted earlier, over the reform decade of the 1980s both the market and commodity compositions of China's merchandise exports have undergone a profound structural change. For one thing, more than 90% of China's global trade in recent years has been with market economies. This is in sharp contrast to what is happening in ex-Soviet Union and Eastern Europe now. Despite their dual reforms of *glasnost* and *perestroika*, the foreign trade of the ex-Soviet Republics and the economies of Eastern Europe remain heavily skewed towards trade, mostly in the form of barter exchanges, with one another, and none of these states have risen to become more important trading nations in the global economy.

In terms of market structure, a large and growing part of China's external trade is trade with Hong Kong. Much of this trade, in turn, is re-export trade. From 1978 to 1992, trade, in terms of US dollar values, between Hong Kong and China grew at a compound annual rate of about 26% with the total volume amounting to over US$58 billion in 1992, according to the most recent Chinese Customs figures on merchandise trade, compared with the Hong Kong Census and Statistics Department figure of some HK$10.8 billion (US$2.3 billion) in 1978. In 1992, Hong Kong accounted for over 44% of China's total exports while imports from Hong Kong accounted for nearly 26% of China's total, making Hong Kong and China the largest mutual trading partners. Much of these increased export and import volumes are due to consignment processing of products by Hong Kong companies in Guangdong province and elsewhere in China and the subsequent re-export of the processed products through Hong Kong to third countries, primarily the United States. By virtue of the booming consignment processing activities across the border, Hong

Kong's re-exports reached some US$88.6 billion in 1992, accounting for about three-quarters of its total exports; during the same year the re-exports destined for and coming from China accounted for some 86% of Hong Kong's total exports. The significance of Hong Kong as an entrepôt for Chinese goods needs hardly be stressed.

According to China's Customs statistics, in recent years Japan and the United States have been the second and third largest markets, respectively, for Chinese exports. In 1992, China exported US$11.7 billion of merchandise goods to Japan, up 14.5% over the 1991 level, and accounting for 13.8% of China's total overseas sales; some US$13.7 billion of Japanese products, on the other hand, were imported by China from Japan last year, up 36.4% over the previous year's figure, and accounting for 17% of China's total imports.[31] Taken together, the total Sino-Japanese trade volume hit US$25.4 billion in 1992. This bilateral trade volume was a 25.3% rise on the 1991 level and accounted for 15.3% of China's total foreign trade.

China's trade with the United States has risen rapidly since the two nations began to establish normalized diplomatic and trade relations in 1979, to reach US$17.5 billion last year, according to China's Customs data. However, by the reckoning of the US Department of Commerce, the Sino-US trade volume stood at over US$33 billion in 1992. According to the US trade statistics, China's exports to the United States jumped more than tenfold in the last decade, from some US$2.5 billion in 1983 to US$25.7 billion in 1992; US shipments to China, by comparison, rose to US$7.5 billion in 1992 from US$2.2 billion in 1983.[32] The large and growing trade imbalances between the two, as recorded by the US Department of Commerce, have caused considerable bilateral tensions and brought incessant calls by members of the US Congress for withholding from China the most-favoured-nation (MFN) trading status, for reasons ranging from alleged unfair trade practices to human rights abuses.

Other major exports markets of Chinese goods in 1992, in descending order of importance, were Taiwan, Germany, Russia, South Korea, Singapore and Italy. Boosted by Taiwanese DFI activitiess on the Chinese mainland, Taiwan's indirect trade with China via Hong Kong, according to Taiwan's Board of Foreign Trade, grew 27.9% to a record US$7.4 billion in 1992.[33] Beyond question, the trade volume between the two sides of the Taiwan Strait will see further rises in 1993 and beyond, as the economies of Taiwan and Fujian province of South China become increasingly integrated via DFI production and Taiwan removes more restrictions on business contacts with China. Since the establishment of diplomatic relations between China and the Republic of Korea in August 1992, the two-way trade volume between the two countries has increased by leaps and bounds during the latter part of the year.[34] Apart from becoming China's seventh largest trading partner, South Korea has also become an important DFI source for China, especially in Shandong province.

As far as China's trade with countries of the European Community (EC) is concerned, China exported some US$7.8 billion of goods to the EC in 1992, while its imports from the latter last year amounted to US$9.8 billion. Germany, followed by Italy and France, took the lead among China's European trading partners with a total bilateral trade volume of about US$6.5 billion in 1992, accounting for over 37% of the Sino-EC total. That makes Germany China's fifth largest trading partner, according to the latest figures released by China's General Administration of Customs.[35] No less significant, Sino-Russian trade also hit a record US$5.9 billion last year, about three times the 1991 level of US$1.9 billion. From the newly-released Customs statistics,[36] it is interesting to note that in recent years Sino-Russian trade was marked by a sharp increase in the proportion of industrial products, which accounted for 82.5%, while primary goods made up the rest; none the less, the current bilateral trade between the two countries was still largely based on barter exchanges, which accounted for 63% of the total two-way trade.

Turning to commodity composition, China's merchandise exports on the eve of the 1980s were roughly divided between primary goods and manufactured products. Primary exportables from China comprised essentially agricultural goods, crude oil, refined petroleum products and other natural resource-based raw materials. After the mid-1980s, however, the share of primary goods began to fall and the share of manufactured products rose continuously and, by 1992, accounted for nearly 80% of total exports. The rapidly evolving commodity composition was largely due to the speedy growth of light consumer exportables, notably textiles, apparels, toys, shoes, travel goods and the like. The fundamental force behind the explosion in China's export trade in light manufactures has, of course, been the reform and opening-up drive to a more market-oriented economy, ongoing over the past decade.

Compared with primary products, manufactured goods are more heterogeneous and price- and income-elastic, and their sale in substantial quantities on highly competitive international markets requires a good understanding of market demands, consumer tastes, quality standards and, above all, their constant changes over time. More importantly, in contrast to the pre-reform years, China's trade specialization since the early 1980s, and more fully so by the late 1980s and early 1990s, has been based on comparative advantage.[37]

Comparative Advantage and External Competitiveness

In the pre-reform decades, China's foreign trade was basically an isolated phenomenon. Indeed, under a rigid system of Soviet-type centrally planned material balances, China's foreign trade was all but an instrument of state policy and was conducted by a handful of specialized foreign trading corporations in accordance with national planning. In plain economics, by neglecting market price signals, trade growth in the pre-reform era was not the results of shifts in domestic demand and supply. To be sure, the absence of market-based relative prices that reflected true scarcity values imposed a grave historical cost on China in the form of industrial structures and production techniques that were inconsistent with comparative advantage. The predominance of heavy, capital-intensive industries in the earlier decades was one obvious result of the disregard of relative factor scarcity values.

All this started to change after the authorities announced in late 1978 the adoption of an open-door policy to renounce the self-imposed economic isolationism of the past and actively sought to expand contacts with the outside world through promotion of foreign trade and investment. Given its vast supply of inexpensive labour, China's comparative advantage in the world markets, according to the Hecksher-Ohlin factor proportions trade theory, has been in the production of exportables requiring large amounts of labour.

A simple descriptive comparison of labour costs underscores China's comparative advantage in labour-intensive manufacturing. In 1992, hourly wage earnings of manufacturing workers in China averaged no more than US$0.25, and those in a foreign-financed, export-oriented firm were about twice that level. Even at this latter level, however, an average manufacturing worker in China earns about one-fifth to one-tenth of the earnings of its competing counterpart in East Asian NIEs, and only about one-twentieth of the earnings of a typical worker in the United States. Reforms in the opening up of China to foreign trade and international production during the 1980s have without question led China to capacitate the comparative cost advantage in labour-intensive production.

In fact, our descriptive perception has been substantiated by the empirical findings of a recent World Bank publication, which concluded that over the last decade or so China has developed a revealed comparative advantage in a relatively broad range of products, and that almost all of these items are labour intensive or require inputs of specialized natural resource materials, and in respect of labour-intensive manufactures China's experience parallels the situation in most of the Asian NIEs in the 1960s and 1970s.[38] This conclusion is also reinforced in Rohwer's survey article for *The Economist*, which notes: "The open-door policy has transformed the Chinese economy, bringing it the same benefits that the export-led growth of the East Asian tigers delivered to them."[39]

The implications of China's evolving comparative advantage in the production of light export manufacturing upon international division of labour and international production of tradables are far-reaching. For one thing, the manifestation that many of the manufactured goods in which China has a revealed comparative advantage often face major forms of hard core nontariff trade barriers (NTBs) — voluntary export restraints (VERs), global quotas, variable import levies, minimum import prices and the like — in the EC and the United States raises the possibility that growing new protectionism in most western countries may constrain further developments in some product lines, particularly in textiles and clothing.[40] Reportedly, China's textiles and clothing industry, for example, is the world's largest and in 1992 exported products worth some US$24 billion, up over 40% above the previous year's figure of US$16.7 billion.[41] Aside from the quantitative limits established under the Multifibre Arrangement (MFA), there should be concern that other forms of NTBs ranging from VERs to special textile quotas negotiated outside the MFA will have adverse effects on China's textiles and clothing sector.

Part of the explanation for the increased external competitiveness and hence the rapid expansion of China's exports rests with its pricing policy of foreign exchange since the late 1970s. In market economies, the foreign exchange rate determines the relative price of tradables to nontradables. In China, as in other centrally planned economies, the official exchange rate, which is administratively set and, therefore, largely a passive policy instrument as such, tends to overvalue the home currency with attendant distortions.[42] As an internal accounting device, the exchange rate had little effect, if any, on the volume of tradables in the pre-reform years. For example, a currency devaluation would seem to increase the profitability of exports and lower that of imports. But since foreign trade profits and losses were all absorbed by the state treasury through a rigid system of exchange control, changes in the foreign exchange rate would impact neither domestic production nor the merchandise trade balance.[43]

For all that, the *Renminbi* — China's domestic currency — was grossly overvalued in the pre-reform era. It is no surprise at all to learn that the domestic currency cost of earning foreign exchange was persistently higher than the official exchange rate by a wide margin, making most exports financially unviable without heavy state subsidies.[44] Beyond question, reforms of the exchange rate system and relaxation of exchange control during the last decade were of crucial importance to China's trade specialization and expansion of exports in world markets. So far as the official exchange rate is concerned, the Chinese authorities devalued the *Renminbi* from a rate that averaged RMB1.5 per US dollar in 1980 to an average of about RMB5.5 per US dollar in 1992, as shown in Table 3. This cumulate devaluation brought the nominal exchange rate index of *Renminbi* to some 27 points in 1992 from 100 points in 1980. This also goes a long way to explain why the Chinese exports have been growing so rapidly in this period.

Table 3. The *Renminbi*–US Dollar Nominal Exchange Rates and Index, 1978–1992

	US dollar per RMB	RMB per US dollar	Index in terms of US dollar (1980 = 100)
1978	0.59	1.68	89.29
1979	0.65	1.55	96.77
1980	0.67	1.50	100.00
1981	0.58	1.71	87.72
1982	0.53	1.89	79.37
1983	0.51	1.98	75.76
1984	0.43	2.32	64.38
1985	0.34	2.94	51.02
1986	0.29	3.45	43.48
1987	0.27	3.72	40.32
1988	0.27	3.72	40.32
1989	0.27	3.76	39.89
1990	0.21	4.78	31.38
1991	0.19	5.32	28.20
1992	0.18	5.49	27.32

Sources: State Statistical Bureau, *Statistical Year-book of China* (Beijing: Statistical Publishing House, selected years); and *Nomura Asian Perspectives* (Statistical Supplement), Vol. 9, No. 5 (December 1992).

Note: Data are period average figures.

Frequent and judicious devaluations over the past decade notwithstanding, it is generally held that the current official rate still overvalues the *Renminbi* by a considerable margin. The extent of overvaluation is given by the premium for foreign currency on the parallel market. Leaving aside the black market rate, in the past decade China has maintained a dual exchange rate system, in which the official rate has been administered as a managed float, while the parallel rate has been basically determined by actual demand for and supply of foreign currency in the foreign exchange adjustment centres (FEACs), otherwise known as foreign exchange swap centres, by eligible participants. The rapid growth of foreign exchange swap centres since the mid-1980s has allowed this premium to be easily observed. Reportedly, by the end of 1992 the official rate of *Renminbi* had drifted down to about RMB5.7 per US dollar, the swap rate, on the other hand, was found to fluctuate in the region of a 30% premium over the then official rate. Although there may be some seasonal or psychological factors accounting for the differential between the two rates, in general terms a premium as large as 30% is *prima facie* evidence of overvaluation.

After all, what has emerged is a burgeoning swap market with rates more or less in line with market demand and supply in parallel to the official market where the rates are administratively set. Thus, while China is still beyond distance of achieving full convertibility of the *Renminbi* in trade transactions, the systematic devaluations and the introduction of limited convertibility via the FEACs over the reform decade have led to a more realistic exchange rate and reduced substantially the bias against exports characteristic of the pre-reform foreign trade regime.

Reforming the Foreign Trade System

From a closed, Soviet-type planned economy with its domestic prices completely insulated from the outside world barely fourteen years ago, China has now emerged as a major economic and trading force, significant within Asia but increasingly so within the global economy as a whole. Much of this impressive economic progress and the spectacular growth of foreign trade particularly can be regarded as achievements of open-door policy and economic reforms, especially of foreign trade and exchange rate reforms.

Decentralization of Foreign Trade

In terms of organizational structure and mode of operation, China's foreign trade prior to the 1978 reform was virtually a complete state monopoly controlled by the Ministry of Foreign Trade (MOFT) and conducted through some fifteen product-specific national foreign trade corporations (FTCs) operating under a near total mandatory trade plan. Bureaucratically, the State Planning Commission first set preliminary annual and long term targets for broad categories of imports and exports. MOFT subsequently prepared more detailed plans on the basis of the State Planning Commission's targets and then transmitted these plans to the FTCs. Correspondingly, the FTCs procured goods from domestic enterprises at fixed prices in accordance with the foreign trade plan, sold them abroad, and surrendered all foreign exchange proceeds to the Bank of China, which was the sole organization authorized to handle foreign exchange. On the import side, the FTCs purchased fixed quantities of foreign goods for domestic distribution at fixed prices, and reimbursed foreign suppliers with foreign exchange obtained from the Bank of China in accordance with the foreign exchange plan. For obvious domestic currency overvaluation reasons, the FTCs usually incurred a loss on exports but earned a surplus over the cost of imports. However, this was not a matter of concern since all the profits of FTCs were turned in to the MOFT and losses were borne by the same agency.

Decentralization of the control and conduct of foreign trade began in 1979 with the partial authorization for provincial and municipal governments and some large state enterprises to establish their own trading enterprises to directly engage in foreign trade. The administration of China's foreign trade was streamlined in March 1982 with the amalgamation of the MOFT, the Import-Export Administration Commission, the Foreign Investment Administration Commission and the Ministry of Foreign Economic Relations into a new formal body called the Ministry of Foreign Economic Relations and Trade (MOFERT), which overlooked the fifteen specialized national FTCs and the local foreign trade bureaus of each province and municipality.

The year 1984 marked a watershed in China's foreign trade reform through a drastic reduction in the scope of foreign trade planning alongside the decisive call by the State Council about ending the monopoly power of the national FTCs in international trade. Since then, the number of FTCs has expanded rapidly. Besides new national FTCs under central government ministries and other state organizations, virtually every provincial and municipal government has its own network of FTCs conducting foreign trade in a large array of diverse fields. The FTCs have also been directed to develop an agency line of business, whereby they can handle foreign trade activities on behalf of domestic clients on a commission basis. Conceivably, this agency system has put the domestic export-producing enterprises in touch with the market conditions abroad and adjusted the prices and quality of their products accordingly.[45]

Following this wave of decentralization, the number of FTCs proliferated from some 15 in 1978 to more than 1,000 in the mid-1980s, and some 6,000 in the latter half of the decade. In many cases, however, the exact status and capacities of these new FTCs were not clearly known. One notable result of this reformist move was that these new FTCs did not report to MOFERT. The rapid growth in the number of FTCs created new problems as well. Unscrupulous activities and harmful competition among FTCs aside, many of the newly-created FTCs were not able to acquire the goods from domestic enterprises they had contracted to export, for reasons of inadequate experience and funding. The adverse developments led to a subsequent rectification of the trading units in mid-1988 and the ensuing months up to late 1989, during which as many as 2,000 FTCs were dissolved, merged or deprived of their rights to foreign trading. Meanwhile, the State Council also took steps to reassert control over the process of approving the creation of new FTCs. For all that, there was still left substantial room for competition among the remaining FTCs. By the end of 1991, there were about 4,000 FTCs, including 500 associated with large state enterprises, that had the right to conduct foreign trade in China.[46]

Together with the expansion in the number of FTCs, the scope of mandatory planning for foreign trade was reduced drastically with the passage of time. Moreover, from the mid-1980s onwards the foreign trade system was replaced by a combination of mandatory planning, guidance planning and market regulations. The 1984 trade reform assigned the mandatory plan exports and imports, which were specified in quantitative terms, to designated national FTCs, and allowed other FTCs to pursue their businesses both within and without guidance plans, which were generally specified in value terms. Besides being more flexible, guidance plans allowed FTCs to take factors of market demand and supply into account when determining the precise mix of tradables within each broad commodity category.

In terms of number of commodities, the export plan, which covered some 3,000 items before 1979, fell to only 112 in 1988.[47] Consequently, by the end of the decade the portion of exports under mandatory or guidance planning accounted for about 34% of total exports.[48] Unlike exports where FTCs were allowed a higher degree of independence, the import system basically remained intact. In addition to import licencing and high tariff on protected products, almost all import users were subject to a series of administrative measures and complicated approval procedures and a rigid foreign exchange allocation system. In the process of reforming foreign trade system, the general scope of mandatory planning for imports was narrowed,[49] however. By 1991, no more than 40% of China's imports were subject to either mandatory or guidance import plans implemented by various levels of jurisdiction.[50]

In a bid to resolve some evident malpractices and other shortcomings existing in foreign trade system, a "foreign trade contract responsibility scheme" has been introduced since 1987 so that the FTCs, export producers and import users would assume greater financial responsibility, and at the same time the central government could limit its commitment to export subsidies.[51] This contractual system in foreign trade was considered as a transitory arrangement on the way towards the provincial and municipal governments and FTCs' full trading autonomy according to the "four selfs" principle: self-management, self-development, self-control and self-responsibility for profits and losses in accord with national interest.[52] The arrangement was of probing significance to China's reforming foreign trade system in view of the still underdeveloped state of the market mechanism and distorted prices in the economy. At any rate, FTCs and export-producing firms would be urged to be more cost-conscious, and import users would be pressed to economize on the use of foreign goods.

Reforming Exchange Control and the Exchange Rate Regime

In the realm of foreign trade incentives, reforms in the pricing of foreign exchange and relaxation of exchange control were among the most important changes in China during the last decade. Starting in 1979, a foreign exchange retention scheme was introduced to allow provincial governments and FTCs to retain a share of foreign exchange from the export proceeds. The right to retain a certain portion of foreign exchange earnings served as a forcible incentive to FTCs and export-producing enterprises. The reason was simple: as the *Renminbi* was considerably overvalued, access to foreign exchange commanded large premia. The retention scheme, which started with a somewhat complicated formula in late 1970s, expanded steadily in several dimensions and remained rather complex during the ensuing years.[53]

Reportedly, the average retention ratio grew from about 10% in 1979 to over 40% by late 1980s. Prior to 1988, the customary ratio was 25% and was divided equally between the foreign exchange earning unit and its provincial or municipal government. The retention ratio was, however, 30% for Guangdong and Fujian provincial governments, and 100% for SEZs. The ratio also differed for different export industries and products and was higher for those which exceeded planned targets. Along with the introduction of foreign trade contract responsibility system, from 1988 onwards all FTCs and other export-earning units, on top of the usual 25% retention of within-target export earnings, have been allowed to retain 80% of their export earnings that exceed planned targets.

To mitigate diversion of exportables from other areas to SEZs, on the one hand, and to promote a fairer competition among different localities on the other, starting in 1989 the State Council duly lowered the retention ratio for SEZs from 100% to 80%. In the past, the large differential in retention ratios among FTCs and export enterprises in different regions and localities, as scarcely needs saying, was one of the major sources of rent-seeking activities in China's foreign trade sector. By unifying inter-regional retention ratios, a major area of administrative intervention in China's foreign trade operation was removed, and this was certainly a right step forward. The move towards equalization of retention ratios among the regions, including SEZs, was completed in early 1991. This notwithstanding, the post-1991 retention ratios have continued to vary by industry and products.

Analytically, the use of differential foreign exchange retention rates on an inter-industry basis is equivalent to applying a multiple exchange-rate system for different export industries, giving rise to another source of distortion in resource allocation. Seen under this perspective, another reformist step is deemed necessary to complete the uniformity of retention rates. But this is not all. The existing retention scheme provides a powerful incentive to foreign traders only to the extent that there exists a serious foreign exchange shortage because of exchange controls and overvaluation of the domestic currency. In other words, the significance of the retention scheme would disappear if exchange control be abolished and exchange rates made flexible.

In respect of the opportunity to trade the foreign exchange use rights, the entitlements were not transferable before 1980, which greatly reduced their use values to export enterprises. Starting in 1980, however, domestic enterprises were allowed limited trading of their foreign exchange entitlements through the Bank of China, and the fixing price was allowed to rise to a maximum of 10% above the official rate. A breakthrough occurred in late 1985 when the first foreign exchange swap centre was established in Shenzhen, where qualified enterprises could buy and sell foreign exchange at prices higher than the official rates, albeit the trading was rather inactive due to an imposed price ceiling.

Since 1988 FEACs have been operating at provincial and sub-provincial levels all over China, with a national swap centre in Beijing. More importantly, also starting in 1988, the swap rates were allowed to float, and foreign investors were allowed to be full participants in these centres, to buy and sell foreign exchange with Chinese counterparts as well as among themselves. Since 1990, local swap rates and the national average rate were quoted publicly to provide traders at each local FEAC on-the-spot information about swap rates at other FEACs, and this created a gradual tendency towards an equalization of swap rates at over 100 FEACs across the nation. Not surprisingly, the reform developments since 1988 have led to a rapid expansion of the volume of foreign exchange transactions in China's burgeoning swap markets. In 1992, the total FEAC transaction volume amounted to US$25.1 billion, compared with US$20.5 billion in 1991 and some US$6.3 billion in 1988, suggesting that the access to FEACs was greatly encouraged in the past years.[54]

Having said this, there can be little doubt that China has already come a long way in freeing itself from administrative exchange controls of the pre-reform era. For all that, China continues to maintain exchange controls. Advocates of free market economy would naturally suggest a floating exchange rate combined with full convertibility of the domestic currency. While the importance of a freely convertible currency and a floating rate regime for the rapidly-expanding Chinese economy can hardly be doubted, it would be somehow premature for China, or any other economies with underdeveloped domestic financial markets, to adopt such a policy. Before this, the Chinese government will need to develop proper monetary weapons to defend its national currency, such as an effective interest-rate mechanism, among others. In the absence of a sound, corrective interest-rate mechanism, and with bank deposits earning less than the inflation rate, it would hardly be possible to stop the wave of selling *Renminbi* for hard currencies, notably the US dollar.

Towards Trade Liberalization and the General Agreement on Tariffs and Trade (GATT) Status Resumption

It is beyond doubt that over the reform years since 1978 the scope of foreign trade planning in China, as discussed previously, has been drastically reduced. Despite this, under a variegated structure of trade restrictions foreign trade in China today remains heavily manipulated by the government. The distinction between trade planning and trade restrictions is an important one. State trading and mandatory planning requires detailed specification of the quantity and price of each tradable as well as the specific state-owned enterprises assigned to produce the exportables or authorized to use the import goods; this naturally distorts the domestic price structure, making it reflective of neither domestic relative scarcities nor world market conditions. By comparison, trade restrictions, such as import tariffs, import or export licencing, are less comprehensive and, therefore, more price flexible with respect to resource allocation. With this understanding, moving from trade planning to trade restrictions should be considered as a step in the better direction. Of course, the right step is the removal of the various restrictions on international trade. This, hopefully, is the next item on China's foreign trade reform agenda in the upcoming years.

As until the late 1980s, China's trade reforms have been driven by the desire to increase foreign exchange earnings to finance technology and materials imports. Following the prevalent emphasis of trade reforms on export promotion to finance "modernization" imports, the import sector has not by and large been seen as a source of competition. Looking forward into the future, however, with China now seeking earnestly to resume its seat in GATT, the current or next reform wave is expected to focus more on liberalizing the import sector and making it more transparent as well.

So far as the history of GATT is concerned,[55] China was one of the twenty-three founding signatories of the GATT treaty when this world trade body was inaugurated in 1947. For more than twenty-odd years after 1950, when Taiwan authority withdrew its membership from GATT,[56] China had no contacts, let alone official relationship, with GATT. Since 1971, the year when the United Nations (UN) General Assembly adopted a resolution to seat China in place of Taiwan in the UN, China has started to develop some indirect relations with GATT.[57] Having joined the International Monetary Fund (IMF) in April 1980 and the International Bank for

Reconstruction and Development (IBRD), better known as the World Bank, in May 1980, China was granted observer status on GATT in November 1984. On 10 July 1986, China filed a formal application for resuming its original status as a contracting party to GATT. Noting that GATT, together with IMF and IBRD, are regarded by the international community as the three pillars that form the foundation of the world economy, membership of GATT thus represents the last step marking China's full return to the world trading system.

Following the usual application procedure, on 13 February 1987 the Chinese authority submitted the "Memorandum on China's Foreign Trade System" to GATT. The pertaining documents embraced China's policy of opening to the outside world, reforms in the domestic economy and foreign trade system, the customs duties and inspection system, the import and export licencing system, the commodity pricing structure, the foreign exchange control system, a report on SEZs and open coastal cities, as well as China's participation in international trade and financial organizations and related treaties.[58] Apparently, when compared to IMF and the World Bank, China's membership with GATT is more difficult and challenging because it requires both a willingness to respond to outside pressures and much greater adjustment of domestic economic policies, especially those relating to foreign trade system and foreign exchange rate regime.

Up to 15–16 March 1993, or the dates when the thirteenth session of the GATT Working Group on China's Signatory Status was held in Geneva, China has as yet not successfully concluded its deliberation with the special Working Group on China's foreign trade system and the protocol that firms up China's obligations and rights after it rejoins GATT. Meanwhile, as told by Douglas Newkirk, Assistant US Trade Representative for GATT affairs, during his discussion with Li Lanqing, the Chinese Minister of Foreign Economic Relations and Trade, about China's re-entry to GATT in Beijing on 2 March 1993, the framework for China's protocol included five main issues: commitment to a market economy; a unified national trade policy; transparent trading rules; elimination of non-tariff trade barriers; and a system to safeguard other GATT signatories from a sudden surge of Chinese exports to their countries.[59] Against this background, it is envisaged that, while China's prospect of joining GATT is by and large a matter of time, negotiation of the protocol for its entry is likely to continue to be a complex and protracted process.

Turning to China's part, since the mid-1980s, especially over the last three years or so, the world trading community has witnessed a reforming China working extremely hard to satisfy GATT's re-entry requirements. To be sure, starting in early 1990, China has launched some genuine efforts to speed up the trade liberalization process. Apart from abolishing state subsidies for exports in January 1991, it has initiated a series of import liberalization measures so as to better conform with GATT standards. To start with, in January 1992 China unilaterally lowered import tariffs on 225 commodity items, including most industrial supplies, semi-manufactures, raw materials and agricultural products.[60] In April 1992, all import regulatory taxes were cancelled.[61] More embracingly, the import tariffs for a total number of 3,371 items were reduced by China's Commission on Tariff Regulation as from 1 January 1993.[62] Moreover, according to Tong Zhiguang, Vice Minister of MOFERT, China will remove more than two-thirds of its import licencing requirements during the next two years and greatly reduce other nontariff administrative measures as well as basically abolish import mandatory plans while domestically introducing reforms, including reforms in state-owned enterprises, finance, taxation, investment, pricing and labour and wage systems, that will make more than 80% of national products subject to market prices.[63]

Further to these, China will make public in a year all those internal documents about import and export management, says Tong Zhiguang, and it will only carry out those laws and regulations known to the public.[64] At the same time, China will exert greater efforts to refine its intellectual property rights system. In this regard, China's Patent Office, which was formally created in 1980, had handled a total of 210,000 domestic and foreign patent applications by the end of 1991; registered trademarks totalled 320,000, including 47,800 foreign items.[65] Among other ongoing revisions of the *Patent Law*, starting from 1993 China has extended the patent-protection period from fifteen to twenty years. After joining the Universal Copyright Convention in July 1992, China is now seeking to gain entry to the Berne Convention on the Protection of Literary and Artistic Works, among others.

In all fairness, while import liberalization has been left to last in the realm of trade reforms, China's latest reform measures, either already adopted or to be mapped out, demonstrate its determination to conform its import system to GATT's requirements. Yet, to genuinely meet GATT's basic tenets, China's import reforms will have to eliminate quantitative restrictions, replacing them, in the first instance, with equivalent tariffs which would then have to be gradually adjusted to a low and relatively uniform level.⁶⁶ The lowering of trade restrictions in general and non-tariff barriers in particular will provide both a better set of relative prices to guide competing resources to their optimal uses as well as the competitive pressure for enterprises to raise efficiency and hence national productivity. In these connections, the establishment of an effective interest-rate mechanism and subsequently currency convertibility, at least for the current account, are two additional steps that will have to be coordinated with decisions regarding the exchange rate regime.

The issue of how China joins GATT is one of paramount importance both for the future unfolding of China's economic reforms and for the world division of labour and trading system as a whole.⁶⁷ Given China's massive size and its capacity to disrupt world markets for light consumer manufactures, it is not surprising at all that many a western country, the United States in particular, continue to have grave doubts over the direction of China's market-oriented reforms and the openness of its markets. Against this global backdrop, one of China's major efforts has been trying to content the US as that hegemonic power of the twentieth century has immense influence on other GATT signatories and has not denied, at least up to the early part of 1993, the MFN status for China — a critically important issue regarding the prospects for the Sino-US commercial relations to which we now turn.

Sino-US Trade Relations and the Case for China's MFN Status

As the world's largest developing country and the world's largest developed country respectively, China and the US economies, for obvious differential factor-endowment reasons, are complementary in nature. Indeed, since the signing of "Sino-US Trade Agreement" in 1979, the bilateral trade volume between the two nations, as noted earlier, has been growing rapidly. The main pillar of the 1979 Trade Agreement was the reciprocal granting of MFN trade status, which allows nondiscriminatory tariff treatment (that is, the lowest tariffs) for Chinese exports to the US, and Export-Import Bank financing for US exports to China.

However, under the Jackson-Vanik Amendment to the US Trade Act of 1974,⁶⁸ as a nonmarket economy country China's MFN status must be certified annually by a presidential determination stipulating that China meets the requirements for emigration freedom at large, or by a presidential waiver of the certification. The decision by the US President to extend

MFN is automatically implemented unless both Houses of US Congress pass a resolution of disapproval. The President can veto such a resolution, and China's MFN status then continues unless the veto is in turn overturned by a two-thirds majority vote in both Houses of Congress.

The stakes are high. If MFN status is revoked, imports from China would fall under the "column two" tariff rates as set out in the US tariff schedule. In some cases, it may be ten times higher than the MFN rate.[69] For instance, the average tariff rate on toys would surge from some 7% to 70%, as Table 4 shows, and those on men's cotton trousers and women's woollen dresses from some 5% and 8% to 60% and 90% respectively. Beyond question, such higher tariff rates would effectively foreclose China's access to vast portions of the US market, especially in respect of those consumer items such as toys and games, clothing and footwear which account for the bulk of China' exports, either directly or via Hong Kong, to the US market. If this occurs, then China is sure to retaliate, probably by imposing similarly high tariffs on US exports to China. For one thing, over 2,000 US DFIs worth more than US$6 billion, which more than equally depend on the two-way Sino-US MFN treatments for their projects in China, would be put at risk.[70] There are, of course, more in these than meet the eye.

Until the June 4 event of 1989 extension of MFN was routine. Since then, the extension of China's MFN status has turned into a perennial battle, fueled by China's trade surpluses, missiles sales and its human rights performance. Despite the annual survival of China's MFN status under the administration of former US President George Bush, Sino-US commercial relations have been becoming a regular, bruising debate over its yearly renewal. Among these, the single most important factor that works against the continuation of China's MFN status is its growing trade surplus with the US. More recently, trade tensions have been further exacerbated by allegations that China fails to provide adequate protection for US intellectual property and adequate US market access to the Chinese market, let alone the US crackdown on imported Chinese textiles with allegedly false country-of-origin labels and allegation that some Chinese exports are manufactured by forced labour. For the purpose of seeing the extension of MFN status, over the past couple of years China has made a great deal of efforts towards resolving these disputations, leading to the subsequent signing in 1992 of three memoranda of understanding on the protection of intellectual property rights, prohibition of forced-labour exports and imports, and market access.

Table 4. Some Selected MFN and Non-MFN Tariff Rates in the United States, 1991

Item	MFN rate (%)	Non-MFN rate (%)	Incremental difference (in times)
Textiles and garments			
Woven fabrics of silk	5–7.8	90.0	14.1
Women's blouses and shirts, wool	6.0	60.0	10.0
Women's briefs and panties	8.1	90.0	11.1
Women's nightdresses and pyjamas	9.0	90.0	10.0
Men's underpants and briefs	7.9	90.0	11.4
Men's trousers, cotton	4.7	60.0	12.8
Cotton overcoats and similar items	4.7	60.0	12.8
Women's dresses, wool	7.7	90.0	11.7
Women's skirts, cotton	8.5	90.0	10.6
Electrical appliances			
Vacuum cleaners and floor polishers	3.4	35.0	10.3
Hair dryers and similar items	3.9	35.0	9.0
Magnetic discs	4.2	80.0	19.0
Burglar or fire alarms apparatus	2.7	35.0	13.0
Toys, dolls and games			
Stuffed toys and electrical trains	6.8	70.0	10.3
Dolls carriages and similar items	7.8	70.0	9.0

Source: Hong Kong Trade Development Council, *U.S. Import Tariff, MFN vs Non-MFN Rates* (July 1991).
Note: Women's clothing items include girls', and men's include boys'.

In the first place, after six rounds of talks since 27 May 1991, an agreement concerning the Special 301 investigation was reached on 17 January 1992. In virtue of this, the US intellectual assets such as computers and medicines are put under protection. No less strenuous, after eight rounds of hard negotiations and joint efforts on both sides, on 10 October 1992 China and US signed an agreement to increase market access for US products to the Chinese market, ending a year-long Section 301 investigation by the US into Chinese trade barriers. Under this second agreement, China has agreed to eliminate import barriers, including licencing requirements, import quota, and other administrative controls and restrictions for a wide range of US exports. The liberalization process, which began on 31 December 1992, will continue until 31 December 1997. In terms of coverage and speed, about 75% of all import barriers will be lifted within two years. In addition, China has pledged to reduce tariffs significantly by no later than 31 December 1993 and make its trade regime more transparent, in line with the requirements under GATT.

At this juncture, a jumbling issue regarding the link between China's prospect of joining GATT and its subsequent MFN status with the US may perhaps need a clarification. To be sure, there is a common misconception, even among high-ranking trade officials in Beijing, that when China rejoins GATT, it will automatically enjoy MFN treatment unconditionally and hence see an end to the annual agony over the debate on MFN renewal. The real world is certainly not that smooth. For one thing, China's joining GATT will necessitate a revision of the US trade laws. For another, the US can still quote Article 35 of GATT that defines special circumstances and refuse to grant China treatment under the GATT legal code. In a word, mechanisms do exist in GATT that allow one contracting party to revoke the MFN status of another. In this regard, "One need only look at the recent wrangle between the US and the EC over oilseed output, or the looming dispute over rice markets pitting Japan and South Korea againt GATT's rice exporting members, to see that there are ample opportunities within GATT for trade tensions to assert themselves," says Edward Paley.[71]

So far as the US global trade policy is concerned, during the past decade and as a result of the huge US trade deficits, US trade policy has become much more controversial and disturbing as it has shifted its emphasis away from free trade and nondiscriminatory multilateralism towards aggressive bilateralism, regionalism and managed trade.[72] Indeed, with the passage of the *Omnibus Trade and Competitiveness Act* of 1988, the US trade laws have given *de facto* legitimacy to unilateralism in defining US trade rights, in determining their violation and in meting out punishment to secure satisfaction. Specifically, under the stated goal of "fair trade," current US trade laws often demand full reciprocity, in the sense of equal access to foreign markets for US products, country by country and product by product, and require retaliation against countries that do not provide market access to US exports equal to that which foreign countries and products enjoy in the US. Having said this, there is little need to further elaborate that China's trade surpluses with US will be the biggest stumbling block over Sino-US trade relations in the upcoming years.

Turning to Sino-US trade balance, since 1983 the US has had a merchandise trade deficit with China and, according to US Department of Commerce data, the US trade deficit grew significantly from some US$31

Table 5. Sino-US Trade, 1979-1992 — According to Chinese and US Trade Statistics (in US$ billion)

Year	Chinese statistics				US statistics			
	Total	Imports from US	Exports to US	Balance as seen by China	Total	Imports from China	Exports to China	Balance as seen by US
1979	2.4	1.8	0.6	-1.2	2.4	0.7	1.7	1.1
1980	4.6	3.7	1.0	-2.7	4.9	1.2	3.7	2.6
1981	5.9	4.4	1.5	-2.9	5.7	2.1	3.6	1.5
1982	5.3	3.7	1.6	-2.1	5.4	2.5	2.9	0.4
1983	4.5	2.7	1.8	-1.0	4.6	2.5	2.2	-0.3
1984	6.1	3.8	2.3	-1.5	6.4	3.4	3.0	-0.4
1985	7.0	4.4	2.7	-1.7	8.0	4.2	3.8	-0.4
1986	7.3	4.7	2.6	-2.1	8.3	5.2	3.1	-2.1
1987	7.9	4.8	3.0	-1.8	9.8	6.3	3.5	-2.8
1988	10.0	6.6	3.4	-3.3	13.5	8.4	5.0	-3.4
1989	12.2	7.9	4.4	-3.5	17.8	12.0	5.8	-6.2
1990	11.8	6.6	5.2	-1.4	20.0	15.2	4.8	-10.4
1991	14.2	8.0	6.2	-1.8	25.3	19.0	6.3	-12.7
1992	17.5	—	—	—	33.2	25.7	7.5	-18.2

Sources: Chinese statistics are as in Table 1; and US statistics are from US Department of Commerce.
Note: The symbol — indicates data not yet available.

million in 1983 to US$6.2 billion in 1989. Despite the post-June 4 disruptions, the volume of Sino-US trade continues to grow and the trade imbalance to widen further. As shown in Table 5, US imports from China totalled US$25.7 billion in 1992, up US$13.7 billion or some 114% higher than in 1989. By comparison, the same US trade statistics indicate that US exports to China amounted to US$7.5 billion in 1992, up US$1.7 billion or some 29% compared to 1989. As a result, in 1992 the US trade deficit with China soared to US$18.2 billion, a tripling of the trade imbalance since 1989. As such, China is now second only to US's trade deficit with Japan.

Closely related to the trade imbalance issue is the problem of discrepancies between the US and Chinese trade data. Official Chinese Customs statitsics differ widely from US reckoning. For example, the Chinese trade statistics for 1991 showed a total of US$14.2 billion in two-way trade, compared to the US Department of Commerce figure of US$25.3 billion. Accordingly, Chinese Customs data disclosed a Chinese trade deficit of US$1.8 billion with US in 1991, while US statistics indicated a US deficit of US$12.7 billion in trading with China. Discrepancies in trade statistics between two trading partners are not uncommon, but the gap between US and Chinese statistics has widened beyond normal statistical errors and omissions since the late 1970s. The difference has increased especially rapidly between Chinese statistics on exports to US and US statistics on imports from China.

The major factor underlying the large discrepancies in trade statistics between the two sides lay in the different way of tackling statistics on Hong Kong's re-export trade. According to Hong Kong Census and Statistics Department's figures, of the merchandise goods from the Chinese mainland exported to Hong Kong and subsequently re-exported to the US since the late 1980s, some 70% belonged to export of products processed or assembled with imported materials and parts by Hong Kong DFI firms in China. The Chinese Customs statistics do not take into account such re-exports through Hong Kong. The US Department of Commerce statistics, in contrast, consider Chinese goods re-exported through Hong Kong to be Chinese exports, but count US goods transhipped through Hong Kong as exports to Hong Kong, rather than as exports to China.[73] As a result, there are wide discrepancies between the two countries' statistics. So far as the outward processing exportables are concerned, the Chinese claim that what they actually earn is only the portion of processing fees, amounting to some 7 to 10% of the total value of these transactions, yet 100% of such Hong Kong entrepôt trade is assigned to China's ledgers by the US. This discordant situation shows how a pure accounting problem can disguise the nature of modern commercial relationships.

Turning to Hong Kong's stake, the growing economic integration of Hong Kong's outward manufacturing and export trade with that of China over the last decade or so has by and large become something of a double-edged sword for the territory. With Hong Kong's economic fortunes being increasingly enmeshed with those of the Chinese mainland, integration has made the territory more vulnerable to the vagaries of China's external commercial relations. Needless to say, Hong Kong has a crucial stake in Sino-US trade relations. Hong Kong's exposure in its China connection is particularly exemplified by the threat to revoke China's MFN status by the US. Taken together, China and the US now account for nearly half of Hong Kong's total foreign trade volume. According to the most recent estimates given by Hamish Macleod, Hong Kong's Financial Secretary, the loss of China's MFN status would cost Hong Kong up to 70,000 jobs and up to three percentage points of Hong Kong's annual GDP growth.[74] Of course, the casualty would not be confined to Hong Kong and China only. Withdrawal of China's MFN status would also cost US consumers some US$14 billion because of higher tariffs, says also Hamish Macleod, while retaliation by China would put at risk over 150,000 US jobs, among others.

Having gone thus far, it is clear that to a considerable extent China's rapid export expansion to the US and the world market since the late 1970s has been attributable to burgeoning outward-processing activity by Hong Kong manufacturers in Guangdong and elsewhere in China. This has enabled Hong Kong to hold down its trade surplus with the US by shifting a good proportion of the surplus onto China's trade books. Following the footsteps of Hong Kong, since the mid-1980s many a foot-loose manufacturing concern from Taiwan have also shifted production base to China, reducing Taiwan controversial trade surplus with the US as well. This trend is driven by sheer economic forces, like rising wage rates and mounting land cost, and will further stretch as South Korean investors join the league in establishing export processing platforms in China.

Leaving aside South Korea, within this growing economic integration what is in fact emerging as a new economic entity is the Greater China Economic Community, comprising the trio of mainland China, Hong Kong and Taiwan. The implications of the advent of the Greater China triangle for US trade policy are far-reaching.[75] For one thing in particular, the growing US trade imbalance with China must be looked at in a broader regional context rather than in isolation. As a matter of fact, while there is increasing attention focused on China's trade surpluses with the US, the US combined trade deficit with Greater China actually declined by some US$3 billion during 1987–1991.

According to a recent economic policy backgrounder document released by the US Information Service,[76] the combined trade deficit of the US with Greater China totalled US$28.3 billion in 1992, up 19.4% in relation to 1991. However, when compared to the 1987 deficit of US$27 billion, as Table 6 shows, the 1992 US deficit with Greater China widened by no more than US$1.3 billion. Specifically, although US trade deficit with China climbed by some US$15 billion during 1987–1992, its deficit with Hong Kong and Taiwan combined shrank about US$14 billion during the same years, confirming the belief that the two small dragons had managed to shift their surpluses and the political burdens that accompany them to China. In 1992, Hong Kong and Taiwan exports to the US were even smaller than their 1987 levels, albeit rather marginally, while China increased its exports to the US by US$19.5 billion to account for all of the incremental growth in Greater China's merchandise sales to the US.

After all, Greater China now accounts for only a small percentage more of US global imports than in 1987. In 1987, Hong Kong and Taiwan combined accounted for almost 9% of all US imports, while China accounted for only 1.4%. By 1992, whereas China's share had risen to about 4.8%, the two dragons accounted for less than 7% of the US total. Taken together, some 11.3% of US imports from the world originated in Greater China in 1987, compared to about 10% in 1987. In respect of US performance in Greater China, US exports grew steadily from US$14.4 billion in 1987 to nearly US$32 billion last year, more than doubling to each of the three Greater China economies during the past five years. Correspondingly, US exports to Greater China amounted to 7.1% of US global exports in 1992, compared to 5.9% in 1987. Altogether, US's share of two-way trade with Greater China has grown from some 8.6% of total US exports and imports in 1987 to 9.4% in 1992.

In a nutshell, US focus on its growing trade imbalance with China has concealed a considerable offsetting shrivelling of the deficit with Hong Kong and Taiwan and a strong US export performance to Greater China. The rapid emergence of Greater China is certainly introducing new challenges and complexities into US commercial policy towards the trio. Yet, on top of lacking a comprehensive appreciation of this historic development, within the US there has been little consensus on appropriate China

Table 6. US Imports, Exports and Trade Balance with Greater China, 1987–1992 (in US$ billion)

Year	Exports to Greater China					Imports from Greater China					US trade balance with			
	China	Hong Kong	Taiwan	Total		China	Hong Kong	Taiwan	Total		China	Hong Kong	Taiwan	Total
1987	3.4	4.0	7.0	14.4		6.2	10.5	24.8	41.5		-2.8	-6.5	-17.8	-27.1
1990	4.8	6.8	11.1	22.7		15.1	9.5	22.5	47.1		-10.3	-2.7	-11.4	-24.4
1991	6.3	8.1	13.2	27.6		19.0	9.3	23.0	51.3		-12.7	-1.2	-9.8	-23.7
1992	7.5	9.1	13.2	29.8		25.7	9.8	24.6	60.1		-18.2	-0.7	-11.4	-30.3

Source: US Information Service, Economic Policy Backgrounder, "Greater China Trade with the United States, 1987–1992: The Trend" (23 March 1993).

policy. Viewed in this light: "One of the first tests of the Clinton administration's ability to develop a forward-looking foreign policy will be the troubled US-China relationship," as Barber Conable and David Lampton, respectively the chairman and president of the National Committee on US-China Relations, correctly wrote.[77]

Before closing, let us add that the term "most favoured nation" is actually a misnomer, since MFN status confers neither "preferential" nor "favoured" tariff treatment. As virtually all countries offer MFN treatment to China, the US is perhaps the only one nation contemplating denial of MFN status to China. The annual ritual of China's MFN status is a charade. Today, there are no more than a handful of nations in the world which do not benefit from MFN. Since the end of the Cold War in the early 1990s, not only the member states of the ex-Soviet Union, but also such former tyrant states as Bulgaria and Albania have been added to the list of MFN beneficiaries. And, irrespective of other sanctions they may suffer, even some of the US's *least* favoured nations — Iraq, Iran and Libya, to name just three — enjoy MFN status without the annual ordeal of a renewal debate.[78] To be sure, a stable Sino-US commercial relationship is not only critical for China's reforming national economy but also crucial for longer-term US interests. The most decisive way to ensure stability is of course, to de-politicize the MFN renewal issue. More important still, the US must recommit itself solidly to free trade, as it did in the 1960s. Notably, the unilateralism of Super 301 goes against the postwar trend of multilateralism and increased liberalization of world trade. Protectionism in the end is a negative-sum game from which the world's economic players will take a long time to recover, as the dire results in the 1930s tell.

In conclusion, there can be little doubt that China has come a long way from the monolithic, centralized and rigidly controlled foreign trade structure and exchange rate regime in the pre-reform era towards a multi-layered, multi-faceted, decentralizing and reforming system. Despite the successes, China's economy remains hamstrung by a good number of institutional or structural factors that will be difficult to reform. These include inefficient state-owned enterprises,[79] difficulties in laying off a massive number of unneeded public employees, and requirements to provide extensive social services to workers, to mention just a few. While it takes time on the part of China to change over a *dirigiste* system that has been in practice for the last forty years or so, the Chinese economy today is too far down the road to a market economy to congeal further reforms, let alone reverse earlier ones. Yet, the process of upcoming reforms, as one can surmise, will be piecemeal and will proceed in stop-go cycles, hopefully not in the mode of two-steps-forward-and-one-backward kind, as it has since the late 1970s.

Notes

1. On top of expounding his ideas about "building socialism with Chinese characteristics" during his political tour of South China last January and February, Deng stressed that "reforms and opening to the outside world offer the only way to lead China to modernization and prosperity." Deng also encouraged Guangdong province to become a "fifth little dragon" in the league with Hong Kong, South Korea, Singapore and Taiwan. In recognition of the significance of Deng's missionary tour and the subsequent "whirlwind" about sparking a nationwide renewal of enthusiasm for market-oriented reforms and the substantially enhanced likelihood that capitalistic reforms in China will be long-lasting, Deng was picked as "Man of the Year" by the London *Financial Times* on 29 December 1992.
2. Qu Yingpu, "Industrial Output Value Hits Record $487.6 Billion," *China Daily Business Weekly*, 14–20 February 1993.
3. See Chinese Premier Li Peng's Government Work Report to the first session of the Eighth National People's Congress on 15 March 1993, as cited in the news piece "Major Progress Made in Past 5 Years — Li Peng," *China Daily*, 16 March 1993.
4. To reconcile the actual economic performance during 1991–1992 as well as to accommodate Deng's insistence on a fast-paced economic growth, in his latest Government Work Report (see Note 3), Li Peng disclosed that the State Council had adjusted the original annual economic growth rate target of 6% for the Eighth Five-year Plan to 8 or 9%. If this revised annual rate for economic growth is attained, says Li Peng, China's established goal of quadrupling the GNP of 1980 by 2000 can be realized two years ahead of schedule. See Chang Hong, "Li Calls for Faster Gains in Report to 8th NPC," *China Daily*, 16 March 1993.
5. In terms of land surface area, China is the world's third largest country encompassing an area of some 9.6 million square kilometres. Besides being the most populous nation on earth, China's 1.18 billion population represents rather more than one-fifth of the world's total.
6. The departure growth rates for Summers' extrapolation are: during the 1980s, China's annual GDP growth averaged about 8.7%, while the US equivalent was 2.3%. By Summers' reckoning, even if that growth differential were cut in half, China's total domestic output would surpass that of the US by 2014.

For details, see his article, "The Rise of China," *International Economic Insights* (May/June 1992). Amongst others, Summers' predictions were cited in "Could China's GDP Surpass That of the United States?" *Washington Economic Reports*, 27 May 1992, p. 2; and Jim Rohwer, "When China Wakes — A Survey of China," *The Economist*, 28 November 1992, p. 5.
7. Summers, see Note 6.
8. Rohwer (see Note 6), p. 3.
9. *Ibid.*, p. 5.
10. To attract foreign capital and expertise, China promulgated the *Law on Chinese-Foreign Equity Joint Ventures* in 1979, the year when the policy of attracting DFIs actually began. And, to monitor enterprises with 100% foreign ownership, the Chinese authority also enacted the *Law on Foreign-Capital Enterprises* in 1986.
11. Hong Kong Trade Development Council, *Status Report on China's Economic Reforms* (August 1992), p. 8.
12. *Ibid.*
13. See Zhang Yu'an, "Economy Looks a Picture of Health," *China Daily*, 31 December 1992; and the Xinhua news piece, "'92 China Foreign Trade Sees Big Rise," *China Daily*, 31 December 1992.
14. For some fuller discussion of the Hong Kong factor in the modernization and internationalization of the Chinese economy, see Yun-wing Sung, *The China-Hong Kong Connection: The Key to China's Open-Door Policy* (Cambridge: Cambridge University Press, 1991); see also Yin-Ping Ho, *Trade, Industrial Restructuring and Development in Hong Kong* (London/Honolulu: Macmillan Press/University of Hawaii Press, 1992), especially Chapter 10.
15. For scholarly work in these areas, see, for example, Nicholas R. Lardy, *Foreign Trade and Economic Reform in China, 1978–1990* (Cambridge: Cambridge University Press, 1992); *idem.*, "Chinese Foreign Trade," *The China Quarterly*, No. 131 (September 1992), pp. 691–720; and Y. Y. Kueh, "Foreign Investment and Economic Change in China," *The China Quarterly*, No. 131 (September 1992), pp. 637–90.
16. A brief account of alternative trade regimes in relation to the reforming Chinese economy can be found in Lardy (see Note 15), pp. 4–15.
17. By comparison, the rate of growth of total world trade between 1980–1992 averaged about 5.5% a year.
18. In a move to realign its foreign exchange reserves statistics with international guidelines, as noted in a recent economic review of *Asian Economic Commentary* (February 1993) by Merrill Lynch, China recently separated the reserves holdings of the People's Bank of China, the country's central bank, from those of the Bank of China. Accordingly, the official foreign exchange reserves were halved to some US$23.2 billion at end-September 1992.
19. Cf. World Bank, Country Operations Division, China and Mongolia

Department, and East Asia Pacific Region, *China: Country Economic Memorandum — Reform and the Role of the Plan in the 1990s*, Report No. 10199-CHA (19 July 1992), p. 30.

20. The first four SEZs, established between 1979 and 1980, are: Shenzhen, Shantou and Zhuhai in Guangdong province, and Xiamen in Fujian province. In 1988, Hainan Island was upgraded to a province, the thirtieth province in China, and made a SEZ the same year. One notable business incentive offered by the SEZs is the 15% preferential income tax rate for enterprises, as compared to 33% elsewhere in the country. The fourteen open coastal cities — Dalian, Qinhuangdao, Tianjin, Yantai, Qingdao, Lianyungang, Nantong, Shanghai, Ningbo, Wenzhou, Fuzhou, Guangzhou, Zhanjiang and Beihai — were opened to foreign trade and investment in 1984. Apart from enjoying some of the preferential policies of the SEZs, special areas in the fourteen cities have been designated as Economic and Technological Development Zones with the aim of concentrating funds on importing advanced technology, and establishing high-tech ventures with foreign enterprises and joint research institutes to develop new technology and high-grade consumer products.
21. Goh Keng Swee, "Why Deng's 'New Revolution' Will Succeed," *South China Morning Post* (Hong Kong, *SCMP*), 31 January 1993.
22. Rohwer (see Note 6), p. 11.
23. *Ibid.*
24. Goh, see Note 21.
25. Wang Yong, "Foreign-funded Firms Do Well," *China Daily Business Weekly*, 14–20 February 1993.
26. "14 Coastal Cities Set a Record," *China Daily*, 15 February 1993.
27. *Ibid.*
28. Wang Yong, "Zones Reap Record in Foreign Exchange," *China Daily*, 19 February 1993.
29. *Ibid.*
30. *Ibid.*
31. "Sino-Japan Trade Hits New Record," *China Daily*, 10 March 1993.
32. These figures were given in "U.S.-China Trade Deficit and Greater China," *Washington Economic Reports*, 3 March 1993, p. 3.
33. These Reuter figures were cited in "Taiwan-China Trade Up 27.9%," *Ming Pao* (Hong Kong), 23 February 1993, the China Business News page.
34. The bilateral trade volume between China and South Korea rose to US$8 billion in 1992, a twofold increase over the 1990 level. This is the figure given by Roh Jae-won, the Republic of Korea's (ROK) Ambassador to China, at a conference on Sino-ROK economic relations, held in Hong Kong in February 1993, as cited in "Sino-ROK Trading Hits $8b," *China Daily Business Weekly*, 28 February–6 March 1993.

35. "Sino-EEC Trade Up by Hefty 15%," *China Daily*, 1 March 1993.
36. Liang Chao, "Sino-Russian Trade Hits Record High," *China Daily*, 25 February 1993.
37. Empirically, it has been revealed that China's trade specialization in the early 1980s was not based on comparative advantage but that by the late 1980s China was exploiting its comparative advantage in international trade more fully, see Zhang Xiaogang and Peter G. Warr, "China's Trade Patterns and Comparative Advantage," in *China: Trade and Reform* (Canberra: National Centre for Development Studies, Australian National University, 1991).
38. Alexander J. Yeats, "China's Foreign Trade and Comparative Advantage: Prospects, Problems, and Policy Implications," World Bank Discussion Papers 141 (November 1991).
39. Rohwer (see Note 6), p. 7.
40. Cf. Yeats (see Note 38).
41. Yuan Zhou, "Textile Exports to Hit Record $24b," *China Daily*, 24 December 1992.
42. For some informative analysis of the Chinese foreign exchange system with respect to its effects on export incentives and import costs, see Sung (Note 14), Chapters 3 and 4; also see Lardy (Note 15), Chapter 3, especially pp. 51–79.
43. Cf. Hang-Sheng Cheng, "China's Foreign Trade Reform, 1979–91," Working Paper 92–01, Center for Pacific Basin Monetary and Economic Studies, Economic Research Department of Federal Reserve Bank of San Francisco (February 1992). Of course, on nontradable transactions between residents and non-residents, such as tourist expenditures and foreign remittances, the exchange rate did have economic significance.
44. The cost in *Renminbi* of earning one unit of foreign exchange varied quite considerably among localities and goods. In Guangdong, for example, the *Renminbi* cost of earning foreign exchange of some goods was ten times the official rate in 1979, over three-quarters of Guangdong exports incurred losses as a result, see Y. Y. Kueh and Christopher Howe, "China's International Trade: Policy and Organizational Change and Their Place in the 'Economic Readjustment'," *The China Quarterly*, No. 100 (December 1984), pp. 844–45. Cf. also Sung (see Note 14), pp. 50 *et sqq.*; and Lardy (see Note 15), pp. 24–29.
45. Cheng (see Note 43), p. 20.
46. HKTDC (see Note 11), pp. 16–17. Cf. also Lardy (see Note 15), pp. 701–702.
47. Cheng (see Note 43), p. 12. Cf. also Liu Xiangdong, "China's Reform on Foreign Trade Administrative Regime," *Intertrade* (October 1992), p. 4.
48. HKTDC (see Note 11), p. 17. According to Wu Shiguo of Economic Research Institute under the State Planning Commission, the number of industrial products produced under mandatory planning has dropped from 123

in 1984 to 54 in late 1992 and, in terms of output value, from about 80% to only 16.2%, see his article "Joining GATT and Acceleration of China's Economic Reform," *Intertrade* (December 1992), p. 10.

49. According to Li Gang of MOFERT's International Trade and Research Institute, mandatory-planned imports only accounted for one-fifth of total imports in 1992, see his article "GATT and Reform of China's Foreign Trade System," *Intertrade* (October 1992), p. 8. See also Wu Yi (Vice-Minister of MOFERT), "Reform of the Foreign Trade Promotes Foreign Trade Development," *Intertrade* (July 1992), p. 18.

50. HKTDC (see Note 11), p. 18.

51. Beyond doubt, the 1988 foreign trade contract system was inspired by the very success of agricultural "Household Contract Responsibility System" introduced a decade ago. At the heart of the agricultural reforms initiated in 1978 was a return of the land to individual rural households on a lengthy lease basis (15 to 25 years), and gave farmers the right to sell their outputs — after fulfilling certain planning quotas and paying other expenses to the state — thus the phrase "Household Contract Responsibility System." It is intriguing to note that prior to the 1978 rural reforms, the constitutional form of grassroots production organization in rural areas were people's communes and agricultural production cooperatives, which no longer exist today with the advent of the Household Contract Responsibility System introduced about ten years ago. To reduce losses and enhance production efficiency, the contract responsibility system, which was introduced nationwide in 1987, was also applied to state-owned enterprises in the same year.

52. Cheng (see Note 43), p. 21.

53. Some fuller account of China's foreign exchange retention scheme and its changes over the past decade are given in Cheng (Note 43), pp. 15–17; Sung (Note 14), pp. 49–53; and Lardy (see Note 15), pp. 707–709.

54. Ren Kan, "Foreign Exchange Balance Declines," *China Daily*, 16 February 1993.

55. In retrospect, the GATT was not intended to be an organization at all, but rather a subsidiary agreement under the proposed International Trade Organization (ITO) Charter. The ITO Charter was adopted in March 1948 at the Havana Conference. In the US, however, the Congress failed to approve the Charter submitted by President Truman. As a result, the proposed ITO was never established. This notwithstanding, since its inception in October 1947 or its entering into force on 1 January 1948, GATT, once known as "the rich men's club," has been the main forum for the liberalization of tariff and nontariff trade barriers and for the settlement of international trade disputes.

56. From the point of view of China, Taiwan's withdrawal was illegal because China has persistently insisted that the Taiwan political regime ceased to be the legal Chinese government in 1949 and, accordingly, Taiwan had no

authority or legal rights to make such a decision. In respect of later developments, Taiwan did return as an observer in 1965 but was driven out in 1971 following China's entry into the United Nations. And, in early 1990 Taiwan filed a formal application to GATT for membership. Taiwan's application, as one can surmise, has met opposition from China, which contends that Taiwan should wait until China has joined GATT before applying for membership.

57. Since the early 1970s, China has joined a number of international organizations which are either affiliated or have some connection with GATT. For example, China has been a member of the Customs Cooperations Council which closely cooperates with the Committee on Customs Valuation under GATT; it has been a member of International Trade Centre, which is joint subsidiary organ of the United Nations Conference on Trade and Development (UNCTAD) and GATT; and after being granted an observer status to MFA, which is part of the GATT system, in 1982, China has been a party to MFA since 1984. See Dehai Tae, "China and Services Negotiations," *Journal of World Trade*, Vol. 25, No. 2 (April 1991), especially Note 2 on p. 23.

58. Feng Yushu, "China Prepares to Restore Its Signatory Status in GATT: Problems and Pitfalls on the Road to Return," *Intertrade* (December 1992), pp. 4 *et sqq.*

59. Amongst these, the contentious issue boils down to whether China will accept a "safeguard system" which will allow other GATT signatories to enact emergency quotas and tariffs should a sudden onslaught of Chinese exportables end up in their countries. This provision would be unique in GATT to China. Conceivably, some GATT signatories, the US in particular, fear that China's lingering socialism and economic clout will combine to subsidize exports and, thereby, unfairly undercut the prices of their domestic products. See James McGregor, "Chinese Talks on GATT Stall over Basic Issue," *Asian Wall Street Journal*, 3 March 1993; cf. also Wang Yong, "Mofert Chief Says Talks Give Impetus to GATT Re-entry," *China Daily Business Weekly*, 7–13 March 1993.

60. Tong Zhiguang, "China and GATT: A Relationship of Mutual Benefit," *Intertrade* (August 1992), p. 16. Cf. also Li (see Note 49), p. 9; and HKTDC (see Note 11), pp. 19–20.

61. Tong (see Note 60), p. 16; and Li (see Note 49), p. 9.

62. "China Striving to Meet Gatt Requirements," *China Daily*, 18 December 1992.

63. *Ibid.* Import subsidies in China had been mostly removed in earlier reforms. In respect of licencing requirements, at present no more than fifty-three kinds of commodities need import licences, see Liu Xiangdong, "Reform of China's Foreign Trade System," *China's Foreign Trade* (October 1992), p. 6.

64. See Note 62.

65. HKTDC (see Note 11), p. 20.

66. Anand Rajaram, "Reforming Prices: The Experience of China, Hungary, and Poland," World Bank Discussion Papers 144, China and Mongolia Department Series (January 1992).
67. For some fuller discussion of the issue of how China joins GATT and its perceivable impact on world trading system, see Harold K. Jacobson and Michael Oksenberg, *China's Participation in the IMF, the World Bank, and GATT: Towards a Global Economic Order* (Ann Arbor: University of Michigan Press, 1990); and Penelope Hartland-Thunberg, *China, Hong Kong, Taiwan and the World Trading System* (London: Macmillan Press, 1990).
68. At its origin, the Jackson-Vanik Amendment was enacted in 1974 to address concerns about the Soviet Union's restrictions on emigration by its Jewish citizens.
69. A detailed comparison of the US MFN and non-MFN tariff rates is to be found in HKTDC, *U.S. Import Tariff, MFN vs Non-MFN Rates* (July 1991).
70. Cf. Donald M. Anderson, "China Policy: Fostering US Competitiveness and the Bilateral Relationship" (a position paper presented by the president of US-China Business Council to Bill Clinton, the then US President-elect, and top members of his administration), in *The China Business Review* (January–February 1993), p. 12.
71. Edward Paley, "Confusion Reigns on the Meaning of GATT," *SCMP*, 14 December 1992.
72. For some fuller account of recent trend in US trade policy, see, for example, Jagdish N. Bhagwati, "United States Trade Policy at the Crossroads," *The World Economy*, Vol. 12, No. 4 (December 1989), pp. 439–79; Dominick Salvatore, "Recent Trends in U.S. Protectionism," *Open Economies Review*, Vol. 3, No. 3 (1992), pp. 307–21; Kimberly Ann Elliott, "United States Trade Policy after the Cold War," *Current History* (April 1992), pp. 162–67; and Biswajit Dhar, "The Decline of Free Trade and U.S. Trade Policy Today," *Journal of World Trade*, Vol. 26, No. 6 (December 1992), pp. 133–54.
73. Harry Harding, "The US and Greater China," *The China Business Review* (May–June 1992), p. 20.
74. Hamish Macleod, *Building on Success: The 1993–94 Budget* (Speech by the Financial Secretary, moving the Second Reading of the Appropriation Bill, 1993) (Hong Kong Government Printer, 3 March 1993), p. 12.
75. For some other discussion pertaining to Sino-Greater China relationships, see Harry Harding, "The Emergence of Greater China: Hong Kong, Taiwan, South China: How U.S. Policy Will Have to Change," *The American Enterprise*, Vol. 3, No. 3 (May–June 1992), pp. 47–55.
76. US Information Service, Economic Policy Backgrounder, "Greater China Trade with the United States, 1987–92: The Trend" (23 March 1993).
77. Barber B. Conable, Jr. and David M. Lampton, "China: The Coming Power," *Foreign Affairs* (Winter 1992/93), pp. 133–49.

78. Editor, "No Need to Pick Out China for Punishment," *SCMP*, 4 June 1992.
79. In China, as in the ex-Soviet Union and East European economies, enterprise reforms in the state sector, which are just beginning, have proved to be the most intractable part of economic reforms. On this issue, see Athar Hussain, "The Chinese Economic Reforms in Retrospect and Prospect," The Development Economics Research Programme CP No. 24, London School of Economics (August 1992), pp. 26–29. According to China's State Statistical Bureau, presently about one-third of state-owned enterprises (SOEs) are operating at a loss and another one-third are suffering from hidden losses. In 1991, the central government paid more than RMB50 billion (US$8.7 billion) to make up for the losses. In addition to the subsidies, the state injects RMB10 billion (US$1.74 billion) every year to improve SOEs' efficiency, see Chen Xiao, "Budgetary Deficit to Be Cut Back in '93," *China Daily*, 26 January 1993. Up to now, SOEs in China are still the principal instruments for the realization of output planning, the principal source of public revenue and the mainstay of social insurance for wage-employed workforce. To be sure, the failure to impose a hard budget constraint on SOEs has an adverse impact on the central government's ability to implement a counter-cyclical macro-stabilization policy and also undermines the viability of the banking system. Yet, a comprehensive SOE reform programme, which is central to the transition from a command to a market economy, consists in not one but a series of interwined reforms, each of which is not only genuinely complex but also decisively demanding.

18

Pearl River Delta Development

Peter Tsan-yin Cheung

Introduction

The phenomenal economic growth of Guangdong province has attracted more business and scholarly attention than any other regions in China in the past few years.[1] If Guangdong's experience suggests a model of reform and development for China, then its Pearl River Delta is undoubtedly its centerpiece. With the countdown to 1997, the flourishing economic links between Hong Kong and the Delta have also assumed growing economic and political significance in China's reform and opening. This chapter will briefly review the growth of the Delta in the 1980s, examine the developments in 1992, and explore its prospects in the 1990s.

The Development of the Pearl River Delta in the 1980s

The Pearl River Delta constitutes the economic core of Guangdong and its economic significance far outweighs other areas (see Table 1). In this chapter, the Pearl River Delta refers to the eleven most important municipalities in the Delta area: Guangzhou, Panyu (formerly a county of Guangzhou), Shenzhen, Zhuhai, Huizhou, Dongguan, Zhongshan, Jiangmen, Foshan, Nanhai (formerly a county of Foshan) and Shunde (formerly a county of Foshan).[2] With only about one-third of the province's population, the Delta accounted for over 61% of its gross domestic product (GDP), about 68% of its total exports and 73% of its total foreign investment in 1991.[3] Half of Guangdong's industries were located in the Delta, contributing 63% of the province's total industrial output.[4] The Delta's investment in fixed assets also amounted to 64% of the provincial total.[5] The average per capita national income of the Pearl River Delta was RMB4,284, almost twice that of the provincial average and more than three times that of the poorer, mountainous areas in the province.[6] While the national average of wage per annum was RMB2,340, the figure for workers in the Delta ranged from RMB3,164 in Jiangmen to over RMB5,000 in Shenzhen.[7] No other area in China is as important as the Pearl River Delta in foreign trade and investment. Guangdong province contributed about one-third of China's total exports and acquired about one-half of its foreign investment, but the Delta's shares in national export and acquisition of foreign investment amounted to respectively one-quarter and over 40%.[8] The significance of the Delta in Guangdong's, as well as China's economy, is evident.

Table 1. Economic Indicators of the Pearl River Delta, 1991

	Population (10,000)	GDP (RMB100 million)	Per capita GDP (RMB)	Total export (million US$)	Foreign investment (million US$)
Guangzhou	630 (10.0%)	386.7 (21.7%)	6,464	1,840.7 (13.5%)	377.4 (14.6%)
Shenzhen	167 (2.7%)	174.8 (9.8%)	7,938	3,179.6 (23.2%)	579.9 (22.5%)
Zhuhai	64 (1.0%)	60.5 (3.4%)	7,477	640.4 (4.7%)	169.8 (6.6%)
Huizhou	229 (3.6%)	61.4 (3.5%)	2,676	425.1 (3.1%)	152.1 (5.9%)
Dongguan	174 (2.8%)	74.8 (4.2%)	5,638	619.7 (4.5%)	148.6 (5.8%)
Zhongshan	124 (2.0%)	52.7 (3.0%)	4,544	467.6 (3.4%)	102.6 (4.0%)
Jiangmen	346 (5.5%)	110.4 (6.2%)	3,112	712.0 (5.2%)	127.7 (4.9%)
Foshan	300 (4.8%)	166.6 (9.4%)	5,911	1,379.8 (10.0%)	226.3 (8.8%)
Total	2,034 (32.4%)	1088.0 (61.2%)	N.A.	9,264.9 (67.7%)	1,884.4 (73.0%)

Sources: *Guangdong Statistical Year-book 1991*, p. 106; *Guangdong Statistical Year-book 1992*, pp. 83, 93, 95, 132, 341, 350 and 369.

Notes: Figures in parentheses are percentages of provincial-level data. All figures are rounded. Statistics of Panyu as well as Nanhai and Shunde are included in the respective figures of Guangzhou and Foshan in 1991. Population statistics are 1990 census figures.

The Pearl River Delta comprises different administrative units and economic entities. Guangzhou, a major political, cultural and economic centre in the nation, is the provincial capital that has enjoyed economic power equivalent to the provincial level since 1984. Shenzhen and Zhuhai include two Special Economic Zones (SEZs) while the rest are part of the Pearl River Delta Open Economic Area that is also endowed with preferential policies. Administrative changes in the past year reflect the dynamic economic forces at work, which lead to growing urbanization as well as expansion of special or development zones. Bao'an county, originally a county under Shenzhen's jurisdiction, was officially incorporated into the SEZ, hence expanding the zone area from 327.5 square kilometers to 2,020 square kilometers.[9] Huizhou's Daya Bay area and

Panyu's Nansha area were also made Economic and Technological Development Zones.[10] Nanhai, Shunde and Panyu were upgraded from counties to municipalities, an action which has enabled them to enjoy more policy-making power.[11] After years of intensive bargaining, Shenzhen's People's Congress has finally been granted legislative power in order to expedite economic legislation that suits its rapid economic growth.[12] Furthermore, these administrative divisions are paralleled by a number of striking economic variations (see Table 1). Guangzhou, Foshan and Shenzhen are the largest areas in size in the provincial economy. Although a former treaty port and a historic city, Guangzhou has long been hampered by an outmoded urban structure and is trying to catch up with other areas in the Delta. The two SEZs are pioneers in adopting the market mechanism and other capitalist practices while other municipalities are noted for their booming export processing sector and their astute strategies in fostering local economic development.

A pattern of Pearl River Delta development can be identified in spite of the intra-Delta differences.[13] First, the Delta has experienced spectacular economic growth in the 1980s. The average real gross domestic product (GDP) growth per annum is in the range of 14% to 16%, which is not only 2 to 4 percentage points higher than the provincial average, but also possibly one of the fastest in the entire world.[14] Secondly, the rapid growth of the Delta has been facilitated by the special policies granted by the central government, which have been exploited to the fullest by the Delta's local governments.[15] Such special policies enable these local governments to offer preferential policies in taxation, land-use, infrastructural support and other areas in order to attract foreign investment.[16] Thirdly, the development strategies of the Delta are outward-oriented. Because of its proximity to Hong Kong and the attraction of preferential policies, the development of the Delta is spurred by a huge inflow of Hong Kong investment to sectors ranging from export processing and infrastructure to real estate, tourism, commerce, and other services. An estimated 40% of China's direct foreign investment in 1991 was invested in the Delta, most of which was in export processing.[17] Fourthly, the local governments in the Delta are noted for their flexibility and efficiency in economic management. Fifthly, the market mechanism is prominent in most aspects of economic activities in the Delta. In addition to extensive links with the world market, the Delta has taken the boldest step in reducing central planning and deregulating prices. Enterprises in the Delta mainly buy and sell through both the domestic and world markets, hence they are far more entrepreneurial than their counterparts elsewhere in China. Similarly, the ownership structure in the Delta comprises a variety of forms, including private, collective, state-owned, as well as foreign-invested firms. Finally, the living standards in the Delta have risen significantly compared to other less well-off areas in the country. The values and lifestyles of the people have also been much more influenced by Hong Kong than by Beijing. The above review can hardly do justice to the diversity and richness of the Pearl River Delta's developmental experience, but this sketch will serve as a point of departure for understanding the developments in 1992.[18]

Major Developments in 1992

An Overview

The year 1992 was eventful yet auspicious for Guangdong province and the Pearl River Delta in particular. Responding to the passive resistance against bolder reforms and faster growth rates under Premier Li Peng's conservative administration, Deng Xiaoping made a surprise tour of the south in late January and stirred up another wave of economic development in China. Reminiscent of his 1984 trip that resulted in the opening of fourteen coastal cities, Deng's rally was matched by enthusiastic responses from localities in Guangdong and elsewhere to speed up economic growth after the three-year long retrenchment. Encouraged by Deng's call to catch up with the "Four Little Dragons" in East Asia in twenty years, Guangdong's leadership was quick to set forth a plan for increasing the pace of growth and the opening of the province in mid-March.[19] According to this plan, the SEZs and Guangzhou would build up industries with more advanced technology. Guangzhou, in particular, would develop into a centre in information, finance, and trade. Various areas in the Delta were picked as key sites for further development, namely Huizhou's Daya Bay area, Zhuhai's western district and Hengqin Island, and Panyu's Nansha area. With the nuclear power plant about to operate, the Daya Bay area would focus on capital-intensive and technology-intensive industries. Zhuhai's western district would promote export-oriented industry and agriculture, trade and tourism while Nansha would develop into a multi-functional economic and technological development zone. In other words, in tandem with the increased opening of the less developed areas in the province, the spearhead of Guangdong's strategy in catching up with the East Asian newly industrializing countries (NICs) in the 1990s ,will still be the strategically situated Delta.

Reflecting the renewed attention of the central government towards Guangdong, a high-powered State Council delegation led by Vice-Premier Zou Jiahua visited the province and studied its experience in late April and early May.[20] Although remaining cautious on Guangdong's developmental lessons, he firmly praised its achievements and endorsed the continued granting of special policies to the province. The summer and autumn of 1992 could well have been a nightmare for the Pearl River Delta and Hong Kong because of the uncertainty surrounding the renewal by the United States of most-favoured-nation (MFN) status to China and the escalation of the Sino-American trade dispute. Had the MFN status not been granted to China, Hong Kong's re-export of China-made products to the US might have fallen by 36 to 49%, employment lost 44,000 to 60,000 jobs, and GDP reduced by 1.8 to 2.5%.[21] Yet the impact on the Delta could have been even more severe because most of Hong Kong's outward processing investment in the Delta targeted the US market. Nonetheless, the subsequent granting of the MFN status and Sino-American agreement over trade issues spelled relief for South China.

A major boost for the Delta in 1992 came, however, from developments in the domestic political scene. The Fourteenth National Party Congress held in mid-October consolidated the special role of Guangdong and the Delta. Not only would the province have more direct access to the power centre, but it would also play a key role in Deng's endeavour at building a socialist market economy. For the first time since 1949, Guangdong's incumbent Party Secretary, Xie Fei, entered the Politburo, the highest policy-making body in the Party, while seven of its officials were elected members of the new Central Committee.[22] In early January 1993, even Premier Li Peng followed Deng's footsteps one year ago by visiting the Delta and praising Guangdong's achievements.[23] Another top Party leader, Li Ruihuan, also followed suit in late January.[24] Hence, the national political environment seemed to be rather conducive to the further development of South China. The Delta's scramble for economic growth, aggressive acquisition of foreign investment and push for economic reform in 1992 were unprecedented, but its efforts were also tarnished by a number of incidents that possibly revealed deeper problems, such as the mishandling of the issuance of new shares in Shenzhen and the frantic development of real estate.

On balance, the Delta should have been satisfied with its accomplishments in 1992. Most areas in the Delta achieved double-digit growth and attracted an unprecedented amount of foreign investment, especially in infrastructural and development projects. For instance, while Guangdong's gross industrial output rose 33.3% in 1992, many of the Delta's cities (such as Shenzhen, Zhuhai, Foshan and Dongguan) registered a growth rate of over 40%.[25] The increases of GDP and national income of the Delta (e.g., in Shenzhen and Huizhou) were also in the range of 20 and 30%.[26] Even more spectacular was the acquisition of foreign (mostly Hong Kong) investment. In the first ten months of 1992, a total of US$217 million of overseas capital was actually invested in Foshan, an increase of 27% compared with the same period in 1991.[27] Panyu absorbed about US$95 million of investment from foreign-funded firms, which was more than the accumulated total in the past thirteen years.[28] Compared with 1991, Guangzhou also attracted a record figure of actual foreign investment of about US$729 million, an increase of 93.1%, while investment in Shenzhen and Huizhou respectively scored an increase of 23.3% to US$710 million and 70% to US$350 million.[29]

The dramatic changes in the Delta in 1992 defy any easy review, hence the following analysis at best offers a glimpse of the massive changes that have taken place in five key areas: export processing industry, infrastructural development, real estate, stock market, and socio-cultural ties between the Delta and Hong Kong.

From Export Processing to the Service Sector

The key source of overseas investment in the Pearl River Delta is Hong Kong, which is responsible for most of the export processing investments. Hong Kong businessmen are already employing more workers in Guangdong (estimated to be about 3 million) than in the colony (about 716,000).[30] The continuing significance of these industries was reflected in Hong Kong's trade figures for 1992. In the first three quarters of 1992, 79% of Hong Kong's re-export came from China's outward processing sector, which rose 42% over the same period in 1991 to HK$216.84 billion.[31] Hong Kong's exports to China for outward processing rose 25% over the same period in 1991 to HK$103.4 billion. Similarly, about 71% of Hong Kong's imports from China was related to outward processing, which increased 32% to $181.11 billion. For the entire year, 58.4% of Hong Kong's re-export came from China, which accounted for about

43.6% of the territory's total export.[32] Since most of these China-made re-exports came from export processing industries in the Delta, the above figures suggest the heavy involvement of Hong Kong investment in the Delta's export processing sector in 1992.

Useful data about Hong Kong's outward processing in the Delta are now available from a survey of members of the Federation of Hong Kong Industries conducted in 1991.[33] The questionnaire survey achieved a response rate of 78.7% among the 1,596 manufacturing members of the Federation, of which 511 (40.7%) had invested in the Delta.[34] The survey data confirmed the widely held profile of Hong Kong investment in the Delta's export processing. These investments were heavily concentrated in Shenzhen (47.7%) and Dongguan (20.3%), which were closer to Hong Kong than other areas in the Delta.[35] Over 43% of the plants were wholly foreign-owned enterprises because it allowed for more autonomy for the owner while 22.6% and 9.1% were respectively equity and cooperative joint ventures.[36] The establishment of these plants tended to be medium-sized with the average of 787 workers per enterprise.[37] The majority (57.5%) of these 511 investors in the Delta were employing less than 500 workers, and another 17.6% employed between 500 and 1,000. The remaining 22.6% employed between 1,000 to 2,000 while 11.7% hired 2,000 or more.[38] The investment of these firms was, however, relatively small. Of the 511 investors who responded, over 60% had invested under HK$10 million; only 17.6% had invested over HK$20 million.[39]

Perhaps more importantly, this survey showed that the factors that led to the growing spread of Hong Kong investment to the Delta were unlikely to vanish soon. "Severe labour shortage" (85.9%) and "high land price" in Hong Kong (52.5%) were ranked the most important push factors that motivated the investors to move to the Delta.[40] On the other hand, the single most important attraction of the Delta identified by 96.7% of the respondents was the proximity to Hong Kong, which facilitated transportation, management as well as technical support.[41] Other attractions included the ample supply of land, the preferential policies and flexible administration of local governments and the relatively cheap labour force. In spite of the continuing interest of Hong Kong businesses in export processing in the Delta, several problems still remained. Among these were included concerns over the unreliable quality of labour, shortage of energy, confusing legislations and regulations, congestion at the Man Kam To border post and under-developed back-up industries.[42] Nonetheless, because of satisfactory performance, over 43% of the investors would like to expand while about 50% would maintain their operations in the Delta.[43] If the Delta wants to keep these outward processing industries, their governments will have to tackle the above-mentioned problems as other neighbouring provinces are also keen to offer similar, if not better, preferential policies to foreign investors. On the other hand, concerned publics in Guangdong have already voiced opposition to the transfer of Hong Kong's polluting industries to the province.[44] Evidently, export processing had helped to generate enormous economic benefits for both the Delta and Hong Kong, but the Delta's governments will have to maintain a conducive investment environment while dealing with the increasing social and environmental problems caused by these industries.

The Pearl River Delta is an attractive site for overseas manufacturing and service sectors alike because of its strategic location and its familiarity with capitalist business practices. The service sector in Hong Kong has begun to take advantage of the low operating costs in China, especially the Delta. If some firms have moved labour-intensive operations north of the border, others have begun importing skilled staff from the Delta. In September 1992, Hong Kong's Cathay Pacific Airline decided to transfer its entire accounting service to Guangzhou because of Hong Kong's rising labour costs and rent.[45] Despite the need to pay extra fees and subsidies, two of Hong Kong's largest banks have planned to import a total of 400 university-educated bank tellers from Guangzhou in 1993 for two-year contracts because of difficulties in local recruitment and high turnover rates.[46] To be sure, this development is only at an initial stage, but it reflects the complementarity and thriving economic integration of the Delta and Hong Kong. Some observers believe that if the trend accelerates, Hong Kong employees in the service sector may suffer the fate of their counterpart in the manufacturing sector.[47] Nonetheless, it seems more plausible that only back office operation, which requires no direct contacts between customers and employees, would be more affected.[48] It would, however, be uneconomic to relocate small operations, in which two-thirds of the employment in Hong Kong's companies fall, as they often have less than one hundred staff. Most of the employment in the civil service as well as in social and personal services will have to remain as it is. While a small percentage of total employment may be relocatable (estimated to be about 4.3% of the total workforce), large-scale transfer of front line services from Hong Kong's service sector to the mainland might not be that feasible, at least in the foreseeable future.[49]

Growing Hong Kong Involvement in Infrastructural Development

The rapid growth of the Pearl River Delta since the late 1980s had compelled long term planning and investment in its infrastructure, but such facilities were soon overtaken by ever faster economic growth. Hong Kong interest in infrastructural projects intensified in 1992 in response to the favourable political and economic environments in China. While a number of Hong Kong firms invested in the Delta's infrastructural development, the master in this area remained Gordon Wu's Hopewell Holdings, which transformed the entire face of the Delta with its construction of highways, bridges and power plants.[50] In 1992, many more Hong Kong magnates developed a keener interest in the Delta's infrastructural projects, and their financing moved with full force.

The improvement of land transport made notable strides in 1992. One of the major developments in rail service was the construction of a RMB180 million new railway station in Foshan. A through-train service between Foshan and Hong Kong began in early January 1993, the second such links in China, which will ease the load on the Kowloon-Guangzhou through-train, especially during the holiday seasons.[51] In early 1993, the State Council also approved the construction of a 147-kilometer Guangzhou-Zhuhai railway as well as another 29.5-kilometer branch between Doumen town and Zhuhai's Gaolan port with a view to connect it with Macau.[52] Perhaps even more important were efforts to improve highway construction in 1992. Despite earlier criticisms from some Guangdong officials of delays in construction, Hopewell Holdings still pledged to finish the 122-kilometer superhighway between Guangzhou and Shenzhen before 30 June 1993.[53] The firm also secured the contracts for the construction of two key projects: a US$1.95 billion contract to build a 110-kilometer section of the second phase of the Guangzhou-Shenzhen-Zhuhai superhighway and a 38-kilometer ring road in Guangzhou.[54] Unlike earlier projects, Hopewell could build the roads without a Chinese joint-venture partner, and land acquisition would be done by Guangdong's provincial government to avoid delays. Even more ambitiously, Zhuhai planned to build a 49.3-kilometer cross-estuary bridge connecting its eastern district with Hong Kong's Tuen Mun, which would cost an estimated RMB10 billion, but the plan has not drawn an enthusiastic response from the Hong Kong government.[55]

Improvement of city transport was also high on the agenda in the Delta administrations because of rapid economic growth and the subsequent urban expansion and redevelopment. Cooperating with a major Hong Kong developer, Shenzhen carried out a feasibility study of a 12.6-kilometer light-rail transit system for the SEZ, although the plan which involved an estimated investment of up to RMB1.2 billion was not yet finalized.[56] Another feasibility study of a RMB11 billion subway system for Shenzhen, which was planned to be operative by 1996, was also underway.[57] Similarly, Yue Xiu Enterprises, Guangzhou municipal government's investment corporation in Hong Kong, was examining the possibility of constructing a light railway in Guangzhou.[58] In all, the project that received the greatest attention in 1992 was the planned construction of a subway system in Guangzhou. Hong Kong businessmen rapidly concluded a series of contracts in property development along the subway while investors from Europe and North America were attracted by the huge construction contracts.

The construction of deep-water ports has been the key development in water transport in the Delta. Reflecting the burgeoning trade, the volume of twenty-foot equivalent units (TEU) in the estuary traffic between Hong Kong and the Delta area in 1992 increased by about 3.8 times.[59] In addition to the inauguration of a container port in Shekou in August 1991, Shenzhen's Yantian port was officially designated open to the outside world in November 1992 and was earmarked for long-term development, while Zhuhai was also planning to upgrade the facilities of Gaolan deep-water port.[60] These two ports are cargo ports with general as well as container facilities, but it may take some time before they can reach full capacity.

Efforts at improving air transport in the Delta were also remarkable. As the construction of the proposed Chek Lap Kok airport in Hong Kong was clouded in uncertainty because of its huge financial cost and the growing Sino-British disagreement over political reform in Hong Kong, Shenzhen's new Huangtian airport inevitably received much attention. The first phase of this two-runway airport was inaugurated in 1992, and the construction of the second phase immediately began, but it will not reach its full capacity for a few years yet.[61] At present, Huangtian has only one runway and handles mainly domestic flights with about 200,000 passengers per month.[62] Its first international passenger flight, to Singapore, will have commenced in April 1993. However, some Chinese officials floated the idea of using Huangtian and other airports in the Delta as replacements for Hong Kong's future airport in view of the Sino-British row.[63] Zhuhai was also keen on improving its Sanzhao airport, a former military airport, which would be completed by 1994 for flights between Zhuhai and Beijing as well as between Zhuhai and Hong Kong.[64] Plans for a second runway for Zhuhai's airport was also raised.[65] With Baiyuan as the sole regional airport in South China, Guangzhou, too, had plans to spend RMB4 billion to build a new airport to cater to the rising domestic traffic.[66] By the end of 1992, there were already five airports in the Delta area, excluding Hong Kong's Kai Tak, and another three new ones (in Macau, Zhuhai, Guangzhou) will be built in the 1990s.[67] Since South China will have rapid economic growth rates in the 1990s, these new airports are unlikely to substitute for a new airport in Hong Kong because they have to absorb the growing passenger and freight needs at home. In terms of international passengers and freight volume, Hong Kong's airport still ranks the fourth in the entire world, and it also has a significant edge in equipment and experience over the budding competitors in the Delta.[68]

One comprehensive development project that deserved special attention concerned the construction of Nansha Economic Development Zone in the southeastern part of Panyu.[69] Strategically located at the mouth of the Pearl River estuary and 70 miles northwest of Hong Kong, Nansha was officially designated a port open to the outside world in early January 1992 and granted various preferential policies in luring foreign investment.[70] With Hong Kong's Discovery Bay in mind, tycoon Henry Fok Ying-tung planned to erect a 22-square-kilometer new town with transportation, residential, commercial, tourist, and even scientific and cultural functions.[71] According to this vision, not only will Nansha's road network be improved, but a 10,000-ton port with a container terminal will also be constructed and ferry service will be increased to relieve the heavy freight load between Hong Kong and the Delta. If the above projects are successfully completed in the 1990s — this requires an injection of an estimated HK$10 billion — it will make Nansha a nexus in the growing trade and transport of the Delta.[72] Similarly, Dongguan and Hong Kong's Hutchison Whampoa have also signed a letter of intent about the feasibility of building a deep-water port and industrial zone in Shatian on the eastern bank of the Pearl River and northeast of Nansha.[73]

An unprecedented number of contracts covering a plethora of infrastructural projects in the Delta were signed in 1992, but many of these proposed projects will not be completed until the mid- or late 1990s. Aside from the above-mentioned developments, other big infrastructural projects that were pending included Guangdong's plan to construct four power plants (of which two will be located in Taishan and Zhuhai) and another nuclear power plant in Yangjiang or Daya Bay, which will use about RMB100 billion of investment.[74] Hopewell also secured a US$750 million syndicated loan to build the Shajiao C power plant.[75] The provincial government already pledged its support for the construction of many of these projects and an estimated RMB17.64 billion will be spent in 1993.[76] Since the upgrading of infrastructural facilities remains a key objective of Guangdong, the role of Hong Kong in these projects is critical. Apart from injecting capital and organizing financing, Hong Kong can offer valuable experience in highway and subway construction, airport management, port development, and even new town planning. However, some scholars have already questioned the wisdom of duplicating basic construction in the area, such as the uncoordinated construction of three deep-water ports (i.e. Shenzhen's Yantian port, Daya Bay's Huizhou port, and Zhuhai's Gaolan port).[77] Whether some coordination in planning among these different projects deserves some serious thoughts, it is certain, however, that Hong Kong will continue to play a strategic role in the Delta's infrastructure in the 1990s.[78]

Volatile Growth of Real Estate Development

In 1992, all localities in the Pearl River Delta from Guangzhou to the SEZs witnessed a year of frenzied commercial and residential property development. Advertisements of Delta real estate conspicuously flooded the front pages of major Chinese newspapers in Hong Kong. These development projects were often carried out by Hong Kong's smaller manufacturers who had close connections with various local governments rather than by major developers who targeted mostly prime real estate.[79] Given the low lending rates in Hong Kong and the high real estate prices in the territory without reprieve in sight, speculation over real estate in the Delta became the latest conduit for Hong Kong buyers, especially the smaller ones.[80] Series of Chinese real estate exhibitions and seminars were held in Hong Kong's exhibition centres and premium hotels in 1992, often attracting sizeable crowds.

China's big cities like Beijing, Tianjin, Shanghai, Wuhan and Dalian joined the foray in luring Hong Kong real estate investors, but the Pearl River Delta apparently enjoyed an edge over other competitors because of its close social ties as well as its geographical proximity to Hong Kong. In the first half of 1992 alone, an estimated HK$ 9.9 billion worth of Chinese real estate with a size of 20 million square feet was on sale in Hong Kong.

Of the total area offered for sale, about 80% was located in the Pearl River Delta.[81] Another estimate suggested that over 80,000 housing units in the Delta had been put on sale in Hong Kong, almost four times the territory's own supply.[82] Consequently, the prices of real estate in the Delta went up considerably. By the end of 1992, the price per square meter in Guangzhou and Shenzhen, for instance, had risen respectively from RMB700 to RMB2,200 and from RMB750 to RMB1,650 compared with late 1991.[83]

By the fourth quarter of 1992, both the central and local governments had recognized the urgent need to impose more restrictions on the overheated development of property in the Delta. In late September, Guangdong's provincial government restricted the total residential area for sales to overseas citizens developed by foreign-invested companies and local firms to respectively under 20% and 10% of the total residential area completed each year.[84] Furthermore, 20% of the total capital for housing projects was to be invested and at least 25% of the construction to be completed before offering for pre-sales.[85] In October, the Land Administration Bureau of the provincial government further ordered that the development of land for agricultural use and for non-agricultural land development above respectively 50 and 100 *mu* (1 *mu* = 0.0667 hectares) of land had to get provincial level approval. Other corrective actions were also taken by the Delta's local governments. Guangzhou, for instance, planned to set up a Property Agent Management Office to strengthen its regulation of the secondary property market.[86] Dongguan, on the other hand, centralized the power to develop real estate from counties and towns to the municipal government.[87] By early December, the provincial government had further standardized land management with a trial measure that aimed to centralize the development of land under various land administration offices.[88] In sum, local governments in the Delta, many of whom had earlier offered bargain prices, were beginning to realize that more regulations were necessary to prevent further speculation, protect their own interests and calm down the overheated market.

The craze over Pearl River Delta real estate in the first half of the year had been subdued by autumn partly because of the above-mentioned administrative intervention and partly because of the growing recognition of the risks involved in such investment among Hong Kong's buyers. Local governments in the Delta were keen on property development, but their management of the land market was not yet mature. For instance, over 96% of Shenzhen's land-use rights had been sold through agreement in 1987–1990.[89] Only in June 1992 did Shenzhen carry out the first public auctioning of land use rights over a commercial and residential lot.[90] While there were only eighteen complaints lodged in Hong Kong's Consumer Council on property sales in China, the dangers of volatile property development in the Delta were obvious for investors and users alike.[91] Several instances of legal suits concerning disputes in the purchase of residential flats reflected the inadequacy of the legal and administrative framework in the Delta. More importantly still, whether the flats were going to be built as scheduled because of rising construction costs was also not entirely clear. One estimate suggested that construction costs had risen from HK$200 per square foot in 1991 to more than HK$350 in 1992 and would possibly be much higher in 1993.[92] Other developments also cast shadows on the frantic market. The growth of supply put pressure on prices and depressed the market, as exemplified by a 10% drop in Shenzhen's property prices between the fourth quarter of 1992 and late February 1993.[93] Therefore, the Delta's real estate market in 1993 will probably enter into a phase of consolidation, rather than repeat the frenzy of 1992. The overheating of the property market reflected the slow development of effective regulation as well as the hazard of collaboration between local governments and overseas investors in real estate development without proper planning. Similar problems were amply reflected in the fever over stocks in the Delta.

Mania over the Stock Market

The desire to develop a flourishing stock market was a major preoccupation of Shenzhen and Guangzhou, the two economic centres in the Pearl River Delta in 1992. Shenzhen's Securities Exchange was opened in December 1990, after Shanghai, but it was rocked by a series of difficulties in 1992. The official suspension of trading of the stocks of a joint-venture with over twenty subsidiaries doing business in textile, trade, real estate was to remain controversial and unsettled as it raised the specter of indiscriminate government intervention.[94] But this was soon overshadowed by the crisis created by the issuance of fourteen new shares in early August that led to an invasion of Shenzhen by an estimated one million frantic share-seekers from all over China.[95]

The scale of the debacle and the lack of crisis management skills of the Shenzhen government aroused much concern and controversy both inside and outside China. The Shenzhen government had priced each of 5 million drawing tickets a substantial RMB100, which was to generate instantly

RMB500 million in revenue. The limited supply of the issue certificates, the police's harsh treatment of the unruly crowds queuing outside selling outlets, the outright abuse of power by police and other staff in pocketing the forms and their quick sell-out stirred up an angry demonstration against the government on 10 August. The fiasco renewed central attention over the dangers of poorly planned reforms as Vice-Premier Zou Jiahua immediately went to Shenzhen in the midst of the incident, an unusual move that reflected the seriousness of the problem.[96] Although the mass uproar abated, and the incident was resolved by additional issues and computerized drawing of the winners, the poor management of the crisis by the most "special" region of China had send a powerful message to Chinese leaders and overseas investors alike.[97] Not only did the incident reflect the dangers of the get-rich-quick mentality and popular ignorance, it also highlighted the incompetence of Shenzhen's authorities as well as the rampant irregularities and corruption among officials and staff of financial institutions. By mid-December, it was known that the scandal had involved over 4,000 cadres and staff working in the financial sector, who had withheld at least 150,399 drawing tickets.[98] The mishandling of the crisis also led to the downfall of its Mayor, Zheng Liangyu, and his replacement by Li Youwei. In sum, the Shenzhen incident aptly revealed the risk of fast-paced market reforms in the absence of a sound legal and administrative system, which may lead to corruption, disruption and reform failure.

Shenzhen's stock market enjoyed a year of rapid growth despite the above-mentioned difficulties. As the only market in South China, Shenzhen attracted investors from all over China and firms that were eager to get listed on the exchange. By the end of 1992, the number of A shares listings traded in Shenzhen's Securities Exchange had increased from 6 to 22 and the number of B shares listings had jumped to 9, which respectively registered a total market value at RMB50 billion and RMB7 billion.[99] The trading volume of the Exchange had increased more than five times over 1991 to RMB43.8 billion.[100] By late 1992, the stock index stood at 241.2055, as compared to only 110.3688 in late 1991.[101] Furthermore, Shenzhen sought to list its B share stocks in the Stock Exchange of Vancouver, Canada.[102] While the People's Bank of China supported the listing of three Shenzhen-listed stocks in Vancouver, the Securities Committee under the State Council remained more cautious about foreign-listing; and the plan had yet to materialize by February 1993.[103] Unlike Shenzhen, Guangzhou failed to achieve its long-stated goal of opening the third securities exchange in China after Shanghai and Shenzhen. Since there was competition from other areas in the north, most notably Tianjin, and the August incident in Shenzhen had further revealed the perils of hasty reforms, the central government was unwilling to open soon the third securities exchange in Guangzhou. Consequently, Guangzhou chose instead to allow its better established enterprises to issue more internal stocks and to list their stocks in Shanghai, Shenzhen or Hong Kong. In fact, Hong Kong has provided a useful reference for financial reform in China. Not only is the issuance of huge amount of new shares often smooth and orderly, which sharply contrasts with what happened in Shenzhen, but the management of the stock exchange also follows internationally accepted standards. Listing in Hong Kong's stock market would provide a useful venue for the Delta to learn from a far more established capitalist stock market.

In spite of the August incident in Shenzhen, the deepening of financial reform gained momentum in 1992. In the wake of the Shenzhen incident, Governor Zhu Senlin made clear that experiments in shareholding and the listing of firms in the stock market would continue.[104] With a booming economy and staunch central level support for building a market economy, the establishment of specialized markets for commodities and capital in the Delta became the next logical step. The first of its kind in China, Shenzhen's Exchange for Heavy Metals was inaugurated on 18 January.[105] Together with three mainland partners, Guangdong Enterprises established one of China's three national brokerage houses in Shenzhen in December with a registered paid-up capital of RMB350 million.[106] Having been granted legislative power in 1992, Shenzhen's new Mayor, Li Youwei, promised to establish the legal framework necessary for a market economy within two to three years.[107] Aspiring to become a major regional financial centre, Shenzhen has formulated an ambitious plan to speed up the establishment of five markets in 1993: a market for transferring property rights, a futures market for major commodities, a foreign exchange market, a gold market, and a market for scientific and technological products.[108] Guangzhou, too, will inaugurate China's first general commodities exchange in August 1993.[109] Whether these markets are actually set up on time and are run well, it is too early to tell, but the emergence of specialized markets has become a top priority of Delta governments. Contrary to the long-held negative view towards market activities, Guangzhou's Mayor, Li Ziliu, even boldly "cleared the names" of speculation (*touji*) and profiteering (*daoba*) arguing that these behaviours were necessary to accord with the laws of prices and were legitimate as long as they were within legal boundaries.[110] In view of the huge amount of cash in the people's hands, their enthusiasm for earning quick money, and the lack of investment outlets, lessons from 1992 strongly suggest that unless a sound legal and administrative framework is established and a high-calibre cadre corps is in charge, financial reforms may not bring about the desired results, but rather chaos and frustration.

Growing Social and Cultural Ties between Hong Kong and the Delta

The extensive social and cultural links between Hong Kong and the Pearl River Delta have been developing rapidly in the reform era. Several important developments in telecommunications, information industry, and consumer culture are worth closer scrutiny. Telecommunications in the Pearl River Delta have progressed by leaps and bounds in the reform era but still cannot keep up with the demand because of its phenomenal economic growth. For instance, about 130,000 people apply each year for telephone installation in Guangzhou, but only 60,000 customers can get the service.[111] Nonetheless, Guangdong province and the Delta are already ahead of the nation in this area. For instance, Guangdong alone boasts of an estimated 60% of China's total number of pagers (1 million) and over 57% of its mobile telephones (about 70,000).[112] Keenly aware of the strategic significance of a sound telecommunication network for economic development, Guangdong's government has decided to invest US$850 million to upgrade its telephone network. An optics fibre cable link between Guangzhou and Zhuhai as well as alongside the existing cable between Guangzhou and Hong Kong will be constructed with a view to extend it further to Macau and connect with that of Hong Kong in the future.[113] A "one-stop shopping" agreement between Hong Kong Telecom and Guangdong's Posts and Telecommunications Bureau has also been concluded to facilitate the efficiency of telecommunication links between the two areas because the province will be responsible for handling technical problems on its side of the border.[114]

Owing to the fierce competition in Hong Kong and the potential of the China market, the Delta has become a battle ground for Hong Kong's telephone and paging companies. In 1992, Hutchison Whampoa became the first foreign company to operate a mobile-phone service in Guangdong while Hong Kong Telecom also planned to expand its card calling service in the Delta because many of Hong Kong's industrial manufacturers were located there.[115] The rapid spread of pagers in the Delta was amazing as well. For instance, Guangzhou doubled the number of pager users in 1992 to 300,000, possibly the highest among China's cities.[116] Shenzhen, too, claimed an estimated 180,000 pager users, about 7.5 pagers per 100 people, while Zhongshan's urban district boasted an even higher average of 14 pagers per 100 people, which is close to Hong Kong's record of 17 per 100 people.[117] In 1992, Hong Kong companies launched cross-border services in Guangdong, covering most of the key cities in the Delta, by using the same frequency in both the Delta and Hong Kong or using pagers that allowed for fine-tuning of different frequencies.[118] A joint venture between Guangdong firms and Hong Kong firms was also set up to launch a three-way pager network on the same frequency covering Hong Kong, Macau and Guangdong.[119] These developments in 1992 aptly reflected the continuing lead of the Delta in telecommunications.

The Pearl River Delta also became the springboard from which foreign investors in information services ventured into the China market. Spending in advertising in Guangdong rose 40% in 1992, of which Guangzhou accounted for a fifth of the total, or about RMB635 million.[120] The Delta had grown more receptive to joint ventures in information services since Deng Xiaoping's visit in early January. Together with Shanghai, Guangzhou emerged as one of China's leaders in advertising as its production and management became increasingly sophisticated.[121] In the first half of 1992 alone, thirteen new joint-venture advertising firms, including many of Hong Kong's advertising giants, were formed in Guangzhou, which brought the total to 43.[122] While still mostly servicing foreign-owned firms and joint ventures, these companies were to promote advertising in the Delta as well as keep themselves well placed for venturing into the entire China market.

Close attention should also be paid to the growing influence of Hong Kong TV in the Delta, which helped make Hong Kong the "entertainment capital" of the Hong Kong–Guangdong–Macau region.[123] An estimated 30% of Guangdong's 63 million population, notably in the Delta, regularly watched Hong Kong TV.[124] This huge audience inevitably caught the attention of businesses on both sides of the border. Guangdong's manufacturers (from medicine and cosmetics to consumer appliances), often not as competitive in the Hong Kong market, were airing commercials on Hong Kong's TV in order to lure consumers in the Delta. With the inauguration of Star TV, which has a *putonghua* channel, the extension of *putonghua* hours in Hong Kong's programming, and the increase in joint

TV productions, Hong Kong's businesses paid increasing attention in their advertising to their potential consumers in South China.[125] Other aspects of leisure life in the Delta was also strongly shaped by Hong Kong. Hong Kong's entertainment industry was boosted by this new market across the border as its pop singers were performing in Guangzhou and Shenzhen far more frequently than before. After holding its first horse-racing last year and with assistance from the Royal Hong Kong Jockey Club, Guangzhou was building a second modern race course with a capacity of 40,000 people.[126] The city would also launch a Hong Kong-styled lottery scheme, albeit both horse-racing and lottery would be for charity purposes rather than for gambling. Evidently, Hong Kong's popular culture is and will continue to exert a strong influence on the Delta.

In view of the relaxation of central policy towards foreign investment in the service sector and the rising purchasing power of people in the Delta, the developments in telecommunications and the emergence of a Hong Kong-styled consumption culture in the Delta have had substantial economic consequences. Since the autumn of 1991, the involvement of Hong Kong in the Delta's retail industry has gained momentum, as exemplified by the creation of special counters selling Hong Kong products in Guangzhou's Nanfang Dasha in November 1991, one of China's largest department stores.[127] While Hong Kong companies had set up specialized counters in department stores in the Delta and had sold wholesale their products through agents for several years, the opening of their own stores became increasingly popular in 1992. Tapping the influence of Hong Kong's styles in the Delta, Hong Kong's fastfood chains and fashion shops set up outlets in Shenzhen and Guangzhou and will soon venture into other areas of the Delta in the future.[128] Four of Hong Kong's banks opened branch offices in Guangzhou in 1992, albeit they were still barred from handling *Renminbi* business for the time being.[129] The Bank of China also set up automated-teller machines in three cities in the Delta and planned to expand the service to four others in 1993 and connect it to its Hong Kong network by the end of 1993.[130] The growing Hong Kong investment in these areas will not only contribute to a faster growth of the Delta's tertiary sector, but also further integrate the consumer markets of the two areas, which will be of significant economic benefits to Hong Kong.

Prospects in the 1990s

What are the prospects of the Delta in view of the rapid changes in China's political economy in the past year or so? Since the Delta comprises localities with different economic potential and strengths, their responses to opportunities and challenges in the 1990s will obviously differ. Hence, my observations are only rather general and tentative. In general, both domestic and external factors still seem to be conducive to the development of the Delta in the 1990s. For instance, the sustained growth of China's economy (12% in 1992), the strength of Hong Kong's economic foundation, and the continued improvement of infrastructural facilities both inside and outside the Delta (such as the planned completion of the Beijing-Guangzhou Highway before the year 2000) will further drive the economic growth of the Delta area.[131] Guangdong Governor Zhu Senlin's report to Guangdong's People Congress in January 1993 highlighted not only the need to speed up reform and opening but also the target of maintaining a GDP growth rate of 13.4% in the 1990s and multiplying by eight times the GDP between 1980 and 2000 in order to reach a per capita GDP of RMB7,200.[132] The Delta will undoubtedly play a critical role in this plan for faster development. Nonetheless, several challenges are looming on the horizon.

First, while the flexibility and ambitions of local governments in the Delta might be key factors explaining its spectacular success in the 1980s, these governments will have to improve their administrative and legal systems if they are to maintain the lead in the 1990s. Flexibility was a virtue in avoiding the malaise of a rigid state bureaucracy in the 1980s, but when the entire country is steering towards a market economy, then only areas that can provide a better legal and administrative framework will succeed in offering a more attractive investment environment. In fact, many legislations on the stock market and property development have been promulgated by both the central and local governments, but their effective implementation remains to be seen. The experience in the real estate and stock markets in the Pearl River Delta in 1992 suggests that the loopholes of the existing system still offer excellent opportunities for official graft and other irregularities.

Secondly, the Delta has to face keener competition in acquiring foreign investment in the 1990s as many areas in China are opening up for foreign investors as well as offering similar, if not more favourable, preferential policies. Although the Delta enjoys the reputation of being a star in reform and Hong Kong's neighbour, the rising labour, rental and other costs will drive some labour-intensive operations out of the Delta and perhaps out of Guangdong in the future.[133] The year 1992 also witnessed the diversion of Hong Kong investment from Guangdong to other provinces with potential for future growth. For instance, Wharf Holdings has already planned to extend Hong Kong's hinterland well beyond Guangdong into central and western parts of China by redeveloping the infrastructure of Wuhan.[134] Other Hong Kong firms like New World, Hutchison Whampoa and even Hopewell have also been extending their investment in China beyond Guangdong to other areas ranging from Guangxi to Beijing and Shanghai.[135]

Thirdly, while the Delta can still claim an edge in producing for the domestic Chinese market, it will face new challenges in the world market in the wake of slow economic recovery among all major capitalist countries. The inauguration of Bill Clinton as the new US President and a Democrat-controlled Congress will inject new uncertainties into Sino-US trade ties because of Clinton's advocacy of human rights and democracy. The date of China's re-entry into the General Agreement on Tariffs and Trade (GATT) is still uncertain. The opening of Vietnam and even Burma would enhance competition for the labour-intensive export processing business while the implementation of the North American Free Trade Agreement may also turn Mexico into a natural site for labour-intensive manufacturing for North America.

Finally, the political and economic significance of the interdependence between Hong Kong and the Delta will grow in the 1990s.[136] Three factors explain the growing significance of this relationship. Governments on both sides of the border have recognized the importance of this interdependent relationship. At present, they have already been cooperating on a number of fronts ranging from water supply, environmental management and border control to anti-corruption and criminal investigation, especially anti-smuggling. In August 1992, the Hong Kong government's urban planners already suggested that its land use, transport and environment plans should take into account the development of the Delta.[137] In January 1993, the Hong Kong government commissioned a HK$3.3 million project to a consultancy firm to study Guangdong's economic and land development with a view to coordinating the overall development planning of the territory with its neighbour.[138] After setting up offices in Beijing and Shanghai, Hong Kong's Trade Development Council opened its third China office in Guangzhou in order to promote trade and provide information and consultation, especially in the Delta area.[139] Such developments, which have not been deterred by the Sino-British split over Hong Kong's constitutional reform, signal an inevitable trend. It has clearly become too costly for one side to ignore the developments of the other.

Further, the economic takeoff in the Pearl River Delta area has contributed significantly to the prosperity as well as social and political stability of the Delta and Hong Kong in the 1980s. On the one hand, the Delta's rapid economic growth has become a crucial asset in legitimizing the still lingering Communist political system. On the other hand, the growth of the Delta has enriched a broad spectrum of Hong Kong's population, ranging from truck drivers and small factory owners to big developers and investors. The economic opportunities in South China have alleviated the social and political uneasiness that would otherwise have been quite substantial in the run-up to 1997. The Delta's economic boom has indeed buffered the impending incorporation of Hong Kong into China. Last but not least, the experience of Hong Kong in a wide range of fields will continue to be valuable for the Pearl River Delta in the 1990s. Aside from acting as a key financier and intermediary in the Delta's trade and investment, Hong Kong still has much to offer in areas as diverse as property development, trade, insurance, finance, international banking, urban planning, media and advertising, telecommunications, as well as public administration and law.[140]

Conclusion

The Pearl River Delta has benefited substantially from the favourable political environment and economic opportunities in 1992. To be sure, the pattern of Delta development is probably a unique example in China's reform era because it enjoys enormous geographical and policy advantages over other parts of China. For some, it seems that its experience cannot be applied to other regions in China. Such a conclusion seems to be premature, however. While the Delta's developmental model may not be wholly transferrable to other areas, different aspects of its experience, such as introducing price and financial reforms, attracting foreign investment and venturing into the world market, will continue to be relevant and useful for China as a whole. Together with the growing economic and social integration between Hong Kong and the Pearl River Delta, the significance of the Delta for China's modernization will increase. The emergence of a greater Delta economic region with Hong Kong as its centre will also take a more definite shape in the 1990s.

Notes

1. See, for example *Business Week*, 6 April 1992, pp. 42–43; *The Economist*, 5 October 1991, pp. 19–22; *Fortune*, 9 March 1992, pp. 71–75.
2. This definition differs from the Pearl River Delta Open Economic Area which comprises twenty-eight municipalities and counties in the Delta while excluding Guangzhou, Shenzhen and Zhuhai. My definition is thus the same as the one used in Pak Wai Liu et al., *China's Economic Reform and Development Strategy of the Pearl River Delta* (Hong Kong: Nanyang Commercial Bank Ltd., 1992).
3. *Guangdong Statistical Year-book 1992*, pp. 93, 95, 350 and 369.
4. *Ibid.*, pp. 184 and 189.
5. *Ibid.*, pp. 229 and 232.
6. *Ibid.*, p. 95. The average per capita national income of the forty-nine mountainous counties was only RMB1,133.5 in 1991.
7. *Guangdong Statistical Year-book 1992*, p. 399; State Statistical Bureau, *A Statistical Survey of China 1992* (Beijing: Zhongguo tongji chubanshe, 1992), p. 45.
8. Liu (see Note 2), p. 3.
9. *Ming Pao* (Hong Kong), 25 February 1993, p. 8; also see 12 December 1992, p. 8.
10. "China Business Review," *South China Morning Post* (Hong Kong, *SCMP*), 27 September 1992, p. 1.
11. For instance, Panyu county could only approve foreign investment under US$5 million, but as a municipality, it can decide on such projects up to US$30 million. See, for example *Hong Kong Economic Journal*, 6 April 1992, p. 3.
12. *Ming Pao*, 20 July 1992, p. 6.
13. The study by Liu et al. (Note 2) is by far the most updated and best treatment of the economic development of the Pearl River Delta. Also see Ezra Vogel, *One Step Ahead in China: Guangdong under Reform* (Cambridge, MA: Harvard University Press, 1989), chaps. 4–7.
14. Liu (see Note 2), p. 2.
15. Vogel (see Note 13), chap. 3.
16. For a useful summary of these preferential policies, see Wan Zuoxin, et al. (eds.), *A Guide to Investment in Guangdong Province* (Tianjin: Tianjin kexue jishu chubanshe, 1990).
17. Liu (see Note 2), p. 38.
18. For a more systematic treatment in English, see Liu (Note 2) and Vogel (Note 13).
19. *Nanfang ribao*, 4 May 1992, pp. 1 and 3.

20. *Nanfang ribao*, 10 May 1992, pp. 1 and 3.
21. Figures are estimates provided by the Trade Department of the Hong Kong Government, see *Hong Kong Economic Journal*, 6 March 1993, p. 5.
22. *Wen Wei Po* (Hong Kong), 7 December 1992, p. 2; also see Willy Wo-lap Lam's analysis in this book.
23. *Nanfang ribao*, 9 January 1993, p. 1.
24. *Nanfang ribao*, 30 January 1993, p. 1.
25. *Nanfang ribao*, 9 January 1993, p. 1.
26. *Nanfang ribao*, 5 January 1993, p. 1; 26 January 1993, p. 1.
27. *Wen Wei Po*, 7 December 1992, p. 2.
28. *Wen Wei Po*, 11 December 1992, p. 17.
29. *Nanfang ribao*, 25, 26 and 28 January 1993, p. 1.
30. *Ming Pao*, 29 June 1991, p. 34.
31. The following statistics are from *SCMP*, 19 February 1993, Business, p. 1.
32. *Hong Kong Economic Journal*, 16 February 1993, p. 6.
33. Industry and Research Division, Hong Kong Federation of Industries, *Hong Kong's Industrial Investment in the Pearl River Delta* (Hong Kong: Hong Kong Federation of Industries, 1992).
34. *Ibid.*, p. 9; The response rate of specific questions varies. Hence the results of the survey are based on the responses of these 511 investors. I suspect that many more small-scale investors are not covered by this survey.
35. *Ibid.*, p. 13.
36. *Ibid.*, pp. 14–15.
37. *Ibid.*, p. 18.
38. Only 2.2% of the respondents did not answer, *ibid.*, p. 31.
39. *Ibid.*, pp. 16 and 32. Respondents who gave no answer amounted to 14.1%.
40. *Ibid.*, p. 11.
41. *Ibid.*, p. 12.
42. *Ibid.*, p. 35. Another survey of the members of the Chinese Manufacturers Association also suggested similar concerns. It should, however, be pointed out that only 5% (180) of the 3,600 members of the association answered the survey. *SCMP*, 8 March 1993, Business p. 3.
43. See Note 33, p. 24.
44. *Ming Pao*, 18 February 1993, p. 59.
45. *International Market News*, Nos. 11–12, 1992, pp. 4–8. Hong Kong Telecom, one of the largest employers in the private sector, was also considering moving its more labour-intensive services such as directory inquiry to China, probably to Shenzhen. *SCMP*, 15 October 1992, Business, p. 1. However, it was suggested recently that the company had decided to abandon the plan because of technical reasons, including the relative unimportant savings and the threat to the morale of Hong Kong employees as a result of the relocation. See *Ming Pao*, 8 March 1993, p. 45.

46. Reported on TVB Jade Channel's news programme, "News Magazine," 27 February 1993. Also see *The Nineties*, April 1993, p. 22.
47. See, for example *Hong Kong Economic Journal*, 19 February 1993, p. 34.
48. *Hang Seng Economic Monthly*, January 1993.
49. *Ibid*. The estimates of the *Hang Seng Economic Monthly* vary across sectors, ranging from the low 1.4% in construction and 4.5% in manufacturing to 8.2% in transport, storage and communications as well as 12.6% in financing, insurance, real estate and business services.
50. For instance, New World Development has invested in the 600-megawatt Zhujiang power plant. *SCMP*, 3 April 1992, Business, p. 6.
51. *Hong Kong Economic Journal*, 6 June 1992, p. 7.
52. *Yue-Gang xinxi bao (GD-HK Information Daily)*, 19 February 1993, p. 1.
53. *SCMP*, 11 October and 24 November 1992, Business, p. 1. Also see *China Trade Report*, January 1993, p. 6.
54. *Ibid*.
55. *Hong Kong Economic Journal*, 9 March 1993, p. 6.
56. *Hong Kong Economic Journal*, 28 March 1992, p. 2; *Ming Pao*, 10 October 1992, p. 37.
57. *Ming Pao*, 9 and 10 February 1993, p. 2.
58. *SCMP*, 27 November 1992, Business, p. 2.
59. *Ming Pao*, 12 February 1993, p. 46.
60. *Ming Pao*, 6 January 1993, p. 2; *SCMP*, 9 August 1993, Money, p. 3.
61. Hong Kong's Kai Tak Airport handles about 20 million passengers per year and the new Chek Lap Kok airport aims for a 35 million capacity, see *Hong Kong Economic Journal*, 3 February 1993, p. 2.
62. *Ibid*. Huangtian's main building claims a handling capacity of 4.75 million passengers per year.
63. *Ibid*.
64. *Ming Pao*, 14 August 1992, p. 81.
65. *SCMP*, 3 February 1993, p. 8.
66. *Ming Pao*, 30 December 1992, p. 8; *Hong Kong Economic Journal*, 3 February 1993, p. 2.
67. *Ming Pao*, 3 February 1993, p. 3.
68. *Hong Kong Economic Journal*, 26 February 1993, p. 2.
69. *Hong Kong Economic Journal*, 11 November 1992, p. 2; *Nanfang ribao*, 6 January 1993, p. 2.
70. *Hong Kong Economic Journal*, 14 December 1992, p. 2; *SCMP*, 20 January 1993, Business, p. 2.
71. *SCMP*, 1 March 1993, Business, p. 2; also see *China–Hong Kong Economic Monthly*, September 1991, pp. 46–47.
72. *Hong Kong Economic Journal*, 11 November 1992, p. 2; see also *China–Hong Kong Economic Monthly*, 15 December 1992, p. 82.

73. *Hong Kong Economic Journal*, 11 June 1992, p. 2.
74. *Hong Kong Economic Journal*, 1 February 1993, p. 2 and 2 February 1993, p. 2; *Ming Pao*, 9 March 1993, p. 57.
75. *Ming Pao*, 17 December 1992, p. 43.
76. *Ming Pao*, 2 February 1993, p. 8; *Nanfang ribao*, 16 February 1993, p. 1.
77. Liu (see Note 2), chap. 8.
78. It was reported that yet another new airport of the size of Hong Kong's Chek Lap Kok may be built in eastern Guangdong. *Ming Pao*, 4 February 1993, p. 7.
79. "China Business Review," *SCMP*, 28 June 1992, p. 5.
80. Real estate prices in Hong Kong rose 60% in 1991 and another 20% in the first six months of 1992. *Far Eastern Economic Review* (*FEER*), 3 December 1992, p. 59.
81. 31.2% in Huiyang (Danshui), 14% in Guangzhou, 11.8% in Shenzhen, 10% in Zhuhai, 4.7% in Foshan, 3.6% in Dongguan, and 2.4% in Zhongshan. The statistics are from *Hong Kong Economic Journal*, 9 September 1992, p. 4. The percentages are calculated by the author.
82. *Ming Pao*, 1 February 1993, p. 2.
83. *Ming Pao*, 29 January 1993, p. 9.
84. *Hong Kong Economic Journal*, 9 January 1993, p. 10.
85. *Ming Pao*, 29 January 1993, p. 9; *SCMP*, 13 January 1993, Property, p. 4.
86. *Ming Pao*, 5 November 1992, p. 9.
87. *Ming Pao*, 6 February 1993, p. 29.
88. *Hong Kong Economic Journal*, 9 January 1993, p. 10; Also see *Ming Pao*, 29 October 1992, p. 64.
89. *Beijing Review*, 9–15 November 1992, p. 16.
90. *Ming Pao*, 28 June 1992, p. 47.
91. *SCMP*, 22 February 1993, p. 3.
92. Owing to nationwide demand for construction materials caused by the acceleration of economic growth, steel and cement prices in southern China rose by 60% and 100% respectively. *FEER*, 3 December 1992, p. 59.
93. *Ming Pao*, 1 March 1993, p. 44.
94. *Hong Kong Economic Journal*, 22 April 1992, p. 6 and 21 July 1992, p. 3; *Ming Pao*, 9 January 1993, p. 8; *SCMP*, 9 July 1992, Business, p. 3.
95. See *Ming Pao* and *SCMP*, 8–12 August, 1992.
96. *SCMP*, 20 November 1992, p. 11.
97. *Ming Pao*, 11 November 1992, p. 9.
98. *Ming Pao*, 17 December 1992, p. 2.
99. *China–Hong Kong Economic Monthly*, No. 18 (15 January 1993), pp. 68–69; also see *GD-HK Information Daily*, 1 February 1993, p. 2.
100. *Ibid.*
101. *GD-HK Information Daily*, 1 February 1993, p. 2.

102. *Hong Kong Economic Journal*, 14 December 1992, p. 3.
103. *SCMP*, 1 March 1993, Business, p. 1.
104. *Nanfang ribao*, 27 September 1992, p. 20.
105. *Hong Kong Economic Journal*, 21 July 1992, p. 6.
106. *SCMP*, 20 January 1993, Business, p. 2.
107. *GD-HK Information Daily*, 19 February 1993, p. 2.
108. *Ming Pao*, 31 December 1992, p. 8, 2 February 1993, p. 8 and 19 February 1993, p. 15.
109. *Hong Kong Economic Journal*, 28 February 1993, p. 3; also see *GD-HK Information Daily*, 2 March 1993, p. 1.
110. *Nanfang ribao*, 28 January 1993, p. 2.
111. *China–Hong Kong Economic Monthly*, 15 August 1992, p. 47.
112. The following draws from information provided in *China–Hong Kong Economic Monthly*, 15 August 1992, p. 43–47.
113. *Ming Pao*, October 20, 1992, p. 54.
114. I owe this point to Mr Henry Lam of Hong Kong Telecom.
115. *The Standard*, 1 January 1993.
116. *Ming Pao*, 28 January 1993, p. 9.
117. *Ming Pao*, 24 February 1993, p. 27; *Nanfang ribao*, 17 January 1993, p. 2.
118. *China–Hong Kong Economic Monthly*, 15 August 1992, p. 45.
119. *SCMP*, 1 January 1993, Business, p. 1.
120. "China Business Review," *SCMP*, 27 September 1992, p. 4.
121. *China–Hong Kong Economic Monthly*, 15 July 1992, p. 28.
122. "China Business Review," *SCMP*, 27 September 1992, pp. 4–5.
123. *SCMP*, 12 November 1992, Business, p. 2.
124. *Hong Kong Economic Daily*, 22 December 1992, p. 10.
125. *China–Hong Kong Economic Monthly*, 15 October 1992, pp. 52–57.
126. *SCMP*, 19 January 1993, p. 8.
127. Research Department, Hong Kong Trade Development Council (HKTDC), *Trade Developments: China's Consumer Market* (Hong Kong: HKTDC, March 1992), p. 33.
128. "China Business Review," *SCMP*, 27 September 1992, p. 1.
129. *Nanfang ribao*, 28 January 1993, p. 1.
130. *Ta Kung Pao* (Hong Kong), 1 December 1992, p. 4.
131. *SCMP*, 7 January 1993, Business, p. 2.
132. *Nanfang ribao*, 10 February 1993, p. 2.
133. *SCMP*, 5 November 1992, Business, p. 3 and 29 November 1992, Money, p. 2.
134. *SCMP*, 6 June 1992, Business, pp. 1–2. Also see *SCMP*, 12 July 1992, Money, pp. 1–2.
135. *Hong Kong Economic Journal*, 19 February 1993, p. 6.
136. In fact, if interdependence can be defined as a high degree of mutual

sensitivity and vulnerability towards changes in two interacting societies, then Hong Kong and the Delta are clearly interdependent. See Robert Keohane and Joseph Nye, *Power and Interdependence* (Boston: Little Brown, 1977).
137. *Ming Pao*, 6 August 1992, p. 2.
138. *Ming Pao*, 8 January 1992, p. 3.
139. *Ming Pao*, 31 November 1992, p. 16.
140. For instance, Shenzhen officials openly acknowledged that they would learn from Hong Kong's laws, see *Ming Pao*, 10 July 1992, p. 6.

19

Population Mobility in the 1980s: China on the Road to an Open Society

Siu Yat-ming and Li Si-ming

I. Introduction

Ever since 1988, hundreds of thousands of migrant workers have periodically flooded the coastal provinces, particularly Guangdong, during the Chinese New Year. The news media have called this stream of migrants "blindfold flow" (*mangliu*). This phenomenon is not new, however. Back in the 1950s there was an even larger scale of spontaneous migration, forcing the Chinese government to take action to stop this unchecked exodus of rural labour population. With the establishment of the commune system in 1958 and the household registration system in 1955 and 1958, peasants were effectively tied to the countryside, and the influx of rural migrants to the cities was controlled.[1] The recent increase in mobile population represents a relaxation of these two controlling mechanisms.

The economic reforms and open policies implemented after 1978 were the major factors contributing to the breakdown of the barriers to population mobility.[2] The contract responsibility system increased the productivity of the peasants, at least in the early days of reform, which led to the abolishment of the commune system in 1983. Peasants were now free to allocate their time, including engaging in non-agricultural activities, as long as they could meet the state production quota. The development of township enterprises funded by the rural collectives promoted nonfarm jobs for surplus rural labour the size of which has been estimated to be in the region of 200 million.[3] The reform of the administrative system in 1983 enabled the city to exercise more direct control over the neighbouring countryside, resulting in closer links between the city and the rural areas. The establishment of special economic zones and the opening of major cities to foreign investment created more job opportunities in the urban areas and thus attracted more rural labour population to migrate into the cities. The policy of allowing certain segments of the population to immigrate and certain parts of the country to speed up reform — specifically, the coastal region with Guangdong and Fujian provinces as pioneers — provided further migration impetus. In response to these changes, the Chinese government carried out several policies in the 1980s to facilitate population mobility, resulting in partial relaxation of the household registration system. These policies testified to and reinforced the increasing mobility of the Chinese society in the 1980s and beyond.

This research is supported in part by Hong Kong Baptist College Research Grant FRG/90–91/II–19.

This chapter attempts to document the changing pattern of population mobility in China, particularly since the launching of the reform policies in 1978. In the next section we shall first describe the major policies enacted in the 1980s to deal with the issue. As the terms migration and mobility have been used in a rather inconsistent manner both in the Chinese language literature and in the official statistical sources, Section III is devoted to a discussion of the data and definition problem. Section IV presents a detailed analysis of the mobility pattern in the 1980s. In the final section we discuss the implications of population mobility for the openness of the Chinese society.

II. Policies Facilitating Population Mobility in the 1980s

Two major policies were formulated in the mid-1980s to address the issue of the increasing need for population mobility induced by the economic reform and open policies.

The first policy tackled the problem by restricting peasants to live in market towns. The State Council issued a *Circular on Peasants Settling Down in Towns* on 13 October 1984, which opened 60,000 market towns below county level for peasants to reside for business purposes.[4] The government encouraged the peasants to move into small or medium-sized market towns to start their own business so as to facilitate urban construction and improve the supply of fresh produce. The migrants were given the status of non-agricultural residents, but they received no subsidy for buying staple food. In sharp contrast to the pre-reform era, they were allowed to build houses in the market towns. This policy opened the avenue for the peasants to move in and settle down, with or without their household registration changed.

The other policy dealt with regulations on population administration. The People's Congress enacted the *Regulations on Identity Cards for Residents of the People's Republic of China* on 6 September 1985. Every resident, aged 16 or above, was given by the Ministry of Public Security an identity card confirming his resident status. In the pre-reform era residents had to obtain permission from their work place before they could move to another place, or even buy a train ticket. The issuing of identity cards allowed the residents to move more freely and to find a new job more easily. All a migrant worker needed to be employed in a non-state-owned enterprise in the Pearl River Delta, for example, was an identity card.[5]

III. Data and Definitions

The major source of data used in this chapter is the Fourth National Census carried out in July 1990. Supplementary information will be taken from migration statistics collected by the Ministry of Public Security and population data collected by the Third National Census carried out in 1982 and the 1987 one per cent population sample survey. For the first time, the 1990 census collected information on migration. These data included household registration status, place of residence five years prior to the census date and the reasons for moving. The 1987 sample survey had also asked similar questions; but due to a difference in defining migration, this information is not comparable to that collected in the 1990 census and, thus, will be used mainly for indicative purpose only.

Migration here is defined as a change in usual residence over a significant distance. Using the census criterion, this distance means crossing a county/city boundary. In China, the major mechanism used to regulate population movement is the household registration. It officially defines and also serves to control migration. Each resident has an official place of residence. To have a permanent change in residence, official permission must be granted by both the places of origin and of destination. Therefore, using household registration as a criterion, we can classify migrants into two groups: permanent and temporary.[6] A migrant is considered permanent if the move involves an official change in the household registration. This is migration *de jure*. A temporary migrant is a person who has been living in a locality which is not his official place of residence for longer than a specified period of time or, though having lived there for less than that specified period, has left his official place of residence longer than that time. Both the 1982 and 1990 censuses used one year as the specified period, but the 1987 sample survey used six months. In a sense, then, the 1987 sample survey yields "inflated" statistics on migration. Regardless of the exact definition of the migrant population, these statistical sources give migration *de facto*.

Migration *de jure* is "permanent" in a sense that changing a registration status may take a lot of time and effort and may be irreversible. On the other hand, moving without a change in registered residence or migration *de facto* means that return migration is possible and, thus, the movement is "temporary."

One of the central issues discussed in current Chinese language literature on migration is "floating population" (*liudong renkou*) which is somewhat different from the temporary migrants defined here. In China, if an individual plans to stay in an urban place for more than three days, a temporary resident registration is required. Most statistics on the floating population measure the number of such temporary resident permit holders. This includes not only the temporary migrants, as defined above, but also those who have stayed in their place of destination (or have left their official place of residence) for less than the specified period of time.

IV. Population Mobility in the 1980s

Composition

Despite what has been said of the increased population mobility in China, the official figures of permanent migration compiled by the Ministry of Public Security showed no growth and remained at a low level in the 1980s. Figure 1 and Table 1 present the permanent migration data.

Figure 1. In- and Out-migration with Household Registration Change, 1954–1989 (Number of movers per 1000 population)

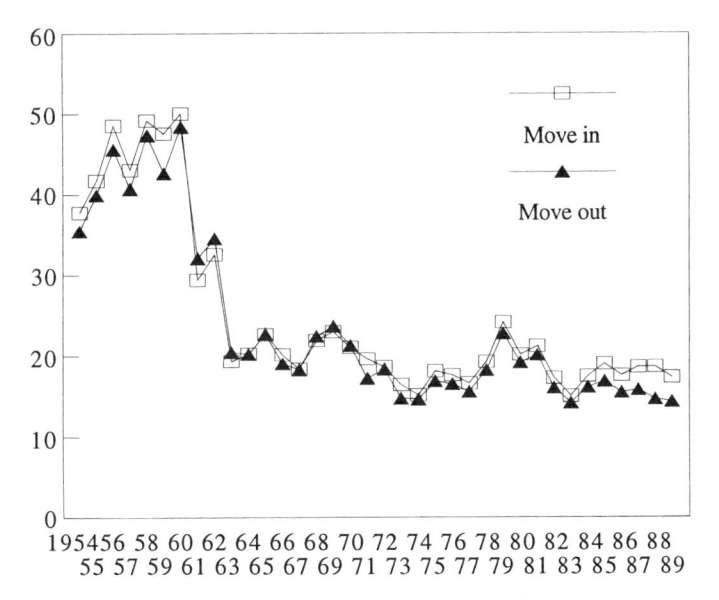

Source: Same as in Table 1.

Table 1. Migration with Household Registration Changed, 1954–1989

Year	Average population	Move in	Rate	Move out	Rate	Net	Rate
1954	590455703	22314496	37.79	20924272	35.44	1390224	2.35
1955	605886796	25296809	41.75	24207925	39.95	1088884	1.80
1956	618634649	30042818	48.56	28212926	45.61	1829892	2.96
1957	637204774	27427621	43.04	25918330	40.68	1509291	2.37
1958	648278039	31884568	49.18	30689857	47.34	1194711	1.84
1959	660249901	31383114	47.53	28167273	42.66	3215841	4.87
1960	661902432	33127135	50.05	32022946	48.38	1104189	1.67
1961	656234818	19311812	29.43	21022044	32.03	-1710232	-2.61
1962	660994675	21509942	32.54	22845520	34.56	-1335578	-2.02
1963	677523708	13093691	19.33	13858620	20.45	-764929	-1.13
1964	693641908	14014973	20.20	14021046	20.21	-6073	-0.01
1965	710485095	16083855	22.64	16100976	22.66	-17121	-0.02
1966	697211098	14047938	20.15	13256689	19.01	791249	1.13
1967	328423582	6006922	18.29	5987902	18.23	19020	0.06
1968	261260065	5725370	21.91	5868619	22.46	-143249	-0.55
1969	265275198	6096515	22.98	6279170	23.67	-182655	-0.69
1970	619406500	13039659	21.05	13162264	21.25	-122605	-0.20
1971	671078823	13144667	19.59	11503519	17.14	1641148	2.45
1972	857490467	15927889	18.58	15654449	18.26	273440	0.32
1973	877292665	14328562	16.33	12878764	14.68	1449798	1.65
1974	895739558	13512341	15.09	13005817	14.52	506524	0.57
1975	911775064	16445466	18.04	15339872	16.82	1105594	1.21

Table 1. Migration with Household Registration Changed, 1954–1989 (continued)

Year	Average population	Move in	Rate	Move out	Rate	Net	Rate
1976	926065276	16241018	17.54	15214946	16.43	1026072	1.11
1977	938829226	15546696	16.56	14547066	15.49	999630	1.06
1978	951534573	18308188	19.24	17295838	18.18	1012350	1.06
1979	964511143	23312813	24.17	21939397	22.75	1373416	1.42
1980	976742780	19641131	20.11	18687935	19.13	953196	0.98
1981	989390583	20980215	21.21	19861223	20.07	1118992	1.13
1982	1003695156	17299087	17.24	16069833	16.01	1229254	1.22
1983	1015942313	15215932	14.98	14352516	14.13	863416	0.85
1984	1025612852	17876015	17.43	16496217	16.08	1379798	1.35
1985	1035798856	19682888	19.00	17428340	16.83	2254548	2.18
1986	1047528603	18352541	17.52	16190143	15.46	2162398	2.06
1987	1061568499	19732083	18.59	16718075	15.75	3014008	2.84
1988	1077852292	20082690	18.63	15775660	14.64	4307030	4.00
1989	1095050500	18951016	17.31	15653801	14.30	3297215	3.01

Source: Department of Population Statistics, State Statistical Bureau, *Zhongguo renkou tongji nianjian 1990* (China Population Statistics Year-book 1990) (Beijing: Kexue jishu wenxian chubanshe, 1991).

Migration here refers to any movement into or out of a city (not including the neighbouring counties under the city's administration), a town or a village. Therefore, both inter-county/city and intra-county/city movements, which involve movements between towns and villages within the same county or municipality, are included. During the Cultural Revolution, the collection and compilation of statistics were disrupted in some provinces, so the data for the period between 1966 and 1971 were incomplete.

Looking at Figure 1, we find that there is an excess of local in-migrants reported over the number of reported out-migrants.[7] Part of the problem is that migration data are not systematically collected. Different provinces may have used different measurement criteria to report move-in and move-out statistics. There could be intentional or unintentional under-reporting of people moving out, as demonstrated by a large gap between the move-in and move-out statistics in the later period. There also may be some deception. For example, some deaths during 1960–1962 in Qinghai had been reported as people moving out and there were incidents in Tianjin that births had been recorded as in-migrants in 1973–1981.[8]

The rate of permanent migration was high in the 1950s with an annual average of 48 per thousand population for the period between 1956 and 1960. Starting from the early 1960s, there was a rapid decline in permanent migration and the move-in rate stabilized at around 18 to 19 per thousand for almost thirty years, with an exception in 1979–1981, when there was a higher rate of migration due to residents returning after "rustication." From these figures we find that permanent migration did not increase in the 1980s but, instead, stayed constant at about an average annual rate of 18 per thousand. Therefore, if there was an increase in mobility in the 1980s, it must be due to a growth in temporary migration.

That this was in fact the case can be demonstrated by compilations based on the 1982 and 1990 population censuses. The two censuses collected data on resident's registration status (Table 2). Using this information, two categories of temporary migrants can be defined: (1) those who had resided in the county/city under survey for more than one year but had registered elsewhere and (2) those who had resided in this county/city for less than a year but had left the registered place for more than one year. The common feature of these two categories is that both had left their registered place of residence for more than one year. In other words, we can define temporary migrants as people who have left their registered place of residence for more than one year. Some scholars in mainland China include those residents with registration unsettled as temporary migrants. This group of residents are newcomers who hold migration permits, veterans, ex-convicts, newborn babies, etc. Clearly some of them cannot be classified as temporary migrants. To be conservative, we exclude this group from our measurement of temporary migrants. Also note that temporary migration as defined here is different from the migration statistics provided by the Ministry of Public Security in two ways. First, migration defined by the census data involves only movement across county/city boundaries, whereas the migration statistics provided by the Ministry of Public Security include both inter- and intra-county/city movements. Secondly, temporary migration involves movement without a change in the household registration whereas Public Security reports only movements involving a change in household registration.

From Table 2 we can find that there is a remarkable increase in the first category of migrants [columns under (2)]. The figure grows from 6.36 million (0.64% of the resident population) to 19.83 million (1.75%), increasing by a factor of 3.12. An even larger increase, at least in relative terms, is found for the second category of migrants [columns under (3)]. The figure grows from 0.21 million (0.02% of the resident population) to 1.52 million (0.14%), increasing by a factor of 7.24. Combining these two categories together, the increase was from 6.57 million to 21.35 million, growing by a factor of 3.25.

Thus, in 1990 there were 21.35 million people, close to 2% of the total population, who had left their registered place for more than one year. According to *Zhongguo renkoubao* (27 December 1990, p. 1), there were about 50 million people who had left their registered place for less than one year. Combining these two figures together, there were about 70 million of the so-called "floating population." This represented some 6% of the total population or for every 16 people, one was in movement.

Size

The 1990 census provided the most comprehensive set of migration data to date. It collected data on the place of residence five years prior to the census date for both permanent and temporary migrants. From these data we can measure inter- and intra-provincial migration for residents who were five years of age or older at the census date. These two figures add up to 33.84 million, which is about 3% of the resident population in 1990.[9] This is an under-estimate of the total volume of migration for the past five year since it excludes migrants younger than five years at the census date,

Table 2. Percentage of People with Various Household Registration Statuses in the 1982 and 1990 Census

	(1) 1982	(1) 1990	(2) 1982	(2) 1990	(3) 1982	(3) 1990	(4) 1982	(4) 1990	(5) 1982	(5) 1990
Beijing	98.02	93.98	1.43	4.51	0.03	0.29	0.38	0.77	0.14	0.45
Tianjin	98.41	97.35	1.34	2.01	0.02	0.07	0.21	0.53	0.02	0.04
Hebei	99.14	98.36	0.57	1.13	0.01	0.04	0.27	0.47	0.00	0.00
Shanxi	98.58	96.56	1.05	2.49	0.02	0.16	0.35	0.79	0.00	0.00
Inner Mongolia	97.65	95.65	1.23	2.62	0.04	0.19	1.08	1.53	0.00	0.01
Liaoning	98.68	97.20	0.77	1.87	0.02	0.20	0.53	0.70	0.01	0.02
Jilin	98.17	96.84	1.07	1.91	0.05	0.12	0.70	1.12	0.00	0.01
Heilongjiang	96.95	94.76	1.62	3.33	0.06	0.22	1.37	1.68	0.00	0.01
Shanghai	97.88	94.98	1.71	3.67	0.03	0.40	0.34	0.45	0.05	0.50
Jiangsu	98.96	97.04	0.55	1.82	0.01	0.11	0.46	1.01	0.00	0.02
Zhejiang	98.96	97.49	0.52	1.60	0.02	0.14	0.49	0.76	0.00	0.01
Anhui	99.12	98.08	0.63	1.28	0.02	0.07	0.23	0.56	0.00	0.01
Fujian	98.04	95.40	0.90	2.42	0.03	0.20	1.02	1.89	0.00	0.10
Jiangxi	98.85	97.67	0.48	1.42	0.02	0.09	0.64	0.82	0.00	0.00
Shandong	98.99	98.19	0.46	0.92	0.01	0.05	0.54	0.84	0.00	0.00
Henan	99.12	98.20	0.57	0.95	0.02	0.09	0.29	0.76	0.00	0.00
Hubei	98.91	97.89	0.61	1.62	0.03	0.09	0.45	0.39	0.01	0.01
Hunan	99.38	98.47	0.37	1.12	0.02	0.07	0.23	0.34	0.00	0.00
Guangdong	99.07	93.94	0.51	4.79	0.01	0.46	0.40	0.79	0.01	0.03
Guangxi	99.33	98.01	0.39	1.33	0.01	0.09	0.27	0.57	0.00	0.00

Table 2. Percentage of People with Various Household Registration Statuses in the 1982 and 1990 Census (continued)

	(1) 1982	(1) 1990	(2) 1982	(2) 1990	(3) 1982	(3) 1990	(4) 1982	(4) 1990	(5) 1982	(5) 1990
Hainan	98.52	95.83	1.05	3.02	0.04	0.28	0.39	0.86	0.00	0.01
Sichuan	99.44	98.47	0.22	1.04	0.01	0.08	0.32	0.40	0.00	0.01
Guizhou	98.62	98.08	0.36	1.24	0.01	0.12	1.00	0.56	0.01	0.00
Yunnan	99.21	98.39	0.31	1.33	0.01	0.13	0.47	0.15	0.00	0.00
Tibet	—	96.82	—	2.63	—	0.20	—	0.33	—	0.01
Shaanxi	99.03	97.81	0.68	1.34	0.03	0.10	0.26	0.74	0.01	0.01
Gansu	98.84	98.11	0.67	1.32	0.02	0.08	0.47	0.49	0.00	0.00
Qinghai	97.13	94.72	1.64	2.98	0.04	1.07	1.19	1.22	0.00	0.01
Ningxia	98.76	97.30	0.81	1.90	0.02	0.15	0.40	0.64	0.01	0.01
Xinjiang	97.24	95.46	2.03	3.42	0.12	0.28	0.59	0.83	0.00	0.01
Total	98.86	97.37	0.64	1.75	0.02	0.14	0.47	0.72	0.01	0.02

Keys:
(1): Resides and holds the household registration in the same county/city.
(2): Resides in the county/city over one year but is registered elsewhere.
(3): Resides in this county/city less than one year but has left registered place for more than one year.
(4): Resides in the county/city with household registration unsettled.
(5): Used to be in county/city; is working/studying abroad with no registration.

Source: *The National Population Census under the State Council, Major Figures of the Fourth National Population Census of China* (Beijing: China Statistical Publishing House, 1991), Table 4.

migrants dying in this period, migration with return migration happening within this five-year period and only one move in multiple movements recorded. We estimate that, if migrants who were younger than five years are included, the total number of ever-movers will be 35.32 million.[10] As reported in the last section, the total number of temporary migrants is 21.35 million. Taking the difference of these two figures, we estimate the number of permanent migrants to be 13.97 million. The ratio of temporary migrants to permanent migrants is, thus, estimated to be 6 : 4. For every ten migrants moving during the period 1985 to 1990, six of them were temporary ones. The temporary migration is estimated to be at least 50% larger than the permanent migration.

Provincial Movements

Table 2 also presents information on the provincial patterns of temporary migration.[11] The temporary residents who held household registration elsewhere were temporary migrants who moved across county boundaries within a province or moved from one province to another. In 1982, Xinjiang ranked first in the relative size of residents who were temporary migrants. More than 2% of its residents were temporary migrants. It was followed by Shanghai (1.74%), Heilongjiang (1.68%), Qinghai (1.68%) and Beijing (1.46%). The national average was 0.66%. The municipalities usually had a higher percentage of temporary migrants and some might have been returned migrants from "rustication." The other three provinces, all located in the border region, were places where the central government was encouraging in-migration so as to assist their development. In 1990, Guangdong became the leader of this category with more than 5% of its residents being temporary migrants. It was followed by Beijing (4.80%), Shanghai (4.07%), Qinghai (4.05%) and Xinjiang (3.70%). Heilongjiang was ranked sixth with 3.55%. The national average in 1990 was 1.89%. The top five provinces in 1982 occupied the second to sixth rank in 1990. The rank order of provinces with temporary migrants, thus, had changed little except for the highest rank. The increase in temporary migrants in Guangdong was very substantial. In 1982, only 0.52% of the Guangdong residents were temporary migrants, and it was ranked 22nd among the 29 provinces (Tibet had no data). With the establishment of the special economic zones and the industrial development in the Pearl River Delta, Guangdong provided a lot of job opportunities to people living in or outside of Guangdong. The strong magnetic forces attracted a lot of people to move to or within Guangdong, both officially with their household registration changed or, more often, unofficially without a change in their household registration, thus increasing the percentage of temporary migrants by more than tenfold. It is a little surprising that Fujian, the neighbouring province of Guangdong and also one of the coastal areas with rapid economic development after the reform, had no change in its rank order (11th), and the increase in temporary migrants was merely by a factor of 2.82, which was lower than the national average of 2.86.

The regional patterns of migration shows a marked change from that of the pre-reform era. The 1990 census also provides us with information on both inter-provincial and intra-provincial migration. Again, migration here refers to both permanent and temporary movements. Using location and economic situation, we classify the provinces into three regions. The first group is the coastal region which comprises Liaoning, Hebei, Beijing, Tianjin, Shandong, Jiangsu, Shanghai, Zhejiang, Fujian, Guangdong, Guangxi and Hainan. The second group is the interior region which includes Shanxi, Shaanxi, Henan, Anhui, Jiangxi, Hubei, Hunan, Sichuan and Guizhou. The remainder are located in the border region and they are Heilongjiang, Jilin, Inner Mongolia, Ningxia, Gansu, Xinjiang, Qinghai, Yunnan and Tibet.

Table 3 presents data on inter-provincial and intra-provincial migration for the period between 1 July 1985 and 30 June 1990 collected by the 1990 census. These data include both permanent and temporary migration. For the inter-provincial migration, we find that Beijing has the highest move-in ratio. It is followed by Shanghai, Tianjin, Qinghai, Xinjiang, Hainan, Guangdong, Ningxia, Liaoning and Jiangsu. Of the top ten provinces with the highest move-in ratio, seven are situated in the coastal region, and three are in the border area. None of them is in the interior region. On the one hand, the opening of the coastal cities to foreign investment and the resulting economic development in the coastal region attract migrants to move in these provinces. On the other hand, the Chinese government always has a policy of sponsoring migration to the border and remote areas for military and economic reasons. Therefore, the border provinces, though having a lower level of economic development, experience a higher rate of economic growth than some of the surrounding interior provinces in the 1980s and are areas benefitting from the government's policy to assist the border and ethnic minority regions, and thus attracting migrants, planned or spontaneous, to move into these provinces.

Table 3. Population Mobility, 1985–1990

	Inter-provincial			Intra-provincial
	In	Out	Net	
Beijing	6.13	1.13	5.00	0.55
Tianjin	3.54	0.98	2.56	0.29
Hebei	0.78	1.10	−0.32	1.37
Shanxi	0.96	0.80	0.16	1.99
Inner Mongolia	1.13	1.32	−0.19	2.86
Liaoning	1.29	0.68	0.61	2.11
Jilin	1.01	1.38	−0.37	2.21
Heilongjiang	0.96	1.71	−0.75	2.84
Shanghai	4.87	1.11	3.76	1.13
Jiangsu	1.23	0.86	0.37	1.91
Zhejiang	0.79	1.53	−0.74	2.05
Anhui	0.61	0.96	−0.35	1.48
Fujian	0.97	0.74	0.23	2.72
Jiangxi	0.59	0.72	−0.13	1.79
Shandong	0.73	0.63	0.10	1.36
Henan	0.57	0.67	−0.10	1.47
Hubei	0.75	0.64	0.11	2.05
Hunan	0.41	0.83	−0.42	2.00
Guangdong	1.84	0.40	1.44	3.99
Guangxi	0.37	1.29	−0.92	2.46
Sichuan	0.42	1.21	−0.79	2.29
Guizhou	0.61	0.95	−0.34	1.69
Yunnan	0.64	0.74	−0.10	2.08
Shaanxi	0.94	1.02	−0.08	2.13
Gansu	0.70	1.17	−0.47	1.81
Qinghai	2.36	2.22	0.14	3.27
Ningxia	1.67	1.19	0.48	2.34
Xinjiang	2.19	1.78	0.41	2.32
Hainan	2.08	1.74	0.34	1.83
Total	0.96	0.95	0.00	2.04

Notes: 1. The figures are expressed in migrants per 100 residents.
2. National figures are weighted averages.
3. No migration data were collected for Tibet.
Source: *Zhongguo renkoubao* (China Population Daily), 8 July 1991, p. 2.

The top ten provinces having the highest move-out ratio, in descending order, are: Qinghai, Xinjiang, Hainan, Heilongjiang, Zhejiang, Jilin, Nei Mongol, Guangxi, Sichuan and Ningxia. Two of them, Hainan and Zhejiang, are in the coastal region. Hainan, which was separated from Guangdong and elevated to the status of a province in 1988, has relatively many of its residents moving out due to the strong attraction of the

Guangdong province. It is quite surprising to many people that Zhejiang, which is a province enjoying a high economic growth, has a high rate of its residents moving out. One of the major reasons for this exceptional movement is that Zhejiang has a high proportion of its residents having a high educational attainment who move, either sponsored by the government or on their own initiatives, to other provinces which need the expertise to assist their development. Six of the provinces having a high move-out ratio are border provinces. Three of these provinces, Qinghai, Xinjiang and Ningxia, are also provinces with a high move-in ratio. It is a common characteristic of provinces with high circular movement, due to planned migration sponsored by the government for military and development reasons. Heilongjiang and Nei Mongol are two provinces where the Chinese government had sponsored a large scale of in-migration in the 1950s and 1960s so as to develop their agriculture and mining. At that time, going together with the planned migrants were an equal or even larger number of migrants moving on their own initiative.[12] As the resources of these provinces had been exploited to their limits, this type of migration stopped in the 1970s, and even some of the previous migrants decided to move back to their original province. The other reason why Heilongjiang has a high move-out ratio, which is also applicable to Jilin, is that its neighbouring province, Liaoning, has a higher rate of economic development, creating a pressure gradient attracting people to move in from the surrounding provinces. The remaining two provinces having high move-out ratio are situated in the interior region. These two provinces, Guangxi and Sichuan, have their people attracted by provinces enjoying high economic development, particularly Guangdong, and large numbers of residents have been moving out to find jobs in these provinces.

Adding both move-in and move-out ratios we get the total mobility ratio. The three centrally-administered municipalities have the highest ratios. Next come the border and then the coastal regions. The interior provinces have the lowest mobility because economic behaviour there is less active than that in the coastal provinces. Furthermore, they have a large population base and thus even a large absolute number of migrants means only a small proportion of their population.

Taking the difference between the move-in and move-out ratios we get the net mobility ratio. The top five provinces having the largest net gain of migrants are, in descending order, Beijing, Shanghai, Tianjin, Guangdong and Liaoning. The three municipalities have reversed their trend in net loss to net gain in migrants. This is particularly true for Shanghai which has experienced a long history of out-migration starting from the early 1950s to the late 1970s.[13] The top five provinces having the largest net loss are, in descending order, Guangxi, Sichuan, Heilongjiang, Zhejiang and Gansu. There is a reverse in the direction of the net inter-provincial movement. Before 1980, the flow was mainly from the eastern coastal provinces to the interior and border regions.[14] In the 1980s most of the coastal provinces became migrant receiving. The notable exception is Zhejiang. In contrast, some of the interior and border provinces, for example, Guangxi, Sichuan and Heilongjiang, previously having net gain in migrants are losing people.

Governed by the law that migration declines with distance, the volume of intra-provincial migration is higher than that of the inter-provincial migration (Table 3). The top five provinces having the highest intra-provincial mobility ratio are, in descending order, Guangdong, Qinghai, Nei Mongol, Heilongjiang and Fujian. The two coastal provinces, Guangdong and Fujian, are the top beneficiaries of the open and reform policies. As their industries develop, especially the township enterprises, peasants in the surrounding counties are attracted resulting in a high volume of intra-provincial movement. Border provinces are more influenced by the government sponsored projects and the roving behaviour of the in-migrated Han Chinese trying to accommodate themselves to the new environment,[15] thus resulting in a higher rate of intra-provincial movements. In contrast, the three municipalities, though having a high level of inter-provincial movement, have a comparatively low level of intra-provincial movement, mainly due to the smaller number of counties within these municipalities when compared to other provinces.

Rural-urban Movements

Ever since the exodus of the rural labour population had brought chaos and instability to the cities in the 1950s, the Chinese government exercised stringent control to prevent the unplanned growth of cities. Basically, there were two types of policies to achieve this aim: policies designed to hold the peasants on the land and policies designed to reverse rural-to-urban net migration.[16] Also due to a lower fertility in the city, the urban growth in China was thus kept low for more than twenty years. The urban population grew from 13.36% of the total population in the 1953 census to 18.4% in the 1964 Census. The speed slackened in the next eighteen years, and the proportion of the population who were urban dwellers grew only slightly to 20.6% in the 1982 census.[17] The Chinese urban growth in the 1980s took up momentum from the increased population mobility caused by the open and reform policies. According to the First Communiqué of the State Statistical Bureau on Major Figures of the 1990 Census, there were 296 million people living in cities and towns in 1990, which accounted for 26.2% of the total population.

The 1990 census data show that rural-to-urban movements dominate the migration streams for both male and female migrants, either in terms of inter- or intra-provincial moves. Table 4 presents information on migrants by sex, type and origin-destination which include permanent migration happening between 1985 and 1990 and temporary migration between 1985 and 1989. The distribution of the rural-urban migration categories is quite similar for male and female migrants in both inter and intra-provincial movements. Rural-to-urban movements rank first followed by, in descending order, urban-to-urban, rural-to-rural and urban-to-rural movements. There are comparatively more women than men moving from rural origins to rural destinations. This is because one of the major reasons to move from a village to another village of a different county is marriage, and, since most Chinese are patrilocal, more women move in the rural areas due to marriage.

Though there are more people moving within a province than between provinces by a factor of roughly 2 to 1, the patterns of rural-urban migration are quite similar for these two types of movements. About half of the movements are rural-to-urban migration and about one third are urban-to-urban migration. Combining the data together, for every five movers there are at least four having cities or towns as their destination. Cities are the most favoured destination for movers when comparing towns and villages. About 62% of all moves are towards the cities, 20% to towns and only 18% to villages (data not shown). The difference between inter- and intra-provincial movement in terms of cities as destination is small. About 58% of the inter-provincial and 64% of the intra-provincial movements are migration into the cities. The policy of encouraging peasants to move to towns for settlement clearly favours rural-to-urban migration within a province rather than between provinces. One of the reasons why cities are more favoured than towns is that in China more people are living in cities than in towns. The 1990 census recorded that there were 18.7% of the population living in cities whereas only 7.5% were living in towns. However, this alone cannot explain the large difference between people moving into cities and into towns. The ratio of city to town population is 2.5 to 1,

Table 4. Migrants by Sex, Type and Origin/Destination of Movement, 1985–1990

	Male N	Male %	Female N	Female %	Both sexes N	Both sexes %
Inter-provincial	6304480	100.00	4531780	100.00	10836260	100.00
Urban-to-urban	2386020	37.85	1366010	30.14	3752030	34.62
Urban-to-rural	348680	5.53	144250	3.18	492930	4.55
Rural-to-rural	737240	11.69	1023040	22.57	1760280	16.24
Rural-to-urban	2832540	44.93	1998480	44.10	4831020	44.58
Intra-provincial	12512950	100.00	10491400	100.00	23004350	100.00
Urban-to-urban	4372410	34.94	3131670	29.85	7504080	32.62
Urban-to-rural	641990	5.13	268410	2.56	910400	3.96
Rural-to-rural	1205110	9.63	1792500	17.09	2997610	13.03
Rural-to-urban	6293440	50.30	5298820	50.51	11592260	50.39
All movements	18817430	100.00	15023180	100.00	33840610	100.00
Urban-to-urban	6758430	35.92	4497680	29.94	11256110	33.26
Urban-to-rural	990670	5.26	412660	2.75	1403330	4.15
Rural-to-rural	1942350	10.32	2815540	18.74	4757890	14.06
Rural-to-urban	9125980	48.50	7297300	48.57	16423280	48.53

Note: Percentages do not add up to 100 due to rounding.
Source: Population Census Office under the State Council and Department of Population Statistics, State Statistical Bureau, *Zhongguo 1990 nian renkou pucha 10% chouyang ziliao* (Ten per cent Sampling Tabulation on the 1990 Population Census of the People's Republic of China) (Beijing: Zhongguo tongji chubanshe, 1991).

but the ratio of city in-migrants to town in-migrants is 3.1 to 1. Though towns have experienced remarkable industrial development in the 1980s, cities seem to be still preferable places to live.

In 1980, the Chinese government developed a new urbanization strategy in view of the situation where the urban population was heavily concentrated at the top (large cities with 500,000 residents or above) rather than at the bottom (small cities with fewer than 200,000 residents). The essence of the strategy was summarized in a slogan: "Strictly limiting the size of big cities, properly developing medium-sized cities and encouraging the growth of small cities and county towns" (*Yange kongzhi da chengshi, heli fazhan zhong deng chengshi, jiji jianshe xiao chengzhen*).[18] Closely tied to this strategy was the policy on migration. The government's position was that migration must fit the needs of the planned economy and any movement to the city must be compatible with the urban economic development. Specific policies formulated to meet these goals were: (1) Rural-to-urban population movement must be strictly controlled. This policy applied especially to movement towards China's three municipalities of Beijing, Shanghai and Tianjin. (2) Movement from towns to cities, from small to big cities, and from rural places to suburbs must be properly limited. (3) Movement between places of similar size did not need control. (4) Movement from large to medium or from medium to small urban places, or from urban to rural places were to be encouraged.[19] Analysis of the 1990 census data presented in the previous section clearly shows that population mobility in the late 1980s were quite contradictory to the government policies. It is worth recalling that, in the analysis of provincial patterns of population mobility, the three municipalities ranked among the top in net inter-provincial movements, which is clearly not where the government wanted them to be. For rural-urban movements, there was a clear trend of rural-to-urban migration. Furthermore, there were more people moving into cities than into towns.

Characteristics of the Migrants

Detailed tabulations of the migrant population by demographic and socioeconomic characteristics based on the 1990 population census have yet to be published. A paper by Zhang Shanyu,[20] however, has reported some of the census findings. Unfortunately, Zhang's paper focuses on inter-provincial migration, and only very patchy information on intra-provincial migration is revealed. Nonetheless, this is the only relevant piece of information from the 1990 census available to us and will form the basis of our discussion below.

(a) Sex Composition

In general, the migrant population is male-dominated. This is especially the case for inter-provincial migrants whose sex ratio, as reported by the 1990 census, was 139.12. This may be compared with a sex ratio of 119.27 for intra-provincial migrants and 105.44 for non-migrants. This finding, although in line with the experience elsewhere, contradicts earlier reports based on small sample surveys conducted in the Pearl River Delta and South Jiangsu Region.[21] A closer examination of the census data reveals that the sex composition of the migrant population exhibits substantial provincial variations. In the prosperous provinces of Guangdong, Jiangsu and Fujian which have benefited significantly from the open policy and which have attracted substantial foreign investment in the processing industries, the female migrants indeed outnumber the male migrants. But in provinces such as Shanxi and Liaoning which are characterized by their heavy industries, male dominance in the migration stream is most apparent. Furthermore, in most areas temporary migrants are male dominated since most of the jobs available to them are manual types such as construction and transportation work. This sex difference in the direction of migration flow, with the bulk of the female migrants moving from the north and west to the southeastern coastal provinces and the male migrants exhibiting a more scattered pattern, is, in a large measure, a response to the difference in labour market conditions across the country.

(b) Age Composition and Marital Status

Table 5 presents the age-specific inter-provincial migration rates reported in Zhang's article. A plot of the data using age on the horizontal axis and the mobility rate on the vertical axis would show an inverted U-shape. As may be expected, young people in the 15–34 age group have the highest mobility rates, with the peak at the 20–24 age category.

As regards marital status, the census data show that singles have higher propensities to migrate than the married. This may be attributable to the difference in opportunity costs between the single and the married involved in the migration decision. Among the intra-provincial migrants, 45.6% are singles; and among the inter-provincial migrants, 41.6%. In comparison, the corresponding figure for non-migrants is 39.7%. Zhang

Table 5. Age-specific Inter-provincial Mobility Rate, 1990

Age	Rate
5–9	5.1
10–14	5.5
15–19	14.4
20–24	29.4
25–29	19.3
30–34	10.6
35–39	9.0
40–44	7.8
45–49	6.4
50–54	5.5
55–59	4.2
60–64	3.9
65–69	3.6
70 or Above	4.1

Source: Zhang Shanyu "Disici renkou pucha shengji qianyi shuju fenxi" (A Data Analysis of Inter-provincial Migration in the Fourth Census), *Renkou yu jingji* (Population and Economics), No. 3, 1992, pp. 13–19.

attributed the higher percentage of singles in the intra-provincial case to the fact that a higher percentage of intra-provincial migrants move because of job transfer and study and training, as compared with that of inter-provincial migrants.

(c) Educational Attainment

In general, migrants have much higher levels of educational attainment than non-migrants. In the case of inter-provincial migration, the census data reveal a consistent and positive relationship between the migration rate and education level. If the rate for illiterates and semi-literates is set at 1.0, then that for primary education will be 1.5, junior high 3.2, senior high 4.0, and sub-degree tertiary education 8.3 and first degree 36.0. Significant spatial variations exist in terms of migrants' educational attainment. Whereas the urban-bound (including cities and towns) migrants had an average of 9.5–9.6 years of education, the county-bound migrants only had 6.5 years. Also, there is a concentration of migrants with higher educational attainment moving to provinces already endowed with a better-educated labour force, such as Beijing, Shanghai, Tianjin, Guangdong and Shaanxi. In the case of Beijing's in-migrants, the average level of education completed is as high as 11.4 years. This is in sharp contrast with some of the

Table 6. Percentage Distribution of Type of Migration by Reasons, 1982–1987 and 1985–1990

	Inter-provincial		Intra-provincial	
	1982–87	1985–90	1982–87	1985–90
Job transfer	19.89	14.55	11.40	10.01
Job assignment	5.26	4.72	6.58	6.51
Job search and trade	9.57	29.44	9.26	21.97
Study and training	9.02	7.76	7.95	15.28
Family reunion	13.35	10.59	8.84	9.52
Retirement	2.54	1.51	2.18	1.58
Dependents	18.66	10.76	15.03	10.19
Marriage	15.54	14.19	30.81	14.34
Others	6.16	6.48	7.94	10.60
Total	99.99	100.00	99.99	100.00
Number of migrants	6,312,600	10,836,260	24,214,500	23,004,350

Sources: Department of Population Statistics, State Statistical Bureau, *Zhongguo 1987 nian renkou chouyang diaocha ziliao: quanguo* (China 1987 One per Cent Population Sample Survey Data: National Volume) (Beijing: Zhongguo tongji chubanshe, 1988). Population Census Office under the State Council and Department of Population Statistics, State Statistical Bureau, *Zhongguo 1990 nian renkou pucha 10% chouyang ziliao* (Ten per Cent Sampling Tabulation on the 1990 Population Census of the People's Republic of China) (Beijing: Zhongguo tongji chubanshe, 1991).

lagging provinces, such as Qinghai and Guizhou in both of which the in-migrants have an average of only 6.6 years of education. To a certain extent, then, migration aggravates the problem of spatial imbalance in development potential.

(d) Employment Status and Occupational Composition

As far as inter-provincial migration is concerned, people without employment have a higher likelihood of migrating than people with employment: the former have a migration rate of 15.1 per thousand whereas the latter 12.6 per thousand. A major factor contributing to this difference is that nearly half of the migrants not at work are students at school. This reflects to a large extent the uneven distribution of education provision in the country. Of course, the expected economic gains associated with migration would be higher for people without work than for people with work, and this could also be a factor leading to the difference in migration rates observed.

Among the employed, clerical workers have the highest rate of inter-provincial migration, at 39.0 per thousand; whereas peasants have the lowest rate, at 4.0 per thousand. Of course, in absolute terms, migration from the rural areas still constitutes the single-most important source — 62.59% (Table 4) because of the distribution of population in China.

Professional and technical workers and government officials/Party cadres have a tendency to move to the more developed coastal regions if they decide to migrate. The centrally administered municipalities of Beijing, Tianjin and Shanghai have a highly disproportionate percentage of migrants in these occupation categories. The migration pattern of production workers correlates with the scale of infrastructure development. Provinces (and centrally administered municipalities), such as Shanghai, Beijing, Guangdong, Xinjiang and Hainan, appear to be the most favoured places of destination. As regards the peasant migrants, migration tends to be associated with marriage and family reunion. Provinces with a high proportion of in-movement because of marriage are also those with a high proportion of peasant in-migrants.

(e) Reasons for Migration

Both the 1990 census and the 1987 one per cent sample survey provided information on the reasons for migration. However, there was a major difference between them in the definition of intra-provincial migration: the former only recorded migration across city or county boundaries, but the latter also included migration between townships within a given city or county. Thus, the intra-provincial migration statistics of these two sources are not directly comparable, as the reasons for short-distance moves may not be the same as those for medium and long distance moves. Table 6 summarizes the 1990 census data on the reasons for migration. The inter-provincial data for the 1987 one per cent sample survey is also presented for comparison. The first four categories of reasons are mainly economic and the fifth to the eighth reasons are social ones. For the economic reasons, the first two, job transfer and job assignment, can be defined as instructive as they are determined by the government. The other two, job search and trade or study and training, are less instructive and can be defined as self-initiated.

A few observations are evident from the table. First, both economic and family-related reasons are of importance in explaining migration. However, the relative importance of these two broad categories differs somewhat between moves within a given province and moves between provinces. In the case of family-oriented moves (i.e., moves due to family reunion, dependents and marriage), the 1990 census data show that they account for roughly the same proportions of inter- and intra-provincial moves (35.54% and 34.05%, respectively). But for the job-related categories, the proportions differ quite markedly between inter- and intra-provincial migration. For example, whereas job transfer accounted for 14.55% of inter-provincial moves in 1985–1990, it only accounted for 10.01% of intra-provincial moves in the same time period. Also, of moves between provinces, 29.44% were due to job search and trade. In comparison, only 21.97% of moves within province were due to this reason. Taken as a whole, the job-related categories accounted for 48.71% of inter-provincial moves but for only 38.49% of intra-provincial moves. Perhaps this reflects a greater degree of variation in the level of economic well-being and, hence, economic incentives for migration between provinces than within a given province.

Secondly, as far as inter-provincial migration is concerned, economic motives seem to be gaining grounds at the expense of social and family reasons. This is especially the case for voluntary economic moves. In 1982–1987, only 9.02% of inter-provincial moves were due to job search and trade. In 1985–1990, the same reason accounted for 29.44%, making it the single most important motive underlying inter-provincial migration. In a matter of just three years, then, there was a three-fold increase in job search and trade's percentage share. Furthermore, individual initiatives were more often quoted as the major impetus to move than government's instructions. In 1985–1990, instructed economic reasons accounted for 19% and 17% of the inter- and intra-provincial movements respectively whereas economic self-initiated reasons accounted for 37% in each of these two types of movements. This was in spite of the economic consolidation measures introduced in the latter part of 1988 and the drastic declines in economic growth rates in subsequent years. With the formal conclusion of economic consolidation in 1991 and the pronouncement of building a "socialist market economy" at the Fourteenth Congress of the Chinese Communist Party in November 1992, it is almost certain that the growing dominance of economic motives in the migration decision will continue in the years to come.

V. Discussion and Conclusion

To recapitulate, our analysis has found that: (1) There was an increase in population mobility in the 1980s. Since there was no growth in permanent migration, this increase was mainly due to the growth of temporary migration which became the major component of population mobility in the late 1980s. This symbolized a shift from planned migration determined by the state to spontaneous migration decided by the individual. (2) There was a reverse in the direction of inter-provincial movement. Before 1980, the flow was mainly from the eastern coastal provinces to the interior and border regions. In the 1980s, most of the eastern coastal provinces became migrant receiving places. Some of the provinces previously having net gain in migrants were losing people. The notable examples were Nei Mongol and Heilongjiang. Most of the provinces in the interior were migrant sending places. This was a consequence of the shifting major component of population mobility from planned to spontaneous migration. (3) There was a clear trend of urban growth due to rural-to-urban migration. More people moved to cities than to towns or villages. This was another indication that the population mobility in the 1980s was less susceptible to the state's decision than during the pre-reform era. (4) Turning to the migrants' characteristics, we found that more men than women moved as there was a shift from social to economic types of reasons to migrate. Furthermore, there was a shift from instructed to self-initiated types of reasons as the decision was mainly made by the individual. In a nutshell, the migration in the 1980s became more spontaneous, less susceptible to the state's influence, and was driven mostly by the individual's economic motives.

One of the implications of this change in population mobility is the wider applicability of western migration theories to explain China's demographic behaviour. In the search for the explanations of population movement, we often encounter the problem of relating the individual to society: of reconciling individual freedom and social constraints. Is migration principally the result of individual choice or is it the product of societal values and constraints? As Skeldon points out, freedom of movement of the individual is guaranteed under most western constitutions, and this democratic right has been transferred, usually implicitly, to much of the analytical writing on migration.[22] Individual's free choice is a major premise in most, if not all, western migration theories. Then, can these theories be applied to explain China's population mobility? When migration is mainly influenced by societal values and constraints, the resource allocation and government policies are the major sources of explanations of population mobility. This was the case of China in the pre-reform era. Any application of western migration theories, which emphasize the individual resources and motivation, without making appropriate adjustment for the role played by the government will only provide partial explanations for the phenomenon. As China's population mobility in the 1980s became more influenced by individual decisions, Chinese scholars[23] are beginning to look at western migration theories, usually micro in nature, for explanations. This application is particularly important when explanations of spontaneous migration, especially "floating population" and "blindfold flow," are being sought.

As the decision to migrate is becoming more volitional, this emancipation of the individual from the collective control should also have an impact on the society. Another implication of the change in population mobility is, thus, the transformation of China from a closed to an open society. The Chinese demographer, Ma Xia,[24] also points out that during the pre-reform era, since occupation and salary were mainly determined by the government, individuals had little economic incentive to move on their own initiative. Furthermore, the tight control of the counter-urbanization policies also prevented peasants from entering the cities. This was a closed population system. The interchange of labour, expertise and knowledge were scarce. This could not be beneficial to a society on the way to modernization. In order to invigorate the economy, more open flow of labour, knowledge and expertise was needed. This inevitably led to a higher level of population mobility and a more open society. In other words, a more mobile population and an open society were essential components of a prosperous economy.

A higher rate of population mobility may also have a negative effect on society. It is possible that a high rate of migration can foster social disorganization or anomie. Elizabeth Bott,[25] in studying a sample of English urban families, introduced the concepts of open and closed social networks. In a closed social network a majority of one's acquaintances know one another; in an open social network this is not so. Newcomers to a community are characterized by an open social network whereas closed social networks are typical of the community old-timers. A community which has few in-migrants is characterized by closed social networks. Group solidarity is high in a closed social network. This type of network, by exercising a strong informal social control, may also be helpful in reducing social pathologies such as crime and, by preventing loneliness, contribute to minimize rates of personal pathologies such as mental illness and suicide. A more mobile population and thus a more open society can be characterized by open social networks. Social and personal pathologies may thus increase with population mobility. This is one of the concerns of the Chinese scholars when they study the effects of the opening and reform policies on the society. In a report on China's social transformation in the 1980s, a group of scholars at the Chinese Academy of Social Sciences[26] point out that China is undergoing a period of social transformation triggered by the opening and reform of the economy. Specifically, China is transforming its economy from a self-sufficiency and semi-sufficiency product economy to a planned commodity economy, from an agricultural society into an industrial society, from a rural society into an urban society, from a closed or semi-closed society into an open society, from a homogeneous and unitary society into a heterogeneous and diversified society, and from a society built on moral principles into a society built on legal principles. A higher rate of population mobility will contribute directly to the transformation of a rural, closed and homogeneous society to an urban, open and heterogeneous society. In this process of transformation, there is a breakdown of old norms, values, regulations, relationships and structures. Put it simply, the old social order is disintegrating and the society is waiting for the building up of a new social order. An anomic situation may develop during this process. The chaotic situation caused by the blindfold flow is one of the examples.

All in all, the increase in population mobility due to the opening and reform policies brings both blessings and misfortunes to China. Though some people call for a tighter control on population mobility and favour *in situ* transformation (*litu bulixiang*), the majority of the Chinese demographers point out a higher population mobility and a more open society are actually helpful to the state's economy, and the ill effects of mobility can be minimized by more proper management.[27] The sociological discussion on problems arising from social transformation can go back to Durkheim's idea of replacing mechanical solidarity with organic solidarity. China is undergoing a rapid social transformation which was experienced by many western countries in the last century. The negative effects of a higher rate of population mobility and a more open society are by-products of social and economic development. A new social order should be established by the time China gets accustomed to the new environment.

Notes

1. Between 1949 and 1960, a total of 73.37 million people moved from the rural to the urban areas in China. On 9 January 1958, the Chinese government announced *The Household Registration Ordinance of the People's Republic of China*, but stringent control of the rural-to-urban migration was only effective after the failure of the Great Leap Forward. See Gu Shengzu, *Fei nongyehua yu chengzhenhua yanjiu* (A Study of De-agriculturalization and Urbanization) (Hangzhou: Zhejiang renmin chubanshe, 1991), pp. 132–33.
2. For a detailed discussion of the policies, see *Institutional Reform and Economic Development in the Chinese Countryside*, edited by Keith Griffin (Armonk: M. E. Sharpe, 1984); Ye Shunzan, "Urban Development Trends in China," in *Urbanization in Asia: Spatial Dimensions and Policy Issues*, edited by Frank J. Costa, Ashok K. Dutt, Laurence J. C. Ma and Allen G. Noble (Honolulu: University of Hawaii Press, 1989), pp. 75–92.
3. See, for example, Chung-tong Wu and Xueqiang Xu, "Economic Reforms and Rural to Urban Migration," in *China's Spatial Economy: Recent Developments and Reforms*, edited by G. J. R. Linge and D. K. Forbes (Hong Kong: Oxford University Press, 1990), pp. 129–43.
4. Deborah Davis, "Urban Job Mobility," in *Chinese Society on the Eve of Tiananmen: The Impact of Reform*, edited by Deborah Davis and Ezra F. Vogel (Cambridge, Mass.: Harvard University Press, 1990), pp. 85–108.
5. Interviews with personnel managers working in the Pearl River Delta area. There are some more certificates needed if the worker is a female. For a single female worker, a certificate proving her single status is needed. For a married female worker, within the age of 15 to 49, a birth-planning certificate is required.
6. This definition is also used by Sidney Goldstein and Alice Goldstein, *Permanent and Temporary Migration Differentials in China* (Paper of the East-West Population Institute, No. 117, Honolulu: East-West Center, 1991) and Gu Shengzu, "Zhongguo lianglei renkou qianyi bijiao yanjiu" (Comparative Study of the Two Kinds of Population Migration in China), *Zhongguo renkuo kexue* (Population Science of China), No. 4, 1990, pp. 16–21.
7. This was also actually pointed out by the Director of the State Statistical Bureau. See Li Chengrui, "Cong renkou pucha gongbao kan Zhongguo renkou de xianzhuang — jianlun Zhongguo renkou tongji shuzi de zhunquexing" (China's Population as Shown by the Population Census Communique, and Some Comments on the Accuracy of the Chinese Population Statistics), *Jingji yanjiu* (Economic Research), No. 12, 1982, pp. 28–38.
8. Zhang Shanyu, "Guanyu woguo renkou qianyi de jige wenti" (Several Problems of Migration in China), *Renkou yanjiu* (Population Research), No. 2, 1992, pp. 16–22.

9. Population Census Office under the State Council and Department of Population Statistics, State Statistical Bureau, *Zhongguo 1990 nian renkou pucha 10% chouyang ziliao* (Ten per Cent Sampling Tabulation on the 1990 Population Census of the People's Republic of China), (Beijing: Zhongguo tongji chubanshe, 1991).
10. From the 1989 and 1990 Sample Surveys of National Population Change, the percentage of permanent migrants aged four or below was 6 to 7%. We assume that this figure was constant for the five-year period prior to the census and the percentage is evenly distributed among the five year groups. For migrants moving four year prior to the census, only those younger than one year at the time of moving were excluded in the census counting of migrants. Following the same logic, we estimate that children younger than five years comprised about 4.2% of the migrants at the time of the census.
11. Province here refers to province, centrally-administered municipality and autonomous region.
12. For detailed analysis of planned and spontaneous migration moving into these two provinces, see Ji Ping and Yan Rui, "Nei Menggu de renkou qianyi" (Migration in Inner Mongolia), *Renkou yu jingji* (Population and Economics), No. 1, 1987, pp. 29–37; Ma Xia, "Heilongjiangsheng zifaxing renkou qianyi diaocha" (A Survey of Spontaneous Migration in Heilongjiang), *Zhongguo renkou nianjian 1985* (Almanac of China's Population 1985), (Beijing: Zhongguo shehui kexue chubanshe, 1986), pp. 1069–79.
13. The inter-provincial net (permanent) migration statistics from 1955 to 1987 (not shown here) are compiled by the Ministry of Public Security, published in Department of Population Statistics, State Statistical Bureau, *Zhongguo renkou tongji nianjian 1989* (China Population Statistics Year-book 1989), (Beijing: Kexue jishu wenxian chubanshe, 1990), pp. 179–93. For a description of the migration trends, see Zhang Shanyu, "Woguo shengji renkou qianyi moshi de zhongda bianhua" (Great Changes in Inter-provincial Migration in China), *Population Research*, No. 1, 1990, pp. 2–8.
14. Ma Xia, "Sanshi duonianlai woguo de guonei renkou qianyi ji jinhou de zhanwang" (China's Internal Migration in the Past Thirty Years and Its Prospects), *Population and Economics*, No. 2, 1987, pp. 3–9.
15. Ma Rong "Renkou qianyi de zhuyao yuanyin he shixian qianyi de tiaojian: Nei Menggu Chifeng qianyi diaocha" (The Main Reasons for Migration and Migrating Conditions: Survey of Migration in Chifeng, Inner Mongolia Autonomous Region), *Population Science of China*, No. 2, 1989, pp. 46–55.
16. Ronald Skeldon, *Population Mobility in Developing Countries: A Reinterpretation* (London: Belhaven Press, 1990), Chap. 6.
17. Population Census Office under the State Council and Department of Population Statistics, State Statistical Bureau, People's Republic of China,

Zhongguo 1982 nian renkou pucha ziliao (1982 Population Census of China), (Beijing: Zhongguo tongji chubanshe, 1985).
18. The slogan was first put forward in a national conference on city development convened in Beijing in October 1980. The major task of the conference was to formulate a strategy for urbanization in the era of the "four modernizations." See *Renmin ribao*, 16 and 17 October 1980. For a detailed analysis of the strategy and its implications, see R. J. R. Kirkby, *Urbanisation in China: Town and Country in a Developing Economy 1949–2000 A. D.* (Kent: Croom Helm, 1985), Chap. 8.
19. For a detailed discussion of the policy, see Sidney Goldstein and Alice Goldstein, *Population Mobility in the People's Republic of China* (Papers of the East-West Population Institute, No. 95, Honolulu: East-West Center, 1985).
20. Zhang Shanyu, "Disici renkou pucha shengji qianyi shuju fenxi" (A Data Analysis of the Inter-provincial Migration in the Fourth Census), *Population and Economics*, No. 3, 1992, pp. 13–19.
21. See, for example, Li Si-ming, "Labour Mobility, Migration and Urbanization in the Pearl River Delta," *Asian Geographer*, Vol. 8(1989), pp. 35–60; Ding Jingxi, "Sunan Taihu diqu chengzhenhua yu quyu kaifa" (Urbanization and Regional Development in Tai Lake Region of South Jiangsu), in *Resources, Environment and Regional Development*, edited by Chi-Keung Leung, Chi-yung Jim and Dakang Zuo (Hong Kong: University of Hong Kong, Centre of Asian Studies, 1989), pp. 272–81.
22. Ronald Skeldon, *Population Mobility* (see Note 16), p. 126.
23. The Chinese scholars are trying to apply some western migration theories, such as those proposed by Ravenstein, Lee, Zelinsky and Todaro, to explain population mobility. Some examples are Wei Jinsheng, "Bashi niandai Zhongguo zhen renkou zengzhang qushi he zhen renkou qianru ji qi jueding yinsu: liangzhong renkou zhuanyi de lishixing huihe" (Population Growth Tendency, Migration and Their Determinants in Chinese Towns in 1980s: Historical Confluence of Two Kinds of Population Transformation), *Population Science of China*, No. 3, 1990, pp. 7–14; Gu Shengzu, "Zhongguo lianglei" (see Note 6); Xie Jinyu and Yu Jing, "Zhongguo jihua chengshihua renkou yu zifa chengshihua renkou duibi yanjiu: cong disici renkou pucha ziliao kan 'liudong renkou' he qianyi renkou zai Zhongguo renkou chengshihua yanjiuzhong de butong diwei" (Comparative Studies of the Planned Rural-urban Migrants and Spontaneous Rural-urban Migrants in China), *Population Science of China*, No. 3, 1992, pp. 6–12.
24. Ma Xia is one of the earliest Chinese demographers to propose and identify the transformation of a closed population system to an open one. For some of his discussion on this topic, see Ma Xia, "Sanshi duonianlai" (see Note 14); and Ma Xia, "Zhongguo qishisi chengzhen renkou qianyi gaikuang" (General

Description of Population Migration in China's Seventy-four Cities and Towns), *Almanac of China's Population 1988*, (Beijing: Jingji guanli chubanshe, 1989), pp. 319–30.
25. Elizabeth Bott, *Family and Social Network* (London: Tavistock Publications, 1957).
26. Lu Xueyi and Li Peilin (eds.), *Zhongguo shehui fazhan baogao* (Report on China's Social Development) (Shenyang: Liaoning renmin chubanshe, 1991).
27. For an example of calling for restricting migration, see Yang Xiaoyong, "Renkou jixie biandong jiqi dui shehui jingji de yingxiang" (Population Mobility and Its Effects on the Society and Economy), *Anhui daxue xuebao (zhexue shehui kexueban)* (Journal of Anhui University [Philosophy and Social Sciences Edition]), No. 2, 1992, pp. 92–96. For views encouraging mobility, see Note 24.

20

The Chinese Family and Gender Roles in Transition

Chong-chor Lau

The family is a basic institution in Chinese society. It is in the family organization that both the values of the members are socialized and the pressures of social change are adapted to. A review of the significant features of the Chinese family in the 1990s provides us with a chance to assess the social impact of the century-long Chinese revolution. It also gives us an indicator of the future with which we may speculate upon the direction of change in Chinese society.

The chapter consists of three main sections. Section one is devoted to a review of the characteristics of the organizational structure. Statistics on the changing size, family form and life cycle will be used to provide background data for a discussion of the emerging principles of family relationships. The typical structure of the Chinese family in 1992 will be summarized with the support of evidence from survey research and case studies.

Three dynamic aspects of the family are discussed in section two. They are the process of family formation, the behaviour and function of fertility decisions, and the pattern of family dissolution. All of them are critical decision-making processes in which the members' power and authority, interests and resources, as well as conflict and accommodation are involved. It is in these dynamics that the family mirrors the distribution patterns in power and resource in the larger society.

The final section considers the new role of the Chinese woman. If the family is the focal point of the turbulent social change in China during the last century, women could be regarded as the centre of the whole transformation. The changing definitions of the female role and her status affect all major aspects of the family organization, from power relationships to fertility choice.

The Changing Structure of the Chinese Family

Family Size

The family size, the number of persons within the organizational membership, is a function of will and possibility. The large, joint-family ideal of traditional China might motivate those who could afford it to increase the size. The reality, however, was that the maintenance of a large family represented a luxury for most Chinese. This was why anthropologist Francis Hsu called it "the myth of Chinese family size."[1] Given the possibility, as Arthur P. Wolf showed in the case of a Taiwanese community, the large size was not only attainable but also attained.[2]

Judging by the national average size in 1911 (Table 1) of 5.17, the sizes reported by Wolf were extremely large, ranging from six to nine, exceeding the traditional norm of between five and seven. The Wolf study, however, is more important on what it takes to support a larger-size farm family. All it took was "sufficient food to eat and sufficient clothes to wear," in other words, whatever material conditions which were somewhat better than miserable.[3]

This insight is important because it helps us to interpret the data in Table 1. Against the urban trend of declining size, the average size of the rural families actually increased during 1953–1982, period in which the first three censuses of the People's Republic of China were taken. The average size of the urban families decreased from 4.66 persons in 1953 to 3.95 persons in 1982, the rural size increased from 4.26 to 4.57.

Table 1. Chinese Family Size (Number of Persons)

Year	National	Urban	Rural
1911	5.17	—	—
1953	4.30	4.66	4.26
1964	4.29	4.11	4.35
1982	4.43	3.95	4.57
1990	3.96	—	—

Sources: *Zhongguo shehui tongji ziliao* (Social Statistical Data of China, 1987), p. 30; *China Daily*, 31 October 1990, p. 1.

One reason for the rural trend in family size was the production requirement of the farm families. According to rural sociologist Zhao Xishun, the production responsibility system implemented in the early 1980s reversed the trend of household division and, in a few cases, motivated family unification in Sichuan province.[4]

With these exceptions in mind, we may conclude that the primary trend in family size in twentieth-century China has been a declining one. The national average size of the Chinese family decreased from over five persons at the beginning of the century to less than four persons eighty years later. The average family size in China's largest metropolitan regions of Shanghai and Beijing today is very close to three persons per family,[5] which may be the trend for the whole China in the future.

Family Form

One central view of the sociology of the family is that there is a dominant family form in advanced industrial societies. This form consists of two types of family composition, the nuclear family type (which is composed of a man and a woman and their dependent offspring) and the one-parent family type. These families may be similarly closed in relation to external kin and community, and they may exhibit similar degrees of relative autonomy in relation to other families.[6] In other words, the theory argues that modern societies tend to be characterized by a distinctive, dominant family form whereby the conjugal family of procreation is prominent.

Table 2 reports the increasing proportion of the nuclear families in a span of almost half a century in China's five major cities. Over two-thirds of the contemporary urban families in these samples were of the nuclear type. The second largest type, the stem family, which is a nuclear family living with one grandparent, accounts for about one-fifth.

Table 2. The Changing Family Form

Family form	Grandparents' generation	Parents' generation	Present generation
Nuclear	53.4	55.4	68.3
Others	46.6	44.6	31.7
Total	100.0	100.0	100.0
(Sample size)	(1,544)	(1,110)	(1,726)

Notes: Grandparents' generation are families of female respondents before they were married in 1938–1953.
Parents' generation are families of female respondents before they were married in 1954–1965.
Present generation consist of families of female respondents before they were married in 1966–1982.
Source: *Zhongguo chengshi jiating* (The Family of Chinese Cities) (Jinan: Shandong People's Press, 1985), p. 484.

The other types, such as extended families and single households, together represented about 10% of the total. The increasing trend and the predominance of the nuclear form of families in Chinese cities confirm the universal pattern that the nuclear family is the most adaptive type in an industrializing society.

In rural China, the level of the nuclear form of families varies, but again quite in line with the level of industrialization. In the suburbs of Beijing and Shanghai, where the level of industrial and economic development is high, almost three-quarters of the families were nuclear in 1986.[7] In rural Sichuan province, where the level of industrialization was comparatively low in mid-1980s, the nuclear families represented only 60% of the total, compared with 70% in the city of Chengdu.[8]

It must be borne in mind that this general increase in the nuclear form of the Chinese family was achieved in a period when the average life expectancy of the Chinese was prolonged by almost a generation (i.e. twenty-five years, see discussion below). Against this demographic force which might have resulted in a growth of the three-generation families, the actual increase in the nuclear form demonstrates that there was significant institutional shift in Chinese society. Central to this shift are the increasing social preference among the Chinese for smaller families and the fact that the nuclear family is the most functional form of family system in an industrial society.

Family Life Cycle

The significant increase in the average life expectancy of the Chinese shown in Table 3 below is a result of two drastic changes:

The rapidly declining death rate, especially the infantile mortality rate, and the general improvement in life quality. Infantile mortality was about 200 per 1,000 population in the 1940s, and remained high (138 per 1,000) in 1955. It was drastically reduced to 35 per 1,000 in the 1981 census, and further improved to 14 per 1,000 in 1985.[9] The rapidly declining death rate was the main reason behind the increasing level of life expectancy of the Chinese.

Table 3. Average Life Expectancy

Year	Survey population	Average	Male	Female
1935	Nanjing	—	29.8	38.2
1950	Beijing	—	53.9	50.2
1957	11 provinces	57.0	—	—
1975	28 provinces	68.2	67.2	69.3
1981	Census	67.9	66.4	69.4
1985	10% census sample	68.9	67.0	71.0

Source: *Zhongguo shehui tongji ziliao* (1990), p. 26.

Partly as a result of the increased life expectancy, and partly as a consequence of the declining birth rates, the Chinese population has been ageing quite rapidly in recent years. The aged population of 65 years and older as a percentage of the total population increased from 4.41% in 1953 (the first census) to 5.58% in 1990 (the fourth census). Even more dramatically, the ageing index, measured as a percentage of the aged population above 64 over the young population under 15, increased from 12.2 to 21.26 in the same period.[10]

Even though China is not yet an ageing society, defined by having 7% or more of the population aged 65 and over, the problem of ageing is a serious one in contemporary Chinese society for the following reasons:[11]

First, the absolute number of the aged population is large. At the moment, the number of people 65 and older exceeds 70 million, and the population of 60 and older is more than 100 million.

Secondly, China's pace of ageing is the fastest in the world. It took Japan fifty years to increase the aged population from the 5% level to the 7% level, it will take China less than twenty years.

Finally, China's aged population is very unevenly distributed. In 1988, Jiangsu became the first ageing province of China, while Shanghai became the first ageing city. Now, most coastal cities have an aged (65 and over) population of over 7%. The proportion of the aged population in the cities is 5% higher than its rural counterpart. Therefore, the ageing problem is concentrated in spatial term.

The ageing problem is aggravated by the nuclear trend in the family structure and the underdevelopment of the social welfare system in China. The lack of public care is less of a problem in rural China as about 95% of the old peasants are cared for by their families. The urban old is very different. A survey in 1986 found that about 60% (18 million) of the aged population in Chinese cities were dependent on government pensions.[12] Since China has a limited welfare budget (in 1990, the welfare expenditure represented only 1.5% of the total budget), the urban old who are dependent on government handouts are very poor indeed. For example, the annual subsidy for an old person without a family living in towns and cities in 1990 was RMB290.7.[13] Nobody can live on this meager income in China today. Indeed, the rates of increase of all kinds of public subsidies have lagged far behind the rate of inflation in recent years.

The Family Structure in 1992

In summary, the structure of the Chinese family today can be approximated as follows:

(1) The average family consists of four persons. Over the century, the mean size has been reduced by 1.2 persons. In general, urban families are smaller than their rural counterparts.

(2) The dominant form of the Chinese families today is the nuclear family. In the cities, almost seven out of every ten families are of this relational form. In the rural areas, about 60% belong to this form. The more industrialized and economically developed the area, the more predominant is the nuclear form in the family structure. Over time, nuclear families have increased by fifteen percentage points in the last three generations, against the trend of rising level of the average life expectancy.

(3) The radical change of the family institution is nowhere more pronounced than in the family life cycle. As the fertility rate is declining drastically and the average life span is prolonged, the older generation as a proportion of the total population or as a percentage of the young increases. Ageing is increasingly becoming a social problem of China. For thousands of years, the Chinese family had been designed to care for its aged members. The differentiation of this function from the Chinese family tells much about the structural transformation and its social source. Like its counterpart in the advanced industrial societies had done before, contemporary Chinese family is adopting a form which is the most adaptive to the change which is taking place in the larger society.

The Processes of the Chinese Family

Marriage

Over this century, the most dramatic change in the marriage pattern has taken place in the choice of mate. The survey results in Table 4 can be further grouped into two categories: those whose marriage was arranged by parents and relatives, and those who selected their spouse on their own and with the help of their friends. The arranged pattern decreased from

Table 4. Patterns of Mate Selection (%)

Arranged by	1953	Married during: 1954–1965	1966–1982
Parents	37.5	7.2	0.9
Relatives	26.8	23.9	17.1
Friends	23.8	41.2	48.1
Self	11.9	27.7	33.9
Total	100.0	100.0	100.0
(Sample size)	2,050	(1,071)	(1,699)

Source: *Zhongguo chengshi jiating*, p. 307.

over 64% for respondents who were married before 1953, to 18% for those who were married after 1966.

Over the years, free mate selection has become the dominant form of family formation. The two marriage laws published in 1950 and 1981 respectively played a role in promoting the modern pattern of free selection in the Chinese marriage institution.

An unintended problem of this success is the increasing number of the so-called "large-age singles," conveniently defined as men and women in the age cohort between 28 and 49 who have yet to find a mate. The third census of 1982 found that this group had over 11 million people, representing 4.36% of the population of similar age. A further analysis found that this was mainly a problem of men, for over 90% of this group were single males, and the "large-age single males" represented 7.78% of the male population of the same age group.[14]

Digging deeper into this problem we may find a key to the changing criteria of mate selection in China. The bulk of the large-age single males are uneducated farmers (almost 80% have an educational level below primary school and almost half of those are illiterate). In contrast, a significant percentage of the single females in this group are highly educated urbanites (about 60% have an education above junior high school). It is easy to see that education and related achievement criteria are high on the mate selection scale in Chinese society today. When decision-making power is shifted from parents to the younger generation, the choice behaviour is drastically altered as a consequence.

The above change in the patterns of mate choice is confirmed by a case study by Martin King Whyte.[15] In this study of Chengdu, Whyte found that 69% of the marriages during 1933–1948 were traditionally arranged. For those married in 1949–1957, only 22% were so arranged. After 1957, arranged marriage had almost totally disappeared. Freedom of mate choice increased markedly during the 1950s, but the social structure that would facilitate the free mating pattern did not change substantially in subsequent years. As a result, youth autonomy was prevented from developing to the level seen in most modern societies.

The sociological theory of family predicts, as the selection of mate becomes freer, the age at marriage is likely to be older.[16] The Chinese case is no exception. The average bride age of China in 1949 was 18.57 years. This was increased to 19.74 in 1965, 21.74 in 1975, and further raised to 22.66 in 1982. Late marriages, defined as women whose bride age is older than 23, accounted for less than 7% in 1949, jumped to 54% in 1987.[17] This national trend is also seen in the case of Chengdu, where the bride age was 15 in 1935 and gradually rose to about 24 in 1985, an increase of nine years in half a century.[18]

This sociological prediction is based primarily on logic. As youngsters are less dependent on their parents in matters such as the choice of mate, they must be at least as old as the employment system forces them to be in order to be independent at marriage. This is particularly true in industrial urban societies. The Chinese case, however, is more complicated.

The primary cause for late marriage in China has been government policy. In the first two decades under communist rule, the bride age at marriage rose only slowly. Since the mid-1970s when the government adopted the present population reduction policy, late marriage has been earnestly promoted. The average bride age at marriage rose sharply from 20 to 22 nationally and from 23 to 25 in the cities. Today, over two-thirds of women in urban China practice late marriage, that is marry after they are older than 23. Thus despite the fact that Chinese marriage behaviour is free from parental control, significant aspects of the marriage pattern are increasingly determined by the state. In decisions concerning the timing of marriage and having children, as well as how many children to have, the influence of the bureaucratic gatekeepers looms very large indeed.[19]

Fertility Behaviour

The sharp decline in the total fertility rate took place in 1975, the year when the population control campaign was officially launched. As in late marriage, fertility decline in the cities were already under way much earlier. However, it was change in rural China that had a significant impact on the national average. As Table 5 shows, when the rural total fertility rate (number of children borne by a woman of 15–49) averages fell from above six to below four in 1965–1975, the national averages had a similar change. In China, government policy actions cast a long shadow over the most private of personal decisions.

Table 5. Total Fertility Rates in China[1] (Number of Persons)

Year	National	Urban	Rural	Fertility-age population[2] (Million of women aged 15–49)
1949	6.13	—	—	—
1952	6.472	5.521	6.667	133.14
1965	6.076	3.749	6.597	151.61
1975	3.571	1.782	3.951	—
1981	2.631	1.390	2.910	248.49
1990[2]	2.250	—	—	306.35

Sources: (1) *Zhongguo shehui tongji ziliao 1990*, p. 34.
(2) *Zhongguo tongji nianjian 1992* (China Statistical Year-book 1992), pp. 80 and 92.

Although it is not possible to weight the effects of governmental action and other socio-economic forces on fertility reduction, the data in Tables 5 and 6 provide a basis for speculation.

Table 6. Total Fertility Rates by Education in China, 1990

Educational level	Total fertility rate
College, degree	1.12
College, non-degree	1.35
Technical school	1.37
Upper secondary	1.52
Lower secondary	2.07
Primary	2.49
Illiterate	2.93

Source: *Zhongguo tongji nianjian 1992*, p. 92.

Together, they show that time, place of residence and education are the most important variables in determining the fertility behaviour of the Chinese women. It may have taken longer for the same reduction without government interference. In due course and given the same conditions, the Chinese couple will arrive at the same decision to have fewer children as their counterparts did in more modernized societies.

Under strong intervention by the state, the adaptive fertility behaviour of the Chinese is an interesting area of study. As there is little research available, we must infer from some survey data. One analysis based on the fourth census of 1990 reveals that, since the adoption of the "one child per couple" measure one decade ago, the sex ratio at birth has been rising, to 114 at the end of 1990. As a result, there are 3.6 million more boys born each year and, in the year 2,000, there will be 70 million more men than women among the marriageable population.[20] These figures indicate that the higher-than-normal sex ratio at birth (generally 106, i.e. 106 boys per every 100 baby girls) is a result of some conscious efforts, may be a compromise between the government's "one child" demand and the traditional value that favours male offspring. The pattern of such adaptive behaviour can only be discovered in case studies.

Divorce

That divorce behaviour is still a taboo in Chinese society even among the social scientists can be seen from the fact that this major source of family disorganization received no attention at all in the "Five-City Family Research" project and its two main reports.[21] In fact, research on divorce was interrupted during the Cultural Revolution which started in 1966 and has not been fully revived since. Of the few published papers on the topic, most are analyses of the background data of the court cases. There is almost no study on the behavioural aspect of divorce.

Divorce court cases in China represent a partial picture of the phenomenon. The first reason is that not all divorces are included in official divorce statistics. For example, divorces by mutual consent are not included, a legacy of Republican China. And this type of divorce is quite numerous. On the other hand, not all court cases result in divorce verdicts. Finally, not all divorce applications are able to proceed to the court.

Therefore, China's divorce statistics can only serve as an indicator of the phenomenon.

With the above limitations in mind, the data in Table 7 show that the divorce trend is a rising one, especially in the reform years since 1979. Analyses of the court data found that the divorcees tended to be younger, the duration of marriage until divorce was shorter, there were more female

Table 7. Divorce Court Cases in China

Year	Number of cases handled	Cases per 1,000 population
1950	186,000	0.34
1979	319,000	0.66
1982	428,000	0.85
1985	458,000	0.88
1987	581,000	1.08
1988	655,000	1.20
1989	763,000	1.36
1990	799,000	1.43

Sources: *Zhongguo shehui fazhan baogao* (A Report on China's Social Development), edited by Lu Xueyi and Li Peilin (Shenyang: Liaoning People's Press, 1991), p. 311.
Population Research Institute, *Almanac of China's Population, 1991*. pp. 83–84.

than male petitioners, and more couples divorced because they found too late that they were not compatible due to rash marriage.[22]

The Family Processes in 1992

To sum up the above study, we may approximately profile the present family dynamics in Chinese society as follows:

(1) Youngsters are free in the choice of mate. In significant aspects of marriage decisions, state intervention has replaced parental control as the new influence in decision-making.

(2) After a sharp drop in fertility rates in the last two decades, the typical Chinese woman today gives birth to a little more than two children in her life, very close to the replacement rate of 2.2 children per couple. Late marriage is practised by two-thirds of the women in the cities and almost half of the women in the rural areas.

(3) Divorce is on the rise. More modern divorce forms are found in China: there are more younger divorcees, more women are taking the initiative, the duration of marriage until divorce becomes shorter, and more people are divorced due to rash marriage.

In summary, today's Chinese family is moving along the direction that the modernization theory of the family has predicted. The dynamics of change, however, have retained some unique Chinese characteristics.

The Gender Roles in Transition

The Role of Women

The most significant impact of the changing structure and processes of the family system is upon the role of women within the family. As the conjugal family becomes the dominant form in Chinese society today, and as it is becoming smaller, simpler, and more independent, the role of the wife changes and her status is drastically altered as a consequence. The trend towards equalitarianism in the family also receives societal boosts in contemporary China, two of the social forces being the legal protection of women and the increasing female labour participation since 1949.

The two marriage laws — the first promulgated on 1 May 1950 and the second on 1 January 1981 — of the Peoples' Republic were the culmination of half a century of public debate, ideological argument and legislative development. Although most of the rights of women protected by the first marriage law were not new, the actual status of Chinese women had not changed appreciably by 1949. It took more conditions than legal promulgation to really change gender roles and improve women's status.

Table 8. Female Labour Participation Rates in Rural China

Year	Percentage of women aged 16–60 participating in agricultural production
1950	20–70*
1953	50–60
1957	60–70
1958	90
1964	95
1987	85–90

Source: Hang Xiyi, "Changes in the Economic Status of Rural Women in the Transformation of Modern Chinese Society," *Social Sciences in China*, Spring 1992, p. 87.

* In new liberated areas, the rate ranged from 20–40.
  In old liberated areas, the percentage was between 50 and 70%.

One great social force is the participation in productive labour. Table 8 shows an extremely high female labour participation rate in rural China today. There are over 200 million female agricultural workers in the villages, representing 43% of the labour force in the rural areas. In the cities, the number of female workers has jumped from 0.65 million in 1949 to nearly 60 million presently, resulting in the near full employment of the whole adult female population.[23] This high female labour participation rate has great impact on the structure of urban family. In 1957, a typical family of 4.3 persons had 1.3 workers. Now the average size of the urban family has shrunk to 3.6 persons, but two members are working. The prevalence of dual-career families has great social consequences for gender roles and the power relationships of the family.

Not only do 90% of the wives work in urban China, their occupational statuses are not lower than their husbands. Among the 3,336 pairs of dual-career couples surveyed in the "Five-City Family Research" project, 22% of the wives were employed as professionals and technicians, compared to 21% for the husbands. Of the remaining female jobs, 49% were production and transport workers, 18% engaged in commercial services and 11% in other employments. The respective numbers for husbands were 42%, 12% and 25%.[24] Judging from this finding, it may be said that there were equal employment opportunities for men and women in the cities.

The high employment and improved status are the result of the rising educational level of Chinese women. As the five-city survey found, the younger the couples, the more similar the educational attainment between husband and wife. The small number of women interviewed who remained at home were mostly old and illiterate. For women who had married after the mid-1970s, 98% worked, as they had received an education equivalent to their husbands'.[25]

As domestic and social changes have brought about more equalitarianism to the Chinese family, the new role patterns do not come without conflicts and strains. The most serious role conflict is between the feminine roles of being nurturant, supportive, passive, and domestic and the expectation to achieve and be equalitarian. The conflict of the traditional role of the Chinese woman with her added social roles is regarded as one of the major sources of family strife in urban China.[26]

The second type of role conflict, that between a career woman and a home-maker, is a universal one. The strains of a career woman in the advanced industrial societies are not less serious than her Chinese counterpart's. In their review of research on the gender roles in the family, Caycedo, Wang and Bahr found that "from 1930 to 1990, family roles have become more equalitarian, with more wives working outside the home and more husbands helping in domestic work. However, behaviour changes have been much less than attitudinal changes and women continue to do most domestic labour."[27] Chinese career women have found themselves in the same situation and are hard pressed by the demand of the professional roles and domestic labour.[28]

The lag of behaviour change behind attitudinal change with respect to equalitarianism in Chinese society has other unpleasant consequences for working women. As a result of reform, Chinese enterprises have adopted a policy of "optimization" (the Chinese equivalent of lay-offs) in recent years. A survey of 660 factories in eleven provinces in 1989 found that, among the laid-off redundant workers, 63 to 80% were women.[29] It is quite clear that implementation of the equalitarianism must be supported by changes in the social structure. Until is completed the development of a free labour market in which the individual is hired for and evaluated on his own skill, Chinese working women cannot expect to be treated equally in fundamental matters in a society which is still male-centred. And that is the main source of the paradox of gender equity in China today: in many apparent ways women are enjoying equal rights and opportunities as men, but in some subtle and important areas they are punished for their sex role.

Gender and Family Relationships in 1992

As in family changes, gender role transformation takes a long time to accomplish. In the case of China, the ideas of the small family ideal, freedom of mate choice and equalitarianism in gender relations were introduced at the beginning of this century. It took half a century for these beliefs to culminate into legal norms. It takes more time to translate the norms into action. That is why we trace so far back into history to understand the present condition of the Chinese family. As a part of an annual review, let us summarize the changes in gender roles and relationships within the family up to 1992.

(1) The status of women has greatly improved as the result of the various trends taking place in society and in the family. The primary relationship is no longer an intergeneration one between father and son, but between that of husband and wife. Since 1949, there has undoubtedly been a trend towards more equalitarian attitudes. However, behaviour changes have been much less than attitudinal changes in many aspects.

(2) As a consequence of the shrinking family size and the unprecedently high female labour participation level, the conflict between occupational and domestic roles is most acute among the working

women. Despite the conscious promotion of equalitarianism in Chinese society for more than four decades, for most Chinese men, behaviour tends to be much less equalitarian than attitudes. In general, women continue to do most domestic labour. Role conflicts of this sort is increasingly a source of family disorganization in China today.

(3) The social roles and status of women in Chinese society have been significantly enhanced after a century of radical change. These new roles, however, are not yet institutionalized and embedded into the social structure. The traditional hierarchical institution of male supremacy has been a constituting part of Chinese society for so long that replacing it with equalitarianism is nothing short of a social revolution. The Chinese gender roles cannot be fully transformed until this social revolution is completed.

Notes

1. Francis L. K. Hsu, "The Myth of Chinese Family Size," *American Journal of Sociology*, Vol. 48, No. 5 (1943), pp. 555–62.
2. Arthur P. Wolf, "Chinese Family Size: A Myth Revitalized," in *The Chinese Family and Its Ritual Behaviour*, edited by Hsieh Jih-chang and Chuang Ying-chang (Taipei: Institute of Ethnology, Academia Sinica, 1985), pp. 30–49.
3. *Ibid.*, pp. 46–49.
4. Zhao Xishun, "Nongcun gaige yu nongcun jiating" (The Reform of the Countryside and The Families in the Countryside), *Journal of Southwest Nationalities College* (Philosophy and Social Sciences), No. 5, 25 October 1990, pp. 24–27.
5. The average size of the Beijing families was 3.2 persons in 1990, according to *Beijing Daily*, 7 November 1990, p. 1. The average size for the Shanghai families was 3.1 persons in 1990, see *Shanghai Family Daily*, quoted by *Press Digest*, 29 January 1991, p. 3.
6. Paul Close, "Family Form and Economic Production," in *Family and Economy in Modern Society*, edited by Paul Close and Rosemary Collins (London: The MacMillan Press, 1985), pp. 9–48.
7. *Zhongguo shehui fazhan baogao* (A Report on China's Social Development), edited by Lu Xueyi and Li Peilin (Shenyang: Liaoning People's Press, 1991), p. 316.

8. Zhao Xishun, "The Changing Structure of the Rural Family in China," *Proceedings of the Second Conference on Modernization and Chinese Culture* (Hong Kong: The Chinese University of Hong Kong, 1985).
9. *Zhongguo shehui tongji ziliao 1990* (Social Statistical Data of China, 1990), p. 207.
10. *Zhongguo nianjian 1991* (China Year-book 1991), p. 421.
11. Wu Jiang and Zhou Xingwei, "Guanyu renkou laolinghua yu shehui he qiye fudan de sikao" (Reflections on Population Aging and the Burden on Society and Enterprises), *Gansu lilun xuekan* (Gansu Theoretical Journal), May 1990, pp. 65–69.
12. *Ibid.*
13. *Zhongguo nianjian 1991*, p. 436.
14. Zhang Ping, "Zhongguo daling weihun wenti ji tedian" (Problems and Characteristics of the Large-age Singles in China), *Zhongguo renkou kexue* (Chinese Demographic Science), June 1989, pp. 53–58.
15. Martin King Whyte, "Changes in Mate Choice in Chengdu," in *Chinese Society on the Eve of Tiananmen: The Impact of Reform*, edited by Deborah Davis and Ezra F. Vogel (Cambridge, MA: The Council on East Asian Studies, Harvard University, 1990), pp. 181–213.
16. William J. Goode, *World Revolution and Family Patterns* (New York: The Free Press, 1963), p. 8.
17. Lu Xueyi and Li Peilin (see Note 7), pp. 302–303.
18. Whyte, see Note 15.
19. According to Anslet J. Coale, "After 1970 Chinese local authorities intervened and did not permit marriage before age 23." See Coale, "Marriage and Childbearing in China since 1940," *Social Forces*, Vol. 67, No. 4 (1989), p. 849.
20. *South China Morning Post* (Hong Kong), 3 March 1993.
21. *Zhongguo chengshi jiating* (The Family of Chinese Cities) (Jinan: Shandong People's Press, 1985); *Zhongguo chengshi hunyin jiating* (Family and Marriage in Urban China) (Jinan: Shandong People's Press, 1987).
22. *Hunyin jiating tansuo* (Explorations of Marriage and the Family) (Guangzhou: Guangdong People's Press, 1985), pp. 310–45. Also see Erika Platte, "Divorce Trends and Patterns in China: Past and Present," *Pacific Affairs*, Vol. 61, No. 3 (1988), pp. 428–45.
23. Lu Xueyi and Li Peilin (see Note 7), p. 321.
24. *Family and Marriage in Urban China* (see Note 21), p. 120.
25. *Ibid.*, pp. 120–22.
26. Wang Jinling, "Zhongguo chengshi jiating chongtu yuanqi xin tedian" (New Causes of Family Conflicts in Urban China), *Zhejiang Journal*, No. 6, 1990, pp. 146–49.
27. J. C. Caycedo, G. Wang, and S. J. Bahr, "Gender Roles in the Family," in

Family Research, A Sixty-Year Review, 1930–1990, edited by S. J. Bahr, Vol. I (New York: Lexington Books, 1991), p. 477.
28. Han Binjie, "Zhongguo nüxing jiaose wenti tantao" (Explorations into the Role Problems of Chinese Females), *Fushun shehui kexue*, Nos. 2–3 (1991), pp. 34–38.
29. Wang Jinling (see Note 26), p. 147.

21

Pro-democracy Movement in the People's Republic of China and Overseas

K. K. Leung

The masses should be encouraged to offer criticisms. There is nothing to worry about even if a few malcontents take advantage of democracy to make trouble.... One thing a revolutionary party does need to worry about is its inability to hear the voice of the people. The thing to be feared most is silence.[1]

Deng Xiaoping (13 December 1978)

Introduction: Democratization in Post-Mao Era

The year 1976 is ranked as a turning point in the Chinese history which marks the persistent restriction of the "ultra-leftist" policy of the "Gang of Four" and the rising promotion of "socialist democracy" encouraged by Deng Xiaoping. The Tiananmen demonstration of April 1976 was a strong protest against the "Gang of Four" who were eventually defeated in October by the new Chairman Hua Guofeng after the death of Mao Zedong in September. Between the third plenary session of the Tenth Central Committee of the Chinese Communist Party (CCP) in July 1977 and the third plenary session of the Eleventh Central Committee of the CCP in December 1978, Deng succeeded in combatting Hua's radical policy. During these eighteen months, socialist democracy was re-written into the 1978 state constitution. As a reaction to Deng's open policy, between November 1978 and March 1979, a democracy movement broke out in the streets of Beijing and subsequently spread across the whole country to demand a more open society. In response to the increasing mass opposition and waves of peasant and "worker" (former Red Guards) demonstrations, Deng declared on 30 March 1979 that modernization must be practised within the bound of the four basic principles (that is: upholding the socialist road, the dictatorship of the proletariat, the leadership of the CCP, and Marxism-Leninism and Mao Zedong Thought) which implied the suppression of the democracy movement.

Despite his suppression of the democracy movement, Deng continued to press for a greater degree of reform and democratization. He encouraged the reform of Party-state division and the "democratic" direct grassroots elections in 1980, 1984, 1987, 1990 and 1993. At the same time, Deng crystallized his power around Hu Yaobang, the then General Secretary, and Zhao Ziyang, the then Premier, to shape up a tripartite ruling group to oust Hua from the political arena at the sixth plenary session of the Eleventh Central Committee of the CCP in June 1981. The years after witnessed the see-saw struggle between reform and rectification, first in the field of literature, then on the campuses and finally the Party. Eventually, between November 1986 and January 1987, student demonstrations broke out across the whole country and were condemned as "bourgeois liberalization," which occasioned the resignation of Hu Yaobang in January 1987. The death of Hu on 15 April 1989 instigated another student movement which led to the June Fourth Incident that alarmed the world, and which resulted in the stripping-off of all of Zhao Ziyang's posts in both the Party and the state in late June 1989.

Reconsideration of the pro-democracy movement echoes in the minds of the democrats both inside and outside mainland China in the years after the June Fourth Incident. Today, suppression by the Party and disintegration overseas are difficulties faced by the liberal intelligentsia, and the solutions are either reformationary or revolutionary. These two extreme approaches are derived from the original conflicts in the Democracy Wall Movement 1978–1979 between the evolutionists (represented by the activists from the underground publications like *Beijing Spring*, *April Fifth Forum* and *Masses' Reference*) and the abolitionists (represented mostly by Wei Jingsheng of *Exploration*).[2]

The Movement inside China

Scattered underground, democracy movements have persisted in China after the crushing-down of the Tiananmen Square demonstration. In 1992, several organizations were reported to be active in promoting democracy in the mainland: (1) The Chinese Alliance for Freedom, protecting workers' economic rights;[3] (2) the Chinese Liberal Democratic Party, supporting political and economic reforms;[4] (3) the Chinese Social Democratic Party, promoting the destruction of the one-party dictatorship and creating a new society full of freedom, justice, humanity and legality;[5] (4) the Inner-Mongolian Alliance for Human Rights Protection, advocating modern democratization in China;[6] (5) the All–China People's Autonomy Alliance, pleading for democratic reform, human rights and freedom,[7] and (6) the Chinese Progressive Alliance and Chinese Liberal Union, promoting the establishment of a free and democratic society.[8]

These secret societies, nevertheless, share certain characteristics. First, they are poorly organized by a handful of dissident students, workers and peasants. Since the crackdown of the June Fourth Incident, dissidents have been chased by the police. Without sufficient resources, organized action is difficult if not impossible to set up. Secondly, because of the aforesaid reason, there is only limited membership in any one organization ranging from several dozens to several hundreds. Because of strict social surveillance in China, members of secret societies are illegally recruited and their identity easily subject to exposure. Thirdly, most of the leaders of the 1989 movement were arrested or are in exile or attempting an escape. Therefore, many pro-democracy organizations lack unified coordination in the absence of capable and daring leaders. Fourthly, all the organizations are isolated and dispersed across cities and the countryside in the absence of a centrally controlled unit, an effective and efficient system of communication and a comprehensively planned movement. Fifthly, weak overseas connection is common. On the one hand, neither resources nor manpower are adequately provided by the overseas pro-democracy organizations. On the other hand, there is no organization to act as a bridge between the mainland and overseas. Lastly, their means of operation are limited to the post, facsimile transmission, circulation of underground papers, dissemination of leaflets, and secret contacts with foreign journalists and overseas democrats. And such measures are either sporadic or malfunctional.

When compared with the underground-publication organizations in 1978–1979, the objective and means of most of the secret societies after 1989 are more radical and more revolutionary. Leaders of the Social Democratic Party, the Chinese Progressive Alliance and the Chinese Liberal Union, and their associates — about six hundred — were arrested around June 1992. The core leaders were charged with the crime of "counter-revolution."[9]

Since the Fourteenth National Congress of the CCP held in October 1992, China has become more stable and prosperous both politically and economically. The immediate future and the prospects of the underground movement are doomed to failure. As the living standards of the workers and the peasants are advancing because of the continuous and determined national open-door policy, the movement will gradually lose mass support. The rising expectations of the general public are, though temporarily, met by the accelerating economic growth. The young, idealistic, but inexperienced democrats without organizational, financial and personnel assistance are fighting the battle alone. The rising frustration of the intellectuals has been occasionally eased with their exile either voluntary or involuntary. The parity of people's expectations and frustrations will be maintained for a certain period of time until a great discrepancy between the two revives on any one or all of the following conditions: (1) economic development being critically hampered; (2) social mobility being tremendously restricted, and (3) political participation being insufficiently channelled.

Unless there is a radical leadership reshuffle and/or an unexpected international economic sanction against China in the near future, it is unlikely that the policy of the socialism-with-Chinese-characteristics economy will be overturned. As long as the upbeat economic growth is stable, upward mobility will be secured by the competent, dynamic and educated youth. Although political participation is often said to be a restricted area in socialist reform, the Party will not be so irrational as to suffocate people's grievances without any pertinent political relaxation after the experience of 1978–1979, 1986–1987 and 1989. Moreover, the blooming of an economy is often accompanied by political demand from the people. The Party has to learn to accommodate a balance between economic output and political input in the course of which it will gain more confidence in handling the non-antagonistic contradictions among the people.

Even though the rising of frustrations has highly exceeded that of expectation in the open reform period, underground pro-democracy movements can at most create minor disturbances. China is hardly as decayed as subjectively considered by the democrats that revolution is inevitable.

The Movement Overseas

There were various problems at the initial stage of development concerning ideology, organization, leadership and ethnics.[10] And a number of reasons have brought the movement to a low ebb after 1989:

1. International pressure for human rights in China is weakening. The most-favoured-nation (MFN) status issue, often used by the United States government and overseas democrats as an economic means to achieve political ends, is losing its importance as a diplomatic tactic to attack the underdevelopment of human rights in China. It is not feasible to impose economic sanctions against China as a permanent policy since most of the developed countries are suffering from economic recession in the early 1990s.

2. The Chinese government has been able to readjust itself socially, politically and economically in response to the challenge of the collapse of

Eastern Europe and the Soviet Union. Socially, the government was able to pacify the emotion of the intellectuals, the proletariat, the peasantry and the general public in the aftermath of the June Fourth Incident. Politically, especially after the Fourteenth National Party Congress, most of the key members in the conservative faction within the Party have been removed and a political crisis has, therefore, been avoided through peaceful power transfer. Economically, the liberal faction within the Party persists with the socialist market system and, therefore, the rising expectations of the people can be satisfied. It appears that "peaceful evolution" was a painful lesson for the disintegrated socialist countries. The rapidly re-established stability and prosperity after the June Fourth Incident is an example in which socialism with Chinese characteristics can compete with capitalism with Russian/Eastern European characteristics.

3. China's economy is flourishing and people's living standard has been relatively raised. It is tactical but not ethical for the overseas democrats to undermine the Chinese economy by advocating foreign economic sanctions and, thus, affect their own people's livelihood. Moreover, the Chinese government has always adopted a hard-line policy on sovereignty issues, ensuring that no foreign intervention is allowed to interfere with its domestic affairs.

4. Domestic dissidents are "exported" and overseas dissidents are "re-imported" back to China to release the tensions of the struggle for human rights both inside and outside. Well-known democrats, Fang Lizhi, who was associate professor of the Physics Department of Peking University (labelled as the "black hands behind the scene"), and his wife Li Shuxian were expelled from China under US pressure. Worker leaders (Han Dongfang and Liu Qing), writers (Bai Hua and Wang Ruowang), scholars (Guo Luoqi, Li Honglin, Liu Xiaobo, Wen Yuankai and Zhou Tuo), and Hong Kong dissidents (Liu Shanqing and Luo Haixing) were or are being approved to leave China. In March 1992, Deng Xiaoping offered amnesty to the exiles regardless of their political views and guaranteed that no reprisal would be taken after their return.[11] Famous nonconformists like Dai Qing (ex-reporter of *Guangming ribao*), Ni Yuxian (ex-Vice-chairman of Chinese Liberal Democratic Party) and Shen Tong (one of the founders of the Chinese Democracy Foundation) were allowed to return to and depart from China notwithstanding their crimes committed under the Chinese law. To a certain extent, the policy of mollification (*huairou zhengce*) is adversely affecting the solidarity of the overseas pro-democracy movement. Nevertheless, overseas dissidents like Chen

Yizi, Liu Binyan, Su Wei, Wu Guoguang, Xu Bangtai, Yan Jiaqi, Yuan Zhimin were in hesitation,[12] especially when they heard of the two Tongs' cases. (Bao Tong, former political secretary of Zhao Ziyang, was sentenced in July 1992 to seven years' imprisonment for committing the crimes of disclosing state secrets and of counter-revolution; and Shen Tong, one of the student leaders in Tiananmen Square, was arrested upon his arrival in China in September 1992 and allowed to return to the United States two months later.)

5. Overseas pro-democracy organizations are draining their financial reserves as their activities are becoming inert. According to the annual reports of the Hong Kong Alliance in Support of Patriotic Democratic Movement of China, the outlay for the sponsorship of overseas organizations' activities were shrinking:[13]

15 June 1989–30 June 1990	HK$1,946,438.72
1 July 1990–30 June 1991	205,939.05
1 July 1991–30 June 1992	431,564.20

Fewer activities mean less funds and, in turn, fewer activities.

If the overseas democracy movement has been described as fractional in the past years, 1993 may be considered the year of unity. In June 1991, the Chinese Alliance for Democracy (the Alliance) announced in June 1991 that the Alliance would unite with the Federation for a Democratic China (the Federation).[14] The two organizations would have combined in October 1992 had it not been for problems over "some organizational details." The union would be delayed until January 1993.[15] The success of the unity depends on the following factors:

1. Leadership. Chai Ling (former leader of Autonomous Union of University Students, AUUS), Wan Runnan (then secretary-general of the Federation and former general-manager of the electronics Stone Corporation in Peking), Wang Bingzhang (former head of the Alliance) and Wuer Kaixi (former leader of AUUS) proved to be incompetent at leading the pro-democracy movement overseas at the initial stage.[16] Fang Lizhi and Liu Binyan were reluctant to shoulder this responsibility. Su Xiaokang (the chief author of television series *River Elegy*), Su Shaozhi (former research fellow of the Institute of Marxism and Leninism of the Chinese Academy of Social Sciences), Hu Ping (former head of the Alliance) and Yan Jiaqi (former research fellow at the Institute of Political Science under the Chinese Academy of Social Sciences) were too scholarly to guide the movement.[17] This leadership vacuum has encouraged the 74-year-old

Wang Ruowang (famous author expelled from the Party in 1987) to campaign for the chairmanship of the Alliance[18] and the chairmanship of the union of the Alliance and the Federation.[19] But as a leader, Wang seems too old and may not be able to strike a balance among the complicated factions.

2. Strategy. The Alliance employs the strategy of "reforming the country from outside" (*tizhiwai gaige*) while the Federation promotes "reforming the country from inside" (*tizhinei gaige*).[20] These two strategies have aroused controversies since 1989.[21] And recently, Wang Ruowang, candidate for union chairman, has declared himself in support of the former, and his three minimum programmes (*zuidi gangling*) are (a) to terminate one-party dictatorship, (b) to implement the freedom of speech, and (c) to rehabilitate the June Fourth Incident and to release all political criminals.[22] Wang, however, has failed to make a compromise between the two organizations unless the supporters of the Federation are ready to abandon their established strategy and totally support that of the Alliance.

3. Organization. Closely related to the strategy issue is whether the merger will become a political party or an ordinary association. Conflict exists between two other potential candidates for the union chairmanship — Wan Runnan (Chairman of the Federation) who supports the establishment of an association, and Yan Jiaqi (ex-Chairman of the Federation) who favours that of a party.[23] As an association, the newly formed organization would function as an overseas pressure group whose objective would be to influence the policies made by the Chinese government. As a party, it would act on a long-term struggle against the CCP and aim, in cooperation with the Kuomintang (KMT) if possible, at replacing the CCP. The nature of the organization determines the future development of the overseas pro-democracy movement.

Revolution, Reformation and "Peaceful Evolution"

Article 3 of the *Charter of the Chinese Alliance for Democracy* states that "The objective of the Alliance are: to abolish one-party dictatorship, to implement democratic constitutionalism, to protect private property, and to promote pluralistic economy." Article 4 of the *Charter of the Federation for a Democratic China* declares that "The programmes of the Federation are: to protect basic human rights, to safeguard social justice, to develop a private economy, and to terminate one-party dictatorship." Institutionally, the two overseas organizations aim not at overthrowing the PRC or the CCP and, therefore, the nature of the pro-democracy movement is reformationary. By the same token, the objective of the seven pro-democracy organizations inside China mentioned above is to encourage political reform without jeopardizing the ruling power of the CCP. It is accordingly safe to say that to establish a multi-party system does not necessarily mean to exterminate the CCP or to overthrow the People's Republic of China.

The CCP, on the other hand, disapproves of reformation directed at "peaceful evolution," using non-violent measures to change the nature of the socialist country.[24] The PRC has accused the western democratic countries of applying to China the tactics which led to the "evolution" of Eastern Europe and the Soviet Union, and it contends that pro-democracy organizations at home and abroad are being manipulated by the Great Powers to force the PRC into the direction prescribed by them. In view of this, the PRC launched the movement of "anti-peaceful evolution" against the "imperialist-capitalist" penetration into the socialist fortress.[25]

In assessing the forms of movement of the pro-democracy organizations inside and outside China, the following points are worth noting:

1. Revolution. No active or visible organization openly advocates the overthrow of the PRC or the abolition of the CCP. It is argued that the present conditions are not yet ripe, and the present pro-democracy groups are not readily organized as revolutionary parties. In the eyes of the democrats who are propagating an independent Taiwan in the Republic of China (ROC), all existing pro-democracy organizations seem to take a much more conservative approach.

2. Reformation. All of the above-said organizations are fundamentally reformationary. By reform, the ultimate objective of the reformers is to replace the position of the ruling group, or to make policies acceptable to the ruler.[26] However, some of the organizations aim at replacing the ruling Party, but their reform programmes cannot in any form be accepted by the ruler. Reformation in the eyes of the CCP means "counter-revolution."

3. "Peaceful Evolution." The only alternative of the pro-democracy organizations is to anticipate *liying waihe* (collaborating within with forces from without) in order to press the CCP for changes towards a westernized democracy.[27] Although their approaches are the same, the aims are different. The domestic dissidents see socialist democracy worth striving after while the overseas democrats regard a multi-party system as the basic programme. However, "peaceful evolution" is deemed by the CCP to be

traitorous collaboration with foreigners and, therefore, to be equivalent to "counter-revolution" too.

The failure of the prevalent pro-democracy movement is foreseeable. On the one hand, the political atmosphere is unfavourable to the democrats. On the other hand, the organizations are not well structured; the leaders of the democrats overlook the crucial alliance with the peasantry and fail in constructing any convincing theory to counter the currently powerful though not popular Party ideology. The reformers are too close to the Party (in the eyes of the people) to gain popular support and too "dissident" (in the eyes of the Party) to gain the Party's trust. The radical opinions of the revolutionists are unacceptable in any countries.

Economic liberalization always comes before political democratization on the Party's list of priorities. Any action contrary to this policy will be condemned as a violation of stability and unity. In fact, democratization itself bears different meanings according to official and unofficial interpretations. The Party deems that democracy has always been a guided "democracy" while, to the democrats, it means a more open form of democracy.

An Evaluation

In June 1957, *Renmin ribao* published the editorial "What Is This All About?" which triggered off the struggle against the "rightists." Almost thirty years later, a new political terminology — "bourgeois liberalization" — emerged. Like "bourgeois rightist" in the anti-rightist movement and "capitalist-roader" during the Cultural Revolution, a new appellation could imply a new movement. It seems that the fear of an ordinary ideological conflict being magnified into a sharp class struggle has not disappeared. As *Guangming ribao* warned in September 1989 right after the June Fourth Incident, "The recent anti-government rioting in Beijing shows that although the class struggle is no longer the main contradiction in Chinese society, its existence is independent of man's will.... One feature of the present class struggle is that representatives of bourgeois liberalization undertake capitalism under the banner of reform and opening to the outside world and adhering to the four cardinal principles ... while changing their essential content."[28]

The framework of the four basic principles excludes anything which does not fit in with the four categories and regards it as "bourgeois," or simply, "hostile." For example, there was initial confusion as to whether the student demonstrations in December 1986 had tacit support from within the Party. When late General Secretary Hu Yaobang "resigned" and a few other prominent Party personnel were sacked or demoted in January 1987 due to their alleged responsibility for the outbreak of "bourgeois liberalization," confusion reigned. Exactly eighteen months later, Zhao Ziyang, the then General Secretary, was sacked for making the "mistakes of supporting the turmoil and splitting the Party." People would ask which Party leadership they were to uphold. If these Party leaders could make such fundamental blunders, how could ordinary people distinguish between "right and wrong"? Thus, even the application of the four basic principles is shown to be arbitrary but, curiously, that is the basis on which "class" enemies are supposedly identified.

The stumbling block of democratization is the four basic principles under which the people have to recognize the restraint on their freedom by the Party. Any attempt to break away from the restraint would be unrealistic; the only outlet for the people who wish to do so would be a revolution which would of course be relentlessly extinguished. It is equally dangerous for the Party to continue to exert boundless dictatorship over the people through unreasonable dogmatism instead of any rational justification, for this can only lead to irretrievable blunders as in the past. If this assumption is true, the June Fourth Incident in 1989 is nothing but an inevitable outcome.

The idea of democratization since Mao Zedong's death has gained tremendous momentum both inside and outside the state apparatus; however, the development has not been like that of western parliamentarism. The traditional Chinese idea of "democracy" always embodies the concept of "for the people" but excludes those of "by the people" and "of the people." The Confucian notion of *minben* (people-as-the-basis) is deep-rooted in the Chinese culture. It means that the people are entitled to welfare, but that is different from *minquan* (people's rights) and *minzhu* (people's rule or democracy).

Andrew Nathan observes that modern Chinese *minben* thinkers "treated political rights as something the ruler should grant rather than recognize. They stressed the advantages of political democracy for the state rather than for citizens. They valued political rights for what they enabled citizens to contribute to the state rather than for what they enabled them to protect for themselves."[29] This tradition can be found in the 1978–1979 democracy movement, the 1986–1987 student movement and the 1989 student occupation of Tiananmen Square, during all of which the Party ignored the political rights and the sovereign power of the people. The principle of "for the people" only gains weight in the context of the economic modernization, one purpose of which is to raise the people's living standards.

In Communist China, democracy is explained in terms of "content" and "form," and the latter must be subservient to the former. Based on the content, class-oriented democracy is only a tool of the vanguard of the proletariat to achieve the goal of the economic base. In this conception, the idea of all-people power is not given any consideration.

Democracy in China remains tutelary in nature. A defined orbit is set by the Party for the people to follow and the centre of that orbit is the four basic principles. Its basis is the exact opposite of the principle of liberal democracy. While the constitution of the PRC provides democracy and liberty for the people, it is often hard to judge which rights belong to the proletariat or the bourgeoisie. When the people strive to be the master of their own affairs and claim the freedom promised by the constitution, they take the risk of being accused of exercising "bourgeois" democracy or "bourgeois" liberty. Thus, members of the working class who clamour for more democracy are said to be "dissidents" because they violate the four basic principles. Consequently, it is not illogical to infer that opinions which are pro-Party must be "democratic" and the election guided by the Party must be "democratic" as well. Party dictatorship is then "legitimately" transformed into the "people's democracy." Virtually, the legitimacy of the Party as the vanguard of the proletariat does not depend on the majority's will, but is rather derived from the correctness of its leadership.

Democracy in China becomes an outlet for political grievances. Since a great discrepancy exists between the views of the democrats and those of the Party, the suppression but not extermination of the pro-democracy movement has caused a further crisis of faith in the Party's ideology after the crises of the Hundred Flowers Movement and the Cultural Revolution. The "lost" generation is further "lost," but its self-consciousness prevails. From November 1986 to January 1987, slogans like "we don't want democracy bestowed"; "we will fight for genuine democracy" and "we want freedom" echoed in the street demonstrations by students.[30] The protest was denounced as "bourgeois liberalization" which denoted "opposing the Communist leadership and opposing the socialist road."[31] With the cumulated anger of the students, the death of Hu Yaobang sparked off explosive demonstrations from April to June 1989. The pro-democracy and anti-corruption campaign was sentenced as "counter-revolutionary rebellion."

If people's democracy is defined as a system in which "the people of the whole country enjoy the supreme right to manage the state's affairs on the basis of common ownership and control, in various forms, of the means of production,"[32] the term "people" is applicable only to those in power in the Party and who entirely submit to the four basic principles which can only be correctly interpreted by the Party alone.

Notes

1. Deng Xiaoping, *Selected Works of Deng Xiaoping* (Beijing: Foreign Language Press, 1984), pp. 155–56.
2. See Kjeld E. Brodsgaard, "The Democracy Movement in China, 1978–1979: Opposition Movements, Wall Poster Campaigns, and Underground Journals," *Asian Survey*, Vol. xxi, No. 7 (July 1981), pp. 768–69 and Jiang Zhengchang, *Zhongguo dalu qingnian minzhu yundong zhi tantao* (Study of the Democracy Movement of the Youth in Mainland China) (Taipei: Youshi, 1981), p. 106.
3. *Express News* (Hong Kong), 18 January 1992.
4. *Ibid.*, 3 April 1992.
5. *Sing Tao Daily News* (Hong Kong), 7 April 1992 and *Hong Kong Daily News*, 16 August 1992.
6. *Oriental Daily News* (Hong Kong), 29 April 1992.
7. *Sing Tao Daily News*, 3 June 1992 and *Hong Kong Daily News*, 22 August 1992.
8. *Wah Kiu Yat Pao* (Hong Kong), 23 July 1992; *Hong Kong Daily News*, 16 August 1992 and 21 October 1992.
9. *Sing Tao Daily News*, 13 July 1992; *Wah Kiu Yat Pao*, 23 July 1992; *Hong Kong Daily News*, 16 August 1992 and 21 October 1992.
10. Winston L. Y. Yang and Ma Yi-yang, *Fengbao zhihou: bajiu minyun ji qi yingxiang* (After the Thunderstorm: The 1989 Popular Movement and Its Impact) (Hong Kong: Pai Shing, 1991), pp. 215–30.
11. *Express News*, 7 March 1992.
12. *Ming Pao* (Hong Kong), 7 March 1992 and 22 April 1992; *Hong Kong Economic Journal*, 3 April 1992.
13. First, Second and Third Standing Committee, Annual Reports, Hong Kong Alliance in Support of Patriotic Democratic Movement of China, November 1990, November 1991 and October 1992.
14. *Ming Pao*, 4 June 1991.
15. *Hong Kong Economic Times*, 1 August 1992.

16. Yang and Ma (see Note 10), pp. 215–30; C. L. Chiou, "Jiebukai de Zhongguojie, zhuabudao de minyun lingxiu" (The Unsolvable Knot in China and the Unavailability of Democratic Leaders), *The Nineties*, No. 264 (January 1992), pp. 82–85; *Oriental Daily News*, 3 June 1992 and *Hong Kong Economic Times*, 1 August 1992.
17. Chiou (see Note 16).
18. *Central Daily News*, 19 October 1992.
19. *Central Daily News*, 16 November 1992.
20. Yang and Ma (see Note 10), p. 227.
21. *Express News*, 6 March 1992.
22. *Central Daily News*, 7 December 1992.
23. *Hong Kong Economic Journal*, 12 May 1992.
24. Li Changxi and Jia Chunfeng, *Lun fandui hepingyanbian* (On Opposing Peaceful Evolution) (Shenyang: Liaoning daxue chubanshe, 1991), p. 21.
25. Niu Jinshan, *Budao de Hongqi* (The Untumbling Red Flag) (Sichuan: Sichuan renmin chubanshe, 1992), pp. 269–85.
26. Zhou Yangshan, *Dangdai Zhongguo yu minzhu* (Contemporary China and Democracy) (Taipei: Tungta, 1986), pp. 128–29.
27. The Federation for a Democratic China suggested the US President-elect, Bill Clinton, to establish an "Advisory Group on the Policy towards Communist China" and "Free China Radio" so as to cultivate a group of qualified democratic personnel. See *Tin Tin Daily News* (Hong Kong), 15 November 1992. Clinton through the Secretary of State-designate openly declared in January 1993 that the new administration would "seek to facilitate a peaceful evolution of China from communism to democracy." See *South China Morning Post*, 15 January 1993.
28. *Beijing Review*, September 1989, p. 44.
29. Andrew J. Nathan, *Chinese Democracy* (Berkeley: University of California Press, 1985), p. 127.
30. *Beijing Review*, 23 February 1987, pp. 18–21.
31. *Beijing Review*, 13 April 1987, p. 21.
32. Lu Cheng and Zhu Gu, "Qieshi baozhang renmin de minzhu quanli" (Effectively Safeguard the People's Democratic Rights), *Hongqi*, No. 17 (September 1980), pp. 9–11, quoted from Brantly Womack, "Electoral Reform in China," *Chinese Law and Government*, Vol. 15, Nos. 3–4 (Fall-Winter 1982–1983), p. 163.

22

The Changing Educational System: Dilemma of Disparity

Leslie Nai-kwai Lo

In the period following the suppression of the student pro-democracy movement in 1989, Chinese education appeared morbid on the surface, sensitive to change that could be misconstrued as deviation from the policies of a suspicious Chinese Communist Party (CCP).

As abhorrence of student defiance of state power grew with escalating official condemnation and returning dissidents such as Dai Qing and Shen Tong were either barred or detained, restraining measures were taken to curb educational practices that were deemed too liberal. The revival of conservative educational policies seemed a strong possibility.

University authorities were charged with the responsibility of identifying and possibly purging from their establishments those students and teachers who actively supported and participated in the student movement. The Party assumed fuller control of the tertiary institutions and schools. The small number of institutions that were still experimenting with the "university president responsibility system"[1] lost their impetus to strive, treading cautiously in order not to arouse the suspicion of conservative officials of the State Education Commission. As the deputy-director of the State Education Commission, He Dongchang, admonished Chinese teachers to purge the nation's schools of capitalist liberalism, safeguard the values of the nation's youths against American influence, and insist on using Marxism as the guiding light in the design of instructional material,[2] other education officials called upon educators to nurture teachers who would be both "red and expert" and scholars who would ensure that educational research would become a stronghold of Marxism.[3]

That the CCP was determined to have fuller control of the education enterprise was evident in its efforts to nip any growth of "capitalist liberal" tendencies in its bud and to re-establish the "socialist road" as the only direction for educational development. However, since the beginning of 1992, educational policies promulgated have been both conservative and liberal, and tentative and bold. To be sure, the reintroduction of conservative educational practice cited above has caused a major setback to the reform efforts initiated in 1978 and again in 1985. Yet the corresponding efforts to restore reformist policies and to introduce new and bold educational practice represent another interesting dimension of Chinese education in transition.

At the beginning of the new academic year in 1992, an editorial of the *China Education News*, the most widely-circulated newspaper devoted entirely to education, urged educators and government functionaries to "speed up reform, speed up development" by, among other means, including institutional autonomy in the scope of educational reform.[4] Months earlier in the past summer, the director of the State Education Commission, Li Tieying, had been counting the ways by which the state could involve others in financing local schooling.[5] Writing on the future of higher education, an education commentator from Shanxi suggested that higher institutions should overcome their fear of instability, abandon their habit of waiting for instructions from above and depending on financial support from the government; instead, they should actively develop their own methods of reforming their institutions.[6] Later on in the year, Li Tieying went so far as to stress that the "good" experience of foreign countries in educational management and instruction, including the experience of capitalist countries, should be "boldly absorbed and borrowed" in order to reform the educational system.[7] By linking education to his aspirations, the deputy-governor of Guangdong urged educators to support the economic development of the prosperous southern province so that it could "overtake the [development] of the 'four little dragons' of Asia in twenty years' time."[8]

Through this haze of contradictory messages, the changing direction from conservative policies to cautious experimentation is discernible in recent educational practice. It may be some time before Chinese education can rebound to the state of conviviality in the mid-1980s when the CCP was willing to loosen its grip on China's education enterprise. Nevertheless, some of the items reintroduced onto the development agenda illustrate a clear departure from the somber apprehensiveness that has characterized Chinese education in the last three years. The deliberation on institutional autonomy is being revived once again. The marketing of research and invention by tertiary institutions and research institutes has been encouraged by the government. Schools have been allowed to have a freer hand in admitting students of their choice, and a major criterion for admission of students beyond the assigned quota is the ability to pay. Despite the apparent loss of precious professional manpower when the US government allowed 70,000 overseas students from China to stay permanently,[9] the CCP has been willing to make concessions to over 100,000 compatriot scholars abroad in order to arrest the brain drain.[10] Moreover, rumours about the dismissal of He Dongchang, the conservative deputy-director of the State Education Commission, have also served to perpetuate an atmosphere of uncertainty, that extensive and rapid alteration of the *status quo* has been imminent. In early 1993, the People's University in Beijing abolished seventeen courses on Marxism and Leninism while introducing fourteen new courses on marketing, international trade, and real estate management. Almost at the same time, the State Education Commission announced the shortening of a full year of military training, which was introduced to the formal curricula of the nations most prestigious institutions after June 1989, to approximately a month.[11]

To many, the change in direction can only be attributed to the will of Deng Xiaoping to reassert himself and to reimpose his vision of development on Chinese society. Indeed, Deng's "southern inspection tour" has been considered by China observers as the turning point in China's post-Tiananmen history, that Chinese politics as well as other contested arenas of the state would henceforth adopt Deng's developmental approach. The Fourteenth Congress of the CCP held in the autumn of 1992 seemed to confirm such speculation when it stressed economic development as its prime concern, adopted "market economy" as the key concept for economic development, and agreed on "openness" as the approach to achieve development. In education, Deng's "southern inspection tour" undoubtedly gave impetus to experimentation. "The strides for reform should be greater, and we should be more audacious," wrote two commentators, "we should have the courage to experiment, and not be like women with bound-feet."[12]

In the following discussion, this chapter will argue that important educational changes which occurred in the last year actually represent the CCP's renewed effort to address inveterate problems that have impeded development — such as meager investment in and rigid deployment of manpower — and emerging problems borne of its post-Cultural Revolution policies, such as regional disparity and illicit practices of schools. Deng's tour, therefore, did not bring about a transformation in education but merely served to highlight some of these changes that have taken place in the recent past. This chapter is an attempt to illuminate the dilemmas confronting an educational system in transition. As stipulated in the *Decision of the Central Committee of the Communist Party of China on the Reform of Educational Structure* of 1985, CCP policies have changed China's educational system through popularization of education, change in financing strategy, and vocationalization of schooling. While these policies have brought about desirable changes, their implementation carried discernible costs. In its effort to provide more educational opportunities to the nation's children and youths in the absence of a concomitant policy of positive discrimination, the CCP has become an unwilling witness to the spread of regional disparity as poorer western provinces have fallen farther behind the richer eastern region in educational development. Moreover, the decentralization of finance of schooling put regional disparity into sharper focus as poor communities lacked the wherewithal to ensure that quality education would be provided in their schools. Furthermore, the move to vocationalize secondary schooling reaffirmed a dual track system of schools which assigned varying degrees of prestige to different kinds of schools. After years of experimentation and growth, the vocational schools and their students are still being considered inferior to those that prepare students for higher education. Schools and higher institutions are trying to grasp the meaning of educational change while engaging themselves in fund-raising endeavours and other kinds of activities that may help them find their place in the educational system. The educational system, in turn, is trying to adjust to dynamics of a rapidly changing society lest it would be left too far behind.

Expansion of Higher Education and Regional Disparity

Expansion of the educational system entails the rapid increase in the number of higher institutions and student enrolment as well as the implementation by regional progression of nine years of compulsory education, starting with provinces of the eastern seaboard and hopefully spreading to the rest of the country. As pointed out earlier in *China Review*:

> Like their counterparts in the West in the 1950s and 1960s, Chinese educational reformers believe that educational expansion will increase educational opportunities which in turn will facilitate development through a more productive citizenry. The continual and rapid expansion of higher education since 1978 is a testimony to the application of this kind of thinking that has dominated educational reform policies in the world for at least two decades in the mid-century.[13]

The expansion of higher education can be seen as a concerted effort to nurture professional manpower for the CCP's ambitious developmental programme. Viewed from a historical perspective, the priority of expansion represents a major shift in the CCP's developmental strategy, from emphasis on the development of inland provinces to that of provinces along the eastern seaboard:

> Before the 1980s, the CCP attempted to narrow the developmental gap between rich and poor provinces through centralized reform policies that

favoured the inland and western provinces. In the 1980s, a more decentralized approach to planning and development allowed many eastern provinces, the major beneficiaries of the 'open door policy,' to choose their own pace of educational expansion and to absorb professional manpower from other provinces.[14]

The advantage of provinces along the eastern seaboard in higher education has been established since the mid-1980s when their increase in student number as well as the growth rate of size of student population per institution clearly exceeded figures for the same categories for the rest of China. As illustrated by the following figures, recent efforts by the CCP to halt the expansion of higher education was successful; however, its efforts have stopped short of rectifying the uneven development of regions that was exacerbated by the reversal of development strategy.

From figures provided in Table 1, higher education in the eastern region as well as in the rest of China has registered negative growth between 1989 and 1991. During this period, across China the total number of institutions decreased from 1,079 to 1,075 as the CCP attempted to control the massive expansion of higher education in the latter part of the 1980s. Taken as a whole, however, the growth in the three categories in Table 1, be they positive or negative, is almost negligible.

Between 1989 and 1991, the eastern region lost three institutions. It also enrolled 28,991 fewer students, a mere 2.5% of the 1989 figure of 1,149,934. The average size of student population in its institutions decreased by 40 students, or a 2% loss.

In the same period, the rest of China lost one institution and enrolled 9,462 fewer students, which is 1% of the 1989 figure of 932,177. The average size of student population decreased by 15.4, or a 0.8% loss.

If we exclude the "educationally advanced" provinces of Sichuan, Hubei, and Shaanxi from the list of "non-eastern" provinces, the "rest of China," composed of poorer inland provinces, lost four institutions and enrolled 5,586 fewer students during the same period. They represent a 1% of the 1989 figure of 562,783. However, the average size of student population in its institutions grew by 3.25, a negligible gain of 0.19%.

The general situation in higher education, then, is that the more developed eastern region has maintained a significant lead over the rest of the country in terms of the number of institutions, student enrollment, and the average size of student population. The widening of the developmental gap between the eastern provinces and the poorer inland provinces during

Table 1. Number of Institutions, Student Enrollment, and Average Size of Institutions by Region, 1984, 1989, and 1991

Regions	1984	1989	1991
Eastern region			
Number of institutions	491	579	576
Student enrollment	764,000	1,149,934	1,120,943
Size of student population per institution	1,556	1,986	1,946
Growth in size		+430	−40
Growth rate		+27.6%	−2%
Rest of China			
Number of institutions	411	500	499
Student enrollment	632,000	932,177	922,715
Size of student population per institution	1,537.7	1,864.4	1,849
Growth in size		+326.7	−15.4
Growth rate		+21.2%	−0.8%
Rest of China, excluding Hubei, Sichuan and Shaanxi			
Number of institutions	266	338	334
Student enrollment	383,000	562,783	557,197
Size of student population per institution	1,439.8	1,665	1,668.25
Growth in size		+225.2	+3.25
Growth rate		+15.6%	+0.19%

Sources: 1984 figures of number of institutions and student enrollment extracted from People's Republic of China, State Statistical Bureau (comp.) *Zhongguo tongji nianjian 1985* (*Statistical Year-book of China, 1985*) (Hong Kong: Economic Information & Agency, and Beijing: China Statistical Information and Consultancy Service Centre, 1985), p. 584; 1989 figures in *Statistical Year-book of China, 1990*, pp. 703, 729; 1991 figures in *Statistical Year-book of China, 1992*, pp. 721, 725.

the period of expansion from 1984 to 1989 has been checked. Yet there is no indication from official figures that the gap is narrowing in any way.

From a strategic point of view, the CCP's effort to check the expansion of higher education is a measure that would eventually ensure an acceptable standard of education provided by higher institutions. In 1991, 30 institutions had to temporarily suspend their admission of first year students because of the quality of their teaching staff, and facilities were considered to be inferior. Another 114 institutions were also asked to decrease the number of first year entrants for the same reasons.[15]

Concomitant with the policy of suspending admission and cutting the admission quota of over 10% of China's higher institutions, the CCP has also attempted to consolidate smaller or substandard institutions with the hope of turning them into stronger institutions. In the western province of Guizhou, for example, efforts are being made to merge various types of colleges of education and to encourage the pooling of resources of regular higher institutions and that of institutions in the adult education sector.[16] In a sense, the gross underutilization of resources at some of Guizhou's higher institutions put into focus the fallacy of expansion that came to characterize higher education in the 1980s. Of the province's 44 higher institutions (including institutions for adult education), some of which enrolled less than 100 students, only 20.8% have managed to maintain the state recommended teacher-student ratio of 1 : 6. Moreover, while the state recommended staff- (including teachers and support staff) student ratio to be 1 : 3.3, ten of its regular institutions still maintained a 1:1 staff-student ratio. In the adult education sector, five institutions have even more favourable staff-student ratios.[17]

The reconstitution of lesser institutions, together with the overall slowdown of the expansion of higher education, should be a policy of the 1990s. From an official outline of educational development in the Eigth Five-year Plan which began in 1991, the estimated number of students in higher education would be increased only modestly. By 1995, the number of students to be admitted into undergraduate programmes of regular institutions will be 650,000, only 24,000 students more than those admitted in 1992.[18]

The suspension of higher education expansion should help prevent the developmental gaps in education between rich and poor regions from widening. Yet suspension alone will not be enough to rectify the unbalanced development among regions. Because of the obviously different levels of economic development attained by the regions and, therefore, their differing standards of living, the "brain drain" from poor provinces to the rich eastern region which occurred in the late 1980s has persisted to the present.[19] The eastward move of professional manpower from the poorer western provinces has perhaps cost them the most valuable asset that they had hoped to retain.[20]

Popularization of Basic Education and Regional Disparity

Regional disparity in educational development is not limited to higher education. Popularization of schooling, which is another form of

The Changing Educational System: Dilemma of Disparity   22.9

expansion of the educational system, is yet another illustration of regional disparity. Again, the regional disparity in the popularization of schooling is a result of imbalance in economic development. According to the deputy-director of the National Research Centre for Educational Development, different regions will attain varying levels of popularization of schooling in accordance with their stages of economic development. In the 1990s, a substantial portion of the eastern region will be popularizing the senior level of secondary schooling (grades 9 to 12), while provinces in Central China will be implementing nine years of compulsory education. The less developed provinces in Western China will first have to popularize primary education in the early 1990s and then attempt to implement nine years of compulsory education in the latter part of the decade.[21]

These varying accomplishments in the popularization of schooling by geographic regions follow roughly the schedule set by the 1985 *Decision* of the CCP to implement nine years of compulsory education. However, corresponding problems experienced by educators in providing schooling to all school-age children and youths, keeping students in schools, and moving them up the ladder of schooling have confirmed not only that the implementation of compulsory education for close to 170 million of the nation's children and youths is a herculean task, but also that the economic strength of a region plays a very important role in determining the chances of success in the popularization of schooling.

Difficulties in extending educational opportunities to all school-age children and youths are encountered by most developing societies. Statistics provided by Chinese official sources customarily emphasize the nation's high rate of access to schooling. In 1992, for example, it was claimed that the entrance rate of first year of schooling had already reached an impressive 97.8%.[22] A closer look at the situation of school enrollment and attrition, however, reveals that schooling remains a remote abstraction for the less fortunate. According to the findings of a recent survey, over 33 million school-age children and youths (ages 6 to 14) are not enrolled in schools. Of this school-age population, 28 million, approximately 83% of the total number, reside in the countryside. The province with the lowest non-attendance rate is Jiangsu, China's richest province, while those with the highest non-attendance rates are Guizhou, Yunnan, and Qinghai, its poorer provinces.[23] Reports on the alarmingly large non-attending number have led quasi-official organizations in China to initiate large scale relief projects to provide schooling for those deprived of schooling.[24]

Student Drop-outs

Difficulties in keeping students in school are shared by all provinces. However, the degree of severity is again determined by the level of economic development of a province. From official sources, the problem of attrition has been alleviated somewhat. The overall drop-out rate for China's primary schools has lowered from 3.3% in 1989 to approximately 2% in 1992;[25] but when the figures are put in the context of regional development, the advances made are less than impressive. In 1992, the drop-out rate in primary schools of the eastern region was reportedly under 1%, while that of the western region was 5.7%. The drop-out rate of Tibet was as high as 18%.[26]

Findings of a study of student attrition problem at the turn of the decade[27] basically substantiate the above depiction of regional disparity, even though its reported figures have put in doubt the aforementioned 1992 figure of 2% drop-out rate for primary education (extracted from an newspaper interview). According to this analysis, the overall drop-out rate for primary education was lowered by 0.1% from 3.3% in 1988 to 3.2% in 1989. Of China's 30 provinces, autonomous regions, and metropolitan areas, only 13 (43.3%) have registered lowering drop-out rates, while 16 (53.3%) have witnessed an increase. As far as regional disparity is concerned, the study's findings depict two different but interesting situations in primary and junior secondary education. In primary education, the drop-out phenomenon is congruent with the overall picture of regional disparity, that the less economically developed the region, the higher the drop-out rate. Thus, drop-out rates in the northwest and southwest regions are found to be the highest. In junior secondary schooling, however, the highest drop-out rates are found in areas where economic development is considered to be at "mid-level." In other words, the junior secondary schools in economically deprived areas do not have the highest drop-out rates while those in the developed regions of East- and Central-southern China have the lowest drop-out rates.[28]

The difference between the drop-out rates for primary and junior secondary education by region can be explained by the fact that in the "mid-level" areas of development, with growing local industries and with commerce being introduced to their economies only recently, students at legal working-age are drawn to activities that promise immediate reward for their labour.[29] In a way, it is a recurrence of the drop-out phenomenon in some of the eastern provinces about three years ago. In 1988, for example, the climbing drop-out rates in some of the so-called "open cities" along the eastern seaboard had caused official concern.[30] With the development of the eastern provinces, the value of professional manpower is obviously on the rise there. The keen recruitment of university graduates by work units in Guangdong and Shanghai, for example, has sent a clear signal to youngsters there that it would be to their advantage to seek higher educational qualifications if they want to succeed in their increasingly modern communities.[31]

Problems of Repeaters

Difficulties in moving students up the ladder of schooling are also shared by all provinces in China, but, like student drop-outs, problems related to repeaters are most pronounced in the less developed regions. Poorer provinces such as Guangxi, Hainan, Gansu, Guizhou, Qinghai and Ningxia are among the most affected areas, while such economically advanced areas as Beijing, Liaoning and Zhejiang (all in eastern China) are least affected.[32] The same pattern is found for both primary and junior secondary schooling.

Like on student drop-outs, research findings on repeaters reveal that the problem is more severe in the rural areas; and in the countryside, the richer areas fare better than the poorer areas.

Research on drop-outs and repeaters points to two important facts. To begin with, emphasis on access without due regard to the repeaters actually clouds the important issue of equality in education because it neglects to address the problems of student survival in schools and the manners in which they survive. Both issues are interrelated and have strong implications for resources. The second fact pertains to the wastage of resources. As student attrition could be counted as losses, repeating should also be considered as a form of wastage since these students fail to complete their studies within a designated period, and more resources have to be invested in order to allow them to graduate. Given this, the problems related to repeaters could be just as damaging to the educational system as student drop-outs. From figures provided for the years 1989 and 1990 on the progression of primary students, only 69% (1989) and 70% (1990) of students managed to complete their first five years of schooling without dropping out or repeating the same grade. In other words, 31% (1989) and 30% (1990) of students failed to complete their studies within a designated period.[33] These students were either drop-outs or repeaters. As expected, the rates of drop-outs and repeaters are related to the level of development of a region.

Problems related to drop-outs and repeaters have seriously affected the popularization of basic education. The problems are especially acute when put in the context of nine years of compulsory education. In 1990, the overall promotion rate of primary students to junior secondary schools in China's eight western provinces was 67%.[34] In the western province of Gansu, for example, the enrollment rate of school-age children in primary schools had already reached 91.37% in 1986. Yet as late as 1989, the enrollment rate in the province's junior secondary school was merely 77.15%. The considerable difference between the impressive enrolment rate of primary schooling in one year and the obviously diminishing rate of junior secondary schooling three years later was reportedly the result of student attrition.[35] Moreover, widespread repetition among students in lower primary grades caused the rapid deterioration of the quality of education in rural schools. With the large number of repeaters sharing space and facilities with their younger peers, some of the primary-one classes in rural schools each had to accommodate 80 to 90 students.[36] Lacking in essential facilities such as desks and chairs, the overcrowded classrooms naturally drained the energy of teachers, easily broke the concentration of students and tested the patience of both. Many students would be required to repeat the same grade as poor pedagogy bred failure. The poor classroom environment would persist, thereby, completing a vicious cycle. In monetary terms, individual provinces had to increase educational expenditures by tens of millions of dollars each year because of the repeater problems.[37]

The popularization of basic education and the implementation of nine years of compulsory education are laudable moves that have met tenacious problems of access and survival. As yet, the dearth of workable solutions casts doubts on the educators' ability to truly implement compulsory education according to the CCP's schedule.

Change in Financing Strategy of Education

For years, educators have decried the acute shortage of funds for education. Mindful of the fact that meager investment in education has presented a major obstacle to educational development, the CCP has attempted to channel more funds into the education sector since 1978. From 1978 to

1988, state appropriation for education, commonly referred to in China as "budgeted funds," increased by 320% to RMB32.1 billion, with an average growth rate of 15.46% per year.[38] Even with the apparent increase in educational funding, state investment in education has continued to be a much discussed topic among educators and officials. The focus of discussion has basically centred on the percentage of the country's gross national product (GNP) invested in education as opposed to the increase in absolute figures.[39]

From figures gathered, state investment in education in recent years has hovered between 2.6% to 3% of China's GNP which puts Chinese education among the world's poorly financed systems. In reality, "guaranteed state investment has been less than the reported figures," thus further diminishing education's expendable income and has forced its share in GNP down to 2.2%.[40] Thus, when the director of the State Education Commission, Li Tieying, claimed that funds for education had reached RMB73 billion in 1991,[41] he was actually referring to a total amount that included funds from the central government, funds from local governments, and aggregated funds acquired through "multiple channels" (*duoqudao*). Since funds from this last category accounted for one-third of the total educational funding,[42] state appropriation was actually RMB48.6 billion, or approximately 2.4% share of the 1991 GNP.[43] The relative reduction of the state's contribution, in terms of its share of the total sum of education investment, has been the result of decentralization in the finance of education.

Decentralization of Educational Finance

Increasingly, decentralization in the finance of education has caused educators to become more dependent on the local governments for funds. In many ways, the central government is playing a diminishing role in financing, as its functions are more confined to planning and control at the national level. As a policy, decentralization has allowed educational planners a certain degree of flexibility and also made them more answerable to local needs. Moreover, the devolution of financial responsibilities to lower level governments, an outcome of decentralization, has given rise to yet another aspect of regional disparity since the finance of education has been determined by the differing economic strengths of provinces and localities.

In higher education, a 1980 decision to change the funding structure for the tertiary sector dictated that the central government be financially responsible for 36 institutions of the State Education Commission and the 300 some institutions of various ministries of the State Council. The majority of the tertiary institutions, depending on their nature, were to be funded by provincial and other types of local governments.[44]

For primary and secondary schooling, education's reliance on local governments and other nongovernmental sources for funds is even more apparent. Under the slogan "sponsorship at three levels, management at two levels" (*sanji banxue, liangji guanli*), senior secondary schools are sponsored by counties and managed by county authorities, junior secondary schools are sponsored by townships and managed by township authorities, and primary schools are sponsored by villages but managed by township authorities because of the absence of government structure at the village level. According to one source, "local contribution amounted to 88.5% of the overall national educational expenditures," while contributions from the local governments accounted for 86.9% of state appropriation in 1990.[45]

Basically, funds for basic education include funds for "improvement of operation conditions in schools" (*gaishan banxue tiaojian jingfei*) and "maintenance funds." Funds for "improvement of operation conditions in schools" cover expenditures for capital construction and purchase of equipment, whereas "maintenance funds" denote such recurrent expenditures as salaries, administrative costs, staff development costs, and expenditures for maintenance and repairs.[46]

Funds for basic education essentially come from the following sources: state appropriation from central and local governments, tuition and miscellaneous fees, education surcharge levied from urban and rural taxes, income generated by school-operated business euphemistically called "work-study programmes," funds raised in localities and collected donations (which usually include donations from local enterprises and individuals, from overseas Chinese and "compatriots" in Hong Kong and Macau), and, in some localities, the recently established "people's education funds."[47] Of these funding sources, only the first kind of income — state appropriation from central and local governments — is considered "budgeted income." The rest is community resources, or non-budgeted incomes. As expected, the kinds and amount of resources that a community can command depend very much on its economic strengths as well as the performance of local functionaries.

Table 2 contains estimated figures on incomes and expenditures of the school system of a township in Hunan province which is planning to

Table 2. Estimated Incomes and Expenditures of Basic Education in Wangling Township, Hunan Province, by Year (1990–1993)

Incomes (in Ten Thousand)	1990**	1991	1992	1993
Budgeted income	51.5	56.7	62	67
Education surcharge	21.5	29.7	31.2	32.7
Student miscellaneous fees	3.4	6.6	6.6	6.6
Work-study programmes	1.5	1.5	1.5	1.5
Collections and donations	(87.1, not included in total)			
Total	77.9	94.5	101.3	107.8
Expenditures (in Ten Thousand)				
Salaries	56.8	62.3	68.2	73.8
Administration and staff development	8.5	9.4	10.2	11.1
Maintenance and repairs	12.7	14	15.2	16.5
Total	78	85.7	93.6	101.4

** 1990 figures are real, not estimated figures.
Source: Figures included in the Table 2 are based on those provided in Zhu Junjie, "Guanyu Hunan Youxian Wanglingzhen 1993 nian shixian jiunian yiwu jiaoyu de kexingxing diaocha baogao" (Investigation Report on the Feasibility of Implementing Nine Years of Compulsory Education in Wangling Township, You County of Hunan Province in 1993), *Huadong shifan daxue xuebao* (*jiaoyu kexue ban*) (Journal of East China Normal University [Education Science Edition]), No. 3, 1992, p. 73.

implement nine years of compulsory education in 1993. At present, Wangling township has 28 schools (three secondary and 25 primary schools) with a student population of 4,846 (1,241 in secondary schools and 3,605 in primary schools). It is planned that in 1993, with the merging of the three secondary schools into two larger schools, the number of schools will be reduced by one. The student population will be increased to approximately 5,000. Taken as a whole, basic education in Wangling township is not atypical of the general situation in townships of China's medium-income provinces.

Education Surcharge and "Multiple Channel Funds"

Of the various types of income mentioned above, education surcharge is perhaps the most interesting addition to the list of possible resources for basic education. Stipulated in the law that formally institutionalized compulsory education in 1986, education surcharge is a certain percentage that local governments can levy from local taxes for use on basic education. In the urban areas, income from education surcharge should be used for improvement of operation conditions in schools. In the countryside, incomes from this source should be used for paying the salaries of community teachers (*minban jiaoshi*) who are not on the government payroll, subsidizing the schools' administrative and operation expenditures, and improving school conditions.[48] Unlike other sources of income such as donations and work-study programmes, education surcharge is tagged to the tax revenues of a locality and, therefore, should be considered a steady source of income for basic education; and depending on the size of a locality's tax revenues, education surcharge could contribute substantially to its basic education. For example, in the Wangling township described above, it is anticipated that education surcharge would consistently contribute about 30% of resources for basic education there.

Education surcharge should undoubtedly alleviate some of the state's financial burden in its quest to popularize basic education, especially among people in the less developed areas. However, the shrinking contribution of the surcharge to the total outlay of basic education, as well as the collection and administration of the surcharge, have caused official concern. Since 1986, the share of education surcharge in the non-budgeted educational expenditures (including funds raised through "multiple channels", "work-study programme," and education surcharge) has been contracting, from 73.57% in 1986 to 45.18% in 1991. Even with an annual growth rate of 17.05%, education surcharge compares unfavourably with other sources of income which combine to record an impressive annual growth rate of 38.19%.[49] Moreover, reports from counties and townships have revealed abuses in the handling of the education surcharge, ranging from the arbitrary percentage of taxes being levied to the misuse of funds for teachers' bonuses.[50]

Even with its problems, educational surcharge and other channels of funding have provided the localities with more incentives to raise funds and more flexibility to deploy their resources for basic education. To be sure, Chinese education is in perpetual need of funds. Schools in the rich Pearl River Delta Area of Guangdong province are still complaining about the lack of facilities and equipment.[51] Nevertheless, as figures in the following table will attest, Chinese schools have benefited from the "multiple channels" of fund raising since its contribution to the improvement of their operational conditions generally exceeds that of the central and local governments.

From Table 3, it is apparent that resources obtained through "multiple channels" have become an important source of funds for improving the quality of schooling in China. In almost all of its provinces and three major

Table 3. Comparison between Contributions by Government Appropriation and "Multiple Channels" of Funding in the Improvement of Operation Conditions in Schools, 1981–1991
(1 = RMB100 million)

Place	Total	State appropriation	"Multiple channels" of funding (MCF)	MCF percentage of total
Total	1,065.91	357.45	708.46	66.47%
Beijing	24.57	10.91	13.66	55.59%
Tianjin	18.87	6.99	11.88	62.96%
Hebei	39.76	8.72	31.04	78.07%
Shanxi	26.53	8.42	18.11	68.26%
Inner Mongolia	15.37	7.65	7.72	50.23%
Liaoning	39.80	17.90	21.90	55.03%
Jilin	24.43	8.03	16.40	67.13%
Heilongjiang	23.22	6.30	16.92	72.87%
Shanghai	39.35	18.95	20.40	51.84%
Jiangsu	39.06	6.35	32.71	83.74%
Zhejiang	45.25	14.37	30.88	68.24%
Anhui	49.80	18.60	31.20	62.65%
Fujian	35.95	11.60	24.35	67.73%
Jiangxi	21.48	6.44	15.04	70.01%
Shandong	55.00	7.28	47.72	86.76%
Henan	102.96	31.07	71.89	69.82%
Hubei	42.02	7.98	34.04	81.00%
Hunan	94.76	13.99	80.77	85.24%
Guangxi	35.48	9.19	26.29	74.09%
Guangdong	106.91	38.07	68.84	64.39%
Hainan**	6.09	3.87	2.22	36.45%
Sichuan	58.00	24.00	34.00	58.62%
Guizhou	16.77	13.67	3.10	18.49%
Yunnan	40.20	28.30	11.90	29.60%
Tibet	2.20	2.00	0.20	9.09%
Shaanxi	25.07	3.98	21.09	84.12%
Gansu	12.65	6.99	5.66	44.74%
Qinghai	8.87	7.03	1.84	20.74%
Ningxia	4.69	1.83	2.86	60.98%
Xinjiang	10.80	6.97	3.83	35.46%

** Figures for Hainan reflect the situation in the 1988–1991 period.
Source: *China Education News*, 8 September 1992, p. 1.

metropolises, resources from "multiple channels" constituted the major share of funds for this purpose, contributing 66.47% of a national total of RMB106.59 billion during the eleven-year period of 1981–1991.[52] From the figures provided in Table 3, it is also clear regional disparity exists both in terms of the size of investment in school improvement and the percentage share of "multiple channels" funds in total investment.

As far as the size of investment is concerned, the prosperous southeastern province of Guangdong, which has ties with overseas Chinese and residents of Hong Kong and Macau, has invested most heavily in school improvement during the eleven-year period. At the other end of the spectrum, Tibet, which is considered to be China's most educationally deprived area, has invested the least in school improvement. To be sure, the number and conditions of schools in each province should determine the size of investment. But even taking into account that Guangdong had 28,455 schools in 1991, and Tibet had 2,712 schools in the same year (both excluding vocational secondary schools), the difference in the sizes of investment in school improvement through time is still very large.[53]

Another observation that could be made about the size of investment in school improvement is the outstanding performance of some of the medium-income provinces. The provinces of Henan and Hunan, for example, have followed Guangdong's lead closely and are ranked second and third in the nation in term of size of investment. The large sums of funds invested by these provinces in school improvement also shed light on the relatively smaller commitment of the more developed provinces, such as Jiangsu and Hebei, and metropolises, such as Beijing and Shanghai. An explanation for this phenomenon is that schools in these areas have been comparatively well-provided for and, therefore, improvement of their operation conditions requires less resources.

Figures on the percentage share of "multiple channels" funds of the total volume of funds invested in school improvement depict another interesting picture of regional disparity. With the exception of China's poorer regions, all of China's provinces have relied more on "multiple channels" funds than on funds appropriated by the state for school improvement. Chiefs among these provinces are the provinces of Shandong, Hunan, Shaanxi and Jiangsu, which have percentage shares of "multiple channels" funds as high as 86.76%, 85.24%, 84.12% and 83.74% respectively. Conversely, poorer provinces, because of their economic situation, have much lower percentage shares of "multiple channels" funds — Gansu 44.74%,

Xinjiang 35.46%, Yunnan 29.6%, Qinghai 20.74%, Guizhou 18.49% and Tibet 9.09%. As it is much more difficult to raise funds for education in poorer provinces, the lower percentage share of their "multiple channels" funds of total investment is understandable. However, this means that poorer provinces are more dependent on state appropriation for school improvement. Thus, unless the central government simultaneously assumes a more active role in the finance of basic education and adopts a policy of positive discrimination in their favour, both of which are unlikely, schools in the poorer provinces will continue to rely on local governments to improve their conditions. When local governments have little resources to spare, which is the situation in poorer provinces, the chances for school improvement will depend on the efforts and fund-raising finesse of provincial and local officials.

With the decentralization of the finance of basic education, regional disparity has been found in expenditures, capital constructions, and work-study programmes.[54] From a comparison of the provinces' budgeted expenditures for primary education, per student expenditures have varied significantly from one area to another. In 1990, for example, per student budgeted expenditures for Beijing's primary schools was RMB289.65, while that for Hubei's was RMB61.46. For the same year, primary schools students in Zhejiang, Shaanxi and Shandong were each budgeted RMB131.98, RMB92.37 and RMB77.05 respectively.[55]

The delegation of financing responsibilities to the local authorities should, at least in theory, allow them to be more accountable to their communities. Yet in some areas, decentralization has caused confusion to the schools and distress to their students and teachers. In order to raise more funds, schools in some areas have found a variety of ways of collecting fees from their students. The situation has become serious enough to warrant a circular from the State Education Commission admonishing local authorities to control their schools.[56] In Sichuan province, because local authorities have failed to collect agricultural taxes from poorer communities, and, therefore, no education surcharge can be levied from taxes, "nearly 7,000 teachers [in one of its counties] have not received a cent since April of this year." An investigation of 12 junior secondary schools in the county concerned has revealed that of the 2,521 students enrolled in 1989, only 1,207 students remained by spring of 1992, a drop-out rate of 48% in less than three years.[57]

Decentralization of the finance of education has born important fruits for basic education. Regional disparity and confusion in the localities are problems commonly shared by developing societies in their efforts to popularize basic education; and as the world's most populous country, China is not immune from their consequences. Thus far, it can be argued that a lot of the accomplishments in basic education can be attributed to the decentralization efforts. What has emerged are problems that are inherent in the economic strengths of different regions and those related to administrative difficulties rather than the effects of conceptual errors that would require another thorough revision of policies to rectify.

Vocationalization of Schooling

To some observers, the vocationalization of schooling, at least in its proposed manner of implementation, is a conceptual problem that would eventually hinder educational development. The CCP's intention to rapidly develop vocational education in the senior secondary stage of schooling was stated in its 1985 *Decision* on the reform of the educational system. The goal of its policy was to have an equal distribution of students in the regular senior secondary schools and vocational and technical secondary schools. It was hoped that by 1990 both kinds of senior secondary schools would be admitting equal numbers of students in most areas.[58] The vocational and technical secondary schools consist of at least three kinds of schools: secondary specialized schools for technical and administrative personnel, schools for skilled workers, and vocational secondary schools for personnel in a variety of recently emerged occupations such as design, services and the like. They are all considered schools at the senior secondary level.

The rationale behind the CCP's policy to popularize vocational education was quite simple. Since there was a strong tendency for regular senior secondary schools to prepare students for further education in the tertiary sector, and the higher institutions could only accept a fraction of those seeking entrance, it would save wastage if some of the students could be channelled through other types of schooling and immediately join the work force upon graduation. This rationale was also supported by the widely shared assumption that secondary vocational and technical schools were more effective than the regular secondary schools in nurturing junior and middle-level personnel for the workplace.[59] With more students entering the senior secondary level of schooling because of compulsory education,[60] the CCP's rationale seemed even more convincing.

At the behest of the CCP, the vocational and technical schools grew rapidly in the secondary sector. By 1992, there were 16,818 schools of the vocational and technical type, with a student population of 6.19 million,[61] or 46.7% of the total number of students in all senior secondary schools.[62] Through administrative means, a large number of graduates from junior secondary schools were successfully channelled into the vocational and technical stream. Some ambitious officials liked to see vocational and technical education advance even further in the secondary sector, claiming that the ratio of student enrolment in these schools and that in regular secondary schools should have reached 1.5:1 by the turn of the century.[63]

The Ambiguous Role and Dubious Accomplishments of Vocational Education

The above achievements notwithstanding, reports from various regions of the country have indicated that the development of vocational and technical education has been impeded by serious problems, some of which have been encountered from the very start of the campaign of popularization. Chief among these problems is the biased views of educators, officials, and members of the public toward vocational and technical education. From the perspective of many educators, vocational and technical schools are inferior to the regular secondary schools. Some view vocational and technical education as a track in secondary schooling that is supplementary to the regular schools, and not as an integrated system that is based on its own educational philosophy with its own clear mission in education.[64] Consequently, the selection of students, curricular design, and pedagogic process of some vocational and technical schools have been placed under the shadow of the regular schools. The general belief, which is often substantiated by facts, is that the best students are admitted to the regular schools while their peers with inferior academic achievements are admitted by the vocational and technical schools. Once admitted to the latter, the chance of pursuing one's further study in higher education is diminished. The tendency exists for some vocational schools, which used to be regular senior secondary schools but were reconstituted after the promulgation of the CCP's 1985 *Decision*, to continue to offer a curriculum very similar to their regular counterparts with the hidden aim of helping their students to gain admission into the higher institutions.[65]

Another problem of vocational and technical education is the ways in which it is managed. In theory, the three kinds of schools — the secondary specialized schools, schools for skilled workers and vocational secondary schools — form an integrated system of their own. In practice, however, the three kinds of schools are hardly integrated. Since the secondary specialized schools are administered by the ministries and their provincial and metropolitan offices, and schools for skilled workers are administered by labour bureaus while vocational secondary schools are placed under the management of education bureaus, all three kinds of schools have their own system of operation. Thus in terms of the school finance and management, and student admission and placement, the three types of schools work independently from one another, with very little coordination among them.

The lack of coordination has resulted in confusion in operation. Schools have been unable to raise their quota of students and, thereby, have been undermining their own cost effectiveness. In Shanghai, where students in vocational and technical schools constitute about 60% of the secondary student population, the average enrolment figures for the three types of schools are still far from meeting the official standards. In 1990, the average enrolment in Shanghai's secondary specialized schools was 560 students while the official standard was 640 students; its schools for skilled workers averaged 141 students whereas the official standard was 200; and enrolment in its vocational secondary schools averaged 320 students when the official standard was 600.[66] In a locality in Inner Mongolia, an agricultural vocational school has had 20 serving teachers and workers but only 31 students enrolled. In a county in the mountainous region in Ningxia, a sizable vocational secondary school was established by money appropriated by the state. It received no application for admission days after it issued formal announcements for that purpose. It finally managed to recruit four students after its principal and teachers were dispatched to "mobilize the masses."[67] In Guangdong and other prosperous areas along the eastern seaboard, students for vocational and technical schools have been hard to come by because of a thriving job market. Youngsters who have decided not to seek promotion to the senior secondary schools can easily find jobs in the localities abounding with industries and commercial activities.[68]

A third problem pertains to the operational conditions and quality of education provided in the vocational and technical schools. Compared to the regular schools, vocational and technical schools require more facilities and, therefore, more investment. The curricula of these schools are usually designed to incorporate into their own major subjects of the regular curriculum. Thus, on top of the facilities required for the teaching of major subjects in regular secondary schools, science laboratories and school libraries, facilities for the teaching of specific vocational or technical subjects are also required. Where there is no clear standard for appropriation of funds for vocational and technical schools, and when there is no consensus among education officials on an acceptable standard, funding for these schools varies from one place to another, with no system of evaluation to follow. As late as October 1991, the State Council was still calling on governments at various levels to decide on a standard sum for per student expenditures in vocational and technical education.[69]

In the absence of a clear funding standard for operation, funds for vocational and technical education are determined by the preference of government bureaus. For those vocational secondary schools with junior secondary schools attached to them, and there seems to be a lot of schools of this type, the acquisition of adequate funding seems especially difficult. This is because the attention of officials is drawn to their duty of popularizing basic education, particularly to the implementation of nine years of compulsory education. Vocational and technical education, which is on the senior level of secondary schooling, does not fall within the compulsory education years and is, therefore, not given the same priority as primary and junior secondary education.[70]

Of the three types of vocational and technical schools, the vocational secondary schools operated by education bureaus are perhaps the most underfinanced since they are not supported by the ministries and labour bureaus, and have to compete with lower schools for funds. These schools are in perpetual shortage of teaching and experimental facilities. Moreover, their meager resources have prevented them from recruiting teachers of high quality. Most of the teachers serving the vocational secondary schools are transfers from the regular schools, with little background in the vocational subjects they teach. Thus, some schools have former physics teachers conducting classes in technology and former music teachers instructing students in fashion design.[71] Few of them have the kind of qualifications and work experience that are required by the positions. Given the situation, it is not uncommon to find schools with no qualified teachers.[72] They often offer certain vocational subjects because of the availability of qualified teachers for those subjects.[73]

Job Opportunities for Graduates

The fourth problem of vocational and technical education is the placement of graduates. With the lack of coordination among the different types of schools and, in the absence of strong linkage between the schools and work units, the placement of graduates has always been difficult for the administrators of vocational secondary schools. Of the three types of schools, the secondary specialized schools and schools for skilled workers have less difficulty finding jobs for their graduates because they still rely on a job assignment system. The vocational secondary schools, however, have to rely on their own contacts for this purpose. In prosperous areas where jobs are in relative abundance, graduates have higher expectations for the kinds of jobs that they can find. Thus, instead of seeking employment in areas for which they are trained, many have resorted to using their families' connections (*guanxi*) in their search for a desirable job. From various reports, there are no dearth of employing units which first select relatives of their own employees to fill vacant posts instead of hiring graduates of vocational secondary schools with relevant training.[74] Another obstacle to placement of graduates is the plethora of short-term training courses offered by different types of government bureaus, or courses contracted by these units to other types of schools, organizations or even enterprising individuals who can convince the units of their ability to operate such courses. The short-term courses have become a major competitor to the vocational and technical schools as they present a cheaper and quicker alternative to vocational education.[75]

Even when employment of graduates of vocational secondary schools are supposedly guaranteed by official quota, the jobs may still not be forthcoming. For example, the majority of counties in five northwestern provinces set aside 20% to 40% of posts for graduates of these schools. When the posts were filled, it was discovered that the employing units preferred graduates of regular schools to those of the vocational secondary schools. In all, only 10% to 25% of their posts were filled by the latter. In 1991, a vocational secondary school graduated 36 students but none was hired by local industries. Another vocational secondary school graduated 246 students in the last five years, but only five found employment through the normal channel of selection thus far.[76]

Difficulties encountered by graduates of vocational secondary schools should not be attributed solely to uncooperative employers. Miscalculation about the availability of jobs and the single-minded pursuance of popular occupations often aggravate the unemployment problem. In Hunjiang city of Jilin province, for instance, there have been over a thousand graduates competing for no more than 300 jobs available in its ten clothing factories. The reason for this surplus of skilled labour is that all of its vocational secondary schools have been offering clothing manufacturing as one of their major vocational subjects.[77] The oversupply of workers for Hunjiang's clothing factories is just one illustration of the kind of mishap shared by graduates in other places because of the ignorance of the school leadership.

In the workplace, graduates of vocational and technical schools are no different from graduates of other types of schools in the sense that they prefer to be able to apply what they have learned. That working in jobs which are relevant to one's training constitutes a major source of job satisfaction and an important factor affecting one's productivity has been substantiated by empirical evidence.[78] Whether vocational and technical schools can develop in such a way as to provide to students relevant education of high quality remains to be seen. The government's insistence on "training before work" (*xianpeixun houshanggong*) for employing units[79] should encourage employing units to recruit more graduates but would not dissuade them from hiring those with the "right" connections.

Aside from the problems of resources and quality of teachers, the most important matter on the development agenda of vocational and technical education is the integration of the three types of schools. With all its promises, vocational and technical education will be doomed without the necessary integration. In the near future, it will be unrealistic to expect a populace which holds the regular school type of education in high esteem to change its attitude toward vocational and technical education. Since the regular schools are seen as the avenue for advancement, it is natural that students and their parents should prefer them to vocational and technical schools. What is important is perhaps for practitioners in the field to acknowledge its present lower status in the eyes of the public and find ways of improving its quality and competitiveness *vis-à-vis* the regular schools.

The Changing Schools

With the state's changing style of educational administration, China's schools now have more control over their own affairs and more responsibilities in management and fund-raising.

The kind of freedom given to the schools to control their own affairs is the result of an evolution of a structure of responsibility in education that began in the higher institutions in the early 1980s, formally sanctioned by the CCP in 1985, and gradually trickled down to the schools. Like the "president responsibility system" found in some tertiary institutions, the "principal responsibility system" of the schools allows school principals to have more control over matters pertaining to personnel and school finance. This policy has given institutions and schools more freedom in operation, but it has not intended to provide them with corresponding enhancement of authority.[80]

Interestingly, it is the schools, rather than the higher institutions, that have finally emerged as the chief beneficiaries of this CCP policy to delegate management responsibilities to the school level. In a sense, the "president responsibility system" for higher institutions came to an abrupt end in the summer of 1989 when the student movement was repressed. To CCP officials who were suspicious of major shifts of responsibilities such as the "president responsibility system," the student movement was but an illustration of its fallacies, that the academics could not even control their own students. The higher institutions have not really recovered the kind of freedom that was bestowed upon them before June 1989, even though there has been a revival of calls for more autonomy to be given to them.[81] Recently the State Education Commission has indicated that the time has come for a fresh look at the issue.[82] In some provinces, higher institutions are once again allowed to take more control of their own affairs.[83]

For the schools, complaints from principals about inflexible state administration and stringent state supervision can still be heard.[84] Yet compared to their counterparts in higher institutions, the school principals in general are given a freer hand in deciding on such matters as personnel, finance, teaching and instruction. Their increased responsibility is accompanied by the diminishing supervisory role of Party functionaries in the day-to-day operation of the schools.[85] The chief benefactors to their administration are no longer simply Party members but also external funding sources on which schools have become increasingly reliant. If a principal can bring in more resources for school operation, it means more than better facilities for the school and admiration from subordinates. It also means that the schools can attract more teachers of high quality to serve and better students to attend. The result is school improvement in form and substance. Getting resources, therefore, has become a major concern of school principals. In a way, it has also become a concern for administrators of higher institutions. It is in this area of work that both have enjoyed considerable freedom.

Fund-raising Efforts by Institutions and Schools

In general, higher institutions rely on several ways of increasing their resources beyond state appropriation — commissioned training courses of various kinds for employees of official workunits and enterprises, consultancy to and cooperation with enterprises, money-making operations and student fees.

As a type of income, the most important of the commissioned training courses are those courses for students admitted beyond the regular admission quota of the institutions. In this so-called "commissioned training" (*weituo peiyang*), the commissioning party is charged a sum of money calculated on an agreed fee for each student it dispatches. The dispatched students are treated like full-time students of the institutions and, depending on the agreement between the work units and the institutions, receive formal recognition of the institutions (in the form of degrees or diplomas) if they successfully complete all requirements. This type of commissioned training courses were started in the early 1980s and have brought much needed revenues to the institutions. In some provinces, such as Zhejiang, there are plans by the provincial governments to lower the admission quota for regular full-time students and to increase the number of students in "commissioned training."[86] Other kinds of commissioned training courses include short-term courses for adults which train needed manpower for occupations with a labour shortage and training courses for highly skilled workers from factories and enterprises.[87] Both are fee-charging courses.

For some institutions, especially the universities and colleges of applied sciences, consultancy to and cooperative efforts with enterprises can bring handsome rewards. In the last two years, more and more higher institutions have approached enterprises with proposals on training, consultancy, cooperative research, joint production, dissemination of new technological information, and sales of prototypes ready for manufacturing. From reports, cooperation between institutions and enterprises has reaped an abundance of products worth billions of dollars when manufactured. In 1991 alone, 3,200 products from this kind of joint efforts were manufactured and the market worth of manufactured products amounted to RMB7.7 billion.[88]

A third source of income for higher institutions is profit-making operations which run the gamut from electronic factories to "industrial companies," from "pharmaceutical companies" to "microcomputing services." With the encouragement of the CCP, academics who choose to turn enterpreneurs now have ample room to test their skills in a field wide-open with money-making opportunities. Such opportunities have tempted not only those in the applied sciences, but also those in the unlikely field of education. In an institution in Wuhan, for example, the staff of the department of education has been mobilized to undertake profitable projects such as developing learning materials for pre-schoolers and providing consultancy service to interested "single-child" parents. To provide the necessary manpower for the growing "technical consultancy company" of the institution, ten members from the large staff of the department have been transferred to work there.[89] A portion of the profits made has been handed over to the institution, the rest of it has been retained by the "company" for its further development. In general, "companies" usually surrender 30% to 40% of the profits to the institutions.[90] According to one official report, the institutions' money-making operations have contributed the equivalent of 20% of state appropriation for "academic activities." For those institutions running thriving businesses, contribution from the money-making endeavours can be as large as state appropriation.[91]

The fourth source of income for the institutions, though considerably smaller than the aforementioned sources, is fees paid by students. Ordinarily, students in higher institutions do not have to pay any tuition fee. For those in "high priority" fields such as education, the state even subsidizes their other expenses with grants. In its plan to allow institutions to raise more funds for their operation, the CCP has allowed them to recruit more students beyond the quota designated by the state. In the last admission exercise in 1992, for instance, 620,000 students were to be admitted as regular students and students for "commissioned training" in accordance with state plan. However, an extra 100,000 "self-financed" students, were admitted to the institutions.[92] Depending on their fields of study and the institutions which they attend, the "self-financed" students have to pay between RMB2,000 and RMB2,500 a year to enrol in the institutions. Some institutions require them to pay the full sum for four years in one payment.[93] Upon graduation, they have to seek employment on their own while regular students are guaranteed employment through a national system of unified job assignments. At the moment, fees paid by students make up only a small fraction (less than 1%) of the total income of the institutions.[94] Officials in education have insisted that the tertiary institutions be not compromising their admission standards since those admitted as "self-financed" students should have examination scores that are respectable but only slightly lower than those admitted as regular students.[95] Moreover, the extra income earned is to be used for scholarships and loans for talented but poor students. Be that as it may, it is anticipated that more "self-financed" students will be admitted to the institutions in the future if the CCP does not withdraw its blessings from such practice.

"Self-financed" students can also be found in the lower schools, especially in the secondary schools, although their presence at this level of schooling is more controversial than in higher education. Some officials think that fee-charging at this level contradicts the basic maxims of compulsory education. Others think that, given the acute shortage of school funds, the acceptance of students who can pay to attend is understandable.[96] As yet, there is no consensus on the matter. In schools, "self-financed" students are admitted into all grades, since they are additions to state allotment. Some schools have classes organized specifically for the "self-financed" students. The schools that attract "self-financed" students are the preferred schools of a locality. These so-called "key schools" usually have a respectable record of getting their students admitted to higher institutions. Through arrangements with parents and work units, students with lower test scores are admitted if substantial fees can be paid to the schools. Consequently, some of these students are labeled "high-priced students" (*gaojiasheng*). The amount of fees paid by these students varies from schools and localities. While earlier estimation of fees paid was RMB2,000 per student,[97] recent reports have indicated a large range of fees being paid — RMB500 to 6,000 for primary schools, RMB3,000 to 5,000 for junior secondary schools, and RMB4,000 to 8,000 for senior secondary schools.[98] For entrance into the best schools in Beijing, parents have to pay up to RMB10,000 (the equivalence of three to four years of an ordinary workers' salary) in order to get their children admitted.[99]

Other sources of income for the schools include agreement with work units to enroll children of their employees, and money-making operations which have come to be known as "work-study programmes." Schools that do not have the prestige and, therefore, the "marketplace advantage" of the key schools cannot expect any extra income through admitting "high-priced students." For them, one way of generating income is agreements with nearby workunits trying to enrol children of their employees in selected schools. Income from this source has been used to improve school facilities, such as the construction of new buildings. Another way of generating extra income from agreement with work units is the offering of "vocational" courses under contract with factories. The fees for students in vocational courses are similar to those paid by the "self-financed" students.[100]

Under the "work-study programmes," a mode of operation sanctioned by the state, schools are engaged in a variety of money-making activities intended to bring in extra income. From large factories that independently hire business managers to handle their transactions to small workshops operating under the supervision of school teachers who are assigned the tasks, these money-making ventures have become a common addition to the schools.[101] Typically, income generated from this source is used for school improvement projects, and, in some cases, for the improvement of living conditions of the staff. The "work-study programmes" were started in the early 1980s with the idea that the availability of a workplace in school should help strengthen the tie between education and labour in the school curriculum and would also bring in extra income for the schools. As they evolved, such "programmes" have become money-making operations, hardly visited by the students and have not contributed to the integration of education and labour. Despite their pedagogical limitations, the "work-study programmes" do provide a steady source of extra income for schools as the enterprising spirit is diffused to all parts of China. In some areas, income from these "programmes" has become an integral part in the long-term planning of basic education.[102]

Selling Ideas and Charging Fees

The changing pattern of income procurement by the higher institutions and the schools has, in successful cases, partially helped to alleviate the shortage of funds. Such financial security is not easy to come by, given the delicate but complicated relations between the institutions and enterprises, and the close official scrutiny of fee-charging practice that has quickly limited the source of income, especially for the key schools.

Despite reports on the flourishing of partnerships between higher institutions and enterprises in developing manufacturable industrial and commercial products, difficulties have been encountered in such cooperative endeavours. A trend has developed from such cooperative efforts: major enterprises, especially those owned by the state, have had little interest in experimenting with new technological ideas because their major concern has been the fulfillment of quota for end products and the submission of profit taxes to the state. Consequently, the institutions have had to turn to smaller enterprises in the rural townships. Being much smaller in size and with limited resources for development, the smaller enterprises usually require ready-made prototypes for immediate manufacturing. Most of the ideas and products developed by the institutions, of sophisticated nature, do not attract the investment of these enterprises which expect immediate returns. Even if cooperative efforts can be forged, the institutions at times suffer losses at the hands of perfidious enterprises which, upon reaping handsome profits, fail to make necessary payments, ignore contractual agreements or even falsely lay claim to products that are not their own invention.[103] The dearth of opportunities for cooperation has led institutions to look abroad for partners. With a growing number of foreign corporations beginning to show interest in the technological accomplishments of Chinese institutions, there is a serious concern that Chinese accomplishments are used to serve the interests of foreign societies.[104]

To education officials, the fee-charging practice of some of the institutions and schools is another reason for concern. Through investigations, it has been discovered that some institutions have admitted additional students beyond state allotment without the knowledge of the relevant official departments. Presumably, the additional students are "self-financed" students whose admission brings extra income to the institutions concerned. This transgression of state regulations has induced a strong response from the State Education Commission. In a circular issued on the subject, higher institutions were instructed to identify those students who were admitted illicitly and take prompt measures to remedy the situation. The students who are being identified are not given any formal recognition of their status in the institutions; but those who can prove genuine need for pursuance of study will be allowed a period of stay of not more than eighteen months. Any institution that fails to comply with these instructions would "have to bear full responsibility for any emerging consequence."[105]

Fee-charging practice in schools has presented an equally thorny problem for education officials. The admission of "self-financed students" has posed a philosophical if not moral dilemma for the schools because of the CCP's promise of providing free basic education to all. The admission of "high-priced students" is clearly a practice that favours the rich and a blatant violation of the principle of fairness.

Upon a closer look, the admission of "self-financed" and "high-priced" students is only the tip of an iceberg of abuses. Along with the illicit admission of students for financial gains, a plethora of miscellaneous fees has also been imposed upon the students. The procurement of money from students through the sales of exercise books, reference materials and mock tests has become so common that it is now considered a steady source of income for the schools. In some areas in Hunan province, primary schools charge from RMB80 to 150 for miscellaneous fees per year while junior secondary schools charge from RMB130 to 200.[106] These miscellaneous charges constitute a substantial portion of the parents' income as the average net income of a family of three in the countryside is only about RMB2,200 per year.[107] In a county in Anhui province, students will have purchased 180 copies of printed material of all kinds by the time they complete their junior secondary education. Of these copies that the students are asked to purchased, only 30% are textbooks.[108] In addition to the sales of unnecessary printed materials and high miscellaneous charges, the schools also reportedly offer additional fee-charging courses such as tutorial classes, classes for repeaters, and other kinds of classes that reportedly have no discernible value. They also issue diplomas without proper authority. In yet another of its circulars warning schools not to abuse their newly found flexibility in procurement of funds, the State Education Commission brands these unwarranted ways of generating income as the "three disorders" (*sanluan*). It threatens disciplinary action against schools, work units, and individual cadres and teachers that knowingly transgress state regulations, and call upon students, parents and members of the public to help in rectifying the situation.[109]

The schools' fund-raising efforts have caused anxiety among all parties concerned. They have also caused considerable tension between the state and schools. A certain irony exists in the case of fund procurement. It is the wish of the CCP to decentralize the system of school finance in order to allow enough flexibility for the localities to contribute to the operation of schools. In doing so, it has also provided opportunities for schools to bend the rules in order to satisfy their wishes. The irony of educational reform will be perpetuated for some time to come.

Concluding Remarks

The preceding sections have depicted recent changes that have taken place in China's educational system. Through discussions of the expanding educational system, change in the CCP's financing strategy, vocationalization of schooling, and China's changing institutions and schools, noteworthy problems in the present system have been highlighted.

Educational expansion is to be taken as a welcomed outcome of the CCP's determination to provide more educational opportunities to the nation's children and youths. However, without the necessary mechanisms to ensure a systematic approach to expansion, educational development has been impeded by underutilization of manpower and regional disparity. Rather than serving as an important impetus to development, the zeal of officials and educators in some areas has in fact retarded the growth of viable institutions and schools. The change in the CCP's development strategy in favour of the eastern provinces has indeed served to widen the developmental gap in education between the rich and the poor provinces; but the absence of a policy structure that protect the poor from the encroachment of the rich has aggravated the problem. Positive discrimination tests the wisdom and will of any political regime that claims equity as its chief operational principle.

The same observation can be made about the change in financing strategy. The decentralization of the finance of education has put regional disparity into sharper focus since funding for individual schools is determined increasingly by the economic strength of a locality. The reliance on local resources to diffuse education and to improve conditions in schools reflects a departure from the burdensome allotment system of old, but masked under the new flexibility is the hardship suffered by schools and students whose community lacks the wherewithal to secure enough funds for ensuring their chances of survival in the system. Its shortcomings notwithstanding, decentralization has provided the much needed incentives for schools to raise funds to improve their own conditions. Such incentives have breathed life into Chinese schooling which has been deprived of vigour and innovation. With the implementation of compulsory education now a reality in the more advanced regions, and with the less developed areas getting ready to follow suit, the pressure is on the CCP to help the poorer regions to popularize basic education. When the old system of centralized allocation of resources can no longer suffice the task, the most logical and convenient way to meet the challenge is to decentralize the system of school finance. If the fund-raising ability of local governments is found wanting, then the next step is to further delegate financial responsibilities to individual schools.

The discussion on the vocationalization of schooling has unveiled issues in vocational education that are shared by most countries that treat it as an integral part of their educational system. Ill-conceived ideas of vocational education being the convenient shelter for low academic achievers are not unique to China but can be heard in other parts of the world. What is peculiar to the Chinese situation is its complicated system of vocational and technical education that has been allowed to survive to this day. The lack of coordination among the three major types of vocational and technical secondary schools, each under the auspices of different kinds of state authority, has caused the operation of the system to be costly and ineffective. Reports of the sad state of affairs in vocational and technical education in some of the poorer areas are almost farcical accounts of educational ill-planning and mismanagement. Without the thorough streamlining of its administrative structure and reevaluation of needs in different regions, vocationalization of education can only be represented by impressive statistics that are in constant search for accomplishments to substantiate.

Finally, China's schools and institutions have tried to increase their revenues in many ways. Some of the methods used are innovative in the Chinese context, such as the partnership between institutions and enterprises, while others are disreputable or even illicit, such as the admission of "high-priced students." Given the present situation in Chinese education — widespread shortage of funds, availability of opportunities for fund-raising, increasing flexibility in the deployment of resources, the diminishing role of the state in school finance — abuse is bound to occur. When fund-raising opportunities avail themselves to school administrators and teachers desperate to improve the operational conditions of their schools, some are tempted to bend the rules, accommodate more students and gain from this exploitation of opportunities. As the educational system expands to accommodate larger student enrolment in the tertiary institutions and schools, more resources will be needed. The CCP will continue to call upon educators and schools administrators to devise innovative plans to raise funds. New abuses of the system will surface to challenge the Party's wisdom and its sense of fairness. Solutions to problems old and new will not be found within China's education enterprise, but in the maturity of the bureaucratic mechanisms and procedures of its state.

In this chapter, discussions have basically focused on changes that have occurred in the educational system and the schools. Little has been said about the individuals within the system, such as the teachers and students. The exclusion of these parties from the discussion, however, does not mean that there is no noteworthy change in the values, opportunities, personal choices, and general situation of teachers and students. To be sure, even a cursive look at reports from China will reveal that school teachers are looking for opportunities in other areas of work which offer better working conditions and salaries,[110] that graduates of the tertiary institutions prefer to begin their careers in such prosperous southern cities as Shenzhen and Zhuhai because of the perceived abundance of opportunities that exist there,[111] that secondary school students no longer worship such CCP sanctioned hero-models as Lei Feng and Zhang Haidi but a *potpourri* of famous Chinese and western personalities such as Zhou Enlai, Deng Xiaoping, Albert Einstein, Ronald Reagan, "Superman" and James Bond,[112] and that primary school students are overburdened by school work to the extent that most of them require parental presence to complete their daily assignments.[113] The new generation of teachers and students will pose new challenges to the development strategy of the CCP. In the years ahead, its strategy will have to include the delicate handling of relations between the central and local governments, rich and poor regions, school and society, and of the development of teachers and students alike.

Notes

1. The "university president responsibility system" was initiated by the CCP in 1985 to allow selected institutions to have more autonomy in managing their own affairs by "eliminating excessive government control over the institutions of higher education ... so that they will have the initiative and ability to serve economic and social development." Under the guidance of centralized state plans, the tasks of student enrolment and career placement of graduates were partially transferred to the institutions. Moreover, the appointment and dismissal of personnel, curricular design, allocation of funds, and linkage with institutions at home and abroad were placed under the purview of the institutions. See, for example, *Decision of the Central Committee of the Communist Party of China on the Reform of the Educational Structure* (27 May 1985) (Beijing: Foreign Language Press, 1985); and Leslie Nai-Kwai Lo, "The Irony of Reform in Higher Education in Mainland China," in *Education in Mainland China: Review and Evaluation*, edited by Bih-jaw Lin and Li-min Fan (Taipei: Institute of International Relations, National Chengchi University, 1990), pp. 52–64.

2. He Dongchang, "Zai quanguo shifan yuanxiao gonggongke jiaoyuxue jiaocai yantaohui kaimushi shang de jianghua" (Speech at the Opening of the National Conference on Instructional Materials for Common-core Courses in Educational Studies of Teacher Training Institutions) (10 March 1991),

Jiaoyu Yanjiu (Educational Research), No. 12, 1991, pp. 3–13; and He Dongchang, "Zai quanguo jiaoyu kexue bawu guihua zhongdian keti pingshenhui shang de jianghua" (Speech at the National Evaluation Meeting on Important Topics in the "Eighth Five-year Plan" of Educational Science) (Excerpts, August 1991), *Educational Research*, No. 1, 1992, pp. 3–5.

3. Chen Mokai, "Guanyu jianshe you Zhongguo tese de shehui zhuyi jiaoyu tixi de jige wenti" (On Several Questions Concerning the Construction of a Socialist Educational System with Chinese Characteristics), *Educational Research*, No. 4, 1992, p. 20.
4. *Zhongguo Jiaoyubao* (China Education News) (Beijing), 1 September 1992, p. 1.
5. Li Tieying, "Jiakuai jiaoyu fazhan yu jiaoyu gaige, wei jingji jianshe fuwu, wei renmin fuwu" (Speed Up Educational Development and Educational Reform to Serve Economic Construction, to Serve the People) (20 June 1992), *China Education News*, 10 September 1992, p. 3.
6. Song Yuyou, "Shenhua gaoxiao gaige yingdang jiejue jige renshi wenti" (Deepen Understanding of Several Problems That Should Be Solved in the Reform of Higher Education), *China Education News*, 6 August 1992, p. 3.
7. *Ming Pao* (Hong Kong), 9 November 1992, p. 6.
8. Lu Zhonghe, "Jiaoyu youwei ganchao yazhou sixiaolong zuogongxian" (Education Should Contribute to Our Overtaking Asia's Four Little Dragons), *Shi Dao* (The Way of Teaching), No. 9, 1992, pp. 3–4.
9. *Ming Pao*, 15 October 1992, p. 9.
10. *Time Magazine*, 28 September 1992, p. 30; *Yazhou zhoukan* (Asiaweek), 19 July 1992, p. 44.
11. *Ming Pao*, 8 February 1993 and 27 February 1993.
12. Zheng Qingdong and Feng Yingbing, "Qianfan jingfa baihe zhengliu — Xiaoping nanxunhou de Zhongguo gaige kaifang xingshi" (Thousand Sails Competing to Push off, Hundred Boats Contending to Surge — The Situation of China's Reform after Xiaoping's Southern Inspection Tour), *China Education News*, 6 October 1992, p. 1.
13. Leslie Nai-kwai Lo, "Higher Education and Professional Manpower," in *China Review*, edited by Kuan Hsin-chi and Maurice Brosseau (Hong Kong: The Chinese University Press, 1991), p. **19**.3.
14. *Ibid.*, p. **19**.9.
15. *China Education News*, 27 February 1992, p. 1
16. *China Education News*, 3 September 1992, p. 1.
17. *Ibid.*
18. The State Education Commission, "Quanguo jiaoyu shiye shinian guihua he 'bawu' jihua yaodian" (Important points of the Ten-year Programme and the 'Eighth Five-year Plan' for the Education Enterprise of the Whole Country),

China Education News, 18 February 1992, p. 2; and *China Education News*, 27 February 1992, p. 1.
19. Gong Fang, "Zhongguo jingji fazhan de quyuhua ji qi dui gaodeng jiaoyu de yingxiang" (The Regionalization of China's Economic Development and Its Effects on Higher Education), *Educational Research*, No. 9, 1988, p. 12.
20. *Ta Kung Pao* (Hong Kong), 24 June 1992.
21. *Ibid.*
22. Ma Li, "Zhongguo jichu jiaoyu de fazhan he gaige" (The Development and Reform of Basic Education in China) (abstract), paper presented at the international conference on "Our Next Generation," organized by the Hong Kong Teachers' Association in Hong Kong, 8–12 December 1992, p. 1.
23. *Ming Pao*, 21 February 1992, p. 7.
24. In 1989, for example, the China Youth Development Fund initiated Project Hope, a large scale relief project to raise fund in China and overseas in order to provide schooling for the deprived. A recent campaign in Hong Kong has successfully raised millions of dollars for that purpose. See, *Ming Pao*, 16 April 1992 and 12 November 1992.
25. 1989 figure cited in "Woguo xiaoxue chuzhong xuesheng chuoxue he liuji wenti de yanjiu" (Research on Problems Concerning Drop-outs and Repeaters among Primary and Junior Secondary Students in Our Country), *Renmin Jiaoyu* (People's Education), No. 11, 1991, p. 16; 1992 figure cited in *Ta Kung Pao*, 24 June 1992.
26. *Ta Kung Pao*, 24 June 1992.
27. "Research on Problems Concerning Drop-outs ..." (see Note 25), pp. 16–17.
28. *Ibid.*
29. The temptation of handsome salaries earned in factories and from commercial activities still lures youngsters away from school in the less developed areas of rich provinces. In Wujing county of Jiangsu province, for example, students who have completed their nine years of compulsory schooling have opted to work in the factories rather than to stay on in school. When workers with higher level of educational attainment are in need, local enterprises pay schools or adult education units to provide the necessary schooling (usually at the senior secondary level) for their workers. Interviews, Wujing county, Jiangsu, November 1992.
30. Leslie Nai-kwai Lo, "The Irony of Educational Reform in China," *China News Analysis*, No. 1377 (15 January 1989), p. 5.
31. *Ming Pao*, 4 June 1992, p. 9; and *Renmin ribao* (People's Daily), 11 March 1992, p. 3.
32. See Note 25, p. 17.
33. *Ibid.*
34. Zhou Wei, "Xibu bashengqu shishi yiwu jiaoyu de zhanlue xuanze he sikao" (Strategic Choice and Thoughts on the Implementation of Compulsory

Education in Eight Provinces of the Western Region), *Educational Research*, No. 12, 1991, p. 37.
35. See Note 25, p. 18.
36. *Ibid.*
37. For example, in 1989, Zhejiang province had to invest an extra RMB26.18 million for repeaters, while Hebei province had to invest RMB24.22 million more for repeaters. *Ibid.*, pp. 17, 18.
38. Li Tieying, "Zhenfen jingshen, ba jiaoyu gaoshangqu" (Rouse Our Spirit, Advance in Education) (17 February 1989), in Zhongguo Jiaoyu Nianjian bianjibu (Editorial Board of Year-book of Education in China), *Zhongguo Jiaoyu Nianjian, 1990* (Year-book of Education in China, 1990) (Beijing: Renmin jiaoyu chubanshe, 1991), p. 8.
39. For example, see, Yuan Liansheng, "Lun woguo jiaoyu jingfei de kuique" (On the Shortage of China's Educational Funds), *Educational Research*, No. 7, 1988, pp. 23–26, 31; and He Cuoxiu and Mao Junqiang, "Woguo jiaoyu jingfei shifou chaoguo tongdeng jingji fazhan guojia de pingjun shuiping" (Is China's Educational Expenditure above the Norm for Countries on the Same Level of Economic Development?), *Hongqi* (Red Flag), No. 9, 1988, pp. 13–21.
40. Qiu Yuan, "Jiaoyu fazhan zhanlue yu jichu jiaoyu" (Educational Development Strategy and Basic Education), *Educational Research*, No. 8, 1990, p. 12, cited in Lo, "Higher Education and Professional Manpower" (see Note 13), p. **19**.12.
41. Li Tieying, "Shenhua jiaoyu tizhi gaige, cujin jiaoyu shiye fazhan" (Deepen Reform of the Educational System, Promote Development of the Education Enterprise) (9 January 1992), *China Education News*, 18 July 1992, p. 1.
42. *Ibid.*
43. Since China's gross national product amounted to RMB1985.46 billion in 1991, the RMB48.6 billion of state investment in education actually had a 2.4% of its GNP; 1991 GNP figure extracted from *Zhongguo tongji nianjian, 1992* (Statistical Year-book of China, 1992) (Beijing: Zhongguo tongji chubanshe, 1992), p. 31.
44. Wang Shanmai and Zhou Wei, "Woguo putong gaodeng jiaoyu jingfei bokuan tizhi" (Fund Allocation System of Regular Higher Education in China), *Jiaoyu yu jingji* (Education and Economics) (Wuchang), No. 4, 1991, p. 52.
45. Cheng Kai Ming, "Education, Decentralization and Regional Disparity: Impact of Financial Reform on Basic Education," paper presented at the international conference on "Education, Social Change and Regional Development," co-organized by the Faculty of Education, University of Hong Kong and the Centre of Asian Studies, University of Hong Kong, 23–25 June 1992, pp. 5–6.

46. Zhu Junjie, "Guanyu Hunan Youxian Wanglingzhen 1993 nian shixian jiunian yiwu jiaoyu de kexingxing diaocha baogao" (Investigation Report on the Feasibility of Implementating Nine Years of Compulsory Education in Wangling Township, You County of Hunan Province in 1993), *Huadong shifan daxue xuebao (jiaoyu kexue ban)* (Journal of East China Normal University [Education Science Edition]), No. 3, 1992, p. 71.
47. Zou Shiyan, "Wei shi woguo jichu jiaoyu maishang xintaijie nuli fendou" (Exert Ourselves in the Struggle for Advancing Our Country's Basic Education to a New Level) (8 September 1992), *China Education News*, 22 September 1992, p. 1.
48. "Zhonghua renmin gongheguo yiwu jiaoyufa shishi xize" (Detailed Regulations on the Implementation of Law of the People's Republic of China on Compulsory Education), *People's Education*, No. 5, 1992, p. 4.
49. See Note 47, p. 2.
50. For example, see, Wang Xibang, "Yiwu jiaoyu zhong de wenti yu jianyi" (Problems of and Suggestions for Compulsory Education), *Qunyan* (Popular Tribune), No. 2, 1992, p. 16.
51. Wu Guanpu and Wu Liuting, "Zhujiang sanjiaozhou jichu jiaoyu fazhan zhanlue yanjiu" (Study of the Development Strategy of Basic Education in the Pearl River Delta) in *Zhujiang sanjiaozhou jiaoyu fazhan zhanlue yanjiu* (Studies on the Development Strategy of Education in the Pearl River Delta), edited by Xu Mingdi and Zhou Guoxian (Guangzhou: Guangdong gaodeng jiaoyu chubanshe, 1992), p. 36.
52. *China Education News*, 8 September 1992, p. 1.
53. In 1991, Guangdong had 28,455 schools (24,633 primary schools and 3,822 secondary schools) and Tibet had 2,712 schools (2,652 primary schools and 60 secondary schools). Figures are extracted from *Statistical Year-book of China, 1992*, pp. 726, 735.
54. Cheng, "Education, Decentralization and Regional Disparity" (see Note 45), pp. 10–16.
55. *Ibid.*, p. 11.
56. *China Education News*, 15 February 1992, p. 1.
57. *South China Morning Post* (Hong Kong), 24 December 1992, p. 8.
58. *Decision of the Central Committee of the Communist Party of China on the Reform of the Educational Structure*, p. 10.
59. The assumption is explicated by Min Weifang, "Zhiye jishu jiaoyu de jingji xiaoyi yanjiu" (Study of the Economic Benefits of Vocational and Technical Education), *Educational Research*, No. 10, 1991, p. 31.
60. In Shanghai, for example, the promotion rate of junior secondary students to senior secondary school was already 75.9% in 1990 (96.9% in the city and 54.6% in its suburban areas). Ying Wenyong, "Jiushi niandai Shanghaishi zhongdeng zhiye jishu xuexiao fazhan he tiaozheng yanjiu" (Study of the

Development and Adjustment of Secondary Vocational and Technical Schools in the City of Shanghai in the 1990s), *Zhiye jishu jiaoyu* (Vocational and Technical Education), No. 4, 1992, p. 9.
61. *China Education News*, 14 July 1992, p. 1.
62. Tang Hua, "Shusong gengduo de zhongchuji shiyong jishu rencai" (Infuse More Junior and Middle-level Applied Technical Talents), *Liaowang Weekly* (Beijing), No. 17, 1992, p. 28.
63. Zhang Rongmao, "Jiefang sixiang, shenhua jiaoyu gaige" (Let Us Liberate Our Thoughts, Deepen Educational Reform), *China Education News*, 28 July 1992, p. 1.
64. Zhang Dianshi, "Yong xitong de guandian shixi Taiyuanshi zhiye jiaoyu xianzhuang yu duice" (An Attempt to Analyze the Present Situation of and Measures for Vocational Education in the City of Taiyuan by Using a Systems Perspective), *Shanxi chengren jiaoyu* (Shanxi Adult Education), No. 7, 1992, p. 26.
65. Feng Qitao, Luo Yunzhu, "Zhujiang sanjiaozhou zhiye jishu jiaoyu fazhan zhanlue yanjiu" (Study of the Development Strategy of Vocational and Technical Education in the Pearl River Delta) (see Note 51), pp. 58–59.
66. Ying Wenyong, see Note 60, p. 8.
67. Yan Xuemin, Cheng Kun, Liu Wenao, "Muqian xibei diqu xianji zhizhong cunzai de wenti jiejue banfa zhi guanjian" (Views on the Existing Problems in Vocational Secondary Schools at the County Level in the Northwest Region and Ways of Solving Them), *Zhijiao luntan*, (Vocational Education Forum), No. 3, 1992, pp. 15–16.
68. Interviews, Chencun township, Guangdong, March 1991. The same situation also applied to a township in Jiangsu where youngsters were reluctant to further their education in senior secondary schools. Interviews, Wujing county, Jiangsu, November 1992.
69. "Guowuyuan guanyu dali fazhan zhiye jishu jiaoyu de jueding" (State Council Decision on the Vigorous Development of Vocational and Technical Education), *People's Education*, No. 1, 1992, p. 4.
70. See Note 65, p. 59.
71. Interviews, Chaoyang district, Beijing, June 1991.
72. Bo Shouxun, "Zhiye jiaoyu yao dabu kuaru jingji jianshe zhuzhanchang" (Vocational and Technical Education Has to Take a Giant Step Forward into the Major Battlefield of Economic Construction), *People's Education*, Nos. 7 and 8, 1992, p. 24.
73. See Note 65, pp. 59–60.
74. *Ibid.*, p. 60
75. See Note 64, p. 26.
76. See Note 67, p. 15.
77. Yu Qingnian, Wu Minghui, "Qianghua zhiye jishu jiaoyu jihua guanli de

sikao" (Reflections on the Strengthening of Planning and Management in Vocational and Technical Education), *Zhiye jishu jiaoyu* (Vocational and Technical Education), No. 4, 1992, p. 28.
78. See Note 59, p. 38.
79. See Note 69, p. 4.
80. For a good discussion of this subject at the school level, see, Brian Delany and Lynn W. Paine, "Shifting Patterns of Authority in Chinese Schools," *Comparative Education Review*, Vol. 35, No. 1, 1991, pp. 23–43.
81. For example, see, Yan Xiange, Yang Hongjie, Yin Huiru, "Jinyibu kuoda gaoxiao zizhuquan, zengqiang banxue huoli" (Take the Expansion of Autonomy for Higher Institutions One Step Further, Strengthen the Vigour of School Operation), *Educational Research*, No. 5, 1992, pp. 23–27; Tang Wenzhong, Wen Hengfu, "Ershiyi shiji Zhongguo jiaoyu zhanwang" (Prospects for Chinese Education in the 21st Century), *Educational Research*, No. 10, 1992, pp. 3–7; and *China Education News*, 29 September 1992, p. 2.
82. Reports on the intention of the State Education Commission to grant a certain degree of freedom to the higher institutions in the management of their internal affairs can be found in *China Education News*, 20 August 1992, p. 1; and 22 August 1992, p. 1.
83. *China Education News*, 1 September 1992, p. 1.
84. *China Education News*, 1 December 1992, p. 2.
85. See Note 80, p. 31.
86. *China Education News*, 1 September 1992, p. 1.
87. Zhu Jiasheng, Hua Pinwen, Yuan Mingfang, "Gaoxiao wei difang jianshe fuwu de jige wenti" (Several Problems of Higher Institutions in the Service of the Construction of Localities), *Gaodeng jiaoyu yanjiu* (Research in Higher Education), No. 2, 1992, pp. 8–11.
88. *China Education News*, 11 August 1992, pp. 1 and 2.
89. Interviews, Hong Kong, November 1992.
90. Findings of an investigation into the conditions of money-making operations of tertiary institutions in ten of China's major cities which are mostly situated along the eastern seaboard. See, Office of Investigation and Research, Central Administration Department of the Communist Party of China, "Dali fazhan xiaoban chanye, jinyibu tigao jiaoxue keyan shuiping" (Vigorously Develop the Estates of the Institutions, Further Raise the Quality of Teaching and Research), *China Education News*, 16 April 1992, p. 1.
91. *Ibid.*, p. 2.
92. *Wen Wei Po* (Hong Kong), 7 August 1992.
93. *China Education News*, 25 July 1992, p. 1.
94. *Ibid.*, 12 November 1992, p. 3.
95. *South China Morning Post*, 8 December 1992, p. 10.

96. For example, see *China Education News*, 3 November 1992, p. 2.
97. See Note 80, p. 35.
98. *Ming Pao*, 25 September 1992, p. 8.
99. *China Education News*, 20 August 1992, p. 1.
100. See Note. 80, p. 35.
101. From the author's observation, the kinds of work that are involved in the schools' "work-study programmes" require rather low level of skills from workers. Of the school factories and workshops that he has visited since 1983, the production processes in such workplaces as soft-drinks factories, sweater factories, printing workshops, etc., involve very few skilled workers, who, if present, act as supervisors to other less skilled workers.
102. For instance, income from the "work-study programmes," which was integrated into its five-year plan, constituted about 1.5% of the total expenditures for basic education in Wangling township of You county in Hunan province in 1992. See Note 46, p. 73.
103. *China Education News*, 26 September 1992, p. 4.
104. *Guangming ribao*, 27 December 1991, p. 1.
105. *China Education News*, 28 November 1992, p. 1.
106. Luo Chunhui, Lai Chunqun, "Zhongxiaoxue shoufei de sikao" (Thoughts on Fee-charging in Secondary and Primary Schools), *China Education News*, 3 December 1992, p. 2.
107. *Statistical Year-book of China, 1992*, p. 306.
108. See Note 50, p. 17.
109. *China Education News*, 15 February 1992, p. 2.
110. *China Education News*, 19 May 1992, p. 4.
111. *Ta Kung Pao*, 8 August 1992.
112. Jin Zhongliang, "Bangyang jiaoyu mianlin yanjun tiaozhan" (Model Education Faces Rigorous Challenges), *Shaonian ertong yanjiu* (Research on Youth and Children), No. 3, 1992, pp. 7–10.
113. *China Education News*, 20 February 1992, p. 1; 25 February 1992, p. 4.

23

Slighting the Needy?
Social Welfare under Transition

Linda Wong

Introduction

Under Mao Zedong, politics was total devotion, to class struggle, and ideological purity took command. This remains true in the Deng Xiaoping era — only that the political goal has become economic construction, and every state activity serves this end. Welfare work obeys the same call and mends its ways to suit the reforms. This chapter begins by examining the relationship between social welfare and social stability. It then reviews the key trends in social welfare during the interregnum from the Tiananmen crisis in 1989 to the end of 1992. Innovations in policies and programmes that are designed to improve the lot of needy groups will be studied. In the process, major problems and policy issues will be drawn out. It is argued that welfare reforms are responses to problems arising from the transformation of society. However, after an initial appraisal of their utility, the author reasons that the desire to enhance social integration through piecemeal social engineering is unattainable. More volatility lies ahead so long as social issues receive inadequate elite attention.

Social Welfare and Social Stability

Chinese leaders likened their reform experience to crossing a stream by planting each new step on slippery river rocks. They were aware that reform was a two-edged sword. On the one hand, it could spell prosperity and progress. On the other, there could be hardship and setbacks. Nevertheless, for open-door and reform policies to succeed, conditions of relative stability would be vital. Herein came the demand that welfare institutions play a shock absorber and stabilizer role in society.

The link between social welfare and social stability can be appreciated in at least three ways. First, welfare programmes assure the livelihood of citizens, in particular of marginal groups, whose chance for unaided survival will be imperiled in the new economic order. Secondly, they address social problems like poverty, old age, disability and unemployment with the attendant dilemmas of inequality and want in the midst of plenty. Efforts at social amelioration prevent distress and gripes from swelling into general discontent, thereby eroding support for the reform. Thirdly, welfare reforms in the direction of enlarging the responsibility of social agencies, local communities and primary groups for self help and mutual aid reduce social burdens of enterprises and the state. Because of these

Slighting the Needy? Social Welfare under Transition 23.3

reasons, reshaping the systems of social security and welfare became part of the agenda in the Sixth and Seventh Five-year Plans. The general aim was to produce a prototype model (*chu xing*) with Chinese characteristics by 1990. The deadline has passed. Obviously, the task proved more daunting than was first thought.

Since 1949, state civil affairs departments and local communities under their oversight have been running relief and welfare programmes for the needy. Citizens who rely on this support system fall into two main categories — "the most adorable" (*zui keai*) and "the most pitiable" (*zui kelian*).[1] The former comprises families of serving soldiers, demobilized personnel, veterans and their dependents, whose contribution to national defence earns them the right to preferential treatment (*youdai fuwu*). The other group are people on the fringes of Chinese society — single elderly, disabled and orphans without family and work ties — as well as households blighted by temporary hardships and natural disasters. However deserving they may be, recipients have scarcely met with respect or generosity. Indeed, client status is often tainted with the stigma of charity because aid is usually given under conditions of selectivity, stringency and low standards.[2] To most people, civil affairs cadres are known more for their ritual visits to veterans and the infirm during Spring Festival and the distribution of alms ("*bai bai nian, pai pai qian*") than anything else.

A good indicator of the residual nature of welfare and relief is the size of the civil affairs programme budget (*minzheng shiye fei*) which includes per capita grants to eligible persons and recurrent expenditure. In the first reform decade (1979–1988), *minzheng shiye fei* averaged only 1.55% of total state spending.[3] During 1989 and 1990, the civil affairs bill rose to RMB4,598 million and RMB5,190 million respectively[4] but gained hardly at all as a share in public spending (1.51% for 1989 and 1.53% for 1990).[5] In 1991, civil affairs outlays went up 20% over the previous year to RMB6,250 million[6] or 1.75% of the state budget. However, this was solely caused by extra allocations for the relief of victims of the East China floods. According to official sources, the deluge was one of the worst in a hundred years; total losses were valued at RMB121.5 billion.[7]

In the period under review, the primary concern of civil affairs agencies has been social stability. This was apparent even on the eve of the Tiananmen crisis. Interestingly, at the Ninth National Civil Affairs Conference held in December 1988, the minister's report bore the name of "Grasping the situation, deepening the reform and serving a stabilizing function to contribute to socialist modernization."[8] Paradoxically, one of the first casualties of the turmoil was the ministry's own newspaper. Caught for its sympathetic coverage of the student demonstrations, *Shehui baozhang bao* was purged of its chief editor and his followers.[9] To reflect a clean break with non-rectitude, the paper was renamed *Zhongguo shehui bao* from 2 January 1990. Since then, utterances from ministry publications all sing the tune of social stability (*shehui wending*) in the time of transition.

Another aspect of the general climate was the programme of economic readjustment and retrenchment. Started during the third quarter of 1988 to bring down inflation and dampen the overheated economy, the austerity drive did not end until 1991. For welfare agencies, tight fiscal policies could only mean even leaner budgets and a hold on service expansion. Thus, consolidation work rather than bold venturing typified the development of much of this period. It was not until the second half of 1991 that more ambitious projects were launched.

Trends in Social Welfare

1. Residential Care for the Needy

In 1989, the residential programme consisted of 738,000 beds in various types of homes catering for some 568,800 residents. Out of the total, non-state provisions, viz. homes run and funded by urban neighbourhoods (streets and residents' committees) and rural collectives (townships and villages) accounted for 80.3% of bed capacity.[10] By year end 1991, total capacity rose to 828,000 beds and the resident population, 646,000; provisions by local neigbourhoods took up 82% of all places.[11]

A number of key trends could be observed during this period.

Shrinkage of state services

Indeed, the shrinkage of state services started in the mid-1980s, when the impetus for programme expansion passed to local areas as a result of government policy and an inevitable outcome of fiscal decentralization. In corollary, the government turned its attention to running larger and more professional facilities, for example through integrating rehabilitative and treatment elements into home care regimes. By acting as models, advanced state units could help community facilities attain higher standards of practice. This was easier said than done since no subsidy was given towards achieving this end.

Open access

Welfare homes went further along the road to open access. This meant that instead of limiting intake to the indigent without families, work unit and means of livelihood (the "three nos"), state institutions allowed needful persons with families and work unit incomes (e.g. pension) to receive care at their own expense. By year end 1991, traditional welfare targets made up only 60% of residents in homes run by civil affairs departments. At the same time, the proportion of self-financed cases went up to 35.19% in old people's homes, 27.52% in children's homes and 58.61% in psychiatric hospitals.[12] A number of factors lay behind the decision to relax eligibility — a natural decrease in the "three nos" population because of high marriage rates and universal employment,[13] unmet needs in the community and the necessity to augment income from fees. For example, voluntary admissions by pensioners were increasingly common. Some sought residential care or sheltered housing because they could not get on with family members. Others had children who were away for study, work or business. Not uncommon were elders "pushed out" to make room for children who got married without their own apartments.[14]

Income generation

In the last few years, most welfare homes had stepped up their efforts at income generation (*chuang shou*). This included catering to self-paying residents as mentioned, offering services — e.g. OPD (out-patient department) treatment in hospitals and homes, temporary care — for a fee and profit-making endeavours. The last ranged from such modest ventures as selling home-grown vegetables, fish and chicken, to bolder undertakings like starting factory production (or leasing land to enterprises) and running holiday camps and restaurants for homes sitting on precious, well-located sites. *Chuang shou* met the needs of stretching paltry state grants, upgrading services and improving welfare for staff, whose incomes were falling behind those of industrial workers. In 1991, self-earned income in state-run institutions accounted for RMB77.4 million (from RMB450.9 million in 1979) or 20.8% of government spending on such homes.[15] However vital extra cash may be, income generation invited two possible evils. One was stratification in the treatment accorded to "free" as against paying clients (in the form of food, accommodation and service standards). Another was service neglect, when home staff were busier making money than tending to people under their care. Such worries were not entirely unfounded. During my 1988 visits to thirteen welfare homes in Guangdong, I found suspicious signs of both dangers.[16] Left unresolved, the ill effects of fund raising may outweigh its benefits to helpless residents.

2. Services for Prostitutes, Drug-users, Abandoned Children and Vagrants

More and more, the authorities were confronted with problems of deviance and "social evils." While traditional programmes existed for frail and harmless persons, they were unsuitable for new clients like abducted women, prostitutes, drug users, rural migrants and "professional" beggars, who feigned ruin to cheat money from unwary citizens.[17]

In the last few years, many big cities, in particular those on the coast, had set up special treatment facilities. Shenzhen opened its first rehabilitation centre for drug abusers on 18 August 1991.[18] The Guangdong province's Civil Affairs Department also ran re-education centres for prostitutes. However, according to press reports[19] and interviews with Guangdong Civil Affairs officials,[20] the effectiveness of rehabilitation could not be assumed. In particular, working with harlots was often frustrating because most were willing operators and resistant to therapy. Some women treated their detention as a temporary respite or even looked forward to being schooled by veteran sisters. Equally taxing was reception and care of unwanted children. The Ministry of Civil Affairs estimated that about one million children were being abandoned each year and the numbers were growing.[21] Not surprisingly, the vast majority were girls, many were disabled and almost always from the countryside. In view of the near impossibility of getting urban resident quotas for them, children's homes were at a loss how to cope.[22]

By far the biggest headache was the relief of vagrants. Around the Spring Festival in 1989, some 2.5 million migrants descended on Guangdong. Vast numbers also flocked to big cities like Shanghai and Beijing in search of work.[23] In subsequent years, such influxes became an annual onslaught during Chinese New Year.[24] Because of their huge numbers, reception facilities were completely overwhelmed. What's more, unlike their predecessors who were genuine victims of poor harvest and disasters and thus grateful to be relieved and sent home, detainees nowadays were of a different breed. Most were not destitute. Many were unruly and stubborn, returning as soon as they were sent away. Obviously, new remedies were direly needed.

3. Management Reforms in Welfare Homes

The shortage of funds was regarded as a key problem which diminished the ability to run enough services. As long as service units relied on meagre state grants, no breakthrough could be envisaged. After Deng Xiaoping's tour of the south in Spring 1992 and especially after the State Council announced the "Regulations Concerning Management Mechanism Transformation of State-owned Industrial Enterprises" in July 1992,[25] welfare centres were asked to follow suit. What this implied was that, in stages and as far as possible, service units had to operate like true economic enterprises, charge fees for their service, open still further to the public and balance their books. Concerning employment practices, staff had to sign responsibility contracts setting out their duties, wages were to be linked to unit income, and both cadres and workers could be laid off.[26] Hopefully, management reforms could enhance responsibility and autonomy so that service agencies could respond quickly and more effectively to new exigencies.

4. Laws on the Protection of Women and Children

The enactment of laws and regulations was another strategy to tackle the worsening social problems. The year 1991 saw the culmination of such efforts that had begun in late 1988. On 18 January 1991, the State Council announced an order to ban the employment of children under 16.[27] The high point came on 4 September 1992 when the Executive Committee of the Seventh National People's Congress passed three decrees.[28] The *Protection of Minors Ordinance*, which became effective from 1 January 1992, set out the rights of minors under 18 to a full range of legal protection. Young persons, who currently made up 33.9% of the population (383 million)[29] were assured protection within the family, school, society and court systems. Acts like child abuse, infanticide, abandonment, forced marriage and child labour were proscribed. Meanwhile, two new regulations laid down a clearer definition of crimes against women and children and provided for stiff penalties. Under the *Resolution Related to the*

Punishment of Persons Committing the Crime of Abduction and Sale of Women and Children, such offences now carried custodial sentence of five to ten years; raping and forcing victims to become prostitutes or organizing such operations were punishable by imprisonment over ten years. Similarly, the *Resolution Related to the Prohibition of Prostitution and Visit of Prostitutes* empowered public security bureaus and other state agencies to pass re-education orders on arrested prostitutes and their customers for six months to two years. More importantly, people who organized prostitution and their abetters — pimps, go-between taxi-drivers, restaurant, guest-house and hotel owners and their staff — were also to receive punishment. Even their superintending agencies or departments were legally liable. If found guilty of condoning illicit acts by their subordinates, they could get fines, administrative censure and suspension of business or, in the extreme case, have their licence revoked.

At the end of 1991, the *Adoption Law* was accepted by the Seventh National People's Congress (to take effect on 1 April 1992).[30] The law addressed prevailing shortcomings. One was the rising number of abandoned children, as mentioned. Another was the exploitation of legal loopholes, for example, dressing up the sale of children and young women as adoptions and "adopting" adults into urban families to beat the system of household registration.[31] In addition, the law tackled the rising demand from foreigners, including Chinese residents from Taiwan, Hong Kong and Macau, to adopt mainland babies. Above all, the gap in legal guarantees and proper procedures to regulate adoption had to be plugged. From 1980 to 1990, a total of 188,620 adoptions had been notarized; in 1990 alone, such cases amounted to 31,045.[32] The new law no doubt gave the authorities the desired weapon to clean up the mess. However, the greatest challenge lay in its enforcement. A great deal needed to be done to educate Chinese citizens and officials to obey the law. Stamping out malpractices linked to corruption may be a bit more difficult.

5. Trends in Community Care

Since 1986, the development of community social services (*shequ fuwu*) had been hailed as the new growth point in social welfare in the cities. The expansion of local amenities took place against the backdrop of urban reforms. The need to enhance the competitiveness of enterprises, create labour markets and relieve work units of excessive welfare burdens called for supplements and alternatives to enterprise welfare. Under new exigencies, local self-catering was "discovered" by the Ministry of Civil Affairs as a cheap and convenient way of meeting social needs, strengthening communal solidarity and solving local problems.[33] Other social trends also contributed to its advent. An important challenge was the "white hair tidal wave" (*baifa langchao*). In 1964, the elderly (aged 65 and above) had made up only 3.6% of the population. By 1990, the proportion had increased to 5.6%. Indeed many big cities like Beijing, Shanghai and Guangzhou had already become aging communities (defined as having 10% of the population over age 60 or 7% over 65). The other was changes in the family system, the major worries being the weakening of family ties and shrinking families. For instance, between 1982 and 1990, the average size of households decreased from 4.41 to 3.96.[34] Finally, the dawn of market society also created novel life styles. Urbanites now wanted a better life. They demanded more and better services to give them time to enjoy their leisure, learn a new skill or make money.

Expansion

In the transitional period, community services continued to expand. At the end of 1988, the programme was still rather small (825 old people's homes catering to 8,713 inmates, 55,000 supervision and care groups for 90,000 elders, 550 work therapy stations for 8,600 discharged mental patients, nurseries and day places for 4,000 handicapped children, 2,370 rehabilitation rooms and 250 consultation centres).[35] These provided social support for priority targets who received help free or at nominal cost. Meanwhile, "convenience services" or *bianmin fuwu*, were open to any resident on a cost basis. Common offerings included milk and coal delivery, home help, repair work, home decoration and supply shops. All these added up to some 69,699 service points across the country as a whole.[36] By 1990, 4,000 street offices (out of 5,600) were operating various forms of *shequ fuwu* through some 85,000 access points.[37] In the last two years the momentum somehow slowed down. As of early 1992, total service outlets amounted to 93,000 only (21,534 units for the elderly; 7,154 for the disabled; 13,728 for soldiers and their dependents; 50,802 community centres and other facilities).[38]

Local diversity

To local areas and civil affairs agencies, the vindication of their efforts was the formal inclusion of community services under the tertiary sector from

January 1992.[39] This meant that *shequ fuwu* became part of the state plan for social and economic development. No doubt a morale booster, this attainment gave no guarantee of smooth sailing. However valiant the goal of community care might be, the prize was still far off.

Until now, most services have been centralized in a few locations, e.g. Shanghai, Beijing, Wuhan, Hangzhou, Dalian and Tianjin. Most medium and small cities have only token facilities. Two scenarios are now typical. On the one hand, forerunners have branched out in all directions and are at pains to redefine their work focus. On the other, laggards worry where they can summon help to make a start.[40]

Further socialization

The current trend points to further socialization of community services. This means opening up services to all residents, mobilizing more volunteers and tapping into local resources. The last implies greater reliance on fee-charging so that most users pay for what they get.[41] At the same time, streets and residents' committees will go all the way to develop tertiary services (*fazhan disan chanye*),[42] a practice that began much earlier. The government is sanguine about the latent power of neighbourhoods. In the October 1992 issue of *Zhongguo minzheng*, a senior official in the Commission for the Reform of the Economic System expressed the belief that the local approach was sowing the seed for social system reform (*shehui tizhi gaige*). When neighbourhoods eventually supplant work units as the basis of social organization and social care, there will be greater specialization of societal functions; duplication of welfare efforts by enterprises will also diminish.[43]

Ultimately, whether *shequ fuwu* flourish or not depends on local resources, including space, human capital and money. As neighbourhoods receive no state subventions and struggle with scarce funds, they lose interest in and capability of offering free care to the needy. Also, the recruitment of volunteers, who provide most of the caring, is getting more difficult. In Guangdong, where capitalism is gaining ground rapidly, the appeal of altruism is wearing thin.[44] New crazes like visiting *karaoke* bars, moon-lighting, buying stocks and shares or pulling deals attract more followers than unpaid labour. Needless to say, the Cantonese can get more and better services in the market than make-do provisions run by residents' committees.

6. Help for the Disabled

In the decade after the reform, there was phenomenal growth in disability employment programmes. This was the outcome of deliberate state policies — tax exemption for work places where 35% of operatives were disabled.[45] In 1981, there were 1,574 welfare factories for the disabled.[46] By 1988, such units had increased twenty-six times (40,496 units), giving employment to 659,000 disabled persons.[47]

Crisis of welfare factories

After 1988, welfare production ran into grave trouble. This was evident from two indicators — the number of facilities and their disabled work force. Regarding the former, there were 41,611 units in 1989, 41,800 in 1990 and 43,758 in 1991.[48] In short, the earlier growth spurt had petered out. As a result, the capacity for disability employment weakened; disabled workers in these places amounted to 719,000, 729,000 and 772,000 respectively.[49] In terms of financial performance, more welfare enterprises, especially government-run ones, were losing money. In 1989, 739 units under state administration made losses of RMB31.18 million; by 1991, 1,144 units had run into deficit, accruing losses of RMB89.84 million.[50] Many others were limping along and making no more than the amount of taxes remitted from the state.

A number of factors were responsible for their decline. To begin with, such places suffered from low productivity because of high concentrations of disabled employees. They were also saddled with pre-modern equipment and welfare bureaucrats more used to running relief centres than true enterprises.[51] Indeed, their only trump card was preferential taxation. When the state eliminated twenty-nine commodities and eight product groupings from exemption in late 1988, the blow was harsh.[52] Their tax edge was further blunted as local areas, eager for fast growth, vied to outdo one another to offer still more attractive terms to lure outside investors. In the meantime, because of paltry state grants, welfare units were forced to use bank loans, often at commercial rates, to meet their capital needs. Without any priority in getting state supplies, welfare factories had tremendous difficulty securing fuel and raw materials. In the face of stiff competition, the future of welfare enterprises looked bleak. Guangdong officials reckoned that such measures as lay-offs, lowering the proportion of disabled persons in each facility, plant mergers, or even closures may become necessary to keep healthy projects afloat.[53] In all probability, dismissed or unplaced disabled persons stood little chance of finding open employment as managers only selected the best from among the able-bodied.

More so than welfare homes and community programmes, welfare factories will have to join the market.[54] Since 1991, a few cities — Beijing, Shanghai, Tianjin, Nanjing and Fuzhou — have started to reform the management system of such units with the aim of turning them into true enterprises and cut their umbilical cord from the state's fiscal womb.[55] In the coming year, the campaign will be pushed into high gear.

Marginalization of the disabled

The plight of China's estimated 51 million disabled persons was not confined to employment alone. They encountered many obstacles in obtaining education, medical treatment, transport, recreation as well as in marriage and social life. In his introduction to the draft bill for the protection of the disabled in 1990, the Minister of Civil Affairs cited the following facts concerning the disabled — illiteracy rate of 68%, schooling for less than 6% of disabled children, unemployment rate of 49% among those with work ability, 46% of adults remaining unmarried, 67% depending on support by their families and 2.7% on the state and local communities, rehabilitation treatment for 4.9 million persons with cataracts, 1.24 million cases with polio and 1.17 million children in need of hearing and speech therapy.[56] The marginalization of the disabled was expected to get worse in a competitive economy.

Social legislation

On 28 December 1990, the Executive Committee of the Seventh National People's Congress promulgated the *Law on the Protection of the Disabled*, which became effective on 15 May 1991. The law was built on the principles of securing equal opportunities for the disabled and their full participation in society. The most important provision was given under Clause 3,[57]

> Disabled persons enjoy rights of political, economic, cultural, social and family life equal to those enjoyed by other citizens. Their civil rights and dignity are protected by law. Discrimination, insult and harm to disabled persons are prohibited.

Specifically, the state and society were obligated to promote services in education, training, work, cultural and welfare for the disabled.

However comprehensive its contents and admirable in spirit, the law's basic weaknesses were its lack of objective targets and authority in enforcement. For example, in the area of education, local areas were asked to work out their own agenda for action. The same applied to employment. The law did not mandate work quotas or designate jobs for the disabled; instead, such tasks were passed to local administrations and relevant departments.

In 1992, experiments (*shidian*) were undertaken to speed up employment programmes for the disabled. Working in concert, the State Planning Commission, Ministry of Civil Affairs, Ministry of Labour and the Chinese Federation of the Disabled picked eight cities (Shanghai, Guangzhou, Qingdao, Shenyang, Dalian, Wuhan, Jiujiang, Wuxi) to serve as test sites to explore multiple placement methods for the disabled. Among them, Wuxi was more advanced; in 1991, the city government announced regulations obliging state enterprises and agencies to employ up to five disabled persons per 1,000 employees or pay a fine. Meanwhile, Guangzhou's approach was to set up a special job exchange scheme.[58] The lesson from past experience was that the journey from policy setting, experimentation to universalization was typically long and arduous. In light of huge needs and the decentralized nature of the implementation process, this and other areas within the law would take a long time to become reality.

7. Aid to the Poor

The "five guarantees"

The mainstay of rural relief was the "five guarantees" (*wubao*). A locally-administered assistance scheme for single elderly, disabled and orphans without families, work and means of livelihood, the programme provided for the subsistence needs of the indigent (for food, clothing, housing, medical care, burial for the old/education for orphans).

At the end of 1989, of the 3.37 million persons eligible for relief, 3.07 million (91%) received the "five guarantees." Among the beneficiaries, 73.25% were given rations and grants in their own home, 12.65% boarded with relatives/neighbours and 14.1% were admitted into local homes for the elderly.[59] After this year, information related to *wubao* was omitted from the annual release of statistics from the Ministry of Civil Affairs. The latest available figure was for 1990, when the number of relieved persons declined to 2.58 million.[60]

Development aid

Since the mid-1980s, the work on poverty had relied more on loans, training and technical support to help poor households develop production (*fupin*) than the issue of relief.[61] In *fupin* work, the Ministry of Civil Affairs played a pioneering role. By the end of 1988, as many as 21 million poverty-stricken households were said to have "escaped from poverty" (*tuopin*) after getting development aid.[62]

In 1989, a total of 3.17 million households out of 9.39 million receiving assistance were said to have regained self-sufficiency; in 1990 and 1991, the relevant figures were 2.61 million out of 7.57 million and 2.14 million out of 7.56 million households. *Tuopin* rates were calculated as 33.7%, 34.5% and 28.3% for these years.[63]

By the end of 1990, the state considered that the basic-needs problems of the vast majority of the rural poor had been solved, the exceptions being mainly minority areas in the southwest and northwest. The State Council's leading group on poverty work, therefore, called for shifting the goal of the anti-poverty campaign from aiming at helping households to long-term development of poor-area economy.[64]

This move may mean a better use of resources. However, poor households not living in designated areas run the risk of being excluded from assistance. Even the very poor within target places may not benefit if help is not tailored to individual requirements.

Persistance of poverty

The question whether mass rural poverty has disappeared or not is a tricky one. Using the official poverty line of per capita net income of RMB200 per year, the number of poor persons declined from 125 million in 1985 to 27 million in 1991,[65] a very impressive achievement. However, this claim is misleading because the benchmark used is problematic. A suggestion has been offered that, had the effect of inflation been counted, the poverty line should have been revised to RMB325 in 1989.[66] Using a per capita net income of RMB300 as the absolute poverty measure and below RMB400 as reflecting precarious sufficiency in 1990, some 9.4% and 43% of the total population would have belonged to these two categories. If the RMB300 yardstick were applied to rural residents, 110 million peasants were in poverty in 1990. This figure of 13.1% of rural poor was similar to the rate in 1985.[67]

Rising inequality

Until now, China has not promulgated a national poverty line. Instead local areas are left to work out their own index in acccordance with local conditions. Without accurate data on income and prices across the country, the magnitude of poverty remains a mystery. What is certain, however, is that more uneven distribution of income exists across occupations, ownership types and geographical areas.[68] There are also suggestions that peasants are not doing as well in material terms as in the early days of the reform. Between 1985 and 1989, real peasant income (after accounting for inflation) grew at an average rate of 4% per year. In 1990 and 1991, it was only 1.8% and 2% over the preceding year. At the same time, the gap widened between urban and rural incomes — from 2.0:1 in 1987 to 2.2:1 in 1990.[69] This was also true of individual savings. Of all bank savings held by individuals, those belonging to urban residents (20% of the population) accounted for 33% of all savings while peasant savings amounted to only 26%. Between February 1991 and June 1992, total savings held by urbanites increased by 1%; those of rural folks fell by 2%.[70]

In addition, peasants had to contend with additional hardships. These included burdensome state taxes and local levies, rising prices of fertilizers, insecticides and agricultural supplies, low farm prices and failure to get payment for produce sold to the government.[71] Taking all things into consideration, the lot of Chinese peasants may have deteriorated since the late 1980s. This does not augur well for agriculture.

8. Rural Social Security

An important consequence of the rural reforms was the abolition of communes and the stripping of the collective welfare umbrella. In 1989, among rural residents, those who were covered by some form of social security, including old age pensions, *wubao* and regular relief amounted to only seven million or 1.7% of the rural labour force.[72] The vast majority of rural masses — farmers, workers in rural enterprises, self-employed and service personnel — were excluded from social security. In terms of annual per capita social security spending, the 1989 distribution was RMB350 per city resident and RMB13 per rural inhabitant.[73] This and other data cited earlier suggested that, despite rosy reports of ten-thousand-yuan households and their lavish life style, dualism was still the dominant feature of Chinese society.

Against the context of rapid aging, the situation of the rural elderly merited public attention. In 1986 the Ministry of Civil Affairs was given the job of starting pilot projects in rural social security. Nevertheless, up to the end of 1989, only 900,000 peasants had taken out contributory old age insurance.[74]

During 1991, such work was pushed to new heights. In May, the ministry drafted a proposal for county-level old age social insurance, which was debated in a special conference convened in October. Thereafter, experimental work (*shidian*) quickened.[75] In the following year, the "Basic Plan on County-level Old Age Social Insurance" was issued for trial implementation. The underlying principles were individual contribution, low premiums, benefits varying with subscription levels and universal coverage without regard to employment status. On top of the basic scheme, local communities and enterprises were encouraged to set up supplementary insurance plans; retirement savings by individuals were likewise supported.

By far, Shandong emerged as the most successful pioneer.[76] As of July 1992, twenty counties in six provinces had introduced pension plans enrolling more than five million members.[77] If one recalls that rural elders numbered some eighty million, the achievement was no more than a drop in the ocean. For the vast majority of rural elderly, family care was still the norm in the absence of appropriate public arrangements.[78]

9. Veteran Welfare

In the review period, preferential treatment through cash payment to families of serving soldiers was universalized. In most places, the collection and distribution of mass levies for the support of soldiers' and veterans' dependents were based on the administrative village/township (*xiang zhen tongchou*) as against the hamlet (*cun*) basis before 1988.[79] In 1989, the state expended RMB1,400 million and local communities RMB920 million for the relief and support of eligible persons. In 1990, the sums were RMB1,620 million (state spending) and RMB1,020 million (local community contribution); in 1991, the figures were RMB1,680 million and RMB1,060 million respectively.[80]

Unequal standards and discrimination

A number of anomalies became apparent with preferential aid. First, cash assistance to soldiers' families was marked by extreme diversity. As rates were determined locally, rich areas could afford annual grants up to several thousand RMB per family; poor places made do with a few hundred or less. Quite naturally the disparity created jealousy and resentment among recruits from different localities. It was not uncommon to find "rich" soldiers getting more cash grants than their salaried officers. Needless to say, the effect on staff morale was negative. Secondly, areas fielding more conscripts were discriminated against. The more soldiers they supplied, the heavier their burden with levies while places contributing less to the military effort got off lightly. This caused ill will between areas. Thirdly, rural residents were unfairly treated. Better-off city residents were not required to chip in to preferential aid; the masses in villages were not exempt.[81] Whether one invoked the criteria of social equity, uniformity of treatment or balance of right and obligation, the shortcomings of the present system were only too obvious. Unfortunately, no solution was yet in sight.

Placement problems

In the last few years, there have been increasing problems in resettling demobilized personnel. As before, rural recruits returning to their native village were not found jobs by the government, a right reserved for urban recruits. Even so, labour offices were having more problems placing urban returnees who did not have a work unit to go back to. This was because enterprises could refuse their assigned quotas if recommended persons did not have the right skill or qualification. Nevertheless, a guaranteed job in the context of fierce competition and over-employment in the state and collective sectors was still attractive. Because of these reasons, the early 1990s saw a "join the PLA" craze (*canjun re*) among city youths who used their army stint as an indirect means of getting vocational training and jumping the job queue.[82] Thus, the higher the number of urban recruits the greater the pressure on labour bureaus.

Issues in Welfare

A number of themes ran through our review of social welfare after June 4. The trends that prevailed did not originate in this period. Rather, they were the products of the 1980s. They only became more prominant as time passed.

The first issue that emerged was the declining role of the government at all levels in service provision. Whether in residential care, welfare production, community services, veteran aid or rural relief, the state component in the total output fell. More and more, maximum mobilization of local communities, groups and individuals in social care took place. A shrinking state sector had serious implications. It meant that other avenues had to be exploited to satisfy needs in the community. It directly aggravated the burden of these agencies. Additionally, the more the state withdrew from catering, the more remote the prospects for uniform standards and welfare rights for all citizens.

Secondly, there was the unmistaken trend towards devolution. In conjunction with the attainment of local autonomy, local administrations also acquired the onus of their own development. In welfare matters, as indeed in education, health and other areas,[83] decentralization — in planning, funding, controlling and delivering programmes — became the dominant mode of policy. Indeed, this step reflected a concession to reality because of vast spatial differences and chronic deficits of central government. Nevertheless, the ability to take up this mantle diverged, creating uneven welfare entitlements. Needless to say, wealthy places fared very well on their own and areas with adequate incomes at least managed. Backward localities suffered. Unfortunately, less help was available from the centre just as it was needed most.

The third issue concerned growing inequality. In a general sense, inequality manifested itself in income polarization, wider gaps between urban and rural social security and the persistence of poverty. It was also apparent in specific aspects like differential standards for aid to veterans, the disabled and community amenities. The disabled presented an interesting case of losers in a race for survival. In particular, the crisis facing welfare factories might portend a similar fate for other overmanned and backward state enterprises when they confront market competition head on. So far, the welfare response proved ineffectual in protecting the weakest; it had still to make an impact in tackling the wider issue of inequality.

From the mid-1980s, the authorities signalled with much fanfare the goal of "socialization of social welfare." From our review, this occurred across the full range of welfare programmes. In terms of service targets, the aim was to widen access to include all people, not just the "three-nos," through an open-door policy and extending the range of community services. In old age support, the duty of families was stressed, as always. Peasants were also encouraged to subscribe to contributary pensions in a spirit of self-insurance (*ziwo baozhang*). The most tangible means to share out responsibility was through diversified funding. All service units and local communities were asked to eschew dependence on the state. Instead, there was increasing reliance on fee-charging, self-financed admissions and income generation. Besides, there were other funding initiatives like raising donations, welfare lotteries and requiring profit-making welfare services (e.g. welfare factories) to make subsidies to relief programmes like welfare homes.[84] As discussed before, entrepreneurship might have brought relief to hard-pressed agencies; it might have been of uncertain value to clients if it took precedence over service delivery.

Pluralism in welfare responsibility,[85] whether in standard setting, funding and administration, brought to mind the concept of privatization in public policy. To what extent was socialization akin to privatization?

According to Alan Walker, privatization refers to the situation "when responsibility for a service or a particular aspect of service delivery passes, wholly or in part, to the private sector and when market criteria, such as profit or ability to pay, are used to ration or distribute benefits and services."[86]

In both Western and Eastern Europe, a key strategy to reduce state social intervention and manage the fiscal crisis has been privatization. According to Oyen, this can take several forms.[87] One is the encouragement of proprietary services. Another is subventing voluntary agencies to produce services rather than direct state provision. A third means is fee-charging. The fourth is de-institutionalization and wider use of family, community and informal care. The fifth form is reducing national economic responsibility and returning nation-wide programmes to local communities. All these, except perhaps the proliferation of commercial provisions, have their Chinese equivalents. In our review, ready examples include the wider use of fee-charging, self-financed admission, encouraging community care, individual contribution to rural pensions, management reforms of welfare homes and income generation to achieve budget balance. Insofar as privatization is still taboo in the mainland, one can argue that socialization in China is a cousin if not the twin to privatization adopted in market societies.

Conclusion

After the 1989 turmoil, maintaining stability became the consuming passion of the government. Although political remonstrations were in abeyance, many social problems were gnawing at society. Such problems as poverty, inequality, abuse of women and children, lack of support for old age, plight of the disabled, erosion of living standards for the needy were old issues of course and were the perennial concerns of welfare agencies. On the eve of the 1990s, such problems had become bigger and more acute.

The institution of welfare was expected to reduce the harm they inflicted on society. In the process of rising to the challenge, welfare agencies and local communities made many valiant attempts at managing the symptoms and finding more lasting solutions, for example, through social legislations. However, their problem-solving capacity remained limited. For example, their work on poverty, rural social security, reception and re-education of deviants and disability employment could only result in minor improvements. The effects of social legislations were harder to predict as the real challenge lay in factors affecting implementation.

In the final analysis, the social problems that emerged were endemic to Chinese society as it stumbled on its way to a socialist market economy. Indeed, the problems developed naturally from fissures in the transforming social structure. They could not be resolved by incremental efforts in multiplying service provisions, passing laws and reforming the way that welfare agencies were organized. The potential of welfare to remove social maladies was also weakened by scarce resources. Returning to the goal of social security, as long as welfare programmes remained half-starved and their development neglected by leaders more concerned with growth than distribution, welfare reforms were unlikely to work wonders. From the angle of citizens in need, namely weak and vulnerable groups who could not enjoy the new prosperity open to those with connections and ability, the reform may have actually increased their sense of injustice and insecurity. In short, welfare improvements, however valuable they were, did not measure up to the needs of recipients. As China entered the 1990s, social integration still remained an important but elusive challenge.

Notes

1. Cui Naifu, *Minzheng gongzuo de tansuo* (Inquiry in Civil Affairs Work) (Beijing: People's Publishing House, 1989), p. 24.
2. Linda Wong, "Social Welfare under Chinese Socialism: A Case Study of the Ministry of Civil Affairs" (Ph. D. diss., London School of Economics, 1992).

3. For statistics up to 1986, see Ministry of Civil Affairs, *Minzhengbu dashiji* (Record of the Ministry of Civil Affairs) (Beijing: Ministry of Civil Affairs, 1988); data for 1987 and 1988 as in *Shehui baozhang bao* (Social Security News, *SHBZB*), 14 April 1989.
4. See *Zhongguo shehui bao* (Chinese Society News, *ZGSHB*), 8 May 1990, for 1989 expenditure and *Zhongguo minzheng* (Chinese Civil Affairs, *ZGMZ*), September 1991, pp. 28–29 for 1990 expenditure.
5. *Zhongguo nianjian 1991* (China Year-book 1991), p. 89.
6. *ZGSHB*, 1 May 1992.
7. *ZGSHB*, 31 March 1992.
8. *ZGMZ*, January 1989, pp. 4–9.
9. Information obtained from personal sources at the Ministry of Civil Affairs.
10. *ZGSHB*, 8 May 1990.
11. *ZGSHB*, 1 May 1992.
12. *ZGMZ*, July 1992, pp. 24–25.
13. *ZGSHB*, 21 January 1992.
14. *ZGMZ*, April 1992, pp. 38–39; *ZGSHB*, 3 July 1992; also from my visits to old people's homes in Beijing in 1990 and Shanghai in 1992.
15. *ZGMZ*, July 1992, pp. 24–25.
16. See Note 2.
17. *ZGSHB*, 30 June 1992; Zhuang Ping, "Guanyu woguo maimai funü shehui xianxiang de fenxi" (Analysis of the Social Phenomenon of Trading in Women), *Shehuixue yanjiu* (Sociological Research), No. 5, 1991, pp. 101–108; Quanguo Renda Neiwu Sifa Weiyuanhui Funü Ertong Zhuanmen Xiaozu (The Special Small Group on Women and Children of the Internal Judicial Committee of the National People's Congress) (ed.), *Weihu funü ertong quanyi zhifa jiandu anlixuan* (Select Resolutions on Law Enforcement and Supervision of the Protection of the Rights of Women and Children) (Beijing: Law Publishing House, 1992).
18. *ZGSHB*, 31 January 1992.
19. *ZGSHB*, 14 February 1992.
20. Interviews were conducted with Guangdong Province Civil Affairs Department officials in November 1991 and September 1992.
21. *SHBZB*, 19 January 1988; *Ming Pao* (Hong Kong), 1 June 1990.
22. *Guangdong minzheng* (Guangdong Civil Affairs), 1991, Issue 4, pp. 18–19; *ZGMZ*, January 1992, pp. 34–35.
23. *The Nineties* (Hong Kong), April 1989, pp. 53–55; *Pai Shing* (Hong Kong), 16 June 1989, pp. 44–46; *Nanfang ribao*, 28 March 1989; *Yangcheng wanbao*, 1 March 1989.
24. *Wide Angle* (Hong Kong), April 1990; *Yangcheng wanbao*, 26 February 1990 and 22 February 1991; *Nanfang ribao*, 24 February 1991; *Ming Pao*, 13 and 14 February 1992; Chen-chang Chiang, "The Influx of Rural Labour

into Mainland China's Major Cities," *Issues and Studies*, Vol. 25, No. 19 (September 1989); Alan Liu, "Economic Reform, Mobility Strategies, and National Integration in China," *Asian Survey*, Vol. 31, No. 5 (May 1991); Dorothy Solinger, *China's Transients and the State: A Form of Civil Society?* USC Seminar Series No. 1 (Hong Kong: Hong Kong Institute of Asia-Pacific Studies, The Chinese University of Hong Kong, 1991).
25. *Beijing Review*, 16–22 November 1992, pp. 13–17; *Hong Kong Economic Journal*, 8 November 1992 and 14 December 1992.
26. *ZGMZ*, October 1992, pp. 1, 4–5, 6–7 and 8.
27. Quanguo Qingshaonian Lifa Gongzuo Bangongshi (Legislation Drafting Office on National Youth) (ed.), *Zhonghua Renmin Gongheguo weichengnianren baohufa jianghua* (Guide to the Protection Laws for Adolescents in the PRC) (Beijing: Law Publishing House, 1992), p. 153.
28. Guowuyuan Fazhiju (Legal System Department of the State Council) (ed.), *Zhonghua Renmin Gongheguo xinfagui huibian* (New Collected Laws and Regulations of the PRC, [3]1991), (Beijing: Zhongguo fazhi chubanshe, 1991).
29. See Note 27, p. 16.
30. See Note 28; *ZGSHB*, 20 March 1992 and 24 March 1992.
31. *ZGSHB*, 24 March 1992.
32. *ZGSHB*, 24 March 1992.
33. *SHBZB*, 18 September 1987; *ZGSHB*, 24 January 1992; Linda Wong, "Community Social Services in the People's Republic of China," *International Social Work*, Vol. 35, 1992.
34. *China Year-book 1991*, p. 422.
35. *SHBZB*, 15 November 1988.
36. *SHBZB*, 14 April 1989.
37. See Note 34, p. 437.
38. *ZGSHB*, 1 May 1992.
39. *ZGMZ*, February 1991, p. 1.
40. *ZGSHB*, 24 January 1992.
41. *ZGMZ*: August 1991, pp. 19–20; February 1992, p. 1; March 1992, pp. 18–19. See also *ZGSHB*, 28 July 1992.
42. *ZGMZ*, October 1992, p. 5.
43. *ZGMZ*, October 1992, p. 12.
44. Interviews with Guangdong Civil Affairs officials in November 1991 and September 1992.
45. Minzhengbu Zhengce Yanjiushi (Policy Research Office, Ministry of Civil Affairs) (ed.), *Minzheng fagui xuanbian* (Selected Laws and Regulations on Civil Affairs) (Beijing: Zhongguo zhengfa daxue chubanshe, 1986).
46. Minzhengbu Zhengce Yanjiushi (ed.), *Minzheng gongzuo wenjian huibian* (Collected Documents on Civil Affairs Work), No. 1, 1984, p. 40.

47. *SHBZB*, 14 April 1989.
48. 1989 figures as in *ZGSHB*, 8 May 1990; 1990 figures as in *China Year-book 1991*, p. 436; 1991 figures as in *ZGSHB*, 1 May 1992.
49. *Ibid.*
50. *Ibid.*
51. *ZGSHB*, 18 February 1992.
52. *ZGMZ*, August 1989, pp. 41–43; December 1989, pp. 12–13; April 1990, pp. 17–19.
53. Interviews with Guangdong Civil Affairs officials in November 1991.
54. *ZGMZ*, December 1991, pp. 8–9; January 1992, pp. 26–27; June 1992, pp. 4–5, 6–8, 9, 10–11.
55. *ZGMZ*, August 1992, pp. 24–25.
56. *Zhonghua Renmin Gongheguo canjiren baozhangfa lifa baogaoshu* (Legislative Report on the *Law on the Protection of the Disabled*), Vol. 1 (Beijing: Huaxia chubanshe, 1991), p. 5; *ZGSHB*, 19 May 1992.
57. *Lifa baogaoshu* (see Note 56), p. 285.
58. *ZGSHB*, 4 August 1992.
59. *ZGSHB*, 5 May 1990.
60. See Note 34, p. 437.
61. Thomas Lyons, *China's War on Poverty: A Case Study of Fujian Province, 1985–1990*, USC Seminar Series No. 7 (Hong Kong: Hong Kong Institute of Asia-Pacific Studies, The Chinese University of Hong Kong, 1992).
62. *SHBZB*, 7 October 1989.
63. 1989 figures from *ZGSHB*, 8 May 1990; 1990 figures from *China Year-book 1991*, p. 436; 1991 figures from *ZGSHB*, 1 May 1992.
64. See Note 61.
65. *Ming Pao*, 14 December 1992.
66. *ZGMZ*, March 1992, p. 22
67. *Ibid.*
68. "Shehui shouru fenpei bugong wenti yantaohui zongshu" (Summary of the Symposium "Unfair Distribution of Social Income"), *Sociological Research*, No. 1, 1992, pp. 80–82; Ge Yanfeng and Yue Songdong, "Dui woguo xianjieduan shouru fenpei wenti de jidian zairenshi" (A Review of the Problem of Income Distribution in Our Country at Present), *Sociological Research*, No. 1, 1992, pp. 83–86.
69. *Wide Angle*, 16 December 1992, pp. 22–26.
70. *Wide Angle*, 16 December 1992, pp. 28–31.
71. *Ibid.*; Robert Ash, "The Peasant and the State," *The China Quarterly*, No. 127 (September 1991).
72. Zhu Qingfang, "Shehui baozhang shiye yu jingji shehui de guanxi" (The Relationship between Social Security and Economic Society), paper

presented at the Conference *China and Hong Kong in the Nineties — Social Welfare Development*, 30 October–3 November 1990, Beijing.
73. Ibid.
74. *ZGSHB*, 16 February 1990; *ZGMZ*, April 1991, pp. 26–27.
75. *ZGMZ*, May 1992, pp. 12–13; *ZGSHB*, 14 July 1992, 4 August 1992, 14 August 1992.
76. *ZGMZ*, November 1991, pp. 6–9; December 1991, pp. 16–17; March 1992, pp. 27–29.
77. *ZGSHB*, 4 August 1992.
78. Joyce Kallgren, *Strategies for Support of the Rural Elderly in China: A Research and Policy Agenda*, USC Seminar Series No. 3 (Hong Kong: Hong Kong Institute of Asia-Pacific Studies, The Chinese University of Hong Kong, 1992). See also Yuan Qihui and Zhang Zhongyu, "Fazhan shehui fuli, cujin jiating yanglao" (Develop Social Welfare, Promote the Family Care of the Elderly), in *Zhongguo neidi ji Xianggang maijin jiushi niandai de shehui fuli fazhan yantaohui baogaoshu* (Report on the Symposium "Mainland China and Hong Kong Are Striding towards Developing Social Welfare for the Nineties"), edited by Xianggang Shehui Fuwu Lianhui (Hong Kong Federation of Social Work Organizations) and Zhongguo Minzheng Lilun he Shehui Fuli Yanjiuhui (Research Association on China's Theory of Civil Affairs and Social Welfare) (Hong Kong, 1991).
79. *ZGMZ*, September 1992, pp. 12–13.
80. 1989 figures see *ZGSHB*, 8 May 1990; 1990 figures as in *China Year-book 1991*, p. 436; 1991 figures as in *ZGSHB*, 1 May 1992.
81. *ZGMZ*, September 1991, pp. 12–13.
82. *ZGMZ*, May 1991, p. 24; July 1991, p. 18; May 1992, pp. 20–21.
83. For discussions on education reforms, see Cheng Kai Ming, "Financing Education in Mainland China: What are the Real Problems?" *Issues and Studies*, Vol. 26, No. 3 (March 1990); Cheng Kai Ming, *Zhongguo jiaoyu gaige: Jinzhan, Juxian, Chuxi* (Reform of Chinese Education: Progress, Limit, Promise) (Hong Kong: Commercial Press, 1992); Leslie Lo, "Chinese Education in the 1980s: A Survey of Achievements and Problems," in *China Modernization in the 1990s*, edited by Joseph Y. S. Cheng (Hong Kong: The Chinese University Press, 1989). On trends in health care, see Gail Henderson, "Increased Inequality in Health Care," in *Chinese Society on the Eve of Tiananmen: The Impact of Reform*, edited by Deborah Davis and Ezra F. Vogel (Cambridge: The Council on East Asian Studies, Harvard University, 1990); also Sheila Hillier, "Healthy Profits? The Road to Privatisation," *China Now*, No. 134, 1990.
84. Linda Wong, "Financing Social Welfare and Social Relief in Contemporary China," *Hong Kong Journal of Social Work*, Vol. 24, Winter 1990.
85. For the concept and practice of welfare pluralism, see Joan Higgins,

"Comparative Social Policy," *The Quarterly Journal of Social Affairs*, Vol. 2, No. 3 (1986); Norman Johnson, *The Welfare State in Transition: The Theory and Practice of Welfare Pluralism* (Brighton: Wheatsheaf, 1987); Richard Rose and Rei Shiratori (eds.), *The Welfare State East and West* (Oxford: Oxford University Press, 1986); and Robert Pinker, "On Rediscovering the Middle Way in Social Welfare," in *The State and Social Welfare: The Objectives of Policy*, edited by T. Wilson and D. Wilson (London and New York: Longman, 1991).

86. Alan Walker, "The Political Economy of Privatisation," in *Privatisation and the Welfare State*, edited by J. Le Grand and R. Robinson (London: Allen and Unwin, 1984), p. 25.

87. E. Oyen, (ed.), *Comparing Welfare States and Their Futures* (Aldershot: Gower, 1986), p. 14.

24

Urban Housing Reform in China amidst Property Boom Year

Lau Kwok-yu

Introduction

According to a report of the State Statistical Bureau, 200 million square metres of new housing were built in metropolitan cities and towns in 1992, a 82% increase over the previous year.[1] If we use the rule of thumb suggested by the Ministry of Construction that the average unit has 56 square metres of constructed space, the equivalent of about 3.6 million urban housing units were built in 1992. Under the urban housing reform and commodification of housing initiatives, investment in commodified housing in 1992 reached the level of RMB48.5 billion, which is about a 93.5% increase over the previous year. (Table 1)

Table 1. Investment in Commodified Housing

Year	billion (RMB)	% increase over previous year
1990	18.5	n.a.
1991	25.1	35.7
1992	48.5	93.5

Source: *People's Daily*, 29 February 1992, p. 2 and 19 February 1993, p. 2.
n.a. = not available

These figures seem to suggest that housing conditions and investment in urban areas have been improving. Statistics in Tables 2 and 3 are consistent with this positive observation. However, critics still argue that urban housing continues to be one of the most pressing problems for the government officials in China's cities.[2]

The extreme shortage of "self-contained" residential accommodations in China's cities was once cited by Lalkaka as reaching a crisis situation, and the problem was acknowledged by Chinese citizens to have been one of the most explosive social issues facing their society in the mid-1980s.[3] Despite the increased production of public sector and commodified housing units, the urban housing crisis stayed with the urban dwellers in the early 1990s.

The rapid development of commodified residential housing projects targetting overseas buyers in 1992 has attracted not only huge amount of overseas investment capitals into the southern coastal areas and some major inland cities located along main inter-city railway network, but it has also created potential problems of "out-of-control" development zones and over-sized infrastructural/fixed capital investment. Excessive investment

Table 2. Per Capita Living Space of China's Urban and Rural Residents

Year	Urban residents (square metres)	Rural residents (square metres)
1957	3.6	n.a.
1960	3.1	n.a.
1963	3.2	n.a.
1978	3.6	8.1
1979	3.7	8.1
1980	3.9	9.4
1981	4.1	10.2
1982	4.4	10.7
1983	4.6	11.6
1984	4.9	13.6
1985	5.2	14.7
1986	6.0	15.3
1987	6.1	16.0
1988	6.3	16.6
1989	6.6	17.2
1990	6.7	17.8
1991	6.9	18.5

Sources: 1957, 1960 and 1963 figures are cited from *China Report — Social and Economic Development 1949–89*, p. 487. 1978–1991 figures are quoted from *Zhongguo tongji nianjian 1992* (Statistical Year book of China 1992), Table 8–32, p. 318.

n.a. = not available

Table 3. Housing Floor Area Completed Yearly (million square metres)

Year	Urban areas	Rural areas	Total
1949–1978 (average)	n.a.	n.a.	100.0
1978–1988 (average)	n.a.	n.a.	765.7
1989	160	710	870.0
1990	180	660	840.0
1991	110	720	830.0
1992	200	620	820.0

Sources: 1949–1988 average figures of completed housing floor area were cited from *China: Implementation Options for Urban Housing Reform* (A World Bank Country Study), 1992, p. 3. (Note: World Bank obtained the figures from the Centre for Policy Research, Ministry of Construction) 1989–1992 figures were based on State Statistical Bureau reports published in *People's Daily*, 21 February 1990; 23 February 1991; 29 February 1992 and 19 February 1993.

n.a. = not available

in fixed capital projects such as housing in turn has become a new concern of the policymakers as it exerts inflationary pressure on the cost of living of the urban dwellers as well as inflates the cost of production (such as cement and steel).

This chapter begins with a brief introduction about China's urban housing problems and is followed by a discussion of the Chinese approach to these problems through urban housing reform measures. A brief review of the property boom in 1992 and its implications for the residential housing provision will also be given.

Urban Housing Problems

1. Poor Housing Conditions and Living Environment

Despite the increased production of urban housing units and marked improvements, the shortage of decent accommodation for many urban households is still acute. In 1991, it was estimated that 4.86 million households experienced difficulties in housing. Among these, 328,000 were classified as very congested households whose per capita living space was below 2 square metres. Among the 4.86 million households, over half were living in non-self-contained units (without private flush toilet, running water and/or kitchen inside housing unit) and about 0.6 million households occupied over 30 million square metres of dilapidated and dangerous buildings in need of major repair.[4] The total area of floor space in danger of collapsing at any moment in early 1980s was around 30 million square metres.[5] In other words, the situation has not been improved despite the increased production of new housing units and urban renewal programmes. In Guangzhou city, the centre of Guangdong province, 40% of 88,000 housing blocks (total construction floor area of over 7 million square metres) are considered dangerous or dilapidated.[6] In Shanghai, there are more than 15 million square metres of dilapidated and primitive housing waiting to be renovated.[7] World Bank experts point out that if adequate maintenance is postponed for another decade, half or more of the urban housing stock could be at risk.[8] Many households live in non-residential structures, and numerous households are classified as "inconvenienced" as some married couples have to share a bedroom with parents and/or teenage children. Poor sewage system, uneven road surface, high population density, lack of open space, etc. are not uncommon in most urban slum areas.

2. Urban Housing Inequalities

There are three different aspects of urban housing inequalities: unequal investment, unequal access to proper housing and unequal rent subsidy.

Unequal investment

One aspect, as Lee[9] points out, is unequal allocation of government investment in housing, which is explained in terms of three major types of ownership in China's cities: (1) housing under the city Bureau of Realty Management; (2) housing under the management of various production units, including (a) state-owned enterprises and (b) collectively-owned enterprises; and (3) private housing owned by individuals. According to Lee, the bulk of the state's housing investment goes to type (2a) housing which is under the management of state-owned enterprises. Ministry of Construction statistics show that in 1990, 60% of China's 455 city residential housing were managed by the work unit. (Table 4)

Most urban households live in cramped public housing units and pay only nominal rents. On average, they devote only 1% of monthly income to housing financed by their work units. But, rent collected do not even pay for the minimal level of maintenance required to preserve the value of the housing stock.[10]

Urban housing is one of the most important in-kind benefits given to urban workers under the low wage policy. World Bank Report shows that enterprises vary among themselves in the capacity to invest. This is due, in part, to accounting practices which allow work units which own large stocks of housing to deduct correspondingly large amounts of depreciation

Table 4. Management Responsibility of Urban Residential Housing in 455 China's Cities and in Shanghai Urban Area, 1990

Management responsibility	Total area (million sq.m.) in 455 China cities	%	Total area (million sq.m.) in Shanghai urban area	%
City Bureau of Realty Management	326.74	16.37	58.55	65.78
Production unit	1186.17	59.40	11.39	12.80
Private	482.62	24.23	19.07	21.42
Total	1995.53	100.00	89.01	100.00

Source: Ministry of Construction, cited in *Zhuzhai yu fangdichan* (Housing and Real Estate), No. 1 (August 1992), p. 51.

funds from gross income before taxes and devote these to housing construction. Obviously firms with few units of housing to their name are likely to be both poor and have little opportunity to generate such depreciation funds.[11]

Housing production depends on the relative economic health of the individual work unit; some workers, therefore, receive much better housing allocation than others. Within any given enterprise, conflicts also emerge between those who benefit from favouritism and those who are in congested housing.

Unequal access

As housing allocation is tied to employment, the fate of workers employed in a profit-generating work unit versus that of workers employed in a loss-making enterprise is very visible and reflected in housing.

In general, workers in key state institutions such as Capital Steel Works and other profitable enterprises usually have better chances to acquire adequate housing than those who are employed by small or non-profitable work units.[12] As housing units are allocated within the work unit, the lack of proper monitoring over the allocation procedure has given rise to malpractice and corruption. Power and connections often count when competing for available housing.[13] "Back-door" lobby for allocation at various levels of government is commonly found.[14] Within-enterprise housing allocation not always conforms with the model whereby housing committees provide housing "scores" for all employees, based on transparent criteria and published for worker scrutiny, and then assign apartments on the basis of those scores. Even if the model were followed, there would still be reasons for dissatisfaction. Since housing is distributed as an in-kind benefit and is not treated as a commercial commodity, workers view it both as a public good (to be equitably distributed) and as a wage good (to be distributed according to rank). Thus, by definition, the administrative distribution of housing is so seriously politicized that the ensuing public dissatisfaction cannot be made less by fine-tuning the existing delivery system.[15]

When newer units of larger size with "self-contained" facilities (kitchen and bathroom available for the exclusive use of the household) become available for allocation, leaders of the work unit responsible for allocation are approached by many sides all hoping to get a share of the new housing. In some cases, leaders just leave the units vacant for two or three years because there is no compromise on which households should get the new units.[16]

Unequal housing subsidy

Lee suggests that another form of housing inequality has occurred as a result of the way rent subsidies are distributed among urban households in China. Workers who live in public-sector housing receive monthly subsidies from the government. The rent subsidies are not distributed according to each household's financial needs. Rather, they are given out by the state on a per-square-metre basis, regardless of the size of household's living area. In other words, the larger the housing unit, the higher the amount of subsidy will be received by the household.[17]

Fong argues that there are fundamental weaknesses in China's urban housing system.[18] The basic problems are primarily due to (1) the lack of regular and adequate funds for housing construction and maintenance, (2) the heavily subsidized rental system, and (3) the lack of comprehensive plans and policies for housing development to meet the needs of the ever expanding urban population and the rising expectation on living standards accompanying increased household income. It is noted that China's housing reform package is formulated to pin-point these crucial problems.

Urban Housing Reform

1. Reform Attempts in the 1980s

In April 1980, Chinese Communist Party leader Deng Xiaoping suggested to the Party that the housing sector should be strengthened and urban households be allowed to build or buy their own homes. Either existing stocks or new housing stocks, selling them to occupying tenants and prospective buyers should be considered. In order to induce urban dwellers to purchase a home of their own, rent increase was inevitable. In his speech to Central Committee members, Deng also suggested that differential rents should be introduced according to location of housing units. As rental charge was revised upward, rental supplement should be introduced simultaneously.[19] Although there was a lack of concrete implementation proposals, Deng's words appeared to be the crucial guideline for the reform. Residential housing is no longer regarded a welfare good, but a "commodity."

Lee summarizes the practical consequences of commercialization of urban housing as follows: "If urban housing is sold to individuals, a much larger part of the initial state investment can be recovered. And when the proceeds from the sale are reinvested in the housing sector, the initial investment money is multiplied, in effect adding to the total amount of housing investment and increasing the rate of housing construction without deepening the state's financial burden. The gradual increase of rents can also relieve much of the state's burden of subsidizing huge maintenance and repair costs. The net result of the commercialization scheme is that the urban housing sector could become financially more healthy and self-sustaining."[20]

The State Council announced in June 1980 that urban residential units should be commercialized gradually.[21] As early as 1979, the state financed the initial capital cost of housing construction and sold residential housing units at cost (RMB120–150 per square metre) to workers interested in home purchase. It was understood that, owing to then low level of income and comparative advantage of continuing living in rental unit of very low rental charge, only several ten thousand square metres of homes were successfully sold to tenants in the 1979–1981 period.[22]

Between 1982 and 1985, a pilot sale scheme was carried out in four medium-sized inland cities: Zhengzhou (in Henan), Siping (in Sichuan), Sashi (in Hubei) and Changzhou (in Jiangsu). Under this scheme, individual purchasers paid one-third of the total construction cost (replacement cost) of a residential unit whereas the government and the purchaser's work unit provided an equal share of the outstanding balance. Property right was to be shared between the purchaser and the work unit. This subsidized sale scheme was reported to have been welcomed by workers.[23] Under this "preferential" homeownership scheme, a small number of new residential units were sold to individuals and small to medium-size enterprises which did not have sufficient resources to build housing for their employees, but the majority were retained for distribution through the usual bureaucratic channels.[24]

By 1985, the sale scheme had been extended to 160 cities and 300 plus county towns throughout the country.[25] By 1986, 4.8 million square metres of housing had been sold, though they amounted to only 3% of the annual production.[26]

Recognizing the limitations of the sale scheme in solving China's urban housing problem, observers argue that the advantage of the sale scheme is that one-third of the initial investment can be recovered and reinvested to build more new housing. This is considered as an advance when compared with the old system of charging nominal rent. It is also observed that buyers were concentrated among younger households with limited entitlement privileges and workers whose work units could not otherwise guarantee easy access to new housing. In 1986, the State Council withdrew this "preferential" sales price scheme as critics argued that its success depended on unequal household access to a form of in-kind wage, forcing the least-favoured to absorb the financial burden of homeownership.[27]

Other than the pilot sales scheme, several cities and towns also adjusted rental charge upward and charged rent according to three factors: depreciation, maintenance expenses and management expenses. The revised rent only applied to those households occupying floor space more than their entitled standard. Other cities set aside some newly-constructed housing units and charged rent according to the same three factors. Realizing the housing problem the newly-wed couples were facing, some cities also reserved some housing units of 25 to 40 square metres construction area and charged monthly rental of RMB1 per square metre of usable area.

The sales scheme proceeded on a limited basis. There was no major attempt to adjust or restructure the overall rent subsidies arrangement. Lee suggests that up to the mid-1980s the government was unable to implement a full housing commercialization scheme because of some deep-rooted difficulty.[28] While the sale of a limited number of new housing benefitted some well-off households and provided an alternative to the hardest-hit households without really hurting anyone, a rent increase or a restructuring of the rent subsidies would have required a total rearrangement of the economic system, and the beneficiaries of the old system would have been adversely affected. As the government understood that rent policy was a politically charged subject in China, stable rents, like stable food and commodity prices, were considered a significant element in preserving the overall economic well-being of China's urban population. Moreover, the fear of inflation caused by rent increase had also kept rents low.

Since August 1987, urban housing reform has been implemented in a number of cities, including Yantai, Bengbu, Tangshan and Shenyang. The Yantai's model appears to have become the "blueprint" for some other cities. In Yantai, rent reform is implemented according to the principle: "raise the rent, issue a certificate, nominal transfer as the first step." Monthly rent is adjusted upward from RMB0.07 to RMB1.28 per square metre (after taking into account the weighted average, the actual increase has been RMB1.17 per square metre). To increase rent of tenants would be impossible without an increase in wage; in order to avoid a sudden wage rise, which would cause difficulties for enterprises, Yantai has chosen to provide rental subsidy in the form of a housing certificate of up to 23.5% of "basic wage." In other words, rent increase is off-set by "basic wage" adjustment. By March 1988 there had been about 4.1% of households in Yantai receiving the exact amount of housing certificate equal to the rent increase; another 49.5% of the households had received more certificates than necessary (these were called "sediment households" whose saved certificates were to be deposited into a special fund); and the remaining 46.4% had to pay more than what they had received from the housing certificates (these were called "households with increased expenses").

The transfer to housing certificates given with one hand and then taken back with the other one is called a "nominal" one. This is only the initial step towards creating the habit of paying higher rents without excessive burden. Gradually rent is to be paid in cash and rental subsidy eventually become part of wage when wage incorporates an element of housing expenses. In such way, commercialization of housing can be realized.

In February 1988 the State Council issued its Plan for Housing Reforms in Urban Areas. The reform plan called for a complete change in the structure, management and performance of the urban housing sector.[29]

There were four main components in the reform: Firstly, there was to be an end to the allocation of enterprise and local government resources to housing construction. Work units would shift from significant reliance on compensation in-kind, including low-rent housing, to higher cash wages and a reform of rents; allowing increase in rents and wages would reduce the current distortion in housing demand. Secondly, the reforms were to allow a complete restructuring of the flow of funds through the housing sector, both for the maintenance of the existing housing stock and new construction. A housing finance system would be developed and the housing sector would become self-financing through the mobilization of household savings; rental housing would be targetted at the "poor." Thirdly, the reforms were to imply a transformation of the housing production system with the development of an independent, consumer-oriented housing industry. This would include the emergence of real estate banking and the development of specialized real estate institutions for the production of new housing, the management of the housing stock and the real estate services necessary for the operation of decentralized commodity housing markets. Fourthly, homeownership programmes, though strongly encouraged, were not to benefit from deep up-front subsidies. As noted, subsidized sales would be banned.

In brief, the housing reform plan required a recomputation of rents on all public-sector housing by including five cost factors: depreciation, maintenance expenses, management expenses, return on invested capital and real estate taxes. Simultaneously, wages of non-agricultural workers were to be adjusted upward to provide offsetting compensation. When the plan was first announced, the average nationwide monthly new rent was arbitrarily set at "about RMB1.56" per square metre of rented space, compared to less than a tenth of that (that is RMB0.13 per square metre on average) before reform. Individual cities could adjust the rent increase according to their unique circumstances. The average enhanced standard rent to be implemented at some unspecified future date targetted RMB3.5 to 4 per square metre of rentable space. This rate was to adopt eight cost factors: other than the above-mentioned five factors, the other three, namely insurance costs, land "fees" and profits were to be included in the enhanced standard rent computation. In general the city-specific adjustments were to yield an average increase in rent per square metre consistent with monthly average unit rents that could just be offset by a per-worker "basic" wage adjustment of no more than 25%. World Bank experts remarked that the maximum permissible wage adjustment in effect constrained the degree of possible rent reform.[30]

Instead of providing a housing certificate or wage compensation to off-set the increase in rent, observers have pointed out that policy-makers could consider not to issue any certificate or wage compensation but adjust rent upward periodically in consideration of workers' affordability.[31] This is seen as a preferred option in time of fiscal constraint. The middle ground is to introduce rent increase by phases and withdraw wage compensation gradually. Ultimately, average households should spend 6 to 10% of their income on housing rent.[32]

Another major objective of the reform plan was to encourage "non-agricultural" workers to buy housing units. The "standard" price for newly-built houses was supposed to include construction costs, on-site infrastructure expenditures, and compensation paid for land requisition. It was supposed to exclude off-site infrastructure fees, construction taxes, "key energy and communication construction project" fees and any financing of support facilities such as stores, post offices, and savings banks. Older housing would be sold at prices that used new construction costs as a standard, discounted to cover depreciation and unit "condition and quality." The plan cautioned against attempts to sell units at "preferential prices" that did not follow these guidelines. An exception to this rule allowed work units to treat favourably households making lump-sum payments for their housing unit, those having relatively long service with the work units and those having relatively low incomes.

Sale of public-sector housing was pursued most actively, and the State Council's directive not to sell housing at "preferential" price appears to have been ignored. World Bank Report pointed out that the typical formula used to price a unit begins by measuring what multiple of annual income a household can be expected to afford to pay for an apartment, often assuming full cash payment. Unit prices to individuals are now often artificially capped at levels that are three to four times the average annual incomes. It is found that in some cases, municipal governments and work units subsidize the remainder of the investment cost.

In times of inflationary pressure in the late 1980s, the government adopted a series of stabilization measures among which was the promotion of homebuying by individuals. The initial plan to adjust rents upward, with compensating wage adjustments, was largely dropped. In August 1988, the policy shifted from a balanced effort to encourage the development of both "market-priced" rental and owner housing to homeownership promotion as the key to the whole urban housing reform programme. Housing sales at "preferential" prices reemerged as the main approach of the reform. By the end of 1988, 7.5% of newly-built, public-sector housing was sold to households, along with 0.3% of the pre-existing stock.[33]

2. Urban Housing Reform in Early 1990s

Up till the early 1990s, rent increase had been modest in most cases. Those having a bigger increase did not recoup much because the work units subsidized households with wage compensation. The modest increase was insufficient to push tenants to purchase their own units. Moreover, it was not uncommon to find work units lowering the sales price to such a level that revenues generated from the sale of one existing unit were insufficient to construct a replacement unit. But, why did the heavily-subsidized sale continue? An illustration about the sale of Guangzhou publicly-owned units may help to shed light on this issue.

Sale price of existing housing units in Guangzhou for tenants was last set in May 1991. It was only after nineteen months that a revised price was introduced with effect from 1 January 1993. The increase is very modest (see Table 5). The new price for housing units built after 1 January 1992 is RMB245.64 per square metre of constructed floor space. The sale price is less than one-third that of the new housing units built to relieve overcrowding of congested households. And it is about one-fifth of the price set for commercial housing sold to domestic buyers.

An observer has criticized that setting such a low price for a public flat to tenants may slow down the process of commercialization and hence turn housing back to welfare housing over time.[34]

Occupying tenants of public housing under the reform have been given favourable treatment since the implementation of the programme. Between 1989 and 1992, about 128,000 public housing units had been sold to tenants in Guangzhou. In 1992 alone, 95,200 units were sold. This is about 52% of all identified public flats for sale in the city. Over RMB1 billion was recovered from the purchasers who were workers of different public sector work units.[35] On average each housing unit costs RMB8,000. A target is set to sell the remaining 48% before the end of 1994.

Subsidy is very obvious. According to estimates, the amount recovered from selling one unit is only able to finance the construction of one-quarter to one-fifth of a new unit.[36]

Table 5. A Comparison of the Different Pricing of Public Sector Housing and of Commercial Housing in Guangzhou, 1993

Type	Year of completion	Price (RMB/sq.m. of construction floor area) in 1993 (percentage increase over last 18 months)
I. Public sector		
Existing[1]	before and of 1991	233.94 (+ 2%)
	after 1.1.92	245.64 (+ 5%)
New[2]	1992	800–900
II. Commercial housing for domestic sale		
New	1992	1,230[3]

Source: *Yue Gang xinxi bao* (GD–HK Information Daily), 23 January, 1993.
Notes: 1. Already occupied public-sector housing units, under the housing reform, they are sold to tenants at concessionary price.
2. New public-sector housing units specially sold to congested households so as to relieve overcrowding in mid-December 1992.
3. Cost of construction materials (end of 1992 price) was about RMB220 per sq.m.

Policymakers of housing reform are caught in the dilemma of either selling public housing cheaply but recovering some cash to finance new construction or carrying on subsidizing tenants because rent increase is not yet able to recover cost.

Let us illustrate this by using the following example:

Households A and B both live in employer-provided housing unit of 56 square metres in Guangzhou. In June 1992, rent was charged at the rate of RMB0.5 per square metre usable/rentable space (versus estimated cost of RMB3.0 per square metre; the cost included five factors: depreciation, maintenance expenses, management expenses, return on invested capital, and real estate taxes). The rate of RMB0.5 per square metre only covers maintenance and management cost. As rent subsidy is also given to households, the actual rent paid by individual households only amounts to RMB0.18 per square metre. On average, the total monthly rental charge, therefore, is roughly equivalent to 1.7% of a household's actual income.[37]

In other words, total subsidy amounts to RMB2.82 per square metre per month or RMB118 per housing unit of 42-square-metre usable area (equivalent to 56 square metre constructed space) or RMB1,416 per annum. This is to say if households A and/or B continue to rent the unit, the amount of subsidy is enormous.

If household A chooses to buy the 56 square metre (constructed space) housing unit at the subsidized price of RMB245.64 per square metre, the total payment amounts to RMB13,756. If the replacement cost is estimated at 4 times the subsidized price, that is RMB55,024, the total subsidy given to household A is RMB41,268, equivalent to 29.1 years of rental subsidy.

The above example seems to suggest that selling public housing cheaply to tenants in terms of subsidy foregone costs more to the government than carrying on providing subsidized rental housing. Moreover, taking into account the location of the sales units which may be on prime site and have great redevelopment potential, the potential return to the buyers may be much greater when the sales units are due for redevelopment by private developers.

Selling public housing units cheaply, though at the expense of government's long-term return, is welcomed by most buyers. In anticipation of upward revision of the sales price, numerous applicants flocked to the Office of Housing Reform in Guangzhou in the second half of 1992. Work units have also been under great pressure from workers who have expressed keen interest in purchasing their own units at subsidized price.

One may wonder why workers are so keen to purchase their own housing units through the sale price (RMB13,756) is equivalent to 113.7 years of rent (rental charge per annum of RMB120.96 at 1992 prices). Under the drive of various housing reform measures, tenants tend to fear that new proposals will be introduced and their existing entitlement will be eliminated. The existing practice is that family members can continue to live in the same housing unit even after the worker entitled retires from his post or even dies. There has been discussion among decision makers that such practice should be discontinued as it creates extra burden on the work unit. As housing allocation is very much related to the ranking and service record of the worker, it is not unusual to find that household heads with longer service enjoy better housing than younger members of the same family. To protect the interest of the younger generation, purchase of existing housing unit is the safest way despite the considerable sum at the time of purchase and the cost of maintenance and improvement. In addition to the security of ownership, the anticipation of price increase and appreciation of asset value can be an inducement to buy. The savings accumulated since 1978 is believed to be another driving force.

The above example shows that, as a result of the sale of housing unit to tenants, total subsidy amounts to RMB41,268 per unit. Could we then argue that housing reform officials have failed to examine alternative options when selling public housing to tenants?

Theoretically speaking, there could be alternative options:

A. to increase the price of sales unit based on the replacement cost concept (that is to reduce subsidy);
B. to discontinue the sales but to increase rental charges.

Both options have been considered by the reformers and found to be impractical. For option A, the price increase may result in turning away many potential buyers who may find it unaffordable to pay over RMB55,000 for the purchase of an existing housing unit without any improvement of their living environment. This is especially valid when the home mortgage banking facilities are still relatively under-developed in China at the moment.

As for option B, it is understood that rental charge of public housing will be increased gradually. Despite the gradual increase in rent, there is still a large element of rental subsidy which drains government coffers. A sharp increase of rent without rental supplement or subsidy would not survive the test of political feasibility especially in urban areas where low rent has been a long-term phenomenon of the public housing market. The discontinuation of the sales scheme may save the government from paying a considerable amount of hidden subsidy (in terms of subsidy foregone and not in real dollar sense). However, the government has to suffer from not being able to collect sizable cash return from the sales of public housing units. As the budget allocation to finance building of additional housing units becomes tighter and the demand for additional housing units is still great, it would be very tempting for people in authority to continue the sales scheme as it is a secured source of finance.

Comparing the options: (1) not selling but subsidizing rental charge without cash return for building additional housing to meet the demand of those in urgent need for accommodation; and (2) selling public-sector housing cheaply with considerable subsidy foregone but obtaining immediate cash return to enable building additional housing units, it is obvious that the latter choice is of a lesser evil nature.

Apart from rent increase and promotion of homebuying, new measures have been introduced in some selected cities. These include:

1. the introduction of substantial rental deposits for newly occupied dwellings, often accompanied by wage-compensated rent increases, to cover all routine maintenance expenditures.[38] The rent deposits vary from RMB40 to RMB80 per square metre, depending on the city and location. In practice, the deposit schemes vary both in terms of required duration and whether interest is paid or not (Beijing, Shanghai, Yantai, Tianjin, Chengdu and Chongqing);
2. the introduction of rental surcharges for households occupying more floor space than their entitled standard (Beijing, Guangzhou);
3. requiring households occupying new premises to pay routine maintenance expenditures directly through higher rents (Beijing);
4. requiring households occupying new rental units to purchase a five-year housing bond carrying nominal interest payments. These bonds are calculated on a per square metre of rented space basis and vary according to unit quality and location (Shanghai);[39]
5. the introduction of a provident fund.

The Shanghai provident fund is modelled after Singapore's Central Provident Fund. In May 1991, Shanghai established a local provident fund, financed by worker and employer contributions, each equivalent to 5% of wages. The fund, which is managed by the Provident Fund Management Centre, earns interests (interest rate equals that of bank savings) and is available at retirement or for housing investment. As such, the contributor's fund can be used by the individual contributors or their work units to finance down-payments, mortgage payments, self-help housing construction, and major renovations.

In Shanghai, the employer's contribution comes from the enterprise's depreciation fund and major repair fund. It is understood that this practice is to minimize the financial burden of the enterprise when the Provident Fund is introduced. The use of depreciation fund to support the employer's contribution means that no new money is obtainable from the work unit for the construction of replacement housing because the original function of depreciation provision is meant for such purpose. Yang argues that a new fund should be available to pay for an employer's contribution which should be accounted for in the cost of production. The loan period is limited to three years for all borrowers of the fund. The maximum loan amount is equivalent to the amount saved. Buying a new house or launching major renovation requires lots of cash and it would take some years before a household is financially capable of borrowing the money. The amount of savings is limited if employees only contribute 5% of their basic wage and not of their total wage.[40]

Guangzhou modified Shanghai's plan and introduced a Housing Provident Fund in April 1992. According to an official estimate, the annual contributions (employee and employer each contributes 5% of basic wages) would amount to RMB173 million in the first year. This sum may enable the government to construct 216,000 square metres of housing, providing relief housing to over 4,000 families with housing difficulties.[41] As we noticed, Guangzhou's fund is specially set up to obtain additional finance for new housing to be built by the municipal authority. Whereas the Shanghai provident fund is also meant for retirement, not only for accelerating homeownership. Moreover, in Shanghai, new housing is not to be built by municipal authority. It is left to individual work units or self-help co-operatives to apply funds to new housing for the contributors. The provident fund in Beijing can be used to pay for the excess rental owing to upward adjustment. This enables rent reform without wage compensation.[42]

The development of urban housing reform since the mid-1980s is given in Table 6. In the first half year of 1992, Jiangsu, Tianjin, Shaanxi,

Table 6. Urban Housing Reform in Select Cities, 1987–1992

City	Date	Major features
Yantai	1.8.1987	Rent adjusted upward to RMB1.28/sq.m., subsidy in form of housing certificate up to 23.5% of "basic wage" (nominal transfer as the first step); rent increase is off-set by "basic wage" adjustment; specialized housing savings bank
Bengbu	1.10.1987	Rent revised to RMB1.18/sq.m., subsidy up to 21%; major features same as Yantai
Tangshan	23.1.1988	Rent reform: in two phases up to RMB1.08/sq.m.; subsidy up to 18% plus fixed cash subsidy of RMB4.8
Chongqing	4.1988	Rent reform: rent of old stocks up in 3 phases: RMB0.55/sq.m. with 8% subsidy; RMB0.95/sq.m. with 16% subsidy; RMB1.35/sq.m. with 25% subsidy; rent of new stocks up in 2 phases: RMB0.95/sq.m. with 10% subsidy; RMB1.35/sq.m. with 25% subsidy
Fomen	4.1988	Rent reform: yearly revision with subsidy; during the 7th Five-year Plan (1986–1990), increase of RMB0.11/sq.m. with 2.8% subsidy; during the 8th Five-year Plan, increase of RMB0.15/sq.m. plus 3.8% subsidy. Phased incremental rent
Jiangmen	1.8.1988	Rent reform in 3 phases with subsidy: RMB0.28/sq.m.; RMB0.80/sq.m.; RMB1.28/sq.m.; policy to encourage homeownership
Chengdu	9.1988	Reform started in enterprises; rent increase up to RMB1.20 with subsidy; increase rent to encourage purchase
Shenzhen	1.10.1988	Rent reform with wage compensation: rent adjusted upward to RMB2.75/sq.m. in one go with 24.9% compensation; encourage homeownership by tenants (note 1); set up housing fund, new policy for occupiers of new housing; comprehensive management in new estates
Guangzhou	10.1989	Started with sale to tenants; rent reform in phases, new policy for occupiers of new housing. Limited increase in rent, revised upward to RMB0.50 per sq.m. on 1.6.92; with compensation average rent per sq.m. is lowered to RMB0.18 and total rent is about 1.7% of total household income (note 2), target to cover five cost factors by 1997
Baoding	7.1990	Sale of units to tenants at "preferential" price; modest increase in rent with modest wage compensation
Zhuzhou	1.1991	Rent deposit by tenants without interest; modest increase in rent

Table 6. Urban Housing Reform in Select Cities, 1987–1992 (continued)

Pingxiang	1.1.1991	Rent increase to RMB1.02 per sq.m. once, but owner of public housing is to subsidize rental in 4 phases over 5 to 8 years: the subsidy is equal to 85%, 75%, 65% and 55% of increased rent, i.e. tenants are to pay increased rent gradually. Work units take over the subsidy gradually
Shanghai	5.1991	Set up provident fund, 100% rent increase with 2% of wage compensation as subsidy; new tenants must buy 5-year housing bond (interest rate is 3.6% per annum); preferential sale of units to tenants; establishment of housing authority to involve community leaders, experts and government officials in policy-making, research, coordination, management and monitoring (note 3); excessive allocated space will not be charged according to cost rent (note 4)
Fuzhou	9.1991	Constructing through collective funding; self-help project with government assistance; modest increase in rent to RMB0.3 per sq.m.; set up provident fund; retain welfare housing to households in difficulty
Tianjin	1.1.92	Set up provident fund; rent increase by phases, initial increase to RMB0.3 per sq.m. with 2% basic wage as compensation; new tenants purchase housing bond; encourage homebuying; develop co-operative projects; set up city and work unit housing funds
Wuhan	11.6.1992	Rent increase to RMB0.32 per sq.m. with 2% basic wage compensation; rental deposit required in new housing; encourage homebuying; set up city, work unit and individual housing funds
Beijing	1.7.1992	Set up government and work unit housing funds, housing provident fund; sale of public housing; gradual rent increase (to RMB0.55 per sq.m. by January 1994 in 3 phases) without compensation; new housing rent at RMB0.55 per sq.m.; rental deposit by new tenants; excessive allocated space at RMB1.34 per sq.m.

Source: *Zhongguo fangdichan* (China Real Estate), No. 141 (September 1992), pp. 49–51. (Note: in October–December 1992 issues of the same journal, some more tables summarized urban housing reform in China's major enterprises (work units), provinces and counties.

Notes:
1. as at 8.1991, 85.9% of reformed housing and 95% of new housing were sold to workers, see *Zhuzhai yu fangdichan* (Housing & Real Estate), No. 3, December, 1992, p. 33.
2. Guangzhou Housing System Reform Office, *Guangzhou fanggai ziliao xuanbian yu wenti jieda* (Guangzhou Housing Reform Resource Book and Questions and Answers), 1992, pp. 296–303.
3. *Zhuzhai yu fangdichan* (No. 3, December, 1992, p. 32).
4. Shanghai Housing System Reform Leading Group Office, *Shanghai zhufang zhidu gaige* (Shanghai Housing System Reform) (Shanghai: People's Publisher, 1991), p. 110.

Henan, Liaoning, Zhejiang and Shandong all had their Urban Housing Reform Plans approved by the State Council Leading Group on Urban Housing Reform. Implementation of these plans is now underway. Up till mid-May 1992, the State Council Leading Group was still examining the plans put forward by Guizhou, Jilin, Fujian, Beijing, Anhui. It is expected that these urban housing reform plans will be in full implementation within 1992 and 1993.

In other provincial cities, in Jiangxi, Hunan, Sichuan and Guangdong, urban housing reform plans, based on previous experimental projects, are being modified or extended. Some other provincial governments are yet to formulate their plans or are now involving people to give feedback on their proposed reform plans. These include cities in Shanxi, Hebei, Hubei, Yunnan, Gansu, Xinjiang, Guangxi, Qinghai, Ningxia, Hainan. Upon the direction of the State Council, these cities are expected to implement their reform plan by the end of 1992. Other than provincial reform plans, other approved plans include those from the Ministry of Railways, and those from the military sector.[43]

3. Assessment of Urban Housing Reform

The State Council Leading Group on Urban Housing Reform gave a summary of China's urban housing reform programmes in May 1992. In its report, the uneven pace of reform in various part of China is noted. Moreover, it is found that many local authorities have not followed State Council's directives when implementing rent reform or sale promotion programmes.[44]

By mid-1992, about 60% of non-agricultural areas had yet to formulate their final urban housing reform plans. Comparing this with the 1988 State Council Housing Reform Plan which called for "the reform ... to be carried out in all cities, counties, and towns in China in 1990, except for some outlying or economically backward cities, counties and towns which may delay the reform one or two years,"[45] the scope of housing reform today is still limited.

In the process of implementation, it is observed that State Council's directives are ignored. For instance, rent increase is too modest when compared with the wage compensation increase; in some cases, wage compensation is also given to workers (tenants and/or owner-occupiers) living in private housing; in other cases, tenants of new housing stocks are not required to pay new cost rent and the sale of publicly-owned units to tenants is at "preferential" low price, etc.

As observers point out, the present approaches, including rent increase in phases, sale of housing unit to tenants at "preferential" price, setting up of provident fund and new tenants to be allocated housing unit upon payment of rental deposit or housing bond, are all targetted at raising additional revenue to finance the construction of new housing. They are basically a conventional and centrally-planned approach, first setting a target of housing production which relates to estimated demand, then measuring the amount of available resources to find out the amount required for the financing of the targetted housing construction programme.[46]

Policymakers of urban housing reform attach greater emphasis to setting up the provident fund, housing bond and rental deposit arrangement, an indication of their anxiety to raise additional funds to finance new housing construction. However, it is questionable whether they have paid adequate attention to more important issues such as raising rent in an initial step to a level covering at least two cost factors (the target of rent reform set by the State Council). It is noted that rent increase on average only reaches the level of RMB0.3 per square metre rentable space which is only half of the two-factor cost. Employees of central government agencies in Beijing paid as low as RMB0.275 per square metre rentable/usable space in June 1992 which was to be further revised on 1 January 1993 to RMB0.41 per sq.m. and further adjusted upward to RMB0.55 per sq.m. on 1 January 1994. The rate of RMB0.55 per sq.m. (just enough to cover maintenance and management charges) has been applied to all new tenants since 1 June 1992.[47]

In the promotion of the sale of publicly-owned housing units to tenants, the State Council Leading Group considers it more advisable to increase rental to such a level that tenants would prefer buying their own unit to carrying on renting at high rent. Again, the State Council's guideline is not followed, and the promotion of sale is done by reducing the sale price to a very low level so that revenues are insufficient to cover basic replacement cost. The reduction of sale price is effectively done by giving discount of one sort or other. Guangdong, Beijing and Sichuan are found to have ignored State Council's guidelines and sold housing units at exceedingly low price.[48] The failure to implement change in the housing system[49] inevitably limits the chance of achieving the stated objectives of urban housing reform.

The Frenzy of Real Estate Market and Residential Housing Provision

The rapid expansion of the real estate market in 1992 has led to the debate over whether the property market is overheated. An unofficial estimate shows that in 1992 about 94,692 housing units in 533 property development projects, with a total worth of 51.7 million Hong Kong dollars, were put on sale in Hong Kong.[50]

Speculative investment in real estate especially in the Pearl River Delta region is believed to have been fuelled by the unfavourable conditions in Hong Kong. With the low savings interest rates and small to medium size residential housing price rising by 53% in 1991 and 30% in 1992,[51] investment in property market or purchase for occupation in Hong Kong have become less profitable. Investing in China's property market has provided local investors with an alternative outlet.

Over 90% of housing units put up for sales in Hong Kong are located in Guangdong province. Out of the estimated 94,692 units, Dongguan has supplied over 21%, Huiyang another 19% and Zhongshan 13% (see Table 7). About 10% of the units are located in Guangzhou, the capital city of Guangdong province. Only less than 5% are located in Fujian (Fuzhou and Xiamen cities), the neighbouring province. Just over 5% of the sale units are located outside Guangdong and Fujian provinces. Some of them are in Beijing, Shanghai, Tianjin and Wuhan.

Because of the close social and cultural ties between the Pearl River Delta cities and Hong Kong and its proximity to the territory, it is understandable that most of the units offered for sale in Hong Kong in 1992 are situated in the Pearl River Delta.

The average price of residential housing units in various parts inside and outside Guangdong province is given in Table 8. It is estimated that about one-third of the real estate units were purchased by Hong Kong investors, and the remaining two-thirds found buyers from overseas or within mainland China.[52]

The development of real estate sector, on the one hand, brings considerable financial income to the state[53] and, on the other hand, it promotes the growth of many other related businesses. Of course, these are valid points to support the further development of real estate industry in China. However, the expansion of commodified residential property market in China is also beneficial to the urban dwellers in China.

The involvement of foreign real estate developers in the urban slum

Table 7. Supply of Commercial Housing for Overseas Buyers in 1992

Location	No. of projects	No. of units on sale in 1992	Percentage of total	Worth (HK$ billion)
Dongguan	77	20,055	21.2	6.6
Huiyang	103	18,014	19.0	5.5
Zhongshan	65	12,085	12.8	6.5
Guangzhou	64	9,148	9.7	6.7
Shenzhen	45	6,719	7.1	5.2
Panyu	29	5,174	5.5	2.4
Zhuhai	26	4,268	4.5	4.7
Fuzhou	19	2,045	2.1	1.2
Xiamen	16	1,875	2.0	1.4
Shantou	12	1,535	1.6	1.0
Other areas in Guangdong	40	8,492	8.9	5.5
Other areas	37	5,282	5.5	5.0
Total	533	94,692	99.9	51.7

Source: *Hong Kong Economic Journal*, 2 March 1993.

Table 8. Average Price of China Urban Housing Units for Overseas Buyers, 1992

Ranking*	City	Price (HK$/sq.ft.)
1	Beijing	1,375
2	Shenzhen Special Economic Zone	1,369
3	Shanghai	1,064
4	Guangzhou (urban)	667
5	Xiamen	582
6	Guangzhou (suburban)	516
7	Shenzhen city	467
8	Zhuhai	456
9	Shantou	399
10	Fuzhou	343
11	Panyu	336
12	Zhongshan	309
13	Dongguan	289
14	Huizhou	264

Source: *Zhongguo fangdichan zhoubao* (China Real Estate Weekly), No. 16 (1 January 1993).
* Ranking according to sale price.

redevelopment projects provides indigenous residents of sub-standard housing a chance to resettle into new housing units with modern facilities. For the lucky few who are given generous resettlement arrangement, the redevelopment of their sub-standard housing area is very much welcome. Other households not being given favourable treatment find the redevelopment project upsetting their present privileges. Social conflicts between developers and residents of urban areas sold by government for property development are a new and difficult issue for government officials.[54]

Neither foreign property developers nor mainland developers involved in real estate business are set up to build welfare housing. Profit is their prime concern. It is natural to expect profits gained, if there are any, from property development will not be used to finance the construction of welfare or low profit housing for the low-pay households with housing difficulty. Unless government is prepared to earmark a certain portion of revenue tax from the real estate business for the construction of new housing for the low-pay households, people in housing difficulty in general are not likely to be beneficiaries of the property boom. On the contrary, they may become the victims of the over-development of (a) luxury villas and expensive apartments for overseas buyers and (b) development zones residents.

1. Problems of Over-development

Wasting public capital in under-developed or unapproved areas

An official with the State Council said that every locality has caught the real estate and development zone fever to the point where some ignore objective conditions, blindly start work while knowing of the problem of duplication. He added there have been too many new projects, their scope too big and the investment structure not justifiable. Zones in the countryside have wasted a lot of money in capital construction but have not been able to attract any capital from overseas because most foreign investors are mainly investing in development zones in coastal areas and major cities.[55]

The official *China Daily* newspaper said government had lost control over the growth of development zones because no government body seemed to know how many there were. The State Economic Planning Commission said there were 1,700 while the Special Economic Zone Office estimated that there were 1,800 whereas the State Land Administration claimed there were 2,700, and the Ministry of Agriculture alleged there were 9,000.[56] Regardless of figures, this was still a major increase from the 117 approved by the end of 1991.

Chinese Vice-Premier Zhu Rongji said there were already too many development zones in China and the central government had decided not to consider any new development zone proposals. Zhu said more than 24 million acres of agricultural land were cleared in 1992, but there was still no sign of any development. This had resulted in a serious waste of resources and the loss of farmland. Zhu expressed concern over the need for putting a huge sum of capital investment in developing the 15,000 square kilometres of land in those over 6,000 development zones. According to his estimate, the state had to invest RMB1.5 trillion while the developer had to borrow and raise RMB3.0 trillion to install the necessary infrastructure before the areas could be used for development. It would take at least six years to properly develop these zones even if the state poured its annual infrastructure development budget of 700 billion into them.[57]

Pushed-up prices of raw materials and services

The rapid growth of development zones helped fixed-asset investment jump 32.5% in 1992 when compared to 1991. This caused prices of raw materials and services to soar, raising more concerns that the country had to face another battle with inflation. For example, in Sichuan province the price of cement quadrupled because of the building boom in 1992.[58] All these showed that before realizing the gains of the property boom, ordinary people and the government had already paid the price, and there was no guarantee that their housing conditions will have been significantly improved or changed for the better in the near future.

Irony of vacant housing units and congested households

The plentiful residential units lying vacant looking for buyers is in great contrast to the poor housing conditions of urban dwellers. Cheung Ching-wan, Hong Kong deputy to the Guangdong Provincial People's Congress warned against the oversupply of luxurious villas in the Pearl River Delta. A lot of these luxurious villas targetted at the Hong Kong and overseas market were not occupied. Their vacancy was in great contrast to acute housing problem faced by the province. Cheung remarked, "It will be an irony for a socialist country if such a situation occurs."[59]

Yuan Zheng, Director of Guangdong Provincial Land Administration, estimated that vacancy rate in some "hot" real estate development spots is as high as 20 to 30%, and developers with limited financial capability may not be able to follow their original plans to develop the real estate as scheduled.[60]

Use of sub-standard construction materials to reduce cost

The flourishing property development activities in the Pearl River Delta and in some large coastal cities such as Xiamen, Fuzhou and Shanghai have also boosted the demand for cement and steel. In autumn 1992, prices for steel were as high as RMB3,800 per ton, compared with international market prices of about RMB2,600. In July and August 1992, cement in Guangdong rose to RMB600 per ton against a normal price of RMB280 to 300. The price increase of construction materials does not only increase the cost of housing for foreigners but also those for domestic use.

To minimize the impact of cost increase, some developers are found to use sub-standard construction materials. Guangzhou authorities conducted two sample tests of cement available and found less than 40% of the cement sampled was of acceptable quality while more than 50% was virtually in the "rubbish" category.[61]

Boost in price for domestic housing units

The increase in land premium, although it may have provided a new source of revenue to the government, has also indirectly pushed up the price of commercial housing. The price of commodified residential housing in January 1992, compared with that at year end,[62] is very alarming: Beijing 110%; Guangzhou and Xiamen 100%; Shanghai 53% and Shenzhen 50%. Li comments that the price of residential housing for domestic sales in Beijing is as high as RMB3,000 per square metre, and it is even higher in Guangzhou, reaching RMB4,000 per square metre. The unrealistically high price, as Li believes, is beyond the affordability of China's urban dwellers.

Besides sub-standard quality, overcharge on domestic sale is another issue of concern to the authority. With the assistance of the Guangzhou Municipal Government, the Guangzhou branch of People's Construction Bank investigated over forty real estate development companies to find out the reasons for the rapid price increase in domestic sales: development companies do not follow government's guidelines and seek high profit margins. The over-charge was also due to the inclusion of many items which should have been excluded from cost calculation.[63]

Under-provision of necessary support facilities and services

The rush to complete housing units is another major cause of concern to buyers. Without proper planning, many housing projects are found to have been completed without timely supply of electricity, water and proper sewage systems. Development of housing without concomitant development of support infrastructural and community facilities is not uncommon in booming areas. Danshui, a boom town near Huizhou, has had difficulties providing supporting facilities to meet the demands of a rapidly growing residential development.[64] The high-rise development of housing blocks is not matched with fire service facilities as fire trucks in China's cities are limited in number and are not yet equipped to fight fire breaking out in high-rise blocks.

2. Concern over Consumer Protection to Overseas Buyers

According to Zou Deci, Director of the country's City Planning and Design Research Centre, the value of property investment has been growing at an average of 26% annually since the adoption of the land leasing policy in 1984. Property investment during the first seven months of 1992 jumped 76% compared with the same period last year, indicating the sector's strong growth momentum. Despite the rapid growth, Zou said, China's property sector needs a long-term master plan and efficient regulation. It is widely believed that a complete set of property rules is necessary to ensure the industry's healthy development and to better complement the country's land leasing policy with market conditions. These rules are designed to avoid land wastage and curb speculative activities.[65]

Regulations and rules are expected to give proper protection to overseas buyers of residential property. The lack of a legal and administrative framework which fails to give consumers proper protection is well reflected in a number of incidents. The Jin Hua Plaza incident in Shenzhen in the summer of 1992 shows that Hong Kong buyers' right were at risk because they had to pay an extra fee as the original developer had not applied for permission to sell the residential units to overseas buyers. In another incident in Huizhou, buyers of Huizhou real estate units were required to pay an extra fee amounting to 15% of the original price to support the city's infrastructural development. After negotiation, buyers who purchased their units from developers whose building plans were submitted before 1 September 1992 were exempted from paying the 15% "city construction charge."[66]

Regulations governing the advance sale of uncompleted housing units are deemed necessary. The procedures for processing presale consent as determined by the Hong Kong government and the requirement of disclosure of information to prospective purchasers as suggested by Hong Kong Consumer Council[67] could be useful references for the concerned authorities in China. There are positive signs that governments of major cities, such as Beijing and Guangzhou, have introduced provisional regulations to give consumers better protection.[68]

For instance, in the 1992 Order No. 18 of Beijing municipal government, the following requirements shall be met in selling houses and buildings in advance after the approval of the municipal real estate management bureau:

1. the payment for the land use right has been made (including the municipal construction fees, resettlement compensation fees and fees for leasing the land use right, the same below) and certificates for using the land have been obtained;
2. the blueprints for construction have been approved and licenses for project plans have been obtained;
3. more than 25% of the total investment for the engineering part has been paid up;
4. the work schedule and the project delivery date have been fixed.

Moreover, after the housing sold in advance is put into use, the buyers shall go through the property right and land use right registration procedures.[69] With these regulations it is hoped that the confidence of overseas purchasers could be rebuilt.

Concluding Remarks

Annual floor space production target and the improvement in average living space per person are the usual production indicators of government policy.[70] According to state plans, China is to speed up the construction of residential housing in the coming ten years. By 1995, non-agricultural population is estimated to reach 260 million, and per capita living area is targetted at 7.5 square metres (which is equivalent to 11.2 square metres of usable area per person). To meet this target, annual production of residential units should reach 150 million square metres per annum in the Eighth Five-year Plan period (1991–1995). Based on 1990 prices, RMB225 billion of investment is required.

By 2000, non-agricultural population is estimated to reach 320 million, and per capita living area is targeted at 8.0 square metres (which is equivalent to 12.0 square metres usable area per person). To meet this target, annual production should reach 180 million square metres per annum in the Ninth Five-year Plan period (1996–2000). Based on 1990 prices, RMB270 billion investment is required.

There is also plan to assist over-crowded households. It is planned that by 1995 families with per capita living area below 4 square metres will have been given relief housing and by 2000 no families should have below 6 square metres per person.[71]

The reform of urban housing in time of property boom is an immense task for the Chinese government. Some of the problems have been leasing too many large lots of land with little regard to actual market demand or the over-development of luxury villas and expensive apartments for overseas buyers, particularly in the coastal regions or in major metropolitan cities such as Beijing, Shanghai and Guangzhou. Yet Chinese officials as well as real estate developers have claimed that there has not been any over-development of affordable residential housing for domestic consumption.[72]

An official with the Ministry of Construction has stated that the housing market is not yet overheated.[73] He has cited urban housing completion figures and claimed that these are still below the targets of the State's Eighth and Ninth Five-year Plans (see Table 9).

Table 9. Housing Floor Area Completed in China Cities (Unit: million sq.m.)

Year	Area completed
1983–1988	140–150
1989 and 1990	100–106
1991	120
1992	130
Target	
1991–1995	150–160
1996–2000	160–180

Source: *Fangdichan kaifa bao*, 16 March 1993.

It is indisputable that the supply of completed flats is still below state's target. But we should distinguish between the supply of affordable housing for domestic consumption from the supply of luxury unaffordable villas originally targetted at foreign investors. The over-provision of expensive villas could be illustrated by the lack of buying support. The denial of an over-heated housing market may do more harm than painstakingly putting the housing market back on a healthy development track.

In view of the slackened demand for residential units designated for overseas buyers and the excessive demand for affordable housing for domestic consumption, governments of metropolitan cities have begun to re-devise their policy towards property development. For instance, Beijing city has decided to allow foreign companies to invest in the reconstruction of the old district and to sell redeveloped property to local companies and individuals.[74]

Guangdong has also taken a series of measures to rectify the province's fledging property market. Yuan Zheng, Director of the province's State Land Administration announced in early 1993 that Guangdong province will restrict the amount of residential property sold to foreign buyers. Local property developers may only sell 10% of their development while joint-venture or foreign developers may sell 20% of the total. The move aims to focus the province's property development activities more on the domestic market. According to Yuan, Guangdong's economic development has grown very fast in recent years, people are eager to improve their living conditions and the demand for housing is great.[75]

It is still too early to speculate whether such change will facilitate the building of additional residential housing units which are affordable to the urban dwellers in China. The preferential treatment given to developers (both local and foreign) to obtain land for housing construction targetted at domestic sale should be continued. To make the housing more affordable, government should review their present practice of charging developers various charges among which the most expensive one is the provision of substitute housing for the previous residents. It is estimated two-thirds to three-quarters of redeveloped housing units are used to house the displaced. Such high costs of redevelopment is believed to be a deterrent to property developers' interest in urban slum redevelopment.[76]

The option of government taking over the responsibility of providing affordable public-sector rental or sale flats to the displaced at concessionary rent or sale price should be further examined.[77] Large-scale public-funded housing programmes in Hong Kong, after forty years of heavy government subsidy, has become financially self-sufficient in the early 1990s. In this regard, is there anything our mainland counterparts can draw upon when developing their urban housing reform programme?

The unique conditions of our mainland counterparts such as low wage, virtually free rent, employment-tied housing allocation and limited provision of home financing mortgage facilities should be taken into serious consideration when devising alternative reform plans as there is no easy solution to the deep-rooted urban housing problems. The comprehensive review of China's urban housing reform and recommendations by the World Bank experts[78] should be seriously considered. Furthermore, delinking housing allocation from employment and providing a legal framework to secure longer-term mortgage facilities as well as reviewing the role of the state in providing public housing only to the low-pay households should be further scrutinized.

Notes

1. *People's Daily*, 19 February 1993.
2. *Guangming Daily*, 24 October 1992.
3. Dinyar Lalkaka, "Urban Housing in China," *Habitat International*, Vol. 8, No. 1 (1984), pp. 63–73.
4. Zhou Ganzhi, "Working Report Given in the National Real Estate Working Conference Held in Beijing on 25 June 1992" (in Chinese), *Zhuzhai yu fangdichan* (Housing and Real Estate), No. 1 (August 1992), p. 9. Results of the 1985 national housing survey show that 10.54 million households, that is 26.5% of all households surveyed, were classified as households with inadequate housing (including all those living in non-residential structures, "inconvenienced" households and those "crowded" households with per capita living space below 4 square metres. See Qiu Zeyuan, Wang Yu and Wang Qian, *Zufang, maifang* (Renting, Buying Houses) (Beijing: People's University Press, 1992), p. 8.
5. Dinyar Lalkaka (Note 3), p. 65.
6. *Hong Kong Economic Journal*, 27 January 1993.
7. *China Daily*, 6 February 1992.
8. World Bank, *China: Implementation Options for Urban Housing Reform* (A World Bank Country Study), 1992, p. xii.
9. Yok-siu F. Lee, "The Urban Housing Problem in China," *The China Quarterly*, No. 115 (September 1988), pp. 387–407.

10. World Bank (Note 8), pp. ix–x.
11. *Ibid.*, p. 21.
12. Peter K. W. Fong, "Housing Reform in China," *Habitat International*, Vol. 13, No. 4 (1989), pp. 29–41.
13. Dinyar Lalkaka (Note 3), p. 65.
14. Peter K. W. Fong (Note 12), p. 31.
15. World Bank (Note 8), pp. 21–22.
16. Qiu Zeyuan, Wang Yu and Wang Qian (Note 4), p. 13.
17. Yok-siu F. Lee (Note 9), p. 399.
18. Peter K. W. Fong (Note 12), pp. 33–34.
19. Guangzhou Housing System Reform Office, *Guangzhou fanggai ziliao xuanbian yu wenti jieda* (Housing Reform Resource Book and Questions and Answers), April 1992, p. 5.
20. Yok-shiu F. Lee (Note 9), pp. 401–402.
21. *Shijie jingji daobao* (World Economic Herald), 26 July 1982, p. 11.
22. Yun Zhiping, Bai Yihong and Tan Chunlin, *Woguo zhufang zhidu gaige de tansuo* (An Exploration of China's Housing Reform System) (Beijing: China Finance and Economic Publisher, 1991), p. 10.
23. *Ibid.*
24. Yok-shiu F. Lee (Note 9), p. 402.
25. Yun Zhiping et al. (Note 22), p. 10.
26. World Bank (Note 8), p. 26.
27. *Ibid.*
28. Yok-shiu F. Lee (Note 9), pp. 403–404.
29. World Bank (Note 8), p. 27.
30. *Ibid.*, p. 28.
31. Yun Zhiping et al. (Note 22), p. 13.
32. *Zhongguo fangdichan* (China Real Estate), No. 141 (September 1992), p. 44; information shows that employees of central government agencies in Beijing can get wage compensation if the rent-to-total household income ratio exceeds 5% after rent increase. The compensation is paid so that rent-to-income ratio is not more than 5%.
33. World Bank (Note 8), p. 26.
34. Lu Ma, "The Slow Progress of Commercialization of Public Housing," *Yue Gang xinxi bao* (GD–HK Information Daily), 23 January 1993.
35. *Yangcheng Evening News*, 25 January 1993.
36. Interviews with officials of Guangzhou and Guangdong provincial governments in September 1992 and February 1993.
37. Guangzhou Housing Reform Office (Note 19), p. 303.
38. World Bank (Note 8), p. 29.
39. World Bank experts point out that this measure, while an improvement over the existing practices, has only a limited impact, when contrasted with

rent-substituting "key" money used elsewhere, such as in Korea. Since the housing bonds are redeemable within five years, their impact on household rental expenditures is limited, when compared to a policy of redemption only on vacating the premises. See World Bank (Note 8), p. 31.

40. Yang Lu, "Zhongguo chengzhen zhufang zhidu gaige de jiben yuanze he youguan zhengce shuping" (Commentary on the Basic Principle and Relevant Policy on China Housing System Reform), *Zhuzhai yu fangdichan*, No. 3 (December 1992), p. 29.
41. Guangzhou Housing System Reform Office (Note 19), p. 312.
42. *Zhuzhai yu fangdichan*, No. 3 (December 1992), p. 32.
43. *Zhongguo fangdichan*, No. 141 (September 1992), p. 32.
44. State Council Leading Group on Urban Housing Reform, "Quanguo zhufang zhidu gaige gongzuo jinzhan qingkuang" (A Progress Report of China's Housing System Reform Work), *Zhongguo fangdichan*, No. 141 (September 1992), pp. 32–37.
45. World Bank (Note 8), p. 28.
46. Guan Jingyu, Hou Ximin and Zhang Jing, "Jiakuai fanggai bufa tuidong jingji fazhan" (Speed up Housing Reform, Promote Economic Development), *Zhongguo fangdichan*, No. 141 (September 1992), pp. 38–42.
47. *Zhongguo fangdichan*, No. 141 (September 1992), p. 43.
48. Guan Jingyu et al. (Note 46), pp. 38–42.
49. Urban housing reform, as suggested, should put system change as the first priority. System change refers to change in housing allocation criteria from welfare housing for everyone to welfare or low-cost housing (for rent or for sale) to the deserving low-income households only. Other households which can afford to pay more should pay higher rental or purchase housing at higher price than the existing heavily-subsidized rent or "preferential" sales price.
50. *Hong Kong Economic Journal*, 2 March 1993. Chinese Real Estate Research Centre (Hong Kong) gives a similar estimate, see *Zhongguo fangdichan zhoubao* (China Real Estate Weekly), No. 16 (1 January 1993), p. 2. On the other hand, Hong Kong Government Rating and Valuation Department estimates in its *Property Review 1993* that there were over 70,000 Chinese housing units on sale in Hong Kong in 1992.
51. Hong Kong Government Rating and Valuation Department, *Property Review 1992, 1993*.
52. *Hong Kong Economic Journal*, 2 March 1993.
53. In 1991, China's incomes from the land use tax, the house property tax and the tax paid by real estate development enterprises hit RMB10 billion, accounting for 2.3% of the country's financial income that year. See *China Market*, No. 2, 1993, pp. 4–5. The Ministry of Construction estimates that real estate related revenue accounts for over one-quarter of

some newly-developed coastal cities. see *Zhuzhai yu fangdichan*, No. 3 (December 1992), p. 8.
54. *Ming Pao* (Hong Kong), 6 February, 29 March and 12 April 1993 about the incidents of disputes in Shenzhen and Dongguan between government/developers and indigenous residents over the rights of redeveloping the areas.
55. *Ming Pao*, 8 February 1993.
56. Vice-Premier Zhu Rongji pointed out that there were over 6,000 development zones, see *Ming Pao*, 26 February 1993.
57. *Ibid.*
58. *Ming Pao*, 8 February 1993.
59. *South China Morning Post* (Hong Kong), 1 February 1993.
60. *Ming Pao*, 22 December 1992.
61. *Ming Pao*, 9 March 1993.
62. Li Guowen, "Dangqian fangdichan re zhong zhide lengjing sikao de jige wenti" (Issues to be Considered with a Cold Head in the Midst of Overheated Real Estate Market), *Zhongguo fangdichan*, No. 144 (December 1992), pp. 67–71.
63. Yang Lu, "Commentary on the Basic Principle and Relevant Policy of China Housing System Reform" (in Chinese), *Zhuzhai yu fangdichan*, No. 3 (December 1992), p. 30.
64. *South China Morning Post*, 1 February 1993.
65. *Ming Pao*, 8 December 1992.
66. *Ming Pao*, 28 November 1992.
67. Consumer Council of Hong Kong. A Study of the disclosure of information to prospective purchasers of units in uncompleted buildings, October 1991.
68. *Zhongguo fangdichan zhoubao*, No. 13 (11 December 1992).
69. *China Economic News*, No. 2 (11 January 1993), pp. 7–8.
70. World Bank experts criticize the adoption of these two principal indicators of housing production since it has ignored the need for monitoring the number of units built and their size and type distribution. See World Bank (Note 8), p. 75.
71. *Jingji xinxi shibao* (Economic Information Times), 16 March 1993.
72. *Ming Pao*, 18 January 1993 and *Xinxi da guan bao* (Information Grand Sight), 16 March 1993.
73. *Fangdichan kaifa bao*, 16 March 1993.
74. *Ming Pao*, 4 November 1992.
75. *Ming Pao* and *South China Morning Post*, 1 February 1993.
76. See Song Qilin, "Mantan woguo chengshi guihua yu zhuzhai jianshe" (Talking about China's City Planning and Housing Construction), *Zhuzhai yu fangdichan*, No. 3 (December 1992), pp. 35–37.
77. To facilitate smooth clearance operation in squatter areas or any occupied

areas earmarked for development Hong Kong government makes good use of its large-scale public housing programme to cater to the resettlement needs of the residents. Private developers obtain land directly from government, pay the premium and concentrate on building new housing. Government will take care of the clearance operation and resettling all eligible residents with government revenue, part of which is developers' land premium.
78. World Bank (Note 8).

25

Commercialization without Independence: Trends and Tensions of Media Development in China

Joseph Man Chan

Introduction

In the field of mass communication in China, 1992 will be remembered as the year of commercialization, which forms the major focus of this review. The importance of media commercialization, I think, paralleled that of the organized demand for freedom of expression as witnessed during the pro-democracy movement in 1989. It represented the lagged diffusion of economic reforms into the ideological and cultural domain and the erosion of the Chinese Communist Party's (CCP) control over ideology. While the mass media had been slowly taking on commercial features since the mid-1980s, it was not until 1992 that media commercialization became more visible in policy and reality. That explains why a more focused examination here is warranted.

Without attempting a comprehensive review, I shall organize the features of media development in China under the following headings: (1) Changes and continuities in ideological and communication policies; (2) the manifestations and processes of media commercialization; (3) the struggle for freedom of expression; (4) the penetration of STAR TV (Satellite Television Asia Region Television) and other overseas media in China; as well as (5) a discussion of the implications of media commercialization.

Although 1992 provides the time frame for this chapter, I have to date back occasionally so as to contextualize some observed trends. The review will extend beyond journalism to the field of mediated entertainment. Illustrative examples will be drawn from both the print and audio-visual media, including newspapers, television, movies, radio and books.

Ideological and Communication Policies

The pro-democracy movement in 1989 marked the culmination of the Chinese people's demands for freedom and democracy since the founding of the People's Republic of China. Among others, it was the first time that journalists marched on the streets for press freedom. But all these calls for freedom and democracy were silenced by the CCP's military crackdown. Attributing the pro-democracy movement to the influence of "bourgeois liberalization" and the western strategy of "peaceful evolution," the CCP tightened its ideological and communication policies in the two years following 1989.[1] Reinforced by the collapse of the Soviet Union and Eastern Europe, policies to combat bourgeois liberalization and peaceful evolution stayed high on the CCP's priority list.

A reflection of this tightened policy was the appointment of conservatives to fill the senior posts in the communication-related areas, including Wang Renzhi, the director of the Central Propaganda Department, Xu Weicheng, the deputy director, Deng Liqun, politburo ideologue, Gao Di, publisher of *People's Daily* and He Jingzhi, acting minister of Culture.[2] Although Li Ruihuan, a liberal, was head of the Central Committee's Leading Group on Ideology and Propaganda, he was overshadowed by Deng Liqun and other members of the group.[3]

The conservative policy also took its toll among journalists and publications. Although precise figures are not available, at least two dozen journalists from newspapers in Beijing and Shanghai were imprisoned.[4] Many other journalists suffered investigation, work suspension and job-reassignment. Some had to hide their bylines even if they were allowed to continue writing. Some publications were closed and some re-organized at the top level. Prevailing in the mass media were orthodox views that criticized the influence of bourgeois liberalization and stressed the importance of the Four Cardinal Principles.

Ideological control began to relax somewhat after Deng Xiaoping had spoken on further economic liberalization during his tour to southern China in early 1992. Brushing aside the conservatives' urge for taking anti-peaceful evolution as the central task, Deng reiterated the primacy of the policy of "one centrality, two basic points": Of central importance was economic construction whereas reform and open-door policy and the maintenance on the Four Cardinal Principles were the two basic points.[5] Deng called for faster economic growth and boldness in experimenting with reforms. At the same time, he directed that practice should take precedence over theoretical debates and that controversies over the nature of Chinese reforms and other historical-political issues should be shelved. While he continued to maintain that rightism was an undesirable tendency, he unprecedentedly emphasized that leftism was posing a more imminent danger. All these ideas were later incorporated in the formal report of the Fourteenth Party Congress that was held in October 1992.

As repercussions of Deng Xiaoping's southern tour were being felt in the economic and political realms, Li Ruihuan, a member of the Standing Committee of CCP Politburo in charge of ideology, began to make obvious headway by the summer of 1992. He pointed out that ideological indoctrination was not the sole aim of arts and literature which should serve multiple functions, including entertainment, aesthetics, cognition and the like. He also asserted that the CCP should not interfere with the creation of culture and arts. While stopping short of touching on the sensitive subject of press freedom, he directed that the key point of propaganda work in 1992 was to give prominence to the task of economic construction, reform and open-door policy and should shy away from dry and empty sermons.[6] On another occasion, he stressed that the news media should increase the volume of information, meet the needs of various audience and shorten news reportage.[7]

Reportedly at the urge of Li Ruihuan, the Ministry of Culture released ten policy guidelines on reforming cultural institutions in 1992.[8] They allowed cultural organizations to form joint-ventures with foreign capital in order to attract investment from Hong Kong, Taiwan and the overseas-Chinese. Life-long employment lacking economic incentives were to be replaced by contractual employment, open recruitment and meritorious salaries. In short, cultural institutions would have to subject themselves to market forces in addition to the political pressures from the Party. These policies were in stark contrast to those released in mid-1991 which had stressed the need to fight bourgeois liberalization with Marxism and Mao Thought.

The policy to commercialize publications was reported to have been formalized at the 1992 National Working Conference on Press Management which recognized the "commodity nature" of the press and produced a schedule for the transformation of the Chinese press.[9] The first phase of transformation was to terminate subsidizing local or non-official publications that mainly carried information about consumption and daily life. The second phase was to subject the national or official press to competition. By 1994, the government was to continue to financially support only the *People's Daily*, the *Economic Daily* and the *Seeking Truth* periodical.

Consistent with this plan was the report that Beijing was set to liberalize Party control over publications that did not touch on ideological and political matters.[10] Censorship standards were to be spelt out in non-ideological and more specific guidelines to be implemented by administrative departments, rather than by the CCP. The new censorship bureaus were to grant greater autonomy to four categories of newspapers: (1) afternoon and evening publications; (2) news digests; (3) papers specializing in culture and lifestyle as well as (4) trade journals. These newspapers were not required to carry ideological propaganda, although political control still applied to Party mouthpieces, army papers and national or municipal general papers.

In the area of book publishing, Beijing authorities announced that some level of autonomy would be introduced to the industry in 1993.[11] Books that carry ideological and political impacts will still be subject to censorship, but publishing houses can have a free hand with other kinds of books. Neither will they be required to limit themselves to publishing a narrowly-defined range of books as they are now. Some will be allowed to transform themselves into enterprises, whereby they can determine their own salary scales and book prices. The book retailing business, now virtually monopolized by Xinhua Bookstore, will be subject to competition from private or collective bookstores.

The resurgence of reforms consequential to Deng's southern trip also had a liberalizing impact on the leaders of China's movie industry who met in 1992 to deal with the continuous decline in box-office receipts. They concluded that reforms and innovative measures should be adopted to meet the entertainment needs of the audience.[12] Movie censorship in 1992 was relaxed as well. The most telling example is the lift of the ban on Zhang Yimou's movies, *Red Lantern*, *Red Sorghum*, and *Judou*. As we shall see later, even the monopoly over movie distribution was to give way to competition.

Media Commercialization

Deng Xiaoping's approach to development has been disjunctive in nature: achieving economic modernization without yielding political control. In the sphere of economics, he has gone as far as being willing to replace China's planned economy with one regulated by the market. But in the realm of politics, he has insisted on the Four Cardinal Principles, the essence of which is to maintain the dictatorial rule of the CCP. Considered to be political-ideological institutions, mass media had been very much shielded from reforms until 1992 when the economic reforms that had been practised in the manufacturing and service industries were more visibly applied to mass media.

China appears to have reached a point when the central government cannot afford subsidizing the old media as well as the new ones that have cropped up in the last decade. To let the mass media finance themselves, therefore, becomes necessary. Besides, economic development has created a huge demand for more effective advertising channels. To form a media market is a natural response to this economic need. Meanwhile, the CCP's disjunction between politics and economics is applied *within* mass media.

By this, the CCP's hold over the less official media and dissemination of non-political information is relaxed while maintaining tight control over the Party mouthpieces and political news. All these changes lead to the commercialization of mass media upon which I am going to elaborate.

Advertising is the economic base of any media commercialization. Complemented by sponsorship and other sources of revenue, advertising is known to have rendered an increasing number of publications self-supporting.[13] Fuelled by an economic growth rate of 12.8% and the legitimation of marketization in 1992, total advertising revenue in China is reported to have exceeded RMB5,000 million, an increase of about 43% over 1991. In some places like Beijing, Jiangsu and Shanxi, the growth rates have been almost as high as 100%.[14] Without the rapid growth of the advertising industry, media commercialization would be just empty talk.

At the strategic level, mass media have included profit-making as a plausible aim. This has meant that mass media have had to reorient themselves to the needs of the market and to increase their financial assets by all legitimate means. The most common practice among newspapers has been to publish what is called "weekend supplements" — dedicating extra pages or a full paper to info-entertainment on weekends. In the past, with the exception of the *People's Daily* which had eight pages, all Chinese newspapers used to have only four pages each. Now, over half of the provincial papers carry eight pages.[15] Meanwhile, *Guangzhou Daily* and *Xinwen Evening Post* publish twelve and sixteen pages respectively. The weekend editions have provided a strong economic incentive for the cadres working in Party mouthpieces because the money thus earned will add to the bonus that they may receive.[16]

Performing public relation functions for enterprises and courting sponsorship are other methods by which mass media increase their revenues. These functions include organizing symposia, shows, competitions, press conferences and any other activities that can promote their "clients."[17] Many media and journalists are known to have gone as far as mixing up news work with advertising and sponsorship. On an institutional level, news media openly charge fees from enterprises for producing a corresponding volume of favourable reportage. This is so commonplace that many journalists do not even regard this as a violation of professional ethics.[18] Trading news space for money is also practised at the personal level. In the spree of stock trading, a common saying that captures the phenomenon is: "The first rate reporters trade stocks; the second rate take 'red packets' of money; the third rate write for outsiders; and the fourth rate write for their newspaper employer." The "red packets," with values ranging from RMB 50 to 200, are often handed out by enterprises to please reporters during press conferences.[19] Some journalists who specialize in finance reporting are known to have reaped great personal gain by providing promotions disguised as news.

Economic opportunity has also lured some journalists and other media workers to desert journalism to start businesses on their own. This trend of moving into business has applied to all intellectuals in 1992. For instance, world-famous writer Zhang Xianliang has been reported to be devoting a quarter of his time exclusively to the "money-making business."[20] Popular writer Wang Shuo has formed his own video production group. Many journalists who have stayed on have taken up side jobs by writing for other institutions. To reduce their employees' economic pressure, some newspapers have even encouraged them to adopt such practice.[21]

Economic development has spawned the need for more financial information and advertising outlets. The need is particularly acute as people from all walks of life have involved themselves in the process of marketization, as entrepreneurs or as consumers. New radio and TV stations that carry mainly economic and commercial information have cropped up in Hubei, Hunan, Shanxi, Sichuan, Beijing, Tianjin, Shanghai and other places.[22] It is expected more "commercial" radio and TV stations as such (see below) will be established in the coming years. The need for economic information has also been felt by the print media. While the newly started economic dailies are selling well, traditional Party newspapers have created special sections on economic news. Among others, the Xinhua News Agency has planned to start China's first newspaper on finance and stocks in 1993.[23]

Analogous to the diversification of investment by media consortia in capitalist societies, the Chinese media have branched out into non-information or entertainment businesses in order to broaden their bases of revenue. The *People's Daily*, for instance, is trying to go into real estate and data businesses.[24] By 1992, the Beijing Movie Studio had already opened twenty-two subsidiaries engaged in a wide range of businesses, including gas retailing, meat processing and video production.[25]

Media commercialization has taken place in tandem with the intensification of competition across media and within media. With the rapid penetration of television sets and the wide attraction of programmes from Hong Kong, Taiwan and elsewhere and the Chinese versions of TV serials (soaps), television has quickly become the most popular entertainment in

China. Movie attendance has suffered as a result. As of 1992, China could produce about 5,000 soap episodes of varying quality per year.[26] Following the lead of the serial "Aspirations" (*Kewang*) in 1991, the most popular local television production has been the "In the Editorial Office" (*Bianjibu de gushi*), a witty twenty-five-part series about a group of magazine journalists filled with humour and satire. The success of these series, coupled with the government's cultural relaxation and revived emphasis on market reforms, has kindled competition among the television stations for audience and advertising. The race has become so intense that China Central Television (CCTV), is reported to have paid Wang Shuo a handsome sum for writing a script for a new forty-one-part series about young romance, "I Love You, Definitely" (*Aili mei shuangliang*).[27]

Private ownership is becoming more common in the manufacturing and service industries, but it has not been officially endorsed in the media field. In reality, the commercialization measures mentioned above and the growing practices of the "contractual system," commercial financing and joint-venturing are effective in granting some autonomy to the media and loosening the CCP's ideological control.

In China, the tightest political control of the media rests upon those run by the CCP's institutions, particulary those at the national level. In 1990, CCP-run newspapers numbered 454.[28] The political directions they take provide the ideological and policy guidance for newspapers operated by non-CCP-institutions such as the democratic parties, the Political Consultative Congress, various central and local departments of the State Council and other units. The majority of Chinese newspapers, numbering about 1,000, are evening dailies, small or specialized papers that are less ideological in orientation than the Party mouthpieces. They serve the info-entertainment function by providing social news, novels of various sorts, adventure and crime stories.

The publishers of these papers can be Party newspapers, enterprises, social organizations or a unit of some sort which have obtained a licence or "publication number" (*kanhao*) from the State Press and Publications Administration in Beijing. The Administration has been very careful with giving out new licences in recent years in spite of a long list of applicants. In face of the keen demand, those institutions holding publication permits can choose to lease their *kanhaos* to individuals or groups that are interested in running media operations, resulting in what is called the "contractual system" (*chengbao zhi*). The typical arrangement is for the contractor to pay the licence-holding institution a fixed sum at the end of a duration for authorization to publish under its name. The contractor is held responsible for the editing, printing, distribution, taxation and all other expenses. The contractor can further sub-contract out parts of its operation. Although the papers so contracted are legally owned by the licence-holding institution, their operative control rests with the contractor. In some cases, it is the medium operator who takes the initiative to persuade an established unit to become a publisher on his behalf. It was through this scheme that the now-defunct *World Economic Herald* got its licence to publish from the Shanghai Academy of Social Sciences and the Chinese World Economists Association.[29]

An illustration of the contractual system and its contradiction with the Chinese media structure is the *Culture Weekly* that was published by *Chinese Culture News*, the official paper of the Ministry of Culture. The contractor in his case was an individual who had assembled a team of his own. He had to pay the *Chinese Culture News* an annual fee of RMB200,000 for using the licence.[30] Should the operation have failed, he would just have paid a penalty of RMB20,000. Launched on 1 January 1993, the weekly was banned after the second issue, presumably because it had touched on the sensitive topic of mediated nudity and had published some nude pictures which appeared to have tarnished the official image of the Ministry of Culture. Realizing that he could not implement his editorial line, the contractor terminated his contract with the Ministry of Culture. While the ban reflects the tight censorship standard of the Propaganda Department in regard to sex, the willingness of the weekly to test such sensitive issues speaks to the pressure of commercialization and the higher autonomy the operator has by virtue of the contractual system.

The contractual system applies not only to the print media but also to the movie, television and other audio-visual media. Associated with the wide attraction of soap operas is the increased competition among television programme suppliers. On the one hand, private or collectively-owned audio-visual production houses have been formed. On the other hand, more than twenty movie studios, including Beijing, Shanghai, Xi'an and Pearl River have set up television departments.[31] There is no coordination among these studios and production houses; they have had to compete for television stations' production contracts. The popular "Aspirations," "In the Editorial Office" and "I Love You, Definitely," for instance, are made by production houses on a contract basis.

The opening of Shanghai East Radio Station in 1992, an offshoot of the Shanghai Broadcasting and Television Administration Bureau, signifies the emergence of an alternative form of media financing in China. Instead of relying on state subsidy, its start-up capital has been a bank loan.[32] Besides, it is contracted out to a team as well. All these commercial arrangements require the radio station to be more responsive to audience needs which, in turn, is conducive to the adoption of management practices, programming policy and programme formats that have proved to be competitive in Guangzhou and other places like Hong Kong. Indeed, the producers at Shanghai East Radio have unprecedently high autonomy in decisions over personnel, finance and content matters. The instant success of this radio station has created immense presssure on media that are more orthodox in their approaches.

Foreign ownership of mass media is one of the most sensitive issues in China. All the requests by media from Taiwan and Hong Kong for full entry into China are to no avail so far. However, forming joint-ventures is becoming more feasible. A symbolic breakthrough was achieved when Sally Au, the Director of Sing Tao Groups originally based in Hong Kong, signed up with the *People's Daily* to co-publish a weekly on economic development, the first newspaper joint-venture in China. If China is to open up further to foreign media investment, it will likely begin with publications that do not touch on ideological issues, rather with those which deal with economics, technology, lifestyle and entertainment.

Numerous negotiations are taking place between Chinese and Hong Kong or Taiwanese media over the formation of joint-ventures.[33] A Hong Kong consortium led by Wharf has announced that it has formed a 50-50 joint-venture with Sichuan Cable Television Development Company to start a micro-wave pay-television system for Chengdu and its neighbouring areas. The system will initially have four channels carrying news, movies, soap operas and general entertainment.[34] In fact, a joint-venture between a Hong Kong tycoon and Wuhan authorities has been operating a cable system in Wuhan since 1992.

Advertising, the key revenue for mass media in capitalist societies, is becoming more important for the Chinese media. More than forty multinational advertising agencies from Japan, USA and Hong Kong have set up joint-ventures with Chinese counterparts in Beijing, Shanghai, Guangzhou and other cities. The growth of the advertising industry is an indispensable part of media marketization. Joint-ventures and the operation of multinational agencies will speed up the diffusion of western advertising culture into China.

Movie co-production between China and foreign capital has been increasing rapidly, totalling twenty-two in the first half of 1992, thirteen of which have been with Taiwan or Hong Kong.[35] The foreign partners are established studios or movie companies, rather than individuals as they were in previous years. Thanks to these co-productions, the audience can now more often see the mixed cast of directors and actors from China, Hong Kong and Taiwan. It is not uncommon for Chinese studios to relax the censorship standards in order to please their co-producers. In cases where they find a film politically too sensitive, they will usually limit its showing to overseas markets. Meanwhile, Chinese studios can learn from their partners the producing of a movie and benefit from the international connections thus established.

Centralized distribution has been a bottleneck of media commercialization because it is too inflexible and ineffective in meeting the needs of market competition. Attempts have been made to break the virtual monopoly of the postal system as the distributor of publications. Newspapers have been allowed to run their own distributional network. A notable example is the system that *Tianjin Daily* has built. It is so effective that it is extending its service beyond its host newspaper.[36] By 1992, as many as 500 (about one-third) of China's newspapers can distribute on their own. Despite China's postal system continuing to play a central role in national distribution, particularly in the rural areas, the growth of alternative distributional networks and media commercialization will feed on one another.

The monopoly over movie distribution by the Chinese Movie Distribution Company has long been seen as a critical factor that has prevented the movie industry from responding more effectively to audience needs. The year 1992 is the seventh consecutive year that has registered a decline in box office. Between 1985 and 1992, the cinema attendance has sharply declined from a count of 27 billion to 16 billion, a drop of about 40%.[37] In late 1992, Chinese movie authorities finally decided to break up the monopoly by allowing studios, local distributors and others to compete in distributing movies. This will likely lead to the diversification of movie capital, the growth of independent producers and intensified competition among movie producers. In addition, it will increase the pressure on the Chinese authorities to relax and repeal the quota system for movie production.

Continuing Struggle for Freedom of Expression

Consequential to the CCP's emphasis on anti-peaceful evolution and the domination of conservatives in the field of ideology and propaganda since 1989, the general atmosphere around the political discourse in China has been suppressive. This has applied not only to the intellectuals and the public at large but also to the liberal faction within the Party as well. Even Deng Xiaoping himself appears to have had some difficulty in having his views on economic reforms published. In 1991, he spoke through the *Liberation Daily* in the form of articles written by a group of journalists who were later criticized and investigated by the leftists within the Party.[38] After he made his liberal views in his southern tour, the first medium to break the news was *Ming Pao*, a Hong Kong daily, to be followed later by *Shenzhen Special Zone News*. Ironically, the *People's Daily*, kept silent until other media had followed suit.[39] Deng's push towards reforms only gained momentum as more and more media promoted his views, particularly after CCTV broadcast a documentary of Deng's southern tour produced by Shenzhen Television Station.

Deng's call to combat leftism during his trip to the south created room for Chinese intellectuals to rekindle the fight for greater freedom of expression. Seminars were held to condemn the evils of leftism in the academia and cultural expression. About 100 prominent Chinese intellectuals attended a seminar that elaborated on the damages that leftism had done to the Chinese people.[40] In another seminar on Supervision by the Media and the Reform and Open-door Policies, the prevailing opinion was that mass media should reflect public opinion quickly so as to create a relaxed and harmonious environment. A supervisory role of the media required the cooperation from officials and people's awareness of their constitutional rights in using the media for criticism and self-criticism.[41] Articles that called for greater press freedom were also published.[42] In a piece printed in the *Liberation Daily*, Qian Bocheng, a representative of the National People's Congress, argued for the journalists' right to report and the public's right to know.[43] He stressed that it was time for implementing these rights. But when *Future and Development*, a bimonthly of the Chinese Technological Society, published a dissenting scholar's argument for greater democracy it was forced to fold.

Anti-leftism never got off the ground in 1992. In the brief period when Deng's warning over leftism was circulated, prominent intellectuals and journalists in China seized the opportunity to publish two books on the subject. Edited and written by liberal Chinese intellectuals, the books *Historical Tides* (*Lishi de chaoliu*) and *The Memorandum on Anti-Leftism* (*Fanzuo beiwanglu*) contained unnamed but sharp criticism of Deng Liqun and other ideologues. High-ranking conservative officials tried to stop both books from publication, but with only partial success.[44] For instance, while limited copies were being circulated among intellectuals, the editor of *The Memorandum on Anti-Leftism* defied the authorities' temporary suspension of the book by distributing 50,000 copies through private book merchants.[45]

There is a growing number of instances in which the Chinese people and media resort to legal channels to assert their rights. *Legal News*, a Shanghai publication, sued a law court in Henan province for violating its right to cover news events by exposing the film and snatching the camera of its reporter before the opening of court trial. This is the first case in China in which a newspaper charges a court for breaching its right. Another case had to do with a shop in Shanghai that tried to sell satellite reception dishes by displaying STAR TV, a satellite television service based in Hong Kong. The Shanghai Audio-Visual Management Bureau imposed a fine on the shop owner who responded by suing the Bureau for infringing upon his legal right to run a business.[46]

The struggle for greater freedom of expression has also continued at the individual level. Zhang Weiguo's experience as an independent freelance reporter is illustrative. Jailed after the June 4 massacre for his active role in the *World Economic Herald*, Zhang was released in early 1991, and he began to write for Hong Kong and Taiwan newspapers on political reform, factional politics and press freedom. In addition, he continued to be interviewed by Hong Kong and overseas media. In spite of threats from the Ministry of Security, he persisted in contributing to overseas media until the authorities acquiesced to the practice. He summed up his experience as follows: "In China, you have first of all to stay alive, not to be engulfed by the threats and machinations of the behemoth. Then you begin to test the limits of its tolerance. Sometimes, the leviathan relaxes a bit due to a change of climate, a chink in its armour, sheer sloth or oversight. After you have pulled off your courageous acts once, twice and three times, a pattern is established. A small victory is won."[47] Finally, Zhang was allowed to leave China for the United States in early 1993. The fact that someone like Zhang could survive as a freelance reporter attests to the growing determination of Chinese journalists to be independent, on the one hand, and to the relaxation of ideological control in China, on the other.

Penetration of STAR TV and Other Overseas Media

As China's entertainment market opened up in previous years, media fare from Hong Kong and China posed increasingly competitive pressure on local productions. This was most severe in the provinces of Guangdong and Fujian because of the respective vicinity of Hong Kong and Taiwan. Television signals from Hong Kong are often received through collectively-operated reception dish and redistributed through rudimentary cable networks. Rebroadcasting is often done without paying dues for copyrights. Overseas movie, television videos and tapes are so popular that public show houses are created for performance. Some of these videos and tapes are imported, but many are pirated or smuggled into China.

Added to this impact of overseas media was the launch of STAR TV in late 1991. It carries five channels, with themes on music television video (MTV), sports and entertainment programming, news (BBC World Service Television) and family entertainment as well as a mandarin-language (*putonghua*) channel, all running on a 24-hour basis. As of 1992, most relevant to China are the mandarin channel that broadcasts programmes made in Hong Kong, Japan, Taiwan, China and elsewhere, and the BBC news channel that broadcasts partly in mandarin. For fear of ideological influence from the West, China generally forbids the reception of all foreign television. However, STAR TV is known to have been picked up by dishes that belong to institutions and community cable networks in China. About 4.8 million households are known to have had access to STAR TV by the end of 1992.[48]

A factor that has contributed to such rapid penetration has been the relaxation of social control consequential to reforms in the last decade.[49] Added to this relaxed control is China's huge size and population which make it difficult for the central authority to monitor the reception of satellite television. The launching of AsiaSat 1 has provided an unintended pretext for some Chinese institutions to receive STAR TV because AsiaSat 1 is also beaming signals for the provincial television stations of Yunnan and Guizhou whose rugged terrains have made microwave transmission difficult. Since it is legal to receive AsiaSat 1 signals with a licence, some institutions can, therefore, access STAR TV while claiming to be tuning in to the provincial television.

The earlier legal case over a shop's right to sell reception dishes for STAR TV in 1992 illustrates the growing tension within China in regard to the reception of STAR TV and other satellite TV services. Not all the government departments have been for the suppression of the shop. At least the Ministry of Machinery and Electronics which manufactures dishes has vested interest in a wider proliferation of reception technology. It is lobbying against the previous ban on the reception of foreign satellite television by the Ministry of Radio, Film and Television on the grounds that it is "good for enriching people's cultural life."[50] This attests to the growing diverging interests among various government departments even when the issue of ideological control is involved.

As it stands now, the accessibility to STAR TV in China can be characterized as what I have called a state of "suppressive openness."[51] It refers to China's intention to fend off foreign culture as evidenced in policy and its imperfect control of access in practice. Given China's deep concern with ideological control, it is unlikely that the accessibility to STAR TV and other overseas media in China will increase linearly and smoothly. The evolutionary path is likely to be interrupted by occasional crackdowns, to be followed by growth spurt each time, until the audience size reaches a point beyond effective policing.

Conclusion

Nineteen Ninety-two has been a year of media commercialization in China. Policies have been made to turn media institutions into enterprises that are scheduled to become self-supporting. Advertising has gained increasing importance to media survival. The contractual system and commercial financing are becoming more common in the field of communication. Joint-ventures with Hong Kong and overseas capital have been formed in advertising, cable television, publications, movie-making and other media. The state's virtual monopoly over media production and distribution is giving way to competition. For the less official and local media, economic consideration has now replaced politics as the editorial guidepost. Meanwhile, the CCP has relaxed its control over the dissemination of non-political information even in Party mouthpieces.

As evidenced by the history of media development in many countries, private media ownership is tied to the development of the media market and notions such as "objectivity" and "media as the watchdog of the government."[52] It can be argued that private ownership is a necessary condition for the birth of a free press. Media commercialization in China has not reached the point of allowing private ownership yet. But it has gone far enough to have somewhat loosened the CCP's control of ideology and to pose structural pressure on the CCP to expand the ideological sphere.

In the past when mass media depended heavily on state subsidy, the costs were high if they wanted to assert their claims to autonomy. In the age of commercialization, profit-making is becoming an alternative if not the overriding goal of media. Coupled with the influence of the contractual system and commercial financing, mass media have become market-oriented. In order to survive, they have had to cater to the needs of the audience and to face up to the competition from domestic as well as overseas counterparts. It is not uncommon for the profit motive to clash with political considerations. Under such circumstances, media operators have to choose one way or the other. Further commercialization will lead many to put economic interest first, thereby distancing themselves from the state.

The demands in the media market have been changing in step with social restructuring caused by reforms in the economic and other social domains. As long as the Chinese society keeps on differentiating and pluralizing, the demands for timely, objective and diversified political information will grow. This is borne out by the frequent complaints from audiences over the omission of important information, the overemphasis on propaganda, news lag, and news redundancy.[53] Such structural tension exists even in the seemingly apolitical field of economic reporting. In the midst of stock value decline in 1992, three main newspapers in Shanghai were ordered not to publish negative comments on the stock market for fear that they would scare off potential buyers.[54] Obviously, the potential buyers would have preferred genuine opinions at that critical juncture. The CCP will have to reckon with all these tensions sooner or later.

The afore-mentioned information demands are being enhanced by marketization and the growth of the private sector. Information about the latest economic and political development at home and abroad can now have immediate implications for people's investments. Decision making at both the institutional and individual levels requires timely and comprehensive information. The traditional communication channels, such as briefing and political study sessions, have become too slow and inflexible for practical purposes. The information needs of the people have to be met openly by the mass media.

From a system perspective, the CCP's disjunctive approach to development has resulted in media reforms lagging behind economic progress. This lag has left many market needs unmet. For instance, there is a general lack of effective advertising channels for developing the consumption market. Even in 1992, it took six to nine months for advertisers to land an advertisement on CCTV.[55] Another systemic need is for mass media to help right the social ills such as corruption and bribery that economic reforms have brought about as side products. Unless the CCP can police these activities effectively through an alternative channel, the pressure for the mass media to exert their supervisory role will likely increase.

All these pressures have already resulted in the increase of communication channels and volume of entertainment and social information, less ideological persuasion, increased autonomy over media operation, as well as a more extensive adoption of western media formats and management practices. As the process of media commercialization spreads and deepens, this erosion of the CCP's control over ideology will intensify.

However, media commercialization has its limitations. Up to now, media commercialization has stopped short of allowing outright private ownership which, as argued previously, is a necessary condition for the development of a free press. Meanwhile, the contractual system has failed to serve as a surrogate for private media ownership because the media market formed in China is severely limited by the small number of publication or broadcasting permits granted by the central government. Besides, the embryonic contractual system is restricted primarily to the info-entertainment domain and to media at the local level. The more important media are still subject to the strict control of the CCP.

In fact, the CCP can jerk its reins over *any* media if it sees the political need. Partisan control in the last instance is the most critical limiting factor of media reforms. In spite of media commercialization, political discourse has to abide by the Four Cardinal Principles as defined by the ruling authorities. In general, the media avoid overstepping the ideological boundaries for fear of penalty. The official news media continue to trumpet the policies of the CCP and to paint a good picture of the state. By all measures, the media are far from being an independent voice of the people and a watchdog of the government. All in all, media reforms in China can be characterized as commercialization without independence.

Media commercialization carries with it other socially undersirable phenomena as well. As mentioned earlier, the profit motive has lured experienced journalists to desert the profession for better-paying jobs. In their effort to expand circulation, many publications are filled with veiled pornography. Infringements of copyright laws happen often. The demarcation between journalism and advertising, at both the institutional and personal level, is so blurred that the audience cannot distinguish news from disguised promotion. These wrongs will ebb and flow but will not disappear overnight. If the experience of developed countries is any guide, improvements can be made if efforts are taken to allow genuine media market competition, to establish professional codes of practice in the media industry, as well as to legislate and to effectively enforce appropriate communication laws.

To conclude, media commercialization represents an erosion of ideological control in China. However, it is not equivalent nor will it necessarily lead to a free press. Democracy is a more fundamental condition. It is the combination of democracy, rule of law and private media ownership that can ensure the practice of the Chinese people's constitutional right to freedom of expression. If the reform experience in the last decade speaks for the future, the development path of a free press in China will likely resemble the swing of a pendulum, oscillating between left and right as political struggles take sudden turns. While media commercialization alone will not lead to a free press, it serves to reduce the amplitude of each pendulum swing.

Notes

1. The CCP's evaluation of and policy on "peaceful evolution" are revealed in its documents published in *The Nineties* (Hong Kong), No. 264 (January 1992), pp. 25–35. For a discussion of the political economy of Chinese media in light of the military crackdown in 1989, see Lee Chin-Chuan, "Mass Media: Of China, about China," in *Voices of China: The Interplay of Politics and Journalism*, edited by Chin-Chuan Lee (New York: Guilford Press, 1990), pp. 3–32.
2. Wei Ping, "Li Ruihuan gao da dongzuo saochu 'zuo'feng" (Li Ruihuan's Significant Measures in Rooting Out "Leftism"), *China Times Weekly*, 30 August–5 September 1992, pp. 9–10. Also see Allinson Jernow, *"Don't Force Us to Lie": The Struggle of Chinese Journalists in the Reform Era* (New York: Committee to Protect Journalists, 1992), pp. 80–81.
3. Willy Wo-lap Lam, "The Media: The Party's Throat and Tongue Defend the Faith," in *China Review*, edited by Kuan Hsin-chi and Maurice Brosseau (Hong Kong: The Chinese University Press, 1991), pp. **20**.1–22.
4. Allinson Jernow, see Note 2.

5. For a transcript of some of Deng's speeches in his southern tour, see *China Times Weekly*, 15–21 March 1992, pp. 10–13.
6. Allinson Jernow, see Note 2.
7. Bi Yi, "Dalu chuanmei fazhan zhangai zhongzhong" (Obstacles to Media Development in Mainland China Are Numerous), *Hong Kong Economic Journal*, 6 November 1992.
8. Lin Fan, "Wenyijie de chuntian heshi daolai?" (When Will the Spring of Arts Arrive?), *China Times Weekly*, 30 August–5 September 1992, pp. 12–13.
9. Chan Ming, "Guonei jueda duoshu baokan jiusinian qi zaiwu butie" (Subsidy Will Stop for the Majority of Chinese Publications by 1994), *Ming Pao* (Hong Kong), 9 December 1992.
10. Willy Wo-lap Lam, "Beijing Set to Liberalize Party Control on Papers," *South China Morning Post*, 28 December 1992.
11. Willy Wo-lap Lam, "Publishing Controls Eased," *South China Morning Post*, 30 December 1992; also see He Zi, "Deng xuanfeng cuijinle wenxuanbumen" (Deng's Influence in the Literature and Propaganda Field), *China Times Weekly*, 27 September–3 October 1992, p. 23.
12. Gu Biling, "Zhongguo dianying zhengce chuxian duozhong biaozhun" (Double Standards in the Chinese Movie Industry), *China Times Weekly*, 23 August–25 September 1992, pp. 82–83.
13. Sun Xupei, "Zhongguo baokan de xianzhuang yu zhanwang" (The Current State and Prospects of Chinese Press) (a paper presented at the Conference on the Press, Beijing: Science, Technology and Social Development in the Asia-Pacific Region, November 1992).
14. *Ming Pao*, 21 January 1993.
15. Sun Xupei, see Note 13.
16. He Pin, "Banguanfang baokan qidongle dalu de xinwenziyou" (Semi-official Publications Started the Press Freedom of Mainland China), *China Times Weekly*, 4 October–10 October 1992, pp. 20–21.
17. Chan Ming, "Yao xiangfu, la zanzhu" (Sponsorship Makes One Rich), *Ming Pao*, 11 November 1992.
18. Yi Shuihan, "Dalu jizhe zhuiqian buzhui xinwen?" (Chinese Reporters Chase after Money But Not News?), *China Times Weekly*, 29 November–5 December 1992, pp. 66–68.
19. Lin Zibin, "Zhongguo yanli zhengdun xinwen renyuan" (The CCP Severely Rectifies Journalists), *China Times Weekly*, 7–13 February 1993, p. 27.
20. Daniel Kwan, "Writer Takes Up Business Challenge," *South China Morning Post*, 23 December 1992.
21. Bi Yi, see Note 7.
22. Sun Xupei, see Note 13.
23. Xu Xing, "Xinwen youle shangye ziyou" (The Press Is Commercially Free), *Open Magazine* (Hong Kong), 18 February 1993, pp. 25–29.

24. Bi Yi, see Note 7.
25. *Ta Kung Pao* (Hong Kong), 13 February 1993.
26. Lian Jie, "Dalu dianshiju 'feitianjiang' gaizai Shenzhen banjiang" (Television Soap Awards Ceremony Held in Shenzhen), *China Times Weekly*, 4–10 October 1992, pp. 82–83.
27. United Press International, "Producers Miss out on TV Cash," reported in *South China Morning Post*, 30 December 1992.
28. Sun Xupei, see Note 13.
29. For an account of the *World Economic Herald*, see Allinson Jernow (see Note 2), pp. 31–50.
30. For a relatively detailed account of the case of *Culture Weekly*, see *Ming Pao*, 18 January 1993, p. 27.
31. Qing Ming, "Zhongguo dianyingjie xin dongxiang" (The New Trends of the Chinese Cinema), *Wide Angle Monthly* (Hong Kong), August 1992, pp. 86–89.
32. Yan Wu, "Tingzhong shizhuzai meiti mingyun de shangdi" (The Audience Is the God of Media), *China Times Weekly*, 10–16 January 1993, pp. 90–92.
33. Kent Chan, "Joint-venture Paper Planned," *South China Morning Post*, 12 January 1993.
34. *Hong Kong Economic Journal*, 8 February 1993.
35. Qing Ming, see Note 9.
36. Bi Yi, see Note 7.
37. Lie Fu, "Dalu duli zhipian de jueqi" (The Growth of Mainland Independent Producers), *Ming Pao Monthly* (Hong Kong), February 1993, pp. 70–72.
38. Deng Xiaoping visited Shanghai in March 1991 and made some liberal comments which were later published in the *Liberation Daily* under the pseudonym of Huangfu Ping. See Zhang Weiguo, "Muqian zhengzai yunniang qidong de dalu xinwen gaige" (Current Ferment for Journalism Reform), *Pai Shing* (Hong Kong), 1 September 1992, pp. 10–13. Also see Hu Jiwei, "Lun fang'zuo' weizhu" (On the Stress on Anti-leftism), *Contemporary Monthly* (Hong Kong), 15 June 1992, pp. 22–26.
39. Yi Ke, "*Renmin ribao* you qi fenglei" (Renewed Movement in the *People's Daily*), *Pai Shing*, 1 May 1992, pp. 16–17; Hu Jiwei, see Note 38.
40. Ting Yi, "Beijing zhishifenzi jilifanzuo" (The Intellectuals of Beijing Vow to Fight Leftism), *China Times Weekly*, 2 June–4 July 1992, pp. 16–18.
41. As recapped in Xue Xinming, "Dalu xinwen meiti jinlaide bianhua" (Recent Changes in Mainland China's Media), *The News Mirror Weekly*, 28 September–4 October 1992, pp. 16–18.
42. Zhang Weiguo, see Note 38.
43. As summarized in Lin Wei, "Xinwengaige, tanherongyi?" (Journalism Reform Is Not Easy), *The Nineties*, October 1992, pp. 32–34.
44. *The Historical Tides* was edited by Yuan Hongbing, a law lecturer at Beijing

University. It was published by the People's University Press in April, 1992. See Xue Yingchang, *"Fangzuobeiwanglu faxing shouzu"* (The Memorandum on Anti-leftism Has Problem in Distribution), *China Times Weekly*, 27 December 1992–2 January 1993, pp. 24–26.
45. Willy Wo-lap Lam, "Publishing Controls Eased," *South China Morning Post*, 30 December 1992.
46. Wang Yuyin, "Dalu minzhong shang fayuan zhengqu weixing tianxian" (Mainland Citizens Go To Court for Satellite Dish), *China Times Weekly*, 27 December 1992–2 January 1993, pp. 66–67.
47. As reported by Willy Wo-Lap Lam, "Dissident Dispatches on the Media's Quiet Revolution," *South China Morning Post*, 10 February 1993.
48. According to figures released by STAR TV, as published in *Hong Kong Economic Journal*, 10 February 1993.
49. For an account of the penetration of STAR TV in China, see Joseph Man Chan, "Satellite Television and the Infosphere: National Responses and Accessibility to STAR TV in Asia," a paper presented at the Ninth World Communication Forum, the Japan Society of Information and Communication Research, Tokyo, Japan, 19–20 November 1992.
50. John Kohut, "Chinese Hear Message From Marketplace," *South China Morning Post,* 28 January 1992.
51. Joseph Man Chan, see Note 49.
52. Michael Schudson, *Discovering News* (New York: Basic Books, 1978).
53. Sun Xupei, see Note 13.
54. Geoffrey Crothall, "Shanghai Papers Facing Stock Market 'Gag Order'," *South China Morning Post*, 18 November 1992.
55. *Hong Kong Economic Journal*, 14 September 1992.

26

A Bird-cage Culture: How Big Was the Cage?

Sylvia Chan

The Politics of Culture[1]

The year began with much sound and fury surrounding Deng Xiaoping's South China tour. Though intellectuals generally supported Deng's push to revive the economic reform, few people in the cultural circles were naïve enough to believe that this would spell the end of ideological control, but they were cautiously optimistic that they could exploit the differences between the Dengists and the hardliners to halt the backtracking to cultural isolationism and ideological dogmatism.

Since the Tiananmen Incident, the sphere of ideological and cultural work has become one of the strongest conservative bastions. Prior to this year, Li Ruihuan, a moderate Politburo member who is supposed to be in charge of this area of work, had failed to make an impact there and had been repeatedly humiliated by the conservatives.[2] Because of this, Deng had clearly lost out to the conservatives in the war of words. His line of taking economic construction as the one and only one central task for the Party and the nation for at least a century to come had been the target of sustained criticism by the conservative-controlled media, and the counter-offensive he had tried to launch from Shanghai in early 1991 had failed to take off.[3] In order to recapture initiatives, Deng had to bring into line the conservative cultural bosses and ideologues, even though cultural diversity and intellectual freedom may not be a high priority in his agenda.

The battleline was drawn during Deng's South China tour. Initially, the conservative-controlled media tried to blockade news of this tour. When the "Deng whirlwind" was finally whipped up by the local press in Zhuhai and Shenzhen with the help of the Hong Kong media, conservative leaders in cultural and ideological work tried desperately to defend their domain against its onslaught, arguing that Deng's line applied solely to economic work and that the central task for ideological and cultural work should be to guard against "peaceful evolution."[4] Their intransigence so provoked the Dengists that Qiao Shi, a Politburo member aligned with Deng, called in the leading cadres of the Chinese Communist Party (CCP) Propaganda Department, the Ministry of Culture and the two leading newspapers, *Renmin ribao* (People's Daily) and *Guangming ribao* to rebuke them for disobeying Li Ruihuan, and threatened to sack them if they did not mend their ways.[5] In May, Deng Xiaoping also threw his weight behind Li, saying that his conservative subordinates were committing not just mistakes but crimes in suppressing artistic creativity.[6] After this, several of them made self-criticism and pledged their support for

Deng's reform programme. This, however, was too late to salvage their political fortune: the conservative head of the Party's Propaganda Department, Wang Renzhi, was replaced by an as yet faceless Ding Guan'gen. Ding will be assisted by his deputy, Zheng Bijian, who is seen to be a liberal because of his former association with Hu Yaobang, but who will probably be neutralized by another deputy head, the infamous ultra-leftist, Xu Weicheng. The Acting Cultural Minister, He Jingzhi, is said to have tendered his resignation early in the year but was officially replaced only after the Fourteenth Party Congress by another faceless bureaucrat, Liu Zhongde. The fact that Liu Zhongde is still an acting minister suggests that the search for an ideal candidate to fill this sensitive post is still going on.

But it was neither Deng's intention nor was it within his power to completely purge his conservative critics. After the experience of the Tiananmen Incident, he will never allow the liberals and democrats to dominate the ideological and cultural sphere and, therefore, needs the conservatives to hold them at bay. The Fourteenth Party Congress was a master-stroke in such politics of checks and balances. While giving free reins to the development of a market economy, the Congress reaffirmed Party leadership in every sphere of activities. The Party was urged to "be tough" in building "socialist spiritual civilization," which entailed "resist(ing) the onslaught of decadent capitalist and feudal ideas," and fostering "correct ideals, beliefs and values."[7] Thus, while notoriously conservative ideologues such as He Jingzhi, He Dongchang and Wang Renzhi lost their seats in the new Central Committee, quite a few personages seen to be sympathetic to the 1989 democracy movement (e.g., Yan Mingfu, Rui Xingwen and Wang Meng) were also excluded.

While the redistribution of power at the highest level in the Congress did not signify a clear-cut victory for the Dengist reformists, to say nothing of the liberals and democrats, it was significant that the Congress endorsed opposition to leftism on the ideological front. This was one of the themes of Deng's South China tour and was immediately seized on by writers and artists to justify their renewed attack on the cultural hardline. Under pressure, the conservatives were forced to shelve a plan to purge all moderates and liberals from the leading organs of various writers and artists' associations. It appears that in the mid-1980s, while Hu Yaobang was in the process of reversing the so-called "anti-spiritual pollution campaign," large numbers of moderates and liberals had been elected to these bodies, and many conservatives had lost their seats. In the aftermath of the

Tiananmen Incident, major reshuffles of leadership took place in all cultural institutions to reinstate the conservatives and oust prominent reformists and liberals. Even though these associations have never had much political clout, positions in their leading bodies are of symbolic significance and financially rewarding. Had there been a general election, many conservatives would most definitely have been voted out of office. They had thus proposed amending the constitutions of these associations to change individual membership to group membership, hoping, thereby, to fill the leading organs with appointed representatives from each province/city. The proposal had met with such strong opposition from writers that the Writers' Congress, originally scheduled to be held in March 1992, was postponed indefinitely.[8]

Another instance of the conservatives' losing control of the cultural sphere was the small-scale rebellion occurring in the middle of the year in the literary journal *Renmin wenxue* (People's Literature), a bastion of conservatism. It was triggered by the unfair dismissal of one of the journal's moderate senior staff members who disagreed with the chief editor's line that the journal's primary objective was to guard against "peaceful evolution." In protest, several editors tendered their resignation and published an open letter to denounce in the strongest terms the "leftism" practised by its arch-conservative chief editor, Liu Baiyu.[9]

Understandably, the Congress was used by intellectuals to give fresh impetus to their cause of combating leftism. Immediately before and after the Congress, prominent cultural figures spoke up publicly for more freedom of expression.[10] Some of them went even further, publishing in the Hong Kong *Ming Pao Monthly* to criticize the leftists in even more caustic language.[11] Apparently, the fear of being seen to be working for overseas anti-communist forces had failed to deter them.

Other articles in this book have referred to the centrifugal tendencies in recent Chinese politics fuelled by the ascendancy of regional leaders and the complex coalescence of forces into interest groups and power blocs. It would, therefore, be wrong to conceive of the cultural scene as a black-and-white picture of confrontation between the reformists and the conservatives. In fact, there is a wide spectrum of political colours among both the Dengists and the conservatives, to say nothing of the large numbers of fence-sitters and non-aligned elements. This has resulted in significant local variations in the actual implementation of the cultural policy. While this may open up more room for manoeuvre for the moderates/liberals, the same can be true for the conservatives. It is not unusual, for instance, for controversial works to be banned in one place and published in another, and vice versa.[12] It seems that, as a rule, control in the provinces has been more lax than in Beijing. Even soon after the Tiananmen Incident, when no journals in Beijing would have dared to print works by such sensitive writers as Wang Meng, Zhang Jie and Liu Xinwu, they appeared freely in a number of provincial publications.[13]

The Wang Meng Saga and Literature of Innuendoes (*yingshe wenxue*)

The former Cultural Minister has become a symbol of resistance to the cultural hardline. He has been the prime target of attack by conservatives who hold him responsible for encouraging "bourgeois liberalization" in culture during his term of office. Their criticism of his humorous short story *Hard Porridge* (*Jianying de xizhou*), however, backfired when Wang Meng filed a libel suit against his critics and won widespread support from both within and outside China.[14] Even though the high court refused to hear Wang's case, the conservatives were ordered by top leaders to stop attacking him.[15]

Wang Meng, however, was not prepared to pull his punches even when his opponents were beating a retreat. Early in the year, he made public a letter written to him on the eve of the Tiananmen Incident by Malaqinfu, the conservative Mongolian writer promoted after the Tiananmen Incident to be the deputy secretary of the Party Group of the Writers' Association.[16] There is nothing unusual for writers sometimes to publish their private correspondence. What is unusual is that this letter, purporting to show the "warm comradeship" between two "friends," was clearly meant to embarrass its writer, for it reveals Malaqinfu to be currying favour in a most obsequious manner from the then Cultural Minister whom he was now denouncing as guilty of "bourgeois liberalization."

As if this was not enough, Wang Meng published another short story in April entitled *The Austrian Porridge Restaurant*.[17] The title itself immediately suggests unmistakable link with his controversial *Hard Porridge*. In fact, Wang's legal saga has already produced many pieces of writing on the topic of porridge with oblique references to this case, written mostly by Wang's cronies as a gesture of support to him.[18] In this sub-genre, Wang's own short story is the most defiant and hilariously mischievous. The story evolves around a very popular restaurant which the author patronized during his visit to Austria. The restaurant, named after its proprietor Mr Porridge, is famous for its porridge. While the Porridge Restaurant is thriving, the Toilet Restaurant across the street run by Mr Toilet hardly has any customers. But how is it possible for a restaurant or for a person to be named Toilet? Wang Meng explains, with a big tongue in cheek, that etymologically "toilet" is related to "toiletry," which means perfume, but that it is the wicked Americans, responsible for most evils in this world, who have given the word the unpleasant associations it has today. At any rate, Mr Toilet is so jealous of his rival's success that he employs a homosexual to spread the rumour that customers taking the porridge served in the Porridge Restaurant have suffered from food poisoning. Lest the reader should miss the political overtone, Wang Meng adds that Mr Toilet's dirty trick has not prevailed until the city is occupied by a foreign army. This is clearly an oblique reference to the armed suppression of the Beijing students and the downfall of the Zhao Ziyang regime. As the story goes, the new rulers, bribed by Mr Toilet, order a sham investigation of the Porridge Restaurant and find it guilty of violation of the Health Act. The Porridge Restaurant quickly loses its business and Mr Porridge dies of a broken heart. Determined to clear her father's name, Mr Porridge's daughter conducts a private investigation during which she interviews the customers alleged to have been food-poisoned. However, only two of them dare to come forward to tell the truth. One may speculate that this is also a reference to the author's personal experience when he lived under a cloud.[19] At any rate, the Porridge case is reopened after the foreign invaders have been driven out. In the end, justice prevails; the notorious Toilet Restaurant is shunned by everybody and soon folds up, while the Porridge Restaurant becomes even more popular than before. The innuendo is so obvious that nobody could have missed its point. That it was published is another indication of how fast the conservatives have lost control of literature. Wang Meng's ingenious tactic of attacking *ad hominem* through exaggerated raillery may also have protected him and his publishers. His enemies would make themselves a public laughing-stock were they to admit to possible resemblance between themselves and the despicable Mr Toilet. But if they could do nothing to the story, they could still retaliate in other ways. They managed to so manipulate the election of delegates to the Fourteenth Party Congress that Wang's name did not even appear on the slate. A last-minute high-level consultation, however, resulted in a decision to invite Wang Meng to attend the Congress as an observer. Wang had to cut short his Australia tour and fly back to Beijing just two days before the Congress was due to open, only to find himself not re-elected to the Central Committee.

Another similar piece of writing which attacks the conservative by innuendo is Zhang Jie's novella *A Disorder Caused by Excessive Internal Heat*.[20] The main characters in the novella are Tang Bingye, the Party secretary of an association for the study of an extinct animal called Mengma, and his cohort, the chairman of that association. It is transparently clear that the fictional association is based on the Chinese Writers' Association in real life, Meng and Ma being the homophones of two characters in the names of the much hated current office-holders of the Writers' Association, Meng Guangjun, Ma Feng and Malaqinfu. Their stubborn adherence to the dead letters of Marxism–Leninism–Maoism is seen to be parallel to the fictional characters' devotion to the study of an extinct species. The novella is full of sarcastic references to their determination to suppress dissent and oppose "bourgeois liberalization," to their inability to produce anything worth reading and their resentment that they have never been invited by foreigners to go abroad. It also explicitly hints at the ideological ties between these people and the Gang of Four headed by Jiang Qing, alias Lan Ping, fictionalized in the novella as the "Lan (Blue) Party." The major event around which the story evolves is the election of the association's leading body, which the Party secretary and the chairman attempt to rig using "post-computer" techniques. The story, thus, has a touch of magical realism, but its predominant mode of narration is one of realism, especially in its treatment of the private life of the characters. It is here that the satire becomes savagely personal and vitriolic. Tang Bingye is portrayed as a half-impotent womanizer having an incestuous affair with his daughter-in-law with the tacit approval of his wife. The naturalistic description of their love-making is meant to shock and disgust. It has been widely rumoured that this sexual episode is also based on real people and events. If this is true, one can understand why those who are believed to be the prototypes of these fictional characters are furious. At the beginning of the year, it was said that Zhang Jie was about to be publicly criticized, but the sudden change in the political climate brought about by the "Deng whirlwind" has probably saved her.[21]

It is inevitable that lack of freedom of speech will force writers to resort to innuendoes to make their points. While one can have a good laugh over Wang Meng's wit and humour and admire Zhang Jie's courage, one cannot but regret the waste of their talent on these trivial word games.

When the topical issues which inspired such writings are forgotten, the stories too may fall into oblivion.

Structural Reform of the Cultural Establishment[22]

The gradual move away from ideological rigidity was not entirely a political decision, or was one only by default. As have been pointed out by a number of authors in this book, Deng's line is to have the best of both worlds: a capitalist economy and a socialist superstructure. It requires culture to contribute to the construction of "socialist spiritual civilization" as well to the coffers of the state, or at least to stop being a drain on the state's scarce resources. Are these two goals reconcilable? According to Marxism, capitalism is intrinsically inimical to artistic development,[23] but nobody is so naïve as to think that Deng is concerned with the development of good art. What he wants is for art to be saleable at the market and at the same time to legitimize the Party's hold onto power. For this purpose, art has to meet certain basic ideological requirements. Under Deng, as would be under the conservatives, culture is essentially a bird-cage culture; the disagreement between them merely concerns the size of the cage. On the question of size, Deng has been quite inconsistent. In the past, whenever "bourgeois liberalization" was perceived to be a serious threat to the state, he joined hands with the conservatives to push for a smaller cage. Now that economic rationality has become his predominant concern, it seems that he has been willing to be flexible with ideological criteria in order to make the cultural institutions and enterprises more cost-effective. The overriding concern of the entire cultural establishment in 1992 was thus to carry out a structural reform. The aim of such a reform is to reduce the government's financial involvement in culture to a minimum, forcing the present state-run cultural set-ups to become self-sufficient and eventually to return a profit, and encouraging private initiatives in the field. To clear the way for this reform, the Deputy Cultural Minister Gao Zhanxiang went so far as to say that culture was a component of the tertiary industry,[24] thereby removing culture from the sphere of superstructure to become a corner-stone of the economic base. The theoretical and ideological implications of such a proposition are enormous, but in their feverish pursuit of profitability, officials and ideologues have not yet had time to worry about them.

The key to reform is to decentralize management of cultural affairs and get rid of or at least reduce political intervention. Rigid control has severely handicapped the ability of cultural institutions to respond flexibly to market demands. For example, the censorship system is so cumbersome that a film or a play often has to be approved by several levels of the bureaucracy before it can go into production and has to go through the same procedure before the finished product can be marketed. Disapproval from even one among the dozens of censors can hold it up indefinitely. In the middle of this year, a decision was finally made to institutionalize censorship by adopting a censorship law, hoping thereby to reduce arbitrary intervention.[25] It was also proposed that censorship be relaxed and decentralized. But any optimism for real liberalization proved to be premature. Before the year came to an end, the monthly *Weilai yu fazhan* (Future and Development) was closed down,[26] and the book *A Memorandum of Anti-Leftism* (*Fang zuo beiwanglu*) was banned.[27] The former was punished for publishing in its October issue articles by liberal intellectuals broaching the taboo subjects of the 1989 military crackdown and political reform. The banning of the latter, however, was somewhat puzzling, for many articles collected here had already appeared in the press.

The second problem in the structural reform is how to streamline the notoriously overstaffed cultural sector without creating too many social problems. Similar reforms had been carried out in a rather haphazard fashion in the mid-1980s, but were ground to a halt by the Tiananmen Incident, when their social costs were thought to far outweigh economic gains. Now the question of social costs is still very much on everybody's mind, though few responsible cadres would want to air it publicly, probably for fear of being seen as obstructing the structural reform. But, while the top authorities seem to be quite determined to carry it out, they have not come up with any concrete proposals to guide it. The only guidelines that local authorities have received are that, short of changing the socialist nature of their respective units and enterprises (whatever that may mean), and short of practising the seven evils (i.e., prostitution, gambling, abuse of drugs and alcohol, drug trafficking, smuggling and tax evasion), they can do whatever they like to achieve economic efficiency. Under the circumstances, all sorts of proposals have been put forward, some of which are nothing if not draconian. These include abolition of tenures, compulsory retirement and retrenchment of staff, and drastic cuts in staff's social benefits. Guangdong province, for instance, has proposed to enforce self-sufficiency by cutting the salaries of employees in cultural institutions by 30% every year starting from 1993, until no one be on the state pay-roll by the end of 1995. In other places, retrenched staff have been paid about 70%

of their former wages for only a fixed period.[28] To open up new channels of employment, the state has agreed to allow a much wider scope for private involvement in the running of culture. For example, control of publications has been relaxed to allow private people to run printing presses and produce newspapers and journals.[29] A form of responsibility system is being tried out among film studios and performing troupes, whereby one or a number of individuals may contract for the production of a show or a film on a fixed budget and, after returning the agreed amount of profit to the studio or theatre, is allowed to keep the surplus. At the same time, all cultural enterprises have been encouraged to diversify their operations. Sometimes, diversification seems to have gone to absurd lengths, such as when opera theatres or drama companies decided to run restaurants, bakeries and even puppy farms, or to convert their auditoriums into places for storing ashes of the dead,[30] but such diversification has apparently become an effective way of generating additional income and redeploying redundant staff.

The structural reform has opened up a rich mine of business talents among writers and artists. An increasing number of them have joined the ranks of cultural private entrepreneurs (*wenhua geti hu*). Confident of earning more in the market, pop musicians have been among the first to either turn down state-assigned jobs or resign from them to go freelancing. Recently, the Writers' Association of the Guangdong province adopted a formal resolution encouraging its members to "diversify" into business, thereby legitimizing the practice of professional writers (*zhuanye zuojia*) having a second job while drawing their full salary as professional writers.[31] One way for writers to make money in their own profession has been for them to be commissioned by corporations and entrepreneurs to write about the latter's virtues and successes. Many pieces of so-called "reportage literature" (*baogao wenxue*) about individual "model" entrepreneurs or enterprises are nothing more than long advertisements, and, as such, their truthfulness must be called into question.

The pace-setter for the commercialization of literature was without doubt the writer Wang Shuo. He was the first writer in mainland China to appoint an agent to handle all commercial transactions relating to his writings.[32] He took the lead in founding the Seahorse Movie and Video Production Centre in Beijing.[33] This Centre gained national fame through its involvement in the production of the scripts for two immensely popular TV series, "Aspirations" (*Kewang*)[34] and "In the Editorial Department" (*Bianjibu de gushi*).[35] The latter series was first shown in late 1991, and was repeated at prime time during the Spring Festival holidays simultaneously in Beijing, Shanghai and Tianjin. But the financial reward these script-writers received was only a pittance compared to the millions of RMB its producers and the TV station earned broadcasting it. Angered by this unfair payment, the group has now demanded being paid a "negotiated price" for its manuscripts. It seems that this demand has been met, for it is revealed that Wang Shuo has recently received RMB10,000 for each part of the script he wrote for an undisclosed TV serial.[36] The action of the Seahorse Group has thrown the "planned cultural economy" into chaos; writers with high market value have now one by one chosen to negotiate payments with their publishers, and the state-fixed prices can no longer apply.

It is too early to tell how successful the structural reform is. The Chinese press, predictably, has reported only individual cases of apparent success. This suggests that some of the measures mentioned above may have been tried out only in a small number of organizations and have not yet been pushed nationwide, but it is not unreasonable to guess that there will be considerable employee resistance to the reform. Clearly, a fundamental solution entails changes in many other areas: the growth of the economy must be such as to create more jobs and pay for the retraining of the retrenched staff; the labour market must be restructured to expedite job mobility, and there must be an improved social security system to back up such a drastic reform. Since it is highly unlikely that these conditions can be met in the near future, structural reform in the cultural sphere is most likely to once again proceed in a piecemeal and haphazard fashion for the time being.

The Film Industry

A decision was adopted in the middle of the year by the Ministry of Culture to formalize official encouragement of foreign investment in cultural ventures.[37] One area most likely to attract foreign and private investment is the film industry. This is why it was among the first areas to benefit from relaxed political control. Without foreign investment, it would have been inconceivable, for example, for permission to be given to shoot a multi-million-yuan-budget TV serial based on the fantastic Ming novel *Canonization of the Gods* (*Feng shen bang*), which had formerly been banned as a book promoting superstition. The serial was funded by a Hong

Kong-based company and made mainly for the overseas Asian markets. Another private venture that attracted a lot of media attention was the film company set up by the famous director Xie Jin and named after him. No sooner had this been announced than Xie was across the strait soliciting Taiwan investments and signing up contracts with Taiwan film stars.[38]

In the middle of the year, bans previously imposed on films such as *Judou* and *Hang High the Red Lanterns* directed by the international-award-winning young director Zhang Yimou were lifted. As if to compensate him, Zhang's new film *Qiuju Goes to Court* was showered with official praises at its *première*.[39] This film is based on the novella *Mrs Wan Files a Lawsuit*,[40] published in 1991. It is a story of a peasant woman who goes through a great deal of trouble, with dogged perseverance, to file a lawsuit against the village head who beat up her husband. With calculated artlessness, the author depicts sensitively the peasant woman's tremendous moral courage in standing up for her simple but humane principle of justice, against a backdrop of callous arrogance and the benighted ignorance of certain officials. Even though the story has a happy ending, with Qiuju winning the court case, thanks partly to the assistance rendered to her by some honest and kind officials, it leaves few viewers in doubt that the Chinese people still have little legal protection against the arbitrary and corrupt exercise of power on the part of the rulers.

It has often been said that Zhang Yimou's films are intended more for foreign than domestic markets. Clearly, they are sophisticated works of art which are never intended to appeal to popular taste either in China or abroad. But even films catering to popular taste these days are facing stiff competition from such popular television drama series as "In the Editorial Department." The series is a situation comedy consisting of twenty-five independent episodes evolving around the six staff members of a certain magazine. It is quite obvious that the series was shot hastily on a low budget. There is too much dialogue and too little action — granted that the dialogue has an important function of its own. Even the script-writers admitted that they had not taken their assignments very seriously and were taken by surprise by its tremendous popularity.[41] Its success thus speaks more of the exceedingly poor quality of most Chinese TV programmes than of its own excellence. But it is not difficult to see why the series was so popular. Situation comedy is still a relatively new genre in China. In a country where every aspect of life is politicized, to cause laughter about anything in everyday life is to trivialize politics, which appeals to a people disillusioned with politics. This is probably the reason why the series has been over-rated as "the most extraordinary social and political satire to have appeared on Chinese television."[42] As I see it, the ideas behind most episodes in the series are so "grey" that they can be interpreted in a number of ways. While many viewers would no doubt interpret some episodes as making fun of such serious political matters as opposition to "bourgeois liberalization" or learning from Lei Feng, others could simply take it as light entertainment with no profound meaning, and miss or knowingly ignore the *double entendre* in the dialogue. This is why the series has been showered with praises from both guardians of the official ideology and its critics. Even if political satire is meant, it is achieved by trivializing Party politics, and, by doing so, it also trivializes its negation and blunts the edge of its criticism. The domestic environment in which such situation comedies are viewed also tends to condition the viewers to take lightly their social and political messages, whatever these may be.[43]

Interestingly, the popularity enjoyed by "In the Editorial Department" was confined to a few big cities in northern China. In Canton, its reception was lukewarm at best. One explanation is that much enjoyment derived from the witty and subtle use of the Beijing dialect was lost upon a Cantonese-speaking audience. Another possible explanation is that Party orthodoxy had become so irrelevant and so increasingly incomprehensible to people in areas where capitalism is most developed that even its very negation failed to make an impact. As a matter of fact, Canton residents can now freely receive Hong Kong TV stations through satellite dishes installed for a charge in their homes by the telecommunication authorities. This has gone a long way towards making Canton culturally more akin to Hong Kong than to mainland China and giving its people a sense of cultural superiority.[44] The situation of "one country, two cultures" may have already come into being ahead of 1997.

The "High" Culture

It is inevitable that with the growth of a commodity economy and consumerism, high or elite culture has gradually been losing out to popular or mass culture. Sales of books and journals of serious literature and attendance rates of traditional opera, modern drama theatres, classical music and dance performances have all reported a sharp drop.[45]

There is a perception that the repressive cultural policy re-imposed after the 1989 crackdown has rendered serious literature (by which is meant literature published in official literary journals) conformist and unreadable. People holding such a view are often nostalgic about "the ten good years" before the 1989 crackdown.[46] They tend to forget that even in the best of those years — 1986 and 1988-May 1989 — the cultural bird was never let out of the cage. If art and literature enjoyed a period of exciting development then, in spite of many restrictions, what reason is there to believe that they have withered under repressive conditions now? Given that freedom is relative and never absolute, both conceptually and in practice, it is theoretically untenable and empirically unfounded to say that art and literature can only flourish in a free — how free? — society.

It is true that since June 1989, there have been few politically explosive texts, whether literary, musical, visual or televisual, that have created an immediate sensation, but this only means that people can no longer rely on newspaper headlines to find out what is going on in art and literature — not that anybody should ever have done so. Those works that made headlines in the past were not necessarily the best Chinese art and literature had to offer. This is not to deny that they were of great social and political significance or that some of their authors were people of high moral integrity. It is likely that writers and artists who are obsessed with topical and sensitive social and political issues and especially those who are given to direct expression of political dissent will find it difficult to work under the present regime, but others of a different artistic temperament do not seem to have been affected. Writers such as Wang Anyi, Jia Ping'ao, Mo Yan, Wang Zengqi and Lin Jinlan, who have always taken a deeper interest in broader philosophical problems and in the formal and technical aspects of fiction writing than in topical issues have continued to publish. Even such a writer as Can Xue has been allowed to continue her experimentation with modernist fiction which evinces a most pessimistic world-view.[47] This is not to say that the tradition of critical realism is now defunct. Zhang Jie is probably the most representative of its practitioners, but the critical intent of the recent fiction of some of her compeers, such as Chen Rong and Liu Xinwu, seems to have weakened. Chen Rong's *How I Keep a Cat*[48] is a delightfully humorous story with occasional jibes at conservative politics. Liu Xinwu's *The Star-singer and I*[49] and *The Star-painter and I*[50] are mild satires of cultural figures said to be based on real people. The spirit of critical realism, however, has been kept very much alive by some younger writers loosely grouped under the label of "neo-realists." Neo-realism has been the target of criticism by conservative critics.[51] It is sometimes said that neo-realism aims at reproducing without adornment "the pristine conditions of life" (*shenghuo de yuansheng zhuangtai*).[52] It is thus simply another term for naturalism, which departs from the orthodox Marxist version of realism in its refusal to tone down the most ugly and unpalatable aspects of life in the name of typification (*dianxing hua*).[53] The term has been applied to a large group of writers of very different artistic styles and moods. What they share in common is probably their authorial neutrality, disinclination for making moral judgement, lack of sentimentality and partiality for the mundane, petty and colourless aspects of the lives of the most lowly and ordinary people. Their world is one where debasement of humanity has become such an accepted norm that it has failed to arouse any strong emotions. For all the matter-of-factness in the tone of narration, their fiction inspires utter despair. For example, Li Xiao's novella *My Maternal Uncle and His Friends and I*[54] is a gruesome tale of how the revolution turns against some of its most loyal children, told dispassionately from the perspective of an uncomprehending child. The tragic irony is brought home most poignantly when the child, now grown up, goes back to the scene where his revolutionary elders once staged an uprising against the Nationalist regime, and finds that the local people are totally ignorant of and indifferent to this piece of history, confusing the uprising with the 1989 "turmoil"! Li Xiao has thus given a completely fresh treatment to a hackneyed theme done to death by "scar literature" of the late seventies and early eighties. Other neo-realists who do not shirk contemporary social and political issues include the two female writers from Wuhan, Chi Li and Fang Fang. Chi Li's novella *Ballad of Vicissitudes*[55] depicts the manoeuvres and counter-manoeuvres by Party officials, professionals and rank-and-file employees of a certain research institute surrounding the appointment of its director. The very theme is a sensitive one, and the seeming authorial detachment does not detract from its powerful condemnation of the current political culture as one that stimulates the basest of human instincts. Fang Fang's *No Escape*[56] deals with the straitened circumstances of underpaid intellectuals. This has been a popular theme since Chen Rong's much-acclaimed novella *At Middle Age*,[57] but Fang Fang's is completely devoid of the latter's sentimentalism and idealism. Possibly under the pressure of competition from popular literature, the story is somewhat melodramatic, and there is no trace of the surrealistic touches and pathological interest in the satanic, morbid and animalistic aspects of human nature which characterize some of her earlier writings.[58] A similar change in style may be discerned in writer Su Tong whose recent fiction has eschewed more sophisticated narrative techniques in favour of a clear story-line and intricate plots. Since the commercial success of his *Wives and Concubines*,[59] on which Zhang Yimou's celebrated film *Hang High the Red Lanterns* is based, Su Tong's fiction has been fetching almost as high a price in the market as Wang Shuo's. Another artist who has moved from "high" to "popular" art is the film director Chen Kaige. His recent film *Farewell to My Concubine* (*Bawang bie ji*) is a far cry from his former films, catering instead unashamedly to the popular taste. On the other hand, a former social realist, He Shiguang, has moved in the opposite direction. Contrary to his former realist mode of writing, his recent short story *A Sequel to "Time"*[60] and lyrical essay *Dreams Left Behind in Mount Qianling*[61] are replete with mysticism and religious transcendence.

Concluding Remarks

The Party's cultural policy in 1992 appears to have followed the familiar pattern of oscillating between the two poles of liberalization and rigid control. Hopes for a cultural thaw raised by Deng's South China tour at the beginning of the year were soon dashed, when the Fourteenth Party Congress turned out to be an uneasy compromise of all political factions. This state of affairs was a logical outcome of the ambivalence in Deng's thinking with regard to the relationship between politics and ideology and the economy. It also reflected the ever-changing coalescence of political forces in a very fluid situation. But such political uncertainties created opportunities for writers and artists to negotiate more space for their activities.

Economic imperatives also militated against a hardline cultural policy. In pursuit of economic rationality, the regime was prepared to privatize cultural activities and, in the course, to loosen its strong grip on culture. If the much-touted structural reform of culture is thoroughly implemented, it will allow the management of cultural activities to be regulated mostly by market forces.

The social and political consequences of a free-market culture have been dreaded by Marxists. While one may disagree with the extreme position some of them take,[62] one can easily see that the effect of a free market on art is not all beneficial. Art is not free if it is subjected to either political tyranny or the dictates of market forces. But, for the time being, most Chinese artists and writers seem to agree that the tyranny of the market is the lesser evil. Exposure of culture to the market has already weakened the Party's political control of it. Even assuming that this is not necessarily conducive to political pluralism,[63] it would be hard to imagine that the Party could still enforce conformity by coercive and repressive methods in a free market situation. There are indications that at least some people in the Party are beginning to learn new ways of soft-selling the Party line in the cultural free market.

In response to market demands, popular culture has been flourishing, often at the expense of elite culture. One must bear in mind, however, that it is controversial whether there is a clear-cut distinction between the two cultures. In terms of their respective ideological role, there is little evidence of a sharp dividing line between the two either.[64] Popular art is not necessarily a site of oppositional values; neither can elite art be equated with officially-sanctioned, conformist art.

Pending a complete political re-orientation, the regime's cultural policy will remain inconsistent and wishy-washy for some time to come. But the increasing dysfunction of the political system and economic imperatives make a return to sterile dogmatism and rigid control unlikely. The size of the cultural cage may vary from time to time, but in the foreseeable future, neither will the birds be let out of it, nor will the cage be so small as to stifle most of them to death. Birds can of course sing in a cage, and at times, some of them can even sing quite beautifully.

Notes

1. Readers are referred to Willy Wo-lap Lam's chapter in this book for a comprehensive analysis of the political scene. While I agree with most of Lam's analysis, my focus, perspective and interpretation are somewhat different.
2. Most notably in the so-called "*Wenhua bao* (Cultural News) Incident" in July 1990. See Sylvia Chan, "Intellectuals and Reform," in *Economic Reform and Social Change in China*, edited by Andrew Watson (London: Routledge, 1992), p. 110. Also, *Summary of World Broadcast* (*SWB*) FE/1301 B2/1 (11 February 1992).
3. *SWB* FE/1280 B2/3 (17 January 1992); FE/1394 B2/2 (30 May 1992).
4. See the speeches by writer Feng Jicai and film director Xie Jin at the National Political Consultative Congress in March 1992, *Zhongguo zhi chun* (China Spring), 6 (1992), p. 25.
5. *SWB* FE/1396 B2/3–5 (2 June 1992).
6. *SWB* FE/1465 B2/2–3 (21 August 1992).

7. Jiang Zemin's political report to the Fourteenth Party Congress, *SWB* FE/1511 C1/13 (14 October 1992).
8. Li Yenan, "Lai zi Beijing wentan de fenbin huaxu" (Tidbits from the Beijing Literary Circles), *Ming Pao Monthly* (Hong Kong), No. 3, 1992, p. 74. Sha Tian, "Dalu zuojia zhengtu zai chufa" (Mainland Chinese Writers Are Getting Ready to Restart Their Journey), *Zhongguo zhi chun*, No. 6, 1992, pp. 25–26.
9. A slightly abridged version of the open letter is reprinted in *Contemporary* (Hong Kong), No. 10, 1992, pp. 32–34.
10. See articles by Bing Xin, Xia Yan, Zhang Guangnian, Wang Meng and others in *Zhongguo qingnian bao* (Chinese Youth Daily), 18 October 1992; Wang Meng's article in *Jiefang ribao* (Liberation Daily), 10 September 1992, and *Yangcheng wanbao* (Yangcheng Evening News), 7 December 1992. Also, *SWB* FE/1528 B2/4–5 (3 November 1992).
11. *Ming Pao Monthly*, No. 12, 1992, pp. 18–35.
12. The publication of such politically sensitive works as *Shan'ao shang de Zhongguo* (China in Crisis) and *Shui lai chengbao* (Who Wants the Responsibility) by provincial publishers and the banning of the book *Lishi de chaoliu* (The Tides of History) are cases in point.
13. In his interview with Li Yi, in *The Nineties* (Hong Kong), No. 10, 1992, pp. 82–87, the writer Bai Hua also referred to regional differences with regard to ideological control.
14. For a detailed account of this "porridge incident" (*xizhou shijian*), see the appendices in the book *Jianying de xizhou* (Hard Porridge) (Hong Kong: Cosmos Books Ltd., 1992), pp. 117–46.
15. *SWB* FE/1530 B2/3 (5 November 1992).
16. *Shouhuo* (Harvest), No. 1, 1992, p. 93.
17. Wang Meng, "Aodili zhou dian," *Xiaoshuo jie* (Fiction World), No. 4, 1992, pp. 26–29.
18. For example, Zhang Kangkang, " Xianhua xizhou" (About Porridge), *Zhuhai wenxue* (Zhuhai Literature), No. 3, 1992, pp. 92–93 and "Xizhou nan bei wei" (Porridge in the Southern and Northern Chinese Cuisines), *Furong* (Hibiscus), No. 3, 1992, pp. 59–61; Zong Pu, "Cong 'Zhou liao' shuo qi" (About the Medicinal Use of Porridge), *Shouhuo*, No. 3, 1992, pp. 101–102; Zhang Jie, "Xiaosa xizhou" (Carefree Porridge), *Ming Pao Monthly*, No. 12, 1992, pp. 39–43. It is said that the Huacheng Publishing House in Guangzhou will publish a collection of these writings.
19. Is it a pure coincidence that apparently only two of his friends took the trouble of writing to him to express their support for his legal action? See *Jianying de xizhou* (see Note 15), pp. 144–46.
20. "Shang huo," *Zhongshan* (Mount Zhong), No. 5, 1991, pp. 25–63.
21. Li Yenan, "Lai zi Beijing wentan de fenbin huaxu" (see Note 8), p. 72.
22. I wish to thank Mr Wen Neng, editor of the literary journal *Hua Cheng*, and

Mr Fan Hansheng, head of the Huacheng Publishing House, for agreeing to be interviewed in Guangzhou on 27–31 December 1992 and share with me their valuable insights into the structural reform.

23. Though Marx never developed a systematic philosophy of art, this idea runs through a number of his writings, e.g., *Capital, Economic and Philosophic Manuscripts of 1844*, and the *Grundrisse*. This theme was elaborated by Lenin, Georg Lukács, and thinkers associated with the Frankfurt School. Also see footnotes 54 and 63.
24. *Wenxue bao* (Literature Press, sic.), No. 599 (17 September 1992), p. 1.
25. See Willy Wo-lap Lam's chapter in this book, footnote 40.
26. *SWB* FE/1581 B2/1–5 (8 January 1992).
27. *Zhongyang ribao*, 11 December 1992, p. 4.
28. *Zhongguo xiju* (Chinese Drama), No. 1, 1992, pp. 50–52.
29. For more on the restructuring of the Chinese media, see Joseph Man Chan's chapter in this book.
30. *Zhongguo xiju*, No. 1, 1992, pp. 50–52. *Contemporary*, No. 10, 1992, p. 43. Another favourite "diversification" has been into the real estate business.
31. *Wenxue bao*, No. 592 (30 July 1992), p. 1.
32. *Ibid*.
33. The Centre counted among its members the writers, Ma Weidu, Su Lei, Wei Ren, Mo Yan, Zhu Xiaoping, Ge Xiaogang, Feng Xiaogang and others.
34. For a discussion of this series, see Geremie Barmé, "The Greying of Chinese Culture," in *China Review 1992*, edited by Kuan Hsin-chi and Maurice Brosseau (Hong Kong: The Chinese University Press, 1992), pp. **13**.4–8
35. "Bianjibu de gushi" consists of twenty-five parts, of which half was written by Wang Shuo and the rest by Wei Ren, Su Lei, Ge Xiaogang and Feng Xiaogang.
36. *Wenxue bao*, No. 590 (16 July 1992), p. 1.
37. *Wenyi bao* (Literary Gazette), No. 33 (22 August 1992), p. 1.
38. *Zhongyang ribao*, 29 December 1992, p. 5.
39. *Wenyi bao*, No. 35 (5 September 1992), p. 1.
40. Chen Yuanbin, "Wan jia susong," *Xiaoshuo yuebao* (Fiction Monthly), No. 8, 1991, pp. 16–30. A pun is intended in the title, which can be taken to mean that thousands of households are lodging complaints.
41. "Bianjibu de gushi" de kanjing (Chatting about 'In the Editorial Department'), *Wenxue bao*, No. 571 (3 May 1992), p. 7.
42. Geremie Barmé, "The Greying of Chinese Culture" (see Note 35), p. **13**.35.
43. This comment is intended to call attention to the aspect of the role of the recipient in communication. It is beyond the scope of this paper to deal adequately with this complicated issue. There is an extensive literature on the reception theory, of which the seminal texts are Hans Robert Jausse, *Towards an Aesthetic of Reception* (Minneappolis: University of Minnesota Press,

1982), and Wolfgang Iser, *The Act of Reading, a Theory of Aesthetic Response* (Baltimore: John Hopkins University Press, 1978). Though both are primarily concerned with readers' response to printed literary texts, they have important implications for other forms of aesthetic response.

44. In my trips to the Guangdong province in the last two years, I noticed that even northerners who either intended to move to Guangdong or had already settled down there proudly referred to Guangdong as "our province."

45. It has not been unusual for performers to outnumber spectators. See *Wenxue bao*, No. 586 (7 May, 1992), p. 2; *Contemporary*, No. 10, 1992, pp. 42–43; *Zhongguo xiju*, No. 7, 1992, p. 44.

46. Helmut Martin's view is fairly representative in this respect. See his "Retrospective Introduction," in *Modern Chinese Writers: Self-portrayals*, edited by Helmut Martin and Jeffrey Kinkley (Armonk: M. E. Sharpe, 1992), pp. xxi–xxxix.

47. For example, "Siyang dushe de xiaohai" (The Child Who Rears Poisonous Snakes), *Shouhuo*, No. 6, 1991, pp. 101–104; and "Yige ren he ta de linju ji lingwai liang san ge ren" (A Certain Man and His Neighbours and Another Two or Three People), *Zuojia* (Writers), No. 5, 1992, pp. 9–30.

48. "Wo shi zenyang yang mao de," *Xiaoshuo jie*, No. 2, 1992, pp. 4–12, 29.

49. "Gexing he wo," *Zuojia* (Writers), No. 11, 1991, pp. 12–15.

50. "Huaxing he wo," *Xiaoshuo yuebao*, No. 7, 1992, pp. 43–50.

51. See, for example, Wang Shide, "Xianshi zhuyi yu 'xin xieshi' xiaoshuo" (Realism and 'Neo-realist' Fiction), *Wenyi bao*, No. 37 (19 September 1992), p. 3, and Zhang Ren, " Xunzhao zhong de guodu xianxiang" (A Transient Phenomenon in the Course of Searching), *Wenxue pinglun* (Literary Criticism), No. 2, 1992, pp. 4–16.

52. This term, together with its many variant forms, has been used by critics since 1988 in connection with neo-realism. See Shen Minte, "Shuo 'yuansheng zhuangtai'" (On the "Pristine Conditions of Life"), *Xinhua wenzhai* (New China Digest), No. 8, 1992, pp. 126–27.

53. In the Marxist literary tradition, realism with its alleged principle of typicality is the ideal mode, while naturalism is an anathema. The consummate expression of such a tradition can be found in a large number of Georg Lukács' writings. See, among others, his *Studies in European Realism* (London: Hillway Publishing Co., 1950); *Essays on Realism* (London: Lawrence and Wishart, 1980) and *Writer and Critic and Other Essays* (London: Merlin Press, 1970).

54. "Shushu a'yi dajiu he wo," *Shouhuo*, No. 1, 1992, pp. 5–23.

55. "Baiyun canggou yao," *Shanghai wenxue* (Shanghai Literature), No. 3, 1992, pp. 4–19.

56. "Wu chu xuntao," *Xiaoshuojia* (Fiction Writers), No. 3, 1992, pp. 37–61.

57. "Ren dao zhongnian," *Shouhuo*, No. 1, 1980, pp. 52–92.

58. Notably her novella "Fengjing" (Landscape), in *Xiaoshuo xuankan* (Selected Fiction), No. 1, 1988, pp. 62–91.
59. "Qiqie cheng qun," *Shouhuo*, No. 6, 1989, pp. 4–27.
60. "'Rizi' xupian," *Xiaoshuo yuebao*, No. 10, 1992, pp. 51–55.
61. "Qianling liu meng ji," *Shouhuo*, No. 2, 1992, pp. 107–12.
62. The strongest critique of what is called the "cultural industry" is found in the writings of the Frankfurt School. See in particular Theodor W. Adorno and Max Horkheimer, "The Culture Industry," in their *Dialectic of Enlightment* (New York: Herder and Herder, 1972), pp. 120–67 and Herbert Marcuse, *One-dimensional Man* (Boston: Beacon Press, 1964). It appears, however, that the "cultural industry" they criticize is not so much a product of market forces but of technological rationality accompanying capitalist industrialization.
63. This is the argument of the Frankfurt school. See the above note.
64. In the study of popular culture, there are in fact two diametrically opposite schools of thought. One school regards popular culture as governed by the ideology and values of the dominant classes and groups. The other school regards it as a site of oppositional ideology and values. For a critique of both these extremes, see Tony Bennett's "Introduction: Popular Culture and 'the Turn to Gramsci'," and "The Politics of 'the Popular' and Popular Culture," in *Popular Culture and Social Relations* (Milton Keynes: Open University Press, 1986), pp. xi–xix, 6–21.

Index

Note: Roman numerals refer to the pages of "Chronology"; the Arabic numerals are composed of two numbers separated by a period; the first in boldface refers to the chapter, the second to the page(s).

Academia Sinica, **9**.8
Administrative Reforms, **4**.3f
Adoption, child, **23**.8
Africa, **8**.4; **16**.25
Agriculture, **1**.14; **14**.*passim*; **15**.7; pricing **14**.4; wool market, **14**.9
Ai Zhisheng, **2**.9
Airports: Baiyuan, **18**.12; Chek Lap Kok (HK), **18**.11; Huangtian, **18**.11; Kai Tak (HK), **18**.12; Sanzhao, **18**.11
Akihito, Emperor, xxvii; **1**.2; **8**.6,10,11
Albania, **17**.33
All-China People's Autonomy Alliance, **21**.3
American Motors, **16**.22
Anhui, **6**.16; **11**.11; **19**.13; **22**.31; **24**.20
Arbitration, **7**.6; China International Economic and Trade Arbitration Commission, **16**.26; Institute of Arbitration, Stockholm, **16**.26; *see also* Law
Arms trade, **8**.6
Arthur Anderson, **16**.27
ASEAN, **6**.20; **8**.14; **9**.18
Asia, **8**.4; **17**.15; Central Asia, **6**.18; East Asia, **18**.5; Southeast Asia, **16**.7,25

Asia-Pacific Economic Cooperation, **8**.5; **9**.18
Asia-Pacific Region, **8**.3,9,10,13; **9**.17
Asian Games, **9**.21
AsiaSat 1 (satellite), **25**.14
Association for Relations Across the Taiwan Straits (PRC), **9**.3,15,22
At Middle Age, **26**.15
Au, Sally, **25**.10
Australia, **9**.18; **16**.25
Austria **16**.19
Austrian Porridge Restaurant, The, **26**.5
Auyang Hsün, **9**.9,13

Ba Zhongtan, **6**.13
Bahr, S. J., **20**.14
Bai Hua, **21**.6
Baker, James, xxi; **8**.6
Ballad of Vicissitudes, **26**.15
Banking: commercial banks, **13**.10; bank credit, **13**.9; loans, **11**.3,4; reform, **13**.*passim*; foreign banks, **13**.13–14;
Agricultural Bank of China, **13**.3; Asian Development Bank, **8**.5; **16**.2; Bank of China, **2**.32; **13**.4; **16**.23; **17**.16; **18**.20; Bank of Communications, **13**.4; Bank of East Asia, **13**.13; Central Bank of

China, **9**.4; China Investment Bank, **13**.4; CITIC Industrial Bank, **13**.5; Commercial Bank of China, **13**.4; Everbright Bank of China, **13**.8; Export-Import Bank (US), **17**.24; Fujian Industrial Bank, **13**.5; Guangdong Development Bank, **13**.5; Huaxia Bank, **13**.8; International Bank for Reconstruction and Development, **17**.21; Long-Term Credit Bank of Japan, **13**.13; Nanyang Commercial Bank Ltd., **13**.13; People's Bank of China, **7**.9,16; **11**.8; **12**.20; **13**.3; **18**.16; People's Construction Bank of China, **13**.4; **24**.26; Shanghai Pudong Development Bank, **13**.5; Shenzhen Development Bank, **13**.5; Société Générale, **13**.13; Sumitomo Bank Ltd., **13**.13; World Bank, **8**.5; **13**.4; **16**.2; **17**.2,13; **24**.4,5,11,12, 31; Xiamen International Bank, **13**.5,13

Bangkok, **9**.18
Bankruptcy, **16**.30
Bao Tong, xxiii; **21**.7
Bao Zunxin, xxviii
Bao'an, **18**.3
Barcelona, xxv
Basic Law (Hong Kong), **10**.7,9,12,14,18,19
Beggars, **23**.6
Beidaihe, **6**.5
Beihai, **16**.30
Beijing, xxii; **1**.10; **2**.19,30,41; **6**.14; **8**.11; **9**.8; **10**.2; **11**.10; **12**.8; **13**.5; **14**.10; **16**.14,26,27; **17**.20; **18**.5,13, 22; **19**.12,13,15,19,21,23; **20**.3,4; **22**.11,18,29; **23**.6,9,10,12; **24**.20,21, 22,26,28,29,30; **25**.3,6,7,10; **26**.5,6,11
Beijing-Guangzhou Highway, **18**.21

Beijing Jeep, **16**.22
Belgium, **16**.25
Bengbu, **24**.9
Berne Convention for the Protection of Literary and Artistic Works, **7**.23; **17**.23
Bo Xicheng, xxiv; **2**.7,39
Bo Yibo, xxiv; xxvi; **2**.7,39
Boshan, **6**.11
Bott, Elizabeth, **19**.26
Bourgeois Liberalism, **2**.9,16; **3**.4,11; **21**.3,11,12; **25**.2; **26**.8,13; *see also* Ideology
Brain drain, **22**.3; regional **22**.8
Britain *see* United Kingdom
Budget, extra ~ revenues, **12**.3 (table)
Bulgaria, **17**.33
Burma, **18**.22
Bush, George, xxv; **6**.16; **8**.7,8; **9**.17; **17**.25
Business and Professionals Association (Hong Kong), **10**.16

Café de Coral, **16**.27
Caithness, Lord, **10**.13
Can Xue, **26**.14
Canada, **8**.3; **9**.18; **16**.25; **18**.16
Canonization of the Gods, **26**.11
Canton *see* Guangzhou
Cao Gangchuan, **6**.11
Cao Pengsheng, xxvii; **6**.13
Cao Qingze, **2**.6
Cao Shuangming, **6**.14
Capital market, **11**.9
Capital Steel Works, **24**.6
Cathay Pacific Airline, **18**.9
Caycedo, J. C., **20**.14
Censorship, **2**.16
Chai Ling, **21**.7
Chan Yuen-han, **10**.8
Chang, P. K., **9**.5
Chang Chien-han, **9**.10

Index

Chang Hsüeh-liang, **9**.10
Chang, John, **9**.14
Changchun, **6**.11; **16**.16
Changsha, xxv
Changzhou, **24**.8
Chao Ching-chi, **9**.10
Chao Yao-tung, **9**.8
Cheffou, Amadou, **9**.14
Chen Fang, **1**.7
Chen Guangzhong, **9**.12
Chen Jinhua, **2**.16
Chen Jinyi, **2**.41
Chen Jung-chieh, **9**.23
Chen Kaige, **26**.16
Chen Kangli, **9**.12
Chen Li-an, **9**.17
Ch'en Li-fu, **9**.10
Chen Ming-chang, **9**.6
Chen Rong, **26**.14,15
Chen Xitong, xxvi;**2**.6
Chen Yizi, **21**.6
Chen Yuan, **2**.7,33
Chen Yun, xxi,xxiv,xxvi; **1**.6,7; **2**.4,7,9,12,33,39,43; **4**.14
Chen Zuolin, **2**.6
Cheng Jianing, **6**.10
Cheng, Joseph Y. S., **10**.5
Cheng Kai-nam, **10**.8
Cheng Yiu-tong, xxiii
Chengde, **6**.13
Chengdu, **6**.9,12,13; **20**.5,8,9; **25**.10
Chenghai, **9**.5
Cheung Ching-wan, **24**.25
Cheung Kong Holdings, **16**.27
Chi Haotian, xxvii; **2**.7,23; **6**.3,8,12,14
Chi Li, **26**.15
Chiang Ching-kuo, **9**.2
Chiang Kai-shek, **9**.2
Chien, Frederic, **9**.14
Children, abandoned, **23**.7f
China International Trust and Investment Corporation, **13**.5
China Light and Power Co. (Hong Kong), **16**.28
China Review, **22**.5
China Strategic Investment Ltd., **16**.29
Chinese Academy of Social Sciences, **2**.10; **9**.12; **19**.27
Chinese Alliance for Democracy, **21**.7,8
Chinese Alliance for Freedom, **21**.3
Chinese Communist Party: 12th congress, **1**.11; **2**.34; 13th congress, **1**.4,11; **2**.7; 14th congress, **1**.2,4,6,11; **2**.2,3,17,31; **3**.3,7,9; **4**.2; **5**.2; **6**.10; **8**.10; **9**.4,13; **13**.10; **14**.9; **16**.5; **17**.2; **18**.6; **19**.24; **21**.4,6; **22**.4; **25**.3; **26**.3,6,16; 3rd plenum 10th Central Committee (CC), **21**.2; 3rd plenum 11th CC, **1**.11; **16**.2,19; **17**.3; **21**.2; 6th plenum 11th CC, **21**.2; 3rd plenum 12th CC, **1**.11; 4th plenum 13th CC, **1**.11; 7th plenum 13th CC, **12**.8; 9th plenum 13th CC, **2**.17; Central Advisory Commission, **2**.7,43; **5**.10; Central Advisory Group, **2**.7; Central Commission for Disciplinary Inspection, **2**.6,25,33; **5**.10; Central Party School, **1**.3; **2**.11,29,34; Collective leadership, **2**.27; Document No. 2, xviii; Document No. 4, **2**.19,21,37; Document No. 7, **2**.5; Gansu faction, **2**.11; General Office, **2**.30,36; **6**.10; leadership succession, **1**.2; Leading Group on Economics and Finance, **2**.28; Leading Group on Foreign Affairs, **2**.33; Leading Group on Ideology and Propaganda, **25**.3; Leading Group on Overseas Propaganda, **2**.10; Organization Department, **2**.4,27,36,39; **5**.6; Party Constitution, **3**.3,5,7,11; **5**.3;

Political and Legal Commission,
2.25,33; Propaganda Department,
2.10,16,30; 3.7,12; 25.3,9; 26.2,3
Secretariat, 2.17; 6.2; Shanghai
faction, 2.30; United Front
Department, 2.36; Zhao Ziyang
faction, 2.16
Chinese Democracy Foundation,
21.6
Chinese Liberal Democratic Party,
21.3,6
Chinese Liberal Union, 21.3,4
Chinese People Political Consultative
Congress, 1.9; 10.7; 25.8
Chinese Progressive Alliance, 21.3,4
Chinese Social Democratic Party,
21.3,4
Chinese Technological Society, 25.12
Chinese World Economists
Association, 25.9
Chiu, Cheyne, 9.14
Chongqing, 2.17; 12.8,9; 13.5
Chu Hsin-min, 9.9
City Planning and Design Research
Centre, 24.27
Civil Affairs Conference, 9th
National, 23.3
Civil Aviation Administration, 5.5
Civil Service, 4.3; 5.*passim*; National
Administration College, 5.9
Clinton, Bill, xxvi,xxviii; 8.3,7,8; 9.6;
17.33; 18.22
Coastal cities budgets, 12.18–19 (table)
Cold War, 8.3; 17.33
Commonwealth of Independent States,
1.2; 16.25
Communist Youth League, 2.36
Conable, Barber, 17.33
Constitution of People's Republic of
China, 16.25; 21.2
Cooperative Resources Centre (Hong
Kong), 10.11,12,14

Copyright, Universal Convention,
7.23; 17.23
Corporatism, 3.10
Corruption, 1.7; 3.14; 4.14; 18.16,22
Court of Final Appeal (HK), 10.11
Credit control, 11.3; 13.12
Cultural Revolution, 2.22f; 3.4,14;
6.2; 16.19; 19.8; 21.10,12; 22.4
Current account balance, 17.7 (table)
Customs Administration, 5.9; 17.8

Dai Qing, xxii; 21.6; 22.2
Dai Xianglong, 13.10
Dalian, 12.9; 13.13; 16.10,30; 18.13;
23.10,13
Danshui, 24.27
Daya Bay, 18.3,5; Nuclear Plant,
18.13
Democracy, 3.5,10; 21.*passim*
Democracy Wall, 21.3
Democratic Alliance for the
Betterment of Hong Kong, 10.16
Democratic Progressive Party
(Taiwan), 9.3
Deng Liqun, 2.4,10,11,12; 25.3
Deng Nan, 2.7
Deng Xiaoping,
xviii,xix,xx,xxi,xxiv,xxvi,xxix,xxx;
1.5,7,9,10,14,16; 2.2,7,16,19,22,30,
35,38,39; 3.*passim*; 4.2,6,12; 5.2,4,
13; 6.2,5,6,13; 7.2,28; 8.2; 9.2,13,
24; 11.5,11; 12.16,17; 13.2; 14.2,7;
15.11,16; 16.5,19; 17.2; 18.5,19;
21.2,6; 22.4; 23.2,7; 24.7; 25.3,5,
12; 26.2,3,8,16
*Deng Xiaoping on Building Socialism
with Chinese Characteristics*, 2.42
Deng Zhifang, 1.7
Diallo, Hamidou, 9.14
Diaoyutai (Senkaku) Islands, 8.10
Ding Guan'gen, xxix; 2.6,10,44; 26.3
Direct foreign investment, 16.*passim*

Index I.5

Disabled, **23**.11–13; Chinese Federation of, **23**.13
Disorder Caused by Excessive Internal Heat, A, **26**.7
Divorce, **20**.11–12; court cases, **20**.12 (table)
Dong An market, **16**.27
Dong Fureng, **2**.41
Dong Xuelin, **6**.13,14
Dongguan, **18**.2,7,8,10,12,14; **24**.22
Dreams Left Behind in Mount Qianling, **26**.16
Drug, illegal use, **23**.6f
Du Tiehuan, **6**.11
Durkheim, Emile, **19**.27

Education, **1**.15; basic education, **22**.8f; its financing, **22**.11f,15 (table); *Decision of CCP on the Reform of Educational Structure*, **22**.4,9,20,21; educational institutions, **22**.7 (table); fund raising, **22**.17 (table); **22**.27–30; higher education, **22**.5; National Research Centre for Educational Development, **22**.9; regional disparity, **22**.5; responsibility system, **22**.2,25,26; teacher-student ratio, **22**.8; work-study programme, **22**.14,30
Einstein, Albert, **22**.35
Elderly, **20**.6; home for elderly, **23**.9
Employment, **7**.5
Energy, **18**.8; Shajiao Power Plant, **16**.28
Entrepreneurship, **2**.21; private, **2**.39
Enterprise, **4**.7; **5**.15; **7**.3; debt chain, **1**.14; ownership, **7**.4; personnel management, **7**.5; reform, **15**.4–11; rights, **7**.4; state-owned, **1**.11,12; **4**.8; **11**.4; **15**.*passim*; taxes and subsidies, **15**.12 (table); village and township, **1**.12; **17**.6
Environment, **1**.15
Equality, **3**.8
Europe, **8**.3,4,6; **18**.11; Eastern Europe, **1**.2; **2**.5,13,23,45; **3**.12; **5**.8,14,17; **9**.15; **16**.25; **17**.9; **21**.6,9; **23**.19; **25**.2; Economic development strategy, **16**.18; European Community, **17**.11,13; European Economic Community, **16**.25; Western Europe, **23**.19
Evans, Gareth, **9**.18
Exchange Rate Regime, **17**.18
External debt, **17**.6

Fairwood Fast Food, **16**.27
Family form, **20**.4 (table); nuclear, **20**.4; size, **20**.2–3 (table); structure, **20**.7
Fang Fang, **26**.15
Fang Lizhi, **2**.45; **21**.6,7
Fang Weizhong, **2**.11
Federation for a Democratic China, **21**.7,8
Federation of Trade Unions, **10**.7
Female role *see* Women
Fertility *see* Women
Film industry, **26**.11–13; Chinese Distribution Company, **25**.11; Beijing Movie Studio, **25**.7,9; Pearl River Movie Studio, **25**.9; Seahorse Movie and Video Production Centre, **26**.10,11; Shanghai Movie Studio, **25**.9; Xi'an Movie Studio, **25**.9
Farewell to My Concubine, **26**.16; *Hang High the Red Lanterns*, **25**.5; **26**.12,16; *Judou*, **25**.5; **26**.12; *Qiuju Goes to Court*, **26**.12; *Red Sorghum*, **25**.5
Fiscal policy, **12**.*passim*;

redistribution, **12**.14–17; **12**.15 (table)
Fok Ying-tung, Henry, xxiii; **18**.12
Fong, Peter K.W., **24**.7
Food Bureau, **1**.13
Foreign exchange, **11**.9; State General Administration of, **13**.4; reserves, **17**.6
Foreign investment by destinations, **16**.11–13 (tables); by sectors, **16**.15 (table); foreign-invested enterprises, **16**.6 (table); leading countries, **16**.8 (table); usage, **16**.4 (table)
Foreign security ties, **6**.16
Foreign trade *see* Trade
Foshan, **2**.38; **8**.2,4,7,10
Four Basic Principles *see* Ideology
France, xxvi; **1**.3; **2**.23,35; **6**.16; **8**.5,13; **9**.9,17; **13**.15; **16**.5,19; **17**.11
Fu Quanyou, xxvii; **2**.7,23,24; **6**.9,14,15
Fu Rui, **2**.7
Fujian, **1**.7; **2**.37; **8**.6; **12**.8; **16**.14,17,27,29,30; **17**.2,3,10,19; **19**.2,13,16,20; **24**.20,22; **25**.14
Futures market, **11**.9; **18**.17
Fuzhou, **13**.13; **16**.30; **23**.12; **24**.22,26

Gaffney, Beryl, xviii
Gang of Four, xxiv; **2**.10; **16**.19; **21**.2; **26**.7
Gansu, xxii; **2**.27; **12**.8; **19**.13,16; **22**.11,12,18; **24**.20
Gao Di, **2**.30; **25**.3
Gao Zhanxiang, **26**.8
GATT, **7**.25,26; **8**.7; **9**.16; **10**.3; **14**.18; **16**.21,35; **17**.21–24,27; **18**.22
Gender roles, **20**.13–16
Germany, **8**.5; **9**.14; **13**.15; **16**.9,10,19; **17**.10–11
Giordano, **16**.26
Goodlad, Alastair, **10**.13

Government *see* State Council
Grain, **14**.7
Great Leap Forward, **2**.13
"Greater China" economy, **17**.30–33
Grenada, **9**.15
Gu Hui, xxvii; **6**.13
Gu Shanqing, xxvii; **6**.12
Guangdong, **1**.13; **2**.17,18,19,20,37; **4**.2; **5**.4; **6**.5; **8**.6; **9**.5; **11**.9,10,11; **12**.8,14; **14**.8,14; **16**.5,10,17–18,28, 31; **17**.3,9,19,30; **18**.*passim*; **19**.2,12,13,15,16,20,21,23; **22**.3,11,16,18,22; **23**.6,10,11; **24**.4,20,21,22,25,30; **26**.9
Guangdong Enterprises (Holdings), **18**.17
Guanghan, **14**.8
Guangxi, **2**.37; **12**.8; **18**.22; **19**.13,14,15,16; **22**.11; **24**.20
Guangzhou, xxi,xxvi; **1**.10; **2**.15,37; **5**.4; **6**.9,12,13,16; **9**.18; **13**.5,13; **14**.10; **16**.10,30; **18**.*passim*; **23**.9,13; **24**.4,12–16,22,26,28,29; **25**.10; **26**.13
Guangzhou-Shenzhen-Zhuhai Highway, **16**.28
Guangzhou-Zhuhai Railway, **18**.10
Guilin, xxviii
Guizhou, **12**.8; **19**.13,22; **22**.8,9,11,19; **24**.20; **25**.14
Gulf War, **6**.4
Guo Haiqing, **7**.5
Guo Luoqi, **21**.6

Haicang Island, **9**.6
Haikou, **16**.30
Hainan, xx,**1**.7; **2**.18,37,38; **6**.16; **12**.8; **16**.2,10,27,34; **19**.13,14,23; **22**.11; **24**.20
Han Dongfang, xxi; **21**.6
Han Huaizhi, **6**.11
Hangzhou, **1**.10; **23**.10

Harbin, **5**.9; **12**.8; **16**.29
Hard Porridge, **26**.5
Hau Pei-tsun, **9**.19
He Dongchang, **2**.9,11; **22**.3; **26**.3
He Jingzhi, xxix; **2**.10; **25**.3; **26**.3
He Qizhong, **6**.11
Hebei, **6**.13; **12**.8; **19**.13; **22**.18; **24**.20
Heihe river, **2**.36; **12**.5
Heilongjiang, **2**.36; **12**.5,8; **19**.12,13,14,15,16,25
Henan, **2**.27; **12**.8; **19**.13; **22**.18; **24**.8,20; **25**.13
Hengqin Island, **18**.5
Historical Tides, **25**.13
Homeownership, **24**.8f
Hong Kong, xxii,xxvii; **1**.3,5; **2**.33; **3**.3; **4**.14; **6**.6; **7**.16; **9**.2,3,7,10,11, 16,19,23; **10**.*passim*; **11**.10; **13**.13; **16**.5,9,10,20,26,27,29,32; **17**.2,5,8,9,25,30,31; **18**.*passim*; **22**.14,18; **23**.8; **24**.22,25,27,28,31; **25**.4,7,10,11,13,14,15; **26**.11,13; Advisers to Beijing, **10**.25 (list); Airport Consultative Committee, **10**.23 (list); Election Committee, **10**.15 (table); Hong Kong Alliance in Support of Patriotic Democratic Movement in China, **10**.9; **21**.7; Hong Kong Bar Association, **10**.12; Hong Kong Federation of Industries, **18**.8; Hong Kong Law Society, **10**.12; Hong Kong Telecom, **18**.18; Hong Kong Trade Development Council, **17**.3,**18**.22; One country, two systems, **9**.2,9,13; Sino-British Joint Declaration, **10**.2,15; Sino-British Joint Liaison Group, **10**.3; Sino-British Land Commission, **10**.3; Sino-British Memorandum of Understanding, **10**.2,11
Hong Xuezhi, **6**.6,15

Hopewell Holdings, **16**.27,28; **18**.10,13,22
Hou Zongbin, **2**.6,27
Housing, commodified, **24**.2 (table); construction yearly, **24**.3 (table); Guangzhou, **24**.13 (table); housing completion, **24**.29 (table); living space, **24**.3 (table); management, **24**.5 (table); overseas pricing, **24**.23 (table); reform, **24**.18–19 (table); sales overseas, **24**.23 (table); subsidies, **24**.7
How I Keep a Cat, **26**.14
Hu Jintao, xxvi; **2**.6,11,14,36,43
Hu Jiwei, **2**.41
Hu Ping, **21**.7
Hu Qili, **2**.17,18
Hu Sheng, **2**.10
Hu Yaobang, xviii; **1**.5; **2**.4,10,14,17, 27,31,36,45; **5**.4; **6**.3; **21**.2,3,11,12; **26**.3
Hua Guofeng, **2**.9,12,28,30; **16**.19; **21**.2
Huang Ju, xx,xxi
Huang K'un-hui, **9**.19
Huang Shunxing, xx
Hubei, **12**.5,8,16; **16**.29; **19**.13; **22**.6,19; **24**.8,20; **25**.7
Huiyang, **24**.22
Huizhou, **1**.7; **18**.2,3; **24**.27
Human rights, **3**.3; **8**.6; **21**.5
Hunan, xxii; **12**.8,16; **19**.13; **22**.14,18,32; **24**.20; **25**.7
Hunchun, **12**.5
Hundred Flowers Movement, **21**.12
Hunjiang, **22**.25
Hutchison Whampoa, **16**.28; **18**.12,18,22

Ideology, **25**.2; conflict **16**.34; Four Basic Principles, **1**.9,11; **2**.29; **3**.2,9; **5**.15,17; **21**.2,10,11,13;

25.3,5,17; Leftism, 2.8; 3.10f;
Maoism, 2.2,42; Marxism, 2.9,35;
3.11; 22.2,3; 25.4; 26.8;
Marxism-Leninism, 2.42; 3.10;
Marxism-Leninism-Maoism, 26.7;
Rightism, 3.11; Rural Socialist
Education Campaign, 3.4; spiritual
civilization, 3.12; ultra-leftism, 21.2
India, 1.2
Indonesia, 8.6,10,12; 16.5,7
Industrial Revolution, 17.3
Industry gross industrial output, 11.5
(table); 15,7 (table); by province,
11.12 (table)
Inflation, 1.14; 11.7,8–9; 20.6; 24.25
Information industry, 18.18; *see also*
Media
Inner Mongolia, 4.7; 12.8;
19.13,14,15,16,25; 22.22;
Inner-Mongolian Alliance for
Human Rights Protection, 21.3
Inoguchi Takashi, 8.11
Insurance, old age, 23.16
Intellectual property, 8.6; 17.25
Interest rates, 11.3
International Monetary Fund, 17.21
Investment, 1.14; 11.3
Ip, Simon, 10.11
Iran, 17.33
Iraq, 17.33
Israel, xviii; 8.6
Italy, xviii; 16.19; 17.10,11

Jackson-Vanik Amendment (US Trade
Act), 17.24
James Bond, 22.35
Japan, xxvii; 1.2; 2.15; 8.3,4–9,13;
9.18; 13.15; 16.9,19,25,26,32;
17.10,27; 20.6; 25.10,14
Jia Chunwang, 2.26
Jia Ping'ao, 26.14
Jiang Chunyun, xxvii; 2.6,19

Jiang Qing, xxiv; 2.12; 26.7
Jiang Zemin, xviii,xxiii,xxvi,xxvii,
xxviii; 1.3,5,13; 2.2,5,6,23,26,28,30,
31,34,35; 3.9; 4.2,6; 6.3,13,14,15;
9.8,13,19,25; 16.21; 17.2
Jiangmen, 18.2
Jiangsu, 11.10,11; 12.8,14; 17.2;
19.13,20; 20.6; 22.9,18; 24.8,17;
25.6
Jiangxi, xxv; 2.9,15; 11.11; 19.13;
24.20
Jilin, 6.11; 11.11; 12.5,8,16;
19.13,14,15; 24.20
Jinan, 6.8,12,13,20
Jiujiang, 23.13
Joint venture, Sino-foreign, 16.*passim*
June 4 *see* Tiananmen Incident

Kaifu, Toshiki, 8.6
Kanter, Arnold, xxi
Kao Kung-lien, 9.4
Kazakov, Valeriy, 6.17
Kennedy, Edward, xxiii
Kinmen (Jinmen) Island, 9.16,23
Kokoshin, Andrey, 6.19
Korea, 8.14; North, xxv; 6.18;
8.4,9,12,13; South, xxv; 1.2,6;
8.3,4,6,11,12; 9.13,15; 16.9,20;
17.2,10,11,27,30
Korean War, 6.7,9; 9.15; 16.9
Ku Chen-fu, 9.23,24
Kui Fulin, 6.11
Kuo, Shirley, 9.2
Kuomintang, 9.2,9,20; 21.8

Labour, Labour Bureau, 7.6; labour
market, 12.6; professional, 22.3
Lalkaka, Dyniar, 24.2
Lampton, David, 17.33
Lan Pin *see* Jiang Qing
Land Administration, State, 24.24
Lanzhou, 6.9,12,13

Index

Latin America, **16**.25
Law, **2**.25; **7**.*passim*; Marxist theory, **7**.2; rule of, **4**.4
  Accounting Law, **15**.16; *Adoption Law*, **23**.8; *Arbitration Law*, **7**.28; *Company Law*, **7**.28; *Copyright Law*, **7**.23–24; *Economic Contract Law*, **7**.28; *Foreign Trade Law*, **7**.24; *Income Tax Law for Foreign Enterprises*, **7**.20; *Industrial Enterprise Law*, **4**.9; **7**.3; **15**.8,10; *Law on Sino-Foreign Joint Ventures*, **16**.21; *Law on the Administration of Taxes*, **7**.19; *Protection of Minors Ordinance*, **23**.7; *Marriage Law*, **20**.8,13; *Omnibus Trade and Competitiveness Act* (US), **17**.27; *Patent Law*, **7**.20–23; **17**.23; *Production Liabilities Law*, **7**.28; *Protection of the Disabled*, **23**.12; *Regulations for Converting Management Mechanisms*, **7**.3; *Regulations for the Implementation of Law on Joint Ventures*, **16**.21; *Regulations of the Working Staff of State Organizations*, **5**.6; *Regulations on Identity Card*, **19**.3; *Regulations on Registered Accounts*, **15**.16; *Securities Law*, **7**.28; *State Budget Management Regulations*, **12**.10; *State Security Law*, **2**.26; *Supplementary Provisions on Tax Evasion*, **7**.19; *Trademark Law*, **7**.20; *Working Staff of State Organizations*, **5**.6
"Leap Forward with Foreign Character," **16**.19
Lee Chu-ming, Martin, **10**.9
Lee Yok-siu, F., **24**.5,8
Lee Kuan Yew, **8**.8
Lee Sang Ock, xxv

Lee Teng-hui, xxix; **9**.3,6,8,10,11,13,20
Legitimation, **3**.12
Lei Feng, **22**.35; **26**.13
Lei Yu, **2**.37
Leung Wai-man, xxviii
Levy, David, xviii
Li Chang, **2**.41
Li Desheng, **2**.35
Li Guixian, **2**.33
Li Hao, **1**.7; **2**.38
Li Honglin, xxi; **2**.16
Li Hou, **10**.16
Li Jinai, **6**.11
Li Jing, **6**.11
Li Jiulong, xxvii; **6**.13
Li Ka-shing, xxiii
Li Lanqing, xix; **2**.6; **17**.22
Li Luoli, **2**.39
Li Peng, xviii,xx,xxii,xxvi,xxviii,xxx; **1**.14; **2**.6,10,13,18,23,27,28,31, 32–33,35,44; **3**.14; **6**.18; **8**.6,14; **9**.8,10; **10**.9,13; **13**.11; **14**.8,13,15; **15**.11; **18**.5,6
Li Ruihuan, xxvi; **2**.6,10,11,30,44; **3**.11; **9**.11; **18**.6; **25**.3,4; **26**.2
Li Shuxian, **21**.6
Li Tieying, xxvi; **1**.15; **2**.6; **22**.3,13
Li Xiannian, xxiii,xxiv; **2**.9,12,27
Li Xiao, **26**.15
Li Xilin, xxvii; **6**.12
Li Ximing, **2**.6,9
Li Xuge, **6**.14
Li Youwei, **2**.38; **18**.16,17
Li Yüan-che, **9**.9
Li Ziliu, **2**.38; **18**.17
Liang Xiang, **2**.38
Liao Chengzhi, **1**.7
Liao Chun, **1**.7
Liaoning, **12**.8,9,17; **19**.13,15,20; **22**.11; **24**.20
Libya, **17**.33

Life expectancy, **20**.5 (table)
Limited Liability Companies, **7**.9,10f
Lin Biao, **2**.28; **6**.10
Lin Jingyao, xxiii
Lin Jinlan, **26**.14
Liu Anyuan, xxvii; **6**.12
Liu Binyan, **2**.17,45
Liu Guoguang, **9**.12
Liu Hongru, xxvi
Liu Huaqing, xxvi,xxvii; **1**.6; **2**.6,7,22,24,30,34–5,43; **6**.3,5,8,10,12,15,19; **9**.17
Liu Jingsong, xxvii; **6**.12,14
Liu Qing, xxi; **2**.16
Liu Shanqing, **21**.6
Liu Tai-ying, **9**.10,13
Liu Xiaobo, **21**.6
Liu Xinwu, **26**.5,14
Liu Zhongde, xxix; **2**.10; **26**.3
Liu Zhongli, **2**.32
Lu Jiamin, **2**.14
Lu Ping, **10**.8,12,15,16
Lü Feng, **2**.4,9
Luo Haixing, **21**.6
Luxembourg, **16**.25

Ma Feng, **26**.7
Ma Xia, **19**.26
Ma Ying-jeou, **9**.6,25
Macau, **7**.16; **9**.16,19; **16**.7,9; **18**.12,19; **22**.14,18; **23**.8
Macleod, Hamish, **10**.13; **17**.30
Major, John, **8**.6; **10**.2,13
Malaqinfu, **26**.5,7
Malaysia, **8**.10; **9**.4; **16**.5
Man Kam To, **18**.8
Manila, **6**.20; **9**.9
Mao Zedong, xxiv; **1**.6; **2**.12; **3**.2,4; **5**.14; **6**.15; **16**.18; **21**.2,11; **23**.2; **25**.4
Mao Zhiyong, **2**.9
Market economy, **1**.10; **11**.2; market mechanisms, **18**.4; reforms, **2**.3; socialist market, **3**.10
Marriage, **20**.7–9; mate selection, **20**.8 (table)
Marx, Karl, **3**.13 *see also* Ideology
Matsu (Mazu) Island, **9**.16
McDonald's Restaurants, **16**.27
McGregor, Jimmy, **10**.12
Media (print), **1**.9; **2**.42; commercialization, **25**.*passim*; Agence France-Presse, **9**.14; *April Fifth Forum*, **21**.3; *Beijing Spring*, **21**.3; *China Daily*, **16**.9; *China Education News*, **22**.2; *China Times*, **9**.7; *China Youth Daily*, **2**.18; *Chinese Industry and Commerce Times*, **9**.8; *Economic Daily*, **25**.4; *Economist, The*, **17**.3,6,13; *Exploration*, **21**.3; *Far Eastern Economic Review*, **9**.25; *Free China Journal*, **9**.4,21; *Future and Development*, **25**.12; **26**.9; *Guangming Daily*, **21**.6,10; **26**.2; *Guangzhou Daily*, **25**.6; *Legal News*, **25**.13; *Liberation Army Daily*, **2**.23; **6**.13; *Liberation Daily*, **25**.12; *Masses' Reference*, **21**.3; *Ming Pao*, **25**.12; *Ming Pao Monthly*, **26**.4; *People's Daily*, **2**.43; **9**.10,14,17,22; **21**.10; **25**.3,4,6,7,10; **26**.2; *People's Literature*, **26**.4; *Red Flag*, **4**.12; *Renmin ribao* (*see People's Daily*); *Seeking Truth*, **25**.4; *Shehui baozhang bao*, **23**.4; *Shenzhen Special Zone News*, **25**.12; *Ta Kung Pao*, **10**.7,17; *Tianjin Daily*, **25**.11; *Time Magazine*, **16**.22; *Wen Wei Po*, **10**.7; *World Economic Herald*, **25**.9,13; Xinhua News Agency **10**.4–6,19; **25**.7; *Xinwen Evening Post*, **25**.6; *Zhongguo*

Index

minzheng, **23**.10; *Zhongguo renkoubao*, **19**.9; *Zhongguo shehui bao*, **23**.4
Memorandum on Anti-Leftism, The, **25**.13; **26**.9
Meng Guangjun, **26**.7
Mental patients, **23**.9
Mexico, **8**.3
Middle East, **8**.4; **9**.17; **16**.25
Migrants, age and marital status, **19**.20–21; age specific, **19**.21 (table); characteristics, **19**.19f; employment, **19**.22; gender, **19**.20; migration, **19**.*passim*; **19**.5 (figure); **19**.6–7 (table); origin/destination, **19**.18 (table); type, **19**.22 (table)
Military *see* People's Liberation Army
Miners, John, **10**.3–4
Mo Yan, **26**.14
Monetary control, **13**.12
Mongolia, **8**.13
Mortality rate, **20**.5
Moscow, **6**.18
Most Favoured Nation (trade status), **8**.7; **17**.24–34; **18**.6
Movie industry *see* Film industry
Mrs Wan Files a Lawsuit, **26**.12
Multifibre Arrangement, **17**.13
My Maternal Uncle and His Friends and I, **26**.15

Nan'ao, **9**.5
Nanhai, **18**.2,4
Nanjing, xxviii; **6**.9,11,12,13,16; **7**.5; **13**.13; **23**.12
Nansha, **18**.5,12
Napoléon Bonaparte, **8**.2
Nathan, Andrew, **21**.11
National Copyright Administration, **7**.23
National People's Congress (NPC), **1**.9; **2**.13,33; **4**.5; **6**.5; **10**.7,16; **11**.5; **13**.11; 5th session 5th NPC, **16**.25; 1st session 7th NPC, **23**.7; 4th session 7th NPC, **16**.32; 5th session 7th NPC, **2**.18; **14**.8; 1st session 8th NPC, **2**.25,44; **12**.20; **16**.3
Nationalism, **3**.12
Nei Mongol *see* Inner Mongolia
Neo-realism, **26**.14
New Hong Kong Alliance, **10**.16
New World Development Company, **16**.27,28; **18**.22
New York, xviii
New Zealand, **9**.18
Newkirk, Douglas, **17**.22
Ni Yuxian, **21**.6
Ni Zhifu, **2**.9
Niger, **9**.14,15
Ningbo, **12**.8; **13**.13; **16**.30
Ningxia, **12**.8,14; **16**.26; **19**.13,14,15; **22**.11; **24**.20
Nixon, Richard, **8**.9
No Escape, **26**.15
Nomenklatura, **5**.16
North America, **8**.4; **18**.11
North American Free Trade Agreement, **8**.3,9; **18**.22
Northeast Asia, **8**.6,12,14

One country, two systems *see* Hong Kong
Organization for Economic Cooperation and Development, **17**.2
Organizational reforms, **4**.6f,10f
Origin of Goods Rules, **7**.26
Ou Guangyuan, **2**.38
Ownership, **3**.8; **7**.8; **14**.2; collective, **15**.4,5,13; private, **15**.4,11–12

Pacific Economic Cooperation Conference, **8**.5
Pacific Power Triangle, **8**.3
Palace Museum (Taipei), **9**.8

Paley, Edward, **17**.27
Panyu, **18**.2,4,7,12
Park'N Shop Ltd., **16**.27
Patent Office, **17**.23
Patriarchism, **4**.3
Patten, Christopher, **1**.3; **10**.2,13,15, 16,19
Peaceful evolution, **1**.2; **3**.3f,13; **21**.6,8; **25**.2; **26**.2,4
Pearl River Delta, **16**.14,27; **17**.3; **18**.*passim*; **19**.3,12,20; **22**.16; **24**.22,25,26; economic indicators, **18**.3 (table); export processing, **18**.7; infrastructural development, **18**.10–13; labour shortage, **18**.8
Peng Zhen, **2**.7,25,27,33,39,43
Penghu Island, **9**.16
People's Armed Police, **2**.25; **6**.4,13
People's Liberation Army, **1**.4,6; **2**.2,22,34,43; **6**.*passim*; Academy of Military Sciences, **6**.9; Air Force, **6**.13,16,19; Air Force Academy, **6**.11; Beijing Garrison Command, **6**.12; Central Military Commission, **6**.2f; demobilized soldiers (*see* welfare); Field Armies, **2**.24; Intelligence, **6**.18; Logistics Department, **2**.24; National Defence University, **5**.9; **6**.7,12; Navy, **6**.11,19; Second Artillery Corps, **6**.12,14; Shanghai Garrison Command, **6**.13
Planning, economic, **2**.12; **7**.7; **11**.2; guidance plan, **5**.4; 6th Five-year Plan (FYP), **23**.3; 7th FYP, **23**.3; 8th FYP, **2**.13,19,24; **12**.9; **16**.32; **17**.2; **22**.8; **24**.29; 9th FYP, **24**.29
Political Reform, **1**.2,4; **4**.*passim*; political rights, **21**.11
Pollution, **1**.15
Population, census, **19**.4; mobility, **19**.14 (table); registration status, **19**.10–11 (table); sex ratio, **20**.11
Ports: Gaolan, **18**.10,11,13; Huizhou, **18**.13; Shatian, **18**.12; Yantian, **18**.11,13
Portugal, xviii
Poverty, **23**.13–15
Press and Publications Administration, State, **25**.8; National Working Conference on Press Management, **25**.4
Price reform, **1**.15; **18**.4; index, **11**.7–8; price and wage index **15**.5 (table); Pricing Bureau, **15**.3
Price Waterhouse, **16**.27
Private economy, **2**.21; privatization, **16**.28
Pro-democracy movement, **25**.2; *see also* Tiananmen Incident
Prostitution, **23**.6f
Public opinion, **1**.10
Pudong, xx; **9**.5; **16**.2

Qi lin, xix
Qian Bocheng, **25**.12
Qian Qichen, xviii,xxv,xxvi; **2**.6,16,34; **9**.18
Qian Zhengying, **2**.9
Qiao Shi, xxvi; **2**.6,11,25,26,27,29,33–34; **26**.2
Qin Jiwei, **2**.6; **6**.3,8
Qingdao, **5**.9; **12**.9; **13**.13; **16**.29,30; **23**.13
Qinghai, **2**.15; **9**.8,12,13,14,15,16,22; **12**.8,14; **22**.9,11,19; **24**.20
Quanzhou, **16**.29

Radio, commercial, **25**.7; Shanghai East Station, **25**.10
Ration coupons, **14**.14
Raw materials, **24**.25
Reagan, Ronald, **22**.35

Index

Real estate, **1**.14; **18**.13–15; market **24**.22–28
Recession, **11**.7
Red guards, **21**.2
Reform policy documents, **15**.14–15 (table)
Regionalism, **12**.13–17
Ren Jianxin, xxix; **2**.26,34
Ren Kelei, **2**.38
Ren Zhongyi, **2**.20,37
Renminbi, value, **17**.14,18; exchange rate **17**.14 (table)
Republic of China, **21**.9
Retail sales, **11**.3
Robinson, Svend, xviii
Roh Tae Woo, **1**.2; **8**.12
Rohwer, Jim, **17**.3,6
Roy, J. Stapleton, **9**.17
Rui Xingwen, **2**.17; **26**.3
Rural market, **14**.*passim*; *see also* Agriculture
Russia, xxix; **1**.2; **2**.36; **6**.8,19,20; **8**.5,6,9,13; **9**.18; **14**.5; **17**.10,11; **21**.6

Sashi, **24**.8
Scar literature, **26**.15
Scott, Geoff, xviii
Second World War, **8**.8
Secret societies, **21**.4
Security, State, **2**.5,25
Seibu Department Store, **16**.26
Self-reliance, **17**.6
Senkaku *see* Diaoyutai
Sequel to "Time," A, **26**.16
7-Eleven Convenience Store, **16**.27
Sha Jianxun, **2**.11
Shaanxi, **12**.8; **19**.13,21; **22**.6,18,19; **24**.17
Shajiao Power Plant, **16**.28
Shandong, **2**.19; **4**.8; **6**.11; **8**.12; **12**.8,14; **16**.9; **17**.2,11; **19**.13; **22**.18,19; **23**.16; **24**.20
Shanghai, xviii,xix,xx; **1**.10; **2**.2,14,16, 19,20,22,27,29,31,34,38; **4**.2,5; **6**.19; **9**.5,8,11; **11**.9,10,11; **12**.8,14, 17; **13**.2,5; **15**.16; **16**.2,27; **18**.13,15, 17,19,22; **19**.12,13,15,19,21,23; **20**.3,4,6; **22**.11,18,22; **23**.6,9,10,12, 13; **24**.4,16–17,22,26,29; **25**.3,7,10, 13; **26**.2,11
Shanghai Academy of Social Sciences, **25**.9
Shantou, **9**.5; **16**.10,30
Shanxi, **12**.5; **19**.13,20; **22**.3; **24**.20; **25**.6,7
Shao Huaze, xxix
Shatoujiao, **16**.30
Shaw Yu-ming, **9**.10
Shekou, **15**.8
Shen Tong, xxv; **21**.6,7; **22**.2
Shenyang, **6**.11,12,13,14; **12**.8,9; **23**.13; **24**.9
Shenzhen, xviii,xix,xx,xxi,xxii,xxv; **1**.7,8; **2**.2,20,38; **5**.9; **6**.5; **11**.10; **13**.2; **15**.16; **16**.2,10,16,30,34; **17**.8; **18**.*passim*; **22**.35; **23**.6; **24**.26,27; **26**.2
Shi Yu, **9**.8
Shi Yuxiao, xxvii; **6**.12
Shih Chi-ping, **9**.5
Shunde, **18**.4
Sichuan, **2**.17,19,37; **12**.6,8,14; **14**.8; **16**.18,29,31,33; **19**.13,14,15,16; **20**.3,5; **22**.6,19; **24**.8,20,21,25; **25**.7
Siew, Vincent, **9**.18
Sincere Company Ltd., **16**.26
Sing Tao Group, **25**.10
Singapore, **1**.6; **2**.15; **3**.12; **4**.14; **8**.3,6,8; **9**.24; **16**.20; **17**.2,10; **24**.16
Sino-Vietnamese Border War, **6**.9
Siping, **24**.8
Skeldon, Ronald, **19**.25

Smith, Adam, **2**.29,39
Social Welfare, **23**.*passim*; social security, **4**.14; rural social security, **23**.15–16; *see also* Welfare
Socialism, **3**.5,6f
Song Keda, xxvii; **6**.13
Song Muwen, **2**.11
Song Ping, xxvi; **2**.4,6,9,11,25,27,36
Song Qingwei, xxvii
South Africa, **9**.15
South China Sea, **8**.14
Soviet Union, **1**.2,3,4; **2**.5,45; **3**.2,4,12; **5**.8,14,17; **8**.3,4,6,9,14; **9**.15; **16**.18; **17**.9,33; **21**.6,9; **25**.2
Spain, xviii; **10**.13
Spratly Islands, xxviii; **6**.16,19,20; **8**.14
Star-painter and I, The, **26**.14
Star-singer and I, The, **26**.14
State Council, **1**.6,14; **2**.4,12,13,15,20,21,31,32,33,40; **4**.6,10,11,15; **5**.5,6,7,9; **7**.3,4,9,15,23; **10**.6; **11**.5,8; **13**.11; **14**.9; **15**.2,6,10,13; **16**.14,21,23,30,33; **17**.16,17,19; **18**.6,10; **19**.3; **22**.14,23; **23**.7,14; **24**.8,9,10,12,20,21,24; **25**.8; Administration of Industry and Commerce, **5**.9; **7**.11; **15**.9; Administration of State-owned Property, **5**.5; **16**.32; Auditing Administration, **5**.9; Bureau of Taxation, **5**.5,9; Economic and Trade Office, **2**.13,15; **4**.15; Environmental Protection Administration, **1**.15; Information Office, **2**.10; Ministry of Agriculture, **14**.9; **24**.25; Ministry of Chemical Industry, **4**.15; Ministry of Civil Affairs, **23**.6,9,12,13,14,16; Ministry of Commerce, **1**.13; Ministry of Communications, **5**.5; Ministry of Construction Materials, **5**.9; **24**.2,5,29; Ministry of Culture, **2**.10; **3**.12; **25**.3,4,9; **26**.2; Ministry of Energy, **15**.3; Ministry of Finance, **1**.6; **2**.32; **5**.5; **13**.4,12; Ministry of Foreign Economic Relations and Trade, **2**.12; **5**.5; **6**.3,23; **17**.16; Ministry of Foreign Trade and Economic Cooperation, **16**.3; Ministry of Justice, **2**.25; Ministry of Labour, **23**.13; Ministry of Labour and Personnel, **5**.6; Ministry of Light Industry, **2**.13; **5**.5; Ministry of Machinery and Electronics, **25**.15; Ministry of Material Supplies, **5**.5; **15**.3; Ministry of Personnel, **5**.6; Ministry of Public Security, **1**.3,10; **2**.25; **6**.13; **19**.3,4,9; Ministry of Radio, Film and Television, **2**.13; **5**.4; **25**.15; Ministry of Railways, **5**.5; **24**.20; Ministry of State Security, **2**.25,26; **25**.13; Ministry of Supervision, **1**.9; **2**.25,26; Ministry of Textile, **2**.13; **4**.15; **5**.5; Production Office, **7**.9; State Commission for Science and Technology Industry, **6**.11,19; State Commission for the Reform of the Economic System, **2**.14; **7**.9; **23**.10; State Commission of Science and Technology, **16**.32; State Education Commission, **1**.15; **2**.9,10; **22**.2,3,13,14,19,26,31,32; State Planning Commission, **2**.12; **4**.15; **5**.4; **7**.9; **13**.11; **15**.3; **16**.14,24; **17**.16; **18**.4; **23**.13; **24**.24; State Statistical Bureau, **5**.9; **16**.7; **24**.2
Stock market, **1**.8; **2**.15,20; **11**.9; **13**.2; **15**.16; **18**.15–18; Shanghai Stock Exchange, **9**.5; Shares, A and B,

Index I.15

7.16; **18**.16; Shenzhen Stock Exchange, **18**.17; State Commission, **2**.15; stock companies, **7**.9,12f
Stockholm, **2**.15; Stockholm Chamber of Commerce, **16**.26
Students, drop-outs, **22**.10; repeaters, **22**.11; self-financed, **22**.29,31
Su Shaozhi, **21**.7
Su Tong, **26**.15–16
Su Wei, **21**.7
Su Xiaokang, **21**.7
Sui Yongju, **6**.14
Suifenhe, **12**.5
Summers, Lawrence H., **17**.2
Sung Hsin-lien, **9**.19
Superman, **22**.35
Supreme People's Court, **2**.25
Sweden, **16**.19
Switzerland, xviii
Szeto Wah, **10**.9

Taipei, **9**.8,10; **16**.9
Taishan, **18**.12
Taiwan, xix,xx,xxvi,xxvii,xxix; **1**.3,6,16; **2**.23,35; **3**.3; **6**.16; **7**.16; **8**.4,6,7,8,11,13; **11**.10; **16**.7,20,29,31,32,33; **17**.2,3,10,21,31; **21**.9; **23**.8; **25**.4,7,10,11,13,14; **26**.12; Council for Economic Planning and Development, **9**.4; Mainland Affairs Council, **9**.3,11,19; Ministry of Finance, **9**.7; National Security Bureau **9**.19; Straits Exchange Foundation, **9**.3,22; Taiwan Institute of Economics, **9**.10
Tam Yiu-chung, **10**.8
Tan Jiazhen, xxvi; **9**.8
Tan Shaowen, xxvi; **2**.6
Tangshan, **24**.9
Tao Siju, **1**.3

Taxation, **2**.20,40; **7**.19–20; **12**.*passim*; **18**.4
Technocrats, **2**.14
Tel Aviv, xviii
Telecommunications, **18**.18
Television, commercial, **25**.7; "Aspirations," **25**.8,9; **26**.10; BBC World Service Television, **25**.14; China Central Television, **25**.8,9,12, 17; "I Love You Definitely," **25**.8; "In the Editorial Office," **25**.8,9; **26**.10,12,13; Shenzhen Television Station, **25**.12; Sichuan Cable Television Development Company, **25**.10; STAR TV, **18**.19; **25**.13, 14–15
Thailand, **8**.10,12; **16**.5
Third World, **1**.3; **8**.15
Three Gorges Hydroelectric Project, xx
Tian An China Investment Company, **16**.27
Tian Chengping, **2**.15
Tian Jiyun, xx,xxvi; **2**.6,11,29,34,44; **14**.9,13; **16**.23,24
Tiananmen demonstration (1976), **21**.2
Tiananmen Incident, **1**.4,8; **2**.26; **4**.5; **5**.8,16; **8**.5,10; **9**.2,3; **10**.2,8,11; **15**.8; **16**.3,16,21; **17**.29; **18**.13; **19**.8,13,15,19,21,23; **21**.3,6,8,10–11,12; **23**.2,3; **26**.2,3,5,
Tianjin, xxii; **1**.10; **2**.15,19,37; **12**.8,9; **13**.13; **16**.30; **23**.10,12; **24**.17,22; **25**.7; **26**.11
Tibet, **6**.12; **12**.8; **19**.12,13; **22**.10,18,19
Tong Dalin, xxvi
Tong Zeng, xxvii
Tong Zengyin, **13**.11
Town, market, **19**.3
Trade, foreign, **11**.8; **17**.5 (table); balance **17**.32 (table); Commission on Tariff Regulation, **17**.23;

Foreign Trade Company, **17**.16–18; Sino-US trade, **17**.28 (table); US import tariffs, **17**.26 (table)
Trade Unions, **7**.6
Tripolar World, **8**.5 (table)
Tsai Wan-lin, **9**.5
Tsang Yok-sing, **10**.8
Tuen Mun (Hong Kong), **18**.10
Tumenjiang, **12**.5; Delta development project, **8**.12

Ukraine, **6**.17
United Democrats of Hong Kong, **10**.9,11,13,14
United Kingdom, **1**.3; **8**.5,6; **10**.2,18; **13**.15; **16**.10,19
United Nations, **8**.12,14,15; **9**.17; **16**.14; **17**.21; Security Council, **8**.2,5
United States, xxii,xxv; **1**.2,3; **2**.23; **6**.16; **8**.3,4,5,6,8,11,14; **9**.9,17,18; **10**.2,4; **13**.14; **16**.9,25; **17**.2,4,9,10,12,13,24–34; **18**.6; **21**.5,7; **25**.10,13
Universities, National Chengchi University, **9**.9; National Taiwan University, **9**.8; Peking University, xxviii; **1**.9; **21**.6; People's University, **22**.3; Qinghua University, **2**.14; Seton Hall College, **9**.2; Tokyo University, **8**.11; University of Law and Politics, **9**.12; Xiamen University, **9**.12
Urbanization, **19**.17,19
Urumqi, xix
USSR *see* Soviet Union

Vancouver, **18**.16
Vanuatu, **9**.15
Vietnam, xxviii; **1**.2; **6**.19,20; **8**.14; **18**.22

Vo Van Kiet, xxviii
Vocational education, **22**.34; job opportunities, **22**.24; schools, **22**.20; *see also* Education

Waigaoqiao, **16**.30
Walker, Alan, **23**.19
Wan Li, **2**.6
Wan Runnan, **21**.7,8
Wan Shaofen, **2**.36
Wang Anyi, **26**.14
Wang Bingqian, **2**.13,32
Wang Bingzhang, **21**.7
Wang Chengbin, xxvii; **6**.13
Wang Chunzheng, **2**.13
Wang Daohan, **2**.30; **9**.23,24
Wang Deying, **2**.6
Wang Dongxing, **6**.15
Wang, G., **20**.14
Wang Hai, **6**.13
Wang Hanbin, xxvii; **2**.6,26,27
Wang Hongwen, xxiv
Wang Jialiu, **2**.9
Wang Jun, **2**.7
Wang Ke, xxvii; **6**.12,15
Wang Meng, **26**.3,5–7
Wang Renzhi, **2**.10,11; **25**.3; **26**.2
Wang Ruilin, **6**.8f,14,15
Wang Ruoshui, xxi,xxiii
Wang Ruowang, **2**.45; **21**.6,8
Wang Shuo, **25**.7; **26**.10,11,16
Wang Tailan, **6**.11
Wang Weicheng, **2**.9
Wang Xianglin, **2**.41
Wang Yung-ching, **9**.6
Wang Zengqi, **26**.14
Wang Zhaoguo, **2**.36
Wang Zhen, **2**.7,39,43
Wangfujing, **16**.27
Wangling, **22**.15,16
Watanabe Michio, **8**.11
Watson's, **16**.27

Index

Wei Jianxing, xxvi; **2**.6,11,26,27
Wei Jingsheng, **21**.3
Welfare, army veterans, **23**.16–17; factories, **23**.11–12; home, **23**.4; income generation, **23**.5
Wellcome Company, **16**.27
Wen Jiabao, xxvii; **2**.6,36
Wen Yuankai, **21**.6
Wenzhou, **13**.5
Wharf Holdings, **16**.27,28; **18**.22; **25**.10
Whyte, Martin King, **20**.8
Wilson, David (Sir), **10**.5,11,13
Wing On Department Store, **16**.26
Wives and Concubines, **26**.16
Wolf, Arthur P., **20**.3
Women, **20**.2,13; female role, **20**.2; fertility, **20**.9–11; fertility rate, **20**.10 (tables); women's protection, **23**.7; work participation, **20**.13 (table)
Wong, Andrew, **10**.11
Wong Kan Seng, **8**.3
Woo, Peter, xxiii
Work-study programme, **22**.14,30
Workers, **1**.12
World Bank *see* Banking
World Intellectual Property Organization, **7**.20
Writers' Association, **26**.4,5,7,10
Wu Bangguo, xxi,xxvi; **2**.6,15
Wu, Gordon, **16**.28; **18**.10
Wu Guanzheng, **2**.15
Wu Guoguang, **21**.7
Wu Jinglian, **1**.14; **2**.41
Wu Mingyu, **2**.41
Wu Quanxu, **6**.11
Wu Shaozu, **9**.8
Wu Shih-kai, **9**.8
Wu Ta-yu, **9**.8
Wu Xiang, **2**.41
Wu Xuecan, xix

Wu Xueqian, xxvi; **2**.6,34; **9**.9,13
Wu Zuguang, xxiii
Wuchang, xviii
Wuer Kaixi, **21**.7
Wuhan, **2**.19; **5**.9; **12**.9; **13**.5; **18**.13,22; **22**.28; **23**.10,13; **24**.22; **25**.10; **26**.15
Wuhan Number 2 Dyeing and Printing Factory, **16**.29
Wuhu, **6**.16
Wuxi, **23**.13

Xi Jing'an, **2**.38
Xiamen, **9**.6,9,23; **16**.2,30; **24**.22,26
Xi'an Incident, **9**.10
Xiang Huaicheng, **12**.3
Xiang Nan, **2**.37
Xiao Ke, **2**.35; **6**.6,15
Xiao Yang, **2**.17,19,36
Xie Fei, xxvii; **2**.6,19,38; **18**.6
Xie Jin, **9**.12; **26**.12
Xinjiang, xix; **6**.12; **12**.5,8,9,14; **14**.9,11,12; **19**.12,13,14,15,23; **22**.19; **24**.20
Xiong Guangkai, **6**.11
Xu Bangtai, **21**.7
Xu Caihou, **6**.11
Xu Huizi, **6**.11
Xu Jiatun, xxii; **10**.4
Xu Qing, **2**.6
Xu Weicheng, **2**.10; **25**.3; **26**.3
Xu Xin, **6**.11

Yan Jiaqi, **21**.7,8
Yan Mingfu, **2**.17; **26**.3
Yan Nian, **7**.5
Yang Baibing, xxvi,xxvii; **1**.6; **2**.5,6,22; **6**.*passim*
Yang Dezhi, **2**.35
Yang Guoliang, **6**.14
Yang Peixin, **2**.40
Yang Rudai, **2**.6,37

Yang Shangkun, xxi,xxvii; **1**.6; 2.5,6,20,39; **6**.2,6,7; **9**.10,13,14
Yang, Winston, **9**.2
Yangjiang, **18**.13
Yangtze River Delta, **9**.5,6; **16**.14,27
Yantai, **16**.30; **24**.9,10
Yao Yilin, xxvi; **2**.9,11,13,33
Yaohan Department Store, **16**.26
Ye Fei, **2**.35; **6**.15
Ye Jianying, **1**.6; **2**.38,39; **9**.2,13
Ye Xuanping, **2**.20,37
Yeltsin, Boris, xxix; **1**.2; **6**.17,18,19
Yip Kwok-chung, **10**.8
You Lin, **2**.11
Yu Chung-hsien, **9**.12
Yu Guangyuan, **2**.41
Yu Haocheng, xxi
Yu Xiaochong, **16**.17
Yu Yongbo, xxvii; **2**.7,23; **6**.9,14
Yuan Hongbin, xxiii
Yuan Zheng, **24**.26,30
Yuan Zhimin, **21**.7
Yunnan, **12**.5,8; **19**.13; **22**.9,19; **24**.20

Zeng Jianhui, **2**.10
Zeng Qinghong, **2**.16,30
Zhang Aiping, **2**.35; **6**.6,15
Zhang Gong, xxvii; **6**.12,14
Zhang Haidi, **22**.35
Zhang Jie, **26**.5,7,14
Zhang Shanyu, **19**.19
Zhang Taiheng, xxvii; **6**.12,14
Zhang Wannian, xxvii; **2**.7,23,24; **6**.8,12,14,15
Zhang Wei, **2**.37
Zhang Weiguo, xxi; **25**.13
Zhang Xianliang, **25**.7
Zhang Yimou, **26**.12,16

Zhang Zhen, xxvii; **1**.6; **2**.7,23,30,35; **6**.7,10,14,15
Zhang Zhiping, **7**.5
Zhang Zhongxian, **6**.9,12
Zhangjiagang, **16**.30
Zhao Haikuan, **13**.10
Zhao Nanqi, **6**.3,9,14
Zhao Xishun, **20**.3
Zhao Ziyang, xviii,xxiii,xxvi; **1**.2,4,5; **2**.4,5,14,27,31,35,36,41,45; **4**.2; **6**.6; **15**.8; **16**.20; **21**.2,3,7,11; **26**.6
Zhejiang **11**.10,11; **12**.8,9; **13**.5; **17**.2; **19**.13,14,15,16; **22**.11,19,27; **24**.20
Zheng Bijian, **2**.10,11,30; **26**.3
Zheng Liangyu, xxv; **2**.38; **18**.16
Zheng Zhongbing, xxiii
Zhengzhou, **24**.8
Zhongshan, **18**.2,19; **24**.22
Zhou Enlai, **2**.18,32; **22**.35
Zhou Jianwei, **12**.16
Zhou Siyu, **6**.11
Zhou Tuo, **21**.6
Zhou Wenyuan, **6**.11
Zhou Yushu, **6**.4,13,14
Zhu Dunfa, **6**.12
Zhu Houze, **2**.10,41
Zhu Rongji, xxii,xxiv,xxvi,xxvii,xxx; **2**.6,14,20,22,27,28,30,31–32,35; **24**.25
Zhu Senlin, **2**.38; **18**.17,21
Zhuhai, xviii,xxii; **1**.7; **2**.2; **16**.2; **18**.2,3,7,10,12,18; **22**.35; **26**.2
Zou Deci, **24**.27
Zou Jiahua, xxvi; **2**.6,20; **16**.28; **18**.6,16
Zou Yuqi, **6**.4,13,14
Zou Zhekai, **9**.23
Zutshi, B. K., **9**.16